War and Progress

BRITAIN

1914–1945

Longman Economic and Social History of Britain

General Editor: J.V. Beckett
Professor of English Regional History, University of Nottingham

This new seven-volume series will become a standard recommendation for students and other readers in search of an authoritative but readable introduction to the economic and social history of Britain from the Norman Conquest to the present day.

Distinctive features will be the commitment to a genuinely British approach, especially from the Union onwards; the openness to new ideas and new approaches; the effective use of instances and examples to animate theory; and a concern with both regional unity and regional diversity, to highlight the development of a national economy and a national consciousness.

The first volume to be published is:

SCOTLAND BEFORE THE INDUSTRIAL REVOLUTION
c1050–c1750
IAN D. WHYTE

WAR AND PROGRESS
Britain 1914–1945
PETER DEWEY

WAR AND PROGRESS
BRITAIN 1914–1945

PETER DEWEY

LONGMAN
London and New York

Addison Wesley Longman Limited
Edinburgh Gate,
Harlow, Essex CM20 2JE,
United Kingdom
and Associated Companies throughout the world.

*Published in the United States of America
by Addison Wesley Longman, New York*

First published 1997

ISBN 0 582 04586 X PPR

British Library Cataloguing-in-Publication Data

A catalogue record for this book is available from the British Library

Library of Congress Cataloging-in-Publication Data

Dewey, Peter, 1944–
War and progress : Britain, 1914–1945 / Peter Dewey.
p. cm. — (Longman economic and social history of Britain)
Includes bibliographical references (p.) and index.
ISBN 0–582–04587–8. — ISBN 0–582–04586–X (pbk.)
1. Great Britain—History—George V, 1910–1936. 2. Great Britain
—History—George VI, 1936–1952. 3. Great Britain—Economic
conditions—20th century. 4. Great Britain—Social conditions—20th
century. 5. World War, 1914–1918—Great Britain. 6. World War,
1939–1945—Great Britain. I. Title. II. Series.
DA576.D46 1996
941.082—dc20 96–16228
CIP

Transferred to digital print on demand 2001

Printed and bound by Antony Rowe Ltd, Eastbourne

CONTENTS

LIST OF MAPS

LIST OF TABLES

IMPERIAL/METRIC EQUIVALENTS

CURRENCY

1 penny (1d.) = 0.42p
12 pennies = 1 shilling = 5p
1 shilling (1s. or 1/–) = 5p
20 shillings = £1.00 = 100p

WEIGHTS

1 ounce (oz) = 28.3 grams (g)
16 ounces = 1 pound
1 pound (lb) = 453 grams
2.2 pounds = 1 kilogram (kg)
2,240 pounds = 1 ton = 1,016 kilograms

ACKNOWLEDGEMENTS

The greatest debt owed by an author is to his family, and in particular to his spouse. Without the interest and support of Hilary, this book might not have seen the light of day. As it is, she has put up with my continuous commentary on the progress of this tome over five years, and deserves medals for sheer endurance far beyond the call of duty. She also suggested 'War and Progress' as a title. On occasion I have also imposed on the patience of my son Nicholas and my daughter Emma, to whom are due my apologies and thanks for their forbearance and willingness to discuss historical topics raised in the course of this work.

Professionally, my thanks are due to the History Department at Royal Holloway, University of London, which provides an environment congenial to, and supportive of, research and writing, and to the libraries which I have used, chiefly those of Royal Holloway (especially its excellent inter-library loan service) and of the University of Reading. I have had nothing but the highest professional expertise and unfailing courtesy from these institutions.

I should like to thank Mrs Sue Macgregor, an undergraduate in the History Department at Royal Holloway, for her computer expertise in converting the Appendix data into graphical form.

Finally, I should like to thank the editor of this series, Professor John Beckett, and Addison Wesley Longman for their expert encouragement, and for allowing me to get on with the book without nagging, in spite of it being distinctly overdue.

The publishers would like to thank the following for granting permission to reproduce copyright material: Blackwell Publishers for Tables 6.2 and 13.7; Oxford University Press for Table 17.8; Cambridge University Press for Table 3.6; Weidenfeld and Nicolson for Table 13.5; Table 14.3 is reprinted by permission of Kluwer Academic Publishers.

CHAPTER 1

BRITISH ECONOMY AND SOCIETY IN THE EARLY TWENTIETH CENTURY

INTRODUCTION

The economy and society of Great Britain are of unique importance in world history. This is because Britain was the first country to experience the 'Industrial Revolution'. This process, which began in the late eighteenth century, and is still going on, consists of the application of more modern and scientific techniques to the economy, so that the labour of human beings becomes more productive, and the efficiency of the economy rises. In the process, economic activity and human settlement change. Men and women now work increasingly in an environment dominated by the machine and the factory, and now live in towns of ever-increasing size. In the process, agriculture and rural life become much less important.

In Britain, these continuing changes had produced by the early twentieth century an economy and society of great complexity. Some idea of the impact of these changes on the regions of the country may be had by considering what people did for a living on the eve of the First World War. This information comes from the decennial population census, conducted in 1911. Of the total British employed population of 18.3 million, the largest employment was in manufacturing, which (together with construction) employed 50 per cent of the total employed population (male and female) in 1911. The next largest was the service sector, which (including transport) employed 35 per cent. These were by far the largest categories of employment. The others were agriculture (8 per cent) and mining (6 per cent). These occupations varied considerably in importance from region to region. The English west midlands was the most reliant on manufacturing, with 56 per cent of its population thus employed, and north Scotland (with 30 per cent) the least. South Wales was the most reliant on mining (32 per cent), and the south-east of England (0.5 per cent) the least. Textiles accounted for almost one-quarter of employment in the northern regions of Lancashire/Cheshire and the West Riding of Yorkshire. Agriculture was of greatest importance in the eastern counties of England, north Wales and north Scotland, where it accounted for about one-quarter of the employed population, and of least importance in the Lancashire/Cheshire region (only 3.0 per cent) (see Map 1).

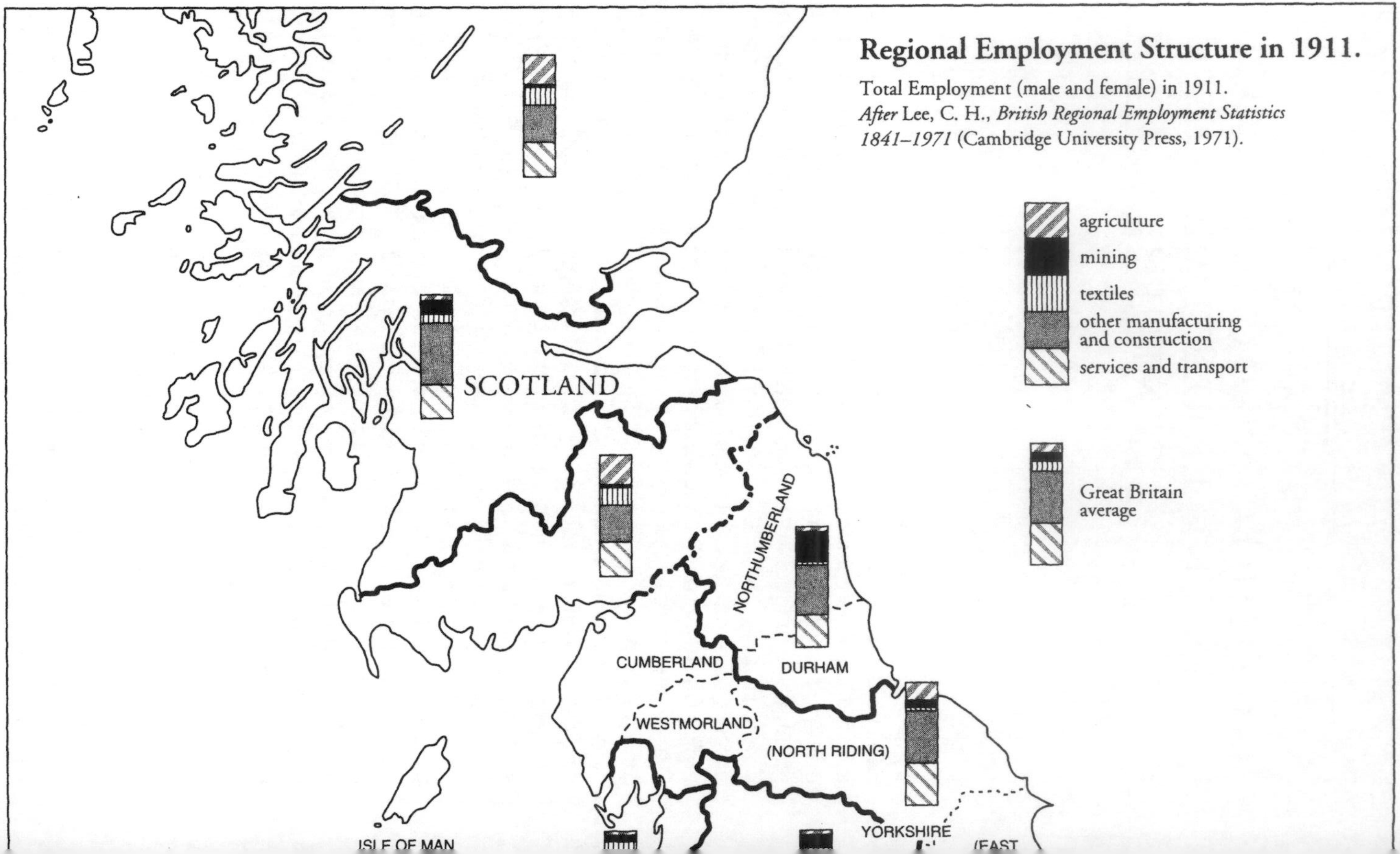

Regional Employment Structure in 1911.
Total Employment (male and female) in 1911.
After Lee, C. H., *British Regional Employment Statistics 1841–1971* (Cambridge University Press, 1971).
agriculture
mining
textiles
other manufacturing and construction
services and transport
Great Britain average
SCOTLAND
NORTHUMBERLAND
CUMBERLAND
DURHAM
WESTMORLAND
(NORTH RIDING)
YORKSHIRE
ISLE OF MAN

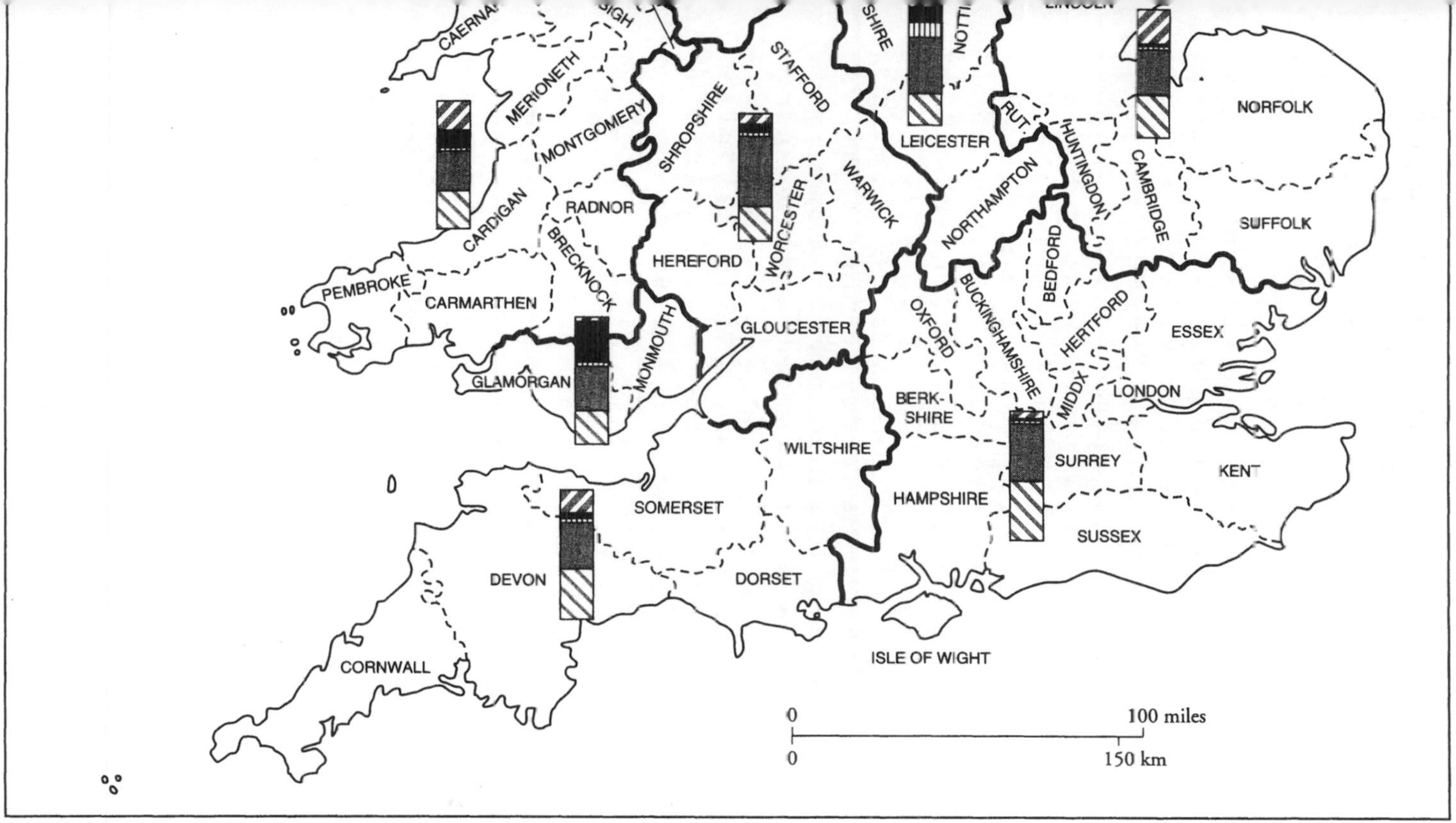

Map 1 Regional employment structure in 1911

These broad classifications concealed much local diversity. The great iron and steel producing centres were few but important. Steel was produced mainly in the north-east of England, south Wales and lowland Scotland. Iron production was carried on in these centres, and also in the east and west midlands, and in the Furness region of Cumberland. Engineering, although spread around Britain, was concentrated in the larger cities such as London, Manchester, Birmingham and Glasgow, and their hinterlands, although few towns of any size did not have their proportion of engineering firms. Some towns depended heavily on a particular variety of engineering; this was most noticeable in the shipbuilding towns along the Clyde, Tyne and Tees, and in Belfast. Coal-mining, employing slightly more than 1 million men in 1911, was largely absent from southern Britain. Apart from the Kent and Somerset coalfields, which were both small, coal was mined only north of an imaginary line from Bristol to the Wash. Coal-mining was heavily concentrated regionally; in 1913, south Wales produced 19 per cent, north-east England (Durham and Tyneside) 20 per cent, and lowland Scotland (chiefly the Glasgow/Lanark region) 15 per cent of total national output.[1]

The greatest effect of the Industrial Revolution had been the spread of modern manufacturing methods, centred on the factory (large or small), using machines and power, usually of steam. These modernised industries covered a wide range by 1911; from the manufacture of furniture to that of bricks and cement, or chemicals, or paper and books. The greatest factory industry was undoubtedly textiles, mainly the cottons and woollens which had been among the first to be modernised and mechanised in the early years of industrialisation. There were 640,000 males in textiles in 1911, but even more females – 870,000. Although found in most regions, textiles were predominantly a northern affair; Lancashire was the main centre for cottons, and the West Riding of Yorkshire for woollens.

Some trades which were important before industrialisation continued to be so into the industrial age. Building and construction employed 1.1 million men in 1911. Although the industry was not located anywhere in particular, the overwhelming dominance of London as a centre of population (7 million out of a total British population of 41 million in 1911) made it the largest centre of building, because of the enormous demand for houses for the still rapidly growing population. Transport, chiefly on the roads and the railways, employed 1.6 million men in 1911. This industry also was largely dominated by London, although every large provincial city was an important railway employer, and there were some towns which depended heavily on railway employment, notably Swindon (Wiltshire), Middlesbrough (Yorkshire) and Crewe (Cheshire).

Finally, there were the service or 'tertiary' occupations. These were second in importance only to the manufacturing occupations. They were found

1. R. Pope, *Atlas of British Social and Economic History since c.1700* (Routledge 1989), Map 4.3.

in a wide range of industries, employing the thousands of (largely male) clerks who kept the accounts and ran the business correspondence of thousands of firms; those engaged in banking, finance, insurance, the professions, administration and the Armed Forces; in wholesale and retail trade; and in domestic service. The service occupations were found in all regions, although the south-east region was the most reliant on them, since it contained London, which was simultaneously the national and imperial government centre, the greatest financial centre, and the largest centre in Britain for entertainment and leisure activities.

ECONOMIC GROWTH AND THE ECONOMY

The Industrial Revolution led for the first time in recorded history to an era of continuous economic growth. Previously, although economic growth had occurred from time to time in different regions of the world, there was no guarantee that it would not be negated by natural disasters such as famine and disease, or the man-made disaster of war. Much effort by historians and economists has been devoted to measuring national rates of economic growth. The calculation is fraught with difficulties, since quantitative evidence becomes less reliable as one goes further back in time. The usual procedure is to measure the money value of national income over a period of time, and adjust this to take account of changes in the price level, thus giving 'real' national income. This is then divided by the number of people in the nation, to give average real income per head of the population. When these calculations are performed, it is found that, once the Industrial Revolution had got under way, real income in Britain grew at a little more than 2 per cent per year (see Table 1.1). When this is adjusted for population growth, it falls to slightly more than 1 per cent per head per year (see the Appendix for the statistical evidence on rates of UK economic growth from 1870 to 1948).

A growth rate of real income per head of about 1 per cent per year may seem hardly revolutionary, but it was much faster than before industrialisation

Table 1.1 Growth rates of British national income, 1700–1913 (% per year)

	Real GDP[a]	*Real GDP per head*
1700–60	0.7	0.3
1761–1800	1.1	0.3
1801–30	2.7	1.3
1831–60	2.5	1.1
1856–73	2.2	1.4
1873–1913	1.8	0.9

Note: a GDP = Gross Domestic Product; see Appendix, pp. 335–9
Source: C.H. Lee, *The British Economy since 1700: a macroeconomic perspective* (Cambridge UP 1986), p. 5

had begun. It must be borne in mind also that these rates are cumulative. Just half a century of growth at 1 per cent per head a year would raise real income per head by almost two-thirds (actually 64.5 per cent). This is what happened in practice. Thus, taking the second half of the nineteenth century, when the statistical data are more reliable, between 1855 and 1913, weekly *real* wage rates in Britain rose by about 55 per cent.[2] Put more simply, the standard of living for wage-earners had risen by more than one-half in little over half a century – an unprecedented achievement.

Since the techniques which lay at the heart of industrialisation could not be kept the exclusive secret of British entrepreneurs, economic growth spread, first to Europe, and then to the Americas and Australasia. By 1900, the diffusion of modern economic growth and its techniques had led to a large gap opening up in real incomes between the 'industrial' and 'non-industrial' world, although some non-industrialised countries such as Australia and Argentina also had high incomes, derived from selling food and raw materials to the industrial regions. In 1900, the richest countries (judged by incomes per head) were Australia and the USA, with $2,923 and $2,911 respectively. The UK followed shortly after, with $2,798. Belgium, Germany and France had incomes per head of $2,126, $1,558 and $1,600 respectively. At the non-industrialised end of the spectrum, Japan's income per head was estimated at only $677, China's only $401, and India's only $436.[3] (Estimates are US dollars at 1980 prices.)

The Industrial Revolution was accompanied by two further changes, which altered the nature of British society decisively. The first was the population explosion after the mid-eighteenth century. The first British census of population (1801) had shown a total British population of 10.7 million. At the census of 1911, it had risen to 40.9.[4] The decades of fastest growth were the 1820s and 1830s. Thereafter the population grew more slowly, but by pre-industrial standards it was still rising rapidly on the eve of the First World War. The second feature was urbanisation; as the British economy was the first to undergo extensive industrialisation, so the British people were the first to undergo extensive urbanisation. By 1911, 78 per cent of the population of England and Wales lived in urban areas; in Scotland, 75 per cent.[5] ('Urban' is here taken to mean people living in urban administrative areas in England and Wales, and, in Scotland, people living in burghs and in certain other districts having a population of over 1,000.)

Industrialisation also produced a profound change in the structure of the economy, as the relative size of agriculture shrank, and industry and the service sector expanded. The greatest change was the relative decline of agriculture.

2. C.H. Feinstein, *National Income, Expenditure and Output of the United Kingdom 1855–1965* (Cambridge UP 1972), Table 65.
3. A. Maddison, *The World Economy in the 20th Century* (Paris, OECD 1989), p. 19.
4. B.R. Mitchell, *British Historical Statistics* (Cambridge UP 1988), pp. 11–13.
5. Census of England and Wales 1931, *Preliminary Report* (1931), p. xv; Census of Scotland 1911, *Report* (1913), vol. II, Cd 6896, pp. xiii, xiv, xli.

Between 1801 and 1901, the proportion of the occupied British population working in agriculture fell from 36 per cent to 9 per cent.[6]

The occupations of the British people on the eve of the First World War were largely of the type to be expected in a highly industrialised and urbanised society (although agriculture was still an important occupation). There were in 1911 five broad groups of occupations employing over 1 million men – metals, transport, agriculture (including horticulture and forestry), building and mining. The other major occupations were in commerce (0.74 million) and textiles (0.64 million). These occupations, all told, accounted for 8.6 million males, out of a total British male labour force of 12.9 million. For females, out of a total labour force of 5.3 million, there was only one outstanding employment, which was domestic and personal service (2.1 million). Apart from this, the two major female occupations were in textiles (0.9 million) and clothing (0.8 million), although 0.3 million were employed in the manufacture of food, drink and tobacco.[7]

Thus, although many people were employed in manufacturing, or in trades deriving their importance from manufacturing (such as coal-mining or railways), the occupational structure was not exclusively industrial. There were some non-industrial occupations such as agriculture (although this was a declining employment), and some such as commerce, transport and building, which were common to both pre- and post-Industrial Revolution societies. For females, the dominance of a completely non-industrial occupation (domestic service) was outstanding. This dominance was the consequence of an employing class whose numbers had risen greatly in the previous century, and a labour supply which was still abundant enough to command only low wages. (There were also many women working part-time, chiefly from home, who did not appear in the census of population as following an occupation.)[8]

SOCIETY

A marked feature of British and other modern societies in the early twentieth century was the high degree of economic inequality, both in income and in ownership of wealth. The extent of economic inequality was uncertain. An early attempt at income classification by an MP, Leo Chiozza Money, in 1908, could specify only three broad categories of household income – 'Riches' (more than £700 a year), 'Comfort' (£160–700 a year), and 'Poverty' (less than £160 a year). The numbers of people living in the three categories of household were 1.4 million ('Riches'), 4.1 million ('Comfort') and 39.1 million ('Poverty'). On this rough basis, the average annual income per head in each of the

6. P. Deane and W.A. Cole, *British Economic Growth, 1688–1959* (2nd edn, Cambridge UP 1959), Table 30.

7. Department of Employment and Productivity, *British Labour Statistics, Historical Abstract 1886–1968* (HMSO 1971), Table 102.

8. S. Pennington and B. Westover, *A Hidden Workforce: homeworkers in England, 1850–1985* (Macmillan 1989).

three classes of household would be £453, £67 and £24. The top 3 per cent of households received 34 per cent of the national income, and the top 12 per cent would receive 49 per cent, leaving 88 per cent of households with only 51 per cent of the national income.[9]

The true distribution was probably even more unequal. An alternative estimate, by Stamp, was that in 1914 the top 1 per cent of income receivers received about 30 per cent of the national income, and the top 5.5 per cent received 45 per cent, leaving the other 55 per cent of the national income to be shared out among nearly 95 per cent of the population. The distribution of wealth would be even more unequal, since in 1911–13 about 1 per cent of the population owned about 70 per cent of total wealth, while the top 10 per cent alone held about 90 per cent.[10]

At the top of the income structure were those rich in their own right, and such public servants as the Prime Minister and High Court judges, both earning £5,000 a year. Few members of the upper-middle class earned even as much as £1,000. The salary of a middle-ranking industrial manager might be from £200 to £500 a year. The dividing line between middle and working class was often taken to be the annual income at which income tax became payable (£160).[11]

For the working classes, those skilled men earning about £100 a year and in regular work could probably bring up a family without too much strain. For those in casual work, or in low-paid occupations like agriculture, whose earnings even in a full week would not amount to more than about £1, poverty was usual and pauperism not unusual. The thirty-one poor families from the Kennington area of Lambeth (London), whose means and expenditure were surveyed between 1909 and 1913, usually had to support their families on £1 or less. Roughly one-third of this went on rent, and the food bill was dominated by bread, which was the cheapest way of surviving. Thus Mr A, who in 1911–12 was a railway-carriage washer, took home 18s. for a six-day week. He made over all his income to his wife: 7s. went on rent, and a further 5s. 11d. on houshold expenses; 8s. 1d. remained for food for the two adults and three children; 2s. 7d. of this went on bread. When allowance had been made for enough food to keep Mr A healthy enough to work, only 2d. per head per day remained to buy food for the four others in the family.[12]

Employment for women was more common in the working and lower-middle classes; the upper-middle-class woman was not encouraged to take up employment. Women's occupations tended to be low paid. Where women

9. L.G. Chiozza Money, *Riches and Poverty* (1911), p. 48.
10. D.H. Aldcroft, *The Interwar Economy: Britain, 1919–1939* (Batsford 1970), p. 388; K.M. Langley, 'The Distribution of Capital in Private Hands in 1936–38 and 1946–47', *Bulletin of the Oxford University Institute of Statistics* 13 (1951), p. 47.
11. G. Routh, *Occupation and Pay in Great Britain, 1906–1960* (Cambridge UP 1965), pp. 170–8.
12. M.S. Pember Reeves, *Round about a Pound a Week* (Bell 1913; Virago 1979), pp. 42–3, 94–6, 132–3.

performed similar work to that of men, their earnings were usually only about 50–60 per cent of those of the men.[13]

Low wages, whether due to casual work, illness, or just low rates of pay, led to considerable poverty, revealed in pioneering social inquiries at the end of the nineteenth century. Charles Booth's survey of the *Life and Labour of the People of London* (1889–1902) concluded that 30.7 per cent of the population were in poverty, and 8.4 per cent in *abject* poverty. Seebohm Rowntree's famous survey of York in 1899 concluded that 9.9 per cent of its population were in 'primary' poverty, that is, with an income that was always insufficient for their needs, and a further 27.8 per cent were in 'secondary' poverty, that is, there would be times when such a state of affairs would occur, either through illness, accident or old age.[14]

Closely linked with the question of wages and earnings was that of unemployment. This fluctuated with the trade cycle, so that a period of near-full employment was followed by a slump, and then a recovery; the period between cycle peaks was usually six to ten years. In slumps, workers were laid off in almost every industry, short-time working rose, and wages were reduced. Most of the unemployment fell on the manual workers, although clerical workers were not immune, and even managers might be unlucky from time to time.

Such figures as we possess on rates of unemployment derive from the records of trade unions; the government did not collect unemployment statistics before 1913. Between 1860 and 1913, at the troughs of the trade cycles, about 8 per cent of trade unionists would be unemployed; at the peaks, about 2 per cent.[15] Since unionists, being drawn from the most skilled ranks of the working class, were less prone to unemployment than the less skilled non-unionists, the *average* rate of unemployment for the working class as a whole must have been much higher both at troughs and peaks. How much higher can only be guessed. A rough estimate is that for wage-earners as a whole, unemployment varied from about 3 per cent in good years to about 10 per cent in bad years. But fluctuating employment affected all sorts of labour:

> In a bad year like 1894, the Scots Blacksmiths had had less than thirteen per cent of their members out of work at any one time, but more than forty-five per cent had had a taste of unemployment at some time during the year. The reader may ask himself, if he had been one of the Scots Blacksmiths then would it have been the thirteen per cent or the forty-five per cent that was the measure of his anxiety?[16]

As well as cyclical unemployment, there was the casual unemployment induced in certain industries by seasonal or short-term trade fluctuations. This was most

13. Routh, *Occupation and Pay*, pp. 7, 104.
14. C. Booth, *Life and Labour of the People of London* (1889–1903, 17 vols); B.S. Rowntree, *Poverty: a study of town life* (1901).
15. (Sir) W.H. Beveridge, *Full Employment in a Free Society* (Allen & Unwin 1944), pp. 42–3.
16. E.H. Phelps Brown, *The Growth of British Industrial Relations: a study from the standpoint of 1906–14* (Macmillan 1959), p. 86.

marked in industries such as dockyard work or building, which were prone to interruption by bad weather.

For those whose means were insufficient to see them through bad times, there were until just before the First World War only two forms of assistance – private charities and the Poor Law. The former were one of the great success stories of the Victorian age, calling on the services of hundreds of thousands of volunteer helpers, and dispensing millions of pounds annually to a variety of ends.

Yet the charities lacked the resources to alleviate all cases of want, and the Poor Law was an important safety net for social casualties. Having its origins in the sixteenth century, the contemporary Poor Law offered help in extreme cases only, and then only after an inquiry into the means and lifestyle of the applicant. The inquisitorial procedures of the Poor Law, the very minimal levels of relief offered, and the general air of grudging charity which permeated its activities made it the last port of call for all but the most desperate. Even so, many people fell onto it. In 1912, 780,000 people in England and Wales were given relief on the Poor Law (average of numbers being relieved on 1 January and 1 July). Of these, 372,000 were inmates in a residential institution such as a hospital, asylum or workhouse, and 408,000 were receiving 'out-relief' in their own homes; in Scotland, some 109,000 of both kinds were receiving relief (average of numbers being relieved on 15 January and 15 September 1912).[17]

The relief offered by charities and the Poor Law was inreasingly seen from the 1880s onwards as insufficient to tackle the mass poverty which was beginning to be revealed by social inquiries. The election of a reforming Liberal government in 1906 provided the opportunity to tackle mass poverty, whether induced by illness, accident or old age. Even before then, an Act of Parliament had been passed (in 1897) to compensate workmen for accidents; by 1906 its provisions had been extended to cover virtually all employments.

The first fruit of the Liberal reforms was the Old Age Pensions Act 1908, which provided non-contributory payments of 5s. per head (25p) per week for respectable persons aged over 69 years. Freed from the stigma of the Poor Law, and paid through the Post Office, it proved unexpectedly popular. By 1913 there were 737,000 recipients in Britain, drawing £9.1 million annually.[18]

The 1908 Act was a milestone in the evolution of social policy. It was followed by a more far-reaching innovation, which laid the foundation for the 'welfare state' after 1945. This was the National Insurance Act 1911, which provided health and unemployment insurance to large sections of the population. Part I of the Act provided health insurance to 13 million people – about seven-tenths of the entire employed population. The main benefits were a sickness payment of 10s. (50p) a week, and free medical treatment from a doctor;

17. Board of Trade, *Statistical Abstract for the United Kingdom . . . 1911 to 1925* (1927), Cmd 2849, Tables 54, 55.
18. Ibid., Table 50.

the greatest omission was that the insured's dependants were not covered. Part II provided unemployment insurance to those engaged in certain occupations of fluctuating employment – building, shipbuilding, mechanical engineering, iron-founding, vehicle construction and saw-milling, comprising together about 2.25 million men (about one-sixth of all industrial workers). The weekly benefit was 7s. (35p), payable for fifteen weeks only in any one year. Both schemes were financed by contributions from state, employer and employee. The use of the insurance principle meant that the schemes were devoid of the taint of private charity or public pauperism; benefit was available as of right to members of the schemes who had paid their subscriptions.[19]

Even before 1914, therefore, the state had intervened substantially to mitigate the economic difficulties of a large section of the poor. In addition, some action was taken to prevent wage exploitation. The Trade Boards Act 1909 specified minimum time and piece rates in such 'sweated' trades as ready-made tailoring, paper-box making, lace making and chain making. By 1913, over half a million workers were covered by the Act. In the coal-mines, a minimum wage (to be settled at district level) was introduced in 1912.[20]

There were other social reforms before 1914. Hours of work in shops were regulated by Acts of 1904 and 1911 (the latter gave the great boon of a half-holiday every week), and coal-miners had got an eight-hour day in 1908. A start had been made in the provision of public secondary education with the Education Act ('Balfour Act') 1902. This was now used as a basis for further social action, in the form of school meals and medical inspection of school-children (1906, 1907). By the First World War, state intervention had begun to transform people's lives in a positive way. Gladstonian Liberalism was dead, and Asquithian Liberalism (with more than a slight bow to the increasing number of Labour Party MPs) ruled the day.[21]

LABOUR AND LABOUR RELATIONS

The Labour Party had been called into being by a combination of socialist societies such as the Independent Labour Party, and the trade union movement, under the auspices of the Trades Union Congress. It began life under the name of the Labour Representation Committee in 1900, changing its name to the Labour Party in 1906. On the eve of the First World War it still depended heavily on the trade unions for funds and parliamentary candidates. The rise of trade unions was one of the most striking industrial and social changes in the prewar years. Between 1900 and 1913, the number of unionists rose from

19. M. Bruce, *The Coming of the Welfare State* (4th edn, Batsford 1968), pp. 198–9, 218–20.
20. Ibid., p. 196.
21. Ibid., pp. 195–6, 225–6; J.R. Hay, *The Origins of the Liberal Welfare Reforms 1906–1914* (Macmillan *SESH* 1975). Abbreviations of journal titles and collected works are listed on pp. 346–7.

2.0 million to 4.1 million. By far the largest union was the Miners' Federation (597,000), the next largest the Amalgamated Association of Weavers (112,000). Aside from mining and cotton, the most important industrial unions were the engineers (100,000), boilermakers (49,000 – mainly in shipbuilding) and carpenters (43,000). Unionism was also strong on the railways (95,000). It had made little headway among domestic servants, agricultural workers or shop assistants, or among the middle classes (except for teachers).[22]

A notable landmark in the history of labour relations was the Trade Disputes Act 1906. This, as well as easing the legal restrictions on picketing during trade disputes, in effect gave unions a legal status above that of other organisations. Henceforth, in an official trade dispute, an action in tort (i.e. for damages arising from a civil wrong) could not be brought against a union. This restored the legal position which had been cast in doubt by the Taff Vale case in 1900. Although this privileged position at law was recognised to be extraordinary, it was passed in recognition that without it unions would be at a disadvantage when considering whether to enter into a dispute.[23]

Industrial relations were profoundly affected by the rise of unions. Collective bargaining and district agreements became well established in many trades as a consequence, and attempts were increasingly made to obtain national agreements on wages and conditions of work. There also occurred in the remaining years before 1914 a period of heightened tension in industrial relations, a considerable increase in disputes, and a sharp rise in social antagonism. This had various causes, which are still debated. Something must be allowed for political and social factors, but underlying these was the fact that the long decline in prices since the early 1870s had come to an end in the late 1890s, and the general level of prices had been rising since then. Thereafter, for real earnings to be maintained, positive action on the part of organised labour was called for in order for wages to keep pace with rising prices. (There is no satisfactory index of wages for the pre-1914 period; these comments are based on the available indices.)[24]

The worst year for disputes was 1912, when over 40 million working days were lost, compared to the previous peak of 15 million in 1898. There were national strikes on the railways (1911) and in coal (1912). In 1913, a sudden outbreak of strikes in midlands engineering boosted union membership considerably.[25] Industrial relations became more embittered; 'blackleg' labour was freely imported by employers. The government tended to react with a show of force, as had been described by George Askwith, a labour conciliator, in the Belfast transport strike a few years earlier (1907):

22. Mitchell, *Statistics*, p. 137; H.A. Clegg, *A History of British Trade Unions since 1889; vol. II, 1911–1933* (Oxford, Clarendon 1985), pp. 2–3, App. Table 9.
23. Clegg, *Trade Unions*, pp. 296–7.
24. Summarised in Feinstein, *National Income*, Table 65. See also C.H. Feinstein, 'What Really Happened to Real Wages?: trends in wages, prices, and productivity in the United Kingdom, 1880–1913', *EcHR* XLIII (1990), pp. 352–3.
25. Mitchell, *Statistics*, p. 144; Phelps Brown, *Growth*, p. 331.

> guards at the railway stations, double sentries with loaded rifles at alternate lamp posts of the Royal Avenue, a very few lorries, with constabulary sitting on the bales and soldiers on either side, proceeding to guarded, congested but lifeless docks, and ten thousand soldiers in and about the city. There had been fights in the streets, charges of cavalry, the Riot Act read, shooting to disperse wrecking mobs, a few men and women killed and scores wounded, and the whole business of the city at a standstill.[26]

Although there were several industries in which the large factory or workplace predominated, workers' experience of the workplace was not merely that of the large factory. Factories themselves need not be large. Even in the mid-1930s, 92 per cent of factories employed under 100 persons, and 76 per cent employed 25 persons or fewer. The 'factory' workplace varied from the large shipyard, cotton mill, iron works or engineering shed, which might employ thousands, to the middling-sized collieries, glassworks and brickyards, or the smaller engineering works. And not everyone worked in a factory; it would be truer to say that, apart from in engineering and textiles, most people did *not* work in factories. There were farms, warehouses, retail shops, tailoring and dressmaking establishments, offices of all sizes, railway stations, docks, and bus and tram depots. The greatest of all non-factory occupations was domestic service, in which the usual workforce was one or two persons in private households.[27]

The hours worked before 1914 were lengthy by post-1945 standards. In manufacturing and building, weekly hours generally averaged fifty-four. In the largest industry, agriculture, they were conventionally fifty-eight, but could be longer.[28] In domestic service, they were seldom defined and varied considerably, being in practice from early in the morning to late at night, for either six or six and a half days a week. In shops, hours could be much longer. Over sixty hours was not uncommon, even after the introduction of a half-holiday; this was not everywhere granted, and shops seldom closed before 7 p.m. on a full day. For the population as a whole, the average weekly hours worked in 1913 were 56.4, having barely altered in the previous forty years. The only substantial exception to this was in coal-mines, where an eight-hour day had been conceded in 1908. In practice, most people in full-time work had to be at their place of work for at least ten hours a day between Monday and Friday, and for about five hours on Saturday.[29]

EDUCATION AND HOUSING

Education had expanded in the nineteenth century. The oldest in the labour force in 1914, say those born in the early 1850s, had had on average perhaps

26. Quoted in Phelps Brown, *Growth*, p. 164.
27. E. Hopkins, *The Rise and Decline of the English Working Classes 1918–1990: a social history* (Weidenfeld & Nicolson 1986), p. 3.
28. Department of Employment, *Labour Statistics*, Tables 1–6, 8, 36.
29. Phelps Brown, *Growth*, pp. 67–8; Mitchell, *Statistics*, p. 147.

about five years of schooling. Those born on the eve of the First World War had in prospect about nine years. Most of the education had been of the elementary sort; in 1914, most school-leavers left at 13. The 6.05 million pupils in elementary schools in England and Wales in 1914 contrasted with the mere 188,000 on the registers of secondary schools. The imbalance was less in Scotland, where 45,000 out of the total of 773,000 children attending school were in secondary schools.[30]

Few members of working-class households had received a secondary education before 1914. This movement really began in 1907 with the introduction of 'free places', whereby up to one-quarter of grammar school places were offered without fees. Private schools, both preparatory (up to age 12–13) and 'public' (13–18 years) accounted for a socially very influential group of pupils, whose numbers are uncertain. Higher education was largely the preserve of the upper and upper-middle classes, with a national student population of about 20,000, comprising only 1 per cent of the national age group in 1914.[31]

The great majority of the British people lived and worked in towns. The enormous expansion of nineteenth-century towns had owed much to the railways, as rail-borne bricks and Welsh slate supplemented the older vernacular stone buildings. The result was that the urban masses were housed, but at a price. The price was the reliance on the speculative builder, whose standards were not universally high. Thus a good deal of the housing stock was showing its age by the end of the century, as well as providing an urban landscape notable for its dreary monotony.

Even before 1914, British housing was deficient in quantity and quality. On the plausible assumption that, to avoid overcrowding, there should be a larger number of dwellings than families, since houses are immobile and there are at any time a certain number of vacant dwellings, it can be said that prewar housing in England and Wales suffered a certain degree of overcrowding, since there were approximately 7.691 million dwellings, but 7.943 million families, or 1.03 families to every dwelling. That the existence of more families than dwellings was undesired by the population concerned is suggested by an estimate that this ratio had been as high as 1.11 in 1861, and had fallen more or less steadily since then.[32] An alternative measure of overcrowding is provided by the proportion of families living at densities of more than two persons to a room, which in 1911 was approximately 5 per cent.[33] (The definitions of 'family' and 'dwelling' are those used in the population censuses (see Chapter 8). The 'rooms' enumerated at the census in both England and Wales and

30. R.C.O. Matthews, C.H. Feinstein and J.C. Odling-Smee, *British Economic Growth 1856–1973* (Oxford, Clarendon 1982), p. 573; Board of Trade, *Statistical Abstract* (1927), Tables 27, 31, 40.

31. G. Sutherland, 'Education', in F.M.L. Thompson (ed.), *The Cambridge Social History of Britain, 1750–1950* (*CSH*) (Cambridge UP 1990), vol. 3, pp. 152–7.

32. Census of Population, England and Wales 1951; *Housing Report* (1956), Table A; S. Glynn and J. Oxborrow, *Interwar Britain: a social and economic history* (Allen & Unwin 1976), p. 216.

33. Census of England and Wales 1931, *Housing Report* (1935), p. xv.

Scotland included bedrooms, living rooms and kitchens, but not bathrooms, kitchenettes, sculleries, closets, landings, lobbies, or any space used for business purposes.)[34]

Conditions in Scotland were very different, and much worse. Here, the predominant housing form in the large towns was the tenement, usually a three or four storeyed building in the form of a terrace, in which were contained 'houses', which were individual apartments, usually of one to three rooms. Detached houses proper were more usually found in middle-class suburbs and smaller burghs. Overcrowding was especially apparent in tenements, and overall it was much more severe than in England and Wales. In 1911, more than one-quarter of the Scottish population was overcrowded on the basis of more than three persons per room; on the English census standard of more than two persons to a room, the total overcrowded was 45.1 per cent of the population.[35]

There is little reliable evidence on the quality of housing before 1914, but it was apparent that many dwellings in Britain lacked basic amenities such as water closets. Few working-class dwellings had bathrooms, and electricity was a rarity (though gas was fairly common). Nor was it unusual to find dwellings without a piped water supply, especially in rural areas. These deficiencies became apparent with the more finely focused attention of housing reformers after 1918; the Census of Population did not inquire into these amenities until 1951.[36]

BRITAIN IN THE WORLD ECONOMY

Although the techniques of the Industrial Revolution spread fairly quickly to Europe and north America, British technology had still dominated the world in the middle of the nineteenth century. Estimates of the degree of this dominance are uncertain. The earliest fairly reliable estimate is for 1880, at which date Britain accounted for 41 per cent of all the world's manufactured exports.[37]

Although the relative position of Britain declined rapidly after 1880, it was still the largest exporter of manufactured goods in 1913, accounting for 30 per cent of the world total. The next largest exporter of manufactures in 1913 was Germany with 26 per cent; France and the USA accounted for only about 13 per cent each. In terms of total exports (not just manufactures), Britain was (also by a short head) still the world's biggest exporter, accounting for 14 per cent, closely followed by Germany and the USA (both 13 per cent).[38]

This relative decline reflected the spread of manufacturing to the rest of the industrialising world. In this sense, the relative decline of Britain was inevitable.

34. Ibid., p. vii; Census of Scotland 1931, vol. II, p. xlii.
35. M. Bowley, *Housing and the State 1919–1944* (Allen & Unwin 1945), App. I, p. 262.
36. (Sir) E.D. Simon, *The Anti-Slum Campaign* (Longmans, Green 1933), App. I.
37. S. Pollard, *Britain's Prime and Britain's Decline: the British economy 1870–1914* (Edward Arnold 1989), Table 1.17, p. 15.
38. H. Tyszinski, 'World Trade in Manufactured Commodities, 1899–1950', *ManS* XIX (1951), Table VIII; Mitchell, *Statistics*, p. 524; Maddison, *World Economy*, Table D1.

But it had been accompanied by a deterioration in relative economic efficiency. Output per head was growing more slowly in Britain than in other countries. If this trend continued, the other countries would become in time more efficient than Britain, and thus achieve higher standards of living (see Table 1.2).

Table 1.2 Comparative growth of UK Gross Domestic Product per man-year, 1873–1913 (annual percentage rates of growth)

	UK (%)	*USA* (%)	*Sweden* (%)	*France* (%)	*Germany* (%)	*Italy* (%)
1873–99	1.2	1.9	1.5	1.3	1.5	0.3
1899–1913	0.5	1.3	2.1	1.6	1.5	2.5

Source: Matthews *et al.*, *British Economic Growth*, Table 2.5

Even though Britain was still the largest exporter of manufactured goods in the world, its export structure was biased towards the old-fashioned and slowly growing trades. Britain was still over-reliant on the staple export sectors of the mid-nineteenth century (textiles, iron, steam engines, coal) and less dependent on the newer technologies of electricity and chemistry. The most obvious example was the great reliance on textiles, especially cottons. In 1909–13, textiles made up 33.3 per cent of all domestic exports (cotton goods being 25.0 per cent). The next largest exports were a long way behind: iron and steel (10.2), coal (9.2) and machinery (7.0). The more modern and faster growing trades of chemicals (4.3), electrical goods (0.8) and vehicles (including aircraft: 0.8) were comparatively small items.[39]

The comparatively slow rate of economic growth after the mid-nineteenth century, and the fact that British industrial exports were rather old-fashioned, has led to a large literature seeking to explain these aspects of British economic history. Contributors to this debate have come to varied conclusions. Some have judged the British performance to be good, given the difficult circumstances of being first to industrialise. Some have seen the relative decline as a symptom of a deeper cultural phenomenon, in which British entrepreneurs turned their back on money-making in order to enjoy a life of snobbish leisure, far from vulgar trade. It has also been suggested that the large annual inflow of interest, profits and dividends from previous foreign investment had bred a complacent, 'rentier' mentality among investors and business people alike. (See the Guide to Further Reading.)[40]

The debate is so far inconclusive. In mitigation of the comparatively weak growth record, it is pointed out that, since Britain had industrialised first, it was

39. Calculated from Mitchell, *Statistics*, pp. 453–83.
40. The best treatment of the debate is by Pollard, *Prime and Decline*.

only to be expected that later industrialisers would avoid Britain's mistakes in the process of catching up. It is also observed that Britain possessed in the long run few natural resources (except coal, and many excellent harbours) on the scale of the USA or Germany (or Russia). By 1913 supplies of iron ore were running out, other mineral mining had been undercut by foreign competition, and even British wool had been supplanted by Australasian imports.

The cultural pessimism has undoubtedly been overdone, on some very thin evidence. As Sidney Pollard remarks:

> There was no lack of commercial spirit in Britain: on the contrary, from the nobility downwards, all were keen to make money. In the services, such as banking, insurance or shipping, Britain led the world. Modern consumer industries, from daily newspapers for the masses to chocolates and cigarettes, had been pioneered in Britain. Even in some of the staples she dominated the world markets still. If there was a lack, it was in certain sectors only, a failure to reach particular decisions, in particular contexts, for particular reasons, not a failure in entrepreneurship as a weakness in British society.[41]

Overall, the concept of 'entrepreneurial failure' has to be treated with care. Ultimately, the test was the market; as long as the profits of domestic producers and exporters were maintained, it seems otiose to blame individuals or firms for not being able to foresee the course of history. Similar considerations apply to the British Empire; criticised by some historians as an irrational diversion of resources, it has been recently reinstated as a rational enterprise on commercial grounds, and as a place where investments earned a higher rate of return than at home.[42]

Even before the middle of the nineteenth century, Britain had a balance of *trade* deficit in goods. This deficit on 'visible' trade was more than offset by the surplus on 'invisible' trade (i.e. intangibles, chiefly the hiring out of ships, insurance and banking earnings, and interest and dividends from previous foreign investment), so that the current balance of *payments* was in surplus. After 1850, the deterioration of British competitiveness meant that the trade deficit grew larger, both absolutely and as a proportion of the national income. However, this was more than counterbalanced by the spectacular growth of invisible income. Estimating invisible earnings is a very inexact process. The best estimate of the Board of Trade was that net invisible income in 1913 (the prewar peak) was £339 million, consisting of investment income (£210 million), shipping hire (£94 million), financial services (£25 million) and other income (£10 million).[43]

The importance of investment income was paramount. However, estimates of investment income depend closely on estimates of the value of the stock of

41. Pollard, *Prime and Decline*, p. 265.
42. A. Offer, 'The British Empire, 1870–1914: a waste of money?', *EcHR* XLVI (1993), p. 221.
43. M.D.K.W. Foot, 'The Balance of Payments in the Interwar Period', *Bank of England Quarterly Bulletin* 12 (Sept. 1972), p. 358, Table C.

Table 1.3 UK current balance of payments, 1870–73 to 1910–13 (annual averages)

	Visible trade balance	*Invisible trade balance*	*Current balance of payments*[a]
	£million	*£million*	*£million*
1870–73	−22	+100	+78
1890–93	−82	+156	+75
1910–13	−87	+291	+204
As per cent of GDP (average GDP)	%	%	%
1870–73 (£1,070 million)	−2.0	+9.3	+7.3
1890–93 (£1,315 million)	−6.2	+11.9	+5.7
1910–13 (£2,102 million)	−4.1	+13.8	+9.7

Note: a Including bullion and specie movements
Source: B.R. Mitchell, *British Historical Statistics* (Cambridge UP 1988), pp. 836, 871–2

British capital previously invested abroad. This is conventionally stated as being some £3,700 million in 1913. This enormous sum was equivalent to about one-third of the entire stock of domestic capital, and almost two-thirds greater than the national income. This figure for overseas capital has been criticised; D.C.M. Platt preferred an estimate for overseas capital stock of £2,632 million of portfolio investment, and £500 million of direct investment, making £3,132 million in all. Yet even this sum would still have been gigantic in contemporary terms, and far outweighed the foreign investment of any other industrial nation. Most estimates suggest that the total stock of British foreign investment *c.*1913 was equal roughly to the combined value of the foreign investments of France, Germany and the USA.[44] (Platt also distrusted the balance of payments figures before 1913 (from Feinstein, *National Income*) used in the present book, describing their original source (A.H. Imlah) as 'weird'.)[45]

The effect of the enormous counterbalancing flow of invisible income was to ensure a substantial surplus on the balance of payments on current account, in spite of the trade deficit in goods (see Table 1.3 above).

Thus by the First World War, the deficit on trade in goods was equivalent to about 4 per cent of the national income. This deficit was offset by a surplus on invisible trade worth about 14 per cent of the national income; the net result was a balance of payments surplus worth about 10 per cent of the

44. D.C.M. Platt, *Britain's Overseas Investment on the Eve of the First World War: the use and abuse of numbers* (Macmillan 1986), pp. 60, 82–3; W. Woodruff, *Impact of Western Man: a study of Europe's role in the world economy 1750–1960* (Macmillan 1966), p. 150.
45. D.C.M. Platt, *Mickey Mouse Numbers in World History: the short view* (Macmillan 1989), p. 19.

national income. This long-term surplus on the current balance of payments resulted in the British economy accumulating funds from abroad. Had these funds remained within Britain, the British economy, as well as the international payments system, might have suffered. There would then have been a shortage of sterling in the world, making it difficult for foreign buyers to find the sterling needed to buy British goods. In addition, the sterling exchange rate might have risen and thus further reduced exports. These consequences were largely avoided by the tendency of British investors to export capital. In the few years before 1914, this increased sharply, to about £200 million a year, or about 10 per cent of the national income.

British overseas investment, unlike that of Germany, France or the USA, tended to avoid industrialising areas. Thus, of the £3,700 million estimated as the stock of British overseas investment in 1913 (*pace* Platt), £1,780 million was in the British Dominions or Empire (mainly India, Canada, Australia and South Africa). Of the rest, the largest amount (£755 million) was in the USA, and something over £300 million in Argentina. The favoured types of investments were the bonds of foreign governments and railway companies; industry, finance, utilities, etc. accounted for only 29 per cent of the total investment. (These are Paish's figures, which have been severely criticised by Platt, but he did not propose alternative estimates.)[46]

The structure of the British balance of trade and payments, and the actions of its overseas investors, played a critical role in the world economy, of which Britain was the functional centre in 1913. Most British imports were food and raw materials, and the overwhelming bulk of British exports were manufactured goods (see Table 1.4 below).

Although most other countries had raised import duties since the 1870s, Britain had stuck to free trade. Partly for this reason, it had remained the world's largest importer of food and raw materials, providing a market for the primary producing regions of the world. This trade also provided these regions with sterling with which they could buy British manufactured goods. In addition, Britain was by the end of the nineteenth century providing a growing

Table 1.4 UK foreign trade structure, 1909–13

Average values, 1909–13	*Imports* (*£million*)	(*%*)	*Exports*[a] (*£million*)	(*%*)
Food, drink and tobacco	269.4	38.7	28.7	6.4
Raw materials	257.4	36.9	57.5	12.9
Manufactured goods	169.8	24.4	359.7	80.7
Totals	696.6	100.0	445.9	100.0

Note: a Including re-exports
Source: Mitchell, *Statistics*, p. 457

46. Platt, *Mickey Mouse*, chs 5, 6.

market for manufactured goods from Europe and north America. As a result, it had large trade deficits with these regions. These deficits were to some extent offset by surpluses on trade with other regions, principally India; invisible earnings then brought the overall British payments into surplus.

The function of Britain in the world economy was thus to act as an open market, accept the concomitant trade deficit, and make up the difference with surpluses earned from third parties such as India, and from invisible income, largely the product of previous investment. Thus the original exporters found a market; British exporters found other markets; and the countries such as India which had import surpluses of British goods had their overall payments balanced by the import of British capital. The role of Britain allowed the development of a multilateral system, so that industrial countries could import large amounts of food and raw materials, without necessarily having to export manufactured goods directly to those primary producing regions where the food and raw materials came from.[47]

In addition to providing a market for the world, and being much the largest source of long-term capital, Britain played an essential role in operating the daily round of world trade. Sterling was the world's major trading currency, since its value was stable, and, Britain being on the gold standard, sterling could readily be exchanged for gold at any time and in any place at an official, fixed exchange rate. Thus sterling was 'as good as gold', which instilled confidence in its use among all who needed to enter the market for foreign exchange. A further medium of payment in sterling was provided by the bill of exchange (the 'bill on London') which was a species of international note of credit in sterling, drawn on a London bank or finance house. Thus London institutions provided much of the world's short-term finance, and found a profitable outlet for their surplus cash. Finally, the hiring-out of British ships, the insurance of cargoes by British insurers, and the provision of financial services by British banks, helped considerably in the efficient and smooth working of the international trading and financial system.

The pre-eminent role of sterling was due to its stability, and to the propensity of the British to funnel large quantities of it abroad, via the trade deficit and overseas investment, so that it was in plentiful supply. Sterling, together with the German mark and the French franc, also formed a significant proportion (about 20 per cent) of the world's official reserves (the rest was usually in gold).[48] Sterling was in such demand that it was used to settle, not merely transactions with Britain, but also transactions between some third-party countries, and even some transactions within these countries. In 1913, therefore, the British economy, as well as being the largest exporter of goods and of investment funds in the world, was the financier of the bulk of daily international trade, as well as supplying the means of exchange.

47. S.B. Saul, *Studies in British Overseas Trade 1870–1914* (Liverpool UP 1960), ch. III.

48. J. Foreman-Peck, *A History of the World Economy: international economic relations since 1850* (Hemel Hempstead, Wheatsheaf 1983), p. 169.

The international position of Britain, although still predominant, was under challenge. The rise of other industrial exporters, and the lagging rate of growth of British efficiency, meant that the British position was bound to be further eroded. Yet this was a very slow and long-term process, and there was no reason to suspect before 1914 that it would be an abrupt one. In the circumstances of the time, and given the particular nature of the British position, the interests of the economy were best served by peace. The worst event to happen would have been a major war, in which Britain was cut off from its markets, and had to diversify into military production, while its competitors made inroads into former British markets. This is exactly what happened after August 1914.

CONCLUSIONS

The early start in industrialisation enjoyed by Britain had enabled it to achieve a high standard of living, and predominance in the world economy by the mid-nineteenth century. Thereafter, its relative lead was reduced, and the British rate of economic growth was less than that of most comparable industrialising economies by 1914. However, industrialisation had set in motion enormous social changes, which continued to operate in British industrial society. The relative importance of agriculture declined, and that of industry and services rose. Socially, the British were now a nation of town-dwellers. There were substantial economic inequalities in society, although these were not new. After the turn of the century, these inequalities were to some extent mitigated by a greater degree of concern for the less well-off, but the majority of the population were vulnerable to economic fluctuations, and had few resources in case of unemployment.

CHAPTER 2

THE FIRST WORLD WAR

The First World War was a turning point in the history of the British economy. The enormous demands of the war, and its vast expenditure, transformed the economy during the war, and caused great economic and financial problems afterwards.

STRATEGY AND TECHNOLOGY

The impact of the war on the economy was due to the nature of the military conflict. The first military turning point was the deadlock on the western front, which had occurred by the end of 1914. The armies on both sides then settled down to the new immobile war of the trenches, which proved very costly of life, and in which neither side could gain more than a temporary advantage. Attempts at breaking this deadlock failed until the summer of 1918. Britain therefore pursued two tactics: continuing to supply the western front with enormous amounts of men and munitions (and imposing a blockade on Germany), while at the same time supplying its allies with money and munitions. The penultimate turning point came in 1917, with the collapse of Russia, the intensification of the German submarine campaign, and the entry of the USA into the war.

There were several reasons for the extraordinary economic and social impact of the war. Most importantly, it was the first major war in which most of the belligerents were substantially industrialised. This made the war enormously destructive of human life simply because of the destructive power of the new technologies which were employed. Second, the nineteenth century had been one of unparalleled population growth. In 1800, the five main belligerents of 1914 had had a combined population of 70 million; in 1910 this had risen five-fold, to 355 million. Thus enormous armies resulted. Third, real incomes had risen as industrialisation proceeded, so that the taxable capacity of nations, and thus their ability to finance the very expensive business of war, was much greater.

These developments ensured that the potential for waging war was vastly increased. That the potential was translated into reality was due to the technological changes accompanying industrialisation. These were seen most clearly in the steel, engineering and chemical industries, to which may be added the new technologies of radio and aircraft. The resultant new weapons were legion: rapid-fire rifles and machine guns, heavy artillery, armoured battleships, submarines, aircraft and poison gas. In addition, the technological changes gave an advantage to the defence: it proved very difficult and costly in human life for foot-soldiers to take positions fortified with barbed wire and defended by machine guns and high explosive shells. Thus the stalemate on the western front continued until 1918.[1]

The extraordinary vulnerability of the foot-soldier to the new concentrations of shell and shot resulted in appalling casualties. The first major British offensive of the war, at Neuve Chapelle in March 1915, lasted three days, and led to an advance of only 1,200 yards on a front 4,000 yards wide, at a cost of 13,000 British and 12,000 German casualties.[2] The awesome power of the shell barrage which preceded an infantry attack on the western front was described by the historian R.H. Tawney, who was an infantry sergeant at the time, about to 'go over the top':

> The sound was different, not only in magnitude, but in quality, from anything known to me. It was not a succession of explosions or a continuous roar; I, at least, never heard either a gun or a bursting shell. It was not a noise; it was a symphony. It did not move; it hung over us. It was as though the air were full of a vast and agonised passion, bursting now into groans and sighs, now into shrill screams and pitiful whimpers, shuddering beneath terrible blows, torn by unearthly whips, vibrating with the solemn pulse of enormous wings. . . . It seemed that one had only to lift one's eyes to be appalled by the writhing of the tormented element above one, that a hand raised ever so little above the level of the trench would be sucked away into a whirlpool revolving with cruel and incredible velocity over infinite depths.[3]

By the end of the war, 722,785 British servicemen had lost their lives.[4]

PRINCIPLES OF THE WAR ECONOMY

From the economic point of view, the essential problem was to move the necessary personnel and military supplies into the Armed Forces as quickly and as efficiently as possible. This, however, would create shortages in the supply of civilian goods and services. This in turn would create inflation, which would distort the allocation of economic resources. The best way to find the necessary real resources for the prosecution of the war, and at the same time avoid excessive inflation, would be to reduce civilian consumption substantially (unless imports could fill the gap).

This is in essence the problem of any war economy. However, things went

1. P.E. Dewey, 'The New Warfare and Economic Mobilization', in J. Turner (ed.), *Britain and the First World War* (Unwin Hyman 1988), pp. 70–3.
2. Ibid., p. 73.
3. R.H. Tawney, *The Attack* (Allen & Unwin 1953), p. 13.
4. J.M. Winter, *The Great War and the British People* (Macmillan 1985), pp. 72–4.

badly wrong after 1914. The reasons for this were that the military demands for men and *matériel* were unprecedently large, and that civilian consumption was not reduced far enough or quickly enough to make economic resources available for military use. The result was inflation of prices and shortages, both for civilians and the Armed Forces. The government did little to overcome these shortages in the first months of the war, preferring to rely on the uncoordinated free market to supply labour and *matériel.* Thus the economy settled into a pattern of resource allocation which proved very difficult to change later on.

There were also financial problems. The enormous cost of the war meant that most of it had to be paid for by raising loans from the public (chiefly in the UK), and the way in which this was done increased the inflationary pressure. The reliance on the USA for munitions, food and raw materials meant that the authorities ran short of US currency, and ran up large dollar debts. Lastly, the finance of the war left large debts (mainly internal, but some external) for future taxpayers to meet.

THE IMPACT OF RECRUITING

Alone of the major belligerents, Britain relied on a voluntary system to supply the majority of the recruits for the Armed Forces. The enormous early rush to the recruiting stations in the first months of the war could not be maintained, but even in 1915, as casualty figures mounted, recruiting was still on a large scale. It was only towards the end of 1915 that the authorities, fearing inadequate military personnel, moved towards conscription. A compromise was the 'Derby Scheme' of October 1915, designed to ascertain whether enough volunteers would be found to make conscription unnecessary. Those willing in future to serve were asked to 'attest' their willingness to do so. Not enough men having attested, conscription was introduced by the Military Service Act of January 1916, for single men aged 18–41. In May another Military Service Act extended it to married men. However, men could still volunteer for the Forces, even after conscription had been introduced.[5] The Army took most of the military personnel, and almost exactly half of its recruits came in the period of voluntary enlistment. Of the total wartime enlistments for the Army of 4.97 million, 2.47 million had enlisted before the end of 1915. The other Services took comparatively few men. Over the whole period of the war, the Navy took 407,000, and the Royal Flying Corps (which later became the Royal Air Force) took 293,000.[6]

There were several sources which counteracted the loss of labour to the Forces. Emigration, which had been running at something over 200,000 persons a year in 1912–14, effectively ceased when the war began. (There is no means of satisfactorily defining an emigrant. The estimate of 200,000 persons a year is a rough one. One study found 573,816 UK citizens migrating to

5. Ibid., pp. 28–40.
6. War Office, *Statistics of the Military Effort of the British Empire, 1914–1920* (HMSO 1922), p. 364.

non-European countries in 1912–14; emigration to Europe was negligible.)[7] After an initial period of trade dislocation, the war brought full employment, and older persons came out of retirement. There were also by the end of the war a large number of men (*c*.0.7 million) who had returned to civilian life from the Forces. Finally, a large contribution was made by the increased employment of women. Between July 1914 and July 1918, there was an increase of 4.6 million men in the Forces. This was counteracted by an extra 2.1 million men and 1.6 million women drawn into civilian industries. Most of the extra male labour (about 1.5 million) went into manufacturing (chiefly munitions), but the extra female labour was divided almost equally between the manufacturing and the service sector. When the Forces are added in, the total national labour force was substantially larger (by about 3.7 million) by 1918.[8]

STIMULATED AND CONTRACTED INDUSTRIES

The part of the economy which received the greatest stimulus from the war was that serving military needs. Commonly labelled 'munitions', it was a protean assemblage of industries, centred on engineering, with important contributions from metal production, chemicals, and textiles, leather and others. The metal and chemical industries had a combined labour force of 2,003,000 in July 1914, but this had risen to 2,684,000 in July 1918. In the government-controlled sector (dockyards, arsenals, National Factories), employment rose from 77,000 to 329,000 in the same period.[9]

Other industries almost always contracted. Coal-mining was hit early on by the reduction in exports, and heavy recruiting. In 1915 it received official protection from recruiting, but its labour force remained below the prewar level. Cotton textiles was also hit by the decline in exports; in the middle of the war, it was also the subject of concern in view of its dependence on dollar imports of raw cotton. Consequently, the government established a Cotton Control Board to ration out the available raw cotton and conserve foreign exchange. Industries which had little protection against recruiting declined; a notable casualty was building, whose labour force fell from 920,000 to 438,000. Woollens also declined, due to the decline in exports and difficulties in importing raw wool. Recruiting was unchecked in agriculture until it received protection from the military in 1917, except that the older average age of farm labourers gave some natural protection. Finally, there was a range of industries which catered more for civilian than military demand, and which accordingly received little protection from recruiting; these were mainly the service sectors

7. N.H. Carrier and J.R. Jeffery, *External Migration: a study of the available statistics* (1953), p. 91.
8. War Office, *Statistics*, p. 364; N.B. Dearle, *The Labour Cost of the War to Britain* (1940), Table IV; Board of Trade, *Report on the State of Employment in All Occupations in the United Kingdom in July 1918* (unpublished), p. 8; A.W. Kirkaldy, *Industry and Finance* (2nd edn, 1920), Table I.
9. Board of Trade, *State of Employment*; Kirkaldy, *Industry and Finance*, Table I.

such as finance and commerce, and such manufacturing industries as paper, food and clothing.[10]

Other sectors replaced their recruits with women, and carried on. In commerce, the 1,225,000 men and 496,000 women of July 1914 had become 746,000 men and 880,000 women by July 1918. Women were also increasingly seen in banking, finance and transport (especially railways and local authority trams, where female employment rose from 12,000 to 66,000, and from 1,000 to 37,000 respectively). A notable feature of the use of women was that employers in the service trades found it comparatively easy to replace men with women, while male opposition (open or covert) in manufacturing made substitution less easy.[11]

THE ROLE OF GOVERNMENT

In spite of the general predisposition of the government to leave private enterprise to supply the needs of the war economy, there were some early official interventions. The most notable was the government's assumption of control of the railways (although the companies were not nationalised) the day after war was declared. In exchange for carrying troops and supplies free of charge, the companies were guaranteed their income of 1913 (a good year). The government also, mindful that two-thirds of the prewar UK sugar supply had come from the enemy countries' sugar-beet producers, set up a Royal Commission on Sugar Supplies to explore alternative sources of supply. Action was also taken to secure a reserve of wheat, to control the Indian grain crop, and to ensure the security of Army contracts for imported meat. For the time being, these were the only positive interventions. Although the government acquired extensive powers of industrial direction and requisitioning under the Defence of the Realm Act of March 1915, they remained for the time being in reserve.[12]

Reliance on private enterprise survived a little longer in munitions. Prior to the formation of the Ministry of Munitions in May 1915, the War Office was distributing contracts to some 2,500–3,000 firms in Britain, and seeking suppliers in north America. But both in Britain and overseas, shortages of labour (partly due to recruiting), delays in machinery deliveries, and trade union restrictions were seriously impeding production.[13]

Bottlenecks in production appeared as soon as the war began. Government factories such as the Royal Arsenals could not meet the demand, and neither could the private manufacturers. Deficiencies in the War Office system

10. P.E. Dewey, 'Military Recruiting and the British Labour Force during the First World War', *HJ* 27 (1984), Table 2.

11. Kirkaldy, *Industry and Finance*, Table I; G. Braybon, *Women Workers in the First World War* (Routledge 1989), ch. 3.

12. H.J. Dyos and D.H. Aldcroft, *British Transport: an economic survey from the seventeenth century to the twentieth* (Pelican 1974), pp. 297–8; (Sir) W.H. Beveridge, *British Food Control* (Oxford UP 1928), pp. 5–15.

13. War Office, *Statistics*, pp. 467–70.

of tendering made things worse; when war broke out, the Army Contracts Department consisted of only fifty-six officials and clerks.[14] The final political straw was the great 'shell scandal' of the spring of 1915, when allegations of shortages and poor quality in the munitions supplied to the Army in France were made. The result was the establishment in May of the Ministry of Munitions, the first Minister being David Lloyd George. By the end of the war, the Ministry managed 250 government factories and supervised the operations of 20,000 'controlled' establishments; it had spent a total of £2,000 million by March 1919.[15]

The intervention in munitions, although substantial, was not followed by a great extension of state control elsewhere (except for conscription). Large-scale state intervention did not occur until the middle of the war. By that time, there were many indications that the still relatively unrestricted private markets were inadequate to meet military needs, and still supply essential civilian requirements. The most telling evidence was the rise in the cost of living, especially food. The Board of Trade's (working-class) cost of living index had risen to 145 by July 1916 (July 1914 = 100); the food index number alone was 161. By the end of the year, general wholesale prices were 90 per cent above those of the first half of 1914.[16]

The rise in price of imports was particularly acute. Shortage of shipping had driven average tramp freight rates in 1916 to 436 per cent above those of 1913. The pound/dollar exchange rate had fallen, and the government had had to support it since September 1915. The final pressure on prices was the expansion of purchasing power, stimulated by full employment and by the government's weak financial policy.[17]

Political discontent with the direction of the war led to a change of government in December 1916, Asquith being replaced as prime minister by Lloyd George. The change in government resulted in a plethora of new ministries and government agencies. The most notable in their impact on popular life were the Ministries of Shipping and Food, although those of Labour and Pensions were also significant. The Department of National Service became a ministry and acquired a more effectual chief, Sir Auckland Geddes. The last important initiative was the establishment of a Food Production Department (nominally a sub-department of the Board of Agriculture, but in effect independent), with the aim of expanding home food production.

These interventions materially expanded the role of government in the

14. E.M.H. Lloyd, *Experiments in State Control at the War Office and Ministry of Food* (Oxford UP 1924), pp. 15–19.
15. S. Pollard, *The Development of the British Economy 1914–1990* (Edward Arnold 1992), p. 17.
16. A.L. Bowley, *Prices and Wages in the United Kingdom, 1914–1920* (Oxford, Clarendon 1921), pp. 9, 106.
17. Freight rates from B.R. Mitchell, *British Historical Statistics* (Cambridge UP 1988), p. 540; E.V. Morgan, *Studies in British Financial Policy, 1914–25* (Macmillan 1952), pp. 40–3.

economy. By the end of the war, as well as controlling military enlistment, the output of munitions, and civilian labour doing war work, it controlled all shipping, rail and canal transport; was responsible for importing about 90 per cent of all imports; marketed about 80 per cent of all food consumed at home; rationed all the major foods (except bread and vegetables), and controlled the prices of most foods.

THE FINANCE OF THE WAR

We don't want to fight, but by jingo, if we do,
We've got the ships, we've got the men,
And got the money, too.[18]

As in the raising of men and munitions for the Armed Forces, the raising of the necessary money to pay for the war was a long saga of government belatedly realising the unparalleled enormity of the task. In all three cases, the lapse of time before effective action was taken led to considerable dislocation.

The war upset completely the pattern of public finance. Before it, only about one-eighth of the national income was spent by government (central and local combined). With the outbreak of war it rose rapidly, to account for more than half the national income in the last three years of the war. Even in 1919, more than half the national income was still being spent by the government (Table 2.1 below).

The growth in war expenditure was carried out by central government. This expenditure, and its main components, is indicated in Table 2.2 opposite.

To find the enormous sums of money required, the government had the yield of taxes (indirect and direct), and the possibility of selling government bonds

Table 2.1 Government expenditure as per cent of UK national income, 1913–19

	Government expenditure (£million)	*Gross National Product (£million)*	*Government spending as % of GNP (%)*
1913	302	2,333	12.9
1914	318	2,362	13.5
1915	690	2,682	25.7
1916	1,690	3,186	53.0
1917	2,331	3,960	58.9
1918	2,839	4,790	59.3
1919	2,744	5,023	54.6

Source: B.R. Mitchell, *British Historical Statistics* (Cambridge UP 1988), pp. 590, 829, 610, 613

18. British music-hall song (by G.W. Hunt) popular during the Russo-Turkish War 1877–78.

Table 2.2 Central government war expenditure, 1914–15 to 1918–19 (£million)[a]

	1914–15	*1915–16*	*1916–17*	*1917–18*	*1918–19*
Fighting services	361	755	854	1,052	1,415
Munitions	b	247	559	715	562
Debt service	23	60	127	190	270
Overseas loans[c]	52	316	545	488	265
Shipping	—	—	8	195	285
War pensions	—	—	2	24	50
Total expenditure	436	1,377	2,096	2,665	2,848

Notes: a Sub-totals may not add up to total due to rounding
b Expenditure under 'fighting services' in 1914–15
c To Dominions and Allies

Source: (Sir) B. Mallett and C.O. George, *British Budgets, Second Series, 1913–14 to 1920–21* (Macmillan 1929), App. Table III

to the public (home or foreign). Selling bonds (i.e. increasing the National Debt) would have the added political advantage of not requiring the war to be paid for by the taxpayer as it occurred, but of shifting the burden onto the post-war taxpayer.

The taxation system proved inadequate during the war. This was partly due to the fact that, although a diminishing proportion before the war, indirect taxes still accounted for a fairly large part of the prewar revenue, and it was difficult practically and politically to raise them very rapidly. In 1913–14, indirect taxes yielded £75.3 million – mainly the customs duty on tobacco (£18.3 million), and the excise duties on spirits and beer (£19.5 million and £13.6 million). Direct taxes yielded £88 million, mainly in income tax (£43.9 million) and estate duty (£21.6 million). Thus 54 per cent of total revenue came from direct, and 46 per cent from indirect taxes.[19]

Clearly there were limits to the rate at which either indirect or direct taxes could be raised; the hope of covering more than a minor part of the total cost of the war by taxation was never very strong. Indirect taxation could be raised, but faced the problem of elasticity of demand if pressed too far on articles of popular consumption. In any case, the supply of some of these was restricted in the latter part of the war. Direct taxation (mainly income tax) had more potential, since full employment and the rise in the national income made it easier to bear. There was also the possibility of taxing war profits.

In the event, it was the direct taxes which proved much more productive, so that the balance swung sharply towards them. In the financial year 1918–19, direct taxes accounted for 79.5 per cent of total taxation revenue.

19. Board of Trade, *Statistical Abstract of the United Kingdom, 1905–1919* (1921), pp. 8–9; (Sir) B. Mallett and C.O. George, *British Budgets, Second Series, 1913–14 to 1920–21* (Macmillan 1929), App. Table I.

By then, a large amount of direct taxation (£284 million) was being contributed by taxation of war profits, in the form of the Excess Profits Duty (EPD). This replaced the first war profits tax, the 'Munitions Levy', which had been imposed on profits made in controlled establishments after July 1915. Its successor, the EPD, had begun in 1915 at 50 per cent of profits above prewar levels. By the end of the war it had risen to 80 per cent. Other forms of direct tax also rose considerably. The standard rate of income tax rose from 1s. 2d. in 1913–14 to 6s. in 1918–19, and the number of income tax payers rose from 1.13 million to 3.55 million. Tax rates also became much more sharply progressive, and discriminatory against 'unearned' (now renamed 'investment') income.[20]

Even with the enormous rise in tax yield, there was still a large gap between revenue and expenditure. In the financial years 1913/14 to 1918/19, Exchequer receipts totalled £2,733 million, but public expenditure totalled £9,647 million. Thus current taxation paid for only about 28 per cent of expenditure. This, though not large, was a better performance than that of France or Germany in 1914–18, or of the British government in 1793–1815. The total deficit was £6,914 million, and this amount had to be borrowed in the course of the war by means of the government selling bonds. The first big War Loan (£350 million) came in November 1914. By the end of March 1919, the National Debt, which had stood at £650 million five years earlier, was £6,142 million. In addition to this internal debt, there was the debt owed abroad which stood at £1,241 million, of which £840 million was owed to the United States government, £113 million to allied governments, and £92 million to the Canadian government. Some relief was to be had from the repayment of loans by former Dominions and allies, but there had been large losses here also. By the end of March 1919, £1,568 million had been advanced to allies; the largest single amount (£568 million) had gone to Russia, and was not retrieved. The Russian debt got bigger after the war. Even in 1926, former allies still owed the UK government £1,534 million, of which the Russian share was £794 million.[21]

In terms of raising the necessary money, financial policy was successful. However, it was an expensive achievement. The government's keenness to attract the savings of the public, coupled with, from 1916 onwards, the need to attract foreign money and thus underpin the exchange rate, meant that the government offered higher interest rates than on the prewar debt. Subscribers were offered favourable terms. While the interest rates offered on most of the issues had a face value of between 3.5 and 5 per cent, issues at less than par or free of income tax raised the effective interest rates. The upshot was that, while the prewar debt had yielded about 3.25 per cent to its holders, the National Debt in 1918–19 paid about 4.65 per cent interest. When this was applied to the enormously swollen total of the National Debt, the result was

20. Mallett and George, *British Budgets*, Tables V, VIII, XX, pp. 324–5, 329–32. See also Committee on National Debt and Taxation ('Colwyn Committee'), *Report* (1927), Cmd 2800, App. XIII.

21. Morgan, *Studies*, pp. 100–5, Tables 10, 48; Board of Trade, *Statistical Abstract*, Table 7; Colwyn Committee, *Report*, para. 149.

to create a large burden of debt service which was to haunt Chancellors of the Exchequer throughout the interwar period.[22]

PRICES, CIVILIAN SUPPLIES AND LIVING STANDARDS

Apart from the expense of the fund-raising, the other major disadvantage of the wartime financial regime was that it was highly inflationary. There seems no doubt that the size of the government deficit was the greatest force making for inflation, and that taxation might have been set much higher than it was without discouraging the necessary effort on the part of entrepreneurs and the workforce.[23] The failure to reduce the deficit is a little puzzling. Partly it was a technical matter; a substantial reform of the income tax system would have been necessary, and wartime was not a propitious time for this. There was also a notable lack of political desire for higher taxation, and a lack of understanding among ministers and the public of the mechanisms involved. It was felt that merely raising lots of money would in some vague way win the war:

> The basic fact that if the Government was to purchase more of the real product of the nation, then private citizens must purchase less, was hardly ever allowed to emerge from the sea of verbiage.[24]

The inflation of the war and early postwar years was by far the greatest experienced since the wars of 1793–1815, and was quite outside the pre-1914 experience. Neither inflation nor deflation had been unknown before 1914, but most people's experience of price changes in the long run had been of the order of 1 or 2 per cent a year. In the four years of the war, the level of retail prices more than doubled. In 1918 the average level of the Board of Trade (working-class) cost of living index was 203 (July 1914 = 100). Inflation continued after the war, until the breaking of the boom in late 1920; the peak in the cost of living index came in November 1920, at 276. Wholesale prices had risen even more rapidly in these six years. As far as consumers were concerned, retail prices in 1914–20 were rising by about 25–30 per cent a year.[25]

To some extent, indices of price changes are misleading, as the national pattern of consumption changed during the war. Apart from the relative strength of military and civilian demand for a commodity or a service, relative prices were affected by the degree of prewar reliance on imports, since wartime importing was difficult and expensive. The degree to which the labour force in a particular industry was attracted away from civilian production into the Forces or munitions also affected the supply of that particular good or service, and thus its price. Finally, the intervention of the government, either to boost or curtail supplies to civilians, could have an effect.

It has been calculated that the real volume of consumers' spending on

22. Morgan, *Studies*, pp. 106–15.
23. Mallet and George, *British Budgets*, p. 381.
24. Morgan, *Studies*, p. 95.
25. Bowley, *Prices and Wages*, pp. 70–1.

goods and services fell by 17 per cent between 1914 and 1918. In this sense, it can be said that the average standard of living (defined as the provision of a given amount and mixture of goods and services per head) fell by the same amount. The largest fall was in the consumption of drink and tobacco (53 per cent), followed by clothing, 'other services' (24 per cent) and durable household goods (23 per cent). Real expenditure on food fell also, but by only 11 per cent.[26]

However, this decline was not shared equally between the social classes. A powerful redistributive force was the rise in wartime taxation. Even though some working-class earners now came into the meshes of the income tax net, the taxation system became for the first time sharply progressive. In addition, the existence of full employment and the high demand for labour meant that real *earnings* probably kept pace with inflation (although weekly wage *rates* lagged behind). Finally, the high demand for labour meant that the wages of unskilled labour rose faster than those of skilled labour. Thus the two great causes of poverty before the war – low wages and unemployment – were temporarily laid aside. This was the personal experience of the young Robert Roberts, whose parents kept a grocer's shop in a slum quarter of Salford [Manchester]:

> One of our customers, wife of a former foundry labourer, both making big money now on munitions, airily enquired one Christmas time as to when we were going to stock 'summat worth chewing'.
>
> 'Such as what?', asked my father, sour-faced.
>
> 'Tins o' lobster!' she suggested, 'or them big jars o' pickled gherkins!'
>
> Furious, the old man damned her from the shop. 'Before the war,' he fumed, 'that one was grateful for a bit o' bread and scrape!'[27]

Although evidence is lacking, it is probable that the real living standards of the poorer sections of the community rose during the war.[28]

In one respect, however, there was a marked deterioration in the standard of living. The quality and sufficiency of the housing stock deteriorated considerably. New housebuilding almost ceased when the war began, and the remaining stock suffered from lack of maintenance. In addition, the large geographical shifts of wartime workers (especially into such industrial centres as the Clyde valley, Carlisle and Gretna, and Woolwich) promoted overcrowding. Early and violent discontent on Clydeside resulted in a national 'rent freeze' in the form of the Rent and Mortgage Interest (War Restrictions) Act 1915, which would have enormous consequences later. But it did little to help the stock of housing, which at the end of the war was insufficient in quantity and quality.

26. C.H. Feinstein, *National Income, Expenditure and Output of the United Kingdom, 1855–1965* (Cambridge UP 1972), Tables 24, 25.
27. R. Roberts, *The Classic Slum: Salford life in the first quarter of the century* (Manchester UP 1971), p. 160.
28. Winter, *Great War*, pp. 230–40.

POPULATION, FERTILITY, FAMILY, MIGRATION

The First World War was a watershed in British population history. Although the rate of growth of population had already slowed down before the war, it was still high by historical standards. The war saw a sharp deceleration. Between 1871 and 1881 the British population had grown by 13.9 per cent, and in 1901–11 it grew by 10.3 per cent. The increase in 1911–21 was only 4.7 per cent, and this rate of growth remained almost unchanged until 1939.

In trying to find the reasons for this sharp slowdown, it is tempting to speculate about a 'lost generation', and to conclude that the enormous number of war deaths in 1914–18 deprived the country of the young, fit males who might otherwise have married and engendered children. The losses were certainly horrifyingly large. The most recent estimate, by J.M. Winter, is of 722,785 British servicemen dying in the war, amounting to about 6.3 per cent of all UK male adults (aged 15–49).[29]

Yet the lack of eligible males was not the only, or even the main, reason for the slowing of population growth. It was also the case that the war accelerated the prewar decline in fertility. Both fertility and mortality had been declining since the late nineteenth century. But during the war, while civilian death rates ceased to fall, birth rates continued to decline (Table 2.3 below).

Wartime death rates were somewhat higher than prewar, especially in 1918, due to the influenza epidemic of that year. But the birth rate fell sharply in wartime, and, after a brief flowering at the end of the war, resumed its rapid

Table 2.3 Birth and death rates, England and Wales, 1900–30[a]

	Birth rate	*Death rate*[b]
1900	28.7	18.2
1910	25.1	13.5
1914	23.8	14.0
1915	21.9	15.7
1916	20.9	14.3
1917	17.8	14.2
1918	17.7	17.3
1920	25.5	12.4
1930	16.3	11.4

Notes: a All rates are per 1,000 of the population
b Civilian deaths only
Source: Mitchell, *Statistics*, pp. 43, 58–9

29. Ibid., pp. 72–4.

long-term decline. Between 1910 and 1930, birth rates declined relatively much more than death rates.

These changes apart, the greatest demographic consequence of the war was to curtail emigration. In 1911–13 (admittedly a peak period), the net loss of population amounted to between 200,000 and 240,000 people annually. In the war, this became a trickle, partly because of a big inflow early on, as émigrés came back to join the Forces, and partly because the outflow died away. Although net emigration resumed after the war, it was only at about half the level of pre-1914.[30]

Although marriage rates remained similar both before and after the war, in one respect the war undermined married life, in that it saw a sharp rise in the rate of divorce. In 1913, there were 827 divorce and nullity decrees in Britain; in 1918, there were 1,596. The average rate in the 1920s was about 3,000; in the 1930s, about 5,000. Some of this rise was undoubtedly due to wartime strains (including over-hasty marriages). The longer-run reasons included legal changes in 1914 which made divorce more affordable for the working class. Even so, divorce remained highly exceptional for most married couples even on the eve of the Second World War.[31]

The wider effects of the war on the position of women in society are still debated. Traditionally, it was held that it represented a great liberation from the servitude of home and children. More recently, historians have moved away from this theme, emphasising instead the reluctance with which employers took women on during the war, and the completeness with which they were eased out of the industrial labour force afterwards.[32] On a political level, the granting of the parliamentary vote in 1918 to women (over 29 years of age) was symbolic of greater equality. On a daily level, the sudden postwar change in women's fashion, to shorter skirts and dresses, lighter fabrics (for both inner and outer wear) and shorter hairstyles, was both a symbol of modernity and a psychologically rewarding push for physical freedom. There was certainly increasing social freedom to use contraception (or, rather, persuade one's sexual partner to do so). On a more mundane level, women took up cigarette smoking, although those bold enough to smoke in the street often encountered social disapproval.

Whether women were now freer in a sexual sense is also debatable. While there appeared to be a more liberal social attitude to female sexual activity, the attitudes of both women and men remained hedged about by ignorance, shame and fear. The letters received by Dr Marie Stopes, the founder of the first birth control clinics, are eloquent evidence of the public's desperate search for sexual education, and, especially, sound and practical advice on contraceptive methods.[33] It is also doubtful if the changes in the occupational structure of the

30. Ibid., pp. 266–7.
31. Ibid., pp. 263–4.
32. Braybon, *Women Workers.*
33. J. Weeks, *Sex, Politics and Society: the regulation of sexuality since 1800* (1981); S. Humphries, *A Secret World of Sex* (1991); R. Hall, *Dear Dr. Stopes: sex in the 1920s* (André Deutsch 1978).

labour force were such as to promote greater female equality. The end of the war saw few long-term gains for women in newer fields of employment, except for office work. That apart, the twin occupations of domestic service and textiles reasserted their dominance of the female labour market between the wars. The only major difference was that a smaller proportion of domestic servants now 'lived in', and thus there was a greater degree of personal freedom.[34]

Nor did the high demand for labour, and consequent high female earnings, outlast the war. Female rates of pay continued to be much below those of males doing similar work in the interwar period. It is hard to escape the conclusion that the First World War was rather a brief experience of women being in high demand, and that it did not lead to any fundamental change in the economic position of women, although certain social and political freedoms were gained.[35]

HEALTH AND SOCIAL WELFARE

There is usually a presumption that wars are inimical to the health of civilian populations. Many reasons may be adduced for this; shortages of food and medical attention are the obvious ones. It is difficult to measure the truth of this presupposition; there are no ready-made indicators of the overall degree of 'health' of a population. In their absence, much reliance has to be placed on mortality statistics.

The war checked the secular decline in mortality rates. They even rose, briefly, in 1918 (due mainly to the influenza epidemic). Yet this may be misleading; the experience of different age groups varied. For males, death rates rose for those aged 5–44 and 65+; rates for other ages fell. For females, the rises were in the age groups 10–24 and 75+. But between 1913 and 1917 (1918 is omitted, due to the influenza epidemic), death rates for children aged 0–4 (both male and female) fell sharply; from 33.3 to 26.3 per 1,000 in the case of females, and from 40.3 to 31.8 (males). Also striking was the fall in the infant (i.e. children up to 1 year old) mortality rate, from 108 to 96 per 1,000 (all figures are for England and Wales). Scottish demographic trends were similar to those of England and Wales, except that Scotland showed less reduction in infant mortality during the war.[36]

There is thus a prima facie case that the health of those most at risk (usually viewed as a most sensitive indicator of changing general social conditions) improved. It has also been noted that deaths due to diarrhoeal diseases, which afflict the very young and old, declined continually throughout the war,

34. D. Gittins, *Fair Sex: family size and structure, 1900–39* (Hutchinson 1982), p. 45.
35. Braybon, *Women Workers*; G. Braybon and P. Summerfield, *Out of the Cage; women's experiences in two world wars* (Pandora 1987); G. Anderson, *The White-Blouse Revolution; female office workers since 1870* (Manchester UP 1988); Humphries, *Secret World*; Gittins, *Fair Sex*; D. Thom, 'Women and Work in Wartime Britain', in R. Wall and J. Winter (eds), *The Upheaval of War: family, work, and welfare in Europe, 1914–1918* (Cambridge UP 1988), esp. p. 317.
36. Mitchell, *Statistics*, pp. 58–9, 61.

indicating improved social, and perhaps sanitational and nutritional, conditions. In addition, mortality due to the complications of childbearing declined. On the other hand, the death rate due to respiratory disease (chiefly tuberculosis) rose, presumably due to the increased overcrowding. Oddly, the absence of doctors on military service seems to have had little effect on the health of the civilian population (although it may have assisted the recorded rise in tuberculosis). There is thus strong evidence that the health of the nation, or at least the poorer sections of it, was actually improving during the war, although this has been disputed.[37]

If the health of the nation in general was at least not deteriorating, some credit must be given to the maintenance of food supplies. For the first half of the war, in spite of food prices rising faster than the general price level, there is little evidence of any material change in the composition of the average diet, with the exception of a shortage of sugar. The calories supplied daily per average 'man' declined only slightly, from 3,442 in 1909–13 to 3,418 in 1916.[38] (The concept of an average 'man' is of the average food consumer, when allowance has been made for the different food consumption levels of different groups in the population.)

In January 1917, fear at the renewed German submarine campaign led to a change of policy. A ploughing-up campaign increased the supply of wheat and potatoes grown at home. By 1918, the area of tillage in Britain was 12.36 million acres, having been 10.46 million in 1909–13 – a rise of 18 per cent. The supply of meat and milk accordingly declined, as pasture was ploughed. To some extent the meat supply was made up in 1918 by imports of bacon and ham from the USA. In 1918 also, food supplies were made to go further by the rationing of all major foods (except bread and vegetables). The proportion of the food supply produced within the UK rose, from 41 per cent of all the calories consumed in 1909–13, to 47 per cent in 1918.[39]

The overall result was a loss of some consumer satisfaction, as cereals and potatoes replaced meat, but there is no evidence that the supply of energy in the national diet was insufficient. The calories supplied per 'man' per day in the UK, having been 3,418 in 1916, fell, but only slightly, to 3,358 in 1918. There were enough calories to go round, and the composition of the national diet did not deteriorate so as to threaten the intake of vitamins. Rationing may actually have improved the diet of the poorest sections of the community, who before the war did not earn sufficient to purchase an adequate diet. In 1918, an official inquiry into working-class living standards collected some 1,300 working-class family budgets, which showed that between 1914 and 1918 the average 'man' in these families experienced a reduction in calorie intake from 3,130 to 3,040, the extra cereals and potatoes being insufficient to compensate for

37. Winter, *Great War*, Table 4.3, pp. 125, 132–5, ch. 5 generally; L. Bryder, 'The First World War: healthy or hungry?', *HWJ* 24 (autumn 1987).
38. Beveridge, *Food Control*, Tables X, XXI.
39. P.E. Dewey, *British Agriculture in the First World War* (Routledge 1989), pp. 201, 227.

the loss of calories due to the loss of sugar. This was a slight, if material, loss, which does not seem to have impaired the physical health of the population.[40]

Social policy also had some role to play in the war. The government encouraged local authorities to improve their services for mothers and babies, and clinics and health visitors proliferated. But it was not until the passing of the Maternity and Child Welfare Act 1918 that local authorities were obliged to establish committees to deal with the subject – and even then they were not compelled to provide specific services. On the other hand, elderly people suffered – as noted, their death rates rose – and they were removed from hospitals and institutions to make way for wounded soldiers. But the treatment of venereal disease improved with new drugs, and although there was no cure for tuberculosis, sufferers who were insured were given free treatment.

There were other indications of more widely diffused prosperity, as the demand for labour created full employment. There was a sharp drop in pauperism. In 1913, the mean number of those receiving institutional relief in England and Wales was 265,410, with 411,575 receiving out-relief. A sharp fall by 1918 reduced these to 199,422 and 303,431 respectively; the Scottish figures were 108,145 and 86,757.[41]

In all, there is a strong probability that the sum of civilian social welfare rose during the war. This was chiefly due to the pressure of the labour market, which acted to benefit the less well-off (and especially the very poor). The losers were the middle and upper classes, who had to pay higher taxes, and lost some of their prewar luxuries.

LABOUR AND LABOUR ORGANISATION

The position of labour changed radically during the war. After an initial brief rise in unemployment due to the disruption of foreign trade, full employment was the rule. The average annual unemployment rate among trade unionists had been 4.1 per cent in 1909–13 and was only 1.2 per cent in 1914–18.[42]

The other main agent of change was the intervention of government in industrial organisation and management. This was especially the case in engineering and coal-mining. In both cases, the imperative need to expand production was bound to conflict with the accepted prewar procedures and rules, which had been designed to protect the position of skilled labour. This had been under threat even before the war, due to the spread of semi-automatic, specialised machinery, which made it possible to 'de-skill' engineering operations. The war speeded up this process. It also brought into industrial

40. Beveridge, *Food Control*, Table X; Working Classes Cost of Living Committee ('Sumner Committee'), *Report* (1918), Cd 8980, para. 23; P.E. Dewey, 'Nutrition and Living Standards in Wartime Britain', in Wall and Winter, *Upheaval*, pp. 206–10.

41. Board of Trade, *Statistical Abstract for the United Kingdom . . . 1911 to 1925* (1927), Cmd 2949, pp. 64–5.

42. Department of Employment and Productivity, *British Labour Statistics, Historical Abstract 1886–1968* (HMSO 1971), Table 159.

bargaining the concern of the government to maintain industrial discipline, to the point of curtailing the right to strike.

The first breach in prewar rules was the Shells and Fuses Agreement of March 1915, between employers, government and the engineering unions, by which the employment of women and semi-skilled men was permitted. More concessions were made under the Treasury Agreement later in the same month, by which the unions gave up their right to strike, agreed to relax all customs which curtailed the output of munitions, and permitted dilution (the employment of labour which had not served a craft apprenticeship) on government work. In return, promises were given that these provisions would apply solely on war work, that they would be in force during the war only, and that profits of firms doing war work would be limited. These provisions were subsequently incorporated in the Munitions of War Act 1915, which made provision for binding arbitration of disputes. It also restricted the right of labour to leave munitions firms without a 'leaving certificate' from their former employers.[43]

The expansion of the munitions industries, and the 'dilution' of skilled labour by the less skilled, permitted a great growth in employment of women. The most spectacular was in the government-controlled establishments, where women's employment rose from 2,000 in July 1914 to 276,000 in November 1918. In the metal industries generally, female employment rose in the same period from 170,000 to 596,000. These were the most obvious new employments for women, all the more striking to the public view because they were largely shopfloor jobs rather than administrative or ancilliary occupations. Women were also largely employed to replace men in finance and commerce, where female numbers rose from 506,000 to 955,000, and in transport (chiefly on the railways, in which female employment rose from 12,000 to 66,000).[44]

The incursion of unskilled (mainly female) labour into jobs which had formerly been the exclusive preserve of the skilled male worker caused some agonising, since it called into question the degree of skill actually possessed by the so-called skilled worker. As Robert Roberts, whose father was a skilled engineer as well as a shopkeeper, recounted:

> the gates of change stood wide open, and the new workers poured through, to the dismay of many a conservative tradesman who saw the 'dummies' acquiring some of his own skills with disturbing ease. My father was typical. In his cups he was wont to boast that, at the lathe, he had to manipulate a micrometer and work to limits of one thousand of an inch. We were much impressed, until one evening in 1917 a teenage sister running a capstan in the iron works remarked indifferently that she, too, used a 'mike' to even finer limits. There was, she said, 'nothing to it'. The old man fell silent. Thus did status crumble![45]

43. J.B. Jefferys, *The Story of the Engineers, 1800–1945* (1945), pp. 175–6; H.A. Clegg, *A History of British Trade Unions since 1889, vol. II, 1911–1933* (Oxford, Clarendon 1985), p. 127.
44. Kirkaldy, *Industry and Finance*, Table I, pp. 96–7.
45. Roberts, *Classic Slum*, pp. 160–1.

It was intended, at least in munitions, that women should be paid the same rate as men doing the same job. In practice, there was no clear definition of what constituted a woman's or a man's job, and women's pay lagged considerably behind that of men. Data on women's pay are sketchy; all that can be safely said is that women's pay in munitions and in most other wartime employments was much greater than in the alternative traditional female jobs. On the whole, little attempt was made to attract married women with young children into factories; it was felt that their place was in the home, and the Ministry of Munitions was reluctant to sponsor factory crèches.[46]

Work in munitions factories could be dangerous and unhealthy. A committee on the subject reported in 1917 that much absenteeism was due to sickness rather than slackness, and that long hours, especially Sunday labour, had a 'pernicious effect' on health, particularly in the heavy trades. In 1916 alone, poisoning by TNT resulted in fifty-two deaths. To serve the welfare needs of labour, the Ministry of Munitions employed fifty-one welfare inspectors for women, and sixteen for boy workers.

The expansion of the labour force, coupled with the need of trade unions to recruit members among the 'dilutees', to protect the interests of their members in the welter of new work, and to monitor changes in payment rates and systems, led to a rapid rise in trade union membership. Trade unionists numbered 3.7 million males and 0.43 million females at the end of 1913, and 5.3 million males and 1.2 million females at the end of 1918.[47]

The rise in the labour force and the pressure to produce caused considerable industrial friction, although the first two years of the war were comparatively peaceful. The largest dispute was in the south Wales coalfield in 1915, mainly owing to the fact that the price of the coal mined had risen much faster than the wages of the miners. But engineering stoppages were many fewer than before the war. It was only in the last two years of the war that engineering and textiles came to the fore as contributors to the national strike record. Even then the general level of strikes was much below the (admittedly unusually turbulent) years of 1910–14. A better comparison would be with the more peaceful years 1900–9, when the annual average number of days lost in disputes had been 3,587,000 (Table 2.4 overleaf).[48]

There were various reasons for the unrest, most of which were induced by war conditions. Rising union membership brought a distancing of members from the official leadership, as national pay bargaining replaced local negotiation, and the number of officials failed to keep pace with the rising

46. Braybon, *Women Workers*, chs 2, 3; *History of the Ministry of Munitions, vol. 6, Manpower and Dilution*, ch. 1, Table I; H. Wolfe, *Labour Supply and Regulation* (Oxford, Clarendon 1923), ch. XIV; Winter, *Great War*, p. 207.

47. Ministry of Munitions, *Health of Munition Workers Committee, Interim Report: Industrial Efficiency and Fatigue* (1917), Cd 8511, PP 1917–18, XVI, para. 61; Winter, *Great War*, p. 206; Department of Employment, *Labour Statistics*, Table 196.

48. Mitchell, *Statistics* (1988), p. 144.

Table 2.4 UK working days lost in industrial disputes, 1915–18[a]

	Annual average days lost (000)				
	1910–14	*1915*	*1916*	*1917*	*1918*
Mining and quarrying	9,330	1,657	326	1,183	1,263
M,E,S[b]	2,012	357	305	3,063	1,499
Textiles	1,766	369	1,161	710	1,704
Transport	1,395	152	103	184	277
Building	842	130	103	68	186
Clothing	200	28	156	142	298
Total[c]	16,484	2,953	2,446	5,647	5,875

Notes: a UK = GB and Northern Ireland
b M,E,S = metals, engineering, shipbuilding
c Total of all industrial disputes, including above industries
Source: Mitchell, *Statistics*, p. 144

membership. The result was the rise in the number of shop stewards, which in many firms became the main way in which workers were represented to the management. Dilution and the undermining of craft status brought a wave of strikes in the major engineering and shipbuilding centres, and out of this activity emerged the famous Shop Stewards Movement. This, which promoted the idea of 'workers' control' of industry, became established in some of the largest munitions centres, but it must be distinguished from the vast bulk of the shop steward population, which remained unpoliticised, winning formal recognition in national engineering agreements in 1917 and 1919.[49]

These broad changes affecting the position of labour meant that labour unrest did not vanish during the war, in spite of agreement between unions and government that it should. Sometimes unrest had wider political implications. The Clyde Workers' Committee (of shop stewards) took the lead in the 'rent strike' of November 1915, which persuaded the government to initiate national rent control. The Clyde region was notable for labour unrest; the strike of March 1916, engendered against the advice of the official leadership, led to the forcible removal by the government of the strike leaders (without charge or trial) away from the region.[50]

A renewed wave of labour unrest, not confined to the Clyde, led to the largest strikes of the war, in May 1917. Although the issues involved were (and remain) ambiguous, the government was sufficiently frightened to set up a commission of inquiry into industrial unrest. Three commissioners – a chairman, an employer, and a labour representative – were to report on the causes

49. J. Lovell, *British Trade Unions 1875–1933* (Macmillan 1977), pp. 52–3; Clegg, *Trade Unions*, pp. 181–92.
50. Clegg, *Trade Unions*, p. 137.

of unrest in each of the eight munitions areas. The inquiry's report took only six weeks to compile, and must be considered as a collocation of hearsay. For what it is worth, it picked out three main causes of unrest: food prices rising faster than wages (coupled with the maldistribution of food supplies); the Munitions of War Acts (especially the leaving certificate), and the proposal to withdraw the 'trade card' scheme; this latter was a scheme to protect skilled labour from military service, by a system of cards issued to workers by the trade unions. Secondary factors were housing inadequacies, liquor restrictions, and industrial fatigue.[51]

The wartime pressure on the labour market was so great that: 'Aged, decrepit men to whom charitable persons used to give occasional light jobs in a garden now form part of the regular body of employees in controlled establishments.'[52] In such a situation, it might be expected that the workforce would establish substantial economic gains. But there were reasons why this might not be so – principally that trade unions had largely abrogated the strike weapon. Indeed, a look at weekly wage rates might suggest that real wages actually fell, since in most cases wage rates rose more slowly than prices. But the spread of systems of piecework payment, and an increase in overtime working, probably kept actual earnings roughly in line with inflation (Table 2.5).

Table 2.5 UK wage rates, wage earnings and retail prices, 1914–18

	Average weekly wage rates	*Average weekly wage earnings*	*Retail prices*
1913	100	100	100
1914	101	101	101
1915	108	117	121
1916	118	133	143
1917	139	170	173
1918	179	211	199

Source: Feinstein, *National Income*, Table 65

The evidence that real wage earnings were maintained is stronger for the war industries than for those whose products were not so much in demand; there is relatively little information on what happened to earnings in the service sector. One industry in which the employees almost certainly suffered a fall in real earnings for most of the war was agriculture. In this, as in other

51. *Commission of Enquiry into Industrial Unrest: summary of the reports of the Commission by the Right Honourable George Barnes, M.P.* (1918), Cd 8696, PP 1917–18, XV, paras 8–12. The strike issues are discussed in Wolfe, *Labour Supply*, pp. 21, 136–7; Clegg, *Trade Unions*, pp. 171–3.
52. Ministry of Munitions, *Health of Munition Workers Committee*, Cd 8511, XVI, para. 3.

industries, weekly rates did not keep pace with inflation. But in farming there was little overtime, and little scope for extra allowances in kind. By early 1918, it is probable that English and Welsh agricultural labourers were earning only about 60 per cent more than in 1914, but the general price level had risen by about 90 per cent. Thereafter the government took action to raise agricultural wages, as part of the drive to increase food production. By the Corn Production Act 1917, Agricultural Wages Boards were set up in every county to implement a minimum wage, and by mid-1918 real wages were more or less restored to the 1914 level.[53]

Before the war, there had been a large gap between the earnings of the skilled worker, who had served an apprenticeship of between five and seven years, or gained the necessary experience in the course of his job, and the less skilled labourer. During the war, various forces combined to reduce this gap. 'Dilution' undermined the position and privileges of the skilled worker, and wartime wages were set high enough to tempt large numbers of the less skilled into employment formerly the preserve of the more skilled. In addition, neither unions nor employers had a coherent view on how to adjust wages in conditions of high inflation. In the event, most did so by offering flat-rate increases ('war bonuses'), which worked automatically to reduce the proportional gap between 'artisan' (i.e. skilled) and less skilled earnings. In the four years from July 1914 to July 1918, engineering artisans' rates rose by 73 per cent, but engineering labourers' rates by 113 per cent. In building, bricklayers' rates rose by 57 per cent, but bricklayers' labourers' rates by 85 per cent. This reduction of differentials, which occurred in many other industries, was not reversed after the war.[54]

The final change in the position of labour and the working classes in general was the political one. The split in the Liberal Party between Asquith and Lloyd George was one of the nails in the coffin of that party, which never again held office. More significant was the rise of the party representing labour, and closely linked with the trade unions, the Labour Party, which gained 22 per cent of the votes (but only 9 per cent of the seats in the House of Commons) in the 1918 general election. Thereafter it was the main opposition party (excluding the temporary ascendancy of Sinn Fein in 1918), and formed its first, although minority government in 1924. Even though it was only once again in government before 1939, in the minority administration of 1929–31, it could not be ignored even while in opposition, and the changing balance of party political power contributed to the drift to more generous welfare policies under administrations of both major parties between the wars.[55]

53. Dewey, *British Agriculture*, pp. 110–13.
54. Bowley, *Prices and Wages*, pp. 105, 113.
55. J. Turner, *British Politics and the Great War: coalition and conflict, 1915–1918* (New Haven, CT, Yale UP 1991); T. Wilson, *The Downfall of the Liberal Party, 1914–1935* (Collins 1966); T. Wilson, *The Myriad Faces of War: Britain and the Great War, 1914–1918* (Cambridge, Polity 1986).

FOREIGN TRADE AND PAYMENTS

For an economy which was highly oriented to the outside world, operating a banking and finance system which was the linchpin of the world payments system, the war could not be anything other than disastrous. However, the more serious adverse effects were not apparent until well into the 1920s.

In 1913, the main continental opponents of Britain – Germany, Austria-Hungary and Turkey – had together supplied 22 per cent of retained British imports, and accounted for about 10 per cent of British exports. The war brought this trade to a standstill. Overseas trade was further impeded by the enormously enhanced cost of shipping. From the start, the Admiralty requisitioned ships at fixed ('Blue Book') rates. The free market in shipping responded accordingly, and freight rates soared. Their average level in 1915 was three times that of 1913; by 1917 they had risen to 1,100 per cent of 1913. Shipping insurance rates also rose. The transition of industry to the war effort, the danger of submarine attack, and government restriction all helped to reduce trade. At the end of 1916 the Ministry of Shipping was established; the U-boat campaign of 1917 brought universal requisitioning of shipping via the Allied Maritime Transport Commission.[56]

While the export trades were seriously reduced, imports flourished, due to the need to buy arms and other war material, chiefly from the USA and Canada. As a result, the balance of trade deficit, which was mainly with north America even before the war, grew substantially. A secondary reason for the continuing reliance on north America was that, to economise on shipping capacity, some imports were redirected onto shorter routes (e.g. Canadian wheat replaced Australian wheat). In 1909–13, the UK overall balance of trade deficit had averaged –£140 million, the deficit with north America being –£103 million. By 1918, the overall deficit was –£784 million, of which the north American deficit was –£602 million.[57]

Describing trade in terms of current values may be misleading at a time of high inflation. On the other hand, since the composition of trade changed so markedly, to describe what happened in terms of volumes (i.e. real values) can also be misleading. There is in any case no satisfactory index of wartime trade volumes. For what it is worth, one estimate of real trade values shows that between 1913 and 1918 exports fell by 59.5 per cent, re-exports fell by 81.8 per cent, but imports fell by only 28.3 per cent.[58]

The collapse of exports (and re-exports) and the relative maintenance of imports made the balance of trade much worse. Whereas this deficit had been previously more than covered by the contribution of 'invisible' earnings, there was also in the war a sharp fall in invisible credits. Their value in 1913

56. Board of Trade, *Statistical Abstract* (1921), Tables 34, 35; Mitchell, *Statistics*, p. 540; Morgan, *Studies*, p. 41.
57. Board of Trade, *Statistical Abstract* (1921), pp. 77–81, 86–9.
58. Mitchell, *Statistics*, p. 522.

Table 2.6 UK current balance of payments, 1914–18 (£million)

	1909–13	*1914*	*1915*	*1916*	*1917*	*1918*
Visible balance	–92	–120	–340	–350	–420	–630
Invisible balance	+283	+254	+285	+440	+470	+355
Current balance	+192	+134	–55	+90	+50	–275

Source: Feinstein, *National Income*, Table 37

has been put at (net) £339 million, most of which was income from previous foreign investment (£210 million), the next largest credit being from shipping hire (£94 million).[59] During the war, although accurate information is lacking, the volume of invisibles must have declined; in spite of the inflation of freights and prices, there was less shipping available for hire, and foreign assets were sold. The most recent estimate of the current balance of payments position of the UK during the war is shown in Table 2.6. (The balance of trade (i.e. visible balance) figures shown here differ from those published by the Board of Trade in 1921 (see note 59).)

On the surface, there seems little cause for concern, since over the whole period 1914–18, the total value of the current deficits (–£330 million) was only slightly greater than the total credits (£274 million), and there was only one year (1918) of serious deficit. But this is to ignore the fact that there had been an enormous decline in the prewar surplus, out of which the prewar foreign investment outflow had been maintained.

The position on the capital side of the balance of payments was even more serious, although the near-cessation of new foreign investment brought some relief. The prewar surplus in short-term credits was wiped out, and London may even have emerged as a net debtor on short-term account at the end of the war. On the long-term capital side, there was disinvestment, chiefly in north America. The government acted from December 1915 to induce private holders of dollar investments to sell them, and make the dollars over to the Treasury; the investors were given sterling in exchange. There were some £207 million of officially sponsored sales in that region, to which should be added a large volume of private sales, amounting perhaps to a further £343 million. Total sales thus amounted to about half the prewar investment in north America, which may have been worth about £1,000 million, or between one-third and one-quarter of the total British prewar investment overseas. There were in addition considerable, although largely unknown, losses of private investment in Russia, Germany and central Europe.[60]

59. Morgan, *Studies*, p. 315; M.D.K.W. Foot, 'The Balance of Payments in the Inter-War Period', *Bank of England Quarterly Bulletin* 12 (1972), p. 358, Table C.
60. Morgan, *Studies*, pp. 327–31, 343, Table 50. See also the comments on the changes in the balance of short-term acceptances in T. Balogh, *Studies in Financial Organization* (Cambridge UP 1947), pp. 247–8.

In addition to the mobilisation of private securities, there were the substantial loans made by the UK to its allies, and the borrowing from the USA. By the end of the 1918/19 financial year, the UK had lent £1,301 million to its allies; £568 million of this had been to Russia, and was never recovered. At the same time, debts had been accumulated to the USA of £1,037 million and to Canada of £73 million.[61]

The external position of the UK at the end of the war was thus much weakened. The current account of the balance of payments had moved from a position of substantial surplus to substantial deficit by 1918. On the capital account of the balance of payments, there had been a substantial outflow in the form of loans to British allies. These had been financed by the cessation of new foreign investment, the repatriation of overseas investments, and the accumulation of British government debts abroad. The overall result was a serious weakening of the international financial position of the British economy. The appearance of wartime sterling crises, which formerly would have been unthinkable, were both testimony to the seriousness of the situation, and symbolic of the end of the supremacy of the pound sterling. There was a run on the pound in December 1916 (induced by political factors), and a more serious potential exchange rate crisis in July 1917. Only loans from the USA allowed the sterling exchange rate to be held reasonably near the prewar level. The international financial position of the UK could have been rebuilt only by a long period of large balance of payments surpluses. These were not to be forthcoming in the postwar world.

THE INTERNAL LEGACY OF THE WAR

The economic and social consequences of the war were considerable. The most obvious economic cost was financial. The cost to the Exchequer had a profound social impact, since the higher rates of taxation, and the sharp shift of taxation to a more progressive system, were continued after the war. To the purely financial cost could be added the considerable destruction of property, chiefly of ships. There was also the accelerated rate of depreciation of industrial and commercial property: the railways and mines suffered from added pressure and inadequate maintenance.

On the social side, the latter had its counterpart in the cessation of housebuilding and the negligible maintenance of the housing stock. The wider social consequences were legion. The altered position of labour had many aspects: the stronger trade union movement, the reduction of wage differentials, the changed political influence of the trade unions and the Labour Party, and the greater acceptance of women in shop and office (although not in the factory). More basically, the war accelerated the decline of fertility, and since the decline of mortality was checked in the interwar period, the rate of population growth slowed down sharply. This was to be one of the most profound differences between the prewar and postwar world.

61. Morgan, *Studies*, pp. 317–20.

THE EXTERNAL LEGACY OF THE WAR

Profound as were the internal effects of the war, it is at least arguable that they were dwarfed by the external consequences. During the war, these were either not immediately discernible, or overshadowed by larger military and international happenings. In a world coming to terms with millions of deaths from war and influenza, the Bolshevik revolution, and the disintegration of the Russian, German, Austro-Hungarian and Turkish empires, to ponder the commercial position of postwar Britain may have been something of an intellectual and emotional luxury.

Nevertheless, the war marked enormous changes in the international position of Britain, and these had enormous repercussions on the domestic economy and society. The most obvious and easily identifiable losses were the losses of investments in the USA, Russia and central Europe. Another form of overseas loss was the roughly £1 billion worth of debt run up, chiefly to the USA. The possibility of restoring the pound sterling to the gold standard, at anything like the prewar parity, was put into question by the weakened balance of payments position of the UK, and the concurrent strengthening of that of the USA.

Finally, and in the event most crushingly, the war led to the disappearance of the formerly enormous British balance of payments surplus. The short-term reason for this was that markets for the main British exports collapsed during the war, and did not fully recover after 1918. There were various reasons for this; a comparative loss of British competitiveness; the rise of domestic manufacturing and Japanese competition in regions such as India and the Far East; the growth of competition from the USA in the American continent; the postwar currency dislocations; the raising of tariffs in Europe; the loss of trade to Russia. In the longer run, the postwar weakness of the balance of payments was due more to the deterioration in the invisible account than in the visible account. This was largely due to the international financial changes brought about by the war. Whatever the reasons, the results for the British people were high unemployment, with all that this entailed in personal misery and economic loss, coupled with a new instability in Britain's international economic position.

CONCLUSIONS

The First World War had enormous effects on the British economy and on British society. The size of the armies raised and the loss of life were unprecedented. The huge impact of the war was due to the new military technologies, and the suddenness with which the war had erupted. In terms of the organisation of the war effort, the result was a constant series of empirical shifts, as the government felt obliged to intervene to a greater extent as time went on. Due to the shifting of economic resources into the war effort, civilian production and exports declined and the population was taxed much more heavily. The bulk of the war was paid for by increasing the National Debt, which would create problems of debt repayment after the war. Partly due to this method of finance, inflation rose to unprecedented levels. Internationally, the British position was undermined by the loss of export markets, the reduction in service income, the loss of overseas investments, and the acquisition of a large foreign debt. There was a sharp slowing-down in the rate of population growth over the period of the war, and this persisted in the interwar period. Politically, the war promoted the influence of organised labour, and of the Labour Party; both of these would have a great effect on social policy after 1918.

CHAPTER 3

POPULATION, SOCIAL CHANGE AND THE LABOUR FORCE, 1919–39

POPULATION

Before the First World War, the British population was still growing rapidly. This process slowed down dramatically after 1914 (Table 3.1 opposite).

Most of the rise in population was due to natural increase, that is, the excess of births over deaths. The contributions of emigration and immigration varied over time. The decade spanning the First World War was a period of high net emigration, due to the intense emigrant activity in the three years before the war and two years afterwards, so that there was a net emigration in those years of 858,000. Even in the 1920s, when entry to the USA was restricted, there was a net emigration of 565,000. But in the 1930s, the flow was reversed, as political tension and political and racial persecution in Europe grew, so that there was a net immigration of 650,000. These were large flows in themselves, but not very large when compared with the increase of population in the long run. Between 1871 and 1941, there was a net emigration of 2.73 million, which was 12 per cent of the whole natural increase of that period.[1]

FERTILITY, MORTALITY AND FAMILY

The slowing-down in the rate of population growth before 1914 was due mainly to the narrowing of the gap between birth rates and death rates. In the early nineteenth century, the death rate had begun to fall, but birth rates had remained high, thus largely accounting for the high rate of population growth of the Victorian period. From the 1870s, death rates continued their (rather slow) long-term decline, but the novel feature was the behaviour of birth rates, which now began to come down, slowly at first, but faster after the turn of the century (Table 3.2 opposite).

The decline in the birth rate was clearly a long-term phenomenon, which cannot be explained merely by (e.g.) the high unemployment of the interwar period. Nor can it be attributed to the military deaths of the First World War;

1. Royal Commission on Population, *Report* (1949), Cmd 7695, p. 9.

Table 3.1 British population at censuses, 1861–1951[a]

	Persons (000)	Intercensal increase (000)	(%)
1861	23,128	—	—
1871	26,072	2,944	12.7
1881	29,710	3,638	13.9
1891	33,029	3,319	11.2
1901	37,000	3,971	12.0
1911	40,831	3,831	10.3
1921	42,769	1,938	4.7
1931	44,795	2,026	4.7
1939[b]	46,467	1,672	3.7
1951	48,854	2,387	5.1

Notes: a England, Wales and Scotland
b Non-census year estimate
Source: B.R. Mitchell, *British Historical Statistics* (Cambridge UP 1988), p. 9

Table 3.2 Births per thousand of the population, 1870–1939

	England & Wales	*Scotland*
1870–74	35.4	34.9
1900–04	28.4	29.4
1910–14	24.2	25.9
1915–19	19.4	21.7
1920–24	21.4	24.3
1925–29	20.5	20.3
1930–34	15.3	18.6
1935–39	14.9	17.7

Source: Mitchell, *Statistics*, pp. 42–6

the 1930s rates were broadly what could have been expected if the prewar trend had continued in the absence of a war.[2] Nor can it be explained by changes in marriage rates, or in changes in the age of women at marriage. The main explanation lies in the behaviour of married couples, who were having fewer children.

The causes of this far-reaching change in social behaviour have been much debated, and remain somewhat obscure. It has been suggested that married couples were becoming more aware that living standards were rising, and that having numerous children threatened the maintenance of these standards. There are also specific factors to be considered, ranging from the expansion

2. J.M. Winter, *The Great War and the British People* (Macmillan 1985), pp. 270–2.

of education, the lessened need for more children as infant survival rates rose, and the introduction of old age pensions in 1908 – thus reducing the craving for many children to be the sustenance of one's old age.[3]

The desire for smaller families, whatever it was due to, was one thing; its realisation was another. The most widely practised method of birth control in the early twentieth century was withdrawal (*coitus interruptus*). In the 1930s, the most popular techniques of birth control were (in order) withdrawal, sheath, safe period and spermicidal pessaries. The increasingly popular method was the condom, or male sheath. Their issue to the Armed Forces in 1914–18 introduced millions of men to their usage, and sheath technology was further improved in the 1930s. By the mid-1930s, the London Rubber Company was producing some 2 million sheaths a year, and the contribution of imports from Germany may have been at least as large. Thus contraceptive devices were now much more readily available. There was also a greater willingness to use them. In a survey conducted for the Royal Commission on Population after the Second World War, it was found that only 16 per cent of women who had married before 1910 had used 'birth control' (i.e. contraceptive devices), but 59 per cent of those married in 1920–24 did so. Contraceptive devices were more likely to be used by the middle class, who tended to use them to space births out on a predetermined plan. Working-class couples tended to have a certain number of children, and when they thought the family was big enough, cast round for some method to limit it.[4]

But even in the 1930s, the subject of birth control was still not one for open public discussion. The sources of contraceptives – chiefly mail order houses and barber's shops – had a clandestine air, and birth control advice was difficult to obtain. This in turn reflected the slowness with which religious and lay opinion towards birth control changed. Traditionally, the Roman Catholic church condemned the entire process. The Protestant churches took a more liberal view. The Nonconformists declined to lay down rules for their members. It was not until the 1930 Lambeth Conference that members of the Church of England were in effect set free to follow their own consciences.[5]

Lay opinion is more difficult to gauge. The more 'advanced' in their opinions would have been aware of the work of the Malthusian League, formed in the aftermath of the Bradlaugh-Besant trial (1876) to disseminate knowledge

3. E.H. Phelps Brown, *The Growth of British Industrial Relations: a study from the standpoint of 1906–14* (Macmillan 1959), pp. 4–9; M.S. Teitelbaum, *The British Fertility Decline: demographic transition in the crucible of the Industrial Revolution* (Princeton, NJ, Princeton UP 1984), chs 7, 9.

4. A. McLaren, *A History of Contraception: from antiquity to the present day* (Oxford, Blackwell 1990), pp. 225, 235; J. Peel, 'The Manufacture and Retailing of Contraceptives in England', *PS* XVII (1963–64), pp. 116–22; Royal Commission on Population, *Papers, vol. I Report of an Inquiry into Family Limitation and its Influence on Human Fertility in the Past Fifty Years*, by J. Lewis-Faning (HMSO 1949), p. 7.

5. F. Campbell, 'Birth Control and the Christian Churches', *PS* XIV (1960–61), esp. pp. 131–6.

of birth control. They may even have attended the lectures on the subject given by Dr Marie Stopes in the Queen's Hall, London, in 1922, or read her book *Married Love*, which sold half a million copies. For the less advanced majority, such things were certainly not to be read, or talked about openly, and they would have been less than amused by the satirical references to 'Malthusian Drill' in Aldous Huxley's novel *Brave New World* (1932). On the whole, however, it seems safe to conclude that contraception had been tacitly accepted by a large part of the population by the 1930s.[6]

The rapid decline in fertility was not matched by that of mortality. Before the war, death rates had declined rapidly, but in the interwar period the decline slowed down (Table 3.3).

Table 3.3 Deaths per thousand of the population, 1870–1939

	England & Wales	*Scotland*
1870–74	22.0	22.3
1900–04	16.6	17.5
1910–14	13.8	15.3
1915–19	15.1	15.6
1920–24	12.2	14.0
1925–29	12.2	13.7
1930–34	12.0	13.2
1935–39	12.0	13.2

Source: Mitchell, *Statistics*, pp. 57–8

The use of these 'crude death rates' understates the extent to which mortality was falling in the interwar period, since they are expressed as rates per thousand persons. This is misleading, since the population was ageing in this period, and thus becoming more liable to mortality. Use of 'standardised' death rates (on the assumption that the age structure of the population was that of 1901 throughout) shows that death rates continued to fall after 1911, being down to 10.3 (standardised rate) in England and Wales by 1931, and 9.6 by 1941. But even the standardised rates fell more slowly after 1911 than before.[7]

Death rates fell most rapidly in the youngest and most vulnerable groups – infants and young children. Between 1913 and 1938, the crude death rate for children aged 0–4 in England and Wales fell from 40.3 to 17.1 (males) and from 33.3 to 13.4 (females). The rate for all infants under 1 year fell from 108 to 53. In Scotland, the crude death rate for males aged 1–4 fell from 16.9 to 7.0, and for females from 16.8 to 6.2. For Scottish male infants under 1 year

6. McLaren, *Contraception*, p. 234.
7. T. McKeown, R.G. Record and R.D. Turner, 'An Interpretation of the Decline of Mortality in England and Wales during the Twentieth Century', *PS* XXIX (1975), pp. 392–3, 398–9.

the rate fell from 122.8 to 81.6, and for females from 112.2 to 65.7. These apart, the greatest falls were in the age groups 25–44.[8]

These improvements had various causes. For infants, one of the great pre-1914 causes of death, infantile diarrhoea (enteritis), fell sharply, as did the incidence of infectious disease (especially measles and tuberculosis). For the population generally, there was a sharp decline in some of the traditional major causes of death, especially tuberculosis, bronchitis and pneumonia. These were offset to some extent by a rise in other causes of death more commonly associated with the twentieth century, such as cancer and heart disease.[9]

The more fundamental reasons for the decline of some of these causes of death have been much debated. Generally, there is little basis for attributing their decline to medical science, since effective drugs for most of these conditions did not exist until the late 1930s – bronchitis, pneumonia and influenza from 1938, tuberculosis from 1947. The fall in death rates from airborne disease is largely attributed to better identification of carriers, and their isolation from the rest of the population in hospitals and sanatoriums. In the case of infantile diarrhoea also, isolation seems to be effective, and the influence of medical advice and sanitation improvements helped to reduce contagious infection. A large part in the decline of non-respiratory tuberculosis (which fell much more than the respiratory type) was played by the pasteurisation of milk. It is also possible that slum clearance helped to eradicate tubercular cross-infection, but the evidence is not clear. More generally, the long-term improvement in the health of the people must have owed a great deal to the steady improvement in nutritional standards, which reduced vulnerability to disease, and helped infected people to resist it.[10]

The decline in the size of families had begun with the upper classes in the 1870s, and had spread to all other social groups by the First World War, by which time the size of the average family had been reduced by one-fifth. But an important gap in social behaviour had opened up; the decline in family size had proceeded furthest in the upper income groups, and was less marked as one descended the social scale. Broadly, the main distinction was between manual and non-manual workers' families, so that by the early twentieth century the families of the former were some 40 per cent larger than those of the latter.[11]

After 1918, the average size of family continued to fall, but the social gap in family size persisted. The average family size of British couples who married in 1920–24 was 1.75 children in the professions, 1.65 in the ranks of salaried employees, and 1.97 for non-manual wage-earners. The families of manual workers were much larger, averaging 2.7 children for all wage-earners' families, rising to a maximum of 3.35 children for the families of manual labourers.

8. B.R. Mitchell, *British Historical Statistics* (Cambridge UP 1988), pp. 61, 64, 66–8, 58–9.

9. W.P.D. Logan, 'Mortality in England and Wales from 1848 to 1947', *PS* IV (1950–51), pp. 138 *et seq.*

10. McKeown *et al.*, 'Interpretation'; J.M. Winter, 'Infant Mortality, Maternal Mortality and Public Health in Britain in the 1930s', *JEEH* 8 (1979), pp. 460–2.

11. Royal Commission on Population, *Report*, p. 29.

Table 3.4 Persons per household, England and Wales, 1911 and 1931

	Per cent of households	
No. of persons in household	*1911* (%)	*1931* (%)
1	5.3	6.7
2	16.2	21.9
3	19.3	24.1
4	18.1	19.4
5	14.4	12.4
6+	26.7	15.5
Average no. of persons per family	4.36	3.72

Source: Census of England and Wales 1931, *Housing Report* (1935), p. xiv

In the long run, this meant a profound change in family size. The 1949 Royal Commission on Population estimated that only 11 per cent of the marriages taking place in 1860 in England and Wales had resulted in only one or two children, but that 50 per cent of the marriages taking place in 1925 did so.[12]

Regrettably, there is little information in the population censuses as to the constitution of the average family; the census first inquired into family composition in 1851, but not thereafter until 1951. The census definition of 'family' was really that of the household, including resident servants and lodgers.[13] On this basis, and deducting those 'families' which were in fact households in institutions (hotels, hospitals, schools, prisons, etc.) the change in the average composition and size of private 'families' (i.e. households) between 1911 and 1931 is shown in Table 3.4 above.

Thus there had been a striking fall in the proportion of large households, and an equally striking rise in the proportion of smaller households. The average size of household declined by about one-fifth in these twenty years. The exact composition of the household remains obscure. An attempt at a longer-term analysis of household composition, which indicates the proportions of blood relations and others, has been made for 1851 and 1947 (Table 3.5 overleaf).

Apart from putting the decline in household size into longer-term perspective, this estimate is a reminder against assuming that all 'families' consisted solely of parents and their children, although they accounted for most of the household's members. In the long run, the number of offspring decline, the numbers of household heads and their spouses rise (presumably due to greater longevity), as do the number of relatives (who may have been adults or children of other relatives), and there are considerable falls in the numbers of servants and lodgers.

The greatest changes are in the servants and lodgers, both of whom had

12. Ibid., Table XVII; A.M. Carr-Saunders, D. Caradog Jones and C.A. Moser, *A Survey of Social Conditions in England and Wales* (Oxford, Clarendon 1958), p. 25.
13. Census of England and Wales 1931, *Housing Report* (1935), p. viii.

Table 3.5 Household composition in England, 1851 and 1947

Status	*No. of persons* 1851	1947
Heads of household + spouses	1.67	1.80
Offspring	2.00	1.34
Other relatives	0.30	0.42
Servants	0.23	0.02
Lodgers	0.37	0.09
Total number in household	4.57	3.67

Note: The original 1851 figures are for rural and urban areas, which have been amalgamated here

Source: Derived from R. Wall, J. Robin and P. Laslett, *Family Forms in Historic Europe* (Cambridge UP 1983), Table 16.2, p. 497

almost disappeared by 1947. Although in most of these categories the 1947 data may also be applicable to the 1930s, this is not likely to be the case for servants and lodgers. While domestic service died out abruptly during and immediately after the Second World War, there were at the 1931 census still over 1 million female domestic servants in England and Wales, and about 60 per cent of them may have 'lived-in'. It was estimated in 1931 that almost 5 per cent of all households had a resident domestic servant. While it is not known what proportion of households took in lodgers, it was a common practice before 1914, and may have continued on a large scale between the wars. It was by no means uncommon on the new housing estates which were built after 1918. An analysis of the 1931 census returns for four estates (72,721 households) in Becontree (London), Birmingham, Liverpool and Manchester, showed that the proportions of households having lodgers varied from 11 to 17 per cent.[14]

These changes had large implications for the economic position of families, and for family life. The decline in the number of children meant that the family income went further. For the poorer families, it meant that the great period of poverty which was due to having young children (which also prevented mothers from earning money) was both eased and shortened. Within the family, individual children may have been assured of a greater share of their parents' attention.

There were thus substantial changes taking place within the family. Families were also becoming more important in society. Between 1911 and 1931, the number of private (i.e. non-institutional) households in England and Wales increased from 7.94 million to 10.23 million (29 per cent), while the population grew only from 36.07 million to 39.95 million (11 per cent). Thus the rate of

14. Census of England and Wales 1931, *General Report*, p. 152; *Housing Report*, pp. xlvi–xlix.

'family' (or, rather, household) formation much exceeded the general growth of population. Some of this excess may have been due to a slight lowering of the age at first marriage, which was to become more marked in the 1930s. It was also noticeable that there had been a brief surge in the marriage rate in 1919–20, although there was little change in other years between 1911 and 1931. But on the whole, changes in the rate and timing of marriage do not help very much to explain the higher rate of household formation, which may have been simply a function of the long-term rise in real incomes which (for those in employment) occurred in the interwar period.[15]

WOMEN AND WOMEN'S WORK

Women benefited greatly from the long-term trends in family formation. It was not just that families were smaller, but also that fewer stillbirths and miscarriages, and a much reduced infant mortality rate, all helped to reduce the number of pregnancies, with their physical danger, and physical and emotional stress. The typical working-class mother of the 1890s, married in her teens or early twenties and experiencing ten pregnancies, spent about fifteen years in a state of pregnancy, and in nursing a child for the first year of its life. By the early 1960s, the time so spent would have been about four years.[16]

In other ways, the position of women did not change so radically. Women did not avail themselves of their smaller families to go out to work in much larger numbers. The total female labour force grew from 5.2 million to 6.3 million between 1911 and 1931, but this was a similar rate of growth to that of the total female population. The proportion of women who were 'economically active' (i.e. in work or actively seeking it) fell slightly, from 35.3 to 34.2 per cent. The female labour force continued to be dominated by single women (77.7 per cent of the female labour force in 1911 and 77.9 in 1931). However, there were some significant changes. Between 1911 and 1931, the proportion of married women aged under 24 in the female labour force rose from 12.1 to 18.5 per cent; the proportion of single women aged under 24 rose from 73.0 to 75.7 per cent. The proportion of widows and divorced women in the female labour force fell from 8.7 to 6.8 per cent, possibly due to the introduction of widows' pensions in 1926. The proportion of older (35+) women at work also fell, possibly due largely to the depressed condition of the cotton industry, which had been one of the largest employers of married women before the war.[17]

15. A.H. Halsey, *Trends in British Society since 1900* (Macmillan 1972), p. 31; Census of England and Wales 1931, *Housing Report*, p. xiv; N.L. Tranter, *Population and Society, 1750–1940: contrasts in population growth* (Longman 1985), p. 52.
16. R.M. Titmuss, 'The Position of Women: some vital statistics', in M.W. Flinn and T.C. Smout (eds), *Essays in Social History* (Oxford, Clarendon 1974), p. 278.
17. Halsey, *Trends*, pp. 115–18; M. Abrams, *The Condition of the British People 1911–1945* (Gollancz 1945), p. 58.

Some social attitudes changed to some degree. As the rise in the proportion of working women who were young and married indicates, the opinion that the place for a married woman was at home (with or without children) may have weakened in some occupations. But married women were frowned on in the teaching profession, and a 'marriage bar' operated to force resignation on marriage in the civil service.[18]

The First World War had not ushered in a new age of expanding employment for women. Most of the women war workers had been employed on the understanding that their jobs were temporary, and most of them were dismissed at the end of the war. Nor had the war ushered in a new age of sexual equality in pay. Throughout the postwar economy, women were paid less than men. Women's pay in all occupations remained at about 55 per cent of that of men between 1913–14 and 1935–36. This was to some extent due to the fact that their occupations were not comparable, and that women were concentrated in jobs which were low-paid. But even in the civil service and teaching, there was a gap between men and women of the same grade; a female clerical civil servant in 1924 earned £206 a year, and her male equivalent £284; the figures for qualified teachers were £272 and £353.[19]

Thus the labour market was not particularly encouraging for women seeking work. This social conservatism may have been reinforced by changing attitudes to the wider role of women in society. It has been suggested that social norms were changing in the first forty years of the century, and that women's roles as wives and mothers were increasingly emphasised. This was due to commercial pressure, which saw the family unit as a fertile marketplace for the increasing flow of consumer goods and leisure services, and to the state, which by emphasising such things as infant and child welfare clinics, the school medical service, and child nutrition, implicitly stressed the importance of bringing up children, rather than going out to work.[20]

The slowing down of population growth had implications for the composition of the population and of the labour force. In the late nineteenth century, the largest age cohorts had been the youngest, gradually reducing in size as one ascended the age-scale. By 1914, the decline in fertility meant that the younger age cohorts were shrinking as a proportion of the total population. At the other end of the age-scale, the oldest cohorts were a growing proportion of the total population, due to their greater survival rate, although they were still a small proportion of the whole. The net result was that the proportion of the population of working age (15–64 years) increased between 1911 and 1931 from 63.9 to 68.4 per cent. Since the total population was still growing,

18. H. Martindale, *Women Servants of the State 1870–1938: a history of women in the Civil Service* (Allen & Unwin 1938), ch. 8.
19. G. Routh, *Occupation and Pay in Great Britain 1906–60* (Cambridge UP 1965), pp. 69, 79, 105.
20. D. Gittins, *Fair Sex: family size and structure, 1900–39* (Hutchinson 1982), pp. 48–52, 181.

the total population of working age also increased, from 26.1 million to 30.7 million.[21]

The national labour force between the wars was thus larger, both absolutely and in proportion to the dependent population, both young and old. In that sense, the economy was potentially more productive, not due to any technical advance, but merely to the change in age-structure. At the same time, the declining proportion of dependants made it easier for society to offer them a wider range of social and personal services. Finally, there were implications for employment; since the interwar period was one of comparatively high unemployment, the growth in the population of working age made the solution of the problem more difficult.

THE OCCUPATIONAL STRUCTURE

The changes in population and family took place within an economy which was undergoing substantial long-term changes, which were reflected in its occupational structure. This is indicated for the census years 1911, 1931 and 1951 (there was no census in 1941): see Table 3.6 overleaf.

Thus the primary sector of the economy shrank considerably; the secondary and tertiary sectors expanded. Some industries (notably agriculture, coal-mining, textiles and clothing) shrank; some (notably engineering and the metal trades) expanded. The declining industries comprised some which had been declining for many decades before 1911, such as agriculture, and some which were badly hit by the loss of markets after 1914 (coal, textiles, clothing, shipbuilding). Some industries expanded because of technical change (motor vehicles, chemicals, electricity), and some as a result of social changes (professional services, public administration, finance). Some, such as building, transport and distribution, changed little in relative importance. One of the largest changes was the shrinkage of 'miscellaneous services', which was due mainly to the decline of domestic service after 1939.

These changes in occupational structure affected the interwar social structure also. Some of the steepest declines had been in the 'heavy' industries, which required hard manual labour – agriculture, coal-mining, shipbuilding. The rising industries (motor vehicles, light engineering, consumer goods manufacture, and the service sector generally) required less physical exertion. Within the manual occupations, there was a shift away from skilled to less skilled labour, as the old crafts, with long apprenticeships, declined in favour of factory or service sector work which required comparatively little training.

More generally, the shift in occupational structure led to a move away from manual to non-manual labour. The newer 'light' manufacturing industries tended to have a higher ratio of supervisory and administrative staff to manual workers than the old 'heavy' industries. Thus the proportion of the occupied population in manual occupations began to decline. The decline was at first slow;

21. Mitchell, *Statistics*, pp. 15–17.

Table 3.6 British economy: occupational structure, 1911–51

	1911		*1931*		*1951*	
Occupied population[a]	*(000)*	*(%)*	*(000)*	*(%)*	*(000)*	*(%)*
Agriculture[b]	1,499	8.4	1,257	6.1	1,142	5.0
Mining, quarrying	1,128	6.3	1,166	5.7	861	3.8
Primary sector totals	2,627	14.7	2,423	11.8	2,003	8.8
Textiles	1,359	7.6	1,338	6.5	997	4.4
Clothing	1,159	6.5	880	4.3	729	3.2
Building	950	5.3	1,122	5.5	1,431	6.4
Engineering, shipbuilding	878	4.9	1,090	5.3	1,801	8.0
Metal manufacturing	509	2.8	524	2.6	579	2.6
Other metal goods	321	1.8	450	2.2	636	2.8
Vehicles	291	1.6	402	2.0	1,009	4.5
Chemicals	147	0.8	239	1.2	442	2.0
Other industries	1,322	7.4	1,627	7.9	1,551	6.9
Secondary sector totals	7,168	39.9	8,164	39.9	9,897	44.1
Transport, communication	1,416	7.9	1,671	8.2	1,734	7.7
Distribution	2,133	11.9	2,697	13.2	2,712	12.1
Finance	199	1.1	366	1.8	439	2.0
Professional services	798	4.4	1,067	5.2	1,543	6.9
Public administration	701	3.9	999	4.9	1,726	7.7
Gas, electricity, water	116	0.6	246	1.2	361	1.6
Miscellaneous services	2,783	15.5	2,865	14.0	2,086	9.3
Tertiary sector totals	8,146	45.3	9,911	48.5	10,601	47.3
Totals	17,941	100.0	20,498	100.0	22,501	100.0

Notes: a Includes employers, self-employed and unemployed
b Includes forestry and fishing
Source: G. Routh, *Occupation and Pay*, p. 40

having been 79.7 per cent in 1911, it had fallen to 76.5 in 1931, but it was to fall faster, to 69.6 per cent by 1951. This and other salient changes in occupational class are indicated in Table 3.7 opposite.

Apart from the decline of manual workers (especially among women), the two other major changes were the rise of the professional and of the clerical occupations. The former may be divided into 'higher' and 'lower' professions, reflecting differences in income and social status. In 1911, the largest of the higher groups were, among males (there were few females in the higher professions), ministers of religion (53,000), doctors and dentists (36,000) and lawyers (26,000). By 1951, the largest of the higher professions was engineering,

Table 3.7 Occupational class of men and women, Britain, 1911–51

	Men		*Women*	
Occupational groups	*1911* *(%)*	*1951* *(%)*	*1911* *(%)*	*1951* *(%)*
1 Professional	2.9	5.7	6.7	8.7
(1a: Higher)	(1.3)	(2.6)	(0.2)	(0.5)
(1b: Lower)	(1.6)	(3.2)	(6.5)	(8.2)
2 Employers, managers, etc.	11.6	12.5	6.6	5.9
3 Clerical workers	5.5	6.3	3.3	20.4
4 Foremen, etc.	1.7	3.2	0.2	1.1
5 Skilled manual	33.0	30.4	24.8	12.7
6 Semi-skilled manual	33.6	27.9	53.4	43.1
7 Unskilled manual	11.5	13.8	5.0	7.9
All manual groups	78.1	72.1	83.2	63.7
Total (%)	99.8	99.8	100.0	99.8
Occupied persons (million)	12.92	15.58	5.42	6.93

Source: Routh, *Occupation and Pay*, pp. 4–5

at 138,000 more than twice the size of the next group, medicine (62,000); the third most important group was the ministers of religion, but this had declined slightly in absolute terms, being reduced to 49,000 men.

In the lower professional group, much of the male expansion was accounted for by the rise in the number of draughtsmen, laboratory technicians and teachers; the female expansion was mainly due to the expansion of nursing, females having been already highly represented in teaching in 1911. Overall, teaching and nursing dominated the female lower professions throughout, comprising 58 per cent of the whole group in 1921 and 48 per cent of it in 1951. For the professions as a whole, the long-term expansion was striking, the higher group rising in numbers by 136 per cent, and the lower rising by 89 per cent between 1911 and 1951. In broad terms, it might be said that the professions had moved away from a nineteenth-century pattern, dominated by the older 'liberal professions' (and medicine) to one in which new occupations had been called forth to serve industrial development, in the form of engineers, draughtsmen and technicians, and to serve a growing demand for education and medical services.

The rise in the clerical group was also striking, from 887,000 in 1911 to 1,465,000 in 1931, and 2,404,000 in 1951 – a rise of 171 per cent. Women played a disproportionately large role in its expansion. Before 1914, clerical work was male-dominated, female 'lady typewriters' were still a novelty, and clerical work was done mainly in decorous clerkly handwritings. In the war, large numbers of women were employed in offices for clerical and administrative work. But, whereas in the rest of industry, the females lost their jobs when peace returned, this was not so in the office; the typists stayed, and male clerks became less common as time went on. In 1931, when typists were first distinguished in the population census, there were almost a quarter of a million, they were almost all female, and they formed 17 per cent of all clerical workers. By 1951, there were over half a million, and they formed almost one-quarter of all clerical workers.[22]

INDUSTRIAL AND COMMERCIAL ORGANISATION

The changes in occupational structure were accompanied by changes in the structure of industrial and commercial organisation. The tendency in both was towards larger-sized firms and places of work. Whereas in 1907 the largest 100 manufacturing firms accounted for 15 per cent of manufacturing net output, this had risen by 1930 to 26 per cent, although it fell thereafter to 23 per cent by 1939.[23]

This increasing concentration reflected technological developments such as the assembly line in vehicle production, and the need for larger units to conduct research and marketing. It was usually achieved through mergers. There were several waves of mergers, especially in 1918–21 and 1928–30. The most notable was that of Imperial Chemical Industries, formed in 1926 by the amalgamation of four of the largest chemical firms. The electrical industry was dominated by 1928 by three firms – General Electric Co., English Electric, and Associated Electrical Industries – who between them controlled 35 per cent of the electrical engineering industry, rising to 60 per cent in heavy electrical equipment. In the food industry, the spur to merger was marketing rather than technological innovation, seen at its most spectacular in the formation of Anglo-Dutch Unilever, by the merger of the continental Margarine Union and the British Lever Brothers in 1929. A final influence making for increasing size was the entry of north American companies, with firms such as Ford consolidating their position, General Motors taking over Vauxhall in 1925, and Proctor and Gamble acquiring Hedley in 1930. Whereas in 1914 there had been perhaps 70 US companies operating in the UK, there were 224 by 1936, and many of these were the dominant firms in their industries.[24]

This increased tendency to industrial concentration had its effect in the workplace. At the 1935 Census of Production, there were 5,694,200 employees in manufacturing, of whom 3,839,300 (67.4 per cent) were employed in establishments of 100 or larger; 1,105,900 (19.4 per cent) were employed in establishments of 1,000 persons or more.[25] The most concentrated manufacturing

22. Routh, *Occupation and Pay*, Tables 1, 10. See also G. Anderson (ed.), *The White-Blouse Revolution: female office workers since 1870* (Manchester UP 1988).
23. L. Hannah, *The Rise of the Corporate Economy* (2nd edn, Methuen 1983), Table A2.
24. Hannah, *Corporate Economy*, ch. 7; C. Wilson, *The History of Unilever* (Cassell 1954), vol. II, ch. XVI.
25. Central Statistical Office, *Annual Abstract of Statistics no. 84 (1935–1946)* (HMSO 1948), Table 145.

industries, with more than 40 per cent of their workforces in plants employing over 1,000 were motor manufacturing, iron and steel, electrical machinery, silk, shipbuilding, newspapers, and cocoa/sugar confectionery.[26] In coal-mining, the degree of concentration was much greater, with 55.1 per cent of miners in 1938 being employed in mines with a labour force of 1,000 or more.[27] But outside manufacturing and mining the large establishment was unusual, particularly in agriculture, retailing and domestic service.

There were also considerable changes in retail trading in the first half of the century, particularly between the wars. The numbers of insured employees in the distributive trades rose from 1,254,000 to 2,324,000 between 1923 and 1939.[28] Although the number of separate shops in Britain is unknown, the 1921 Census of Population recorded 614,579 shop premises in England and Wales. The bulk of these remained, as ever, single-unit enterprises, which might range from the substantial family business in a high street, to the front room of a backstreet terrace house, pressed into service to eke out the occupiers' dole or pension. George Orwell described lodging in a particularly unpleasant backstreet house (selling tripe) in 1937.[29] But there were considerable changes. The main one was to a concentration of ownership and larger firms, through the expansion of the multiple chain, the cooperative society shop, or the large department store. Between 1900 and 1939, the multiple retailers' share of all retail trade rose from about 4 per cent to about 19 per cent; the share of the cooperative societies rose from about 6 to about 11 per cent; the share of department stores rose from about 1.5 to about 5 per cent. All these newer ways of retailing had thus made headway, at the expense of the more traditional retailers (usually the one-family, one-shop concern).[30]

Although a wide variety of goods were found in each type of outlet, the cooperatives were particularly strong in food, household stores, clothing and footwear; the department stores in women's and children's clothes and drapery. The multiple retailers acquired their own specialisms. Notable examples of the latter were F.W. Woolworth, stocking a wide range of inexpensive merchandise, Marks & Spencer (mainly clothing), Boots the Chemists (pharmaceuticals) and Timothy Whites (household goods). There were also large multiple retailers in meat, groceries and fish.[31]

26. P.S. Florence, *The Logic of British and American Industry* (rev. edn, Routledge & Kegan Paul 1961), Table 1D.
27. B. Supple, *The History of the British Coal Industry, vol. 4, 1913–46: The Political Economy of Decline* (Oxford, Clarendon 1987), Table 9.2.
28. Department of Employment and Productivity, *British Labour Statistics, Historical Abstract 1886–1968* (HMSO 1971), pp. 210–11.
29. G. Orwell, *The Road to Wigan Pier* (Gollancz 1937; Penguin 1962), pp. 6–7.
30. J.B. Jefferys, *Retail Trading in Britain, 1850–1950* (Cambridge UP 1954), Table 18.
31. Jefferys, *Retail Trading*, pp. 54ff.; P. Mathias, *Retailing Revolution: a history of multiple retailing in the food trades based upon the Allied Suppliers Group of Companies* (Longman 1967); G. Rees, *St Michael: a history of Marks & Spencer* (Weidenfeld & Nicolson 1969).

While concentration led to larger units and more impersonal service, at a greater distance (the larger shops were usually in town centres only), there were also forces making for the survival of the small shop. In the interwar period, resale price maintenance spread rapidly. In 1900 it may have covered 3 per cent of consumers' expenditure, and in 1938 30 per cent. Since this reduced the ability of shops to compete on price, they resorted to other devices, notably the provision of frequent delivery services, even for small orders. In this respect, the small shop could compete with the large, and the local shop was still very much a part of everyday life, in town, suburb and country, on the eve of the Second World War.[32]

SOCIAL STRUCTURE AND SOCIAL CLASS

Since the occupational structure of a society is closely associated with the concepts of social structure and social class, it is worthwhile enquiring how far occupational changes led to changes in the social structure of Britain. Although the concept of social class is a relatively modern one, the language of class was well enshrined in social analysis by the end of the nineteenth century. Different observers emphasised different characteristics as determining class, but occupation, and the income derived from it, was central to the discussion.

It is unfortunately very difficult to analyse changes in social class structure by the obvious means, that of the population census. Although the 1911 census attempted it, the method of classification changed at subsequent censuses, making later comparison difficult. An alternative classification is offered in Table 3.8, based on Routh's occupational categories in Table 3.7.

Table 3.8 British social classes by occupation, 1911 and 1951

Social class	*Occupational groups*	*1911 (%)*	*1951 (%)*
Upper and upper middle	1a	1.0	1.9
Lower middle	1b, 2	13.1	15.2
Upper working	3, 4, 5	36.6	38.2
Middle working	6	39.5	32.6
Lower working	7	9.6	12.0
All occupied persons (%)		99.8	99.9

Note: Occupational groups are the same as those in Table 3.7
Source: Based on Routh, *Occupation and Pay*, pp. 4–5

Although change was slow, it was perceptible. There was a general upgrading of society. The upper class, middle class and upper-working class combined rose from 50.7 to 55.3 per cent of the occupied population in 1911–1951,

32. Jefferys, *Retail Trading*, p. 54.

most of this increase being in the lower-middle/upper-working class. The decline of the middle-working class is striking, although it was offset to some extent by the rise of the unskilled working class.

INCOMES AND WEALTH

The social changes of the period were accompanied by changes in the structure of incomes and wealth-holding. Here, the broad process was one of levelling. Colin Clark estimated that in 1929 the top 1.5 per cent of income-earners accounted for 23 per cent of all UK income, and the top 10 per cent accounted for 42 per cent of all income, so that the other 90 per cent accounted for 58 per cent. Some redistribution had clearly taken place since 1914.[33] (For data on pre-1914 income distribution see pp. 7–8.) In 1938, the top 1.4 per cent of income-earners are estimated (by Dudley Seers) to have accounted for 32 per cent of all incomes, and the top 13 per cent to have had 46 per cent, so that the remaining 87 per cent had 54 per cent of all income. Given the uncertainties of such calculations, it can be concluded that little change in income distribution took place between 1929 and 1938.[34]

These changes in incomes are pre-tax, and take no account of the increases in taxation, which affected chiefly the well-off, and the redistribution through public expenditure of monies which on the whole increasingly benefited the less well-off. To the well-off, the most evident change was the rise in income taxation. Before 1914, even the highest incomes had not paid more than 10 per cent of their income in direct tax. During the war, rates rose substantially, and did not revert to their prewar level afterwards. Income tax was also made much more progressive. As a result, the proportion of an income of £1,000 a year taken in tax in 1937–38 was 8.7 per cent, compared with 4.0 per cent in 1913–14. On an income of £20,000, the tax yield was 47.5 per cent, compared with only 8.1 per cent prewar.[35]

The income of the better-off was also adversely affected by the decline in income from property abroad. Before the war this had been very considerable, amounting to about 8.3 per cent of GNP. Over the whole interwar period, the income from overseas property averaged about 4.1 per cent of GNP. Since the recipients of this income were (either directly or indirectly), it may be assumed, overwhelmingly middle and upper class, this was another blow to their incomes.

The higher taxation of the well-off was offset to some extent by higher indirect taxes, which bore most heavily on those with lower incomes. Although the lower incomes escaped most direct taxation, a married man with three children, earning £200 a year or less in 1937–38 contributed on average 8–10 per

33. C. Clark, *National Income and Outlay* (Macmillan 1937), p. 110.
34. D. Seers, *The Levelling of Incomes since 1938* (Oxford, Blackwell 1951), p. 35, Table V.
35. D.H. Aldcroft, *The Inter-War Economy: Britain, 1919–1939* (Batsford 1970), p. 388.

cent of his income in indirect taxation, this being about double the prewar proportion.[36]

The higher indirect taxation of lower incomes was more than offset by the redistributive effect of public spending. Some of this benefited the better-off also, in the form of interest payments on the National Debt, roadbuilding, educational provision and state pensions, but on the whole the working classes were the gainers. The extent of the gain is arguable. Barna's estimate was that in 1937 the net effect of the tax structure was to redistribute between £200 million and £250 million annually, representing about 5–6 per cent of the national income, from the well-off to the less well-off. Colin Clark thought the gain was less, amounting to a net redistribution in 1935 of £91 million (about 2.2 per cent of the national income) from the middle and upper classes to the working classes.[37]

By the late 1930s, then, the social distribution of income had changed perceptibly. Much of this change was due to higher taxation and public spending which benefited the poorer rather than the richer groups in society. But there were other causes also. One was the steady, if slow, upgrading of the social structure already referred to. One aspect of this was the rise in salaried occupations. In 1911 in the UK there had been 15.2 million wage-earners and 1.7 million salary-earners. By 1938, the number of wage-earners had fallen by 170,000, but the number of salary-earners had more than doubled, to 3.8 million. Before the war the latter had accounted for 11 per cent of the gross national product, but by 1935–38 this had risen to 16 per cent.[38] The lower ranks of the salaried groups (female and young male teachers, junior clerks and draughtsmen) might earn less than a skilled manual worker; in 1935 the median salary of male clerks ranged from £103 to £368, averaging £192; the rate for engine drivers averaged £258, and for carpenters and bricklayers £176. But on the whole the transition to the salaried class led to a rise in average earnings.[39]

The First World War saw a change in the distribution of wealth, though less than that of income. Estimates of wealth-holding from estate duty returns, although incomplete, give some idea of how wealth-holding changed (Table 3.9 opposite).

While the decline in the preponderance of wealth-holding by the richest group was marked, the *proportionate* changes in wealth-holding affected the poorest groups most, since their share of the national wealth increased by about one-half by the end of the 1930s, compared with the position before 1914. In social terms, the fact that a much larger proportion of the less well-off had any wealth to leave (at least, enough to come within the scope of estate duty, whose threshold was £100) was as striking as the sudden diminution of the

36. J. Marchal and B. Ducros (eds), *The Distribution of National Income* (1968), pp. 116, 372.
37. Aldcroft, *Inter-War Economy*, pp. 372–3; Clark, *National Income*, pp. 146–8.
38. Marchal and Ducros, *Distribution of National Income*, pp. 119–20.
39. Routh, *Occupation and Pay*, pp. 79, 88.

Table 3.9 Distribution of personal wealth, England and Wales, 1911–13 to 1936–38 (adults aged over 25 years)

	Shares of personal wealth		
No. of estates	*1911–13 (%)*	*1924–30 (%)*	*1936–38 (%)*
Top 1 per cent	69	62	56
2–5 per cent	18	22	23
6–10 per cent	5	7	9
11–100 per cent	8	9	12

Source: Royal Commission on the Distribution of Income and Wealth (1975), p. 97

wealth of the very rich. (Calculations from estate duty records assume that estates not paying duty were not eligible for it. This is a source of error, since a large proportion of the poorer estates are not examined by the probate authorities, and the incidence of estate duty avoidance (or evasion) is difficult to assess.)

CONCLUSIONS

The interwar period saw the working-out of substantial long-term changes in the population and in the labour force. The greatest changes were the sharp slowing-down in the rate of population growth and the reduction in the size of the average family. The rate of household formation rose, as it became more feasible for married couples to set up a household independent of their parental homes. The occupational and social structures of society changed. Non-manual work became more prevalent, and the professional and clerical classes with which it was associated became more important in society. These changes were linked to changes in industrial and occupational structure which reflected the decline of older industries and the rise of newer ones. Finally, there was a sharp shift in the distribution of income, and to a lesser extent of wealth, as taxation rose to pay for the First World War and the higher level of social welfare spending which took root after 1918.

CHAPTER 4

GOVERNMENT IN THE 1920s:
ECONOMIC FUNCTIONS AND POLICIES

GOVERNMENT EXPENDITURE AND FUNCTIONS

Government expenditure after the First World War remained as a much higher proportion of the national income than before, even after the end of the fighting. In 1910–13, total government spending (central and local) had been 12–13 per cent of GNP, but by 1916 it had risen to over 50 per cent of GNP. Postwar governments never reduced it below 24 per cent, a level which was reached in 1923. Thereafter it fluctuated, rising to 29 per cent in the depression of 1929–32, and falling thereafter, to rise again with the rearmament programme of the late 1930s, reaching 35 per cent in 1939.[1]

The real incidence of government spending and of taxation had thus more than doubled by the early 1920s. Before 1914, public expenditure had been dominated by social (chiefly education and poor relief) and military spending. By the mid-1920s, the military budget had declined substantially, and the social budget had risen, but the largest rise in expenditure had been in the service of the National Debt (Table 4.1 opposite).

The real incidence of debt service rose further after the collapse of the postwar boom in 1921, with its accompanying fall in the national price level. The capital value of the debt had been determined by the high national price levels in 1916–19, when much of it had been issued. Since the interest rates offered on the debt remained fairly stable, the income which it yielded also remained stable in money terms. The sums payable to debt-holders hardly varied; £349.6 million in 1920–21 and £358.2 million in 1925–26.[2] Meanwhile, the national level of prices had fallen considerably; the Board of Trade (working-class) cost of living index by 30 per cent and the Board's wholesale price index by 48 per cent (1920–25).[3] Thus the real value of the debt, and the relative burden of debt service on government finances, had increased sharply

1. A.T. Peacock and J. Wiseman, *The Growth of Public Expenditure in the United Kingdom* (Oxford UP 1961), pp. 164–5.
2. Board of Trade, *Statistical Abstract for the United Kingdom 1911–1925* (1927), Cmd 2849, p. 109.
3. B.R. Mitchell, *British Historical Statistics* (Cambridge UP 1988), pp. 729, 739.

Table 4.1 UK government expenditure (central and local), 1910–35

	1910 (%)	*1920* (%)	*1925* (%)	*1930* (%)	*1935* (%)
Military defence	27.3	32.6	12.5	10.4	12.6
Social services	32.8	25.9	36.3	42.3	46.5
Economic services	13.9	12.8	12.3	11.6	11.2
National Debt service	7.4	20.4	28.4	25.4	18.5
Environmental services	5.3	1.6	3.0	3.3	3.7
Administration	8.1	4.5	4.6	4.1	4.3
Law and order	4.7	2.1	2.8	2.8	3.0
Overseas services	0.4	0.2	0.1	0.1	0.1
Total expenditure (£million)					
At current prices	272	1,592	1,072	1,145	1,117
At 1900 prices	264	565	525	602	643

Source: A.T. Peacock and J. Wiseman, *The Growth of Public Expenditure in the United Kingdom* (Oxford UP 1961), pp. 164–5, 186–7

by the time that the price level stabilised in 1923. Continuing deflation in the later 1920s, although at a slower rate, increased the real burden of the debt further. Keynes wrote in 1927 that: 'More than a third of the burden of what is now owed in respect of the war-debt is due not to the expenses of the war, but to the fall in prices since this debt was incurred.'[4]

This rise more than outweighed the effect of the debt redemption policy (via a Sinking Fund) pursued by successive Chancellors of the Exchequer in the 1920s. Relief from the debt service burden came only in the depression after 1929, when the decline in the long-term market rate of interest enabled the government to convert a large portion of the debt to a lower rate of interest.

This enormously increased National Debt was a new nightmare for postwar Chancellors of the Exchequer, who were very concerned to raise revenue to service it. Thus the search for economy was a constant theme of the Budget after 1918. It also entailed a great burden for the taxpayer, as it was the main reason for the retention of high wartime rates of taxation into the postwar period.

Military expenditure proved more amenable to cost-cutting in the 1920s. This was partly due to the changed nature of warfare. Of the £72 million spent on the Armed Services in 1912–13, the Navy had spent £44 million, and possessed 66 battleships, displacing 1.1 million tons. The disappearance of the German Navy, and the Washington Naval Agreement of 1921, provided an opportunity for economy. By 1925, the battleships had been reduced to 22, displacing only 0.58 million tons. Reductions in the Army were also possible

4. J.M. Keynes, 'The Colwyn Report on National Debt and Taxation', *EJ* XXXVII (1927), p. 212.

Table 4.2 UK government social expenditure (central and local), 1910–35

	1910 (£million)	*1920 (£million)*	*1930 (£million)*	*1935 (£million)*
Education	33.5	88.8	104.2	111.7
Unemployment	a	10.8	101.6	99.0
Poor relief	16.1	34.2	42.5	51.8
Pensions war	a	100.9	49.2	40.4
old age and other	7.4	20.7	72.1	88.4
Health care	4.3	44.9	58.1	63.6
Housing	0.9	4.7	40.0	48.2
Totals	62.2	305.0	467.7	503.1

Note: a Not applicable
Source: HM Treasury, *Public Social Services* (1937), Cmd 5609, pp. 6–7

with the end of the British military presence in Southern Ireland after 1921, and the liquidation of some of the occupying armies in Europe and the Middle East. However, even in 1921 the total Army strength was still, at 297,000, above its prewar level of around 250,000. Both services fell under the scrutiny of the Committee on National Expenditure of 1921–22 (nicknamed the 'Geddes Axe', after its chairman, Sir Eric Geddes), which sought economies in public spending. It recommended that the services contribute £45.5 million of its proposed economies of £86.8 million. By 1925–26, the cost of all three services came to £119 million, which was in real terms only slightly higher than in 1913. The increase was mainly due to the creation of the Royal Air Force, which cost £15 million in that year.[5]

The expansion of social expenditure as compared with prewar was very considerable (Table 4.2 above). The rise in social spending was much more rapid than that of government spending as a whole, even when allowance has been made for price changes. Much of the basis of higher expenditure had been laid before the war, in the shape of old age pensions (payable at 70), the national health insurance scheme, and the beginning of the unemployment insurance scheme. War pensions were an unavoidable commitment, which weighed heavily on the Budget in the early 1920s, but then declined fairly rapidly. Postwar 'reconstruction' added to spending commitments in the shape of the extension of unemployment insurance to most of the working population in 1920, the beginnings of house-building subsidies in 1919, and the raising of the school-leaving age under the Education Act ('Fisher Act') 1918. The most significant new commitments in the 1920s were the adding of dependants' allowances to unemployment benefit in 1921, and the inauguration of contributory pension schemes for insured persons reaching the age of 65 (in

5. Board of Trade, *Statistical Abstract* (1927), pp. 100–1, 104, 110–11; Committee on National Expenditure, *Third Report* (1922), Cmd 1589, pp. 168–9.

1928), and for the widows and orphans of insured men (in 1926). In addition, both the health and education budgets expanded steadily, in response to technical developments and changes in professional thinking.

Higher social expenditure was thus part of a broader process of social reform, which had been well under way before 1914, and continued into the 1920s. But there were other reasons for the greater social spending. In particular, the rise in unemployment after the breaking of the postwar boom meant that the unemployment insurance fund ran up large deficits, which had to be borne by the Treasury, and the cost of poor relief was also increased. There was also the continued ageing of the population, with the numbers eligible for old age pensions rising from 705,678 in 1911 to 1,010,684 in 1925 (number of pensioners on last Friday in March in both years).[6]

While the social functions of government expanded greatly in the first quarter of the century, the economic functions remained relatively constant. Government spending on economic functions was largely accounted for by the trading services of local authorities. These services were a heterogeneous array, which included the provision of

> water, gas and electricity, trams and buses, markets and cemeteries. In addition, there are such rarer birds as Birmingham's Bank, Hull's telephone, Colchester's oyster fishery, Doncaster's race-course, Bradford's wool-conditioning house, and Wolverhampton's cold storage. Watering-places frequently own pavilions and piers; municipal aerodromes are becoming increasingly common. In short, there are no limits to the variety of local investment except those set by the imagination of town councillors and their ability to get parliamentary sanction for experiments.[7]

Trading services accounted for slightly over one-half of the economic expenditure of central and local government combined before 1914, when it totalled £102 million. The Post Office accounted for a further one-quarter, and road-building and maintenance for about one-fifth; the small residual was taken up by aid to trade and industry. In the interwar period, total economic spending rose considerably, and by the late 1920s was running at about £280 million a year. However, this expansion did no more than keep it at a constant proportion of total government spending. Local trading services and the Post Office now occupied a slightly smaller proportion of the whole, the difference being made up by greater spending on the roads, and on aid to trade and industry.[8]

Spending on the roads had begun to rise before the war, as the advent of the motor vehicle necessitated the reconstruction of routes (especially long-distance ones) which had been built and maintained for horse-drawn traffic. Neglect during the war led to arrears of maintenance, and a new Road Fund was set up in 1920, to collect motor taxes for road improvement. Total road

6. Board of Trade, *Statistical Abstract* (1927), p. 58.
7. U.K. Hicks, *The Finance of British Government, 1920–1936* (Oxford, Clarendon 1938; 1970), p. 106.
8. Ibid., p. 381, Table 4.

expenditure had been only £16 million in 1913, and had risen to £59 million in 1926; it remained at roughly that figure for the rest of the interwar period.[9]

Direct aid to trade and industry, which had been a very small part of government economic spending before the war, remained minor; in normal years, around 2–4 per cent of the whole. The abnormal years were those when, by design or accident, certain industries were very heavily subsidised. Coal was subsidised in 1920 (£15 million) and 1925 (£19 million). A large payment (£20 million) was made to farmers in 1921, following an unforeseen large fall in cereal prices, as compensation for the repeal of the guaranteed prices enshrined in the Agriculture Act 1920.[10] These apart, relatively small sums were involved, such as those for overseas settlement and colonial development, the Empire Marketing Board, export credit guarantees, and some support for civil aviation, none of which exceeded £1.2 million a year in the 1920s. A pointer to the future was the funding for the Department of Scientific and Industrial Research; still only £0.3–0.4 million in the 1920s, but destined to expand greatly thereafter.

Rural enterprise was also favoured. The Forestry Commission was established in 1919 to make good the wartime timber losses. By 1929 it had a grant of around £0.5 million a year. The state also encouraged the sugar-beet industry, to reduce dependence on imported sugar. An Act of 1925 granted a ten-year subsidy, and by 1934 the industry had received about £30 million. The attempt to settle ex-servicemen on the land enjoyed a brief postwar vogue, absorbing £13.4 million before coming to an end in 1925.[11]

Government spending thus played a much more important role in the economic life of the nation in the 1920s than before 1914. This was partly due to the rise in National Debt service, but even omitting this, total spending had risen by 189 per cent between 1913 and 1929, whereas GNP had risen by only 97 per cent.[12] The rise of government spending also meant that government was now much more important as a paymaster for capital investment projects. Whereas in 1910–13, the expenditure of central and local government combined had provided 18 per cent of national capital formation, this had risen by 1925–29 to 31 per cent. (These figures are of Gross Domestic Fixed Capital Formation.) Most of this was done by local authorities, in their housing, educational and roadbuilding roles.[13]

The increased reliance on centrally administered direct taxation also had implications for the fiscal balance between central and local government. Between 1914 and 1925, the proportion of public spending (current and capital) accounted for by central government rose from 50.8 to 62.4 per cent. The

9. C.I. Savage, *An Economic History of Transport* (Hutchinson 1959), p. 174.
10. E.H. Whetham, *The Agrarian History of England and Wales, vol. VIII (1914–39)* (Cambridge UP 1978), p. 140.
11. Hicks, *Finance*, pp. 66, 90, 381.
12. Ibid., p. 380; C.H. Feinstein, *National Income, Expenditure and Output of the United Kingdom 1855–1965* (Cambridge UP 1972), Table 1.
13. Feinstein, *National Income*, Table 86.

local authorities were themselves more reliant on the central government, which had provided 13.4 per cent of their income in 1914, and provided 19.3 per cent of it in 1925. While government was providing a higher proportion of the nation's capital investment between the wars, most of this continued to be channelled through the local authorities (chiefly for housing programmes), and this partly accounts for their increased reliance on central government funding. In effect, the authorities were increasingly acting as agents for the capital spending projects of central government.[14]

GOVERNMENT INCOME

Higher spending had to be paid for, and so the incidence of taxation increased. The annual burden of central taxation (Inland Revenue and Customs and Excise) per head rose from £3.57 in 1913–14 to £15.07 in 1923–24. This rise (of 322 per cent) was only partly accounted for by the rise in the general price level (about 90 per cent between 1913 and 1923), so that the rise in the real level of taxation per head was about 220 per cent.[15]

The national tax structure had moved sharply from indirect to direct taxation. Before the war direct taxes had contributed only 32 per cent of total taxation, but they had risen by 1924–25 to 47 per cent. The chief rises were in the supertax/surtax and income taxes. Income tax, having been 1s. 2d. (6p) in the pound in 1913–14, had been as high as 6s. (30p) in 1920–21, and never fell below 4s. (20p) between the wars. Before 1914 it had not been payable on incomes under £160 a year. Although the threshold was raised after the war, first to £200 in 1920, and then to £250 in 1925, this did not keep pace with the inflation of incomes, so that, in spite of more generous dependants' allowances to be set against tax, the number of income tax payers rose from 1.2 million in 1913–14 to 2.4 million in 1924–25. The number of supertax/surtax payers rose from 14,008 to 96,682, and their tax rates became more steeply progressive. Taken together, the yield from income tax, surtax and death duties combined had provided 28.5 per cent of all government revenue (central and local) in 1913–14; in 1924–25 it had risen to 43.0 per cent.[16]

Indirect taxation was mainly provided by Customs and Excise duties. As in 1914, a small number of articles provided most of the revenue. Excise duties on spirits and beer, and import duties on tobacco, tea and sugar, accounted for 87 per cent of customs and excise revenue in 1913–14, and 90 per cent in 1924–25. Between these years, rates of duty were raised sharply; that on spirits

14. Mitchell, *Statistics*, pp. 610, 623–4.
15. Committee on National Debt and Taxation ('Colwyn Committee'), *Report* (1927), Cmd 2800, p. 74; Feinstein, *National Income*, Table 133 (index of prices of consumers' goods and services).
16. (Sir) B. Mallet and C.O. George, *British Budgets, Second Series, 1913–14 to 1920–21* (Macmillan 1929), pp. 398, 400; *British Budgets, Third Series, 1921–22 to 1932–33* (Macmillan 1933), pp. 561, 564, 566; C. Clark, *National Income and Outlay* (Macmillan 1937), p. 140.

from 1s. $11\frac{1}{2}$d. to 8s. $5\frac{1}{2}$d. a bottle; that on beer from roughly $\frac{1}{4}$d. to $2\frac{1}{4}$d. a pint; tobacco from 3s. 8d. to 8s. 2d. a pound; and sugar from $\frac{1}{4}$d. to $1\frac{1}{4}$d. a pound. These increases did not raise the tax yield commensurately, since there was a sharp fall in the consumption of spirits and beer, only partly offset by rising consumption of tobacco.[17]

ECONOMIC AND FINANCIAL POLICIES

The economic weight of government was thus much greater after 1918, mainly because of the cost of debt service, the expansion of social programmes, and much higher unemployment. In such a situation, it might have been thought that a reconsideration of the traditional role of government in the economic affairs of the nation could or should have taken place. Such a reconsideration took place among economists in the 1930s, following the lead of Keynes. Whether governments had by the late 1930s come round to the ideas of Keynes is still debated. Later historians have often condemned the governments of 1918–39 for not anticipating Keynes, especially in view of his suggestions that the government should take a more active role in overcoming unemployment, by raising its expenditure further in order to make up for the lack of demand from the non-government side of the economy. Yet for most of the interwar period, and especially in the 1920s, there was little support among economists or politicians for radical new policies.[18]

In broad terms, the economic aims of governments at all times have been very similar. The list of priorities changes somewhat over time and place, but the list of basic objectives remains similar; economic growth (or 'prosperity' in pre-1939 language); high employment; stable prices; and a balance (or preferably a surplus) in foreign payments. There have, however, always been great differences of view as to how these aims (especially if they were seen to conflict with one another) were to be achieved. These differences give scope for great variations in policy.

Before 1914, the dominant view of the economic role of government was that it should try to ensure an environment of stability – in trade (domestic and foreign), prices, and employment – within which private enterprise could flourish. In practical policy, this meant the maintenance of the gold standard and free trade, coupled with action by the monetary authorities to smooth out the trade cycle. It was also axiomatic that public spending should be balanced by taxation. These views still held the field after 1918. Thus policy in the 1920s was directed to the re-establishment of the gold standard and the maintenance of free trade, while bringing the central government budget back into balance from its wartime and postwar deficits. (See the Note on the gold standard at

17. Board of Trade, *Statistical Abstract* (1927), pp. 112–15; Colwyn Committee, *Report*, App. IX.
18. K.J. Hancock, 'Unemployment and the Economists in the 1920s', *Economica* 27 (1960); R. Middleton, *Towards the Managed Economy: Keynes, the Treasury and the fiscal policy debate of the 1930s* (Methuen 1985), esp. pp. 173–4.

the end of this chapter, p. 84, and the Guide to Further Reading at the end of this book.)

THE RETURN TO THE GOLD STANDARD

During the war, the pound sterling had been detached from the gold standard; the import and export of gold had ceased, and the sterling exchange rate had declined. The US dollar being the only substantial currency remaining on gold, the dollar became thereafter the customary standard of comparison when the sterling exchange rate was being considered. The abandonment of the external gold standard was accompanied by its abandonment for domestic transactions. The paper currency ceased to be exchangeable for gold at the banks, and the supply of paper currency, unbacked by gold reserves in the banking system, grew substantially.

Before the war, the official dollar exchange rate had been £1 = $4.86. The exchange rate having fallen, it was pegged at $4.76 in 1916, and supported at that level by government intervention. The exchange rate system was henceforth a managed one. The discipline formerly exerted on domestic credit creation by the gold standard was now inoperative, and inflationary forces were no longer checked by a restricted money supply. British prices rose rapidly, propelled by the rise in the National Debt and shortages of all kinds. By 1918, the general price level had roughly doubled, government spending was greatly in excess of revenue, and the money supply had expanded considerably. There was also developing a substantial current balance of payments deficit.

It was in these circumstances that the decision was taken to return to the gold standard. Recommendation of this course was made by the Committee on Currency and Foreign Exchanges after the War ('Cunliffe Committee') in its interim report of August 1918, and reiterated in the final report of December 1919. The committee's case was that the absence of the standard permitted excess credit creation, which in turn facilitated inflation, thus threatening exports and the exchange rate of sterling. This might 'jeopardize the convertibility of our note issue and the international trade position of the country'. As remedies, the committee proposed that government borrowing should cease as soon as possible, that a Sinking Fund should be created to pay off accumulated debt, that the fiduciary note issue should be restricted, and that steps should be taken to make Bank Rate once more effective. In essence, the committee proposed to reduce the supply of credit (and hence money), in order to lower prices and thereafter keep them stable. This in turn would permit the restoration of the gold standard and a stable exchange rate.[19]

The Treasury and the Bank of England endorsed these proposals, but their

19. Committee on Currency and Foreign Exchanges after the War ('Cunliffe Committee'), *First Interim Report* (1918), para. 47, and *Final Report* (1919), para. 2, both in T.E. Gregory, *Select Statutes, Documents and Reports relating to British Banking 1832–1928*, vol. 2 (Oxford UP 1929; Cass 1964), pp. 361, 366. There is also a large extract from the *First Interim Report* in Eichengreen, *Gold Standard*, pp. 169–83.

implementation had to be postponed. In March 1919 the cost of supporting sterling proved too much, and the pegging of the exchange rate was abandoned. The following month the export of gold was legally prohibited, and the gold standard was now formally abandoned, having been de facto suspended since 1914. The exchange rate then fell sharply, reaching a low of $3.20 in February 1920. Meanwhile, it took time to reduce government spending, although the deficit of 1919–20 was much smaller than that of 1918–19. A large budget surplus was realised in 1920–21, and smaller ones in the next two years. Inflation was still rapid until 1920. The Board of Trade (working-class) cost of living index, which had risen from 100 in July 1914 to 203 on average in 1918, continued to rise after the end of the war, when price controls and rationing were removed. In 1920 it peaked at a yearly average of 249, until the sharp economic recession at the end of the year precipitated a rapid fall in prices. The recession also helped to reduce the money supply, and steps were taken to reduce the volume of short-term government debt, and the issue of fiduciary notes.

It should be explained that the fiduciary note issue was originally only the issue of Bank of England notes, unbacked by gold. The limit of this issue had been set at £14 million by the Bank Charter Act 1844. The rest of the Bank's note issue was to be backed pound for pound by gold in the Bank's reserves. By 1913 the fiduciary issue had risen to £19 million, as the Bank took over the note issues of amalgamated banks. By 1918, the fiduciary issue was still £19 million, but there was also in circulation £249 million of Treasury banknotes, unbacked by gold – in effect, a new form of fiduciary issue, and a new form of paper currency in its own right.[20]

The recession of 1920–21 was one of the most severe, if short-lived, in British economic history. A deflationary Budget in April 1920 was followed by a sharp rise in unemployment, from an average of 3.9 to 16.9 per cent of insured employees between 1920 and 1921. The rise was most acute in the first half of 1921; between January and May, the proportion of insured workers unemployed rose from 11.2 to 23.4 per cent. Even at the end of the year it was still 18.0 per cent.[21] Between 1919 and 1922 the UK GDP fell in real terms from £4,580 million to £3,992 million (13 per cent).[22] (Feinstein allows a loss of 4 per cent UK GDP in 1920 due to the secession of Southern Ireland from the UK.)

The extent to which this decline had been desired by the government, as part of the mechanism for reducing the British price level, and thus creating the conditions for the restoration of the gold standard, is still debated. The initial raising of Bank Rate (from 6 to 7 per cent in April 1920) was a panic

20. Mitchell, *Statistics*, pp. 583–5, 739; D.H. Aldcroft, *The British Economy, vol. I, The Years of Turmoil 1920–1951* (Harvester 1986), ch. 1; Cunliffe Committee, *First Interim Report*, para. 13.
21. Mitchell, *Statistics*, p. 682; Department of Employment and Productivity, *British Labour Statistics, Historical Abstract 1886–1968* (HMSO 1971), Table 160.
22. Mitchell, *Statistics*, p. 124; Feinstein, *National Income*, Table 5 (GDP at 1938 market prices).

measure, which helped to precipitate the slump, which seems to have begun in the last quarter of 1920.[23] The rate was kept at 7 per cent for twelve months, and even then reduced by only 0.5 per cent. Even by the end of 1921, which was the trough year of the recession, it was still at 5 per cent. There is little doubt that rates were kept at these high levels for longer than economic conditions warranted, if the aim had been merely the conventional one of smoothing out economic activity.[24]

The recession saw a sharp fall in output, and in prices. By December 1922 the Board of Trade wholesale price index and the Ministry of Labour cost of living index had fallen by 51 per cent and 35 per cent respectively below their peak 1920 levels.[25] The final act of government economy also came in 1922, with the reports of the Geddes Committee, which recommended savings on government spending of £86.8 million, amounting to about 8 per cent of central government expenditure in that year.[26]

By the end of 1922 most of the preconditions for return to the gold standard envisaged by the Cunliffe Committee had been fulfilled. Not only had internal prices been lowered, and the money supply been brought under control, but also the current balance of payments had been in surplus since 1920, and the Budget had been brought into balance. Severe deflation in Britain had led to UK prices falling more than those in the USA (which had also experienced a recession), and so the dollar exchange rate had risen to an average of $4.43 in 1922.[27] This was still lower than the prewar rate of $4.86, and it was the government's intention that restoration of the gold standard should be at that prewar rate. However, the fall in British prices and costs had not offset the fact that US costs and prices had risen less than the British during 1914–19, so that in comparison with 1914 British prices and costs were still higher than those in the USA. A further rise in the exchange rate would seem to depend upon either a further fall in British prices, or a rise in US prices.

These relative price changes did not take place. British wholesale prices hardly altered for the next three years, although the cost of living index fell slightly; US prices remained stable. Whereas between 1920 and 1923 the sterling/dollar exchange rate had been influenced principally by such price changes, it was thereafter more dependent on relative interest rates and speculation. The Bank of England, in an effort to increase the dollar rate by attracting foreign funds, raised Bank Rate from 3 per cent to 4 per cent in July 1923, and, when the Federal Reserve Bank of New York lowered its rate in 1924, did not follow suit. The return of a Conservative government at the general election in

23. F. Capie and M. Collins, *The Inter-War British Economy: a statistical abstract* (Manchester UP 1983), pp. 20, 48.
24. J.A. Dowie, '1919–20 is in Need of Attention', *EcHR* XXVIII (1975).
25. D.E. Moggridge, *The Return to Gold 1925: the formulation of economic policy and its critics* (Cambridge UP 1969), p. 15; Capie and Collins, *Inter-War British Economy*, pp. 32, 36.
26. Committee on National Expenditure, *Third Report* (1922), Cmd 1589, p. 169.
27. Mitchell, *Statistics*, p. 703.

October 1924 heightened speculation of a return to gold at the prewar parity, thus offering potential capital gains for investors in sterling securities.[28] By April 1925 the pound had reached almost its old dollar parity, and the Chancellor of the Exchequer, Winston Churchill, announced the return to the gold standard at the prewar parity in his Budget speech of that month.

FREE TRADE MAINTAINED

The return to gold had been a difficult process; the maintenance of free trade was easier. This was partly because, in spite of the exporting difficulties of the 1920s, there was no great demand from manufacturers for the imposition of protection, and the electorate, as the general election result of 1923 showed, was firmly in favour of free trade. However, several breaches in the principle had been made in the war and immediate postwar years. The McKenna duties ($33\frac{1}{3}$ per cent *ad valorem*) of 1915 on 'luxuries' (motor cars and cycles, watches and clocks, musical instruments, cinematograph films) had been imposed mainly to save shipping space and foreign exchange. Since they had by the end of the war become useful as sources of revenue, they were retained. Although briefly abandoned by the Labour government in 1924, they were re-imposed, and extended in 1926 to cover commercial vehicles and parts.

Certain 'key' industries, dependent on imported parts or materials before the war, had been protected by import licences in the later years of the war, and this protection was formally ratified by Acts of Parliament in 1920 (dyestuffs) and the rest of the 'key' industries by the Safeguarding of Industries Act 1921. In wartime, the products concerned had been certain chemicals, scientific instruments, laboratory glassware and magnetos. These were now given the same tariff as the McKenna goods. The Safeguarding Act's provisions were extended in 1925 to include certain imports which might be thought to benefit from unfair advantages such as currency depreciation or subsidies. Thus such industries as cutlery, pottery, lace, buttons, wrapping paper and some other minor industries were also protected.

Special protection was given to the British film industry in 1927; the Cinematograph Films Act established a compulsory minimum quota of British pictures, beginning at 7.5 per cent for renters and 5 per cent for exhibitors, to rise by stages to 20 per cent for both in 1936–38. The quota system was a success, since the British industry soon exceeded the minimum quota at home, and developed an export trade. However, the quality of the 'quota quickies' spawned under the Act left something to be desired.

These measures hardly constituted overall protection; in 1930, only 17 per cent by value of all British imports were dutiable, and most of these fell under the heading of revenue rather than protective duties. However, the principle of protection had been accepted, and it assisted several nascent industries

28. N.H. Dimsdale, 'British Monetary Policy and the Exchange Rate 1920–1938', *OEP* 33 (1981), Suppl., p. 313.

(principally dyestuffs and motor vehicles) to grow relatively unperturbed by import competition.[29]

FREE TRADE, THE GOLD STANDARD AND UNEMPLOYMENT POLICY

By the mid-1920s, therefore, the presuppositions of prewar economic policy had been restored. The gold standard had been resurrected, and free trade, although breached in principle, was still in practice the normal mode of commerce. However, it had also by that time become apparent that Britain had serious economic problems. In particular, unemployment failed to decline as expected when production picked up after 1922. By 1924 the average proportion of the insured labour force out of work had fallen, but only to 10.3 per cent. The other worry was exports. At their lowest level in the postwar slump, in 1921, they had sunk to 50 per cent of their 1913 level. Some recovery had taken place after this, but by 1924 they had reached only 76 per cent of their 1913 level.[30]

Both the maintenance of free trade and the restoration of the gold standard, it was thought, would assist to solve these problems. Free trade was indicated because it was held to be the best way of promoting international efficiency, including that of Britain. In addition, while the current balance of payments was still in Britain's favour, there was little to be said for protection, which was further ruled out by electoral considerations.

It was also thought that the restoration of the gold standard would help exports to recover. To later generations, mindful of Keynes' strictures on sterling overvaluation in 1925, this line of thought has seemed somewhat perverse. However, the gold standard restoration was, as Sayers has emphasised, 'essentially an employment policy'. The thinking behind it was that, in a world beset by hyperinflation and currency collapse (as many European countries were in 1919–24):

> Britain's unemployment problem was due to the depression of world export markets; this was partly due to currency disorganization; therefore get the world's currency instability removed, the former exchange stability restored, and export markets could be expected to revive and unemployment would dwindle.[31]

The gold standard and free trade were, in essence, the 'rules of the game' which governments set for the economy; within them, private enterprise, it was held, would have to find its own salvation in the form of greater economic efficiency. This might involve cutting costs, higher levels of investment or the 'rationalisation' of individual industries. Whatever the course chosen, the decisions to be taken were essentially those of private entrepreneurs and boards

29. S. Pollard, *The Development of the British Economy, 1914–1990* (4th edn, Edward Arnold 1992), pp. 65, 193–4, for the preceding paragraphs.
30. Mitchell, *Statistics*, pp. 124, 519.
31. R.S. Sayers, 'The Return to Gold', in S. Pollard (ed.), *The Gold Standard and Employment Policies between the Wars* (Methuen 1970), pp. 89–90.

of shareholders; they were not within the customarily defined boundaries of government action.

INDUSTRIAL POLICY

However, this general predisposition to *laissez-faire* did not preclude some specific interventions, either to relieve unemployment or to stimulate industry. Measures to relieve unemployment first manifested themselves in the slump of 1920–22, in the setting up of the Unemployment Grants Committee (UGC) in December 1920. This allocated Exchequer funds to assist local authorities' public works projects. There was also a separate public works programme employing about 73,000 men in the winter of 1920–21.[32]

The work of the UGC went on until 1932, and the total capital value of the projects which it approved was considerable, being some £191 million, chiefly on sewerage projects and local road and electricity supply schemes. However, it is unlikely that more than about £60 million of this was actually spent by then, and the total employment provided by these schemes in 1920–32 cannot have been large. The UGC estimated that £1 million spent on these schemes created 2,500 'man-years' of employment, so that spending £60 million implied the creation of only 150,000 jobs for one year only (or about 12,500 a year).[33]

While the UGC was the only body charged specifically with relieving unemployment via public works, the road schemes undertaken by central and local authorities may have had some effect in relieving unemployment. However, they did not total more than £77 million by 1932, so that their direct effect on unemployment would have been little greater than that of the UGC, even assuming that they attracted into their workforces the previously unemployed.[34]

A logical alternative to providing public works to relieve unemployment was to encourage labour to move away from depressed areas. Such a policy was not attempted until the end of the decade, after the report of the Industrial Transfer Board in 1928. Three types of transfers were attempted – single men (mainly from colliery districts), families, and boys and girls. Some success was recorded initially, 32,000 single men and 2,850 families being thus transferred in 1929, but the numbers had fallen to 8,000 and 605 respectively in 1933. This comparative failure was in spite of encouraging the transfer of workers from the depressed areas into employment on UGC schemes, 4,500 men being thus employed at the peak of this movement in July 1930.[35]

Some direct intervention in industry was also seen in the 1920s. Some of this represented an effort to promote external trade, in the form of the creation of

32. S. Howson, 'Slump and Unemployment', in R. Floud and D. McCloskey (eds), *The Economic History of Britain since 1700, vol. 2, 1860 to the 1970s* (Cambridge UP 1981), p. 275.
33. Unemployment Grants Committee (UGC), *Final Report* (1933), Cmd 4354, pp. 22–5, App. III; Hicks, *Finance*, pp. 199–201.
34. Howson, 'Slump', p. 281; Hicks, *Finance*, p. 194.
35. Hicks, *Finance*, pp. 203–4; UGC, *Final Report*, p. 10.

the Department of Overseas Trade, the promotion of colonial settlement and development, and the creation of the Empire Marketing Board in 1926. None of these initiatives came to very much, although the Department of Overseas Trade played an important part in the operation of the new system of export credit guarantees which was brought in after 1918.

Internally, a notable innovation was the introduction of interest guarantees for industry. Initially brought in under the Trade Facilities Acts 1921–26, the object was to enable industrial concerns to borrow cheaply at a time of high interest rates. Although applicable generally, its main purpose was to assist the export industries; that these were also industries with high unemployment doubtless provided another reason. By March 1927, £74.3 million had been guaranteed, principally in transport, shipping and shipbuilding, and other heavy industries. In view of the difficulties of these industries at the time, and of the subsequent failure of some of the concerns involved, this policy must be regarded as essentially a form of export subsidy.

Postwar governments were also more directly concerned in industry through the promotion of research. This was not only through the Department of Industrial and Scientific Research, which had been created in 1916, but also via various bodies such as the Medical Research Council, the prewar Development Commission (1909), and the Empire Marketing Board. In addition, other government departments responsible for transport, mining and the Post Office also commissioned research. Although the sums involved were small, they represented a new and growing area of government activity. Government was also involved with the new industry of civil aviation, which was first subsidised in 1920.

None of these industrial forms of intervention really amounted to a determined effort to reduce costs in industry as a whole. The nearest approach to such a policy came in 1929, when the de-rating provisions of the Local Government Act gave substantial assistance to many industries. 'Productive' industry (difficult to define) was relieved of 75 per cent of its local rates liability; this was equivalent to a subsidy from the Exchequer of about £21 million. The intention had been that this form of aid should mainly benefit 'heavy' industries, since it was known that they suffered from particularly high unemployment. In the event, relief was more generally spread. Agriculture also benefited. Farmers had previously been relieved of rating obligations to the extent of 75 per cent of their agricultural land and all their buildings; relief was now available for the last 25 per cent of agricultural land. Finally, railways also benefited from de-rating, to a similar extent as in industry, although this took some years to establish.[36]

THE SUCCESS OF ECONOMIC POLICY

To some extent, economic policies were successful in a broad sense; economic growth continued, and was faster in the 1920s than in the 1900–13

36. Hicks, *Finance*, pp. 64–79 for the three preceding paragraphs.

period. The more specific aims of the restoration of the level of exports, and the reduction of unemployment to the prewar level, were not attained. In the case of exports, their volume had reached a postwar low of 50 with the slump in 1921 (1913 = 100). Although they recovered afterwards, most of their recovery came before the return to the gold standard, and their 1920s peak (in 1929) was only 81 per cent of the 1913 level. In the case of unemployment, the 1920s levels remained much higher than those before 1914. After the boom, slump and recovery of the early 1920s, the lowest recorded level of unemployment of insured labour was 10.3 per cent (in 1924); the rates for 1925–29 varied between a low of 10.4 (1929) and a high of 12.5 (1926).[37] (See the Appendix to this book on UK rates of economic growth.)

There had also been some specific successes, chiefly in the field of public finance. The government's budget deficit had been eliminated; inflation had been brought to an end; the National Debt had ceased to grow. The world had been made safer for the rentier and capitalist, but less so for the industrial worker (particularly if in one of the major pre-1914 export trades). Whether such successes outweighed such failures was a matter of political rather than economic judgement.

ECONOMIC POLICY: WELL OR ILL-FOUNDED?

For good or ill, policy in the 1920s was constrained by the acceptance of the need to return to gold, and by the limited view which governments (of all political hues) held as to their responsibility for direct intervention in economic affairs. With hindsight, the policies adopted failed; exports did not recover their prewar level; unemployment remained much higher than prewar; and the restored gold standard (or, rather, gold exchange standard) had a short life, collapsing in 1931. The failures of the 1920s have lent an edge to subsequent historical judgements. Yet in a sense, criticism of the restored system for its failure is misplaced. British governments thought that it was the best way forward, did not wish it to fail, and worked hard to sustain it. Given the presuppositions of policy-makers in the 1920s, it remains to ask whether these were reasonable in the circumstances, and whether the policies adopted were well founded and managed.

From the standpoint of exports and the balance of payments, it was held to be better to have an international system of fixed, rather than floating exchange rates, since this would instil confidence in international traders and investors. There was nothing wrong with this presupposition, and subsequent history with both fixed and floating exchange rate regimes does not provide clear evidence that it was wrong in the circumstances, especially since British trade was still an important element in total world trade. However, the concept was flawed if it was thought that it would by itself counteract any deterioration in British competitiveness during the war. In the long run, exchange rates are determined by relative international efficiencies, not the other way around. To

37. Mitchell, *Statistics*, pp. 124, 519.

see the gold standard as a solution to British inefficiency was to put the cart before the horse.

For the purpose of returning to gold, the only acceptable standard for comparison was the US dollar, which had alone of the major currencies remained on the gold standard, with its prewar parity unchanged. But there was a fatal error; during the war, technical efficiency in the UK (and Europe) had deteriorated severely in relation to that of the USA.[38] Thus, instead of trying to reduce costs by a process of general deflation, in a vain attempt to restore competitiveness with US industry, it should have been accepted that Britain was now less efficient in relation to the USA, and, if the return to gold were still insisted upon, it should have been at a lower than prewar parity.

In this situation, the early decision to return to gold, taken in 1918, and the use of the US dollar as a benchmark for the restoration of the sterling exchange rate, were considerable errors. While a case could be made for the use of the dollar in this way in the early 1920s, there was less justification after 1923–24, when many European currencies had been stabilised. But the authorities pressed on *à outrance*. In refusing to accept devaluation, they had the great bulk of informed opinion on their side. Even Keynes did not suggest that the prewar parity should have been allowed to slip by more than 10 per cent. Even in 1931, when the system was crumbling, the Macmillan Committee (of which Keynes was a member) firmly rejected devaluation:

> But, while all things may be lawful, all things are not expedient, and in our opinion the devaluation by any Government of a currency standing at its par value suddenly and without notice (as must be the case to prevent foreign creditors removing their property) is emphatically one of those things which are not expedient.[39]

This refusal to contemplate devaluation was maintained in spite of the committee's recognition that the restoration of 1925 had been at too high a parity.

The technical aspects of the return to gold can also be criticised. It was odd that, in the discussions which led up to the return to gold, little use was made of balance of payments statistics, even if the contemporary figures were a little rough.[40] The authorities may also have been misled by reliance on nominal exchange rates. It has been suggested that when real exchange rates are calculated, rather than nominal rates, the pound was in fact overvalued in 1920–21 by 6–10 per cent, so that the policy of deflation was already squeezing exporters severely during the sharp recession of those years.[41] (The real exchange rate is the nominal exchange rate, adjusted for price changes in the countries concerned.) It has also been shown that policy-makers were misled by relying solely on the dollar rate as a comparator. After 1925, comparison of the pound,

38. M.E. Falkus, 'United States Economic Policy and the "Dollar Gap" of the 1920s', *EcHR* XXIV (1971).

39. Committee on Finance and Industry, *Report* (1931), Cmd 3897, para. 256.

40. Dimsdale, 'British Monetary Policy', p. 316.

41. S.N. Broadberry, *The British Economy between the Wars; a Macroeconomic Survey* (Oxford, Blackwell 1986), p. 121.

not with the dollar alone but with a basket of currencies (including the dollar), shows that the pound was probably at least as overvalued as Keynes had suggested, and possibly much more (5–25 per cent) depending on the price measurements adopted.[42] In defence of the authorities, it may be said that some of the overvaluation was due to the fact that some countries (notably France and Belgium) had returned to the gold standard after 1925 at much lower exchange rates than prewar; the German mark was also undervalued in relation to sterling in 1925.[43]

Acceptance of the thesis that sterling was overvalued in 1925 involves also acceptance of the view that the balance of trade was injured thereby. While calculations of the hypothetical level of such an injury are very speculative, Moggridge estimated that a lower parity, of $4.38, might have improved the balance of (visible) trade in 1928 by £52 million, with a further £15 million due to an improvement in the invisible balance. This would have also reduced unemployment, although by how much is unclear. This suggestion is of particular interest since, after 1925, British exports grew more slowly than world exports, so that the British share of the total fell, and the current balance of payments surplus was small. It is hard to escape the conclusion that the return to gold was in practice misplaced, and contributed to the failure of exports to revive.[44]

Finally, domestic policy may be considered. It was notable that interest rates in the 1920s were higher than prewar. In 1909–13 the average yield on 2.5 per cent Consols (long-term government securities) had been 3.17 per cent. In 1920–24 it was 4.73 per cent, and in 1925–29 4.52 per cent. Thus the level of interest rates was on average about 45 per cent higher than before the war. It has to be borne in mind also that the price level was falling throughout the 1920s, and thus the real level of interest rates was much higher than this nominal level indicates.[45]

High interest rates were the intentional policy of the Bank of England and the Treasury. Before 1924, the Bank was concerned to assist the deflation of prices as a necessary prelude to the restoration of the gold standard. After restoration, rates were not reduced unless there was no danger of an outflow of gold or foreign exchange. This in turn depended on the interest rates in New York and Paris, so there was not much room for manoeuvre, although Montagu Norman was concerned not to tighten home credit conditions too much. The Treasury was preoccupied with the problems of maintaining the debt funding programme, and for this, fairly high interest rates had to be maintained; otherwise much of the debt, contracted at the high interest rates of 1914–20, would be sold by its holders back to the authorities, who were in

42. J. Redmond, 'The Sterling Overvaluation in 1925: a multilateral approach', *EcHR* XXXVII (1984), pp. 528–9.
43. Moggridge, *Return to Gold*, p. 82.
44. Ibid., p. 95.
45. London and Cambridge Economic Service, *The British Economy: key statistics, 1900–1964* (Times Publishing Co. 1965), Table G.

no position to buy much of it. In addition, the weakness of the foreign exchanges required high interest rates in London. The upshot was a high interest rate regime. This presumably did not encourage business investment, even if most firms relied rather on their undistributed profits than on the capital market for their capital investment requirements.[46]

In sum, therefore, it can be said that economic policy on conventional lines was only partly successful, and governments in the 1920s were reluctant to adopt unconventional policies. Constrained to limit themselves to one large policy, the authorities had no remedy when it did not work. Perhaps it was the case that, as Moggridge remarked, the restoration of gold was 'ultimately an act of faith in an incompletely understood adjustment mechanism undertaken largely for moral reasons'.[47]

Such a policy is understandable by the light of contemporary thought and feeling. Less easily understandable is the lack of thought as to the remedies for its failure, which was apparent by 1928–29, with lagging exports and continuing high unemployment. But the logical immediate remedy, that of devaluation, aroused fear and repugnance in the responsible authorities. This possibility excluded, they had nothing more to offer. It was their lack of boldness which condemned the policy-makers to rely on the conventional wisdom, even when it had failed. Keynes' words, written in support of Lloyd George's public works proposals of 1929, are apposite here also:

> There is no reason why we should not feel ourselves free to be bold, to be open, to experiment, to take action, to try the possibilities of things. And over against us, standing in the path, there is nothing but a few old gentlemen, tightly buttoned-up in their frock coats, who only need to be treated with a little friendly disrespect and bowled over like ninepins.
>
> Quite likely they will enjoy it themselves, when once they have got over the shock.[48]

CONCLUSIONS

The economic functions of government were not in principle changed after 1918, but certain of these functions were enormously expanded. The chief of these were the repayment of interest on the much higher National Debt, and the expansion of social spending. To pay for these, the level of taxation rose sharply. This affected chiefly the higher income earners. Thus the central government budget became a much greater matter of political concern. This apart, the attitude of government to economic affairs changed little. In particular, there was a determination to stick to what were felt to be the tried and tested foundations of economic policy – the gold standard and free trade.

46. S. Howson, *Domestic Monetary Management in Britain, 1919–38* (Cambridge UP 1975), pp. 32, 49–50; D.H. Aldcroft, *The Inter-War Economy: Britain, 1919–1939* (Batsford 1970), pp. 332–3.
47. Moggridge, *Return to Gold*, p. 81.
48. J.M. Keynes, *Essays in Persuasion* (Hart-Davis 1951), pp. 133–4.

Apart from the attractions which politicians and bankers discerned in their intrinsic virtues, it was thought that these policies would provide the best chance of remedying the higher unemployment and lower exports which were apparent by the mid-1920s. These hopes were not fulfilled. In retrospect, there is one clear error; the return to gold, if persisted with, should have been at a lower exchange rate. That apart, it is difficult to see what else could have been done, since government retained the *laissez-faire* instincts of pre-1914. Given this constraint, government had little else to offer as the decade wore on, and the failure of policy became clearer.

A NOTE ON THE GOLD STANDARD

There is still much debate as to how the prewar gold standard operated. It is perhaps best approached by considering the following (rather idealised) description of the course of events in a pre-1914 boom. For a slump, the sequence of events is reversed; the reader may substitute the opposite terms throughout the following description to see what probably happened in a slump.

Due to a boom developing in the later stages of the trade cycle, there is a tendency for prices to rise. Thus exports become less competitive. At the same time, rising incomes increase demand for imports. Thus the balance of payments deteriorates. An export of gold then occurs, to pay for the increased foreign obligations. This external drain of gold has two consequences. The banking system, deprived of some of its cash (i.e. gold) reserves tries to restore the previous ratio between its issue of paper money and its gold reserves, by calling in old loans and declining to renew old ones. Thus a credit squeeze is initiated. At the same time, the Bank of England, which has lost reserves of gold and foreign exchange, raises Bank Rate in order to attract an inflow of gold and foreign exchange. The higher Bank Rate accentuates the credit squeeze. Interest rates rise in general; firms find finance scarce and expensive; economic activity is lowered generally; unemployment rises and incomes decline; the general price level comes down; the prices of exports are restored to a competitive level; imports fall as incomes are lowered; the balance of payments improves; the outflow of gold is checked; the system is restored to equilibrium. Thus the gold standard performed its twin functions of stabilising both the balance of foreign payments and the value of the internal monetary unit (i.e. prices).

CHAPTER 5

GROWING AND DECLINING INDUSTRIES AFTER 1918

THE NATIONAL PATTERN

In spite of the losses of output due to the war, and to postwar unemployment, the British economy as a whole was larger at the end of the 1920s than before 1914. Taking UK GDP in 1913 as 100, it has been estimated that GDP in 1929 was 107.8 in real terms. This annual rate of growth of national output (0.5 per cent a year) was about the same as that of the years 1899–1913, which had been the slowest-growth years of the half-century or so before 1914. That it was not higher may be attributed to losses of output in the war and in the postwar recession, and the severing of Southern Ireland from the UK in 1921. The loss of national product due to the latter has been estimated at 3.6 per cent.[1]

Manufacturing remained the largest single source of national output. Together with mining and building, it accounted for 37.0 per cent of national income in 1907, and 40.2 per cent in 1924.[2] There were profound changes under way in manufacturing by the end of the 1920s. Some industries were expanding relative to industry in general, some were declining relative to the general run of industries, and some were declining absolutely. A listing of the major groups of industries indicates the variations in growth (Table 5.1 overleaf).

The outstanding expansion was in vehicles, reflecting the arrival of the motor car, lorry and bus for the first time on a large scale in British society. The other major expansion was that associated with electricity and building. That apart, the rise of the consumer industries of tobacco and food (largely processed) was also striking. Industries such as chemicals, mechanical engineering and ferrous metals showed below-average growth. At the bottom of the scale was a small group of large industries (essentially cotton textiles, coal and shipbuilding) which were in decline. Not only was their output less than it had been in 1913, but also for the most part it either declined further or was fairly static between the wars.

1. C.H. Feinstein, *National Income, Expenditure and Output of the United Kingdom 1855–1965* (Cambridge UP 1972), Table 19.
2. B.R. Mitchell, *British Historical Statistics* (Cambridge UP 1988), p. 822.

Table 5.1 Indices of UK industrial production, 1920–38 (1909–13 = 100)[a]

	1920	*1929*	*1938*
Above-average growth industries			
Vehicles	203.7	384.4	647.6
Electrical engineering	169.7	217.0	389.0
GWE supply[b]	141.4	204.7	338.0
Building and contracting	101.1	217.1	262.3
Tobacco	163.2	198.8	243.2
Food	123.2	162.6	232.1
Non-ferrous metals	96.5	152.6	226.2
Timber and furniture	87.8	174.1	218.2
Paper and printing	131.4	170.6	207.2
Below-average growth industries			
Chemicals	121.0	134.0	168.5
Mechanical engineering	104.4	132.3	142.5
Leather	86.3	107.5	125.4
Ferrous metals	99.4	106.8	121.1
Clothing	72.2	102.4	116.2
Declining industries			
Mining and quarrying	85.8	98.8	90.4
Shipbuilding	123.8	87.2	77.0
Textiles	97.4	86.7	100.5
Drink	96.3	82.0	92.5
All manufacturing industries	111.4	136.3	175.9
All industries	108.3	138.8	175.5

Notes: a Southern Ireland is excluded throughout
b GWE = gas/water/electricity

Source: K.S. Lomax, 'Production and Productivity Movements in the United Kingdom since 1900', *JRSS* ser. A, 122 (1959), pp. 192–3. The original figures are based on 1924 = 100, rebased here on 1909–13 = 100

To this list may be added two non-manufacturing industries, the railways, which were declining in both activity and profitability, and agriculture, which, although not experiencing declining output, was in a very poor financial position.

DECLINING INDUSTRIES: COTTON, COAL, SHIPBUILDING

It was in the immediate postwar years that the problems of certain large industries first became apparent. After the postwar boom had broken in 1920, the ensuing partial recovery left them with lost markets and high unemployment. The consequences for these industries, and the devastating effects on their local communities, form two of the major themes of the period. It is also apparent that their problems were not solved before 1939. The high-unemployment industries of the 1920s were identical to those of the 1930s, being consistently worse-off than others in the slump of 1929–32 and the recovery of 1932–37. Even the rearmament programme of the late 1930s failed to raise them to the status of average-unemployment industries. It is to the 1920s, then, that we must look for the reasons behind the industrial failure and unemployment of the interwar years.

Cotton textiles

The cotton textile industry's problems were essentially those of lost export markets. In 1907, 83.4 per cent of the industry's output had gone for export, and the UK was the largest producer in the world, possessing 39 per cent of the world's cotton spindles. In the 1920s, the best year for piece goods exports (1925) saw them at only 72 per cent of the 1909–13 level. The next largest export, yarns, fell less, but in their best year (1922), exports were 7 per cent less than in 1909–13.[3]

The greatest loss of markets was in the Far East. The imposition of a tariff of 7.5 per cent *ad valorem* on imports by the Indian government in 1917 (raised to 11 per cent in 1921) was a particularly severe blow to Lancashire. By 1925, the Far Eastern market accounted for only 42 per cent of British exports of piece goods, compared with 62 per cent in 1913. In the Indian market, Japanese imports had made substantial headway at the expense of the British, aided by favourable exchange rates. Whereas the UK had 97 per cent of the Indian import market for piece goods in 1913–14, this had fallen to 75 per cent by 1928–29, and most of this decline was made up by Japanese piece goods. Such had been the dependence of the prewar industry on foreign markets, that the overall course of production almost exactly echoed the export figures. In 1909–13, the industry consumed an average of 1,934 million lb of cotton a year, and this had fallen in 1929 to 1,498 million lb, or 77 per cent of the previous level.[4]

The decline of exports was not due to a decline in world consumption. World raw cotton consumption rose by 28 per cent between 1913 and 1929, and the number of spindles in the world rose from 143 million to 164 million. But the number of spindles in Britain was almost the same in both years (56 million). It was clear that the capacity of the industry was little changed, and that the loss of output had been mainly due to loss of world markets. Although cotton consumption within Britain rose in the 1920s, it could not offset the loss of exports.[5]

To some extent the industry compounded its problems. The brief postwar boom, after several years of restricted output, stimulated a speculative movement

3. A.E. Kahn, *Great Britain in the World Economy* (Pitman 1946), pp. 68, 93, 95; Mitchell, *Statistics*, pp. 356–7.
4. G.W. Daniels and J. Jewkes, 'The Crisis in the Lancashire Cotton Industry', *EJ* XXXVII (1927), p. 38; L. Sandberg, *Lancashire in Decline* (Columbus, Ohio State UP 1974), pp. 185–7; Mitchell, *Statistics*, p. 332.
5. Kahn, *Great Britain*, p. 95; Mitchell, *Statistics*, p. 332.

within the spinning section of the industry, which resulted in many firms being taken over at excessively high valuations, and then refloated. The new firms were then burdened with high capital charges, which proved a liability when exports failed to recover to the expected levels. Profits in recapitalised and refloated companies were much lower than in those which had not been reorganised.[6]

In addition, for most of the 1920s, those in charge of the industry failed to see the decline in output as a permanent fact of life, to which adjustment should be made. Instead, they preferred to introduce a substantial element of short-time working, partly to keep their workforce intact against better days, partly for charitable reasons, and partly as a response to trade union pressure. In this course, they were aided by the rules of unemployment benefit, which enabled benefit to be claimed even if interrupted by several days' work (the 'OXO' system: see pp. 255–6). Finally, the industry set its face against shift working, so that its machinery was worked much less intensively than in some other countries. In 1926, the economist J.M. Keynes estimated that, due to shift work, the average Japanese spindle was being worked between 4.5 and 5 times more intensively than a comparable Lancashire spindle.[7]

In this situation, of chronic over-capacity, excess employment and wage costs, and minimal profitability, the only long-term solution would have been the amalgamation of firms, and the scrapping of surplus capacity. But this solution was opposed by the directors of the cotton firms, who feared the loss of their independence and possibly their salaries. A less drastic course was to organise a cartel. This was attempted in January 1927, with the formation of the Cotton Yarn Association, whose object was to fix minimum prices for the coarser yarns, via a market-sharing scheme, with provision for production quotas to be transferred from weaker to stronger firms. In spite of having the support and encouragement of Keynes, the association collapsed in November of the same year.[8]

By the end of the decade, the government was taking an interest. The Bank of England had formed an agency in 1929 to administer the large industrial properties which had come into its possession as a result of postwar commercial failures. This, the Securities Management Trust, was enlarged in 1930 into the Bankers' Industrial Development Company (BIDC), with a capital of £6 million, one-quarter provided by the Bank, and the rest provided by other large banks. The BIDC sponsored the formation of the Lancashire Cotton Corporation, whose objects were to buy up excess spindles (through a levy on the more profitable firms), and scrap them. Formed in January 1929, its initial target was the acquisition of 10 million spindles, mainly in the American (coarser)

6. Daniels and Jewkes, 'Cotton Industry', p. 46.

7. J.M. Keynes, 'The Position of the Lancashire Cotton Trade', in *The Nation and Athenaeum* (13 November 1926), in D. Moggridge (ed.), *The Collected Writings of John Maynard Keynes* (Macmillan/Cambridge UP), vol. XIX (1981), pt 2, p. 583.

8. R. Skidelsky, *John Maynard Keynes, vol. 2, The Economist as Saviour 1920–1937* (Macmillan 1992), pp. 260–2.

section. In June 1929, Combined Egyptian Mills was formed to acquire 3 million spindles in the Egyptian (finer) section of the industry. But on the eve of the great depression of the 1930s, the industry had hardly been touched by reorganisation. Companies staggered on with low profits. Dividends had averaged 6.6 per cent in 1909–13, and, after high profits in 1920–21, fell to an average of 2.9 per cent in 1923–29.[9]

Coal-mining

The second of the great prewar industries which suffered particularly badly after 1918 was coal-mining. Here, although declining exports were a considerable problem, they were compounded by the decline in the use of coal in the UK, and an increasing degree of relative technological backwardness. In 1909–13, the UK had produced an average of 270 million tons, of which 88 million (33 per cent) had been exported. In 1921–29 the average output was lower by 15 per cent (at 230 million tons), and average exports by 20 per cent (at 70 million tons), indicating that, although both home and foreign markets had been lost, the loss of the export markets was somewhat more important.[10]

The industry had other problems, chiefly of extreme fluctuations and low profits. Output was considerably reduced in 1921 by a three-month strike, and by the six-month strike of 1926 which was accompanied by the General Strike. On the other hand, output and especially exports were stimulated by the effects of the US coal strike in 1922, the occupation of the Rhineland by France and Belgium in 1923, and the subsequent strike of Ruhr miners. Briefly, in 1923, both output and exports were higher than in 1909–13. It was not until after the General Strike that the industry settled down, with output at about 250 million tons, and exports at *c.*75 million. Paradoxically, this was the worst period for profitability, as coal prices, both home and export, were insufficient for profitable working. The industry as a whole made a loss in 1927 and 1928, and had made only a small profit in 1925 and 1926 because of the government subsidy.[11] (Export figures in the two preceding paragraphs include bunker fuel.)

Abroad, the rise of protectionism, and the emergence of Poland as an exporter curtailed the market. The return to the gold standard in 1925 forced exporters to cut their prices, with adverse effects on profits. Finally, the export effort was undercut by the failure of British productivity to rise in line with that of competing nations. British output of coal per man-shift was almost the same in 1929 as in 1913, but that of the Ruhr had risen by 34 per cent, of Polish Upper Silesia by 12 per cent, and that of the Pas-de-Calais by 10 per cent.[12]

The relative decline in British productivity was bound to lead to exporting difficulties. But both exports and the home market were undercut by the main

9. R. Robson, *The Cotton Industry in Britain* (Macmillan 1957), pp. 215, 338, for the two preceding paragraphs.
10. B.E. Supple, *The History of the British Coal Industry, vol. 4, 1913–46: The Political Economy of Decline* (Oxford, Clarendon 1987), pp. 174–5.
11. Mitchell, *Statistics*, pp. 249, 257; Supple, *Coal Industry*, pp. 389, 391.
12. Supple, *Coal Industry*, p. 192; coal prices in Mitchell, *Statistics*, p. 749.

weakness of the world coal industry; it was being left behind as consumers shifted to other forms of energy. In the century down to 1914, world demand for coal had risen at about 4 per cent a year; in the interwar period it grew by only about 0.3 per cent a year. The chief competing forms of energy were oil and electricity, whose consumption rose much faster than that of coal.[13] Within Britain, between 1913 and 1930, the proportion of national energy consumption supplied by coal directly fell from 89 to 83 per cent. Against this could be set a rise in the use of coal for electricity, from 3 per cent to 5 per cent of total energy consumption in the same period. The proportion of energy supplied by oil and petrol rose from only 1 per cent in 1913 to 5 per cent in 1930. Thus, although coal was still the supreme energy source, its position was being slowly eroded.

Competition from the new sources of power was felt in various ways. The rise of the motor car and lorry adversely affected the railways, and thus the demand for coal. The spread of the electric motor for industrial power affected the demand for coal for steam engines. In 1905, it was estimated that industry consumed 52 million tons of coal to provide power, and this had fallen to 36 million tons by 1930. The shipping industry also rapidly converted to oil. The world tonnage of coal-fired vessels fell from 44 million in 1914 to 32 million in 1937; the tonnage of oil-fired and diesel vessels rose from 1 million to 34 million.

Even in traditional markets, considerable fuel economies were being made. Major savings were achieved in the railways, the gas industry and in iron and steel. In iron and steel blast furnaces, a saving of one-fifth of coal consumption for each ton of pig-iron smelted was achieved between 1913 and 1936. Nor were economies confined to the traditional industries. Electricity generation, although it provided a new market for coal, became much more efficient. Coal requirements per million kilowatt hours declined by 55 per cent in the relatively few years between 1920 and 1935. The stagnation of output in traditional coal-using industries compounded the problems of the coal suppliers.[14]

In neither cotton nor coal was the structure of the industry conducive to the elimination of excess capacity. The coal industry was very fragmented. In 1924, there were 1,411 coal-mining undertakings, controlling 2,507 mines, with an average output of only 106,000 tons from each mine. This was much below the average output per mine of comparable regions in Germany and the USA. The average British mine was also a small employer; 31 per cent of the mines in 1924 employed fewer than 100 miners, although they accounted for only just over 1 per cent of the total labour force in the industry. This fragmented and small-firm structure stood in the way of large-scale amalgamation. Although some notable amalgamations took place in the prosperous years of the early 1920s, these stopped after the market for coal collapsed in 1924. They were

13. N.K. Buxton, 'Coalmining', in N.K. Buxton and D.H. Aldcroft (eds), *British Industry between the Wars: instability and industrial development 1919–1939* (Scolar 1979), p. 50.
14. Buxton and Aldcroft, *British Industry between the Wars*, pp. 52–4.

tentatively resumed after 1926, when the Mining Industry Act of that year gave some encouragement to the process, but only 20 were recorded between 1926 and 1929, and most of these, except in south Wales, were little more than recognitions of pre-existing amalgamations.[15]

Amalgamation to achieve economies of scale was often recommended as a cure for the troubles of the industry. The mine-owners were resolutely opposed to such a course, although it received strong endorsement from the Samuel Commission in 1925. Whether such a course would have yielded such economies is still debated. There were 'abundant instances of small undertakings which were very profitable and large colliery firms which did very badly'.[16]

The lack of enthusiasm for amalgamation in the 1920s reflected the general lack of profitability of the industry; there was little to be gained by taking over an inefficient mining company, short of a mass programme of capacity reduction via the closing of the less efficient mines. Failing this, which would have presupposed a powerful government or industry initiative, firms fell back on securing their own positions, via marketing agreements or interlocking directorships, which were already widespread before 1914.

Regardless of the parlous state of the industry's finances as a whole, there were always some mines making a profit, sometimes a very good one, especially if favoured by grades of coal which were particularly marketable, or coal-getting conditions which were more favourable than average. Investment to increase efficiency did not cease in the 1920s, and the use of machinery in coal-cutting rose. Before the war, only 8 per cent of output was cut by machine; this had risen to 14 per cent in 1921, and rose to 23 per cent in 1927. Less interest was shown in conveying coal by machinery, the proportion of output thus conveyed being only 11 per cent in 1927. Paradoxically, mechanisation did little to raise efficiency per man-shift for the industry as a whole, but merely offset the deteriorating geological conditions faced by any deep-mining operation, as seams worked became thinner, and the distances from mine-shaft to workface greater.[17]

Neither amalgamation nor mechanisation provided an easy way out of the industry's difficulties. For most of the 1920s, the companies fell back on the more immediate course of reducing costs. Since the largest cost item was wages, these bore the brunt of this policy. The reduction of money wages throughout the economy was considerable after the price level began falling at the end of 1920, but miners' wages had fallen further than the national average by 1924. Miners' real earnings continued to fall in the later 1920s, when real wages elsewhere in the economy were rising slightly. Whereas real

15. Supple, *Coal Industry*, p. 303; British Association, *Britain in Depression: a record of British industries since 1929* (Pitman 1935), p. 159.

16. Supple, *Coal Industry*, p. 231. The arguments on economies of scale are found in N.K. Buxton, 'Entrepreneurial Efficiency in the British Coal Industry between the Wars', *EcHR* XXIII (1970), and B. Fine, 'Economies of Scale and a Featherbedding Cartel?: a reconsideration of the interwar British coal industry', *EcHR* XLIII (1990).

17. Supple, *Coal Industry*, pp. 306–8, 380.

wages (of fully employed workers) in the economy as a whole fell by 4 per cent between 1920 and 1924, the real earnings of miners fell by 19 per cent. In the succeeding five years to 1929, the national average real wage rose by 6 per cent; the miners' real wages fell by a further 5 per cent. Nevertheless, wage reductions by themselves did not suffice to restore the industry's international competitiveness.[18]

Shipbuilding

Before the First World War, Britain dominated world shipbuilding, accounting for 58.7 per cent of the world tonnage launched in 1909–13. British-registered ships also dominated the world fleet. In 1914, they accounted for 18.9 million (41 per cent) of the world total of 45.5 million tons, and the next largest fleet (Germany, 5.1 million) was a long way behind. This dominance, already being slowly diminished before 1914, was substantially eroded after 1918. Between 1920 and 1929, Britain accounted for only 44.7 per cent of world output. By 1930, the British fleet, although slightly larger than in 1914, at 20.3 million tons, represented only some 30 per cent of the total world fleet of 68 million tons.[19]

At the root of the problem lay the great oversupply of ships which emerged at the end of the First World War. The substantial losses of shipping during the conflict were remedied by a greatly increased building programme in the UK and the USA. However, the programmes did not get under way until 1918–19, and due to the length of time required to build ships, world output peaked in 1920–21. In those two years, slightly over 10 million tons was added to the world's shipping stock.

Partly due to this sudden surge in carrying capacity, and partly due to the sharpness of the slump of 1920–21 (which badly affected the USA also), freight rates, which were naturally volatile, collapsed, falling almost four-fifths from their inflated 1918 level by 1921. They drifted down further by 1925, recovered somewhat, and then fell again to the end of the decade. In relation to general commodity prices, they were slightly higher in the 1920s than in 1909–13, but this was small consolation to owners burdened with expensive ships. At the height of the postwar boom, in March 1920, the price of a new cargo steamer of 7,500 tons was estimated at £259,000; by the end of 1920, it had fallen to £105,000.[20]

18. Money wage *earnings* in Supple, *Coal Industry*, pp. 176–7; cost of living index and national wage rates from B.R. Mitchell and P. Deane, *Abstract of British Historical Statistics* (Cambridge UP 1972), p. 345; Buxton, 'Coalmining', pp. 56–7.
19. L. Jones, *Shipbuilding in Britain: mainly between the two world wars* (Cardiff, University of Wales Press 1957), pp. 50, 64; A. Slaven, 'British Shipbuilders: market trends and order book patterns between the wars', *Journal of Transport History*, 3rd ser. 3 (1982), Table 4, p. 43.
20. Jones, *Shipbuilding*, p. 64; Mitchell, *Statistics*, p. 540, for tramp freight rates (Isserlis' index) and general commodity price level (Sauerbeck/Statist index); *Fairplay* (trade journal) ship prices from D.H. Aldcroft, 'Port Congestion and the Shipping Boom of 1919–20', in Aldcroft, *Studies in British Transport History, 1870–1970* (Newton Abbot, David & Charles 1974), p. 170.

The position was worsened by the slow recovery of world trade. Before 1914, the rate of growth of the world fleet had approximated roughly to the rate of growth of world trade in primary products. By 1920, the world fleet had grown faster than primary product trade, which lagged throughout the interwar period, so that the carrying capacity of the world was continually greater than the demand for shipping. In this situation, the industry was permanently depressed financially. In January 1922, almost 11 million tons of world shipping were laid up; 4 million tons were still laid up six years later.[21]

A particular disadvantage for the British industry was the loss of naval orders. In 1909–13, they had accounted for an average of 166,000 'displacement' tons a year. This amounted to only 9 per cent of the gross tonnage of all ships launched from British yards. However, when allowance is made for the much greater labour content of the 'displacement ton' in which naval launchings were measured, as compared to the 'gross ton' of the merchant fleet, the proportion of naval launchings was 18 per cent of the total gross tonnage-equivalent in 1909–13. Naval orders dried up after the Washington naval agreement of 1921, accounting for only 4 per cent of all the tonnage launched from British yards in 1920–29. The average total British launchings in 1904–13 had been 1,728,000 gross tons-equivalent annually. This fell in 1920–29 to 1,314,000, a reduction of 24 per cent. Of this total decline of 414,000 tons, the loss of naval orders accounted for 196,000; the reduction in home orders 128,000, and the loss of foreign orders, 90,000 gross tons-equivalent.[22]

Even if the largest single factor in the decline of construction was the naval, this does not explain the decline in output in the other sectors, since world shipping tonnage rose in 1920–30 by 26 per cent. Some of this was admittedly inactive, being composed of US ships built at the start of the decade, and thereafter laid up. One calculation is that the total world fleet had risen between 1913 and 1930 by 48 per cent, but the 'active' fleet had risen by only 40 per cent. But it was clear that the merchant side of the British industry was in decline relative to the rest of the world. This was not due to a reduction in potential capacity, since the number of construction berths had increased by 18 per cent between 1914 and 1925, and improvements in yard organisation and technique meant that the potential increase of capacity was even greater, so that one estimate put the prewar capacity of the industry at 3 million gross tons, and the 1920 capacity at 4 million tons.[23]

The decline of home orders can be explained largely by the slow recovery of world and British foreign trade in the 1920s. Contrary to popular belief, British shipowners placed few orders abroad, and the home market remained the preserve of home shipbuilders. But there seems no doubt that exports were reduced by foreign competition. To some extent this may have been a

21. J.R. Parkinson, *The Economics of Shipbuilding in the United Kingdom* (Cambridge UP 1960), Fig. 2, p. 51; Jones, *Shipbuilding*, p. 29; Committee on Industry and Trade (Balfour Committee), *Survey of Metal Industries* (1928), p. 385.
22. Slaven, 'British Shipbuilders', Table 3, p. 41.
23. Ibid., Table 3, p. 41; S.G. Sturmey, *British Shipping and World Competition* (Athlone 1962), p. 65; Jones, *Shipbuilding*, pp. 123–4.

matter of higher British wages. But it was also due to more expensive materials. Before the war, builders had relied heavily on imports of cheap European steel, but in the 1920s tended to use the more expensive British steel, partly because of the fusion of steel and shipbuilding interests which had occurred during the postwar boom, and partly due to the policy of 'loyalty' rebates offered by the British steel producers. More generally, the average postwar British yard was still relatively small, labour relations were poor, and the organisation of shipyard work was on a craft basis which left little scope for rationalisation of work methods. Lack of product standardisation discouraged yards from expanding their scale of production. Externally, the industry was seriously disadvantaged by the growth of subsidised output in mainland Europe and in Japan, as foreign governments tried to increase their merchant fleets.[24]

A contributory factor was what may be described as 'product inertia', or the sticking to traditional ship types. In the world at large, the oil-fired steamship or diesel-engined ship was replacing the traditional coal-fired steamship, and there were more oil tankers being produced. In the case of tankers, the British record was not unimpressive, since the proportion of British output accounted for by tankers in the 1920s was almost the same as the proportion of tankers in world output. But there was some slippage as regards motor-ships, since in the 1920s 45 per cent of British output was motor-ships, compared with 52 per cent in the world. Some of this inertia was due to shipowners, who were comparatively unenthusiastic about diesel ships and tankers. The tendency of British shipowners to build in Britain when better or cheaper ships could have been built abroad may have disguised from the shipbuilders the full seriousness of their postwar position.[25]

OTHER DECLINING INDUSTRIES: RAILWAYS AND AGRICULTURE

Railways

The railways were declining because they faced a market in which competition from road transport was increasing rapidly. In 1921–28, they carried on average 6 per cent fewer passengers and 40 per cent less freight than in 1909–13. After the war, the system had been forced into an amalgamation by the government, as a compromise between *laissez-faire* and nationalisation. By the Railways Act 1921, some 120 separate companies had been merged into four groups. The counterpart to this attempt to enhance the network's degree of monopoly was a system of regulation to act in the interest of the public. The rates which railways could charge for various classes of traffic were to be fixed by a Railway Rates Tribunal. The rates were also published, which gave rival

24. Jones, *Shipbuilding*, pp. 73–83; Slaven, 'British Shipbuilders', p. 39; E.H. Lorenz, *Economic Decline in Britain: the shipbuilding industry 1890–1970* (Oxford, Clarendon 1991), chs 2, 3.
25. Slaven, 'British Shipbuilders', p. 45; Sturmey, *British Shipping*, ch. IV, pp. 400–1.

forms of transport the opportunity to undercut the railway rates on forms of traffic in which they were particularly able to compete.[26]

However, the railways were not in a monopoly position, and the market for their services was shrinking. Thus they were unable even to earn the average net revenue (i.e. revenue after the subtraction of working expenses) of pre-war. This had been £45.4 million in 1909–13, and was only £39.2 million in 1922–29, falling far short of the intention of the Tribunal that it should amount to £51.4 million. In these circumstances, the decision of the companies in 1928 (the first full year of operation of the new system) not to apply for an increase in rates can be explained only as a recognition of their competitive weakness; in fact, no increase in rates was applied for until 1937.[27] (The year of the General Strike, 1926, is excluded from these figures. In the year of the other major railway strike, 1921, the railways' net revenue was negative.)

The competitive weakness of the system led to low profits. The average dividend return on ordinary railway shares in 1913 had been 3.75 per cent. In the 1920s it was similar, but then fell sharply, and the average of 1933–38 was only 1.2 per cent. In spite of fighting back with new faster steam services, the electrification of the Southern Railway, and some forays into running their own road transport operations, the railways were shrinking. Between the wars, 240 miles of track and 350 stations were closed to all traffic, and 1,000 miles of track and 380 stations were closed to passengers but retained only for goods traffic. Although in 1938 there were still 20,007 miles of railway route mileage in Britain, much of the system was of dubious financial viability.[28]

Agriculture

The decline of agriculture was relative rather than absolute. The proportions of national income and the national labour force accounted for by agriculture continued to fall, as they had since before 1914. By 1924 agriculture accounted for only 4.1 per cent of the national income, and, by 1931, only 8.7 per cent of the male UK labour force.[29]

The relative decline of the labour force was also an absolute one; the numbers of farm workers had been declining since the 1870s, and they continued to fall after 1918. Between 1921 and 1938, the number of full-time workers on British farms fell from 789,000 to 697,000. Low wages and the attractions of the towns were more than sufficient inducements for labour to leave the land.[30]

The decline of the labour force did not mean that output was declining,

26. C.I. Savage, *An Economic History of Transport* (Hutchinson 1959), ch. 5.
27. Ibid., pp. 109–10; Mitchell, *Statistics*, pp. 547–8.
28. G. Walker, *Road and Rail* (2nd edn, Allen & Unwin 1947), p. 267; Mitchell, *Statistics*, p. 542; M. Freeman and D.H. Aldcroft, *The Atlas of British Railway History* (Beckenham, Croom Helm 1985), p. 93.
29. P.E. Dewey, *British Agriculture in the First World War* (Routledge 1989), pp. 240–1.
30. Ministry of Agriculture, *A Century of Agricultural Statistics: Great Britain 1866–1966* (HMSO 1968), p. 62; A. Armstrong, *Farmworkers: a social and economic history* (Batsford 1988), ch. 8.

because farmers continued to mechanise; by 1938 there were 38,500 wheeled tractors on farms in England and Wales (although they would not go very far among the almost 250,000 or so farms in Britain). Although the real output of the industry was fairly static between the early years of the century and the late 1920s, it rose more rapidly thereafter. By 1927–28 it was about 5 per cent higher than in 1906–8; by 1937–38 it was about 21 per cent higher.[31]

Slow growth in output, and sharp fluctuations in product prices, spelled financial difficulties for farmers throughout the interwar period. The brief expansion of output in 1917–18 was followed by a sharp recession after 1920, as British and world agricultural prices began to fall rapidly. Frightened by the prospect of paying out large amounts in compensation, the government repealed the Agriculture Act 1920, which had promised a system of guaranteed prices to farmers, in April 1921. Between 1920 and 1923 the index of agricultural product prices in England and Wales fell by 46 per cent. The decline was much more marked in cereals than in livestock products, so farmers reconverted wartime tillage back to grass; the area of tillage in Britain fell from the wartime peak of 12.36 million acres to 9.78 million in 1925.

Arable farming profits, which had been very high in the war and post-war boom, collapsed. Former tenant farmers who had purchased their farms at the high land prices ruling in 1919–20 were particularly badly hit, as were those landowners who still retained agricultural estates, since land prices fell sharply after 1920. The value of farmers' working capital (mainly livestock and machinery) fell in similar proportion. The tenant of a large farm in Wiltshire, A.G. Street, wrote in 1931 that the working capital of any tenant who came into farming in 1920 would have lost about 60 per cent of its value by 1927. The recession after 1929 brought a further loss of income and capital values. Street thought that by 1931, 'every thousand pounds invested in farming in 1920 is today worth only two hundred and fifty pounds'. The financial problems of farming were eased with the change of government policy to protectionism and price support after 1931, but farm incomes and capital values remained historically very low until 1940.[32]

SLOW-GROWTH INDUSTRIES

Chemicals

Although commonly referred to by historians as a 'new' (and by implication dynamic) industry, the performance of the chemical industry was disappointing, since it grew more slowly than the average of all industries. This was partly due to some bad commercial miscalculations, which resulted in

31. Board of Agriculture, *The Agricultural Output of Great Britain* (1912), Cd 6277, p. 25; E.H. Whetham, *The Agrarian History of England and Wales, vol. VIII, 1914–1939* (Cambridge UP 1978), p. 260; Ministry of Agriculture, *A Century*, p. 85.
32. Whetham, *Agrarian History*, ch. X; Ministry of Agriculture, *A Century*, Table 38; R.R. Enfield, *The Agricultural Crisis 1920–1923* (Longmans, Green 1924), ch. 1; A.G. Street, *Farmer's Glory* (Faber & Faber 1932), pp. 210–11.

overinvestment in some sectors, and consequent oversupply. This seems to have been the case in dyestuffs immediately after the war, and in artificial fertilisers in the 1920s. The plant erected by ICI at Billingham to produce ammonium sulphate for fertiliser was a commercial error, which turned to disaster when the world fertiliser market collapsed after 1929. A later scheme (1936) to produce oil and petrol from coal at Billingham was costly and of dubious benefit to the chemical industry as a whole. But ICI (which dominated the industry after its formation in 1926) survived, and made impressive scientific progress, which may be symbolised by its development of modern plastics. By the late 1930s both perspex and polyethylene (polythene) were in production.[33]

Mechanical engineering

Mechanical engineering is a very heterogeneous industry, comprising the manufacture and installation of all kinds of machinery, boilers and engines. Its chief products before the war had been engines, boilers, textile machinery, and marine engineering. Together, these made up 60 per cent of its output at the 1907 Census of Production. The industry was highly export-oriented, sending approximately 60 per cent of its output abroad.

After 1918, such products were relatively less in demand, both at home and abroad. The output of the industry, which had been worth £85 million in 1907, was £158 million in 1924 and £165 million in 1930. While this represented some increase in real terms, after allowing for inflation, it was much lower than the average for manufacturing industry, or for the economy as a whole.

The greatest single problem was the decline in exports. At the Censuses of Production of 1924 and 1930, they represented only 28 and 31 per cent of the industry's total production. Some of this was due to the closure of markets (the Russian market was effectively lost), or the raising of tariffs in postwar Europe, forcing manufacturers to seek a haven in Imperial or Dominion markets. Some of it was due to technological backwardness, as demand for steam engines and steam-powered machinery declined. Some of it was due to the rise of competing centres of production overseas, as in the case of the Japanese textile machinery industry. The reduction of exports emphasised the importance of the home market, yet even here there were problems, notably the depressed nature of some major customers such as the coal-mines, the cotton industry and shipbuilding. Salvation, such as it was, came through diversification, largely in the home market, where the expanding sectors were internal combustion (chiefly oil) engines, constructional engineering, machine tools and a wide range of miscellaneous products.[34]

33. L.F. Haber, *The Chemical Industry, 1900–1930* (Oxford, Clarendon 1971), pp. 252–3; W.J. Reader, *Imperial Chemical Industries: a history*, vol. II (Oxford UP 1975), chs 5, 10; W.J. Reader, 'The Chemical Industry', in Buxton and Aldcroft, *British Industry between the Wars*, pp. 170–2.
34. T.R. Gourvish, 'Mechanical Engineering', in Buxton and Aldcroft, *British Industry*, pp. 130–42.

Iron and steel

The problems of the iron and steel industry were also partly those of lower exports, combined with higher imports. But these came on top of a series of existing problems, whose resolution posed great difficulties. Even in the early years of the twentieth century, it had been apparent that the efficiency of the British industry lagged behind that of the two other great iron and steel producers, the USA and Germany. This was due to the antiquated nature of many British plants, which in turn was due to the way in which the industry had grown up, unplanned, and unable to take advantage of the latest economies of scale as technical progress made them feasible. Iron and steel works had a long physical life, and, even if not the most efficient, there was little incentive to scrap them and reinvest in best-practice plants as long as they were still profitable.[35]

On this inefficient industrial structure was superimposed during the war a great expansion. At the behest of the Ministry of Munitions the industry increased its capacity considerably. Blast furnace capacity rose from the prewar level of 11 million to 12 million tons a year; steel works capacity rose from 8 million to over 12 million tons; rolling mills and forges from 7–8 million to 10–11 million tons annually. In all cases, this extra capacity was built at existing works, or so near as to be capable of operation with them.[36] The expansion of capacity continued into the postwar boom, as firms, buoyed up by optimism, extended their works and issued further share capital to finance these extensions. Thus the industry became burdened with fresh obligations to its shareholders. A notable example of this was the Ebbw Vale Steel, Iron and Coal Co., which issued £3 million of debenture shares in 1920, bearing an interest rate of 8 per cent. Interest payments were suspended in 1926.[37]

The extra capacity proved a deadweight on the industry after the war. In 1909–13, the average make of pig-iron had been 9.6 million tons a year. After the postwar boom broke, and the industry had settled down, average output in 1923–29 (excluding 1926, the year of the General Strike) was only 7.1 million. The steel sector was more flourishing; the 1909–13 production of 6.6 million tons was exceeded in 1923–29 (again, excluding 1926), at an average of 8.5 million. Yet this was far below capacity, and even below the wartime peak of 9.5 million tons produced in 1918.

The problems of the industry were compounded by a sharp rise in imports after the war. In 1923–29 they were 57 per cent higher than prewar (1910–13), and exports were 17 per cent lower. The result was that whereas before the war exports had been more than double the level of imports, they were now only about one-third greater. The foreign markets for constructional steel and railway material were much reduced, as was the market for iron; the rise in

35. K. Warren, 'Iron and Steel', in Buxton and Aldcroft, *British Industry*, pp. 103–6.
36. Committee on Industry and Trade, *Survey of Metal Industries*, p. 18; Warren, 'Iron and Steel', p. 105.
37. J.C. Carr and W. Taplin, *History of the British Steel Industry* (Cambridge, MA, Harvard UP 1962), pp. 358–9, 372.

imports was mainly accounted for by semi-finished iron and steel. One of the few large exports to maintain its prewar level was tinplate, but that was small consolation in view of its world overproduction and low prices.[38]

Some home markets were also unsatisfactory after the war; in particular, shipbuilding, which before 1914 had taken 30 per cent of steel ingot production. On the other hand, there was a rising demand for tinplate from the food canning industry, and for steel for the rapidly expanding motor vehicle industry, so that overall home demand for steel was rising in the 1920s.

The industry was in a poor way in the 1920s. Capacity was so great, and the market was so small, that works were producing at much less than capacity, with consequent high unit costs. The comparative inefficiencies of the British industry continued, and, since imports were unrestricted, the industry was continually undermined by external competition. In addition, companies had the burden of the high fixed costs shouldered in the postwar boom. All these factors restricted profitability. One of the largest firms, United Steel Companies Ltd, was the third largest producer in 1920, and rose to be the largest in 1929, yet was drained of profit in 1924–27 by its 'high capacity, unamortized investment, and high fixed charges'. Although it made a trading profit in every year except 1927, its fixed charges meant that it actually lost £796,801 in the three years, and was forced to negotiate a moratorium with its creditors in 1927.

Solutions to these problems were not found in the 1920s. Low profits restricted investment which might have reduced costs to allow the industry to compete more effectively. Excess capacity reduced the incentive for mergers; the top five producers' share of output remained almost constant between 1920 (36 per cent) and 1929 (38 per cent). While there was a rapid growth of concentration in tinplate in the 1920s, the rest of the industry had to wait until after 1929 for the rationalisation which it failed to achieve in the 1920s.[39]

RAPID-GROWTH INDUSTRIES

Motor vehicles

Of the newer industries, the one which expanded fastest was that of vehicles. On the eve of the First World War, there had been 106,000 private cars and 64,000 commercial vehicles on British roads. Even during the war, these numbers had increased, and by 1921 had almost exactly doubled. In the 1920s, growth was extremely rapid. By 1930, there were 1.06 million private cars, and 348,000 commercial vehicles in use. Motor cycles had also proved extremely popular, peaking at 724,000 in 1930 before undergoing long-term

38. Mitchell, *Statistics*, pp. 283, 288–9, 295–6, 301; Committee on Industry and Trade, *Survey of Metal Industries*, pp. 52–3; Carr and Taplin, *Steel Industry*, pp. 369–70; W.E. Minchinton, *The British Tinplate Industry: a history* (Oxford, Clarendon 1957), pp. 139–49.

39. Warren, 'Iron and Steel', pp. 107–8; S. Tolliday, *Business, Banking and Politics: the case of British Steel, 1918–1939* (Cambridge, MA, Harvard UP 1987), pp. 157–8, Table 4, p. 32.

decline thereafter. But cars in use doubled again in the 1930s (to 1.94 million), and commercial vehicles rose to 495,000 by 1938.

The success of the motor industry was due to the tapping of a new, mass market, due to rising real incomes and the decline in the real price of vehicles. The latter reflected the adoption of production methods which were much nearer to those pioneered by Henry Ford than those of the prewar British industry, which had been those of hand-building comparatively expensive cars for the upper classes. Ford had outlined his production policy as early as 1903:

> The way to make automobiles is to make one automobile like another automobile, to make them all alike, to make them come through the factory just alike; just as one pin is like another pin, when it comes from the pin factory. . . . You need not fear about the market. The people will buy them all right. When you get to making the cars in quantity, you can make them cheaper, and when you make them cheaper you can get people with enough money to buy them. The market will take care of itself.[40]

British producers had a chance to evaluate the Ford principles of mass production, moving assembly lines, and interchangeability of parts when the Ford assembly plant at Old Trafford, Manchester, opened in 1911. After the war, aided by the 'McKenna' protective tariff of 1915, British producers such as Morris and Austin copied Ford techniques, and opened a new market by progressive reductions in price. Between 1924 and 1929, car prices fell by an average of 25 per cent. By 1929 three producers (Morris, Austin, Singer) accounted for 75 per cent of the industry's total car output. Along with mass production went a reduction in the number of firms, as capital requirements rose and smaller producers failed. The number of car-producing firms fell from eighty-eight in 1922 to thirty-one in 1929, and interlocking interests meant that by 1939 there were only about twenty truly independent producers, six firms accounting for 90 per cent of all car output.[41]

Electricity supply

As in motor vehicles, the pioneering origins of the electricity supply industry lay as far back as the 1880s. Electricity initially faced stiff competition from the long-established gas lighting industry. In addition, the technical problems of establishing large-scale plant, which would lead to a reduction in price through economies of scale, were not solved until generating companies adopted the steam turbine of Charles Parsons. By 1914, the industry had passed its technical infancy, and was supplying almost 2,000 million kilowatt-hours (kWh) of power. The price had also fallen; the 9d.–10d. per kWh for lighting of the pioneer days had been reduced to about 4d. by 1912.[42]

40. K. Richardson, *The British Motor Industry, 1896–1939* (Macmillan 1977), pp. 63–4.
41. Mitchell, *Statistics*, pp. 557–8; G. Maxcy and A. Silberston, *The Motor Industry* (Allen & Unwin 1959), pp. 13–15.
42. L. Hannah, *Electricity before Nationalisation: a study of the development of the electricity supply industry in Britain to 1948* (Macmillan 1979), ch. 1, pp. 428–9.

The potential advantages of electricity had been apparent to its pioneers: cheap, clean, convenient power, which did not depend on proximity to the coalfields for its cheapness. As a source of industrial power it had the advantage that even the smallest workshop could install a suitable engine, since electric motors came in a wide variety of sizes. In addition, there were by the 1920s new markets opening up, in the form of suburban housing, the cinema, and the radio and domestic appliance industry. Thus by 1918 the industry was poised at the beginning of new market opportunities. In so far as there were barriers to progress, these lay in the large number of undertakings, both private and municipal, supplying power, with consequent inefficiencies. In 1917, there were some 600 supply undertakings in Britain, with an average generating plant of only 5,000 horsepower (hp), whereas efficient generation required units of at least 20,000 hp, placed on carefully selected sites. But the haphazard development of the industry had led to the use of many ill-located sites.[43]

By 1924, about half of all industrial power used was electrical. But by then the chaotic nature of the industry, which lacked even a standard generating frequency, had prompted a series of inquiries. These culminated in the report of the Weir Committee in 1925, which recommended the interconnection of the existing generating plant in a national 'grid'. This would enable savings to be made in capital and operating costs, as well as encouraging frequency standardisation. Such a scheme would be best administered by a public body. Accepted by the government, the recommendations were embodied in the Electricity (Supply) Act 1926, and the Central Electricity Board (CEB) came into being in the same year. In 1927 the construction of the 'national grid' and the standardisation of frequencies were commenced, both being practically completed by the end of 1936, so that lines of steel towers ('pylons') marched across the countryside, to the annoyance of the environmentalists.[44]

As in motor vehicles, expansion of the market produced economies of scale, consequent price reductions, and further extensions of the market. Continuing technical efficiency was encouraged by the CEB, which favoured the more efficient suppliers when drawing supplies into the national grid. The price per kWh fell from an average of 2.48d. in 1921 to 1.04d. in 1938, and between those years electricity usage rose from 3,242 gigawatt-hours (GWh) to 20,404 GWh (1 GWh = 1 million kWh). In 1920, there had been only 730,000 electrical consumers, but by 1938 there were 8,920,000, and the national grid was recognised to be technically superior to the distribution systems of other countries.[45]

The prewar chaos of electricity supply had had unfortunate consequences for electrical engineering, which had been underdeveloped in comparison with the industries of Germany and the USA. The disappearance of German competition during the war had proved a useful stimulus. After the war the

43. L. Gordon, *The Public Corporation in Great Britain* (Oxford UP 1938), p. 87.
44. M. Compton and E.H. Bott, *British Industry: its changing structure in peace and war* (Lindsay Drummond 1940), pp. 243, 94–9; Hannah, *Electricity*, pp. 117–18.
45. Hannah, *Electricity*, pp. 430–3; R.E. Catterall, 'Electrical Engineering', in Buxton and Aldcroft, *British Industry*, p. 244.

industry made rapid progress. Although subject to severe short-term fluctuations, and badly affected by the General Strike, output grew rapidly, from a value of £13.9 million in 1907 to £70.3 million in 1924, and £106.9 million in 1935. At the same time, it became more efficient, the real value of output per employee rising by 28 per cent between 1924 and 1935. While most of its output throughout the period was composed of machinery and cables, the new category of radio rose very rapidly, from a negligible amount in 1907 to £13 million worth in 1935.[46]

Rayon

Perhaps the industry which best deserves the term 'new' was that of the synthetic fibre known as 'artificial silk' or 'rayon'. Based on cellulose fibre, it was first produced in 1905 by the Courtauld Co. Largely used for hosiery before the war, the industry turned to dresses, underwear, clothes linings, shirtings and furniture fabrics afterwards. Fabric made from rayon had the advantage of feeling and looking smooth and lustrous, and retaining dirt less readily than natural fibres.

In 1919, the UK had been Europe's largest producer, although it was overtaken by Germany and Italy in the 1930s. Between 1924 and 1935 the industry was protected by customs duties, which were lowered in 1935. Protection did not inhibit the larger producers such as Courtaulds from following an aggressive policy of price reduction, which helped the industry to find new markets. Between 1927 and 1937, the price of rayon fell by more than half. Growth was very rapid in the interwar period; UK production of yarn was 5.5 million lb in 1919, rising to 52.4 million in 1929, and 169.0 million in 1939. Like the chemical industry, rayon production was highly concentrated, being dominated by two firms, Courtaulds and British Celanese. The switch to rayon gave a boost to the ailing cotton industry; by 1937, it was thought that about one-fifth of the active looms in Lancashire were working on mixed cotton/rayon fabrics, the average rayon content of which was probably about 50 per cent.[47]

Aircraft

The last two 'new' industries to be considered are aircraft and consumer electrical goods. The former, although progressing rapidly in a technical sense, was comparatively small. The 1920s had been lean years; at the end of the war, military orders had dried up, there were too many firms, and many of them had to diversify to stay in business. Orders remained patchy even in the early 1930s, and exports were an important factor enabling the industry to keep going; by 1935, about 25 per cent of airframes and 20 per cent of engines were exported. In 1934, before rearmament began, the industry provided directly fewer than 24,000 jobs. The lean years came to an end with

46. Catterall, 'Electrical Engineering', pp. 246–55.
47. J. Harrop, 'Rayon', in Buxton and Aldcroft, *British Industry*, pp. 276–7, 280–3, 288; A. Plummer, *New British Industries in the Twentieth Century* (Pitman 1937), pp. 215–26.

the announcement by Baldwin in March 1934 that Britain was to have parity with the German air force. By May 1936 the existing firms' production facilities were obviously inadequate, and the 'shadow factory' scheme was inaugurated. Thereafter, rearmament spending rose rapidly, and the Royal Air Force was completely re-equipped with the latest monoplanes such as the Hurricane and Spitfire by the time war broke out in 1939.[48]

Consumer electrical goods

The expansion of the consumer electrical industries was most spectacular in the case of radio. Its spread was closely linked to the development of public policy on radio receiving, following the inauguration of the British Broadcasting Co. (BBCo.) in 1922. This was largely controlled by six manufacturing firms, the largest of which was Marconi. In all, the BBCo. had 1,700 shareholders, most of whom were engaged in the manufacture or assembly of sets, often under licence from one of the 'big six'. The success of the BBCo. led to its transformation in 1926 into the British Broadcasting Corporation (BBC), under the chairmanship of John (later Lord) Reith. The reason for the transformation of broadcasting into a public body was that the government had been appalled by the low quality of commercial radio output in the USA, and wished to avoid such a situation in Britain. The choice of Reith was perfect; he was willing to entertain audiences, but wished to uplift them also, and was concerned to provide quality programming.

In the early days the radio industry enjoyed conditions of near-perfect competition, being easy to enter. Many manufacturers were little more than assemblers, and often did not understand the technicalities. The result was a lot of poor-quality sets on the market. As time went on, the sets became more reliable, complex and expensive, but this did not stifle the industry, which still enjoyed a sellers' market up to 1939.

The radio industry expanded rapidly; the turnover of the radio section of the electrical industry rose from £7.8 million in 1926 to £30 million in 1931. The number of broadcast receiving licences grew in every year of the interwar period, reaching 8.97 million in 1939. Radio firms often produced allied products. In 1935, alongside the 1.7 million radio sets manufactured there were also produced 126,000 radio-gramophones and 743,000 gramophones. The industry remained fragmented, although some large combines emerged, notably Electrical and Musical Industries Ltd (EMI) in 1931, whose factory at Hayes, Middlesex, was easily the largest radio and gramophone factory in the UK.[49]

The sales of other domestic electrical appliances were dependent upon the expansion of the electricity network. Whereas in 1921 only about 12 per cent of UK households were wired for electricity, this had risen to 65 per cent by 1938. Other factors stimulating the appliance industry were the building of the

48. P. Fearon, 'Aircraft Manufacturing', in Buxton and Aldcroft, *British Industry.*
49. S.G. Sturmey, *The Economic Development of Radio* (Duckworth 1958), pp. 147ff.; Catterall, 'Electrical Engineering', pp. 260–4; Plummer, *New British Industries*, pp. 44–9.

many new houses in the suburbs, and the rise in real incomes, together with the spread of the habit of instalment buying ('hire-purchase'). Finally, the change to protective tariffs in 1932 boosted home production considerably. The most notable example of this was in the vacuum cleaner section. Before 1932, only about 20 per cent of the cleaners sold annually had been made in the UK, but following the imposition of the tariff, Hoover established manufacturing in Britain (at Perivale, Middlesex, where its factory is now preserved as a building of historic architectural importance). By 1935 97 per cent of cleaners sold were home-manufactured.

Adoption of the new consumer durables was patchy. The most successful was the electric iron, and the least successful were the few (rather primitive) washing machines. In 1939 there were in use an estimated 6.5 million irons, 2.3 million vacuum cleaners, and 1.5 million electric cookers. These apart, the most widespread product in use was probably the electric fire, used as supplement to the coal fires which still provided the bulk of British domestic heating. Yet most of these apparatus would have been in upper-class and middle-class households. Even as late as 1948, it was estimated that about 80 per cent of AB (upper- and upper-middle-class) households had an electric vacuum cleaner, but only about 25 per cent of DE (unskilled working-class) households had one.[50]

CONCLUSIONS

The interwar period may be considered as one of sudden shocks to the economy. The war and postwar changes in the world economy brought considerable problems to certain very large British industries – chiefly cotton textiles, coal, and shipbuilding. Their markets (largely foreign in the case of cotton; more balanced between domestic and foreign in the case of coal and shipbuilding) were lost or disrupted, and technological change worked to their disadvantage. Technological change also acted to promote the more rapidly expanding industries, which were technically more modern. Their greater reliance on the home market was to prove a source of strength; not only did they avoid the exporting difficulties which continued to haunt the more old-fashioned industries, but also they benefited from rising real incomes and changing patterns of expenditure on the home market.

These new patterns of development were being laid down before 1914; the next ten years were to emphasise them strongly. They were reinforced by the slump of 1929–32 and its effects. In the 1930s the formerly dominant industries found it even more difficult to survive, and the newer industries found that the home market was to be even more buoyant. No solution was found to the problems of the older industries before 1929. After 1929, the economic environment was even less propitious for the finding of effective remedies for their problems.

50. T.A.B. Corley, *Domestic Electrical Appliances* (Cape 1966), pp. 16–34; Catterall, 'Electrical Engineering', pp. 265–6.

CHAPTER 6

EXTERNAL TRADE AND FINANCE, 1918–29

THE BALANCE OF PAYMENTS

The financial transactions of an economy with the rest of the world may be thought of in terms of a current and of a capital account. In a given period of time, a certain flow of income will accrue to the economy through its sale of 'visible' goods and 'invisible' services to the rest of the world. There will be also an income derived from previous foreign investment, in the form of interest, profits and dividends. The sum of these income flows will be offset by flows of the same types of income from this economy to the rest of the world. At the end of the period, if the flow of income from the rest of the world to this economy exceeds the flow of income from this economy to the rest of the world, there will be a balance of payments surplus on current account; if the latter exceeds the former, a current balance of payments deficit.

These surpluses or deficits become translated, through the mechanism of foreign exchange markets, into accumulations of foreign capital. Thus a surplus on current account will lead to the building up of a stock of capital (or credit) in foreign currency, and a deficit on current account to the reduction of any stock of capital or credit in foreign currency already existing. (Alternatively, current deficits may be financed by borrowing in foreign currency.) Taken together, the current and the capital accounts of the balance of payments should add up to zero. However, statistical omissions in balance of payments estimates can be substantial even at present, and there is always a 'balancing item' (i.e. errors and omissions) in the accounts.

For the British economy before 1914, the large annual deficit on visible trade was more than offset by the sale of shipping, banking, insurance and other services to overseas residents, and by the income from previous foreign investment. The result was a large balance of payments surplus on current account. This surplus was more or less matched by the outflow of investment abroad, so that the current and capital accounts more or less offset each other (as they always do in economic theory).

The result was that Britain was steadily increasing its stock of overseas capital, which even in the mid-nineteenth century had been much bigger than that held by any other nation. The traditional view, based on estimates by Sir

George Paish, was that the value of British overseas investment in 1913 was *c.*£4,000 million, comprising £3,700 million of portfolio investment, and £300 million of direct investment. These figures have been criticised by D.C.M. Platt, who estimated a lower total, of £2,630 million for portfolio and £500 million for direct investment, making £3,130 million in all. But even if this revision is accepted, Britain still dominated the world of foreign investment. The traditional estimates show British investors as owning about 40 per cent of all the foreign investment in the world in 1913; the Platt revision would bring this down to about 34 per cent.[1]

After the war, the balance of payments surplus was diminished seriously. The current balance over the whole period of the war had been only slightly in deficit. In the boom of 1919–20, it was strongly in surplus, as demand for exports was high, and income from 'invisibles' (especially the hiring out of ships) very buoyant. But from then on, it declined steadily, being barely in surplus by 1924–25, when European economic reconstruction could be said to have taken effect. The coal dispute in the year of the General Strike (1926) produced the first peacetime deficit on record. In the later 1920s, there was some recovery, but the surpluses were, in real terms, much lower than before the war, and they began to fall off sharply as the world depression took effect in 1929 (Table 6.1 opposite).

Consideration of the changing balance of trade in visibles and invisibles, and of the current balance of payments, reveals the extent to which the war and the events of the early 1920s had weakened the British external trading position. Before the war, the visible trade gap had been more than covered by the substantial invisible earnings, leaving an overall payments surplus which amounted to about 8 per cent of national income (GDP) in 1909–13 (although less in 1900–09).

In the 1920s the current surplus was reduced to about 2 per cent of GDP. Taking the 1920s as a whole is in fact flattering to the British position, which was favoured by the factors described above. A more representative comparison, even allowing for the effects of the General Strike, is with 1924–29. In these years, the balance of payments surplus was only about 1 per cent of GDP. Even this conceals the adverse trends in trade volumes; by 1929, the volume of exports was about 19 per cent below that of 1913, while the volume of imports was about 15 per cent above it. That these changes did not damage the balance of payments even further was due to the improvement in the terms of trade (the ratio between import and export prices) by about 19 per cent between 1913 and 1929. This was due mainly to the decline in the world prices of raw materials, relative to world industrial products, of 15 per cent by 1929.[2]

1. D.C.M. Platt, *Britain's Investment Overseas on the Eve of the First World War: the use and abuse of numbers* (Macmillan 1986), pp. 5–6; United Nations, *International Capital Movements during the Inter-War Period* (Lake Success, NY, United Nations 1949; New York, Arno 1978), p. 2.

2. B.R. Mitchell, *British Historical Statistics* (Cambridge UP 1988), pp. 519, 527; W.A. Lewis, 'World Production, Prices and Trade, 1870–1960', *ManS* XX (1952), p. 118.

Table 6.1 UK current balance of payments, 1900–29

	Visible balance (£m)	*Invisible balance (£m)*	*Current balance (£m)*
Average 1900–09	–120	+204	+83
Average 1909–13	–92	+283	+192
1920	–148	+463	+315
1921	–148	+322	+174
1922	–63	+244	+181
1923	–97	+259	+162
1924	–214	+272	+58
1925	–265	+296	+31
1926	–346	+307	–39
1927	–270	+348	+78
1928	–237	+341	+104
1929	–263	+339	+76
Average 1920–29	–205	+319	+114
Average 1924–29	–266	+317	+51
% of GDP 1900–09	–5.8%	+9.9%	+4.0%
% of GDP 1909–13	–4.0%	+12.2%	+8.3%
% of GDP 1920–29	–3.8%	+5.9%	+2.1%
% of GDP 1924–29	–5.8%	+6.9%	+1.1%

Sources: R.G. Ware, 'The Balance of Payments in the Inter-War Period: further details', *Bank of England Quarterly Bulletin* 14 (1974), Tables A, B
1909–13 averages from C.H. Feinstein, *National Income, Expenditure and Output of the United Kingdom 1855–1965* (Cambridge UP 1972), Table 82
GDP ratios calculated from Feinstein, *National Income*, Tables 10, 11 and Tables 82, 83, using GDP at market prices

VISIBLE EXPORTS AND IMPORTS

Considerations of trade balance apart, the failure of British visible exports to recover after 1918 was a watershed in the history of Britain's place in the world economy (Table 6.2 overleaf).

Thus the war accelerated the relative decline of the UK. It is particularly striking that the relative fall of the UK proportion between 1913 and 1929 was similar to that of Germany, and that it was faster than the relative decline of the UK in the 1930s. Overall, although smaller manufacturers such as Japan gained relatively most during 1913–29, the greatest absolute increase was recorded by the USA.

While the export problems of the older industries contributed substantially to Britain's weakened trade position, this was not the whole story. In the longer run (1899–1937), Britain lost its share of trade in sectors whose world trade was growing, such as iron and steel, industrial equipment, and electrical goods, and in relatively stable groups such as chemicals, as well as

Table 6.2 Country shares in world exports of manufactures, 1899–1950

	1899	*1913*	*1929*	*1937*	*1950*
UK	32.5	29.9	23.6	22.4	25.0
USA	11.2	12.6	20.7	19.6	29.1
Germany	22.2	26.4	21.0	22.4	7.1
France	15.8	12.9	11.2	6.4	10.2
Belgium	5.6	4.9	5.5	5.9	5.8
Italy	3.7	3.6	3.7	3.6	3.8
Japan	1.5	2.4	3.9	7.2	3.3

Note: Tyszinski's total of 'world' trade in manufactures in reality comprised data from only eleven countries. This has laid his estimates open to criticism from D.C.M. Platt, *Mickey Mouse Numbers in World History: the short view* (Macmillan 1989), p. 44. In fairness to Tyszinski, he acknowledged that his world 'total' would cover only about 80–85 per cent of total world trade in manufactures. Estimates of the value of world trade are uncertain, even today, and calculations to one decimal place may mislead by a spurious air of precision. But there is no doubt that the British share of world trade in manufactures fell sharply in 1913–29

Source: H. Tyszinski, 'World Trade in Manufactured Commodities, 1899–1950', *ManS* XIX (1951), p. 286

in declining sectors such as textiles. It was not so much that Britain had been caught out in 1914 by being too much concentrated on the 'older' industries, but that they were special cases of a general decline in British competitiveness. This was particularly marked in 1913–29, but was part of a longer-term decline. Over the longer period 1899–1937, the British share of world manufactured exports declined from 32.5 per cent to 22.4 per cent. Tyszinski estimated that this decline was mainly (85 per cent) due to general competitive weakness, rather than merely possessing an inappropriate export structure.[3]

The failure of visible exports to recover in the 1920s was in contrast to the rising volume of imports. As in the late nineteenth century, these mainly consisted in food and raw materials (with the important twentieth-century addition of petroleum). In 1913, food/drink/tobacco had accounted for 42.2 per cent of the value of total imports, and raw materials 33.5 per cent. In 1928 the proportions were 47.1 and 28.6 respectively. Between 1913 and 1929, the volume of retained imports of food had risen by 32 per cent, and that of petroleum by 292 per cent, although the volume of raw materials had fallen by 4 per cent. Overall, retained imports had risen by 24 per cent.[4]

3. H. Tyszinski, 'World Trade in Manufactured Commodities, 1899–1950', *ManS* XIX (1951), pp. 283, 289.
4. R.E. Baldwin, 'The Commodity Composition of Trade: selected industrial countries, 1900–1954', *Review of Economics and Statistics* 40 (1958), p. 61; M. Fg. Scott, *A Study of United Kingdom Imports* (Cambridge UP 1963), pp. 244–5.

The general rise in imports reflected the fact that the population was still rising, and so were average living standards. Food was still the main import. Since British farming remained unprotected from foreign competition, this meant that the total cost of food imports continued to rise (although lower wheat prices in the 1920s provided some relief). Higher living standards were also reflected in the rise in imports of meat, butter and margarine.

In the 1920s, the geographical distribution of trade shifted, with a greater concentration of both imports and exports on Empire countries, and a relative decline in trade with north America and Europe. One consequence of the decline in British industrial competitiveness, perhaps also aided by the rise of postwar protectionism in Europe and the USA, was the rise in the deficits with north America and Europe, with whom Britain already had deficits before 1914. Thus the trade deficit with the USA rose from –£66.7 million to –£144.3 million between 1909–13 and 1924–29, that with British north America from –£2.8 million to –£27.8 million; with north and north-east Europe from –£39.5 million to –£81.4 million, and with western Europe from –£18.2 million to –£52.1 million. In addition, the deficit with central and south America rose from –£13.4 million to –£55.0 million, as the USA retained markets gained after 1914.

Whereas before 1914 these deficits had been partly offset by surpluses with Asia (chiefly India) and Africa, the Asian and African surpluses now failed to grow correspondingly. This failure raised the overall trade deficit, and meant that in addition it was now increasingly concentrated in dollar countries, with a resulting potential strain on the sterling–dollar exchange rate. This weakness was undoubtedly enhanced by the return to the gold standard at the prewar sterling–dollar exchange parity in 1925.[5]

INVISIBLE TRADE

Expressing the balance of payments as a proportion of GDP (Table 6.1) makes it clear that the greatest reason for the weaker current balance of payments after the war was not the failure of visible exports, in spite of the well-known weaknesses of the major exporting industries; it was the decline of invisible income. The relative decline in this aspect of the current balance was much greater than that of the visible deficit, regardless of which of the prewar or postwar periods from Table 6.1 one uses for comparison.

Estimates (especially before the Second World War) of invisible earnings are rather rough, but the net surplus on invisibles in 1913 was probably about £300 million, about two-thirds of which was composed of interest on existing foreign investments, and the profits and dividends of British companies operating overseas. The remainder was mainly earnings of shipping and financial services. After 1918, the main components of the invisibles surplus remained much the same in money terms, but this did not take account of inflation, and their real value was much reduced. The extent of the reduction may be debated.

5. Trade figures from Mitchell, *Statistics*, ch. IX, Table 16.

A rough indicator is the Board of Trade wholesale price index, which rose by 45 per cent between 1913 and 1925–29, implying a fall in the real value of the invisibles of roughly that amount (Table 6.3).[6]

Table 6.3 UK invisibles surplus, 1913 and 1920–29 (annual averages)

	1913 (£m)	*1920–24 (£m)*	*1925–29 (£m)*
Investment income, profits, dividends	210	194	238
Shipping	94	71	23
Financial services	25	41	44
Other items	10	26	42
Total invisibles surplus (net)	339	332	347

Sources: For 1913: M.D.K.W. Foot, 'The Balance of Payments in the Inter-War Period', *Bank of England Quarterly Bulletin* 12 (1972), p. 358
For 1920–29: Feinstein, *National Income*, Table 84

The greatest postwar surplus was still that on investment (including profit and dividend) income, but it was in current money terms only slightly higher than prewar, and then only in the latter half of the 1920s. In constant money terms it was substantially less, reflecting the reduction in the stock of overseas capital during the war. The greatest proportionate fall had been in (net) shipping income, which was adversely affected by the fall in postwar trade, and the very low freight rates after 1920–21, as well as the declining proportion of the world merchant fleet under the British flag. The result was that shipping income was less, and a much greater expense was incurred by hiring foreign-owned ships. These large relative declines were offset inadequately by higher earnings on financial services and other items (chiefly tourist spending, and payments on government account). (Contemporary estimates showed a net balance of over £100 million a year on the shipping account in the 1920s, but Feinstein's revisions, accepted by Ware, show a substantial offsetting debit on the shipping account.)[7]

THE STOCK OF OVERSEAS INVESTMENT

Before 1914, the invisible surplus had sufficed to pay for the deficit on visible trade, and provide a supply of investible capital, amounting to some £200

6. Ibid., p. 729.
7. M.D.K.W. Foot, 'The Balance of Payments in the Interwar Period', *Bank of England Quarterly Bulletin* 12 (1972), Table C; T.C. Chang, 'The British Balance of Payments, 1924–1938', *EJ* 57 (1947), App.; Feinstein, *National Income*, Table 84; R.G. Ware, 'The Balance of Payments in the Interwar Period: further details', *Bank of England Quarterly Review* 14 (1974).

million annually, which flowed overseas and expanded the already large stock of British overseas investment. In the 1920s, this investible surplus was much smaller. Table 6.1 shows it as only £114 million per annum in 1920–29. However, the predisposition of British investors and finance houses to invest abroad was still strong. Estimates show that in 1920–29 an average of £118 million a year went abroad as new investment. Thus it appeared that the new foreign investment was more or less exactly paid for by the current surplus. However, this decadal average conceals a serious weakness: while new overseas investment was more than covered by the balance of payments surplus in 1920–24, it was higher than the current surplus in 1925–29. Thus in the second half of the 1920s, British investors were investing more abroad than was warranted by the strength of the current balance of payments.[8]

While in the 1920s, fresh overseas investment took place, it had not sufficed to rebuild the prewar stock. The traditionally accepted estimate of British overseas portfolio investment in 1913 is *c.*£3,700 million. By 1928, it has been estimated at £3,380 million. While this was not much less in terms of current money values, it was substantially less when inflation is considered. Since between 1913 and 1928 the general British (wholesale) price level had risen by about 40 per cent, the real value of the stock of overseas investment in 1928 may be said to have been only £2,028 million – a decline of 45 per cent compared with the stock in 1913. While the rate of return in 1913 and 1930 was about the same (slightly over 5 per cent), investment income had not kept pace either with the national income or with the rise in prices.[9]

The partial rebuilding of the overseas investment stock also had certain disadvantages. The loss of investments in the USA was not made good, so that dollar income remained lower than before the war. Investors preferred to invest in the British Empire, and especially in the Dominions (Canada, Australasia, South Africa). The avoidance of investment in the USA may be partly explained by lower rates of interest in New York than in London. The preference for the Empire seems to have owed something to the fact that many Empire securities enjoyed 'trustee' status in law. This in effect allowed Imperial borrowers to have access to the London capital market more cheaply than many UK borrowers, boosting Empire investment. By 1930, the pattern of overseas investment had altered substantially. Whereas in 1913 47 per cent of all overseas investment had been located in the Empire, and 20 per cent in the USA, by 1930 the Empire proportion had risen to 59 per cent, and that of the USA had fallen to 5 per cent. Relative distribution elsewhere had changed very little.[10]

The pattern of postwar investment was less appropriate to the external trading and payments position of the UK than it had been before 1914. Apart from a slightly higher presence in Europe, the pattern of investment had shifted

8. Ware, 'Balance of Payments', Table B.

9. Royal Institute of International Affairs, *The Problem of International Investment* (1937, Cass repr. 1965), pp. 153, 160; Mitchell, *Statistics*, pp. 728–9; C.H. Feinstein, 'Britain's Overseas Investments in 1913', *EcHR* XLIII (1990), p. 294.

10. Royal Institute of International Affairs, *International Investment*, p. 144.

away from the industrial countries, with which the UK now had much greater balance of payments deficits. Thus investment income was going to play a smaller part than before 1914 in offsetting these deficits directly. In order to obtain foreign exchange to settle these deficits, the UK was going to have to rely on running larger surpluses with the primary producing areas within the Empire. However, these areas were now suffering from a decline in their terms of trade, *vis-à-vis* the industrial regions of the world, and thus found greater difficulty in earning surpluses in the appropriate currency. To make matters worse, the UK itself found it more difficult to earn surpluses with those primary producing regions such as south America and India which had developed their own manufacturing industries after 1914.

THE OUTFLOW OF NEW LONG-TERM INVESTMENT

The continuance of a relatively high level of overseas investment in the 1920s raised the question of whether too much capital was going abroad, either from the point of view of the capital needs of domestic industry, or from the point of view of maintaining the sterling exchange rate. Keynes drew attention to this as early as 1924.[11] From one point of view, it may be said that it was unlikely that British industry was deprived of capital by the continuing popularity of foreign investment, since home capital issues were a higher proportion of total capital issues after the war. In 1910–13, of the average of £221 million raised annually on the new issue market, only 19.9 per cent was for home issues; in 1926–30, out of a total of £284 million raised annually, the proportion was 57.9 per cent. Thus the £177 million raised annually before the war for overseas borrowers shrank in the later 1920s to only £119 million.[12] Even when account is taken of the fact that a substantial proportion of annual investment came from firms' retained profits, and thus was not derived from the new issue market, the importance of overseas investment can still be shown to have fallen substantially; in 1907, overseas investment accounted for some 56 per cent of the nation's total annual investment, but in 1924 and 1929 the proportions were 31 and 33 per cent.[13] (Henry Clay thought that about four-fifths of all new industrial and commercial investment in 1924 came from the retained profits of business.)[14]

Nor, for most of the 1920s, was the government concerned that the balance of payments surplus was inadequate for the level of foreign lending. Although for most of the decade the Treasury operated (via the Bank of England) an unofficial restriction on foreign capital issues in London, this was

11. J.M. Keynes, 'Foreign Investment and National Advantage', *The Nation and Athenaeum* (9 August 1924), in D. Moggridge (ed.), *The Collected Writings of John Maynard Keynes* (Macmillan/Cambridge UP), vol. XIX, pt 1 (1981), pp. 275–85.
12. A.E. Kahn, *Great Britain in the World Economy* (Pitman 1946), p. 139.
13. C. Clark, *National Income and Outlay* (Macmillan 1937), p. 185.
14. H. Clay, 'The Financing of Industrial Enterprise', *Transactions of the Manchester Statistical Society* (1931–32), p. 215.

initially (1921–24) designed to make it easier for the government itself to borrow, to place the National Debt on a more permanent footing. It was only in 1924, in the run-up to the return to gold, and in 1929–31 (when funds were flowing out in large amounts to the USA and Germany) that the Treasury used the restrictions to bolster the sterling exchange rate.[15]

In spite of the higher proportion of home capital issues after 1918, and of the government's reluctance to contemplate effective exchange control, it could be said that in effect the level of foreign investment was indeed too high to be financed by the balance of payments surplus of the 1920s. While contemporary estimates of the size of the surplus erred, chiefly in overstating the visible deficit and the invisibles surplus, the net effect was that official estimates of the overall surplus were not too dissimilar to those prepared more recently. It is clear that the current surplus was not financing the long-term capital outflow at any time after 1923, and that this fact was apparent at the time.[16]

SHORT-TERM CAPITAL

But the great statistical gap of the 1920s was the estimation of short-term capital movements. Before the war Britain had had a surplus of assets over liabilities on short-term capital account, chiefly in the form of bills of exchange accepted for discounting on the London discount market. After the war, Britain had a deficit on such short-term capital. The feeling that, in effect, Britain was financing long-term overseas investment by means of an increase in its short-term capital liabilities was widespread. However, the size of such net liabilities was unknown. The Committee on Finance and Industry of 1931 ('Macmillan Committee') provided the first public inquiry into the matter. On balance, the committee thought that there was indeed a net liability, which varied between 1927 and March 1931 from £254 million to £302 million.[17] While more reliable figures were not collected until after 1931 (and not published until 1951), there were those who felt even at the time that this was an understatement of the liability. A year later, Keynes estimated the net liability in June 1931 at £500 million.[18] A more recent estimate is that the net liability in June 1930 was as high as £760 million, although this had been run down to £640 million in June 1931, and to about £411 million by December 1931, after the financial crisis of the autumn.[19] However, it should be stressed that all estimates of the value of short-term international capital movements were (and still are) approximate only.

15. J. Atkin, 'Official Regulation of British Overseas Investment, 1914–1939', *EcHR* XXIII (1970), pp. 324–31.
16. Compare the contemporary (interwar) estimates in Foot (1972), Table C, with those of Ware (1974), Table B, which are largely derived from Feinstein, *National Income.*
17. Committee on Finance and Industry, *Report* (1931), Cmd 3897, para. 260, App. I.
18. J.M. Keynes, 'Reflections on the Sterling Exchange', *Lloyds Bank Review* (April 1932), pp. 143–59.
19. D. Williams, 'London and the 1931 Financial Crisis', *EcHR* XV (1962–63), App.

The tendency of British investors to send abroad an amount of long-term capital at least equal to the current balance of payments surplus was thus offset by an increased tendency for short-term foreign funds to be drawn into Britain. Some of this followed naturally from the financial changes of the war and recovery period. But some was the product of policy. In particular, the return to the gold standard in 1925, apart from reducing the future current balance of payments surplus by an unknown amount, was at a parity which was difficult to maintain. After the return to parity the sterling exchanges were perpetually weak.[20] To defend sterling, the authorities were forced to keep interest rates higher than would have been warranted by the domestic state of the economy. Between 1925 and 1928, Bank Rate varied between 4.5 and 5.0 per cent, while the Federal Reserve Bank of New York discount rate ranged between 3.25 and 4.25 per cent. These differences may seem small, but they amounted to an average excess UK interest rate of 27 per cent.[21] The maintenance of relatively high short-term rates in London served to attract 'hot' money from abroad, so that policy was storing up potential trouble for the future.

Even with the short-term interest rate differential, the authorities had a hard time holding the sterling parity. Montagu Norman, the Governor of the Bank of England, admitted to the Macmillan Committee that Bank Rate had been mainly influenced by international considerations, and that in the previous few years: 'we have been continuously under the harrow'.[22] This reflected the dilemma in which the monetary authorities found themselves. Having returned to gold at a parity which proved to be too high, they were faced with the choice of abandoning the parity or defending it. The former course being ruled out, high interest rates were a logical course of action. The only other feasible solution would have been to restrict the outflow of investment funds. This was attempted even before 1925, but only intermittently, and was largely abandoned between 1926 and 1928.[23] Any greater degree of exchange control would have been anathema on grounds of economic theory, and was ruled out politically. Thus caught, the outflow of foreign investment continued to be financed by the rise in London's short-term liabilities.

CONCLUSIONS

The external position of the UK after the war was very different from before 1914. The volume of exports was reduced, due in particular to the weaknesses of the former major exporting industries, and to the general decline of British competitiveness in the world as a whole. But the decreased volume of exports

20. D. Moggridge, *The Return to Gold 1925: the formulation of economic policy and its critics* (Cambridge UP 1969), p. 83.
21. London and Cambridge Economic Service, *Key Statistics of the British Economy, 1900–1964* (Times Publishing Co. 1965), Tables F, I.
22. Quoted in R.S. Sayers, *The Bank of England, 1891–1944* (Cambridge UP 1976), vol. I, p. 211.
23. Atkin, 'Official Regulation', p. 331.

was largely offset by the improvement in the terms of trade, so that the balance of trade deficit did not change very much as a proportion of the national income.

The decline in the current balance of payments surplus was mainly due, not to the weakness of visible trade, but the decline in the invisibles surplus. This constrained the ability of the economy to lend abroad on the prewar scale. The continuance of foreign lending, although at a much reduced level, reflected former habits and the presence of institutions specialising in that sort of business. Although the surplus on the current balance of payments was adequate to finance new foreign investment in the first half of the 1920s, this was not so in the second half of the decade. As a result, net short-term liabilities built up, whose size was unknown, and whose instability posed a potential threat which became a reality in the crises of 1929–31.

CHAPTER 7

EMPLOYMENT AND UNEMPLOYMENT IN THE 1920s

THE LABOUR FORCE

In spite of the losses of life during the First World War, and the declining birth rate, the population of Britain was still growing, although less rapidly than before 1914. The total UK population of 40,831,400 in 1911 had become 44,795,400 in 1931, an increase of 9.7 per cent. Between these dates there was a slight increase in the proportions of both males and females occupied (i.e. stating their occupation at the Census of Population, even if unemployed at the time). The ratio of males thus 'occupied' rose from 65.5 per cent in 1911 to 68.9 per cent in 1931, the ratio for females being 25.4 and 26.8 per cent respectively.[1]

These slightly higher ratios were due to a change in the age structure of the population, rather than a greater tendency for individuals to seek employment; indeed, the rates of participation in the labour force of men and women of working age fell slightly in this period. But the demographic changes of 1911–31 resulted in a lower proportion of young persons (under 15) in the population, and this was only partly offset by the rise in the proportion of those above working age. Thus the proportion of the males of working age (here taken as 15–64) rose between 1911 and 1931 from 63.4 to 67.9, and of females from 64.4 to 68.9 per cent. This comparatively sharp change meant that the occupied population grew more rapidly than the total British population; between 1911 and 1931, the number of occupied males rose from 12.58 million to 14.79 million, and occupied females from 5.22 million to 6.25 million, making a total rise of 3.24 million, or 18.2 per cent.[2]

Within this enlarged labour force, most persons were employees. In 1911, employers and proprietors of businesses had accounted for only 6.7 per cent of the occupied population, and this proportion was almost the same in 1931. The 1.25 million employers and proprietors were found in a very limited range of industries. In 1931, some 40 per cent were in the distributive trades, and 20

1. B.R. Mitchell, *British Historical Statistics* (Cambridge UP 1988), pp. 9–10, 15–17.
2. A.H. Halsey (ed.), *Trends in British Society since 1900* (Macmillan 1972), p. 115; Mitchell, *Statistics*, pp. 15–17.

per cent were farmers; only 12 per cent were in manufacturing and mining. Female employers and proprietors had an even more limited range of occupation. Self-employment was in fact a severely constrained affair; as Abrams remarked, for men who wished to be self-employed, the choice was usually between running a shop, farm or garage; for women, it was usually a shop or boarding-house. Although this was probably true of most working-class and many middle-class people, it would not apply to the higher professions (law, medicine, accountancy, etc.), where in 1931, 34 per cent of all persons were either employers or self-employed. The overwhelming majority of employees were manual workers. In 1911, 85.1 per cent, and, in 1931, 82.5 per cent of all employees were in manual occupations.[3]

The changing occupational structure of the economy (which is analysed in Chapter 3) had implications for the sexual division of labour. Overall, the proportions of men and women in the occupied population changed very little. In 1911, males formed 70.7 per cent of the occupied population, and 70.2 per cent in 1931. Although a population census was not taken in 1941, an estimate by Frankel of the occupied population in July 1939 placed the proportion of males in the occupied population at 69.9 per cent.[4]

Within the occupied male population, changes between 1911 and 1939 reflected the longer-term changes in industrial structure. The greatest decline was in agriculture (including forestry and horticulture), where numbers fell from 1.436 million to 0.934 million. This was a decline of 35 per cent, and was much larger, both in absolute and relative terms, than the next largest decline, textiles and clothing, where numbers fell 25 per cent, from 1.071 million to 0.806 million. The only other declining sector was mining and quarrying, where numbers fell by 9 per cent, from 1.202 million to 1.097 million. In all, these three sectors lost 872,000 males between 1911 and 1939.

Since the total occupied male population rose in these years from 12.93 million to 16.01 million, or just over 3 million, there were available almost 4 million males for redistribution to the expanding industries. The greatest expansion was in the commercial and financial sector. The 1911 census had recorded 739,000 males in 'commercial occupations'. This had rather more than doubled by 1921 (if clerks and typists are included), and reached 2.399 million at the 1931 census; Frankel's estimate for 1939 was 2.525 million. The next largest expansion was in the metal and engineering sector, which rose from 1.795 million to 2.650 million. The only other industry to show a large absolute increase was building, which rose from 1.140 million to 1.387 million.[5]

Changes in female employment also reflected the changing fortunes of certain industries, but with the difference that women's employment was concentrated

3. G. Routh, *Occupation and Pay in Britain, 1906–60* (Cambridge UP 1965), pp. 4–5, 7, 18, 20; M. Abrams, *The Condition of the British People 1911–1945* (Gollancz 1945), p. 65.
4. Mitchell, *Statistics*, pp. 104–5; H. Frankel, 'The Industrial Distribution of the Population of Great Britain in July, 1939', *JRSS* CVIII (1945), Table XLI.
5. Mitchell, *Statistics*, pp. 104–5; Frankel, 'Industrial Distribution', Table XLI.

in 1911 in a relatively small number of industries, and, in spite of the changing occupational structure, remained so in the interwar period. In 1911, of the 5.356 million occupied females, 2.127 million were engaged in 'domestic offices and personal services', and textiles and clothing accounted for 1.695 million. Thus 71 per cent of the occupied females were in either personal service or textiles/clothing. These were by far the dominant occupations, the next largest being the 308,000 recorded in the food, drink and tobacco industries.

By 1939, there were still 2.052 million females recorded in personal service (institutional and private), although the textiles/clothing group had fallen to 1.269 million. Thus the two major employers had declined substantially in relative importance, losing some 500,000 women, and now employed only 48 per cent of occupied women. Even so, the number of female private domestic servants had been only slightly reduced, from 1.26 million in 1911 to 1.20 million in 1931. The greatest fall was to come during and after the Second World War; by the time of the next census of population, in 1951, there were only 343,000 female domestic servants.[6]

Since the total female labour force had risen to 6.906 million by 1939, there remained some 2 million more to account for. On the whole, the extra numbers employed were not to be found in manufacturing industry (although metals in 1939 were an exception), but in commerce and government service. Female commercial employment rose from 157,000 in 1911 to 1,188,000 in 1939. Most of this was probably an increase in clerical workers. In 1911 only 179,000 female clerical workers had been recorded (out of a total of 887,000 clerical workers), but this had risen to 648,000 in 1931. Slightly over one-third (239,000) of the latter were typists. Before the war, these had been a negligible category. Now the female typist had largely replaced the male clerk. In 1911, women had accounted for 20 per cent of all clerical workers; by 1931 they were 44 per cent of all clerks. The other great expansion was in government service (again, largely in clerks and typists), which was almost negligible before 1914, but was employing 435,000 women by 1939.[7]

The expansion of women's employment was thus mainly in the service occupations. It was also at the lower end of the pay and prestige scale. Numbers of women in the 'lower professions' such as teaching and nursing changed very little; female teachers actually declined by 4,000 between 1921 and 1931, although the nurses rose from 113,000 to 141,000. In 1931, there were more women employed as cleaners or 'charwomen' (158,000) than nurses (141,000).[8] Few women occupied high positions in administration, commerce or the professions, and domestic or personal service continued to be the largest employment for women until the Second World War.

6. Census of England and Wales 1931, *Industry Tables* (1934), p. 714; Routh, *Occupation and Pay*, p. 33.
7. Mitchell, *Statistics*, pp. 104–5; Frankel, 'Industrial Distribution', Table XLI; Routh, *Occupation and Pay*, p. 25.
8. Routh, *Occupation and Pay*, pp. 17, 37.

THE GEOGRAPHY OF THE POPULATION

The economic difficulties of the interwar period had implications for the geographical distribution of the population. Between 1921 and 1939, the UK population rose by 8.5 per cent, but there were sharp differences in regional experience. Three English regions showed much faster growth than average; the south-east (18.6 per cent), the west midlands (13.8) and the east midlands (13.1). Most of the rest of the UK grew at between 3 and 6 per cent, but two regions lost population, albeit by small amounts (see Map 2): English northern counties (−0.1 per cent) and Wales (−0.7 per cent).

Locally, there were sharper variations. Between 1921 and 1937, in south Wales, Glamorganshire and Monmouthshire lost 9 per cent of their combined populations. In northern England, Northumberland and Durham lost 1.4 per cent. Mid-Scotland grew by slightly less than 4 per cent; Lancashire grew by slightly less than 1 per cent. The population of the six counties of Northern Ireland, having fallen from 864,000 to 842,000 between 1911 and 1926, then remained almost unchanged, being 843,000 in 1937. Most of these changes were due to migration rather than to regional differences in the balance of fertility and mortality, which were small. Even in the single decade 1921–31, the south-east of England gained 615,000 persons by net migration, while Scotland lost 392,000, Wales lost 259,000, and the northern region 231,000.[9] (The regions are slightly modified versions of the official Standard regions of 1966–74.)[10]

There were three main internal migratory movements in the interwar period. The first reflected prosperity rather than depression, as London lost population to the home counties. But the remaining two were clearly correlated with depression. From south Wales, migrants moved to north Wales, the counties bordering London, some eastern counties and the midlands. From the northern English counties (chiefly Northumberland and Durham), migrants moved to eastern, south-eastern and southern counties. Some of these movements went far to explain the population changes in some regions; between 1911 and 1931, about 30 per cent of Middlesex's population growth and almost 25 per cent of Surrey's growth were due to migration, as was about 17 per cent of Warwickshire's, while migration reduced the combined population of Durham, Monmouth and Glamorgan by about 12–13 per cent. Total migration was split about equally between those moving to adjacent counties and those going further. On average, migration to an adjacent county involved a movement of about 46 miles, whereas movement to a non-adjacent county involved travelling about 126 miles.[11]

9. C.M. Law, *British Regional Development since World War I* (Newton Abbot, David & Charles 1980), pp. 58–60; Royal Commission on the Distribution of the Industrial Population, *Report* (1940), Cmd 6153, Table I; Mitchell, *Statistics*, pp. 33–4.
10. Law, *British Regional Development*, pp. 28–31.
11. D. Friedlander and R.J. Roshier, 'A Study of Internal Migration in England and Wales, Part I: Geographical Patterns of Internal Migration 1851–1951', *PS* XIX, 3 (1966), pp. 260, 265, 267, 278.

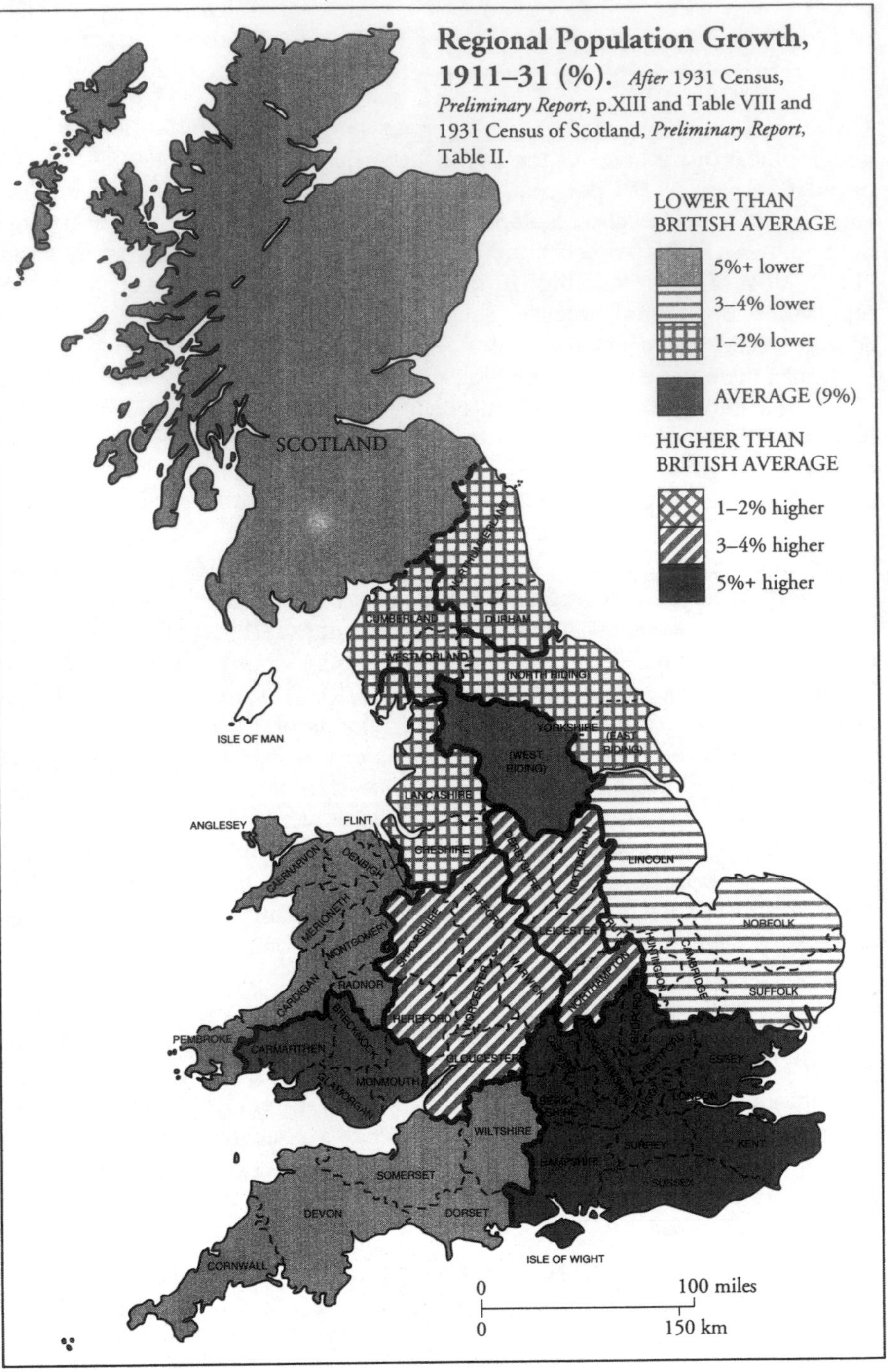

Map 2 Regional population growth, 1911–31

A further indication that much migration was a response to depressed economic conditions is found in the fact that most migrants were young adults. In a study of Durham and south Wales for 1921–31, it was found that nearly 20 per cent of all the residents aged 15–29 migrated out of these counties, and that they comprised 53 per cent of all the out-migrants of these counties. Another study of migrants from south Wales to Oxford in the 1930s showed that 79 per cent were aged 16–34, and that 33 per cent were aged 20–24.[12]

POSTWAR UNEMPLOYMENT

The sudden emergence of lost markets and excess capacity in some of the major prewar industries, coupled with the fact that the most dynamic industries were still too small to dominate industry as a whole, meant that substantial unemployment was likely to emerge after the postwar boom had broken. That this was so, and that it was concentrated in the less dynamic or declining industries, is confirmed by the statistics of the insured unemployed (Table 7.1).

Table 7.1 UK insured workers unemployed in 'old' and 'new' industries, 1923–29[a]

	1923[b] (%)	*1924* (%)	*1925* (%)	*1926* (%)	*1927* (%)	*1928* (%)	*1929* (%)
'Old' or declining industries							
Coal-mining	3.0	5.8	11.5	9.5	19.0	23.6	19.0
Cotton textiles	21.6	15.9	8.8	18.3	15.4	12.5	12.9
Wool textiles	9.5	8.4	16.9	17.4	11.0	12.0	15.5
Shipbuilding	43.6	30.3	33.5	39.5	29.7	24.5	25.3
Iron and steel[c]	21.2	22.0	25.0	40.4	19.4	22.4	20.1
'New' industries							
Chemicals	11.8	9.9	9.1	10.9	7.2	6.1	6.5
Cars & aircraft	9.7	8.9	7.1	8.2	8.1	8.1	7.1
Gas/water/electricity	7.2	6.3	6.2	6.0	5.4	5.8	6.1
Electrical engineering	7.3	5.5	5.6	7.5	5.9	4.8	4.6

Notes: a January/July averages; persons under 16 excluded
b For all industries, 1923 figures are for July only
c Steel smelting, iron puddling, iron and steel rolling/forging
Source: Department of Employment and Productivity, *British Labour Statistics, Historical Abstract 1886–1968* (HMSO 1971), Table 164

For the UK as a whole, average unemployment in these years varied between 10.6 and 12.7 per cent of the insured labour force, averaging 11.3 per cent over

12. H.W. Singer, *Transference and Age Structure of the Population of Special Areas* (Pilgrim Trust Unemployment Enquiry, Interim Report no. 3, 1937); G.H. Daniel, 'Labour Migration and Age Composition', *Sociological Review* 32 (1940), pp. 216–23.

1923–29. In absolute numbers, unemployment varied between 1.13 million and 1.38 million.[13]

These statistics, being the percentage of insured workers registering themselves as unemployed, do not tell the whole story. The unemployment insurance scheme did not cover the whole of the workforce. Employers and the self-employed were excluded, as were employees in agriculture (until 1936), forestry, horticulture, private domestic service, teaching, nursing, the police forces, the established civil service, certain local authority employments, the railways and military service. The liability of these groups to unemployment is presumed to be much less than those covered by the national unemployment insurance scheme, which was broadly restricted to manual employees, and non-manual employees earning less than £250 a year. It probably accounted for only about 64 per cent of the total labour force in 1931.[14]

How much allowance should be made for the lower propensity of these groups to unemployment when calculating a national unemployment rate is debatable. Feinstein's estimate, based on an inquiry in the 1931 population census, is that the 1923–29 average should be reduced from 11.0 (for the insured groups) to 8.4 per cent for the proportion of employees unemployed in the economy as a whole.[15] More recently, it has been suggested that even Feinstein's estimate may exaggerate the percentage of the total workforce unemployed:

> one could suggest that the national unemployment rates for *most* of the interwar period, while very different in pattern, were not very much worse than the national average rates which prevailed before 1914 with, of course, the major exception of the depressed years 1921–22 and 1931–33.[16]

This hypothesis is difficult to test, since unemployment figures under the national insurance scheme began only in 1913. The much older unemployment statistics for trade union members, which continued until 1926, are probably vitiated by the limited numbers of employees in unions before the war, and the fact that most of them were skilled workers, who were less prone to unemployment than the unskilled. In the 1920s, when the numbers of trade unionists were much greater, and included a larger proportion of unskilled workers, the trade union and national insurance series showed very similar levels, but in the prewar period unemployment among unionists was probably much lower than general unemployment.[17] Beveridge's view was that the

13. Mitchell, *Statistics*, pp. 128–9.
14. W.R. Garside, *British Unemployment 1919–1939: a study in public policy* (Cambridge UP 1990), p. 4.
15. C.H. Feinstein, *National Income, Expenditure and Output of the United Kingdom 1855–1965* (Cambridge UP 1972), Table 128.
16. A.E. Booth and S. Glynn, 'Unemployment in the Interwar Period: a multiple problem', *JCH* 10 (1975), p. 614 (original italics).
17. Garside, *Unemployment*, pp. 6–7. See also J. Hilton, 'Statistics of Unemployment Derived from the Working of the Unemployment Insurance Acts', *JRSS* 86 (1923).

recorded unemployment rate among trade unionists between 1883 and 1913 of 4.8 per cent might be equivalent to a rate of about 6 per cent for the labour force as a whole. On this basis, unemployment in the 1920s was either about one-third higher than prewar (if one takes the total number of employees in the economy), or almost double it (if one takes insured employees only). Such general statements are probably the best permitted by the statistical data.[18]

THE CAUSES OF UNEMPLOYMENT

The causes of unemployment after 1919 were much debated at the time, and still give rise to differences of opinion. In a proximate sense, one can explain unemployment either by supply factors (inefficiencies leading to excessively high costs and thus product prices) or by demand factors (loss of markets, lack of effective demand). In the interwar period, attention among economists and politicians was concentrated mainly on supply factors. In a broad sense, it could be said that if unemployment occurred, then by definition British real wages (which accounted for the bulk of industrial costs) were too high; whatever the state of the market for goods, there must be a point at which all that is produced can be sold, if costs (and, by implication, wages), are low enough. This is not to say that comparative British real wages had necessarily risen excessively for internal industrial reasons alone; real wages in other countries might have fallen, or new, low-cost producers might have entered export markets (as was the case in cotton textiles). Alternatively, British real wages might have been rendered too high by a generally too-high British price level, or a too-high exchange rate. But these were immaterial considerations in the face of the allegation that the solution to unemployment lay in cutting costs (which meant largely wages).

Economists in the 1920s concluded that the single most important explanation for unemployment was that British real wages were too high. Pigou explained most of the unemployment after 1921 as due to excessive wage costs, emphasising that trade unions were in a much stronger position after 1918 than before 1914.[19] Clay considered that the extension of collective wage bargaining, and of the system of unemployment relief, had

> interfered with the harsh but effective correctives of wages-demands that restrict employment, namely, the loss of income by unemployment and the expansion of employment where wages are not held up. Either, therefore, we must devise alternative correctives, or we must expect unemployment on a large scale from this cause alone.[20]

In coming to this conclusion, Clay was not necessarily saying that real wages were generally too high; it was rather that the war had caused a maldistribution

18. W.H. Beveridge, *Full Employment in a Free Society* (Allen & Unwin 1944), pp. 335–7.
19. A.C. Pigou, 'Wage Policy and Unemployment', *EJ* XXXVII (1927), p. 355.
20. H. Clay, 'The Public Regulation of Wages in Great Britain', *EJ* XXXIX (1929), pp. 341–2.

of labour, and that this maldistribution was not being corrected, since labour markets were less flexible than before the war. Thus some industries had excessively high wages, which were not being reduced by the forces of the labour market, as had been the case before 1914.[21]

But, in making such judgements, economists also were aware that real wages in Britain had in fact increased since 1914, partly because of the general reduction of working hours in 1919–20, and partly because prices fell more than wages after the postwar boom broke in 1920. As a result, hourly real wage rates in 1924 were 28 per cent higher than in 1913, while output per head had risen only by 5 per cent. Thus the real cost of labour had risen by 23 per cent per average unit of output.[22]

Internationally, British price competitiveness had declined. An index of export unit values in 1929 (of all manufactured exports) shows a value of 159 for the UK, compared with a weighted average of 134 for twelve major industrial countries (1913 = 100).[23] On that estimate, relative British export prices were about 19 per cent higher than in 1913. Thus the charge that excessively high real wages were at least part of the reason for unemployment has a strong foundation. Beveridge went further, having no doubt that excessive real wages were at the root of the unemployment problem of the 1920s.[24]

The effect of historically high real wages on employment was probably worsened by the exchange rate policies of the 1920s, which had the effect of raising the price of exports (in sterling) higher than was warranted by the level of domestic costs. The return to gold in 1925, at the prewar dollar parity (£1 = $4.86), certainly overvalued sterling. The accusation of overvaluation was made by Keynes in a polemical pamphlet ('The Economic Consequences of Mr. Churchill') in 1925, and has been confirmed by the work of Redmond. It has also been pointed out that, when international price changes have been taken into account, the pound had an even higher real exchange rate in 1920–21 than in 1925–26, and presumably this had severe effects on exports in those years as well.[25]

Contemporary economists referred also to the extension of the system of unemployment benefits after 1918, as tending to raise real wages, in comparison with prewar. This is theoretically feasible, since a wider and more generous system of benefits would reduce both the opportunity-costs of unemployment, and the incentive for unemployed people to search for fresh employment. This approach has been elaborated by Benjamin and Kochin, who suggested that

21. H. Clay, 'Unemployment and Wage Rates', *EJ* XXXVIII (1928), pp. 5–6, 10–11.
22. N.H. Dimsdale, 'Employment and Real Wages in the Inter-War Period', *NIER* 110 (1984), p. 94.
23. A. Maizels, *Industrial Growth and World Trade* (Cambridge UP 1963), pp. 509–10.
24. W.H. Beveridge, *Unemployment: a problem of industry* (Longmans, Green 1930), pp. 369–71.
25. J. Redmond, 'The Sterling Overvaluation in 1925: a multilateral approach', *EcHR* XXXVII (1984); S.N. Broadberry, *The British Economy between the Wars: a macro-economic survey* (Oxford, Blackwell 1986), p. 122.

unemployment after 1918 can be explained largely by the scale of unemployment benefits:[26]

> the persistently high rate of unemployment in interwar Britain was due in large part not to deficient aggregate demand but to high unemployment insurance benefits relative to wages.[27]

This view has some plausibility, both on theoretical grounds, and because the rates of unemployment benefit rose in real terms after 1918, especially in 1921–22, so that by the late 1920s they were about double the level of 1920–21. On the other hand, benefits were much lower than the wage levels of all except the very poorly paid. The rate of benefit for a man, his wife and two children was 22s. in 1922, rose by several stages to 30s. in 1930, and was then reduced to 27s. 3d. in 1931.[28] This may be compared with (weighted) average earnings (in 1924) of about 70s. a week for skilled men, and about 51s. 6d. a week for unskilled men.[29] There was thus a large gap between the incomes of those in work and those on unemployment benefit. It may also be the case that the average benefit received was even lower than these comparisons indicate. It has been suggested that average unemployment benefit *actually paid* per unemployed person was less than one-third of the average wage in the 1920s, rather than about one-half, as suggested by Benjamin and Kochin.[30]

The ideas discussed above, which dominated the policy debates of the 1920s, and which were revived in the mid-1980s, led in effect to the conclusion that unemployment after 1918 was largely voluntary. But they did not take demand factors (e.g. loss of markets, or lack of effective demand) sufficiently into account. Thus they largely missed the fundamental point that the few big industries in which unemployment was concentrated were suffering from a sudden and sharp decline in demand – whether due to overexpansion in 1914–19, falling exports, outdated products, a decline in government orders, a generally depressed state of home demand, or a combination of all of these. (Eichengreen comes to a balanced conclusion between the two schools of thought on the causes of unemployment – the 'voluntary' and the 'involuntary'.)[31] The fact that these industries had been large employers of labour meant that they accounted for a high proportion of total unemployment (Table 7.2).

26. The *Journal of Political Economy* (1982) contains articles mostly critical of this proposition, with a further defence of their position by Benjamin and Kochin.

27. D.K. Benjamin and L.A. Kochin, 'Searching for an Explanation of Unemployment in Interwar Britain', *JPE* 87 (1979), p. 474.

28. Royal Commission on Unemployment Insurance, *Final Report* (1932), Cmd 4185, p. 20.

29. Routh, *Occupation and Pay*, pp. 88, 98.

30. P.A. Ormerod and G.D.N. Worswick, 'Unemployment in Interwar Britain', *JPE* 90 (1982), pp. 407–8.

31. B. Eichengreen, 'Unemployment in Interwar Britain: dole or doldrums?', *OEP* 39 (1987), reprinted in N. Crafts, N. Dimsdale and S. Engerman, *Quantitative Economic History* (Oxford, Clarendon 1991).

Table 7.2 UK unemployment in high-unemployment industries, 1923–29 (thousands)[a]

	1923	*1924*	*1925*	*1926*	*1927*	*1928*	*1929*
Insured unemployed in							
Mining and quarrying	41	68	325	150	240	184	270
Shipbuilding[b]	119	74	84	95	51	55	45
Textiles[c]	194	151	179	318	107	158	163
Metals[d]	288	219	223	395	174	170	156
Totals	642	512	811	958	572	567	634
% of UK unemployed in these industries	49%	47%	58%	55%	53%	44%	54%

Notes: a Total insured population (male and female) at mid-year, less insured population employed at mid-year; 1923–27 figures include all aged 16 or over; 1928–29 figures are those aged 16–64
b Shipbuilding = shipbuilding and ship repairing
c Textiles = all textiles
d Metals = metal manufacture, engineering, other metal industries and trades

Source: Department of Employment and Productivity, *British Labour Statistics*, Tables 111, 114

THE NATURE OF UNEMPLOYMENT

Such comparisons suggest that the great problem of postwar unemployment was not so much the 'intractable million' referred to at the time, but the intractable two-thirds of a million represented by these industries in an average year of the 1920s. Their unemployment was disproportionate to their importance in the labour force. In 1923 they comprised 40 per cent of all insured workers; this fell steadily, to 36 per cent in 1929. Thus, while the shrinkage of these industries offset the impact of their high unemployment on the national workforce, unemployment became more heavily concentrated in them by the end of the decade.

The causes of excessive unemployment in these industries were various. The chief cause was undoubtedly reduced exports, if only because it was the greatest cause of the problems of the cotton industry, and a large part of the reason for the difficulties in iron and steel and mechanical engineering. But the problems of the latter two were compounded by import penetration also. In coal, the decline in demand came almost equally from home and overseas. In shipbuilding the greatest problem was the decline of naval orders.

Unemployment was not confined to this short list of large industries, which comprised 51 per cent of recorded unemployment in 1923–29. How may one account for the other 49 per cent? Here, the notable fact is that there were very few *manufacturing* industries, other than those in Table 7.2, with high rates of unemployment. The only one which was notably above the national unemployment average rate in the 1920s was pottery, which was not a large

Table 7.3 Regional insured unemployment rates, 1923–29

	1923	*1924*	*1925*	*1926*	*1927*	*1928*	*1929*
London	9.9	8.6	7.1	6.3	5.5	5.2	5.3
South-east	9.2	7.1	5.5	5.0	4.8	5.2	5.6
South-west	10.4	8.7	8.0	7.8	7.3	8.1	8.3
Midlands	9.9	8.3	8.5	10.4	8.3	9.8	9.2
North-east	11.5	10.4	14.6	16.8	13.9	15.5	14.1
North-west	14.2	12.3	10.9	14.0	10.6	12.5	12.3
Wales	6.3	9.0	16.9	18.2	20.7	23.2	19.9
Scotland	13.8	13.3	14.7	15.8	10.4	11.6	12.3
N. Ireland	16.4	15.5	22.8	21.1	12.3	16.3	14.0
UK	11.7	10.3	11.3	12.5	9.7	10.8	10.4

Source: Mitchell, *Statistics*, pp. 124–5

industry. Most of the residual unemployment was in industries with high rates of casual unemployment, notably, on average in 1923–29, the waterside trades (docks, harbours, canals – 28.0 per cent), building (12.4), fishing (13.2) and road transport (13.8). If these rates are applied to the numbers of males in those industries at the 1921 population census, an unemployment total of 267,000 for these industries alone is indicated on average in 1923–29. For the rest, unemployment was either frictional, or derived from those sectors which had very low recorded unemployment rates, such as commercial services and administration.

Since unemployment was concentrated in the 'old' industries, which were regionally imbalanced, unemployment was also regionally imbalanced (Table 7.3 above).

By 1924, when the economy had recovered from the depression of 1920–21, it was clear that the unemployment problem was also a regional problem, becoming more marked as one travelled north and west. This was the reverse of the prewar pattern. In 1912–14, rates of unemployment derived from the national insurance scheme had showed London to be the great unemployment region, with more than twice the national rate; the other southern divisions were also above the national average, and it was the rest of Britain which had below-average rates.[32]

The concentration of certain industries in limited regions had serious consequences for employment. Thus, even in 1931, Lancashire and the West Riding of Yorkshire accounted for 81 per cent of all male, and 78 per cent of all female textile workers in England and Wales. Durham, Lancashire, the West Riding and Glamorgan had together accounted for 59 per cent of all males in coal-mining in 1921, and the ratio was almost exactly the same ten years later. Thus it was hardly surprising that in 1931 all these counties had above-average

32. Beveridge, *Full Employment*, p. 73.

unemployment rates, ranging from only 2 per cent above (West Riding) to 35 per cent (Lancashire), 77 per cent (Glamorgan) and 105 per cent above the national average (Durham). The overvaluation of the pound sterling in 1925, which must have made exporting more difficult, may have contributed to this strongly regional pattern of unemployment.[33]

There was also considerable variation within regions. Thus in Lancashire in 1931, the average county unemployment rate for men (as a proportion of the whole male occupied population) was 13.9 per cent, but this covered substantial variations, from 24 per cent in Oldham to only 10.3 per cent in the seaside and residential town of Southport. In south Wales, the coal-mining town of Merthyr Tydfil had a rate of 35.8, but the administrative and business city of Cardiff recorded 20.1 per cent. The lowest proportions were found almost entirely in the southern counties and London boroughs, such as Hendon (4.7) or Finchley (4.3). The only non-southern counties with especially low rates were Radnor and Westmorland, which had high proportions of agricultural workers, who had low unemployment rates.[34]

Unemployment thus varied industrially and regionally. It also varied over time. Among the insured population, the peak of unemployment in the 1921 depression was reached in May, when it was 23.0 per cent. With partial recovery, it fell to 9.2 per cent in June 1924. The lowest level of the later 1920s was 8.6 per cent, reached in May 1927. With the beginning of the world depression in 1929, it rose sharply, and had reached 22.4 per cent by September 1931.[35]

The fact that the insured unemployed figure did not fall below about 10 per cent a year on average (the lowest annual average, 9.7 per cent, was in 1927), and that this was equivalent to slightly over 1 million unemployed, led to much discussion of 'the irreducible million'. Yet this was a misleading expression; the unemployed did not consist of 1 million permanently unemployed persons, joined by greater or lesser numbers of temporarily unemployed persons from time to time. There was a comparatively small core of the more or less continuously unemployed – probably only about 100,000 – who were joined at various times by a substantial proportion of the insured population. In the nearly seven years between October 1923 and July 1930, some 65 per cent of the insured population had drawn unemployment benefit at some time. Yet the periods of benefit claim were not usually great in total, taking the period as a whole. Of those who drew benefit, 59 per cent did so for less than 10 per cent of the period, and 21 per cent for between 10 and 20 per cent of the period. In other words, about three-fifths of the drawers of benefit had done so for less than eight months in total in the seven-year period, and four-fifths of them had done so for less than fifteen months.

33. Census of England and Wales 1931, *General Report*, pp. 119–23, 133–5, 143; M.E.F. Jones, 'The Regional Impact of an Overvalued Pound in the 1920s', *EcHR* XXXVIII (1985).

34. Census of England and Wales 1931, *General Report*, pp. 161–2.

35. Royal Commission on Unemployment Insurance, *Final Report* (1932), Cmd 4185, para. 109.

A further light on the liability of the insured population to unemployment is cast by a consideration of the number of benefit claims made. Since a claim, once made, remained in effect for a year, it was possible in the years 1923–30 for each insured person to make eight claims. Of those who were insured throughout this period, 35 per cent made no claim, 15 per cent made a claim in only one year, and 12 per cent in two years; only 17 per cent made a claim in more than four years, and only 1 per cent in every year of the eight.

Thus it can be said that continuous unemployment was exceptional in the 1920s, at least, as far as the insured population is concerned. We are ignorant, except in the broadest terms, of the experience of the uninsured population. Most unemployment was occasional, punctuating a life of almost continuous employment. However, unemployment at some time or other was to be expected by the majority of the insured population. There was also a comparatively small number of people who suffered prolonged or very frequent spells of unemployment, and they accounted for a large part of total unemployment.

Experience of unemployment also varied according to gender and age. The incidence of unemployment was slightly greater for men than for women. In 1923–30, 66 per cent of the insured male population claimed benefit at some time, but only 61 per cent of insured women did so. Men were also liable to draw benefit for longer periods. In 1923–30, 22 per cent of men making claims drew benefit for more than one-fifth of the eight-year period, but only 11 per cent of women making claims did so. Generally, the risk of unemployment was higher for older men, and young men between the ages of 21 and 25; juveniles under 18 probably suffered more temporary, short-term unemployment than did other persons. Among adult males, those aged 30 to 39 appeared to suffer the lowest risk of unemployment. Unemployment rates rose with age, partly because of the greater risk of unemployment, but also because of the greater difficulty older men found in getting re-employed. This higher risk of prolonged unemployment was found in all regions, but especially in the depressed areas.[36] (The data come from a survey of a 1 per cent sample of the insured population in July 1930; the above calculations include only those who had been insured for the whole seven-year period.)[37]

The plight of the older unemployed man was described by a south Wales miner who had lost his job at the age of 41, in 1926, and was still unemployed eight years later:

> Since that day I have never been able to get back to work again, although I tramped the mountains three times a week for some two years till I got properly fed up with meeting refusals. Every time it was 'We are full up'. My brother, who is in work, tried to find a job for me, and the boss sent me a message through him to come up in the morning; but the first question he asked me was how long I had been idle, and when I told him the truth his comment was that I had been out of work too long, and that he was sorry, but he had already started a man working where he had intended to start me. Actually, this was the very place where I had formerly worked

36. Calculated from ibid., paras 113, 115.
37. Garside, *British Unemployment*, p. 12.

for seventeen years. I was received with the same sort of story at other pits: 'There are younger men than you out.'[38]

Finally, unemployment varied according to occupational status. Employees, manual workers and the less skilled were more likely to be unemployed than employers, the self-employed, non-manual workers and the more skilled. This is apparent in the case of males from Colin Clark's analysis of the 1931 census inquiry (Table 7.4).

Table 7.4 Male unemployment by occupational status, England and Wales, 1931

Proportion of unemployed males to total occupied males	*(%)*
Unskilled manual workers	30.5
Skilled and semi-skilled manual workers	14.4
Personal service workers, barbers, waiters, etc.	9.9
Salesmen and shop assistants	7.9
Agricultural workers	7.6
Clerks and typists	5.5
Higher office workers	5.1
Professions[a]	5.5
Retail traders, innkeepers, bookmakers, etc.	2.3
Farmers	0.5
Proprietors and managers of other businesses	1.3

Note: a 'Of the unemployment among professional men, 11,500 is accounted for by actors and musicians, put out of work by cinemas, and in other professions the percentage rate of recorded unemployment is only a little over 2 per cent.' (original note by Colin Clark)

Source: C. Clark, *National Income and Outlay* (Macmillan 1937), p. 46

THE RELIEF OF UNEMPLOYMENT

Prior to the First World War, the relief of unemployment had been usually a matter for individuals and their families. Unemployed people were expected to subsist by a combination of reducing spending, using up savings, and obtaining assistance from family and friends, from any friendly societies or savings clubs to which they might belong, or from private charity. There was also the insurance scheme of 1911 for certain trades prone to cyclical or seasonal unemployment, covering about 2.25 million men (about one-sixth of the male labour force). Finally, there was the Poor Law to relieve clear cases of distress.

After 1918, the position changed radically. To the existing sources of relief was added the generalisation of the unemployment insurance scheme to cover the bulk of the working population. This was combined with more generous conditions and scales of benefit, so that the state had in effect agreed to

38. H.L. Beales and R.S. Lambert, *Memoirs of the Unemployed* (Gollancz 1934), p. 65.

maintain the unemployed, rather than, as envisaged in the 1911 Act, merely augment the resources of the individual. However, this new approach coincided with the unforeseen arrival of large-scale, long-term unemployment. This exposed the contradictions and inadequacies of the unemployment insurance scheme, led to unexpected expenditure, and ensured that unemployment and its relief were in the forefront of political controversy.

The origin of the more generous postwar treatment of the unemployed lay in the 'out-of-work donation' adopted at the Armistice. Originally intended for ex-servicemen, it was extended to civilians in order to cope with the unemployment widely expected with the demobilisation of the Armed Forces. It set two important new precedents. First, it offered a level of benefit which was distinctly more generous than that offered by the National Insurance Act 1911. Benefit under that Act had been 7s. a week (about one-third of the wages of the lowest-paid urban worker), which in the prices of the end of 1918 would be equivalent to about 15s. 6d. The out-of-work donation was fixed (for an adult male) at 24s. (women received 20s.). Second, for the first time, dependants' allowances were offered (6s. for the first child under 15, 3s. for all others).[39]

The donation had been adopted in a hurry. The government did not yet have a general scheme of unemployment insurance to put forward. But, mindful of the Bolshevik revolution, it feared popular violence if nothing were done to cope with the considerable unemployment which it expected during the demobilisation of the Forces. Without some new scheme, unemployed people would have only the ungenerous assistance provided by the Poor Law to fall back on. Thus the donation was put forward as a short-term expedient. Although expensive, it was extended (the civilian scheme to November 1919 and the military scheme to March 1920), while a general scheme of unemployment insurance was put together.

The scheme finally adopted was enshrined in the Unemployment Insurance Act which became law in August 1920. It covered all manual employees, and other employees earning less than £250 a year, with certain industries excepted (chiefly agriculture and private domestic service). Other exceptions were teachers, nurses, police, established civil servants, certain local authority employees, and those in railways and military service. Special schemes were envisaged for some other industries, although in the event only two (banking and insurance) were set up before the provision to contract out of the scheme was suspended in 1921 (and finally revoked in 1927). The result was that, while the Act had been intended to cover the same population as that covered by the health insurance scheme (about 17 million), it covered only 11.75 million.[40]

As in 1911, the principle of the 1920 Act was insurance. Weekly contributions by employees, employers and the state were intended to build up a fund

39. B.B. Gilbert, *British Social Policy 1914–1939* (Batsford 1970), p. 62; A.L. Bowley, *Prices and Wages in the United Kingdom 1914–1920* (Oxford, Clarendon 1921), p. 70.
40. Royal Commission on Unemployment Insurance, *Final Report*, paras 22–4; Gilbert, *Social Policy*, pp. 68–9; Garside, *Unemployment*, p. 4.

which would tide the unemployed over spells of unemployment. It was thus a vital principle of the scheme that it would be self-financing. But this aim was made difficult of achievement by the actuarial errors in the scheme. Most notably, it rested on a calculation of expected unemployment which was too optimistic – 5.32 per cent, or nearly one-third less than that assumed in the 1911 Act. In addition, although benefit rates were higher than in 1911 (raised from 7s. to 15s. for men, and from 7s. to 12s. for women), with dependants' allowances also, the rates of contribution were not (at first) raised proportionately. In addition, expenditure was raised by cutting the waiting period before benefit could be drawn from six days to three. The scheme was actuarially weakened also by the exclusion of the trades less prone to unemployment such as agriculture and domestic service.[41]

The scheme thus had certain financial weaknesses, even without the miscalculation as to future unemployment rates. But it was the latter which effectively made it unworkable almost as soon as it became law. It had been evolved, as in 1911, to deal with periodic unemployment of workers who had built up a record of contributions; benefit was limited to fifteen weeks in one year, and one week's benefit could be drawn for every six contributions previously made. Yet these conditions were inapplicable to many claimants. By March 1921 the rate of insured unemployment had risen to 11.3 per cent (having been 3.7 per cent in November 1920). Benefit rates, initially raised to keep pace with inflation, were now cut, and contribution rates were raised, but the Unemployment Fund, which had begun with a surplus of £22 million, was in deficit by £16.5 million at the beginning of 1923.

Although the Fund was in deficit, it was politically impossible to deny benefit to large numbers of unqualified claimants, since this would have thrust them on to the Poor Law as their sole support. At first the giving of benefit to unqualified claimants was justified by labelling it 'uncovenanted benefit'. The theory was that although claimants would draw benefit to which they were not entitled by reason of their contribution record, when once again employed they would pay these sums back by way of their insurance contributions. 'Uncovenanted' benefits were replaced by 'extended' benefits in the Labour government's remodelling of the system in 1924, when benefit rates were increased and the conditions relaxed. As a political set-off, it was agreed that applicants for standard benefit should be questioned to see if they were 'genuinely seeking work'. Thus the onus for proving the genuineness of a claim was now on the claimant (although applicants for extended benefit faced the less harsh test of merely proving that they were making 'all reasonable efforts' to obtain work).[42]

These tinkerings with the system were on an *ad-hoc* basis, and failed to come to terms with the fact that the insurance scheme was a failure. By 1925, about half of all claims authorised for payment were for extended benefit, which had come to be known popularly as 'the dole'. In effect, a new system of outdoor relief had been built up, outside the Poor Law.

41. Royal Commission on Unemployment Insurance, *Final Report*, para. 20; Gilbert, *Social Policy*, p. 74; Garside, *Unemployment*, pp. 37–8.
42. Garside, *Unemployment*, pp. 38–46.

Politically, reform of the system was caught between the pressures from the left to provide maintenance to all unemployed people without further conditions, and from the right to curb the costs of extended benefit. A compromise was sought by the Blanesburgh Committee, whose deliberations were enshrined in the Unemployment Insurance Act 1927. This reduced male adult benefit slightly (but increased dependants' rates). The most important change was that standard benefit was to be granted as of right and for unlimited duration, as long as the condition of thirty contributions in the previous two years was fulfilled, provided the applicant was 'genuinely seeking work'. Those unable to fulfil this (not particularly stringent) condition would be granted 'transitional' benefit for up to a year, as long as they had made eight contributions in the previous two years, or thirty at any time. 'Extended' benefit was to be abolished and replaced by 'transitional benefit', which would itself be ended in April 1929.[43]

The Blanesburgh compromise, like the original insurance scheme, was fatally flawed by overoptimism, basing its recommendations on an estimated future rate of unemployment of 6 per cent. The committee generously intended that as many unemployed people as possible should be entitled to standard relief, but it proved impossible to abolish 'transitional' relief. Moreover, the abolition of the previous restrictions on benefit (the 'one in six' rule, and the limitation of benefit to twenty-six weeks in one year) moved the focus of financial control to the 'genuinely seeking work' test, which was now applied to both standard and non-standard claims. The test was tightened in the ensuing years. By June 1929, nearly two-thirds of all benefit disallowances were accounted for by failure of the test.[44]

The history of the unemployment insurance scheme in the 1920s is one of failure. The scheme was inappropriate to the times, and it was not recognised that structural unemployment was going to be a long-term feature of the labour market. Governments were thereafter condemned to tinker with the system, caught between the desire to make provision for unemployed people outside the Poor Law, and to control expenditure. Yet the system had become more generous in the decade, and came closer to the idea of maintaining the unemployed, rather than merely assisting them along the lines of the 1911 Act (Table 7.5 overleaf).

The rate of benefit in 1913 has been estimated as about one-third of the wage of an unskilled urban workman. This may be an overestimate. Routh estimated that the average wage of unskilled labour in 1906 was about 23s. a week, and wages had risen by 1914; the rate for a bricklayer's labourer in July 1914 is shown by Bowley to be 29s. 1d. By 1924, Routh estimated unskilled male earnings at 51s. 6d. a week. On this basis, a single man could get about 35 per cent of his former wage in benefit, and if married with two children, about 52 per cent. It is also noticeable that the increases in benefit in 1924

43. Royal Commission on Unemployment Insurance, *Final Report*, paras 41–2; Garside, *Unemployment*, pp. 46–7.

44. Garside, *Unemployment*, p. 48; see also A. Deacon, *In Search of the Scrounger: the administration of unemployment insurance in Britain, 1920–31* (1976).

Table 7.5 Unemployment benefits, cost of living and wage levels, 1913–28

	Rates of benefit (shillings per week)				
	Single adult man	*Adult man, wife and two children*	*Single adult woman*	*Cost of living index*[a]	*Relative wage index*[b]
Jan. 1913	7s.	7s.	7s.	100	100
Nov. 1920	15s.	15s.	12s.	276	270–80
Mar. 1921	20s.	20s.	16s.	241	210–15
June 1921	15s.	15s.	12s.	219	210–15
Nov. 1921	15s.	22s.	12s.	203	210–15
Aug. 1924	18s.	27s.	15s.	171	170–75
Apr. 1928	17s.	28s.	15s.	164	170–75
Mar. 1930	17s.	30s.	15s.	161	170–74

Notes: a July 1914 = 100; cost of living calculated at beginning of month
b July 1914 = 100; wages calculated at end of year
Source: Royal Commission on Unemployment Insurance, *Final Report* (1932), Cmd 4185, PP 1931–2, XIII, para. 29

(under a Labour government) were only slightly reduced in 1928 (by a Conservative government), and were in any case bolstered slightly in real terms by the continuing deflation after 1924. While postwar unemployment benefit would not allow the maintenance of previous standards of living, it was much more generous than the pre-1914 scheme, and grew more generous by the end of the 1920s in both money and real terms.[45]

In spite of the relative rise in the real level of unemployment benefits, the high unemployment of the 1920s meant that the insurance system could not achieve the aim of keeping the needy from recourse to the Poor Law. The number receiving Poor Law relief was much greater than before the First World War. In 1912–14, the total number relieved in Britain had averaged 873,577 annually. High employment in wartime reduced this to a low of 634,582 in 1919, but the postwar depression saw a sharp rise to levels much higher than before 1914; the peak was 1922, with 1,926,432 relieved. Even with the partial economic recovery, the figure was still 1,543,216 in 1924. (Figures are averages of numbers relieved on 1 January and 1 July.) Most of the relief was the 'outdoor' kind; the population of workhouses and other Poor Law institutions fluctuated between 200,000 and 300,000.[46]

The extent to which the population relieved by the Poor Law overlapped with the unemployed insured population is unknown, since the Poor Law statistics for England and Wales included the dependants of insurance claimants in the total of paupers. The Webbs thought that dependants accounted for

45. Routh, *Occupation and Pay*, p. 97; Bowley, *Prices and Wages*, p. 113.
46. Board of Trade, *Statistical Abstract for the United Kingdom . . . 1911–1925* (1927), Cmd 2849, pp. 63–5.

three-quarters of the recorded paupers. In Scotland, where the Poor Law statistics made the distinction between claimants and dependants, the ratio of the two groups in 1921–26 was about 1:1. It seems likely that, when the dependants are omitted, there were in the 1920s between 100,000 and 200,000 persons receiving Poor Law relief who also received unemployment benefit or assistance, although this must remain a very rough estimate.[47]

The sudden rise in Poor Law relief strained local government finances, which had to pay for most of it, via the 'poor rate' levied on local property. Whereas in 1911–14, total expenditure on poor relief in Britain had averaged £16.4 million a year, of which central government provided £2.7 million, in 1921–25 it averaged £40.6 million, of which central government provided £3.1 million. The result was that poor rates rose substantially.[48]

The problem was compounded in areas of high unemployment, which often had a lower taxable capacity than areas of low unemployment. In addition, in certain areas, Labour Party control of Boards of Poor Law Guardians led to a determination to pursue a policy of generous relief, regardless of central government disapproval. The most famous example was in Poplar, in East London. The council leader, George Lansbury, who had been elected a Guardian as long ago as 1892, was pledged to a policy of 'decent treatment and hang the rates'. The resulting conflict with authority led to the Poplar Borough Council being imprisoned briefly in 1921. 'Poplarism' continued, and was not confined to Labour Boards of Guardians. The problems were increased in 1926 by the General Strike, during which 2.5 million people in England and Wales alone received poor relief, and the rickety finances of the Guardians crumbled further. The government then took powers to discipline recalcitrant Guardians. Under the Board of Guardians (Default) Act 1926, the Minister of Health acquired the power to dismiss a board and replace it with his own nominees. This fate was meted out to the Boards of West Ham (London), Chester-le-Street (Durham) and Bedwellty (south Wales).[49] In theory, Guardians were still expected to enforce the workhouse test or the labour test on the head of a family seeking relief. In practice, this duty was suspended.[50]

EARNINGS, TRADE UNIONS AND LABOUR RELATIONS

Wartime inflation and the subsequent deflation after 1920 meant that, in current values, postwar incomes were very different from prewar. By 1922–24,

47. Ibid., p. 65; the above 'informed guess' is derived from a consideration of the statistics in S. Webb and B. Webb, *English Poor Law History, Part II, The Last Hundred Years* (App. II, English Poor Law Statistics) (Longmans, Green 1929).
48. Board of Trade, *Statistical Abstract* (1927), p. 68.
49. M.E. Rose, *The English Poor Law, 1780–1930* (Newton Abbot, David & Charles 1971), pp. 292–4, 303–4, 309–11.
50. M.A. Crowther, *The Workhouse System 1834–1929* (Methuen 1981), pp. 100–12. See also P. Ryan, 'The Poor Law in 1926', in M. Morris (ed.), *The General Strike* (Pelican 1976).

when the post-1920 deflation had almost ceased, men's average earnings are estimated to be some 94 per cent higher than in 1913–14, and women's some 104 per cent higher. Among men, the largest gains had been achieved by foremen and managers, whose average earnings had risen by 137 and 140 per cent respectively. The greatest relative losers had been the higher professions and the skilled manual workers (only 77 and 81 per cent). Among women, the greatest gainers had been the forewomen and the unskilled, whose earnings had risen by 170 and 161 per cent respectively; the skilled and semi-skilled women showed the least gains (only 98 and 96 per cent).

In terms of annual income, the spectrum of male earnings ran from the higher professional, earning £582 a year, to the unskilled man earning £128 a year. The range of women's earnings ran from the lower professionals (e.g. teachers) with an income of £214 to the unskilled worker earning £73 a year; there were too few women higher professionals (e.g. lawyers, doctors, engineers) for their earnings to be estimated. Women were still paid less than men for similar work, although women's pay had risen slightly in relation to that of men. The overall average of women's pay rose from 54 per cent of male average pay in 1913–14 to 57 per cent in 1922–24.[51]

The rise in money incomes meant that real incomes also rose. The cost of living index of the Ministry of Labour for the average of the years 1922–24 stood at 174 (1913 = 100), which suggests a rise in real incomes of about 11 per cent for men (194/174 × 100) and 17 per cent (204/174 × 100) for women.[52]

In addition, there was a further form of increase in real income, in the sense that hours of labour were reduced. During the postwar boom many sections of organised labour pressed successfully for reductions in working hours. The result was that manufacturing industry gained a general reduction in the working week, for the most part in 1919, from an average of fifty-four hours before the war to forty-eight. This change was the result of organised labour exploiting a period of high labour demand for other than purely financial ends. Although the change led to complaints by employers of higher costs, little was done to reverse the process, and the hours achieved remained little changed until the next major round of reductions in 1945–46.[53]

A major change in the environment in which labour operated was the strengthening of trade union organisation. The union movement had grown spectacularly since the early 1890s; by 1913, the total membership was 4,135,000. The doubling of membership to 8,348,000 by 1920 was even more spectacular. Thereafter, however, there was an almost continuous decline, especially in the depression of 1920–22; by 1929, the number was down to 4,858,000. The General Strike and its consequences seem to have had little impact on this process.[54]

51. Routh, *Occupation and Pay*, pp. 104–5.
52. Feinstein, *National Income*, T140.
53. M.A. Bienefeld, *Working Hours in British Industry: an economic history* (Weidenfeld & Nicolson 1972), chs 5, 7; Garside, *Unemployment*, pp. 90–4.
54. Mitchell, *Statistics*, p. 137.

Between 1913 and 1929, then, union membership had risen by only 17 per cent. But the impact of labour organisation on industrial relations was very much greater than this slight growth might suggest. In 1910, about 3 million workers had been covered by collective bargaining agreements, either national or local. Collective bargaining was boosted during wartime by government control of large sectors of engineering, chemicals and transport. Although after 1919 some unions ceased to press for collective bargaining, and some employers left the employers' organisations which recognised unions for the purpose of wage bargaining, collective agreements made headway. Most national and local authorities adhered to them, and in private industry the emergence of many national employers' associations ensured the use of national wage agreements, even when union membership declined in the years of unemployment, so that in 1933, collective bargaining may have covered between 8 million and 9 million workers.

The rise of union membership and collective agreements had implications for industrial disputes, a much higher proportion of which now became national rather than local. While industry-wide stoppages had not been unknown before 1914, they had accounted for only about one-quarter of total working days lost through strikes and lockouts in 1901–10. In 1919–26 the proportion was four-fifths, even excluding the General Strike. The General Strike apart, there were between 1919 and 1926 four industry-wide stoppages in shipbuilding, three in coal-mining, two each in cotton and the railways, and one each in building, docks, engineering, foundries, printing and wool.[55]

The tendency for national negotiation to replace plant or individual negotiation was strengthened by union amalgamations, the most important of which produced the Amalgamated Engineering Union (1921), the Transport and General Workers Union (TGWU: 1922), and the National Union of General and Municipal Workers (1924). The TGWU grew further in 1929 when it merged with the Workers' Union. At the apex of the movement was the General Council of the Trades Union Congress (TUC), whose organisation was strengthened and reformed in the early 1920s. Yet the General Council had limited influence and powers on the trade union movement as a whole; the authority which it was given in the General Strike far exceeded its constitutional powers, and in most disputes negotiations were conducted by individual unions.[56]

Increasing centralisation could also be seen on the employers' side. Attempts to create a central employers' organisation succeeded in 1916, with the formation of the Federation of British Industries (FBI). However, the FBI was not permitted by its members to deal with labour relations. It was joined in 1919 by the newly formed National Confederation of Employers' Organisations (NCEO),

55. H.A. Clegg, *A History of British Trade Unions since 1889, vol. II, 1911–1933* (Oxford, Clarendon 1985), pp. 547–50.
56. H. Pelling, *A History of British Trade Unionism* (3rd edn, Pelican 1976), pp. 168–72; C.J Wrigley, 'The Trade Unions between the Wars', in Wrigley (ed.), *A History of British Industrial Relations, vol. II, 1914–1939* (Brighton, Harvester 1987), pp. 71–2.

intended to present the employers' side of things at the National Industrial Council (NIC) which Lloyd George proposed to establish. The NIC failed to be established, and the NCEO, dominated by employers in engineering, coal-mining, railways, shipping, and iron and steel, was limited by them to a subordinate role in labour relations.[57]

The course of industrial relations in the 1920s was chequered. While most workers, as usual, had their disagreements with their employers settled by negotiation, either personal or collective, strikes and lockouts did occur, and they indicate a period of considerable turbulence in industrial relations. The unsettled years of 1911–14, when an average of 17.7 million working days a year had been lost in industrial disputes, had been succeeded by the comparative tranquillity of 1915–18, when the average number of days lost was 4.2 million. In 1919–29, the average rose to 32.0 million a year, thus easily exceeding the prewar level. The great bulk of these losses in 1919–29 (72 per cent of the total) were in the coal-mining industry, mainly during the strikes of 1921 and 1926.[58] (These estimates of lost days exclude strikes held in sympathy with the coal-miners in the General Strike of 1926.)

After 1918, industrial conflicts grew considerably. In 1919, 35.0 million, and in 1920, 26.6 million working days were lost. These high levels reflected in part the high demand for labour in the postwar boom. Strikes over hours – either in pursuit of fewer hours or as a result of disputes over the implementation of an agreement to proceed to a shorter working week – increased substantially. In addition, there was a movement away from district to national agreements on pay and hours, which proved a fruitful source of industrial conflict. Finally, there was the threat of 'direct action' against the government; in this case, it took the form of the coal-mining unions pressing for nationalisation of their industry, since they feared the consequences of decontrol once the boom had broken. The government purchased peace by the offer of the Sankey inquiry into nationalisation, but the miners struck successfully on the question of wages in October 1920.[59]

Having won a brief victory, the miners were faced with the decision of the government to hand back the mines to the owners from the end of March 1921. There followed an immediate attempt by the owners to reduce wages, and a strike by the miners, in the course of which the 'Triple Alliance' (of Miners, Transport Workers and Railwaymen) collapsed. The miners' strike alone guaranteed that 1921 would be an exceptionally heavy strike year (85.9 million working days lost), but elsewhere things were quiet, the mine dispute accounting for 73.0 million of these days.[60]

Like 1921, 1922 was a quiet year apart from engineering, where employers

57. H.F. Gospel, 'Employers and Managers: organisation and strategy 1914–39', in Wrigley, *Industrial Relations*, p. 161.
58. K.G.J.C. Knowles, *Strikes* (Oxford, Blackwell 1952), pp. 307–10.
59. Clegg, *Trade Unions, vol. II*, pp. 266–75.
60. Knowles, *Strikes*, pp. 307–10.

were trying to impose wage reductions following the severe slump. At the same time, they were trying to reimpose what were seen as managerial prerogatives lost in the war and the postwar boom. The rejection of the wider managerial demands by the Amalgamated Engineering Union provoked a national lockout, so that engineering accounted for 17.5 million of the 19.8 million days lost through strikes in all industries.[61]

Industrial disputes were declining steadily by 1925, when 7.9 million days were lost. In 1926 the coal industry's problems resurfaced, in the form of a further attempt by the owners to reduce wages and increase working hours, following a renewed fall in coal sales in the summer of 1925. The TUC offered its support to the miners, to the extent of being prepared to call a general sympathetic strike. Faced with this threat, the government agreed to establish a Royal Commission on the coal industry (the Samuel Commission), and offered a temporary subsidy to allow the owners to pay existing wage rates. At the end of April 1926, the subsidy was terminated, the owners locked the employees out, and the strike began. Certain important trades, chiefly in transport, printing, heavy industry, building, electricity and gas, were called out in sympathy by the TUC, and the coal dispute became the General Strike on 3 May. The response was very complete; a total of 1.58 million insured workers came out (excluding the miners). But the TUC, uneasy from the start, was outmanoeuvred by the government, and after nine days the miners were left to continue their strike alone, which they did for almost eight months. The General Strike apart, it was a very peaceful year, since only 0.6 million working days were lost through disputes unconnected with coal or the General Strike. But the strike accounted for the enormous loss of 161.6 million working days, of which coal-mining contributed 146.4 million.[62]

After 1926, the numbers of days lost through disputes fell sharply; 1.1 million and 1.4 million in 1927 and 1928 respectively. This has sometimes been taken to mean that the General Strike was a watershed in the industrial relations of the 1920s; a watershed symbolised a little later by the Mond-Turner talks of 1928–29. Yet this may be misleading. Of greater importance may have been the fact that the early 1920s had been unusually turbulent, due to the sharp inflation and subsequent deflation, and that the comparative economic stability of 1927–29, with stable unemployment, and a slight deflation which allowed employers to contain their costs without launching a fresh wage-reduction offensive, made it unnecessary for them to engage in industrial conflict.[63] On the other hand, the NCEO and employers in metals, engineering and textiles had supported the coalowners in their dispute in 1925–26,

61. Ibid., pp. 307–10; Wrigley, *Industrial Relations*, pp. 95–7.
62. Morris, *General Strike*, pp. 221–8; Knowles, *Strikes*, pp. 307–10. See also G.A. Phillips, *The General Strike* (Weidenfeld & Nicolson 1976); Clegg, *Trade Unions, vol. II*, ch. 10.
63. Clegg, *Trade Unions, vol. II*, p. 257; J. Lovell, *British Trade Unions 1875–1933* (Macmillan 1977), pp. 56–8.

hoping that cheaper fuel would result. Since the price of best coal in London fell from 29s. 8d. in 1925 to 23s. 1d. in 1927, their aims may have been achieved already.[64]

In this situation, employers concentrated on parliamentary rather than industrial action. The main fruit of this was the Trade Disputes and Trade Union Act 1927, which made sympathetic strikes outside the industry concerned illegal, prohibited established civil servants from joining unions affiliated to the TUC, and changed the system of trade union members paying their political levy to the Labour Party to a system of 'contracting-in' rather than 'contracting-out', as formerly.[65]

The industrial relations of the 1920s have been long recognised to be particularly bad. It is perhaps most appropriate to see them as the concluding phase of a period of unrest, which had begun before the war. Between 1910 and 1925 (1914–18 apart), there was no year in which some major sector of the economy did not lose at least 3 million days in industrial disputes. Existing tendencies to unrest were severely exacerbated by the inflation and deflation of these years, by the increased proportion of labour unionised, by the rise of national agreements on both sides of industry, by rank-and-file militancy, and by the general air of class confrontation which characterised the immediate postwar period. In this situation, the coal industry, with its special economic and technical problems, and its critical role in British economic life, was perhaps bound to play a leading role. The General Strike, however, was something of a *coda* played after the rest of the industrial relations world had settled down to a somewhat precarious stability by the middle of the 1920s.

CONCLUSIONS

The national labour force continued to grow in the interwar period, partly through natural increase, and partly through a rise in the proportion of the population of working age. The occupational structure altered, reflecting the changes in the fortunes of industries and service trades. There was a notable shift to 'white-collar' and clerical occupations, for both men and women. There was also a shift in the relative weight of population from 'outer Britain' (Wales, Scotland, the north-west and north-east of England) to 'inner Britain', as depressed industries were found chiefly in the former. Unemployment was undoubtedly higher than before 1914 over all Britain, though chiefly concentrated in the outer regions. The causes of this higher unemployment are still controversial; due allowance must be made for the sudden loss of markets due to the war, as well as for the longer-term decline in British competitiveness which had been apparent before 1914. But contemporary diagnoses

64. W.R. Garside, 'Management and Men: aspects of British industrial relations in the inter-war period', in B. Supple (ed.), *Essays in British Business History* (Oxford, Clarendon 1977), pp. 251–2; Mitchell, *Statistics*, p. 749.
65. Pelling, *Trade Unions*, p. 187.

concentrated chiefly on more obvious 'supply-side' factors, pointing especially to the rise of trade union influence, and the rise in the real level of unemployment benefits since 1914. For the employed, real incomes rose also in comparison with pre-1914. However, this did not prevent substantial labour unrest after 1918, chiefly in the coal industry.

CHAPTER 8

ECONOMIC AND SOCIAL WELFARE IN THE 1920s

ECONOMIC GROWTH

In the long run, the whole interwar period may be seen as one in which the rate of economic growth was more rapid than in the period between 1900 and 1913, and restored the British economy to the rates of economic growth which had characterised the later nineteenth century. This may be seen from the national income data assembled by C.H. Feinstein, which is presented in the Appendix to this book. These data are most easily appreciated in the form of a graph. From this it appears that interwar economic growth was higher than in the couple of decades before the First World War. It is also possible that it was higher than the average for the period 1870–1910, although this is less certain. When it is appreciated that the interwar period included two particularly severe depressions, and that output throughout these years was less than its potential (indicated by the higher level of unemployment than before 1914), the achievement is the more impressive (see the Appendix).

For the 1920s, the pattern is less simple. During the war, national output rose substantially, aided by the rise in the labour force and full employment. While the wartime estimates of national output are not comparable with those of peacetime, owing to the altered structure of wartime output, it may be noted that GNP in 1914–18 (at constant factor cost) averaged about 9 per cent above that of 1913. During the recession of 1920–21, national output fell sharply. In addition, the detachment of Southern Ireland from the rest of the UK led to a loss of national output of about 4 per cent. Industrial production did not exceed the 1913 level until 1924, but grew rapidly thereafter, checked briefly by the effects of the General Strike. For the rest of the decade, economic growth was fairly rapid, although total national income did not exceed the prewar level until 1927.

The picture of the 1920s is thus of a relatively buoyant economy, which overcame the disadvantages of the loss of Eire, a very sharp recession in 1920–21, the coal strike and General Strike of 1926, continuing high unemployment, and the loss of foreign markets, and yet managed a very respectable rate of growth. Between 1924 and 1929, the growth of national output averaged 2.2 per cent per year. This was an uneven process, ranging from a decline in the output of mining and quarrying, to average growth of 7.4 per cent annually in construction and 5.8 per cent in electricity, gas and water. The average output of all manufacturing rose at 2.8 per cent per year; the average growth of national output as a whole was 2.2 per cent a year. For the population of the UK as a whole, real income per head in 1929 was some 8 per cent above the 1913 level.[1]

GROWTH IN REAL INCOMES

The extent to which this rise in average real incomes was shared by the working class can be only tentatively estimated. A rough indicator of changes in the standard of working-class living may be had from comparing changes in money wages and the cost of living (Table 8.1). This is not quite the same as an index of real wages, since the cost of living index used is that of the Board of Trade, which was based on a sample of working-class budgets taken in 1904. There is no doubt that it was out of date by 1929, when it would have been more appropriate to the family of a low-paid, unskilled worker than an average working-class family, but there is no readily available substitute.

The proximate reason for the rise in 'real wages' was that they had been maintained in the war by the high demand for labour, and the postwar boom raised them further. The subsequent decline in both prices and wages reduced real wages, but not below the 1920 level. Subsequent to 1924, a gradual fall in prices led to a continued, though not large, rise in real wages. The result was that by the end of the decade real wages were almost one-fifth higher than before the war.

Table 8.1 Money wages and the cost of living, 1910–14 to 1929 (1914 = 100)

	Money wages	*Cost of living*[a]	*'Quotient'*[b]
1910–14 av.	97	99	98
1924	194	175	111
1925	196	175	112
1926	195	172	113
1927	196	167	117
1928	194	166	117
1929	193	164	118

Notes: a Board of Trade cost of living index
b Bowley declined to use the term 'real wages' for this column, because of 'the numerous qualifications with which it must be used' (p. 30)
Source: A.L. Bowley, *Wages and Income in the United Kingdom since 1860* (Cambridge UP 1937), Table VII, p. 30

1. J.A. Dowie, 'Growth in the Inter-War Period: some more arithmetic', *EcHR* XXI (1968), Statistical App., Table 1; C.H. Feinstein, *National Income, Expenditure and Output of the United Kingdom, 1855–1965* (Cambridge UP 1972), Table 17.

The rise in real earnings was accompanied by an important redistributive effect: the earnings of unskilled labour had risen faster than those of skilled labour. This movement had taken place in the war, when flat-rate cost-of-living increases were awarded to workers in a wide variety of industries. Thus, for example, the time rates of labourers in engineering and shipbuilding had risen by 1920 to 309 (1914 = 100), whereas those of fitters and turners had risen only to 231. In the building industry, the increase for labourers was 365 (by December 1920), and that of bricklayers was 278. This movement survived the postwar recession of 1920–21. Routh's more comprehensive analysis compares earnings in 1924 with those of 1906, and concludes that between those dates the earnings of skilled men had risen by 88 per cent, those of semi-skilled men by 100 per cent, and those of unskilled men by 126 per cent.[2]

THE REDUCTION OF POVERTY

The few social surveys which were carried out in the 1920s provide strong evidence for the poverty-reducing effects of the rise in real wages. The most relevant is that of A.L. Bowley and M. Hogg, who in 1923–24 carried out a survey of the working-class populations in five towns which had been the subject of social surveys in 1912–14 – Reading, Northampton, Warrington, Bolton and Stanley (County Durham). In the 1923–24 survey a definition of poverty based on Rowntree's 1899 survey of York was adopted. This envisaged just enough food to avoid starvation, and allowed for fuel, lighting, clothing and house-cleaning materials, but nothing for entertainment or social spending. It was thus a very minimal and to a certain extent unrealistic standard.[3] On this minimal basis, poverty was found to have substantially diminished (Table 8.2).

The disparity in 1923–24 between the full week and the week of the invest-

Table 8.2 Persons below the poverty line: five English towns, 1912–14 and 1923–24

	1912–14 (%)	*1923–24* Full week[a] (%)	*1923–24* Week of investigation (%)
All persons	12.6	3.5	6.5
All men (over 18)	7.2	2.0	4.2
All women (over 16)	9.4	2.7	5.0
Children under 14	21.6	6.4	11.3

Note: a Assuming that all persons capable of work received their full income
Source: A.L. Bowley and M. Hogg, *Has Poverty Diminished?* (P.S. King 1925), p. 18

2. A.L. Bowley, *Prices and Wages in the United Kingdom, 1914–1920* (Oxford, Clarendon 1921), pp. 114, 131; G. Routh, *Occupation and Pay in Great Britain, 1906–60* (Cambridge UP 1965), pp. 88, 92, 97.
3. A.L. Bowley and M. Hogg, *Has Poverty Diminished?* (P.S. King 1925).

igation was usually a product of short-term difficulties: 'Thus in Stanley the mines are closed now and again for a week, the suspension averaging one week in eight.'[4] But even with these problems, it was clear that the incidence of acute poverty had diminished to about half the prewar level, although it was still highest among children, reflecting the difficulties of households with large, young families. However, the authors of the survey admitted that their sample of towns reflected the national incidence of unemployment inadequately.

The relative decline in poverty was clearly due to improved real wages, whose effects, as the above survey suggests, had not been offset by unemployment (the income figures include all forms of income except poor relief, and thus include unemployment benefit or assistance). Similar trends in the cost of living, money wage earnings, and the reduction of differentials between skilled and unskilled labour were observed in London in the *New Survey of London Life and Labour* (carried out between 1928 and 1930), which suggested that the real wage rates of unskilled labourers had increased by one-quarter since the time of the original *Survey* by Charles Booth, in 1886–1903. On the other hand, the rise in real wages would have done little to help those casually employed, notably in the docks, where unemployment was especially high. Even in 1929, 24 per cent of London dockers were registered as unemployed, and the waterside trades generally (docks, canal and harbour services) had a level of unemployment in the 1920s which was more than twice the national average of all insured workers; the industry was hit badly by the depressed level of foreign trade after 1918.[5] (There were nine volumes in the *New Survey*, published between 1930 and 1935.)[6]

The comparatively prosperous London region had only 9.8 per cent of its working-class families in poverty in 1928. The more depressed Merseyside region (again, much affected by unemployment in docks) had, on a similar standard, 16 per cent of its working-class families in poverty in 1929. Although clearly affected by unemployment, it was not the main reason for poverty: 'If all the families in receipt of public assistance were given enough relief to raise them above the poverty line, 10 per cent of the families sampled would still be below the poverty line.'[7]

THE IMPACT OF UNEMPLOYMENT

By the end of the 1920s the general standard of living, and especially that of the less skilled workers and their families had been raised. This judgement

4. Ibid., p. 16.
5. (Sir) H. Llewellyn Smith, *The New Survey of London Life and Labour* (P.S. King 1930), vol. I, pp. 105, 122–3, 142, 356; G. Phillips and N. Whiteside, *Casual Labour: the unemployment question in the port transport industry 1880–1970* (Oxford, Clarendon 1985), pp. 176–80.
6. The *New Survey* is discussed by C.A. Linsley and C.L. Linsley, 'Booth, Rowntree, and Llewellyn Smith: a reassessment of interwar poverty', *EcHR* XLVI (1993).
7. D. Caradog Jones (ed.), *The Social Survey of Merseyside, vol. I* (Liverpool UP 1934), p. 153.

must be tempered in the case of those occupations which were prone to a pattern of sharp swings in labour demand, or operated on the basis of casual hiring. Such was a large proportion of the building trade, and, notably, dock labour. It must also be tempered in the case of unemployed people. The scales of relief offered both by the unemployment scheme and the Poor Law system were much below the wages of an unskilled labourer, and approximated to the minimal 'poverty line' adopted in the social surveys referred to in Table 8.3 opposite.

The loss of income attendant on unemployment was thus very great, particularly for families with dependent children. It was notable that Poor Law children's rates were more generous than those under national insurance, which were fixed at 2s. per child in 1924 until raised to 3s. by the Unemployment Assistance Board in 1935. After 1924, as prices fell further, poor relief scales probably became less generous. The Liverpool scale in 1929–30 ranged from 22s. a week for a couple with one infant, to 35s. for a couple with two infants and three schoolchildren, but was still preferable to exclusive reliance on insurance benefits; of course, a family on unemployment benefit could still make a claim for relief to the local Guardians.[8] In the circumstances it was not surprising that poor relief grew in popularity; in London, out-relief was about three times its prewar level by 1929, and it was held that attitudes to it were quite changed:

> Thus large numbers of people in the industrial quarters of London have come to regard the Poor Law as one social service among many, which specialises in certain more personal domestic benefits, is readily available, and appears to them no less honourable than the various health, education and insurance services – something which they feel themselves equally entitled, and in particular, something to which they may turn when the benefits to be provided by those other services fall short of their needs.[9]

Loss of earnings, and consequent reliance on either unemployment relief or the Poor Law, would reduce an average family to destitution, if no other source of income were available. Carr-Saunders and Jones estimated the cost of providing the 'bare physical efficiency' standard of living for a family consisting of husband, wife and three children (two aged 5–14, one under 5 years) on 1 January 1927. Based on the prewar Rowntree standard (as modified by Bowley), an income of 43s. 5d. would be required; on the more humane 'human needs' standard proposed by Rowntree in 1918, an income of 63s. 6d. was necessary. Comparison of these estimates with the income and relief rates above indicates not only that unemployment meant effective destitution for those without alternative resources, but also that even the worker in work, if in the lower ranks of the unskilled, had a standard of living not much above that required to maintain bare physical efficiency.[10]

8. Ibid., p. 150.
9. *New Survey of London Life and Labour*, vol. I, p. 379.
10. A.M. Carr-Saunders and D.C. Jones, *A Survey of the Social Structure of England and Wales as Illustrated by Statistics* (Oxford UP 1927), pp. 186–9.

Table 8.3 Wages and relief scales, 1924 (per week)

Wages, 1924

Skilled			*Unskilled*		
Men	*s.*	*d.*		*s.*	*d.*
Railway engine driver	106	1	Building labourer	55	5
Bricklayer	73	6	Local authority labourer	53	0
Coal-face worker	69	3	Railway porter	51	2
Engineering fitter (time rates)	60	4	Engineering labourer	44	7
Women	*s.*	*d.*	Average for female unskilled trades in 1924 = 27s. to 29s.		
Wool and worsted	36	0			
Cotton weaving	35	10			
Hosiery	28	10			

Relief scales

Unemployment benefit, August 1924	
Single adult male	18s.
Single adult female	15s.
Adult male, wife, 2 children	27s.
Adult male, wife, 3 children	29s.
Adult male, wife, 4 children	31s.
Poor Law relief rates, 1922 (London)[a]	
Single adult living with parents or relative	10s.
Single adult not living with parents or relative	15s.
Man and wife or 2 adults living together	25s.
Man and wife + 2 children[b]	36s.
Man and wife + 3 children	41s.
Man and wife + 4 children	45s.

Notes: a The Poor Law relief rates (sometimes referred to as the Mond scale, after the then Minister of Health, Sir Alfred Mond) were not intended as scales of benefit, but maxima, beyond which the local (London) Guardians of the Poor would not be reimbursed by the Metropolitan Common Poor Fund. However, in many cases the Guardians did treat them as relief scales

b Children = aged under 16

Sources: Routh, *Occupation and Pay*, pp. 88, 90, 97, 100; Royal Commission on Unemployment Insurance, *Final Report*, p. 20; Smith, *The New Survey*, vol. I, 375. Unemployment insurance benefit rates for the whole interwar period are given in W.R. Garside, *British Unemployment 1919–1939: a study in public policy* (Cambridge UP 1990), App. 3.2

The failure of the unemployment benefit rates to reach even the meagre pre-war Rowntree/Bowley standard was hardly surprising, since it was not intended that they should. In 1927, the Minister of Labour, Sir Arthur Steel-Maitland, said that the unemployment insurance scheme had never been intended to provide maintenance, but to provide 'a help and a very material help indeed – for people to tide over a period of unemployment'. The Blanesburgh Committee produced a similar argument in the same year.[11] On the other hand, it might be said that, in spite of the actuarial failure of the unemployment insurance scheme, it did serve to prevent starvation, and, since most of the unemployed did not remain so for long periods (especially in the 1920s), the original conception of the level of benefit was not, by its own scheme of things, deficient.

SOCIAL WELFARE: HEALTH CARE, PENSIONS, EDUCATION

In several important aspects of life, social welfare became more widely diffused during the 1920s. There was a wider and more comprehensive supply of health services, more generous pension provision, and educational provision was made more available and improved in quality.

Health care

The major collective effort in health care remained the national health insurance scheme inaugurated in 1911. Those who did not consult a general practitioner privately could be put on a doctor's 'panel' of a local insurance committee, which would allow them to have free consultations with a general practitioner and paid for medicines prescribed. A period off work due to sickness involved the doctor signing a 'sick note', which would entitle the patient to draw sickness benefit. The level of sickness benefit had been raised to 15s. at the end of the war, and it remained at that level throughout the interwar years. The sickness scheme was resorted to on a large scale, particularly, it has been alleged, by married women, as a means of supplementing family income in hard times.[12]

This alleged tendency of insured married women to claim benefit on exiguous grounds was partly due to one of the signal omissions of the 1911 Act, in that sickness and medical benefits were available to the insured person only; dependants remained uninsured. The development of the unemployment insurance scheme after 1918 to include allowances for dependants exposed the inequity of the health insurance scheme. However, governments concerned with retrenchment did not feel able to extend the scheme in this way. One consequence of this omission was the growth of a movement for family allowances, which was finally put into effect in 1945.[13]

The national health insurance scheme had other defects: its administration, largely via the artificially created 'Approved Societies', was cumbersome and inefficient. But the greatest omission lay in its neglect of any provision for treatment in hospital. This remained in the 1920s a bifurcated system. On the one hand, the public Poor Law and local authority institutions; on the other, the private 'voluntary' hospitals, provided by local effort and philanthropy.

11. Both quoted in M. Bruce, *The Coming of the Welfare State* (Batsford 1968), p. 263.
12. D. Fraser, *The Evolution of the British Welfare State* (Macmillan 1973), p. 184.
13. Fraser, *Evolution*, p. 184; J. McNicol, *The Movement for Family Allowances, 1918–45: a study in social policy development* (Heinemann 1980).

Nearly all the more prestigious hospitals, including almost all the teaching hospitals, were voluntary, but voluntary institutions provided a minority of beds for the physically ill (56,550 in England and Wales in 1921). Far more were provided by the Poor Law authorities (120,278), chiefly in the form of the sick wards of the workhouses, and almost as many by municipal authorities (51,720), mainly as isolation hospitals for specific diseases such as tuberculosis, under various Acts of Parliament.[14]

Hospital provision was patchy, and less available in working-class areas. In addition, the voluntary hospitals, in spite of deriving about one-quarter of their income (in 1920) from government sources, had difficulty in making ends meet. The result was a variety of fund-raising initiatives, and many hospitals abandoned their practice of not charging patients. Hospitals got by with charitable fund-raising activities (such as flag days), covenanted gifts (made possible by an Act of 1922), but largely by contributory schemes (mainly in London) by which local people could, on payment of a small weekly sum, receive treatment without further payment.[15]

There was also no overall coordination of medical services, such as had inspired those pressing for the establishment of a Ministry of Health before 1918. This ministry was established in 1919, but its responsibilities were awesome and varied: national health insurance, the public health work of local authorities, housing, and the entire Poor Law administration at national level. For the ministry to take stock of the situation, as well as cope with the novel and pressing housing problem, required time. It was not until after 1924 that ministers stayed long enough in the job to consider long-term planning.[16]

While the deficiencies of the scheme of national health insurance were manifest (and were voiced by a Royal Commission in 1924–26), it was successful in its primary aim, which was to ease the financial and psychological cost of accident and illness (of wage-earners) for the bulk of the working-class population. By 1925 the scheme was paying out £25 million a year to 15.6 million insured persons, chiefly in the form of sickness (£10 million) and medical (£9 million) benefit. Although the administration was inefficient and costly, the scheme as a whole was financially viable, and by then had accumulated enormous surplus funds, worth £126 million.[17] This allowed the state to reduce its contribution to the fund in 1922 and 1926, until it stood at about one-sixth of the cost of the scheme, a lower proportion than in the unemployment and pensions schemes. On the negative side, it was widely felt that the 'panel patients' got an inferior service from the general practitioner (GP), and suspected they were being condescended to. Since for each patient the GP received only a capitation fee of 9s. a year, there may have been justification

14. A.H. Halsey, *Trends in British Society since 1900* (Macmillan 1972), p. 349; Acton Society Trust, *Hospitals and the State* (1955), pp. 8–13.
15. B. Abel-Smith, *The Hospitals 1800–1948* (Heinemann 1964), ch. 20.
16. Bruce, *Welfare State*, pp. 243–4.
17. Board of Trade, *Statistical Abstract for the United Kingdom . . . 1911 to 1925* (1927), pp. 56–7.

for this suspicion. More basically, it could be argued that the medical benefit assisted those who needed it least, while ignoring those who needed it most – notably families with young children.[18]

Pensions

The provision of pensions was further extended in 1925. The original scheme (means-tested, and not paid until the age of 70) was felt to be inadequate, yet it was also becoming more expensive. There was a growing number of old people, and the original pension of 5s. a week (at the age of 70) had been raised to 10s. in 1920. The solution proposed in a 1925 Act by the Minister of Health (Neville Chamberlain) was to introduce a supplementary scheme, whereby a pension could be paid at the age of 65, but on a contributory basis, thus relieving the Exchequer of the full cost of the scheme. The scheme covered everyone already in the national health insurance scheme, and required additional contributions of 9d. a week for men and 4½d. for women, shared equally between employer and employed. This ensured a pension of 10s. a week at age 65, with no means test, payable both to the insured person and his wife; beyond the age of 70 the same pensions would continue on the same terms. To spare the Treasury some of the initial cost, the new contributory pensions would not be paid until 1928.

A more radical departure of the 1925 Act was the provision, for the first time, of pensions for widows and orphans, whose only recourse in difficulty had been the Poor Law. The pensions were fixed at 10s. a week for widows and 7s. 6d. for orphans, and were paid from 1926; on reaching the age of 70, the widows' pension was to be replaced by an old age pension of 10s. a week.[19]

Thus the expansion of the population of pensionable age was provided for; the 764,000 old age pensioners of 1913, who had drawn pensions worth £9.5 million, had by 1930 risen to 1,373,000 (of whom 447,000 were included under the contributory scheme) drawing pensions worth £34.9 million. In addition, there were by 1935 some 755,000 women drawing widows' pensions.[20]

Education

The 1920s saw also some interesting educational developments, although in most cases these did not reach fruition until after 1945. The chief of these was the continuation of the expansion in secondary education begun in 1902. By contrast, there was comparatively little change in the pre- and post-secondary spheres. Although 'elementary' education was universal by 1918, few ex-elementary pupils entered separate secondary schools. Fewer still went on to higher and further education, which was largely the preserve of the upper and

18. Bruce, *Welfare State*, p. 244; Fraser, *Welfare State*, p. 184.
19. Bruce, *Welfare State*, pp. 246–7, 250–1; Political and Economic Planning (PEP), *Report on the British Social Services* (1937), pp. 118–19, 131–2.
20. Board of Trade, *Statistical Abstract* (1927), pp. 58–9; PEP, *Social Services*, pp. 120, 131–2.

middle classes, whether educated at one of the comparatively new grammar schools, or in the independent, 'public' schools.

For the elementary school pupils entering adolescence, and intending to leave school at the official age of 14, there was little choice but to stay in the higher class of a school which was essentially a primary school. Thus 'school' for the overwhelming majority of children meant the elementary school. In 1920–21, there were (in England and Wales) 5,861,000 children in elementary schools, and only 355,000 in grant-aided secondary schools, to which may be added some 263,000 in the independent sector, whether at pre-adolescent ('preparatory' or 'prep') schools or secondary ('public') schools. Ten years later, there were fewer elementary schoolchildren (reflecting the declining birth rate) – 5,570,000 – and the numbers in grant-aided secondary schools had risen to 411,000, together with an estimated 254,000 in the independent sector. While most children left school at the age of 14 in the 1920s, there was an increase in the proportion going on to secondary level; about 12 per cent (84,000) did so in 1920–21, and about 16 per cent (104,000) in 1935. By 1938, the numbers of children in grant-aided secondary schools had risen to 470,000.[21]

This mild expansion of secondary education was a matter for local education authorities, under the stimulus of prodding from the Board of Education, some of which was obligatory, and some merely permissive. The most notable example of compulsion was the Education Act 1918, sponsored by the President of the Board, H.A.L. Fisher. This raised the school-leaving age to 14, finally abolished all fees in elementary schools, and promoted the establishment of 'continuation' schools, which pupils would attend for 320 hours a year, from the age of 14 to 18, to bridge the gap between school and employment. Apart from its educational merits, this system would have had a particular value in Britain, with its limited development of secondary schools. This provision was not compulsory, however, and in most localities continuation schools fell a victim to the government's economy drive of 1921–22; one school survived at Rugby, where it was especially useful to the local electrical works and their apprentices.[22]

The loss of the continuation schools was certainly due to the economy drive which followed the reports of the government's committee, set up in 1922 under Sir Eric Geddes, in order to find savings in national expenditure. However, the rest of the education system survived the cuts fairly painlessly. While it is true that the 'Geddes Axe' (as the committee was dubbed) recommended large cuts in educational expenditure – £18 million out of total cuts of £87 million – most of the cuts in practice fell on the Armed Forces, and most of the educational cuts were not proceeded with. The parliamentary grant for education did reduce, but only from £48 million in 1922 to an annual average of £41 million in 1923–25. Of this, the share going to local education authorities

21. Carr-Saunders and Jones, *Social Structure*, pp. 120–1, 125; ibid. (2nd edn, 1937), pp. 115–17, 119; Halsey, *Trends*, p. 164.

22. M. Sanderson, *Educational Opportunity and Social Change in England* (Faber & Faber 1987), p. 26.

(LEAs) fell from £36 million to £33 million. However, since the rest of the LEA income came from local sources, and was little changed in money terms, LEA spending on elementary education fell only from £62 million in 1922 to £60 million in 1925.[23]

Apart from the Education Act, Fisher's tenure of office was notable for two important innovations. The first was that teachers' salaries were raised, and a fixed scale system introduced, regularly reviewed by the Burnham Committee (1919). In addition, teachers were offered a superannuation scheme under an Act of 1918, which secured the position of retired teachers. Both schemes to some extent fell victim to the Geddes cuts. The salaries of teachers were reduced by 5 per cent in 1922, and the superannuation scheme, which had originally been non-contributory, was made contributory in the same year, so that teachers had to contribute 5 per cent of their pay to the scheme. But much had been done to enhance the attractiveness of teaching for the more able and highly qualified, and to give it the status of a profession.[24]

Even with the expansion of secondary education since 1902, the supply of places lagged behind the demand. At the beginning of the academic year 1919–20, it was estimated that 10,000 applicants for admission to secondary schools as fee-payers were denied places, together with a further 10,000 who would have qualified as free place scholars. Even these figures paled into insignificance before more than 2 million, who, it was thought, would be capable of profiting from a secondary education.[25]

The plea for 'Secondary Education For All' made by R.H. Tawney in a famous Labour Party pamphlet of 1922 was beginning to obtain wide support, and received indirect support from Sir Henry Hadow's Committee on the Education of the Adolescent, which reported in 1926 (Tawney being a member of the committee). The Hadow Report deplored the small proportion of children aged 11–16 currently receiving a secondary education, and proposed a reorganisation of the system; a break should be made at the age of 11+, and the adolescent should be educated in a separate, secondary school, with a suitable curriculum. Selection for secondary education should be by means of the existing '11+' examination, which usually incorporated an intelligence test. Thus at least three years of post-primary education would be assured. The report called for a further raising of the school-leaving age to 15 years. With expansion, the report recommended reorganisation of secondary education, chiefly into three types: the existing grammar schools (for academic, literary and scientific studies);

23. Committee on the National Expenditure, *Third Report* (1922), Cmd 1589, p. 168; Board of Trade, *Statistical Abstract* (1927), pp. 44–7. See also G. Sherington, *English Education, Social Change and War 1911–20* (Manchester UP 1981), pp. 164–6, on the resistance to the Geddes proposals put up by Fisher.

24. S.J. Curtis, *History of Education in Great Britain* (7th edn, University Tutorial Press 1967), pp. 345–6; Routh, *Occupation and Pay*, p. 69.

25. G.A.N. Lowndes, *The Silent Social Revolution: an account of the expansion of public education in England and Wales 1895–1935* (Oxford UP 1937), p. 115; Sanderson, *Educational Opportunity* (1987), p. 26, gives slightly different figures for 1919–20.

new, 'modern' types, for 'realistic or practical' studies; and the existing 'Junior Technical Schools' (with entry at 13).[26]

The Board of Education encouraged such reorganisation by LEAs, although, since it entailed much new building work, it did not really accelerate until the 1930s, when building costs had fallen. By the end of 1938, 64 per cent of all pupils aged 11 and over were in reorganised schools.[27] However, development in rural areas was slower than in towns. In 1936, about 65 per cent of rural schoolchildren were still being educated in all-age schools.[28] Further reorganisation was envisaged by the Spens Committee in 1938, which thought that a further type of secondary school should be provided, the 'Technical High School', which, although having 'parity of esteem' with the more academically inclined grammar school, would have a more practical curriculum. For pupils over 13, it would provide 'a liberal education with Science and its applications as the core and inspiration'.[29]

The economies made in the slump of 1929–32 had one marked effect: the 'free places' in grammar schools were abandoned, being replaced with 'special places', with contributions from parents based on their income. Thus, instead of reserving a defined proportion of places for the brightest pupils, grammar school places were open to all, dependent on ability and parental means. Thus ability alone was no longer enough to move an intelligent child from a poor background to a grammar school. Finally, the school-leaving age was raised to 15 by the Education Act 1936; the date of implementation was to be 1 September 1939. Not surprisingly, this proved abortive, and the school-leaving age was not raised to 15 until 1947.[30]

Standing outside the state-run system of schooling were the private schools. These covered a wide range: infant and kindergarten schools; 'preparatory' schools which usually served as feeders to private secondary schools, and many others, some (at secondary level) constituting the misleadingly named 'public' schools. The latter were difficult to define, since in practice only membership by the headmaster of the Headmasters' Conference (a forum for discussion of mutual problems and policies, limited to 200 members) served to differentiate them from other private schools. The public schools offered considerable variety, ranging from the dozen or so famous ones, such as Eton, Harrow, Charterhouse, Marlborough and Rugby, to many lesser known ones. But the demand for them

26. R.H. Tawney (ed.), *Secondary Education for All: a policy for labour* (Allen & Unwin 1922); Board of Education, *The Education of the Adolescent: Report of the Consultative Committee* (HMSO 1927), para. 200.
27. Curtis, *History of Education*, p. 353.
28. A. Armstrong, 'The Countryside', *Cambridge Social History of Britain* (Cambridge UP 1990), vol. I, p. 143.
29. Board of Education, *Report of the Consultative Committee on Secondary Education with special reference to Grammar Schools and Technical High Schools* (HMSO 1938), ch. XI, paras 112, 132.
30. Lowndes, *Social Revolution*, p. 118; Sanderson, *Educational Opportunity*, pp. 27–9; Carr-Saunders and Jones, *Social Structure* (1937), p. 118; Curtis, *History of Education*, p. 353.

was certainly there; in the 1920s two new ones (Stowe and Canford) were founded. What they had in common was the provision of boarding-school education; a high level of scholastic achievement; an official ethos based on Christian worship and values; a stress on self-discipline and *esprit de corps* via such things as the house and prefectorial systems, and a strong emphasis on organised games. They dominated the supply of undergraduates to the older universities (chiefly Oxford and Cambridge), although their products could be found to some extent in other universities.[31]

There was a slow expansion in higher education between the wars. The number of students at universities, teacher training colleges, and other forms of higher education rose from 61,000 in 1924–25 to 69,000 in 1938–39. University education was a rarity for the great mass of school-leavers. The number of full-time university students in Britain was about 42,000 in 1924–25, and rose, but slowly, to about 50,000 in 1938–39. Even at the latter date, only about 1.7 per cent of the relevant age group entered university, a further 0.7 per cent entering teacher training (some via universities, most via training colleges). About one-third of university entrants in those years came from LEA secondary schools; the rest came from non-grant-aided schools (roughly coterminous with the 'public schools'). Thus undergraduates came mainly from the upper and upper-middle classes. In 1938–39, only 19 per cent of Oxford entrants came from maintained (i.e. state) schools, although the civic and provincial universities relied largely on local grammar schools. Apart from university study, the only real avenue for the working-class adult to obtain higher education was to obtain a place at the trade-union supported Ruskin College, Oxford (founded 1899), or to take a series of tutorial classes organised by the Workers' Educational Association, and taught by a university lecturer.[32]

The universities were still dominated by a small number of older universities (in England, Oxford, Cambridge and London; in Scotland, St Andrews, Aberdeen, Glasgow and Edinburgh), although there were also some new or expanding foundations. Some new university colleges were founded between the wars – Nottingham, Southampton, Exeter, Leicester and Hull. These did not have the power to give their own degrees, but awarded London University degrees. The only new university was the former Reading University College, which became a university in 1926. The great 'civic' universities such as Manchester, Birmingham, Leeds, Liverpool, Sheffield and Bristol, which had been established before 1914, continued to expand slowly.[33] Finally, there was London

31. Sanderson, *Educational Opportunity*, pp. 38–42; Carr-Saunders and Jones, *Social Structure* (1937), p. 117; H.C. Barnard, *A History of English Education from 1760* (2nd edn, University of London Press 1961), ch. XXVII.
32. Halsey, *Trends*, p. 206; V.H.H. Green, *The Universities* (Pelican 1969), pp. 127–30; M. Stocks, *The Workers' Educational Association: the first fifty years* (Allen & Unwin 1953).
33. (Sir) J. Mountford, *British Universities* (Oxford UP 1966), pp. 18–34. On universities generally, see Green, *Universities*, and 'Bruce Truscott' (pseudonym), *Red Brick University* (1943).

University, a federation of colleges, which finally acquired its central administration and library site in 1929, although building continued until 1937. By 1931, over 3,000 Bachelors' degrees annually were being awarded, compared with slightly over 1,000 before 1914. Expansion was especially rapid at one of its constituent colleges, the London School of Economics (LSE), which had been founded by Sidney and Beatrice Webb in 1895. Sir William Beveridge, the director of the LSE from 1919 to 1937, was fond of claiming that he ruled over an empire on which the concrete never set.[34]

Thus in the interwar period, educational opportunity, in the sense of the availability of forms of education suitable for all who wished to use these opportunities, was increasing (although sometimes from a low starting point). In spite of the check to free secondary education in the 1930s, the more academically able working-class children were increasingly provided for, and this provision would continue to expand after the Second World War.

CONCLUSIONS

In spite of the brief postwar recession, and continuing high unemployment afterwards, the 1920s was a decade in which, for those in work, real incomes and living standards rose. Thus a large part of the poverty revealed in prewar social surveys had disappeared. However, in spite of the more generous unemployment insurance benefits, unemployment would reduce most households to near-destitution. In other ways, social welfare was more widely diffused. The health insurance system continued in being, although it had serious limitations. The state pension system became more comprehensive, with the provision of contributory pensions in 1928, and pensions for widows and orphans in 1926. Educational provision expanded, with the raising of the school-leaving age to 14, the final abolition of fees in elementary schools, and the development of separate secondary schools. The number of university students also grew, although the opportunities to advance to higher education were still very limited. In all, the 1920s was a period of economic and social improvement for most – with the notable exception of unemployed people.

34. N. Harte, *The University of London, 1836–1986* (Athlone 1986), p. 197 and ch. 6. See also R. Dahrendorf, *The London School of Economics, 1895–1995* (Oxford UP 1995).

CHAPTER 9

TOWN, COUNTRY AND HOUSING, 1918–39

THE GROWTH OF TOWNS

By the early twentieth century, British society had become highly urbanised, some four-fifths of the population living in towns. In England and Wales in 1911 the urban proportion of the population was 78 per cent, and in Scotland it was 75 per cent.[1] ('Urban' here is taken to indicate people living in urban administrative areas in England and Wales; in Scotland, it indicates people living in burghs and certain other districts having a population of over 1,000.)

Within this highly urbanised society, towns were getting larger. Between 1901 and 1931, the greatest growth was in towns of between 50,000 and 200,000 people, whose proportion of the total population of England and Wales rose from 21.6 to 27.3 per cent. The proportion of the population living in towns of fewer than 10,000 declined from 12.4 to 8.5 per cent.[2] But merely counting numbers of people in towns (i.e. local government urban areas) understates the urbanness of everyday experience, since by this time a high proportion of the population lived in 'conurbations', or groups of towns whose suburbs had expanded so far beyond their local government boundaries as to reach out to one another to form a more or less continuously built-up area. The greatest by far was the London region, which even in 1911 had a population of 7.25 million. The other major conurbations came a long way behind, but together they accounted for a high proportion (40.4 per cent in 1931) of the British population (Map 3 opposite).

Between 1911 and 1931, the population of the conurbations grew by 12 per cent, while the total British population grew by only 10 per cent. Some grew much faster than others. The most spectacular was the west midlands, which grew by 18 per cent, and even the relatively depressed regions such as Clydeside and Merseyside grew by 16 per cent. Below-average growth was seen in south-east Lancashire and west Yorkshire (both 4 per cent) and Tyneside (9 per cent). Greater London grew by 13 per cent; by 1931 its population had

1. Census of England and Wales 1931, *Preliminary Report* (1931), p. xv; Census of Scotland 1911, *Report* (1913), vol. II, Cd 6896, pp. xiii–xiv, xli.
2. A.H. Halsey, *Trends in British Society since 1900* (Macmillan 1972), p. 277.

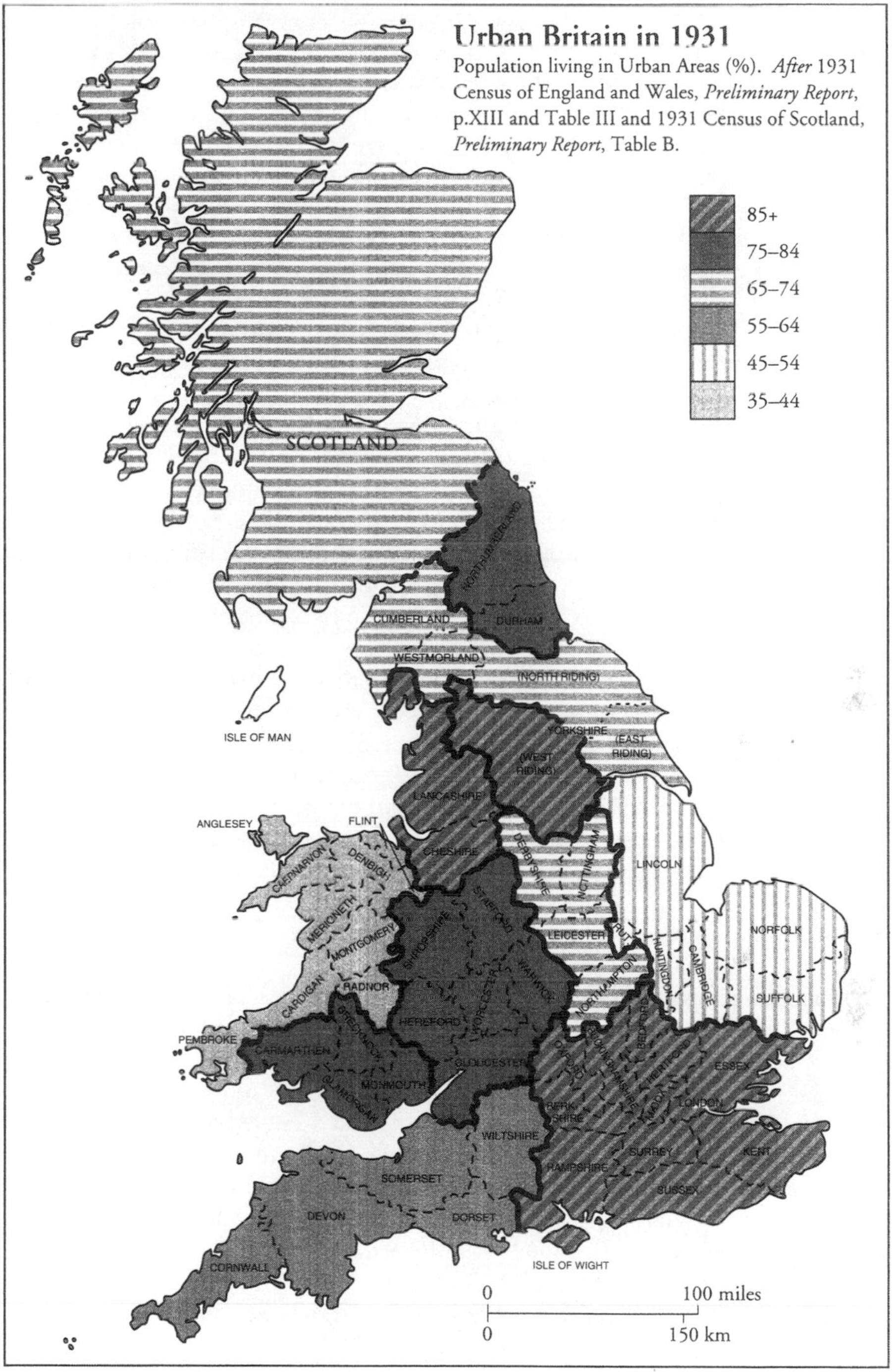

Map 3 Urban Britain in 1931

reached 8.2 million, and it remained by far the biggest urban agglomeration, the next largest being south-east Lancashire, with only 2.4 million people.[3]

Within the conurbations, a substantial change was occurring, as their inner centres lost population to their suburbs. Over the whole interwar period (1921–38), the seven great conurbations gained in population by 12 per cent, but their inner centres experienced a decline of 2.5 per cent, and their suburbs expanded by 32 per cent. In total, almost two-thirds of the entire national increase in population in those years was concentrated in the suburban parts of these seven conurbations. This movement was particularly striking in the London and west midland conurbations. Over the same period, their inner centres lost 1.5 per cent of their population, while their suburbs gained 51.3 per cent. In terms of total numbers, this meant that the populations of their inner centres remained almost unchanged, while their suburbs grew by slightly over 2 million people, from 4.01 to 6.07 million.[4] (The southern and midland conurbations listed here include minor ones. The full English list is London, Birmingham, Bristol, Nottingham, Stoke-on-Trent, Portsmouth, Leicester, Brighton, Plymouth, Coventry, Southampton, Bournemouth and Medway (Gillingham).)

Thus, while the urban population comprised about four-fifths of the total British population, and about two-fifths of the urban population lived in a greater or lesser conurbation, the most striking movement of people was to the suburbs. Suburbanisation was not of course a new phenomenon; the Victorian middle classes had long ago turned what were then the outer suburbs into commuting bases. After 1918 the process went much further, greatly assisted by transport developments. The chief of these were motor buses and cars, suburban railways, and, in the case of London, the Underground railway.

Even before 1914, London horse buses had been largely replaced by motor buses. The postwar buses and coaches were more reliable and ranged further. Since owning a car even in the 1930s was still a middle-class affair, suburban expansion was reliant chiefly on motor bus and rail services. In the face of this competition, tramcars stagnated; by 1929, there were 50,000 buses or coaches operating in Britain, but only 14,000 trams.[5]

Urban transport services, however, were in a state of chaos by the end of the 1920s. In all but a few rural areas, anyone could start a bus service without a licence. The result was excessive competition for passengers, characterised by such dubious practices as 'tail chasing', 'leap frogging' and 'hanging the road'. This situation was ended by the Road Traffic Act 1930, which imposed a new and comprehensive licensing system on public transport operators. In London, regulation was to go further and became outright public ownership (of both surface and Underground services), by the London Passenger Transport Act 1933.[6]

The rise of motor transport, which could provide 'feeder' services to and from railway stations, gave a new boost to suburban rail services and thus suburban development. This was most notable in London, whose effective commuting

3. B.R. Mitchell, *British Historical Statistics* (Cambridge UP 1988), p. 25.
4. M. Abrams, *The Condition of the British People 1911–1945* (Gollancz 1945), p. 36.
5. Mitchell, *Statistics*, p. 557.
6. C.I. Savage, *An Economic History of Transport* (Hutchinson 1959), ch. 6.

boundaries were pushed out to 10–15 miles from the centre: to Ilford in the east, Surbiton and Croydon in the south, Staines and Uxbridge in the west, and Watford, Barnet and Enfield in the north.

The physical features of a not untypical suburban development (Stoneleigh, between Worcester Park and Ewell West, in outer south-west London) have been described as they appeared to the young John Osborne (later to be a famous playwright) in 1936:

> Stoneleigh itself was a station surrounded by groups of housing estates. Coming off the concrete railway bridge on either side were 'Shopping Parades'. In the middle was the Stoneleigh Hotel, which was not an hotel at all, but a by-pass Tudor pub where my mother was to work throughout the war and for several years after. The Parades consisted of a small Woolworth's, the dry cleaners, newsagents and a two-penny library, butchers, florists and empty shops which had not yet been sold, gaps in the townscape, corners which had not yet been built on, patches of fields and stubble between houses and shops. It was not Stockbroker's Tudor but Bankclerk's Tudor. The ribbons of streets were empty most of the day except for occasional women on their way to the Parades, pushing prams along the clean pavements with their grass verges, fresh as last week's graves.[7]

Some of the movement to the suburbs owed its origin to public housing programmes. Between Barking and Dagenham in the eastern suburbs of London, the enormous and entirely new estate of Becontree, developed by the London County Council, accommodated 103,328 people by 1932.[8] In addition, London had the advantage of underground railways, which, running above ground outside the central area, were greatly extended after 1918. The Northern Line reached to Edgware in 1924, the Piccadilly Line to Cockfosters by 1933, while the Metropolitan Line reached Watford in 1925, and extended into Hertfordshire as far as Chorley Wood and Rickmansworth, and into Buckinghamshire as far as Amersham. The Metropolitan Line was associated with substantial speculative housing developments for the middle classes; 'Metroland' (the prewar nickname for this process) spread into new territory. Finally, the rapid electrification of the Southern Railway stimulated the developing commuter villages in Surrey and as far afield as Brighton.[9]

RURAL AREAS

The British rural population grew very slowly between the wars, being 8,349,000 in 1911 and 8,963,000 in 1931.[10] Under the largely unregulated pressure of suburban and industrial expansion, farmland was shrinking. The area of agricultural crops and grass in Britain fell from 31.7 million acres in 1918 to 29.2

7. J. Osborne, *A Better Class of Person: an autobiography 1929–1956* (Faber & Faber 1981), pp. 38–9.

8. T. Young, *Becontree and Dagenham: a report made for the Pilgrim Trust* (Becontree Social Service Committee 1934), p. 78.

9. J. Burnett, *A Social History of Housing 1815–1970* (Newton Abbot, David & Charles 1978), p. 252.

10. Central Statistical Office (CSO), *Annual Abstract of Statistics no. 84 (1935–1946)* (1948), Table 12.

million in 1939.[11] A notable change in social relationships in the countryside occurred with the large sales of country estates after 1918; about 25 per cent of the agricultural land of England changed hands. Although some went to speculators initially, most went finally to the previous tenant farmers. In 1909, only about 13 per cent of agricultural holdings had been owned by their occupiers; by 1927, the figure was 37 per cent. In effect, it may be said that a new class of yeomen had been created, although the economic conditions of agriculture for much of the interwar period meant that it was financially hard-pressed.[12]

The rural population was becoming less dependent on the land, as the agricultural workforce continued to fall under the twin pressures of farm mechanisation and the low pay of farm workers. Between 1921 and 1938, the numbers of agricultural workers in Britain fell from 996,000 to 697,000. In 1911 about 36 per cent of those living in rural districts in England and Wales were employed in agriculture, and in 1931 about 30 per cent.[13] Expansion of service trades made up some of the loss. To some extent, tourism replaced agriculture in the more scenic parts of Britain, as the spread of motor transport eased access to areas away from the main railway lines, and as the custom of paid holidays spread. In addition, better transport allowed an increasing number of people to live in the countryside and work in towns; already in 1921, 14 per cent of the economically active population in rural districts travelled to work in urban areas, and the proportion was growing.[14]

To some extent, town and country were drawing together; on the one hand, the urban fringe expanded; on the other, transport developments meant that personal communication was easier. The rise of the motor bus and the continuing diffusion of the bicycle and motor cycle brought the urban amenities of shopping and amusement more within the reach of country dwellers. On the other hand, the countryside continued to lack many amenities enjoyed in towns. The quality of rural housing was noticeably inferior. Most agricultural workers could not afford to rent or buy any of the 871,000 new houses built in rural areas (usually adjacent to towns) between 1919 and 1943, and most of them relied on farmers' tied cottages, which were of older stock. Even in 1939, 25 per cent of English parishes lacked a piped water supply, and more lacked mains sanitation; wells, cess-pits and earth closets were all too prevalent.[15]

11. Ministry of Agriculture, *A Century of Agricultural Statistics: Great Britain, 1866–1966* (HMSO 1968), Table 41.

12. S.G. Sturmey, 'Owner-Farming in England and Wales, 1900–1950', in W.E. Minchinton (ed.), *Essays in Agrarian History* (Newton Abbot, David & Charles 1968), vol. II, pp. 287–96; F.M.L. Thompson, *English Landed Society in the Nineteenth Century* (1963), p. 332; A. Howkins, *Reshaping Rural England: a social history 1850–1925* (HarperCollins 1991), pp. 279–81.

13. Ministry of Agriculture, *A Century*, p. 62; Halsey, *Trends*, calculated from Table 9.8, p. 280.

14. Halsey, *Trends*, Table 9.10, p. 281.

15. W.A. Armstrong, 'The Countryside', in F.M.L. Thompson (ed.), *Cambridge Social History of Britain* (Cambridge UP 1990), vol. I, pp. 143–4.

HOUSING

House-ownership was the exception before 1914. Most houses were rented from private landlords, although a few had been provided by local authorities. This *laissez-faire* policy was transformed by the war. Two events were responsible for this change – the introduction of rent control, and the cessation of housebuilding. Rent control began as an emergency measure, following an outcry in Glasgow against rising rents, which were being driven up rapidly by general inflation and the influx of munition workers into Clydeside. Fearing the revolutionary overtones of the agitation, and conscious of the threat to munitions production, the government passed a general Act, the Increase of Rent and Mortgage Interest (War Restrictions) Act 1915, which in effect fixed working-class rents (and mortgage interest payments) at their prewar levels. Intended to be a temporary measure, the rent control scheme was prolonged long afterwards.[16]

The other reason for the transformation was the lack of new building. Rapid inflation, the movement of skilled building labour into the Forces, shortages of materials and disruption of the usual pattern of household formation combined to reduce housebuilding. Finally, rent control made the building of houses to let unprofitable. Thus new construction virtually ceased; whereas on average in 1909–13 72,000 houses annually had been built in Britain, this had fallen to 17,000 in 1916 (national figures were not collected for the rest of the war).[17]

In spite of war losses, the British population grew between 1911 and 1921 by 4.75 per cent, and the number of families rose, so that the housing shortage increased. A reasonable estimate for England and Wales alone is that there was a further shortage of 805,000 houses by 1921, compared to 1911.[18] (In making these calculations, account has been taken only of the *extra* gap between the rise in the number of families and the rise in the number of dwellings between 1911 and 1921; the gap already existing in 1911 has been ignored.)

Thus by the end of the war the housing position had been transformed. The shortage was much greater, but rent control and inflated house prices made it unattractive for private builders to build houses for renting. Even if they had been willing, there was a shortage of materials and skilled labour (especially bricklayers). In this situation, the logical solution seemed to be some form of state subsidy, which would stimulate the production of houses until the housing shortage had been overcome. Free market rents would then decline to a level at which rent control could be abandoned. This line of thought was given

16. M. Bowley, *Housing and the State, 1919–1944* (Allen & Unwin 1945), pp. 5, 39–40; J.P. Lewis, *Building Cycles and Britain's Growth* (Macmillan 1965), pp. 225–6.
17. Mitchell, *Statistics*, p. 390.
18. Census of England and Wales 1931, *Housing Report* (1935), ch. 5; Bowley, *Housing*, pp. 262, 269–70; R. Rodger, 'Crisis and Confrontation in Scottish Housing, 1880–1914', in Rodger (ed.), *Scottish Housing in the Twentieth Century* (Leicester UP 1989), p. 48.

added force by the political pressure for the government to build 'Homes for Heroes'.[19]

The result was the first substantial state intervention in the construction market, in the form of the Housing and Town Planning Act 1919, popularly named the 'Addison Act', after the President of the Local Government Board, Dr Christopher Addison. Intended to result in the provision of 500,000 houses, it amounted to an open-ended subsidy to local authorities, who were to contract for the houses with private builders. The authorities were to prepare plans to meet the housing needs of their localities and submit them for approval by the Ministry of Health. The crucial financial provision was that all losses made by the local authorities in excess of the amount provided by a penny (1d.) rate were to be borne by the Treasury. The level of rents, however, was to have regard mainly to the current level of controlled rents. It was hoped that the housing shortage would have sufficiently abated by March 1927 to permit economic rents to be charged. It was thus not contemplated that government should play a permanent role in the housing market. In addition, under the Housing (Additional Powers) Act 1919, a lump sum subsidy per house could be provided to private builders.[20]

At a time of rapidly rising prices, which did not start to fall until the postwar boom broke in the autumn of 1920, the Addison subsidy had no upper limit, and nothing was done to increase the supply of skilled labour and materials. Thus the programme proved to be expensive, and was abandoned in July 1921. However, some progress had been made; by the time that the houses commenced under the Acts had been completed, in March 1923, 213,821 houses had been built in England and Wales. In addition, 53,800 unsubsidised houses had been built privately. But these additions to the housing stock had been outweighed by the formation of new families; thus the overall shortage has been estimated at 822,000 in England and Wales in March 1923.

The next, more cautious attempt to tackle the housing shortage, was the Housing Act 1923 ('Chamberlain Act'). This offered a fixed subsidy, of £6 a house per year for twenty years, whether built by local authorities or private enterprise, and whether for sale or for rent. Again, it was assumed that the problem was a temporary one, the Act being designed to apply only to houses built by 1 October 1925. The Act was designed to encourage private builders rather than council provision, since local authorities were to provide houses only if they could convince the Ministry of Health that this was preferable to leaving it to private enterprise. There were also provisions designed to encourage home ownership; the authorities were permitted to advance money to people who wished to buy, but lacked the necessary initial down payment required by the building societies.

Policy changed again in 1924, with the Housing (Financial Provisions) Act ('Wheatley Act'). The Chamberlain subsidies were extended until 1939, and a

19. M. Swenarton, *Homes Fit for Heroes: the politics and architecture of early state housing in Britain* (Heinemann 1981), pp. 77–81.
20. Bowley, *Housing*, pp. 16–18, 21–2; Swenarton, *Homes*, pp. 80–1.

new, more generous subsidy, of £9 a house per year (£12 10s. in rural parishes) for forty years was offered. The Act was notable for two things – the restoration of the position of the local authorities, and the development of a long-term housing policy. The former was achieved by dropping the need to show that private enterprise could not do the work better; the latter by means of a compact with the building trade unions, by which they would relax their apprenticeship rules so that the number of skilled men could be increased, and by extending the life of the Chamberlain subsidy. Finally, to ensure that the emphasis would be on the provision of working-class housing, the Wheatley subsidy would be available only on houses built to rent.[21] (The capitalised value of the subsidy, reckoned at 5 per cent interest, was £75; the local authorities could pay out the subsidy as a lump sum to the builders, and recoup it from the annual payments made to the authority by the Treasury.)

Under the Acts of 1923 and 1924, further progress was made, although the rates of subsidy on both were reduced in 1927, and in 1929 the Chamberlain subsidy was ended. The Wheatley subsidy ran on until 1933. The net result was that between 1924 and 1931, 1,408,000 houses were built in England and Wales. Local authorities had built 431,000, subsidised private enterprise (chiefly under the Chamberlain Act) 370,000, and unsubsidised private enterprise 607,000.[22]

Although this represented an annual rate of building far above that of prewar, the continued creation of new households meant that there was still a shortage, although less than in 1918. In England and Wales by 1931, there were 2,187,000 more families than in 1911, but only 1,708,000 more houses, giving a further shortfall of 479,000 houses, above that of 1911. In Scotland, the housing shortage had been almost eliminated, but only 12,500 houses had been built to reduce the overcrowded slums, which were almost as widespread as before 1914. ('House' is used in the Scottish sense, to include tenement dwellings as well as terraced or semi-detached 'cottages' in the English working-class style.)[23]

The housing schemes of the 1920s had been intended mainly to improve the supply of working-class housing. In practice, this aim was only partly achieved. Whereas at the end of the war, about 68 per cent of the housing stock in England and Wales may be described as working class (i.e. having a rateable value of less than £14 a year), houses in this category accounted for only 42 per cent of all houses built between 1919 and 1934, and there was a shortage of working-class housing by 1934 which has been estimated (roughly) at 500,000. In addition, local authorities, mindful of the need to avoid rent arrears, tended to set rent levels which were affordable only by the artisan class, rather than the unskilled working class. Also, in 1923, rent control was removed from houses which became vacant. Henceforth, families wishing to move within the private housing sector lost the protection of the Rent Acts.

21. Bowley, *Housing*, pp. 21–4, 36–7, 40–1.
22. Ibid., App. II, Table 2.
23. Ibid., pp. 262–4, 269.

Thus the ability of slum dwellers to improve their housing condition was limited.[24]

Thus the initial aims of postwar policy had been only partly fulfilled; the poorest section of the population probably benefited little from the housing programmes of the 1920s. Those who moved into the new council houses were the upper echelons of the working class and the lower sections of the middle class, who found the rent more affordable, could pay for the longer travel distances to work which living on a suburban estate entailed, and could demonstrate that their income was stable.[25]

In spite of the vacillations of housing policy, a considerable start had been made in improving the quality of British housing in the 1920s. By 1931, there were about 1.77 million postwar houses, compared with about 8.60 million prewar houses, or a proportion of just over one-fifth. The ratio was higher in England and Wales (21.8 per cent) than in Scotland (11.9).[26] These postwar houses were of superior quality compared to the older houses. The Ministry of Housing set a new standard for working-class housing, following the recommendations of the Tudor Walters Report of 1919. The result was that local authority houses were laid out at low densities (about twelve per acre, compared with the more usual forty of the prewar towns) on 'garden city' lines, with wide roads and more generous garden space. Internally, an attempt was made to provide a bathroom or, at least, a fixed bath in the kitchen/scullery area, more generous bedroom space (very often three bedrooms), a piped hot water supply and WC. Gas cookers were frequently installed, as was electric lighting.[27]

For the middle classes, such improvements were already standard, but they benefited further from such things as electric hot water heaters, perhaps electric cookers, and (at the end of the decade) refrigerators. In one sense, middle-class families benefited from the decline of living-in servants, since more family space was thereby created, and there were now various labour-saving devices, chiefly electrically powered, from vacuum cleaners to kettles, irons and toasters. These sold mainly to a middle-class and upper-middle-class clientele, even by the later 1930s.[28]

SLUM CLEARANCE

The early 1930s saw a sharp shift in housing policy. In 1928, it had been announced that the Chamberlain subsidy was to be discontinued except for

24. Ibid., pp. 40, 53–4, 96–9, 265.
25. Young, *Becontree and Dagenham*, pp. 118–20.
26. Calculated from Bowley, *Housing*, p. 265, App. II, Table I; Census of Scotland 1911, *Report*, vol. II, c.
27. S. Glynn and J. Oxborrow, *Interwar Britain: an economic and social history* (Allen & Unwin 1977), pp. 238–9; Young, *Becontree and Dagenham*, pp. 105–6.
28. A.A. Jackson, *The Middle Classes 1900–1950* (Nairn, David St John Thomas 1991), pp. 117–23. See also T.A.B. Corley, *Domestic Electrical Appliances* (Cape 1966).

houses completed before 30 September 1929. The Chamberlain and Wheatley subsidies were both reduced at the same time; a further reduction in the Wheatley subsidy was prevented by the incoming Labour government in 1929. By this time, the Ministry of Health was convinced that the general housing shortage had been overcome. The obvious inference was that private building would suffice for general demand in future, and that the role of the state would be more appropriately directed to areas of special need such as slum clearance and the abatement of overcrowding.[29]

The new policy was enshrined in the Housing Act 1930 ('Greenwood' Act). This offered a subsidy to local authorities in both urban and rural areas which varied according to the number of persons displaced *and rehoused*. This was designed to prevent schemes for slum clearance merely rendering people homeless, leaving them to find their own accommodation. It also gave an incentive to deal with large families, since the size of the subsidy would rise with the size of the family rehoused. Provision was also made for a higher subsidy where, because of high land and clearance costs, rehousing had to be by building flats.

There was no doubt that the problem of the slums was very large. Even in 1935, after the new building of the postwar period, it was estimated that over 3 million houses in Britain (more than one-quarter of the total stock) were at least eighty years old. Many of them would have been built by speculative builders, whose standards fell far short of those envisaged in the Tudor Walters Report. The extent of the slums was a matter of conjecture; one of the most active campaigners considered that the 'really bad slums' amounted to about 1.75 million houses, and that the total approached 4 million.[30]

Examples of bad housing were legion, and were not confined to the towns. George Orwell noted the condition of one house in Mapplewell, a mining village near Barnsley (Yorkshire):

> Two up, one down [i.e. a three-storey house with one room on each storey]. Living-room 14 ft. by 12 ft. Sink in living-room. Plaster cracking and coming off walls. No shelves in oven. Gas leaking slightly. The upstairs rooms each 10 ft. by 8 ft. Four beds (for six persons, all adult), but 'one bed does nowt', presumably for lack of bedclothes. Room nearest stairs has no door and stairs have no bannister, so that when you step out of bed your foot hangs in vacancy and you may fall ten feet on to stones. Dry rot so bad that one can see through the floor into the room below. Bugs, but 'I keeps 'em down with sheep dip'.[31]

The initial impact of the Greenwood Act was muted; by December 1933, only 11,796 houses in England and Wales had been built under its subsidy. This slow progress was largely attributable to the stringency in local government finance at the time; councils preferred to continue building under the

29. H.W. Richardson and D.H. Aldcroft, *Building in the British Economy between the Wars* (Allen & Unwin 1968), p. 179; Bowley, *Housing*, p. 45.
30. E.D. Simon, *How to Abolish the Slums* (Longmans, Green 1929), pp. 63–5; E.D. Simon, *The Anti-Slum Campaign* (1933), p. 125.
31. G. Orwell, *The Road to Wigan Pier* (Gollancz 1937; Penguin 1962), p. 49.

Wheatley subsidy, and ignore the complex problems posed by slum clearance and rehousing.[32]

This relative inertia was ended by a ministry circular in April 1933, asking every authority with a population over 20,000 to prepare programmes under the 1930 Act with a view to abolishing their slums in five years. Concurrently, the Wheatley subsidy was ended. In 1934, the authorities put forward their plans, which proposed the demolition of 266,851 houses in England and Wales and 66,417 in Scotland.[33] This was but a small proportion of the total housing stock – 2.8 per cent of that in England and Wales, although the relatively higher Scottish figure reflected the relatively worse situation north of the Border.[34]

There is little doubt that the local authorities were conservative in assessing their slum clearance programmes; the London County Council condemned only 33,000 out of 749,000 houses; Newcastle, 2,253 out of 61,000; Manchester, 15,000 out of 180,000.[35] In Manchester, the Medical Officer of Health had estimated that there were 30,000 houses unfit for human habitation.[36] The overall programmes were revised in March 1937 and March 1939, when the England and Wales total rose to 377,930 and 472,000; at the latter date, the Scottish total had risen to 132,417, so that the total British programme had risen by 82 per cent on the original one of 1934.[37]

The slum clearance targets of the early 1930s were largely met, although the achievement fell short of the revised targets of the later 1930s. From 1930 to the end of March 1939, in England and Wales, 272,836 houses had been closed or demolished, and replaced by 273,389 houses; 1,092,526 persons had been rehoused. In Scotland, 66,417 houses had been demolished, and 315,578 persons rehoused. (The greater proportionate effort in Scotland reflected the larger role played by local authorities; between March 1919 and March 1940, they accounted for 67 per cent of housebuilding in Scotland, but only 25 per cent in England and Wales.)[38] Overall, 339,253 houses had been demolished, compared with an original target of 333,268 demolitions. This compared very well with the 1934 target, though ill with the revised target of 604,417, which had come to be accepted by March 1939.

On the other hand, the programme could be presented as an historic breakthrough, in that more people had been rehoused in the 1930s than in the fifty

32. Bowley, *Housing*, pp. 148–9.
33. Richardson and Aldcroft, *Building*, pp. 181–2.
34. Census of England and Wales 1931, *Housing Report* (1935), Table 1; Census of Scotland 1931, vol. II (1933), p. xliii.
35. Burnett, *Housing*, p. 238; Burnett gives 'just over 1,000' for Newcastle; here I give the figure used by J.L. Marshall, 'The Pattern of Housebuilding in the Inter-War Period in England and Wales', *SJPE* 15 (1968), App. B.
36. Marshall, 'Pattern', p. 194.
37. Richardson and Aldcroft, *Building*, pp. 181–2.
38. R. Baird, 'Housing', in A.K. Cairncross (ed.), *The Scottish Economy* (Cambridge UP 1954), p. 205.

years preceding 1930, and in addition some 751,000 houses had been reconditioned. But the programme had been tackled in a patchy way. The problem was largely one of the 'big five' (London, Leeds, Liverpool, Manchester and Sheffield), which had accounted for 37 per cent of the original demolition target, and 43 per cent of the original rehousing target. These all (except Leeds) fell short of the 1934 target; aiming at 98,937 demolitions, they had carried out only 55,896 by the end of 1938. The greater achievements of other authorities masked the failures of the large towns. Authorities determined to defy the ministry and Parliament could do so by understating the original problem and by failing to carry out the programme in full.[39]

THE RELIEF OF OVERCROWDING

The problem of overcrowding was tackled in the Housing Act 1935, which called on local authorities to eliminate it within five years. The subsequent Overcrowding Survey (1935–36) reported on the inspection of some 10 million (mainly working-class) dwellings in Britain, revealing 342,000 (3.8 per cent) overcrowded dwellings in England and Wales, and 259,000 (22.6 per cent) in Scotland. For the first time, the Act gave a definition of overcrowding, but the standard was not rigorous. Although based on the 'two persons to a room' norm (five persons in three rooms, ten persons in five rooms, and so on), children under 1 year were not counted, children under 10 years counted only as half a person, and living-rooms were included as potential sleeping rooms. Provision for segregation of the sexes was made only at 10 years old. Thus at the higher end of the scale, a couple with seven children under 10, of which one was under 1 year, might not be classed as overcrowded in a three-room dwelling. If a slightly higher standard had been adopted, requiring that living-rooms should not be used for sleeping purposes, the number of overcrowded families in England and Wales would have been 853,000, roughly 9.6 per cent of the total.[40]

The extent of overcrowding varied enormously over Britain. The most overcrowded areas were in London, north-east England and north-west Wales. In London the areas affected most were the central boroughs of the East End – Shoreditch (17.2 per cent of families in overcrowded accommodation), Stepney (15.4), Finsbury (15.2) and Bethnal Green (14.9). Of the overcrowded county boroughs outside London, the top six were all in Durham or Northumberland; the most overcrowded was Sunderland (20.6), and the least was Newcastle (10.7). The least overcrowded areas were the more middle-class towns and districts in southern England, such as Bournemouth (0.3), Croydon (0.9) and Oxford (1.0), although some of the larger industrial cities had average rates (Manchester 2.1; Birmingham 3.7; Leeds 3.3). In rural areas, the most overcrowded districts

39. Bowley, *Housing*, pp. 152–9; Richardson and Aldcroft, *Building*, pp. 181–2; Marshall, 'Pattern', App. B.
40. Richardson and Aldcroft, *Building*, pp. 185–6; Ministry of Health, *Report on the Overcrowding Survey in England and Wales 1936* (1936), pp. v, x, xvi.

were likely to be mining areas, again in the north-east, such as Norham (Northumberland, 22.2) or Chester-le-Street (Durham, 13.2).[41] In Scotland, local rates of overcrowding were much higher. In Lanarkshire (outside the burghs), 36.8 per cent of families were overcrowded; in Coatbridge and Motherwell over 40 per cent; in Clydebank (Glasgow), 44.9, and in Edinburgh 17 per cent.[42]

Since the problem of overcrowding was largely coterminous with that of the slums, most overcrowding was dealt with as part of slum clearance programmes. The degree to which actual overcrowding was relieved is thus unclear. Bowley thought that by 1938 overcrowding had reduced by one-third. In Scotland little progress had been made; by the end of 1938 only 34,500 families, or about 13 per cent of the total, had been removed from overcrowded houses. The slower progress in Scotland was due to the fact that the overcrowding had been due, not to the large size of families (as in England and Wales), but to the small size of dwellings; thus merely moving families out would not solve the problem.[43]

FLAT-DWELLING

A feature of the public housing programmes of the interwar period was a revived interest in flat-dwelling. By the end of the 1920s, the flat had, in architectural and housing reform circles, lost the opprobrious connotation of the pre-1914 working-class tenement. Influenced by continental examples (notably the Viennese experiment of the 1920s), architects became interested in large schemes of flats. This interest was boosted by the extra subsidy available under the Greenwood Act, which became attractive to local authorities after the Wheatley subsidy was withdrawn in 1933.[44]

The move towards flats in England was most pronounced in London and Liverpool, where flats constituted 40 and 20 per cent respectively of all new local authority housing between the wars. Manchester built over 9,000, Liverpool over 5,000, Leeds nearly 1,000, and Newcastle over 500 flats. In London, lofty blocks towered over the former slums in areas such as Southwark, Lambeth, Shoreditch and Wandsworth. The most spectacular single block was the Quarry Hill estate in Leeds (938 flats). Some of the local authority flats were showpieces, but, being usually built in blocks of up to five or six storeys high, usually without lifts, and relying for the most part on solid fuel fires, some were little better than the nineteenth-century workers' tenements erected by private

41. Ministry of Health, *Report on the Overcrowding Survey in England and Wales* (1936), Tables IX–XI; G.D.H. Cole and M. Cole, *The Condition of Britain* (Gollancz 1937), pp. 161–5.
42. C.L. Mowat, *Britain between the Wars* (Methuen 1955; repr. 1968), p. 510, quoting Political and Economic Planning, *Report on British Health Services* (1937), p. 36.
43. Bowley, *Housing*, pp. 151, 160–1, 265; Richardson and Aldcroft, *Building*, pp. 185–7.
44. A. Ravetz, 'From Working-Class Tenement to Modern Flat: local authorities and multi-storey housing between the wars', in A. Sutcliffe (ed.), *Multi-Storey Living: the British working-class experience* (Beckenham, Croom Helm 1974), pp. 133–6; Bowley, *Housing*, p. 136.

philanthropy such as those of the Peabody or Guinness housing trusts. In Scotland, the tenement building was still popular. In the interwar period, 25,537 tenement buildings were built by Glasgow Corporation and a further 15,552 'flatted houses' (small blocks, usually containing four flats) were provided out of the total of 49,366 houses built by the corporation in 1919–39.[45]

THE HOUSING BOOM OF THE 1930S

The housing boom of the 1930s was a much stronger movement than the 1920s housebuilding. Between 1920 and 1939, 3,977,700 houses were built in England and Wales, of which 2,723,200 (68.7 per cent) were built after 1929; 2,079,100 of the latter (76.3 per cent) were built by private enterprise. The reasons for the housing boom are still debated. On the side of demand may be adduced the housing shortage, the rise in real incomes, the availability of finance, population movements, and changes in tastes; on the side of supply may be adduced the fall in costs, together with the ability of builders to provide a suitable product.[46]

There is no doubt that there still existed a housing shortage at the end of the 1920s. Housebuilding in the 1920s had failed to keep pace with the rise in the number of families, and those seeking separate accommodation. One estimate of the rise in the number of UK families between 1920 and 1929 is 1,898,000, yet only 1,623,000 houses were built in the UK in those years.

In the early 1930s, the cost of housebuilding came down. Maywald's index of building costs shows them as falling from 1925, chiefly due to falling materials prices; after 1927, wages costs also fell. The fall in costs accelerated after 1929, so that the total index fell by 8.5 per cent between 1925 and 1928, and 10 per cent between 1930 and 1933. By then, the overall index stood at 90.0 (1930 = 100), having been 111.1 in 1925. In effect, therefore, housebuilding costs had fallen since 1925 by some 19 per cent. After 1934, costs began to rise, and rose faster in 1936–37, but this seems to have had little effect on the rate of building. In 1934, 336,700 houses were built in Britain, but in 1935–38 an average of 359,000 a year were built.[47]

The fall in costs may be taken in conjunction with the continuing rise in real incomes for those in work. This had antedated the depression, and continued in the 1930s. The fall in the cost of living in the early 1930s raised real incomes further. A rough estimate of weekly real wage earnings (1925 = 100) suggests that they had risen to 106 by 1929, and to 118 by 1936.[48]

45. Mowat, *Britain*, p. 512; Ravetz, 'Working-Class Tenement', pp. 141–3; Burnett, *Housing*, pp. 239–42; T. Brennan, *Reshaping a City* (Glasgow, House of Grant 1959), p. 37.
46. Bowley, *Housing*, p. 271, Table 2.
47. Mitchell, *Statistics*, pp. 390, 394; Richardson and Aldcroft, *Building*, pp. 52, 75, 86, 251.
48. Calculated from C.H. Feinstein, *National Income, Expenditure and Output of the United Kingdom, 1855–1965* (Cambridge UP 1972), Table 140. Feinstein's indices were based on 1913 = 100, and have been rebased as 1925 = 100 here. See also notes to Feinstein, Table 141.

Since housebuilding was (and is) an activity which depends crucially on the rate of interest, from the point of view of both the housebuyer and housebuilder, it is also possible that the boom owed much to the policy of 'cheap money'. While it is unlikely that the boom was initiated by the sharp reduction in Bank Rate from 6 per cent to 2 per cent between February and June 1932, it is likely that cheap money sustained the boom thereafter. Low interest rates reduced the cost of purchase, increased the attraction of buying houses as an investment to rent out, and eased the availability of finance for the builder, as well as raising builders' profits.[49]

The fall in the capital cost of a house and of the mortgage interest rates translated into reduced weekly mortgage payments for the housebuyer. The fall in capital and mortgage costs (for an average three-bedroomed house) from £510 in 1925 to £361 in 1934 implied a fall in weekly payments from 12s. 1d. to 7s. 10d. (35 per cent) on a typical twenty-year mortgage worth 70 per cent of the house value.[50]

Prior to the boom, building societies seldom advanced more than 75 or 80 per cent of the purchase price of a house; the rest had to be found as a deposit by the purchaser. In the 1930s, societies found ways to reduce this. Sometimes the society would advance a higher proportion of the price. But the most important innovation was the 'builders' pool', an arrangement under which the society advanced up to 95 per cent of the purchase price, finding the difference partly through its own resources, and partly by the builder putting up some cash as collateral. In effect, the system was a joint effort by builders and building societies to stimulate the flow of new business. By 1938 the system was so widespread that up to half the business of some large societies was on the pool basis.[51]

Societies also encouraged buyers by extending the repayment period from a maximum of twenty years to twenty-five years or even longer. By the middle of the decade, houses worth £500 could be purchased with a down-payment of £25–£50, and the weekly cost of mortgages had fallen to bring them within the reach of the upper-working class; the monthly payments of one large London society (presumably the Abbey Road) fell from £4 17s. 6d. in 1932 to £3 13s. 10d. by 1936, a decline of 20 per cent for most income groups.[52]

Building societies were the novel element in house purchase finance. Whereas in 1929 the societies had £268.1 million outstanding on mortgages, this had

49. E. Nevin, *The Mechanism of Cheap Money: a study of British monetary policy 1931–1939* (Cardiff, University of Wales Press 1955), pp. 275–81; Richardson and Aldcroft, *Building*, pp. 201–4, Tables 1, 4.

50. Bowley, *Building*, p. 278.

51. Richardson and Aldcroft, *Building*, pp. 205–7; (Sir) H. Bellman, *The Thrifty Thirty-Three Millions: a study of the building society movement and the story of the Abbey Road Society* (1935), pp. 125, 127, 130–1; A.T.K. Grant, *A Study of the Capital Market in Britain from 1919–1936* (Cass 1967), pp. 245–6; Bowley, *Housing*, p. 175.

52. Richardson and Aldcroft, *Building*, Table 6, p. 205; H. Bellman, 'The Building Trades', in British Association, *Britain in Recovery* (Pitman 1938), p. 429.

risen to £686.8 million in 1938. New mortgages amounted to £74.7 million in 1929 and £137.0 million in 1938. Societies benefited from cheap money by keeping their deposit and share interest rates comparatively high, thus stimulating the inflow of investors' funds. Nor were the societies the only finance agents for house purchase, although they were by far the most important. There were banks (who also lent to builders), insurance companies, property companies and private individuals (and sometimes local authorities), whose contribution cannot be quantified with any certainty, but yet played a role in the finance of the housing boom.[53]

Finally, the investment market for houses picked up in the 1930s, as interest rates and building costs fell, but house rents continued to rise. Thus investment in housing to rent became more attractive. In addition, the yields from Consols, bank deposits, foreign investments and the stock market fell (or became more uncertain) relative to the potential return from property. Thus building to let became more attractive; between October 1933 and March 1939, 351,131 houses were built for letting by private enterprise, accounting for 28.0 per cent of all the houses built by private enterprise.[54]

Interwar population movements played their part in the boom, which was heavily concentrated regionally, depending on the degree of regional economic buoyancy. The outstanding expansion was in the south-east region: between 1918 and 1940 houses built were 76.2 per cent of the number of houses occupied in 1921. The only other region where housebuilding amounted to more than half the 1921 housing stock was the midlands. Wales had a notably low proportion (28.5 per cent). For England and Wales as a whole, the proportion was 53.6 per cent. It was not so much interregional population movements which accounted for the preponderance of south-eastern building, but the shifts in population within the region, notably the expansion of the counties nearest London, as the suburbs and housing estates developed. Thus Surrey, Hertfordshire and Middlesex built more houses in 1918–40 than had been occupied in 1921. Outside the south-east, the depressed regions and the rural counties hardly participated in the boom at all, reflecting depressed older industries and agriculture, and low incomes generally.[55]

In effect, the housing boom may be considered as the expresion of changing tastes. Bellman wrote that the driving force had been 'an almost revolutionary conception of what are tolerable housing standards among a vast section of the population', adding 'It is undoubtedly the womenfolk who are the motive force behind this changed conception of housing standards'.[56] Thus lower-income consumers were demanding more spacious accommodation; the more well-off required houses which were more economical to run in an age of higher taxation and fewer resident domestic servants. Both groups

53. Bellman, *Thirty-Three Millions*, p. 139; Richardson and Aldcroft, *Building*, Table 6, pp. 53–4; Grant, *Capital Market*, pp. 240–3.
54. Richardson and Aldcroft, *Building*, p. 102; Marshall, 'Pattern', Table II.
55. Marshall, 'Pattern', Table I, App. A.
56. Bellman, 'Building Trades', pp. 432–3.

Table 9.1 Housebuilding in Britain, 1919–39

	England & Wales	*Scotland*	*Great Britain*
Houses built 1919–39 by			
Local authorities	1,112,505	212,866	1,325,371
Subsidised private enterprise	430,327	43,067	473,394
Unsubsidised private enterprise	2,449,216	61,444	2,510,660
Totals	3,992,048	317,377	4,309,425
Houses in 1911	7,691,000	1,010,531	8,701,531
Houses built 1919–39 as % of 1911	51.9	31.4	49.5

Sources: Royal Commission on the Distribution of the Industrial Population, *Report* (1940), Cmd 6153, p. 67; Census of England and Wales 1931, *Housing Report* (1935), p. x; Census of Scotland 1931, vol. II (1933), p. xlii

wished to benefit from the domestic freedom to be had by the use of electricity; both also wished to take advantage of motor and improved rail transport so as to be able to live further away from their work, in more agreeable surroundings. As the advertising of one London builder put it:

> Live in Ruislip where the air's like wine,
> It's less than half an hour on the Piccadilly Line.[57]

Both therefore underpinned the overwhelmingly suburban nature of the 1930s housing boom. But it was the changes in real income and the relative cost of housing which permitted the realisation of these aspirations, and this was a process shared very unevenly over the whole of Britain.

In quantitative terms, the interwar housebuilding was very substantial (Table 9.1 above).

Thus, had there occurred no demolition, there would have been about 13 million houses in Britain in 1939. However, roughly 700,000 were demolished between the wars, so that there were in 1939 some 12.3 million, of which about 35 per cent had been built since 1918.[58] (Demolitions, especially in the 1920s, can only be estimated, and this is a high estimate; Richardson and Aldcroft estimate 548,000 for the UK in 1922–38.)[59]

The extent to which interwar building reduced the housing problem which existed before 1914 is uncertain. There is agreement that by 1931 the problem was much worse than it had been before 1914. Bowley estimated an additional shortage of 479,000 houses in England and Wales by 1931; Richardson and Aldcroft estimated 1,044,000 in the UK. In the 1930s, the shortfall was reduced. By 1938, there were an extra 1,676,000 families in the UK since 1931, and an

57. Quoted in A.A. Jackson, *Semi-Detached London* (Allen & Unwin 1973), p. 204.
58. R.L. Reiss, *Municipal and Private Enterprise Housing* (Dent 1945), pp. 15–16.
59. Richardson and Aldcroft, *Building*, pp. 60–1.

extra 2,528,000 houses had been built, so that the pre-1930s shortage had been reduced by 852,000. Thus, compared to 1914, the absolute shortage had either been reduced or was somewhat worse, depending on which estimate of previous shortage is accepted.[60]

However, even assuming that the interwar building kept the relative degree of shortage in 1914 from getting worse, it had been unbalanced. After 1918, it was realised that the great shortage was of cheaply rentable accommodation; this had been the reason for retaining rent control after the war. By 1937, rent control had been to some extent withdrawn from the more expensive houses, but still covered 44.1 per cent of the houses in Britain, and the relative shortage of affordable accommodation meant that rents in uncontrolled properties were about 50 per cent above those of controlled properties.[61] Most of the new houses built (which were not subject to rent control) had been in the higher, rather than the lower rateable bands. In England and Wales, 41.6 per cent of all new houses were in the lowest (working-class) rateable band, yet in 1914 this band had accounted for 67.6 per cent of all the existing houses.[62]

In practice, the provision of housing for the poorer-paid was done largely by local authorities; 1,393,000 houses had been built by them to rent, but private enterprise built only about 850,000 for renting. For the families of the skilled working class, whose income was less than £5 a week, local authority housing may have provided about 60 per cent of their housing needs; for the less skilled, with an income of less than £3 a week, local authority housing probably accounted for almost 90 per cent of their housing.[63]

Thus the interwar housebuilding, although probably restoring the overall degree of shortage to no more than the pre-1914 level, failed in accommodating the lowest-paid people and their families, who had to rely on controlled tenancies, and lost the protection of rent control if they moved house. On the other hand, the overall quality of the housing stock improved. The postwar houses were of higher relative quality, as measured by rateable value; in 1919, it is estimated that 67.6 per cent of the houses in England and Wales were in the lowest rateable band (below £14); in 1939 the proportion was 59.3 per cent. Nor is there much doubt that the new houses were better equipped, having indoor sanitation, fixed baths and electricity; this was also true of older houses improved by local authorities. But the slum clearance programme had revealed how much needed still to be done; in the mid-1930s, about 3 million houses were more than eighty years old, and even by contemporary standards, between one-third and one-half of the houses in the larger cities (Manchester, Glasgow, Liverpool, Birmingham, Leeds) could be classified as slums.[64]

60. Bowley, *Housing*, p. 269; Richardson and Aldcroft, *Building*, p. 172.
61. *Report of the Inter-Departmental Committee on the Rents Restrictions Acts* (Ridley Committee) (1937), Cmd 5621, pp. 16–17.
62. Bowley, *Housing*, p. 273.
63. Reiss, *Municipal and Private*, pp. 68–9.
64. Glynn and Oxborrow, *Interwar Britain*, p. 235; Richardson and Aldcroft, *Building*, p. 180.

Although the national level of provision of basic amenities is uncertain, it was estimated that in Britain in 1944 50 per cent of the working classes and 14 per cent of the middle classes had no indoor sanitation. Scattered local evidence suggests that for Britain as a whole, roughly about one-third of the population did not have bathrooms; in 1947, a national survey indicated that 13 per cent of all urban households had no bath of any sort, while 29 per cent had only portable baths. In rural areas, provision was undoubtedly worse, since mains water was rarer. The Ministry of Health estimated that about 30 per cent of the rural population of England and Wales lacked a mains water supply at the end of the 1930s, and nearly half the rural households in Britain lacked a bathroom and fixed bath in 1947.[65]

OWNER-OCCUPANCY

In the interwar period, there was a large rise in the proportion of houses owned by their occupiers. This had been exceptional in 1914. It is commonly stated (although on no very precise grounds) that on the eve of the First World War only 10 per cent of the housing stock of Britain was owner-occupied. Working-class ownership was most usually found in certain industrial towns, such as the cotton towns of Lancashire, mining regions in south Wales, shipbuilding towns such as Jarrow, some Yorkshire woollen districts, and some south-east London suburbs. Middle-class ownership was more often found in large towns which had suburban areas newly developed by speculative builders. Thus, for example, Cardiff had an average level of ownership of 7.2 per cent, but in the new middle-class districts to the east and west of the city it was 25 per cent.[66]

Nationally, in 1938, the level of ownership is estimated to have risen to 'somewhat below 35 per cent'. An analysis of the probable distribution of home-ownership in 1938 gives some idea of how this sudden rise had occurred (Table 9.2 opposite).

From this, it seems that home-ownership was much more common in postwar than prewar housing, and was more common in the more expensive properties. The lowest band of gross value corresponded closely to working-class housing, so that the home-ownership movement of 1919–39 seems to have passed by most of the working class. To obtain a house costing £500–600 with a building society mortgage in 1939, the minimum income would have been £3 8s. 9d. a week, thus confining the process to the lower-middle class and the very top echelons of the working class. Such a mortgage involved outgoings of £1 0s. 5d. a week, fitting in well with the contemporary view that house-owning involved an outlay of at least £1 a week. For the skilled working-class household to take on such a commitment was possible, but only with self-

65. Glynn and Oxborrow, *Interwar Britain*, pp. 236–44, using data in R.M. Titmuss, *Problems of Social Policy* (*HSWW*, HMSO 1950), pp. 131–2, 177n. 3.
66. M. Swenarton and S. Taylor, 'The Scale and Nature of the Growth of Owner-Occupation in Britain between the Wars', *EcHR* XXXVIII (1985), pp. 374–80.

Table 9.2 Estimated distribution of home-ownership in Britain, 1938

		Percentage owner-occupied		
Gross value (£pa)	*Purchase price (£)*	*Prewar dwellings (%)*	*Postwar dwellings (%)*	*All dwellings (%)*
Under 20.5	Up to 417	17.2	24.5	19.0
20.5–40	417–816	38.8	60.3	50.5
40–60	816–1,224	62.8	84.7	72.0
60–100	1,224–2,040	74.1	87.9	78.5
Over 100	Over 2,040	79.3	91.0	81.3
	Average	27.1	49.1	35.0

Notes: 'Gross value' = estimated annual rent, including repairs, insurance, etc. The GV has been roughly converted to a 1938 purchase price. The data on which the table was based cover only about 73 per cent of British dwellings, excluding tenements and flats; since these were less likely to be owned than houses, the national ownership figure must have been less than 35 per cent, though it is unlikely to have been much less

Source: M. Swenarton and S. Taylor, 'The Scale and Nature of the Growth of Owner-Occupation in Britain between the Wars', *EcHR* XXXVIII (1985), p. 383

sacrifice and thrift – not unusually it involved taking in a lodger. Building societies promulgated a 'safe rule' that total outgoings on house purchase, including rates (3s. to 6s. weekly on a small to medium house) should not exceed one-quarter of net income. It was therefore highly unlikely that anyone earning less than around £3 to £3 10s. a week would be able to manage it. The evidence is overwhelming that the great majority of the new home purchasers of the interwar period came from the middle or lower-middle classes. Jackson remarks: 'It was from the salaried class earning upwards of £260 a year that the vast majority of the new London house owners came'.[67]

TOWN PLANNING

The enormous building effort which marked the interwar period was largely unplanned and unregulated. This was the more remarkable, since the first Town Planning Act dated from 1909. Further Acts followed in 1919 and 1925. The last prewar Act was that of 1932, which attempted to make up for the deficiencies of former ones by conferring the force of law on town-planning regulations made by the Ministry of Health. By April 1939, approved planning schemes covered 1,093,785 acres. However, town planning had had very little effect before the outbreak of the Second World War.

67. Swenarton and Taylor, 'Owner-Occupation', p. 185; Jackson, *Semi-Detached*, pp. 190–2.

The result was a spate of inappropriate development which came in many forms, not least the comparatively new phenomenon of 'ribbon' development, in which a major road leading out of a city became lined with shops, factories and houses; the spaces between these outgoing arteries remained undeveloped and marginalised. This situation was not alleviated by the Restriction of Ribbon Development Act 1935. The reasons for failure were various. The Ministry of Health exercised little positive direction, and there were many local authorities, from county councils down to rural district councils, with town planning functions. In the London Transport area alone, there were 133 different authorities exercising planning functions, and there was little coordination between those planning new developments and those responsible for new road and rail services, with the single exception of the London County Council (LCC). As Ashworth observed:

> Whatever changes took place after 1918 in the statutory basis and in the concept of town planning, there was very little change in its practice. Almost everywhere the period saw an enormous multiplication of the low-density residential suburbs which had been the admired symbol of statutory town planning in its original form, and this happened whether the districts concerned were subject to town-planning control or not.[68]

HOUSING ESTATES AND TRADING ESTATES

The novel social feature of interwar housing was the housing estate. By 1939, several million people lived on them. The estates were largely provided by local authorities for working-class tenants. Middle-class development tended to be either in a small-scale 'ribbon development' along a main or suburban road, or in small groups of houses. Some of the council estates, however, were enormous. The greatest was Becontree, which had 90,000 residents by 1934, and was the largest planned residential suburb in the world. There were many other smaller ones, such as the Watling estate, near Hendon (Middlesex), with a population of 4,000. The LCC alone built about 61,000 'cottages' (small houses) and flats on fifteen estates in the interwar period, of which 26,000 were at Becontree. Outside the immediate LCC area, the county and municipal boroughs built many thousands of houses. The largest single venture was Croydon's New Addington Estate, with a planned total of 4,000 houses, of which 1,000 had been completed by 1939.[69]

There is no doubt that the majority of council tenants approved of their new accommodation.[70] As one tenant said:

68. W. Ashworth, *The Genesis of Modern British Town Planning* (Routledge & Kegan Paul 1954), p. 207.
69. Young, *Becontree and Dagenham*; Burnett, *Housing*, p. 231; Jackson, *Semi-Detached*, pp. 162–5.
70. See A. Rubinstein, A. Andrews and P. Schweitzer, *Just Like the Country: memories of London families who settled the new cottage estates 1919–1939* (Age Exchange 1991).

> The thing that pleased us most when we first moved here was to have a house of our own, with electric light and a bathroom and scullery with running water. We'd been in two rooms in Bethnal Green, with a tap and W.C. three flights down and shared with two other families. . . . I thought [the new house] was just like a palace.[71]

This satisfaction was confirmed in a survey by Mass-Observation just before the Second World War; of the many types of working class housing examined, satisfaction was greatest with the housing estate, and lowest with privately rented older houses. Even at Becontree-Dagenham, which the authors of the report described as a one-class suburb 'devoid of imagination', where 'a hundred thousand people have been dumped down', 85 per cent of tenants liked their houses, 62 per cent liked the neighbourhood, and 14 per cent wanted to own their own houses.[72] On the other hand, there were disadvantages. There was little accommodation for single people or for unusually large families, so that overcrowding was not absent from the new estates. The *Overcrowding Survey* of England and Wales in 1936 revealed that 5.1 per cent of council housing was overcrowded, but only 3.7 per cent of privately owned housing.[73] Social facilities were often inadequate; especially in the early days of construction, schools and shops were rare. Even when estates were completed, there was usually a lack of local employment, so that men and women had to commute to work, very often back to the inner-city neighbourhood which they had left in the first place. For Becontree, employment prospects were transformed by the opening of Ford's Dagenham factory in 1932, but few estates had such luck. On the Watling estate (Hendon) in 1937, only 26 per cent of the tenants worked in Hendon; 50 per cent worked in inner London.[74] Nor was there much for adolescents to do, and public houses were rare. In Glasgow, the city corporation was prohibited from selling alcohol on its property; thus the thousands of estate dwellers by 1939 had to do their drinking elsewhere.

The greatest criticism from a social point of view is that the new council housing did not serve well the poorest groups in society, who tended to be paying disproportionate rents in the inner cities. Because councils feared rent arrears, they preferred to rent to the upper strata of the working class. When tenants had moved from poor inner-city accommodation to the new estates, they usually paid more in rent than before, and thus went into debt. Finally, when more successful efforts were made in the later 1930s to move erstwhile slum dwellers out to the new suburban estates, the older-established families tried to move out.[75]

71. Burnett, *Housing*, p. 231, quoting from P. Willmott, *The Evolution of a Community* (1963).
72. Burnett, *Housing*, p. 232, quoting a Mass-Observation report, *An Enquiry into People's Homes* (1943).
73. Ministry of Health, *Overcrowding Survey of England and Wales* (1936), Table XIV.
74. R. Durant, *Watling: a survey of social life on a new housing estate* (P.S. King 1939), p. 9.
75. D.C. Jones (ed.), *The Social Survey of Merseyside*, vol. I (1934), pp. 277–80, 283; R. Jevons and J. Madge, *Housing Estates: a study of Bristol Corporation policy and practice between the wars* (Bristol, Arrowsmith 1946), pp. 44, 68–70.

An aspect of suburban development which received a boost in the interwar years was the development of the 'trading estate', usually run by a commercial company, providing industrial premises and necessary services. The oldest one, Trafford Park (Manchester), dating from 1896, had by 1939 some 200 firms, providing work for 50,000. The greatest of the post-1918 developments was at Slough, where the trading estate had by 1939 210 firms, providing 28,500 jobs, with considerable welfare facilities. The success of the estate helped Slough to grow from a population of 20,285 in 1921 to 50,620 in 1938 – although the insufficiency of housing meant that many workers had to commute in each day. A later development was the use of trading estates in the Special Areas, the most notable of which were Team Valley (Gateshead, County Durham) and Treforest (Cardiff), which employed 2,520 and 1,870 in May 1939.[76]

Both housing estates and trading estates tended to suffer from imbalance – a deficiency of either jobs or housing. The garden city movement attempted to avoid this problem, in pursuance of its ideal of providing healthy and pleasant living and working conditions. The first garden city had been Letchworth (Hertfordshire) in 1903; by 1938 the population was about 17,400. In 1920 the second, Welwyn Garden City, was established nearby, and had a population of 15,000 in 1939, of whom more than one-quarter were employed locally. A sort of suburban garden city was tried by Manchester Corporation, at Wythenshawe, but, although it developed rapidly in the 1930s, having 7,649 houses in March 1939, it provided few jobs. The largest and most successful attempt to marry houses and jobs was in Cadbury's company housing at Bournville (Birmingham); this expanded greatly after 1918, and by 1939 had 2,400 houses.[77]

CONCLUSIONS

Between the wars, the state intervened for the first time on a large scale in the provision of housing for the British people. The result was the creation of a new social form, the local authority housing estate; the improvement of a large part of the national housing stock; the reduction of the slums. In addition, the period was a buoyant one for private housebuilding and owning. The more rapid rate of interwar housebuilding generally made it easier to improve the housing amenities enjoyed by the population as a whole. Thus a higher proportion of households had the benefits of piped water, indoor sanitation, and light and power provided by electricity and gas. Even so, the quality of much older urban housing remained poor, rural areas had generally poor housing and amenities, and the slums were by no means vanquished.

76. Royal Commission on the Distribution of the Industrial Population, *Report* (1940), Cmd 6153, paras 283–7. The Slough population is from Jackson, *Semi-Detached*, p. 328. The comment on Slough housing is from Richardson and Aldcroft, *Building*, p. 314.
77. Royal Commission on Distribution of Industrial Population, *Report*, pp. 280–2; Richardson and Aldcroft, *Building*, p. 314.

CHAPTER 10

LEISURE BETWEEN THE WARS

The reduction in the working week, the slow rise in living standards, and the growth of holidays with pay meant, at least for those in employment, an increase in the demand for ways of filling 'leisure' time. ('Leisure' is understood in this chapter to mean the occupations and amusements of people when not at (legitimate) work.) In addition, technological change offered new avenues of amusement and pleasure.

SPECTATOR SPORTS

Pre-eminent among the organised leisure activities were the mass spectator sports such as football, rugby, cricket, hockey, and racing. Association football was by far the biggest. Already a major activity before 1914, it was growing even larger between the wars. In 1908–9, English First Division League matches had been watched by 6 million people, with an average crowd size of 16,000; by 1937–38, there were 14 million spectators, with an average crowd size of 30,000. Almost exclusively a male pastime, it was strongest in lowland Scotland, northern and midland England, and to a lesser extent London, whose clubs, especially Arsenal, achieved national repute in the 1930s. A notable landmark was the first radio broadcast of a football match (Arsenal v. Sheffield United at Highbury) on 22 January 1927. Attendance at all forms of League matches probably peaked in the late 1930s at around 40 million.[1]

Rugby League (especially strong in Yorkshire and Lancashire) and Rugby Union (stronger in southern England, and ousting football as the game for public schoolboys) were also expanding, but more slowly, and probably accounted for about 5 million spectators each by the late 1930s. Wales was notable for its enthusiasm for Rugby Union, but the game was badly hit by the decline of the coal industry after the First World War; the crowds were still large, but the best players were tempted away by offers from the Rugby League clubs.[2]

1. H. Cunningham, 'Leisure and Culture', in F.M.L. Thompson (ed.), *The Cambridge Social History of Britain* (*CSH*) (Cambridge UP 1990), vol. 2, pp. 314–15.
2. H. Durant, *The Problem of Leisure* (George Routledge 1938), pp. 156–7; R. Holt, *Sport and the British: a modern history* (Oxford, Clarendon 1989), pp. 248–52.

Cricket presented many paradoxes. As a national game, it was essentially an English sport, having much less of a Scottish or Welsh following. In addition, it was, in the upper echelons, a notably elite affair, dominated by the Marylebone Cricket Club (MCC), whose members came from the top social ranks. Yet the game spanned the class divide in a more effective way than some of the other large spectator sports, having a large middle-class and working-class following. Nor, although strongest there, was it confined to southern England. Two of the largest county clubs were Lancashire and Yorkshire. Their style differed from that of the southern counties; the doyen of twentieth-century cricketing journalists, Neville Cardus, contrasted the 'dour, shrewd' ways of north-country cricketers with the 'suburban and genteel' flavour of southern cricket.[3]

Fewer spectators watched cricket than football or rugby, and interwar gate numbers were probably much less than the probable twentieth-century peak for county matches of around 2 million in the late 1940s. In the 1930s, declining gates caused several counties financial embarrassment. Attendances in different counties varied markedly. In 1926, nearly 326,000 people paid to watch Yorkshire's home matches (the county's highest interwar attendance), and in 1935, nearly 183,000. Those for Essex in the same seasons almost certainly did not exceed 40,000 and 22,000.[4] However, it is possible that numbers watching non-first-class games were even larger than those coming to county matches. At the national level, interest in the Test matches reached great heights, spurred by newspaper reporting and BBC commentaries; Howard Marshall's coverage of the 1934 Test made his voice one of the best known in Britain.[5]

The mass spectator sports were mainly male preserves. The only field game which had even before the war had a high proportion of female players was hockey. Between the wars, some success was had in reviving women's cricket, with the formation of the Women's Cricket Association in 1926, but the sport was largely confined to former public school pupils, and there were probably no more than fifty active women's clubs. Lancashire and Yorkshire were particularly active in women's cricket in the 1930s, both having county federations of women's clubs.[6]

TENNIS AND GOLF

Female participation in games was more promoted between the wars by the rapid growth of lawn tennis and golf. In 1920 the Lawn Tennis Association had 423 associated clubs, and this had risen by 1938 to 3,220. Tennis could be played on the rising number of suburban club courts, the lawns of large

3. N. Cardus, *Autobiography* (Readers Union/Collins 1949), p. 153.
4. Holt, *Sport*, p. 178; J. Williams, 'Cricket', in T. Mason (ed.), *Sport in Britain: a social history* (Cambridge UP 1989), pp. 116–21; Cardus, *Autobiography*, p. 153.
5. Williams, 'Cricket', p. 121; A. Briggs, *The History of Broadcasting in the United Kingdom, vol. II, The Golden Age of Wireless* (Oxford UP 1965), p. 120.
6. Holt, *Sport*, p. 129; Williams, 'Cricket', pp. 140–1.

private houses, or the newly built municipal courts (whether grass or asphalt). The tennis club became part of the normal fabric of middle-class suburban life, and a popular way for young men to meet young women. The high level of female participation aroused great interest, especially in the matter of dress; Miss Tomblin became the first lady to play tournament tennis in shorts at Chiswick in 1932. Nationally, the Wimbledon championships retained their social and professional cachet, being boosted by the opening of the new courts in 1922. The Wimbledon championships were broadcast by wireless in 1927, and televised in 1937.[7]

Golf was already well established by 1914, when there were 1,224 clubs in Britain. The interwar period added another 373, of which 252 were founded in the 1920s. By the end of the decade, total club membership may have been about 352,000. Cheap agricultural land was one factor in this expansion; the growth of the suburbs another. As Richard Holt has written:

> In the Home Counties, in particular, the golf club helped consolidate the new routines of suburban life. Its trees, fairways, and greens epitomized *rus in urbe*. Calling in at 'the club' for tea or a drink after the shopping or a drive in the car was part of a new middle-class style of life.[8]

A notable feature of golf, as tennis, was its almost exclusively middle-class nature. Most clubs were firmly barred to working-class players, partly out of a desire to maintain social exclusiveness, and partly due to the high cost of the joining fees and annual subscriptions. Although an Artisan Golfers' Association was founded in 1921, and boasted 15,000 members by 1937, its progress was severely limited by the lack of municipal courses. Unlike Scotland, where they were comparatively common, London had only two municipal courses by 1929, which were badly overcrowded. The other notable feature was the game's accessibility to women, either in their own right or as associates of their husbands. In addition, there was the (prewar) Ladies' Golf Union. Within clubs, women led a quasi-segregated existence, both socially and sportingly, although the extension of handicapping encouraged the sexes to play together. The liberalisation of dress codes after the First World War was a great encouragement to women's golf, and culminated in the first appearance of a woman in trousers at a championship, in 1934.[9]

HORSES, GREYHOUNDS AND FISHING

Team games apart, the only other activity which generated mass audiences from all social classes was horse racing. Apart from those who travelled widely

7. A.H. Halsey (ed.), *Trends in British Society since 1900* (Macmillan 1972), p. 562; H. Walker, 'Lawn Tennis', in Mason, *Sport in Britain*, pp. 250, 261–5.
8. Holt, *Sport*, p. 133.
9. J. Lowerson, 'Golf', in Mason, *Sport in Britain*, pp. 188, 201–9; A. A. Jackson, *The Middle Classes, 1900–1950* (Nairn, David St John Thomas 1991), p. 288; Holt, *Sport*, p. 132.

to race meetings, there were the very large crowds which assembled intermittently for the Derby or Grand National, at which numbers could exceed a quarter of a million. As an essential topic of male pub conversation, it was exceeded in importance only by the fortunes of the local football team. Enjoying something of a boom after 1918, its image was marred by a rise in on-course robbery and violence, which led to the Jockey Club instituting its own effective policing arrangements on courses in 1925. But in the 1930s the industry did not keep up with the expectations of the consumers; an internal Jockey Club inquiry of 1943 revealed antiquated courses, often with poor catering and betting facilities – the latter only marginally improved by the introduction of totalisator betting in 1929.[10]

Smaller audiences, but with many more meetings per year, were provided by the novelty of greyhound racing, which suddenly sprang to prominence in the 1920s. Two notable constructions were the tracks at Belle Vue, Manchester (1926) and White City, London (1927). In 1927 alone, sixty-two companies with a capital of £7 million were registered for greyhound racing, and by 1932 the annual attendance at licensed tracks in London alone had risen to 6.5 million. In Scotland, it was by the late 1930s the second most popular spectator sport after football, with big tracks in all the major cities. In addition, there were makeshift local tracks in and around many smaller cities and towns. Less organised, but very popular in mining villages, was whippet racing, but even this was slowly giving way to the larger greyhound in the 1930s. Dog racing owed its popularity to cheap or free admission (the owners being satisfied with profits from the totalisator), the fact that it took place in the evenings after the working day was over, and that the tracks were more easily reached than horse-racing courses.[11]

Only one other sport could be labelled 'mass entertainment', although not attracting large audiences – fishing. While the upper and middle classes retained their interest in 'game' trout and salmon fishing, usually on expensively rented stretches of rivers such as the Hampshire Test or the Spey in Scotland, other types of fish provided the 'coarse' fishing beloved of the urban worker. The two great coarse 'angling' centres were London and Sheffield. Regional match fishing competitions were keenly contested. The full number of anglers in Britain is not known, but it must have been in the millions, even if many did not belong to clubs. In 1931, there were 13,510 club members in Birmingham alone. Unemployment in the 1920s cut down some clubs, but new ones were founded, not least those sponsored by the new car firms in the midlands, and they became as solid a symbol of worker pride as the works brass band had formerly been. In fact, while recession cut down the travel to matches, it probably promoted angling for unemployed people, at least on waters easily

10. Holt, *Sport*, p. 181; B.S. Rowntree, *Poverty and Progress: a second social survey of York* (Longmans, Green 1941), p. 359; W. Vamplew, 'Horse-Racing', in Mason, *Sport in Britain*, pp. 220–3.
11. Holt, *Sport*, p. 186; Durant, *Problem*, pp. 175–6.

accessible by foot or bicycle; even the Wigan of George Orwell's depressing survey could boast 1,900 anglers on its local canals.[12]

CARS AND MOTOR CYCLES

One of the greatest developments of the period was the rise in personal mobility. This was particularly marked for the middle classes, who took to the motor car with alacrity. On the eve of the war there had been 132,000 private cars in use in Britain. Numbers fell during the war, but had risen to 187,000 by 1920. By 1930 there were 1,056,000 in use. By then, it could be said that the upper-middle class and most of the middle ranks of the middle classes had been motorised. They were helped in this by the decline in the cost of cars, which continued after the initial postwar deflation had ended. The average price of cars has been estimated at £684 in 1920, but only £294 in 1929. The price of motor cycles and bicycles also came down substantially in the 1920s, and their use rose; the numbers of motor cycles in use peaked at 724,000 in 1930, by which time bicycle production was 635,000 a year.[13]

In the 1930s, car ownership spread further. A leading role was taken by the manufacturers, who continued to reduce their prices, as larger-scale production and amalgamations of firms led to reductions in unit costs. They were assisted by the rising real incomes of consumers, the fall in raw material costs, and the continuance of import duties. A large second-hand market also developed. The upshot was that car ownership rose sharply; by 1937 there were 1,798,000 private cars in use, but only 488,000 motor cycles.[14] Although the larger cars (14 hp and above) remained expensive, the 'baby' cars of 8–10 hp were now just within reach of the lower-middle-class singles, and those marrieds whose responsibilities allowed them to save the capital or make the hire purchase payments. The Ford 8 hp two-door Popular saloon, selling at £120 in 1933, £100 in 1936, and £125 in 1939, was much appreciated by the lower-middle class, as was the tiny 'baby Austin', first introduced in 1922 and selling at £122 in 1938; among its devotees, schoolteachers were said to be numerous.[15]

Even with the spread of car ownership, it remained a middle-class affair. Running costs were low; an 8 hp car was taxed at £8 a year in 1933, shortly afterwards reduced to £6; comprehensive insurance cost a similar amount, and petrol was slightly under 2s. a gallon. But the capital cost was a deterrent. A survey of middle-class (civil servant) incomes in 1938–39 showed that those earning £350–500 spent on average only 3s. 4d. a week on private transport (including purchase costs), which suggests that they did not run cars, and

12. J. Lowerson, 'Angling', in Mason, *Sport in Britain*, pp. 19–23.
13. B.R. Mitchell, *British Historical Statistics* (Cambridge UP 1988), p. 557; R. Stone and D.A. Rowe, *The Measurement of Consumers' Expenditure and Behaviour in the United Kingdom 1920–1938*, vol. II (Cambridge UP 1966), pp. 52, 58.
14. Mitchell, *Statistics*, p. 557.
15. Ibid., p. 557; Jackson, *Middle Classes*, pp. 104–9.

motoring did not figure at all in a national survey of working-class expenditure carried out by the Ministry of Labour in 1937–38. It seems unlikely that more than a minority of the lower-middle class ever bought a new car. For the working class it must have been a rarity.[16]

The smaller cars were probably not used for anything much more than local trips and Sunday jaunts. Annual holidays continued to be taken by rail. There were technical reasons for this. Cars were underpowered, and hills often presented an insurmountable obstacle. Breakdowns were frequent, and cars handled badly (most had steering that veered to and fro alarmingly). Night motoring was particularly perilous, not least due to the lack of road discipline, being only partly improved by the insertion of 'cats' eyes' reflectors in the road surface, and the painting of white lines down the middle of roads. Most cars did not have heaters, so winter motoring was a test of endurance. It was not until 1935 that motorists were required to take a test of aptitude to drive, or that a speed limit (of 30 m.p.h. in built-up areas) was imposed.[17]

For the middle classes, the car was soon a prime means of recreation, in the form of day excursions (perhaps with picnic), or the visit to a cinema, golf club or 'roadhouse'. The latter was a new version of the traditional roadside inn, usually situated at important road intersections, or on one of the few bypasses. With a variety of amenities, and usually in neo-Tudor style, the latter, and some of the new large 'superpubs' in the commuting regions, brought a new dimension to middle-class life.[18]

CINEMA, MUSIC HALL AND THEATRE

More wide-ranging in its appeal was that other great innovation, the cinema. It had become a mass entertainment medium before 1914, with perhaps 400 million seats filled a year, and with 4,000 cinemas. By 1934, when reliable attendance records are first obtainable, the number of admissions had more than doubled, to 903 million. By 1938 they had risen to 987 million; the cinema industry estimated its weekly admissions at 23 million. Increasingly, cinemas were purpose-built, and the smaller independent houses were now being replaced by very large cinemas, each seating about 2,000. The archetype of the large cinema buildings were the 'Odeons', which, with their streamlined curves and art deco embellishments, were the quintessence of the Modern Movement in mass architecture, and are inextricably linked to the 1930s in popular memory.[19]

16. P. Massey, 'The Expenditure of 1,360 British Middle-Class Households in 1938–39', *JRSS* CV (1942), p. 185; *Ministry of Labour Gazette* XLVIII, 12 (1940), 'Weekly Expenditure of Working-Class Households in the United Kingdom in 1937–38'.
17. W. Plowden, *The Motor Car and Politics: 1896–1970* (Bodley Head 1971), pp. 278–81.
18. Jackson, *Middle Classes*, pp. 283–6.
19. Cunningham, 'Leisure and Culture', p. 312; J. Richards, *The Age of the Dream Palace: cinema and society in Britain 1930–1939* (Routledge & Kegan Paul 1984), pp. 11, 21.

Film distribution was now partly oligopolised by two (later three) major distribution chains. The extent of 'monopoly' can be exaggerated; even in the 1930s almost two-thirds of cinemas were independent. Located mainly in urban centres, and notably absent in the new suburbs, cinemas relied on imported films from the USA, whose products were further boosted by the introduction of the 'talkies' in 1928. British films accounted for only 5 per cent of the output by 1926, and the protective legislation (Cinematograph Films Act 1927), which was to produce a rash of low-quality 'quota quickies' raised it only to 20 per cent by 1933. The industry remained dominated by films from the USA; the great age of Hollywood was coming to its peak. The 1927 Act was re-enacted in 1938, since it was apparent that the British industry could not survive unprotected, but even in the year ending in March 1939, only 16 per cent of all feature-length films shown were home-produced.[20] A not untypical programme from a London East End cinema in 1935 consisted of

> 1. NEWS REEL
> 2. MICKEY MOUSE in 'PLUTO'
> 3. 'POSSESSED' (Star – Clark Gable)
> 4. 'THE LITTLE GIANT' (Star – Edward G. Robinson)
>
> On the Stage; MASU, famous Japanese entertainer.[21]

The cheapness of the seats (ranging from 6d. to 1s.) and the fact that cinemas were open from around midday to about 11 p.m. made it easy for people to attend several times a week, regardless of age, domestic situation or working hours. In practice, the bulk of the audiences were working class, especially young males. In 1934, 43 per cent of all admissions cost less than 6d., and another 37 per cent less than 10d. In London, the cinema operators estimated that the weekly attendance in 1935 was equivalent to one-third of the entire London population. In Liverpool in 1934, it was estimated that 40 per cent of the population went to the cinema at least once a week, and about two-thirds of those (about one-quarter of the whole population) went twice or more a week.[22]

The cinema certainly provided an escape from the tedium or turmoils of daily life. In York in 1936, Seebohm Rowntree estimated that there were 50,000 attendances (from a total population of only 90,000) at the cinemas each week.

> They play a great part in relieving the monotony of countless lives. At a cost of 6d. or so a working woman, bored to death by a never-ending round of humdrum

20. Cunningham, 'Leisure and Culture', p. 332; Political and Economic Planning, *The British Film Industry* (1952), p. 82.

21. (Sir) H. Llewellyn Smith (ed.), *The New Survey of London Life and Labour*, vol. IX (1935), pp. 43–7.

22. Smith, *New Survey*, IX (1935), p. 47; D.C. Jones, *The Social Survey of Merseyside*, vol. 3 (Liverpool UP 1934), p. 281; Cunningham, 'Leisure and Culture', p. 312. See also P. Wild, 'Recreation in Rochdale, 1900–40', in C. Clarke, C. Critcher and R. Johnson, *Working-Class Culture: studies in history and theory* (Hutchinson 1979), pp. 148–58.

household chores, or a factory worker oppressed by the monotony of his work, can be transplanted, as if on a magic carpet, into a completely new world: a world of romance or high adventure.[23]

Although the cinema had been subject to censorship since 1913, when the British Board of Film Censors had been formed, its influence was still feared as having a pernicious effect on moral conduct (especially among young people). But the cinema had the merit of providing a cheap and enjoyable alternative to the public house or the race track, or even to criminal activity. It also provided an alternative for those who shrank from courting the opposite sex in the front parlour or living-room of their parents' terraced house. The new 'super-cinemas' were even provided with cafés and/or dance floors, providing further innocuous (and non-alcoholic) entertainment.[24]

The cinema competed against the established entertainments provided by the music hall and the theatre. The music hall entered on a long decline as a result; in Liverpool between 1913 and 1934, the number of cinemas rose from thirty-two to sixty-nine, while the number of theatres fell from eleven to six. Most of the theatres which closed had been music halls. The halls were more the preserve of middle-aged people and family parties (although appealing to all classes); the seating was less luxurious, and the programmes shorter than those of the cinema, although admission costs were similar. The theatre proper continued in existence, but had little appeal to working-class audiences.[25]

RADIO

The final novelty in twentieth-century entertainment was the radio, or 'wireless'. A rash of enthusiasts' magazines in the early 1920s encouraged the building of 'crystal' sets, which were cheap, but had poor reception. With the formation of the British Broadcasting Company (BBCo.) in 1922, and the building of new transmitters, reception improved; with the opening of the BBCo.'s Daventry station in 1925, national broadcasting was feasible for the first time.[26]

From the beginning, a licence fee had to be paid to the BBCo. for operating a radio receiver. By the end of 1922, 36,000 licences had been issued. However, there were probably many more unlicensed sets in operation, since home construction from a kit of parts supplied by a manufacturer was simple and

23. B.S. Rowntree, *Poverty and Progress: a second social survey of York* (Longmans, Green 1941), p. 470.
24. A contemporary debate on morals and the cinema is analysed in J. Richards, 'The Cinema and Cinema-Going in Birmingham in the 1930s', in J.K. Walton and J. Walvin (eds), *Leisure in Britain, 1780–1939* (Manchester UP 1983), pp. 31–52. The 'super-cinemas' are referred to in Smith, *New Survey*, IX (1935), p. 45.
25. Jones, *Merseyside*, pp. 278–9; Smith, *New Survey*, IX (1935), p. 48.
26. M. Pegg, *Broadcasting and Society 1918–1939* (Beckenham, Croom Helm 1983), pp. 7, 18, 36–8, 46–7.

cheap. It was estimated that about 3 million sets were in use in July 1925, against 1.4 million licences issued.

The fate of home construction and of the crystal set was sealed with the development of the more expensive valve radios, which continually improved in quality and fell in price. By the end of 1930, there were 3.4 million licences, equivalent to about 30 per cent of all households, and probably about 13.6 million people were able to listen to the radio. By 1939, there were 8.97 million licences. Even so, set ownership was not within everyone's reach. The crystal sets of the 1920s had retailed at an average of £1–2; the average valve sets of the 1930s cost at least £5–6, or about two weeks' wages for an unskilled manual worker. In addition, there was the annual BBC licence fee of 10s. to pay. A cheaper service could be provided by relay systems, but these had only 271,000 subscribers by the end of 1939.[27]

Programmes were now dominated by the British Broadcasting Corporation (BBC) (the successor to the BBCo.), which had been established in 1926, although foreign stations such as Radio Luxembourg or Radio Normandie provided a certain amount of competition. Although firmly marked with the policy of the first Director-General, John Reith, which sought to instruct and uplift as well as to entertain, the BBC provided a wide variety of programmes. In terms of air time, music dominated; in a sample week in 1930 one-third of the output was light music, and a further 20 per cent was dance music. By then, the Corporation had become also the accepted medium for news, and its forays into 'outside broadcasts' of sporting events had made it immensely popular. A notable feature of radio was that for the first time the voices of public figures could be heard in the home. The Christmas broadcast made for the first time by King George V in 1932 was greatly appreciated, the more so since it was broadcast throughout the British Empire.[28]

The pronunciation employed by the BBC remained resolutely 'Standard English' and the style of delivery was formal (announcers wore dinner jackets), and thus the BBC never found it easy to fully penetrate the working-class world. Nevertheless, the Corporation could claim to be one of the great cultural successes of the first half of the century, providing a good variety of programmes, with some regional variation. At the same time, it became a symbol of cultural and national unity which still provided for diverse tastes. The variety on offer could be sampled in the pages of *Radio Times*, which had reached a circulation of 2.6 million in 1939, and was never merely a programmes listing. For the more leisured and erudite, *The Listener* (circulation 50,000 in 1939) reprinted radio talks, and became renowned for the quality of its book reviews.[29]

27. S.G. Sturmey, *The Economic Development of Radio* (Duckworth 1958), pp. 155, 248.
28. Pegg, *Broadcasting*, pp. 7, 19–20, 38–9, 194; Briggs, *History of Broadcasting, vol. II*, pp. 35, 112–13.
29. Pegg, *Broadcasting*, p. 194; Briggs, *Golden Age*, pp. 35, 40–1, 280–92.

RELIGION

A major use of 'leisure' time for many people was religious observance. It is clear that before the war, religion was an important activity, though not a majority one; the major religious denominations in 1901 could probably claim no more than about 7.3 million adherents, and this may be an overstatement. In the interwar period, the major denominations were more than holding their own. The number of Easter communicants of the Church of England was almost static between 1914 and 1939, at about 2.2 million; the estimated Roman Catholic population of Britain rose from 2.0 million to 3.0 million between 1900 and 1940. A notable feature of the latter's history was the high number of adult conversions, which in the interwar period ran at over 10,000 a year in England and Wales alone, and included some prominent intellectuals and writers, such as Ronald Knox, Compton Mackenzie, Graham Greene and Evelyn Waugh.[30]

Scottish figures held up even better, and were probably strengthened by the amalgamation of the Church of Scotland and the United Free Church of Scotland in 1929. Actual decline was largely confined to the Congregational Union of England and Wales, and the Wesleyan Methodist Church. The combined membership of these two denominations fell from 2.2 million to 1.8 million between 1901 and 1931. In all, the total British church membership may have risen from about 7.3 million in 1901 to about 8.7 million in 1939, or about 19 per cent, compared with a rise in the total British population of about 16 per cent between those years (British refers to England, Wales and Scotland).[31]

However, the superficially satisfactory statistics concealed certain weaknesses. The Church of England (although not the Roman Catholic Church) was finding difficulty in recruiting new clergymen, whose numbers fell from 23,193 in 1911 to 21,309 in 1931. There was also a widespread feeling that the responses of the Christian churches to the theological and moral problems posed by the war of 1914–18 had been less than satisfactory.[32] Among the upper classes, agnosticism and atheism were making notable advances. It has been suggested that by the 1920s the principal intellectual (if not as yet social) orthodoxy was not any form of Christianity, but a confident agnosticism.[33]

Finally, it has been suggested that the apparent maintenance of formal religious observance concealed the extent to which the churches were failing to recruit from the wider world, and that they were being undermined by the

30. Halsey, *Trends*, pp. 421, 449; R. Currie, A. Gilbert and L. Horsley, *Churches and Churchgoers: patterns of church growth in the British Isles since 1700* (Oxford, Clarendon 1977), pp. 25, 128–9.
31. Currie *et al.*, *Churches*, pp. 427, 446, 448, Table 2.4; Mitchell, *Statistics*, p. 9.
32. Halsey, *Trends*, p. 424; A. Wilkinson, *The Church of England and the First World War* (SPCK 1978). See also E.R. Wickham, *Church and People in an Industrial City* (Lutterworth 1957), pp. 208–9.
33. A. Hastings, *A History of English Christianity 1920–1985* (Collins 1986), p. 221.

increasing secularisation of society. The latter process was well under way before 1914, but was masked by 'religion's inherited social prominence and continuing involvement in mainstream politics'. Thus the symptoms of long-term decline were for the time being concealed.[34]

ASSOCIATIONS

An important indicator of leisure activity was the membership of associations, clubs or societies. For adults, these usually reflected an existing interest in a sport or hobby, or in a particular political or religious outlook. Such associations came and went as their members' interests fluctuated. Perhaps the only such movement which was truly novel in the interwar period was the Women's Institutes (WIs), a Canadian innovation, which began in Britain in 1915, and flourished especially in the countryside. Although often led by women of the upper and upper-middle classes, they were a popular movement, having a membership of 328,000 by 1939, when there were nearly 6,000 separate WIs. They, and other rural social activities, were greatly encouraged by the building of village halls after 1918; although still far from universal even by 1939, they had made a great impact on village life.[35]

For younger people, provision of associations to some extent followed on sporting or religious lines. The most notable new development was the rapidly growing interest in 'hiking' – walking, often in groups, in the countryside. Provision for these groups to have somewhere to stay overnight came with the formation of the Youth Hostels Association in 1930. But young people also benefited from the widespread provision of youth clubs. In addition, there were associations such as the Boys' Brigade, which had a military flavour, and had some 121,000 members in 1930. With fewer quasi-military trappings, the Boy Scout (founded in 1908) and Girl Guide (1916) movements were growing very rapidly. By 1930 they dominated the provision of youth associations, having together almost exactly 1 million members. Much of the growth was due to inspiration of the founder, Baden-Powell, who managed to create a youth ideology which 'was more broadly based than its imperial and military origins'.[36] The extent to which the prewar organisations such as the Boys' Brigade (and, more controversially, the Scout movements) promoted militaristic and nationalistic sentiment is examined by Blanch.[37] There was a left-wing minor antidote to the Scout movement, in the form of the Woodcraft Folk.[38]

34. A.D. Gilbert, *The Making of Post-Christian Britain: a history of the secularization of modern society* (Longman 1980), pp. 78–9.
35. S. Goodenough, *Jam and Jerusalem: a pictorial history of the Women's Institute* (Collins 1977), pp. 16–17; W.A. Armstrong, 'The Countryside', *CSH* 1, pp. 143–4.
36. R.J. Morris, 'Clubs, Societies and Associations', *CSH* 3, pp. 423–5; Halsey, *Trends*, p. 568.
37. B. Blanch, 'Imperialism, Nationalism and Organized Youth', in Clarke *et al. Working-Class Culture.*
38. D. Prynn, 'The Woodcraft Folk and the Labour Movement, 1925–70', *JCH* 8 (1983).

NEWSPAPERS, BOOKS AND LIBRARIES

Since the spread of general literacy in the late nineteenth century, and the diffusion of the popular press, reading newspapers had become a very popular British pastime. In the interwar period, this became even more marked. According to a newspaper reading survey of 1939, 69 per cent of the population aged over 16 years read a national newspaper, and 82 per cent read one of the national Sunday papers. Even in 1920, the total circulation of all daily papers had reached almost 15 million, and the Sunday and weekly newspapers sold 20 million. Since there were at the time only about 9 million private 'households', many of them were taking more than one paper. By 1939 the total dailies circulation had reached 19.5 million, and the total Sundays/weeklies was 23.4 million.[39]

A notable change was the decline of the provincial press, and the concentration of mass circulation in the national daily and Sunday press. Between 1920 and 1930, the circulation of national and London daily papers rose from 7.4 million to 10.6 million, while the provincial daily paper circulation remained static. In 1921 there had been forty-one provincial morning titles, and eighty-nine evenings. By 1937 there were only twenty-eight mornings. Three more closed by 1947, by which time the number of provincial evenings had dropped to seventy-five. Even in the 1920s, three national or London titles had disappeared (*Daily Chronicle*, *Daily Graphic* and *Westminster Gazette*). The provincial Sunday press held up better, but most of the growth in Sunday and weekly papers was provided by the national titles. By 1937, the national dailies were selling 9.9 million, and the national Sundays 15.7 million copies.[40]

This concentration was accompanied by a rise to new circulation heights. The famous 'mass circulation' of the *Daily Mail* in 1914 was in fact only 800,000. By Lord Northcliffe's death in 1922 it was 1.75 million. By 1937 there were three national dailies with a circulation of over 1 million (*Daily Mail*, *Daily Mirror* and *News Chronicle*) and two with over 2 million (*Daily Express* and *Daily Herald*). Circulations of the leading Sunday papers were much higher than the dailies. In 1937 the largest, the *News of the World*, had a circulation of 3.8 million, and the *People* had 3.4 million; the next three largest sold 1.3–1.4 million.[41] The self-important world of Fleet Street was effectively satirised in Evelyn Waugh's novel, *Scoop*, in 1938.

Much of this mass circulation had been obtained by a more popular style of journalism, the use of more pictures, and more attractive layouts, but it was partly bought by aggressive marketing. The 'circulation war' had begun in the

39. J. Stevenson, *British Society, 1914–45* (Penguin 1984), p. 402; N. Kaldor and R. Silverman, *A Statistical Analysis of Advertising Expenditure and of the Revenue of the Press* (Cambridge UP 1948), p. 84.

40. Kaldor and Silverman, *Analysis*, p. 84; Political and Economic Planning (PEP), *Report on the British Press* (1938), pp. 84, 95; G. Boyce, J. Curran and P. Wingate, *Newspaper History from the 17th Century to the Present Day* (Constable 1978), p. 132; Royal Commission on the Press 1947–1949, *Report* (1949), Cmd 7700, App. III.

41. PEP *British Press*, pp. 84–90; Royal Commission on the Press, *Report*, App. III.

1920s, with the *Mail* and *Express* offering reader incentives. The purchase of the *Daily Herald* by Julius Elias in 1929 raised the stakes. He offered a much wider range of 'gifts' to new subscribers – pens, teasets, clothes, kitchen equipment – and (in 1933) complete bound sets of Dickens. Some novel and popular innovations also boosted circulations – notably the craze for crossword puzzles, which began in 1924. An even bolder step was to offer free insurance against accident; by 1937, about three-quarters of the readers of the popular national dailies were so insured. The circulation drive was driven by the commercial imperative that high circulations permitted the charging of greater fees for a given amount of advertising space. Thus the popular press became even bigger business. The quality press was a much smaller affair. In 1937 *The Times*' circulation was only 192,000, that of the *Morning Post* 132,000, and the combined *Daily Telegraph/Morning Post* 637,000, but higher advertising rates per page (justified to advertisers by the higher incomes of their readers) kept them in profit.[42]

The British tended to read newspapers rather than buy books. Even in 1939, only 7.2 million books were sold. Of the 14,904 new titles published in that year in the UK, 4,222 were fiction. While it is unlikely that popular fiction was any more or less popular than before, there was a change in its composition. The most striking development was the rise of the crime or 'detective' novel, exemplified in the works of Edgar Wallace (a prewar writer, but still going strong), Dorothy L. Sayers and Agatha Christie. The doyenne of 'the little world of Mayhem Parva', as Colin Watson has dubbed the genre, was undoubtedly Agatha Christie, who published nineteen novels featuring her Belgian detective, Hercule Poirot, between 1920 and 1939.[43]

Agatha Christie's *The Mysterious Affair at Styles* was one of the two detective novels among the first ten titles republished by the newly formed Penguin Books in July 1935; the other was *The Unpleasantness at the Bellona Club* by Dorothy L. Sayers. Thus Penguin inaugurated a paperback revolution. By the autumn of 1938, the Penguin list had grown to two hundred titles, including forty Pelicans, about half a dozen Penguin Specials, and about half the Penguin Shakespeare. Penguins were modestly priced (6d.) and attractively presented reprints of well-known books. Together with the non-fiction Pelicans and the Penguin Specials (some specially commissioned) on topical matters, Penguins represented a new mass market in publishing, whose members are best described as intelligent, serious, eager to educate themselves, and to possess, rather than borrow, books.[44]

42. Boyce *et al.*, *Newspaper History*, p. 131; PEP, *British Press*, pp. 84–90, 130; F. Williams, *Dangerous Estate* (Longmans 1957), pp. 151, 172; H.W. Steed, *The Press* (Penguin 1938), ch. VI.
43. Halsey, *Trends*, p. 565; C. Watson, *Snobbery with Violence* (Eyre & Spottiswood 1971), ch. 13.
44. H. Schmoller, 'The Paperback Revolution', in A. Briggs (ed.), *Essays in the History of Publishing* (Longman 1974), pp. 297–304. See also the history of Penguin and its founder, Allen Lane, by J. Morpurgo, *Allen Lane, King Penguin: a biography* (Hutchinson 1979).

Of greater importance in most people's reading habits were the libraries, public and private. The expansion of public libraries was very striking. In 1913–14, only about 60 per cent of the British population lived in an area served by a public library; by 1934–35 almost everyone did so. Although the book stock in public libraries had risen only slightly, it was circulated much more quickly. In 1913–14 54 million books were lent out, and in 1934–35, 166 million. Much of this expansion was due to the Public Libraries Act 1919, which abolished the previous 1d. rate limit on local authority spending on libraries. In addition, it gave the counties powers to develop library services, so that the rural areas were now to be provided for, having been almost completely neglected before 1914. All but three counties had a rural library service by 1931, usually by distributing book-boxes to village schools. In 1934–35 under these arrangements over 48 million issues were made to 2 million registered borrowers.[45]

There was also some private library provision, in the shape of the chain of libraries run by Boots the Chemists ('Boots Booklover's Library') which had a clientele of between a quarter and half a million in the 1930s. A similar service was provided by W.H. Smith and Son, which may have served some 100,000 customers in the same period. Borrowings from both public and private libraries were dominated by fiction.[46]

TOBACCO AND ALCOHOL

Tobacco and alcohol had for centuries proved popular as stimulants, relaxants and aids to sociability. The two had differing fortunes between the wars. Tobacco was the gainer. In 1909–13, average UK consumption had been 2.04 lb per head annually. In the First World War, consumption rose sharply, and continued to rise, although more slowly, thereafter. By 1930 it was 3.31 lb a head, and the rise was only briefly interrupted during the ensuing depression, reaching 4.00 lb in 1938. The real price of smoking rose sharply, due to higher taxes. Before the war, the tax was 3s. 8d. per lb; by 1925–26 it was 8s. 2d. By 1938, about 47 per cent of the retail price of a packet of cigarettes went in tax. Expenditure on tobacco and tobacco products accounted for 2.0 per cent of total UK consumers' spending in 1910–14, and 3.9 per cent in 1935–38.[47]

The main agent of the rise in tobacco consumption was the growing popularity of cigarettes. Between 1920 and 1939, UK cigarette consumption rose from 36,240 million to 73,810 million a year. Most of this extra consumption was by men. Consumption of tobacco products by women had been negligible

45. T. Kelly, *A History of Public Libraries in Great Britain 1845–1965* (Library Association 1973), p. 491, ch. VIII; Armstrong, 'The Countryside', p. 143.
46. Watson, *Snobbery*, pp. 30–1; Q.D. Leavis, *Fiction and the Reading Public* (Chatto & Windus 1932; 1965), pp. 3–4.
47. Mitchell, *Statistics*, pp. 710–11; Committee on National Debt and Taxation (Colwyn Committee), *Report* (1927), Cmd 2800, p. 223, App. IX, p. 42; B.W.E. Alford, *W.D. & H.O. Wills and the Development of the U.K. Tobacco Industry 1786–1965* (Methuen 1973), Table 60; Stone and Rowe, *Consumers' Expenditure*, p. 122.

Table 10.1 UK alcohol consumption, 1909–35

	Beer production (GB) ('000 standard barrels)[a]		*Spirit consumption (UK) ('000 proof gallons)*	
1909–13 av.	30,486	100	30,067	100
1914–18	21,265	70	25,690	85
1919–23	20,899	69	18,745	62
1924–28	20,246	66	13,026	43
1931–35	15,148	50	9,476	31

Note: a 36 gallons at 1,055 degrees proof
Source: G.P. Williams and G.T. Brake, *Drink in Great Britain 1900 to 1979* (Edsall 1979), Tables I/1, I/7, pp. 354, 360

in 1920, although it was still rising more rapidly than total consumption, and was 10 per cent of the total by 1939. By 1939, average adult male consumption is estimated at 3,630 a year and female consumption at 500 a year. In effect, the average man smoked about ten cigarettes per day, and the average woman between one and two.[48]

Generally, it may be said that by the Second World War cigarette smoking had come of age. Most adult males smoked them, and a large number of juvenile males, for whom they represented something of a *rite de passage*, having the added attraction of being illegal under the age of 16 years. As for female cigarette smoking, only a little residual embarrassment attached to the woman who wished to smoke in public, although smoking in the street was still frowned on, especially in middle-class circles.

Drink, on the other hand, had a declining market, in spite of the continuing growth of the population. In fact, there had been a slow and steady decline in alcohol consumption per head even before 1914. This accelerated during the war. After the war, consumption continued to fall. The decline was very sharp, especially in the case of spirits (Table 10.1 above).

The reasons for this large change in the habits of the British people may be debated. The number of outlets selling drink fell after 1918, but only slightly. More relevant were the restrictions on drinking hours and on juvenile drinking, the reduction in the alcohol content of beer (a wartime innovation which remained to some extent afterwards) and the steep rise in tax. The tax on spirits was raised by 486 per cent, and that on beer by 1,290 per cent between 1913–14 and 1925–26. Before the war, tax had taken about 25 per cent of the national drink bill; afterwards it was about 45 per cent.[49] It may be that the

48. Alford, *Wills*, Figs 13, 14, Tables 42, 45, 51; G.F. Todd, *Statistics of Smoking in the United Kingdom* (4th edn, Tobacco Research Council 1966), Tables 1.3, 1.4.
49. Colwyn Committee, *Report*, App. IX, pp. 43–5; G.P. Williams and G.T. Brake, *Drink in Great Britain 1900 to 1979* (Edsall 1979), Tables 13–16, pp. 368–71. Data on alcohol content from G.B. Wilson, *Alcohol and the Nation* (Nicholson & Watson 1940), pp. 58–9.

rise of the cinema provided a useful social outlet without requiring alcohol. Yet, had the desire to drink remained unimpaired, it is difficult to see why these changes alone should account for the decline. It may be more to the point that heavy manual labour was declining (thus less beer drinking) and that the rise in real wages provided some sort of psychological leeway in the poorer sections of the working class, so that less need was felt to take the 'shortest way out of Manchester' by getting drunk. Robert Roberts, growing up in a slum area of Salford (Manchester) before 1914, had had vivid memories of his father's drinking – never less than four quarts (eight pints) of beer a day, because, he said, it kept his strength up. This behaviour was now less usual.[50] Whereas alcohol had accounted for about 15 per cent of total consumers' expenditure in 1910–14, it fell substantially, to 9 per cent in 1925–29, and to 6.5 per cent in 1935–38.[51]

Even with the decline in alcohol consumption, the public house remained a mainstay of British social life, although now having to compete with the cinema and the entertainment provided in the home by the wireless. Yet the 'pub' was still a unique institution, especially for the working class:

> These public-houses are still the community-centres, where everyone meets, arranges most of his common activities, lays his personal cares aside, and satisfies some of his social cravings. To the women who go there, they serve, though to a lesser extent, the same purpose. The public-houses are recognised exchanges of news, and a man who wishes to get in touch with another, or find out what has happened to him, naturally goes in, has a drink, and asks, 'Seen so-and-so lately?'[52]

After 1918 there was a great growth in licensed clubs. There had been some 8,000 (in England and Wales) before the war, and by 1935 there were 16,000. Some of these were night-clubs, some working men's or ex-servicemen's clubs. The greatest new growth was in working men's clubs and sports clubs. However, they did not compete with the public house in the provision of social amenity, being for specialist occasions or purposes.[53]

GAMBLING

A very popular form of recreation was betting. Before the war, this had been almost entirely on horse racing. Since cash betting was illegal unless actually taking place on the racecourse, a large part of betting took place surreptitiously, by passing the bets and the cash to a 'bookies' runner'. The prohibition on off-course cash betting remained in force between the wars, so that in effect horse racing was split into two sections. Those who could attend the races or who could afford to maintain a credit account with a bookmaker had

50. R. Roberts, *The Classic Slum: Salford life in the first quarter of the century* (Manchester UP 1971), pp. 92–6.
51. Stone and Rowe, *Consumers' Expenditure*, Table 56, p. 125.
52. Smith, *New Survey*, IX (1935), p. 257.
53. Wilson, *Alcohol*, pp. 140–3.

little difficulty in pursuing their interest; those who fell into neither category had continual difficulty, and were dogged by police inquiries.[54]

There is no doubt that large sums went on betting. Calculations of the total depend on many assumptions, because a great deal escaped record. One estimate is that by 1925 almost £99 million annually was being wagered in the UK, chiefly on horses. In the 1920s, there emerged two new forms of gambling, which grew rapidly – the football pools and betting on dog races. By 1938 the total wagered on all forms of betting has been estimated at £221 million in the UK, which was over five times greater than the total spent by the public on cinema admissions.[55]

Most of this betting was conducted from a distance. By the late 1930s, a rough estimate of the numbers of people engaging in any form of betting would be 10–15 million, but the numbers attending race meetings (horse or dog) were very much smaller. Most of the betters would be 'doing the pools'; the promoters of the football pools had 10 million people on their books by the late 1930s. In most cases the sums wagered on any of these forms of gambling were comparatively small: between 6d. and 2s. 6d. probably covered the majority of off-street bets and football pool entries. Apart from the hope of financial gain, betting brought excitement; as one inveterate gambler told Seebohm Rowntree's investigator in York in 1936, he would rather have sixpence worth of hope than sixpence worth of electricity.[56] There was also the excitement of illegality; 'bookies' runners' (some of them children) were in constant danger of police pursuit.

HOLIDAYS

Increasing leisure permitted a greater amount of holiday time. By 1914, most middle-class families would have been able to take an annual holiday, and the habit was spreading to the better-paid manual workers. To be paid while on holiday was still exceptional, whatever the class of the family. The main seaside resorts had been long established, and sometimes catered for whole industrial groups at a time, as in the migration of Lancashire workers to Blackpool during Wakes Week.[57]

After the war, the custom of paid holidays spread. The Ministry of Labour estimated that in March 1925, 1.5 million manual workers enjoyed paid holidays under collective agreements. By 1937, this may have risen to around 4 million of the manual workers earning less than £250 a year, to which may be added perhaps another 1 million earning more than this. In total, about 15

54. R. McKibbin, 'Working-Class Gambling in Britain, 1880–1939', *Past and Present* 82 (1979), pp. 147–8.

55. Stone and Rowe, *Consumers' Expenditure*, Tables 36–7, p. 91.

56. McKibbin, 'Working-Class Gambling', pp. 154–6; Rowntree, *Poverty and Progress*, p. 403.

57. J.K. Walton, *The Blackpool Landlady: a social history* (Manchester UP 1978), pp. 101–2.

million people may have taken a holiday of some kind, so that the paid holiday was not normal, and holiday-makers must have been drawn disproportionately from the middle classes.[58] The length of the holiday can only be guessed, but sample surveys of London elementary schoolchildren in 1926, 1929 and 1932 indicated that about half took a holiday, usually with their parents (although some went with the Scouts or other organisations), and that most spent between eight and fourteen days away from home. The annual hop-picking in Kent was a unique and very popular form of working holiday for thousands of London East End families.[59]

A notable change was occurring after 1918 due to the spread of the motor car, coach, motor bicycle and cycle. The traditional excursion to the seaside was now being challenged by inland resorts, so that many inland villages were providing facilities for tourism:

> Derelict hotels and inns were rejuvenated, cottage parlours blossomed forth as tea-rooms, the village blacksmith became a motor mechanic and a petrol station sprang up where once the village smithy stood.[60]

Even so, since most holiday-makers still did not have the use of a car, most travelled by train.

A portent for the future was the development of the large 'holiday camp', accommodating several hundred people or more at a time. Although these had their precursors in the 1920s, the movement rapidly expanded with the opening of Billy Butlin's first large camp at Skegness in 1937. Providing accommodation, food and entertainment for a modest inclusive charge, they rapidly proved very popular. Even by 1939, there may have been about 200 camps on the coast, providing in season for some 30,000 guests per week.[61]

The total numbers taking holidays, even if brief, were very large. Rough estimates for the 1930s were that Blackpool had 7 million visitors annually, Southend 5.5 million, Hastings 3 million, Bournemouth and Southport 2 million each. These totals included daily 'excursionists'.[62] Bank Holidays (especially in August) were notable for the great numbers of city-dwellers who poured out (mainly by train), usually to the nearest seaside resort; Southend, near London, and Blackpool, were favourites. The period was notable for the large investment made by municipalities, especially seaside ones, in all sorts of improvements and attractions. Thus at Blackpool between the wars seven miles of promenade were rebuilt, with sunken gardens and other amenities, at the cost of over £1.5 million, and another £250,000 was spent on improvements to the Winter Gardens. At Hastings over £100,000 was spent on the

58. E. Brunner, *Holiday Making and the Holiday Trades* (Oxford UP 1945), p. 9.
59. J.A.R. Pimlott, *The Englishman's Holiday: a social history* (Faber & Faber 1947; Hassocks, Harvester 1977), p. 214; Smith, *New Survey*, IX (1935), p. 84.
60. Pimlott, *Holiday*, p. 257.
61. Brunner, *Holiday Making*, p. 5; Cunningham, 'Leisure and Culture', p. 314.
62. E.W. Gilbert, 'The Growth of Inland and Seaside Health Resorts in England', *Scottish Geographical Magazine* LV (1939), p. 20.

White Rock Pavilion, which was opened in 1927. Lest it should be thought that this was all designed purely to attract the masses, it may be mentioned that the Winter Gardens in Bournemouth was rebuilt to house the Municipal Orchestra, which became the Bournemouth Symphony Orchestra, with a full complement of seventy players, and that even in 1928 the town was spending £20,000 a year on the orchestra, regarding it as money well spent.[63]

Finally, there were the more organised day trips. Those organised by firms and works, churches, Sunday schools and clubs had a long pedigree, and were by train or horse-drawn wagon before 1914. After the war these forms of transport were augmented or replaced by the motor coach. An early version was called the 'char-a-banc', or 'charabanc', a single-deck vehicle (usually open to the weather) with bench seating for about thirty people. These could cover large distances. The poet Laurie Lee recalled an annual choir outing by charabanc, probably in the late 1920s, from Slad (Gloucestershire) to Weston-super-Mare (108 miles return). (Lee does not give the date, but he was born in 1915.) By the 1930s the enclosed coach was usual, and the range greater; in 1938–39, Southdown Motor Services of Brighton ran day excursions to Oxford and as far as the Bristol area.[64]

CRIME

The changing patterns of life and leisure after the war brought also new levels and patterns of crime. In retrospect, the late Victorian and Edwardian era had been a plateau of low criminal activity. By the First World War, serious crime was on the increase, and although it was to increase much more rapidly after the Second World War, there was sufficient cause for concern. In 1901 there had been 80,962 indictable (i.e. serious) crimes recorded in England and Wales; this had risen to 97,171 by 1911, to 159,278 by 1931, and 283,000 by 1938. It was particularly alarming that a higher proportion of persons coming before the courts on indictable charges was juvenile (under 17 years). Neither the institution of the borstal system nor the introduction of juvenile courts (both in 1908) seem to have obviated this trend. However, part of this increase was probably due to a change in the law; the Children and Young Persons Act 1933 may have increased the number of juveniles found guilty by reducing the reluctance of the authorities to take children to court.[65]

Juvenile crime apart, there was less cause for concern. Even for indictable offences, there was little change in the nature of the offence. Crimes against

63. Smith, *New Survey*, IX (1935), p. 87; Pimlott, *Holiday*, pp. 244–5; R. Nettel, *The Orchestra in England* (Cape 1946), p. 240.
64. A. Delgado, *The Annual Outing and Other Excursions* (Allen & Unwin 1977), pp. 113, 152–3; L. Lee, *Cider with Rosie* (Penguin 1962), p. 190.
65. F.H. McClintock, N.H. Avison and G.N.G. Rose, *Crime in England and Wales* (Heinemann 1968), pp. 20, 26; A.M. Carr-Saunders and D.C. Jones, *A Survey of the Social Structure of England and Wales* (2nd edn, Oxford, Clarendon 1937), pp. 185–6; A.M. Carr-Saunders, D. Caradog Jones and C.A. Moser, *A Survey of Social Conditions in England and Wales* (Oxford, Clarendon 1958), pp. 266, 268.

property, without violence, accounted for 80 per cent of known indictable offences in England and Wales in 1900–04 and 77 per cent in 1925–29. It was also of some comfort to know that the number of murders declined slightly, averaging around a hundred per year. The more novel features of crime were those affecting non-indictable (less serious) offences. Here, there were two major changes; a great decline in drunkenness, and a great rise in the number of offences against the Highway Acts. In 1900–09, 218,459 persons had been tried for drunkenness, and this fell to 73,451 in 1925–29, and to 52,700 in 1938. The highway offences rose from 55,633 convictions in 1910 to 157,875 in 1920, and 475,124 in 1938 (in England and Wales). This largely reflected offences by motorists; for the first time, the middle classes experienced in large numbers the novelty of being on the wrong side of the law. There was also a great decline in begging offences; in 1900–13 these had fluctuated between 11,000 and 33,000 a year, but between the wars hardly ever rose above 5,000 a year. Crime, as ever, reflected social values and social changes.[66]

CONCLUSIONS

Between the world wars, the reduction in the average working week and the rise in real incomes increased the demand for leisure activities. This rising demand was satisfied to some extent by the expansion of existing types of activities, such as the cinema, spectator sports, and newspaper reading; to some extent it was met by the technological innovations of the time, notably radio and the motor vehicle. In addition, there were some rapidly developing novelties, such as cigarette smoking and the football pools, which had become more or less universal by the end of the 1930s. Some more traditional activities, such as religious worship and drinking in pubs, retained their historic attractions for a large part of the population. Finally, the idea of taking an annual holiday spread, and a larger part of the working population could afford to do so by 1939. However, unemployed people were excluded from a large part of these pleasures and pastimes. In sum, for the majority of the population, the balance between work and leisure swung to the latter, and more variegated amusements and occupations were available outside working hours.

66. D.C. Marsh, *The Changing Social Structure of England and Wales 1871–1961* (Routledge & Kegan Paul 1958), p. 242; Carr-Saunders and Jones, *Social Structure* (1937), p. 192; Halsey, *Trends*, p. 530; H. Mannheim, *Social Aspects of Crime in England between the Wars* (Allen & Unwin 1940), pp. 127–8.

CHAPTER 11

SLUMP AND DEPRESSION, 1929–31

CAUSES OF THE WORLD DEPRESSION

The depression which began in 1929, and continued to deepen in most countries until 1932, was the most severe international depression which had ever been recorded. Apart from its severity, it was notable for two features; it affected both industrial and primary producers, and it was rapidly transmitted around the world by the mechanisms of international trade and payments. By 1932, there were about 30 million people recorded as unemployed, chiefly in the industrial economies. In the agricultural regions of the world, the depression was felt more in the shape of falling incomes, in both domestic and export markets, and unemployment either went unrecorded or took the form of higher underemployment. For all economies exposed to it, the depression reduced national incomes. In the process, prices also dropped precipitously. The USA, which was the industrial economy most severely affected, saw its GDP fall (in real terms) between 1929 and 1932 by 28 per cent. For the industrial economies as a whole, average GDP in those years fell by 18 per cent in real terms.[1]

Superimposed on the depression, and mainly brought into play by it, were a series of financial crises. Some were internal, such as the waves of bank failures in central Europe and the USA. Some were external, such as the defaulting on interest payments in south America, or the German banking crisis which followed the flow back to the USA of the investment funds exported since 1924. Finally, there were exchange rate crises and devaluations, of which those of the UK in 1931 were the most notable.

The causes of the depression are still debated. While space forbids extensive discussion here, it can be said that the main elements were the weak position of primary producers, in both agrarian and industrial economies; the ending

1. A. Maddison, *The World Economy in the Twentieth Century* (Paris, OECD 1989), pp. 51–3; G.M. Walton and H. Rockoff, *History of the American Economy* (7th edn, Harcourt Brace 1994), p. 516.

of the industrial boom in the USA; destabilising capital flows; the decline of world trade; the decline of investment.[2]

The cumulative effects of the depression between 1929 and 1932 were enormous. The collapse in industrial production was deepest in the USA and Germany, at 47 and 46 per cent repectively. The total import volume of the industrial – later OECD (Organisation for Economic Cooperation and Development) – countries fell by one-quarter, and consumer prices in the worst hit, the USA and Germany, fell by one-fifth. The value of exports of the primary producing regions collapsed, sometimes by as much as 80 per cent (Chile), but in most cases by at least 30–45 per cent (Lithuania, Philippines, Turkey, Venezuela). Along the way, international lending dried up completely; the gold standard was abandoned; most countries adopted protectionist policies.[3]

THE NATURE OF THE DEPRESSION IN BRITAIN

There seems little doubt that the British depression was largely the result of external influences. Unlike in the USA, there had not been a strong domestic boom in the late 1920s, whose collapse would precipitate a depression. Between 1924 and 1929, real GDP rose by about 13.7 per cent, which was slow by the standards of other industrial economies. Nor, on the other hand, had there been an export boom; between 1924 and 1929, the volume of domestic exports rose only by 7 per cent, and the current value of exports in 1929 (£729 million) was almost the same as it had been in 1928 (£724 million).[4]

There were, in fact, signs before 1929 that British exports were weakening due to the lowered incomes of primary producers. These were important markets for Britain; in 1928, British India, the British colonies, south America, Canada and the Far East accounted for 42 per cent of British exports. In all these cases, British exports turned down in 1928. Thus there is the suggestion that even without the world depression which began in 1929, Britain might have had an independent recession. Once the depression began, these primary producers found that their export markets declined much further, and thus they absorbed fewer British exports.[5]

In the depression, the British economy emerged relatively unscathed in comparison with other industrial economies. By 1932, industrial production had fallen by 11 per cent, GDP and GNP also by 11 per cent, and employment by 4 per cent. The Board of Trade wholesale price index had fallen by 16 per

2. B. Eichengreen, 'The Origins and Nature of the Great Slump Revisited', *EcHR* XLV (1992); Eichengreen, *Golden Fetters: the gold standard and the Great Depression* (New York, Oxford UP 1992).

3. C.P. Kindleberger, *The World in Depression, 1929–1939* (Penguin 1987), p. 189; Maddison, *World Economy*, p. 53.

4. C.H. Feinstein, *National Income, Expenditure and Output of the United Kingdom, 1855–1965* (Cambridge UP 1972), Tables 19, 26; B.R. Mitchell, *British Historical Statistics* (Cambridge UP 1988), pp. 453, 518.

5. D.C. Corner, 'Exports and the British Trade Cycle: 1929', *ManS* XXIV (1956), pp. 133, 136.

cent, and the (working-class) cost of living index by 12 per cent. But even this relatively mild experience had been devastating to employment, business confidence and foreign trade. The percentage of insured workers unemployed (seasonally adjusted) had in 1929 varied between 11.9 and 9.4 per cent; at its peak in the depression it reached 22.5 per cent (August September 1932). Net domestic fixed capital formation (i.e. new investment in the fixed capital of buildings, industrial equipment, vehicles and ships) fell from £145 million in 1929 to £59 million in 1932, or by 59 per cent. For industrial investment alone, the position was even worse, since investment in manufacturing, mining and transport was actually negative, so that there was disinvestment in those industries; thus their fixed capital stock was falling in value. The overall position would have been worse had not this negative investment been offset by investment in dwelling houses (£89 million of the total in 1929) which fell only slightly. In foreign trade, the most obvious effect of the depression was the collapse in the value of exports, from £729 million in 1929 to £365 million in 1932.[6]

The mildness of the depression in real terms is emphasised when allowance is made for the fall in prices in 1929–32. When this is taken into account, the 'real' decline in GDP was only 4.5 per cent. The severe fall in invisible income from abroad (and thus development of a balance of payments deficit) meant that total national income (GNP) fell slightly more than this. A large part of the economy was hardly affected when price changes have been taken into account. In real terms, the service sector's output barely changed, and agricultural output fell only slightly (2.2 per cent). The transport sector's output declined rather more (8.8 per cent), chiefly due to the decline in railway traffic, both passenger and freight; the numbers of private cars and goods vehicles on the roads continued to rise during these years. The sector most affected was mining and manufacturing (a decline of 10.8 per cent) and in particular the exporting industries (decline of 38 per cent, at 1929 prices).

It is the severe decline in manufacturing which has coloured subsequent accounts of the depression after 1929. But manufacturing industry did not dominate the whole economy; rather, it was a large minority interest. In the 1920s, manufacturing (together with mining and building) accounted for 40 per cent of UK national income, and this ratio was almost the same at the end of the 1930s. Thus, given the relatively slight decline in the non-manufacturing sectors after 1929, the impact of the depression on the national economy as a whole was mitigated. But the extreme decline of industrial production led to a sharp rise in unemployment, and the deflation of prices severely affected profits and investment.[7]

6. F. Capie and M. Collins, *The Inter-War British Economy: a statistical abstract* (Manchester UP 1983), Table 4.5; C.H. Feinstein, *Domestic Capital Formation in the United Kingdom 1920–1938* (Cambridge UP 1965), Tables 3.40, 3, 51, 57; Mitchell, *Statistics*, pp. 453, 729, 739.

7. P. Deane and W.A. Cole, *British Economic Growth 1688–1959* (Cambridge UP 1967), p. 291.

One industry which had an exceptional experience was agriculture. Although agricultural product prices fell by a similar amount to other wholesale prices, farmers had less scope for reducing output. Thus most of the losses of the industry were those of income rather than output; the value of the gross output of farming in England and Wales fell from £221.5 million to £182.5 million between 1928–29 and 1932–33.[8]

Within the mining and manufacturing sector, the experience of different industries varied widely (Table 11.1).

Table 11.1 Industrial output in Britain, 1929–32 (1929 = 100)

% change since 1929	*1930*	*1931*	*1932*
Mining and quarrying	−4.9	−14.3	−18.7
Chemical industries	−5.1	−8.9	−2.8
Metal manufacture	−9.8	−29.9	−28.2
Engineering industries	−5.5	−20.4	−24.3
Textiles, leather, clothing	−8.1	−5.2	−0.1
Food, drink and tobacco	+0.1	−1.9	−2.0
Other manufacturing industries	−1.9	−4.6	−3.5
Building and contracting	−7.6	−12.7	−17.7
Gas/electricity/water	+1.8	+4.5	+7.2
Total industrial production	−4.3	−10.5	−10.8

Source: Feinstein, *National Income*, Table 112

In most industries, output declined continuously until 1932. There were exceptions; chemicals and textiles began to recover in 1931. The 'gas/water/electricity' sector continued to expand during these years, chiefly via the building of the national grid. But in the larger and most affected sectors of mining, metals, engineering and building, the decline grew more marked until 1932.

The decline in activity was largely due to the fall in exports, especially in the traditional large exporting industries. Overall, UK domestic exports fell by 50 per cent in 1929–32 (Table 11.2 opposite).

THE RISE IN UNEMPLOYMENT

The vulnerability of the major exporting sectors to the depression meant that they were particularly prone to high unemployment. Unemployment varied enormously according to the industry; outstanding was shipbuilding and repairing, in which registered unemployment reached 62 per cent in 1932. The next worst cases were steel (47.9) and pig-iron (43.8). But there were also very large industries in which it was at around 30 per cent or more – notably

8. Ministry of Agriculture, *A Century of Agricultural Statistics, 1866–1966* (HMSO 1968), Table 43; E.H. Whetham, *The Agrarian History of England and Wales, vol. VIII, 1914–1939* (Cambridge UP 1978), pp. 230–1.

Table 11.2 UK domestic exports, 1929–32

	1929 (£m)	*1932 (£m)*	*% Decline*
New ships and boats	15.5	3.9	75
Non-ferrous metals	18.3	6.9	62
Iron and steel	68.0	28.0	59
Electrical goods	13.2	5.8	56
Textiles	213.9	98.8	54
Machinery	59.6	30.3	49
Vehicles and aircraft	20.7	13.3	36
Coal	52.9	34.3	35
Chemicals	26.6	18.5	30
Total domestic exports	729.3	365.0	50

Source: B.R. Mitchell and P. Deane, *Abstract of British Historical Statistics* (Cambridge UP 1972), pp. 284, 306

coal (34.5), pottery (36.2), general engineering (29.2), linen (29.7), cotton (30.6) and building (30.2). Dock work was unusual, in that it was a service industry with high unemployment (33.3 per cent), due to the decline of external trade.[9]

Apart from the general increase in unemployment, there was a disproportionate rise in long-term unemployment (twelve months or more). In September 1929, only 10.7 per cent of male applicants for unemployment benefit had been unemployed for a year or more. By September 1932, this had risen to 18.6 per cent. This caused the average length of time spent unemployed by all male applicants to rise, from 22.3 to 33.2 weeks.[10]

Even before the beginning of the world depression, British unemployment had been a regional matter. The impact of the depression after 1929 served to raise unemployment in all regions by similar proportions. Although there was a slight increase in the relative unemployment of London and the south-east of England, the general regional distinctions in unemployment already established in the 1920s continued (Table 11.3 overleaf).

It may be re-emphasised that the official figures of unemployment covered to the insured population only, and that it is likely that the uninsured sections of the working population had a lower propensity to unemployment than the insured. This was brought out in the 1931 Census of Population, in which, for the first time and only time between the wars, the entire working population was asked whether it was employed or out of work. The results of the 1931 inquiry are presented on Map 4. This shows that the national unemployment

9. Department of Employment, *British Labour Statistics, Historical Abstract, 1868–1968* (HMSO 1971), Table 164.
10. W.R. Garside, *British Unemployment 1919–1939: a study in public policy* (Cambridge UP 1990), p. 16, Table 6.

Table 11.3 Regional insured unemployment rates, 1929 and 1932[a]

	London	*South-east*	*South-west*	*Midlands*	*North-east*	*North-west*	*Scotland*	*Wales*	*GB*
1929	5.3	5.6	8.3	9.2	14.1	12.3	12.3	19.9	10.6
1932	12.9	14.3	17.2	19.6	28.8	25.6	28.2	36.8	22.1

Note: a Unemployment as a percentage of all insured employees
Source: B. Mitchell, *British Historical Statistics* (Cambridge UP 1988), p. 125

rate was not as high as the insurance figures indicate. It also shows that the areas most severely affected by unemployment were relatively small, being the north-east (Northumberland and Durham), the north-west (Lancashire and Cheshire) and south Wales (chiefly Monmouth and Glamorgan).[11]

The fairly uniform rise in regional unemployment rates after 1929 concealed the fact that 'Outer Britain' (Scotland, Wales and northern England) suffered disproportionately from the rise in long-term unemployment. By June 1932, the proportions of long-term (male) unemployed were 21.1 per cent in Wales, 27.6 per cent in Scotland and 19.6 per cent in northern England (the north-east and north-west divisions of the Ministry of Labour), but as low as 4.4 per cent in London, 3.8 per cent in the south-east, and 8.8 per cent in the south-west divisions.[12]

THE DETERIORATION IN PUBLIC FINANCE

The rise in unemployment, and in particular long-term unemployment, had serious implications for the stability of public finance. The ground for this had been laid in 1927, when the Insurance Act 1927 had permitted new claimants unable to fulfil the strict contributory requirements of the scheme to draw 'transitional payments' for one year (to April 1929), if they had paid eight insurance contributions during the previous two years or thirty at any time. The pending general election and mounting unemployment persuaded the outgoing Baldwin government to extend this provision (in March 1929) for a further year. The new Labour government, caught by the substantial rise in unemployment in 1929–30, was equally reluctant to thrust unemployed people on to the Poor Law, and agreed in March 1930 to extend the transitional payments system for a further year (to April 1931). Further, the cost of transitional payments, hitherto confined to the Unemployment Fund, was now to be borne directly by the Exchequer, thus entrenching a system of direct state dole. Finally, in the Unemployment Insurance Act 1930, the system was further liberalised, as the 'genuinely seeking work' test was abolished; in effect, the onus of proof was transferred from the individual to the Employment

11. Census of England and Wales 1931, *Industry Tables* (1934), Table 2.
12. Garside, *Unemployment*, p. 17, Table 7.

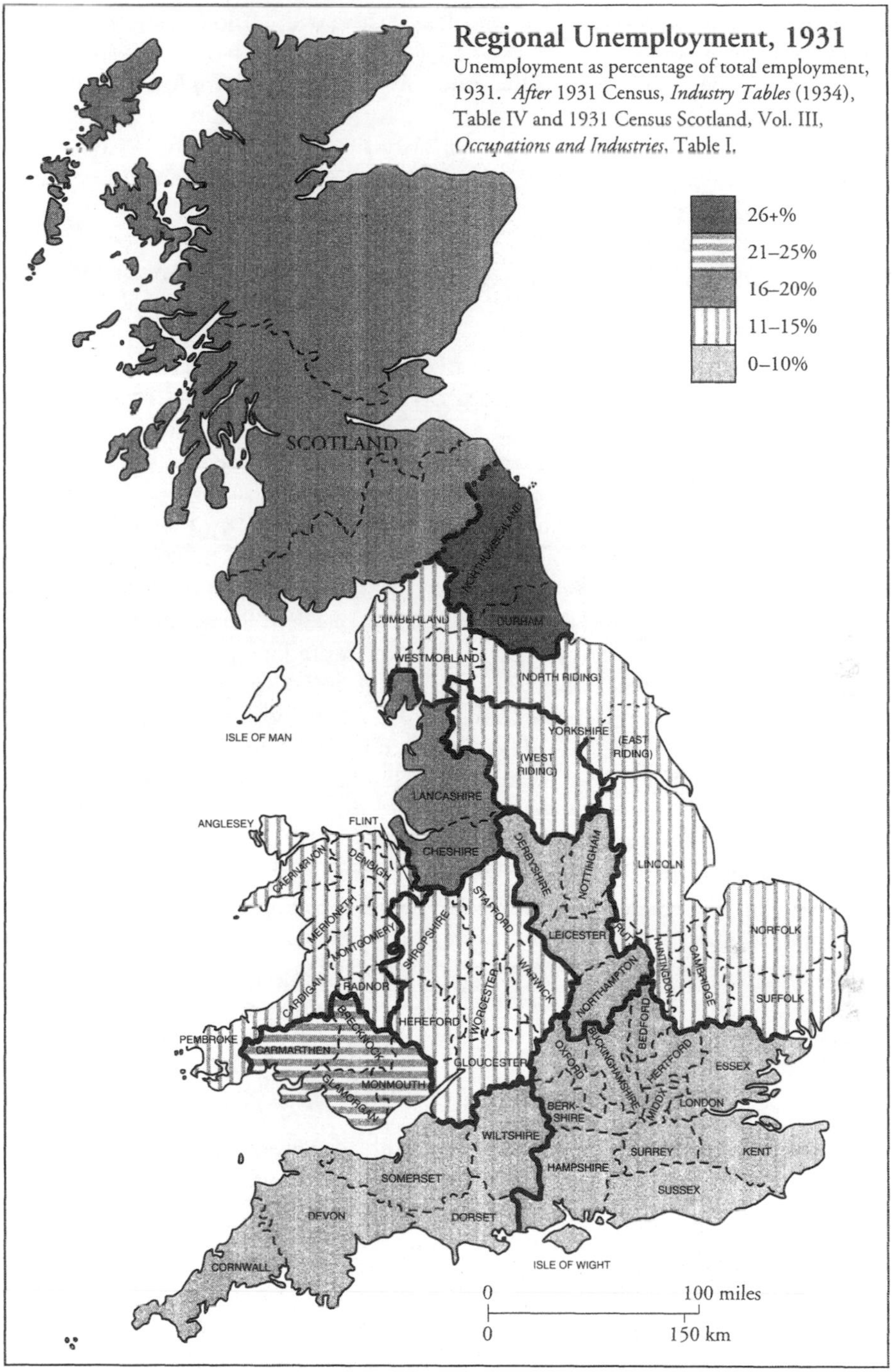

Map 4 Regional unemployment, 1931

Exchanges, making benefit a right unless just cause could be shown why it should not be paid.[13]

The successive relaxation of the rules for claiming unemployment benefit provoked much controversy, chiefly in the form of allegations of 'spongeing', or abusing the system. There is little evidence that this took place on any scale. Nor did the relaxation of the 'genuinely seeking work' clause entail an enormous increase in expenditure; its cost has been assessed at no more than £5 million between March 1930 and October 1931. But a desire to deflect political criticism impelled the government to react, in the form of the Anomalies Act of July 1931, the chief effect of which was to exclude most married women from unemployment benefit; by the end of March 1932, over 82 per cent of married women's benefit claims had been disallowed.[14]

There is no doubt that expenditure on unemployment relief rose pro rata with the numbers unemployed, rather than being spurred by the relaxation of the rules; in 1929 it had totalled some £47 million, and rose to about £92 million in 1931. This rate of increase was slightly less than the rate of increase in the number of insured unemployed in those years. By the end of 1932 there were almost as many persons receiving transitional benefit (1,039,000) as insured benefit (1,200,000), although the cost of transitional benefit was only £19 million, compared to insured benefits of £73 million. But even before the depression, the Unemployment Fund had accumulated a deficit of £36 million; by March 1931 this had risen to £75 million.[15]

The result of the increased expenditure, largely on unemployment relief, was that central government budget deficits rapidly became larger. Even in the later 1920s, central government had run deficits, but these were small, and were offset by surpluses in local authority accounts. They now became much larger. The combined current surplus of central and local authorities in 1929 had been £12 million; by 1931 this had developed into a deficit of £28 million (the central deficit alone had risen from £33 million to £82 million). The deterioration in the public finances, and in particular the politically sensitive central government deficit (and the even more politically sensitive total cost of unemployment relief) led to a search for economy, which was to find its fullest expression in the May Report of 1931.[16]

GOVERNMENT POLICIES IN THE DEPRESSION

Apart from anguishing over the details of the unemployment relief schemes, the period from 1929 to 1931, when the Labour government was hampered by its parliamentary reliance on Liberal support, saw little in the way of economic

13. Ibid., pp. 49–51.
14. E.M. Burns, *British Unemployment Programs, 1920–1938* (Washington, DC 1941), p. 70; Garside, *Unemployment*, pp. 55–6; A. Deacon, *In Search of the Scrounger: the administration of unemployment insurance in Britain, 1920–31* (1976).
15. Burns, *Unemployment Programs*, pp. 56, 69, 361 (App. IV).
16. Feinstein, *National Income*, Tables 31, 33.

or social legislation. An attempt at cutting through the maze of the unemployment relief system was made in the form of the setting up of a Royal Commission on Unemployment Insurance in 1930, but this did not make its final report until 1932. The most notable social intervention came in the field of housing, when the Housing Act 1930 ('Greenwood Act') began to make subsidies available to local authorities for slum clearance.

Nor, in the brief tenure of office of the Labour government, was anything very fundamental done to solve the problems of over-capacity and unemployment in the older industries. The most notable intervention was in the coal industry, in the form of the Coal Mines Act 1930. This was partly a political matter; one result of the General Strike had been the lengthening of the miners' working day from 6.5 to 7.5 hours. The Labour Party came to power committed to reducing the working day to 7 hours, and this provision formed Part III of the Act. More fundamentally, the Act attempted a temporary palliative, in the form of compulsory cartelisation, and a more permanent reorganisation. The cartelisation formed Part I of the Act, under which a Central Council, composed of the owners, would determine the allocation of sales quotas between seventeen districts into which the country was divided, and subsidiary quotas would be determined for individual collieries. However, this scheme was not backed up by an effective system of national price maintenance, and so fierce inter-district competition continued. However, the scheme did something to control output and keep up prices and profits, and since quotas were transferable, it led to some concentration of production.

The longer-term rationalisation of the coal industry was, under Part II of the Act, entrusted to a Coal Mines Reorganisation Commission, charged with promoting amalgamations and the concentration of production. However, opposition from the industry ensured that this did not take place. The Commission's powers were eventually transferred to the Coal Commission by the Coal Act 1938, which also nationalised coal royalties, a process concluded in 1942 at the cost of £66.5 million.[17]

The hand of the government was felt more indirectly in the case of the two other depressed major industries of the 1920s, cotton and shipbuilding. In April 1930, J.H. Thomas, the minister charged with responsibility for unemployment, and Montagu Norman, the Governor of the Bank of England, were instrumental in forming the Bankers' Industrial Development Company (BIDC), to bring City capital and industry together. Supported by many of the most influential banking and finance institutions in the UK, it was yet not designed to risk its own capital; it was essentially a vetting and guaranteeing body for projects deemed financially sound. Nor was it equipped with any money from the government. In the circumstances, it was perhaps surprising that any progress at all was made.

17. M.W. Kirby, *The British Coalmining Industry 1870–1946: a political and economic history* (Macmillan 1977), chs 8 and 9; B. Supple, *The History of the British Coal Industry, vol. 4, 1913–46: The Political Economy of Decline* (Oxford, Clarendon 1987), pp. 301–2, 334–6.

Under the auspices of the BIDC, the Lancashire Cotton Corporation was formed, which quickly bought up 9 million spindles in the American section of the industry; it proceeded to scrap these over the next few years, but in 1932 the UK still had 51.9 million spindles, compared with 55.9 million in 1929.[18] In shipbuilding, an organised scheme of restriction was set up in 1930, in the form of National Shipbuilders' Security Ltd (NSS), which had the backing of the BIDC. It was empowered to raise funds, to be repaid by a levy of 1 per cent on the sales of participating firms, in order to purchase obsolete or redundant shipyards, dispose of their assets, and sell off the sites with a restriction on their further use for shipbuilding. For these purposes the Bank of England advanced £2.5 million. By the end of 1932, NSS had purchased ninety-nine berths, although over-capacity was not thereby solved, as the shipbuilding crisis was to deepen in 1933–35, and little had been done even by the late 1930s to promote amalgamations and concentration of production.[19]

The last great industry to have suffered in the 1920s had to weather the new crisis alone. By 1932, pig-iron production had fallen by 53 per cent, and steel output by 45 per cent, compared with 1929. The formation of a British Steel Exports Association in 1929 was not able to stop exports falling precipitously; between 1929 and 1932, total iron and steel exports fell by 57 per cent. Relief was not to come until the introduction of a tariff in 1932. Meanwhile, the industry survived by writing down its capital, and undergoing forced amalgamations under the pressure of the commercial banks.[20]

EXPLAINING THE FAILURE OF POLICY

These policies were restrictionist answers to the problem of excess production in particular industries. They were not designed to be a general way of counteracting the depression, which had begun shortly after the government assumed office. Nor, in their limited nature, could they give much relief. In practice, the British economy experienced the depression without any coherent or substantial effort being made by the government to counteract its effects. The reasons for this were much debated at the time, and still arouse controversy.

In essence, the choices were between policies entailing expansion of demand (and a recovery in the price level), or those leading to the reduction of prices and costs (i.e. deflation) in order to raise profits and thus stimulate entrepreneurial activity. In practice, there were a limited number of possible policies which could have been adopted to these ends; a protectionist tariff; deflation (cutting public spending, to reduce the price level, thus reducing costs and restoring competitiveness); devaluation (to restore competitiveness

18. R. Skidelsky, *Politicians and the Slump* (Macmillan 1967), pp. 152–3; Mitchell, *Statistics*, p. 370.
19. S. Pollard, *The Development of the British Economy 1914–1950* (Edward Arnold 1962), p. 118; E.H. Lorenz, *Economic Decline in Britain: the shipbuilding industry 1890–1970* (Oxford, Clarendon 1991), pp. 30–1.
20. Pollard, *Development*, pp. 115–16; Mitchell, *Statistics*, p. 301.

by reducing export prices); public works (to reduce unemployment directly); finally, a policy of inactivity, until conditions improved by themselves.

However, there were strong objections to all of these except the last. These objections were not on grounds of economic theory. All of these possible policies could have been justified to some extent on economic grounds. Indeed, they were all suggested as part of the recommendations of the Economic Advisory Council (EAC), set up to provide the government with just such professional advice by economists (the Council included Keynes). But in practice the government declined to adopt the EAC advice, for reasons which were essentially political. A protectionist tariff was anathema to the Liberal Party, on whose support in Parliament the government relied. Deflation, which would involve another offensive to reduce wages, was not favoured by the government, as the self-perceived representative of the working classes. Devaluation was unpopular with most shades of political opinion. Public works on any greater scale were held in horror by conservative financial opinion, which the government did not wish to antagonise unnecessarily. There remained only the last option.[21]

In retrospect, the government has been much criticised for failing to strike out on a bold new policy to combat the depression. Such criticism became commonplace after the Second World War, when 'Keynesian' economic theory and full employment formed the intellectual and historical background against which history was written. But, it has been pointed out, this is to be guilty of hindsight; there did not exist in the early 1930s anything in the nature of a 'Keynesian' orthodoxy. The predominant 'classical' school of economic thought, derived from Alfred Marshall and developed by Pigou, Robbins and Clay could offer no new insights into the causes of depression and its remedies. Keynes himself was not to produce his General Theory of Employment, Interest and Money until 1936; one of its central theories, the concept of the 'multiplier', according to which a stimulus to demand via public works could occur as a multiple of the original spending, had been formulated (by Kahn) only in 1931, and was at the time of the economists' report hardly a central feature of Keynes' thinking.

More immediately, any public works programme on a large scale risked destroying business confidence (or so business people maintained), as well as raising questions of how large-scale direction of investment was to be reconciled with democratic government. Thus, party political constraints aside, a large-scale public works programme was ruled out in 1930–31, regardless of which party was in power.[22]

It may also be noted that studies have thrown doubt on the plausibility of Lloyd George's claim, in the Liberal pamphlet written for the 1929 general

21. Skidelsky, *Politicians*, pp. 203–25; S. Howson and D. Winch, *The Economic Advisory Council, 1930–1939* (Cambridge UP 1977), pp. 46–79; the report of the Committee of Economists is reproduced on pp. 180–243.

22. R. McKibbin, 'The Economic Policy of the Second Labour Government 1929–31', *Past and Present* 68 (1975).

election campaign, *We Can Conquer Unemployment*, that the solution to unemployment could come through a large programme of public works. This postulated a large programme of public works, costing an extra £100 million a year for five years, chiefly on roadbuilding, but also on electrical supply, telephones and housing. The calculation was that this would reduce unemployment to 'normal proportions' (taken as the pre-1914 level of 4.7 per cent) by the end of the first year, implying a reduction of about 2 million in the insured unemployed. Simulations by M. Thomas suggest that this programme would not have worked, that the reduction in unemployment would have been no more than 286,000 in the first year (rising to 359,000 in the fifth year) and that any attempt to push forward an even larger programme would have led to a greater balance of payments deficit. Thus the only way (Thomas contends) in which a large public works programme could have succeeded would have been if combined with a 'closed economy', that is, one in which the state controlled foreign trade and the export of capital. This, akin to what was to develop in Germany in the 1930s, would have been a far cry from a Keynesian expansion programme.[23] (So much did the government fear the influence of this pamphlet that, rather unconstitutionally, it enlisted the aid of civil servants to draft a reply.)[24]

To some extent, however, a deflationary policy was pursued. Churchill's last Budget had realised a deficit of £14.5 million. Snowden's first Budget (1930) attempted to eliminate this by raising taxation (although spending was not reduced); the standard rate of income tax was raised from 4s. to 4s. 6d. in the pound, and surtax and estate duty was raised. But this device failed, and the official realised deficit was £23.3 million. The continuing deterioration in the balance necessitated a tighter budget in April 1931 (again, to be achieved through higher taxation rather than cutting spending), which was designed to bring the budget back into balance. This move failed, as unemployment continued to rise, reducing tax yields and raising expenditure. Between 1929 and 1931, total central government receipts rose only from £785 million to £802 million, but expenditure rose from £818 million to £884 million. The result was a rise in the budget deficit from (–)£33 million to (–)£82 million.[25]

The picture for the whole public sector was not so worrying, since local authorities achieved a surplus in these years, thus achieving a combined (central and local government) public sector surplus of £15 million in 1929, and deficits of only (–)£15 million in 1930 and (–)£28 million in 1931.[26] But political attention focused on the budget of the central government, and the rapidly

23. D. Lloyd George, *We Can Conquer Unemployment* (Cassell 1929).
24. *Memoranda on Certain Proposals relating to Unemployment* (1929), Cmd 3331. The analysis of the Liberal proposals is by M. Thomas, 'Aggregate Demand, 1918–45', in R. Floud and D. McCloskey, *The Economic Hisotry of Britain since 1700*, vol. 2 (1981), pp. 337–8.
25. (Sir) B. Mallet and C.O. George, *British Budgets, Third Series, 1921–22 to 1932–33* (Macmillan 1933), pp. 444–50; Feinstein, *National Income*, Table 31.
26. Feinstein, *National Income*, Tables 31, 33.

rising total spending on unemployment was causing concern by early 1931. While the deficit could in theory have simply continued being added to the National Debt, this was not favoured by financial orthodoxy (of which Snowden was an exemplar). Nor would orthodoxy take kindly to abandoning or reducing the annual payment to the Sinking Fund (designed eventually to pay off the National Debt, or at least provide a token of the government's desire to do so); this was running at about £50 million annually in 1929–30. In addition, the Treasury wished to reduce the spending on debt service, which remained the largest cost of central government, and to increase government borrowing carried the risk of driving up market interest rates, thus making debt service more expensive.[27]

CONCLUSIONS

The years 1929–31 may be summed up as follows: the depression which began in 1929 was externally induced, having its greatest effects on exports. Although relatively mild by international experience, it impinged very severely on the traditional large exporting industries, which were already suffering from lost markets and higher than average unemployment in the 1920s. But even the newer and more technologically up-to-date industries such as vehicles and chemicals lost severely in export markets. The most obvious consequences were the doubling of unemployment, the rise of long-term unemployment (particularly in northern Britain) and the deterioration of the public finances. In the absence of a coherent body of economic opinion and theory to indicate the way out of the depression, policy remained inert, apart from some restrictive measures applied to certain industries. These measures had little effect, either in the short or the long term.

27. Ibid., Tables 31, 33; Mallet and George, *Budgets*, pp. 444–7; Howson and Winch, *Advisory Council*, p. 276.

CHAPTER 12

THE 1931 CRISIS AND CHANGES IN POLICY

THE POSITION BEFORE THE CRISIS

The position in the spring of 1931 was therefore that the depression had led to a fall in exports and in the national income, a rise in unemployment, a fall in the price level, and a deterioration in public finance. These had largely been brought about by external forces, as international trade and the prices of internationally traded goods fell. Although very serious by historical standards, and socially the more distressing since unemployment was concentrated in those industries and regions which had already been suffering in the 1920s, the British depression was relatively mild by international standards. However, at this point, the depression in the real economy became the background to a series of financial crises, which in turn led for the first time to a radical shift in policy.[1]

One of the emerging financial crises was that associated with the growing central government budgetary deficit, and the reactions of politicians and financiers to this. The second crisis was the deterioration in the foreign balance of payments. When the depression began, exports of manufactures (the largest single category of exports) fell sharply. By 1931, the total volume of exports had fallen by 38 per cent. The total volume of imports was unchanged. While the unit prices of imports had fallen more than those of exports (thus improving the terms of trade by 20 per cent), this did not prevent a deterioration in the balance of trade.[2] There was an even larger deterioration in the invisible balance, as shipping and investment income fell substantially. The result was that in 1931, for the first time since the year of the General Strike (and thus only the second time on record), the British economy had a deficit on the current balance of payments (Table 12.1 opposite).

1. The British financial crises of 1931 have been much discussed. The most useful recent contributions are A. Cairncross and B. Eichengreen, *Sterling in Decline: the devaluations of 1931, 1949 and 1967* (Oxford, Blackwell 1983); and D.B. Kunz, *The Battle for Britain's Gold Standard in 1931* (Beckenham, Croom Helm 1987). Both of these are referred to extensively in this chapter.
2. B.R. Mitchell, *British Historical Statistics* (Cambridge UP 1988), pp. 519, 527.

Table 12.1 UK current balance of payments, 1929–31

	1929 (£m)	*1930 (£m)*	*1931 (£m)*
Visible trade			
Exports	854	670	464
Imports	1,117	953	786
Visible balance (A)	–263	–283	–322
Invisible trade			
Government services and transfers	+14	+19	+10
Private services and transfers	+78	+60	+31
Interest, profits and dividends	+247	+219	+167
Invisible balance (B)	+339	+298	+208
Current balance of payments (A) + (B)	+76	+15	–114

Source: R.G. Ware, 'The Balance of Payments in the Inter-War Period: Further Details', *Bank of England Quarterly Bulletin* 14 (1974), Table B

The slump was thus much greater in invisibles than in visible trade. It has been estimated that income from shipping deteriorated by £50 million, and net investment income by £70 million between 1929 and 1931. On this estimate (by Moggridge), the total deterioration of the invisible balance between those years was –£180 million, rather than the more modest –£131 million shown above. Whatever the true figure, it seems clear that the major force behind the balance of payments crisis of 1931 was the invisible account rather than visible trade.[3]

Thus by the beginning of 1931, there were two deficits – a budgetary one and a balance of payments one. (The deterioration in public finances 1929–31 was discussed in Chapter 11.) Much confusion has been caused by the association of both types of deficits with the crisis of 1931. The importance of the balance of payments deficit is obvious, in that it was thought likely to provoke a sterling devaluation, and holders of sterling were understandably nervous. The attention given to the budget deficit is harder to explain. While, in certain conditions, a budget deficit might contribute to hyperinflation, as in Germany in 1923, such conditions did not exist in Britain in 1931; the budget deficit was comparatively small, and could have been absorbed into the National Debt without much difficulty. In practice, however, financial markets reacted with extreme nervousness; the budget deficit seems to have raised fears of government insolvency and currency collapse in the minds of holders of sterling. Thus the link between the two types of deficits was that they both acted on sterling holders in the same way – psychologically. This in turn became a politicised lack of confidence in the government, which was in any

3. D. Moggridge, 'The 1931 Financial Crisis: a new view', *The Banker* (1970), p. 833.

case already suspect in the minds of the holders of capital (British and foreign) simply by being a Labour government. The situation is full of ironies, not the least being that the government tried very hard to appear 'respectable' (i.e. conservative) in financial matters.

Since the government had ruled out any expansionary measures, was committed to defending the existing sterling parity, and remained resolutely opposed to protection, its only option was to continue with its mildly deflationary budgetary policy and hope that things would improve in the course of time. This hope was misplaced. By this time, fears as to the sterling parity had already surfaced. The Economic Advisory Council had been aware for some time of the danger of a sterling crisis. In December 1930 the gold reserve had fallen below the 'Cunliffe minimum' of £150 million. In January 1931 Snowden drew the attention of the Cabinet to the disturbing implications of the transfer of funds abroad, warning that this could lead to a panic flight from sterling. Readers of the French journal, *Revue d'économie politique*, were alerted to the danger of a sterling crisis in the first issue of 1931. In the first week of March 1931 Montagu Norman warned the Committee of Treasury of the danger of forced devaluation.

In the absence of alternatives, Keynes' remedy was the controversial one of a mild ('revenue') tariff, which he proposed in an article on 7 March 1931. This drew no response from the government. On 13 July 1931 the report of the Committee on Finance and Industry ('Macmillan Committee') was published. This surveyed the working of the international gold standard, and of the British financial and monetary system. It found the remedy for the slump to lie in the raising of producers' prices internationally, relative to wages and other costs. Some members of the Committee thought that a British remedy might involve a revenue tariff combined with export bounties (tantamount to devaluation).[4]

But the Macmillan Committee firmly rejected unilateral devaluation:

> But, while all things may be lawful, all things are not expedient, and in our opinion the devaluation by any Government of a currency standing at its par value suddenly and without notice (as must be the case to prevent foreign creditors removing their property) is emphatically one of those things which are not expedient. . . . Moreover, considering the matter from another point of view, in the environment of the present world slump the relief to be obtained from a 10 per cent devaluation might prove to be disappointing. . . . in the atmosphere of crisis and distress which would inevitably surround such an extreme and sensational measure as the devaluation of sterling, we might well find that the state of affairs immediately ensuing on such an event would be worse than that which had preceded it.[5]

This firm commitment to the sterling parity may have reassured some holders of sterling. But it is also possible that, since in the report there appeared for the first time an estimate of the size of British *short-term* foreign liabilities, it may have suggested to investors that now was the time to sell their sterling

4. Cairncross and Eichengreen, *Sterling*, pp. 55–61.
5. Committee on Finance and Industry, *Report* (1931), Cmd 3897, paras 256–7.

holdings. Those interested could also trace in the appendices of the report the deterioration in the current balance of payments.[6]

THE DEVELOPMENT OF THE CRISIS

The report was quickly overshadowed by the financial crisis in mainland Europe, which was soon to spread to British financial institutions. In May, the Credit Anstalt, an Austrian bank which was small by international standards, but held two-thirds of the total deposits of the Austrian banking system, had collapsed. The illiquid state of this bank created panic in European banking circles. Within weeks the banking crisis spread to Germany and eastern Europe. The international scramble to liquidate doubtful assets held abroad proved fatal for the German banking system. On 13 July, the day of publication of the Macmillan Report, the Darmstadter Bank, one of the largest German financial institutions, failed. Three days later it was able to reopen, but only under government guarantees, and with the benefit of exchange control. This latter provision froze in Germany some £70 million owing to British banks.

The pressure on bank deposits was thus immediately transferred to Britain. On 13 July the Bank of England suffered an external outflow of gold. On 15 July sterling fell sharply against the dollar and French franc, and gold losses resumed. Over the two and a half weeks from 13 July to 1 August, the Bank of England was to lose more than £33 million in gold and at least £21 million in foreign exchange. About 60 per cent of the £38 million of gold lost in July went to France and 30 per cent to the Netherlands. The only action that the authorities took was to raise Bank Rate by one point to 3.5 per cent on 23 July and another point, to 4.5 per cent, on 30 July. No further rises occurred until the crisis was over. The reasons why the rate was not raised further to reduce the outflow from sterling are still obscure.[7]

At this point, attention on the part of foreign holders of sterling switched to the budgetary position. Sir Richard Hopkins, Controller of Finance and Supply Services in the Treasury, sent the Chancellor of the Exchequer a memorandum in the last week of July, warning that Britain would be driven off the gold standard unless dramatic action were taken:

> Nor can we control the fact that foreign nations have immense sums of money in London and will try to get them away if distrust of the pound extends. . . . the first thing at which foreigners look is the budgetary position. Whether it is reasonable that they should do so may be open to debate. That they do so is beyond question. When on Monday the Governor sounds J.P. Morgan as to the possibility of an American loan to support the pound, the first question the latter will ask, in my belief, is: 'Will steps be first taken about the dole and the budgetary position?'[8]

6. Cairncross and Eichengreen, *Sterling*, Table 11, App. IV.
7. Ibid., pp. 62–3; D. Williams, 'London and the 1931 Financial Crisis', *EcHR* XV (1963), p. 524.
8. Undated, but probably 24 July 1931; quoted in Cairncross and Eichengreen, *Sterling*, p. 64.

This tendency on the part of overseas investors was not wholly irrational. Many had vivid recollections of the great European inflations of the early 1920s, driven by budget deficits financed by the issue of government bills and of paper currency unbacked by gold. The French drew similar lessons from their own inflationary experience in the mid-1920s. The fact that the underlying British financial position was quite different escaped them. Britain was experiencing an outflow of short-term funds, which was small in relation to the total of British capital invested abroad, but the latter could not be mobilised in a short period. Likewise on the budgetary position; the deficits contemplated were small in relation to the existing National Debt, and could have been used to swell the latter without overburdening the finances of central government. Nor was the internal banking structure unsound, although the clearing banks had had to allow many firms to run up overdrafts. But these subtleties did not sway those who feared a run on the pound, culminating in devaluation and the loss of their capital.

At this point, two further events happened. First, between 25 and 30 July the British government arranged loans ('foreign credits' in bankers' language) from the central banks of France and the USA, amounting to £50 million in foreign exchange (£25 million in francs and £25 million in US dollars). These foreign loans/credits were required due to official reluctance to raise Bank Rate further. Given this reluctance to strengthen the sterling exchange rate by raising Bank Rate, the only alternative was to intervene directly on the foreign exchange markets. With these foreign loans, the Bank would now be able to defend sterling by buying it on the foreign exchange markets, paying for these purchases with the foreign exchange thus borrowed. The US credits began to be used for this purpose on 7 August, the French credits on the following day.

The second event was the release on 31 July of the final report of the Committee on National Expenditure ('May Report'). This had been set up on 17 March with a view to recommending reductions in public expenditure. Barely concealing its disapproval of the spending policies of the Labour government, the report made recommendations for substantial savings, totalling £96.6 million, of which £66.5 million were to come by savings on unemployment insurance (mainly through cutting benefits by 20 per cent and raising insurance contributions); the rest was to come mainly from savings on education and the road programme.[9]

THE MAY REPORT AND THE FORMATION OF THE NATIONAL GOVERNMENT

The May Report caused a sensation, not least because it predicted a budget deficit of around £120 million; this was a particularly gloomy view, obtained by assuming that no further borrowing for the benefit of the Unemployment Fund should be allowed, but that all the expenditure of the Fund would be

9. Cairncross and Eichengreen, *Sterling*, pp. 65–9; Committee on National Expenditure, *Report* (1931), Cmd 3920, ch. VIII.

covered by taxation. (The central government deficit for 1931 was in fact £82 million, and the combined central and local government deficit only £28 million.)[10] The report, and revelation of the recent foreign exchange losses, further dented foreign confidence. Keynes was scathing about the report, on the grounds that its deflationary recommendations would reduce domestic demand and thus increase unemployment, and thus also paradoxically further reduce government income. But such criticism was in a sense misplaced, in that it would not weigh with foreign holders of sterling, and from then on until the fall of the government the struggle to defend the gold standard centred on the measures to balance the budget.[11] (The impression should not be given that all the sellers of sterling were foreign; British holders were 'rushing to get out of sterling' in July and August, as were French and German; the only holders who did not join the rush were those of the USA.)[12]

The struggle was conducted in the Cabinet, which set up an Economy Committee to consider what cuts could be made. Its initial meeting was told by Snowden that the budget imbalance would be £170 million, rather than £120 million. The committee proposed expenditure cuts of £79 million, and £89 million of new taxation. These proposals were considered by the Cabinet on 19 August, by which time more than £28 million of the £50 million of foreign credits had been spent. Fresh discussion in Cabinet failed to reach agreement; the proposed cuts in unemployment benefit were too little for the financiers, and too much for the representatives of organised labour. By this time only one-third of the foreign credits were left. Thus further defence of sterling would require fresh credits. The government's agents in New York, J.P. Morgan and Co., indicated that a private credit of £20 million–25 million might be possible, if the government's economic programme had the support of the Bank of England and the City of London (although the tone of the telegram was very tentative). Fortified by this, Macdonald told the Cabinet that such a credit would require cuts of £70 million. On this the Cabinet split, and the National Government was eventually formed on 24 August.[13]

The formation of the National Government did not save sterling. Fresh credits of unprecedented size, amounting to the equivalent of £40 million each, were arranged in New York and Paris, via the commercial banks, but the pressure on sterling continued. The final cuts were presented to Parliament in Snowden's Emergency Budget of 10 September. This envisaged a rise in tax yield of £40.5 million (mainly through raising the standard income tax rate from 4s. 6d. to 5s., and surtax rates by 10 per cent) and a reduction in total spending of £35.7 million. Actual cuts in spending programmes (presented in an Economy Bill the next day) were to be £70 million, of which £25.8 million was to come from

10. C.H. Feinstein, *National Income, Expenditure and Output of the United Kingdom, 1855–1965* (Cambridge UP 1972), Tables 31, 33.

11. J.M. Keynes, 'The Economy Report', *New Statesman*, 15 August 1931; Cairncross and Eichengreen, *Sterling*, pp. 67–9.

12. Kunz, *Battle*, p. 94.

13. Cairncross and Eichengreen, *Sterling*, pp. 70–1; Kunz, *Battle*, pp. 104–5.

unemployment benefit, the standard rate of which was to be reduced by 10 per cent.

THE END OF THE GOLD STANDARD

The Budget did not relieve the situation, and on the same day the final run on sterling began. Matters were not helped by rumours of a 'mutiny' in the Navy at Invergordon (actually a series of mass meetings by ratings protesting against pay cuts proposed in the Budget), which prevented the Atlantic Fleet departing on manoeuvres. The pressure culminated on 18–19 September, when £25 million of foreign exchange was lost. On the evening of 20 September the government announced the suspension of the gold standard. The possibilities of remaining on the gold standard and merely devaluing sterling were not seriously considered, probably since this might have resulted in a wave of devaluations elsewhere. The pound immediately fell in the foreign exchange markets. For the rest of the year, the sterling–dollar rate averaged only \$3.69, a reduction of 24 per cent on the previous parity. In 1932 the average rate was to be \$3.50, a reduction of 28 per cent on the gold standard parity.[14]

The causes of the financial crisis have been much debated. Contemporary opinion was much influenced by the idea that it was a conspiracy by the financial establishment in Britain and the USA (a 'bankers' ramp'), an idea proposed by the *Daily Herald* newspaper (which supported the Labour Party). In fact the origins of the crisis were laid down in 1925; the overvaluation of the pound and the failure of British exports to rise further than they did meant that sterling was dangerously overexposed to sudden short-term movements across the foreign exchanges. The deterioration of the balance of payments after 1929 clearly began to stimulate such movements; London's gross short-term liabilities fell from £760 million in June 1930 to £640 million in June 1931, as holders of sterling converted to other currencies.

Once this movement started, sentiment was further affected by the growing budget deficit. There is no evidence that either the British or US financial establishment or the Bank of England conspired to discredit MacDonald's government. Although bankers were conservative financially (and politically), and thus not predisposed to favour a Labour government, there was a strong feeling in banking circles that the balancing of the Budget was in the interests of the government, and, after a period of necessary stringency, of the British people as a whole.

The authorities also made some mistakes; the low level of Bank Rate in 1930 weakened confidence in London, and the failure to raise Bank Rate earlier and higher in 1931 made it difficult to counter the external drain once the crisis

14. Kunz, *Battle*, ch. 5; Cairncross and Eichengreen, *Sterling*, pp. 66–72; (Sir) B. Mallett and C.O. George, *British Budgets, Third Series, 1921–22 to 1932–33* (Macmillan 1933), pp. 450–1; Mitchell, *Statistics*, p. 703; *Memorandum on the Measures Proposed by His Majesty's Government to Secure Reductions in National Expenditure* (1931), Cmd 3952, pp. 1–11.

started, for fear of alarming sentiment further. On the other hand, once the crisis had got under way, it has been suggested that, paradoxically, confidence in sterling was already too weak for a high Bank Rate to have the usual effect:

> With liquidity tight abroad and confidence in sterling shaky, it is doubtful whether the crisis could have been corrected by a 10 per cent bank rate, which, according to tradition, would draw gold from the moon.[15]

Also, the handling of the sterling support operation in August could have been better. Finally, the available information was almost entirely in the hands of the Bank of England, which consulted with only a handful of Cabinet ministers. This probably made political agreement more difficult when the matter was brought to the whole Cabinet.[16] (The secretiveness of the Bank was revealed during the crisis, when it used some of its secret reserve of foreign exchange to defend the pound. The government had been unaware of the existence of this reserve.)[17]

The abandonment of the gold standard, after so much effort, was an anti-climax. The fears of bankers and the financially conservative that it would presage currency collapse and hyperinflation did not materialise. It represented, from the domestic point of view, a recognition of reality; that the pound could not be sustained at the pre-1914 parity. Internationally, it contributed to the break-up of the gold standard system, as a sharp distinction emerged between those countries remaining on gold and those which joined Britain in leaving it.

THE RESULTS OF THE ABANDONMENT OF THE GOLD STANDARD

The result of the crisis was a watershed in policy. The abandonment of gold freed the government to develop new financial policies and instruments. This possibility had been recognised by Keynes immediately after the abandonment. Having been in favour of maintaining the standard while it seemed possible to do so, he nevertheless welcomed the decision when it seemed inevitable, and looked to the future. (Keynes had had the opportunity, as the director of an investment trust, to speculate on a large scale against sterling in the days before devaluation, but declined it, writing on 18 September that 'What you suggest amounts in the present circumstances to a frank bear speculation against sterling. . . . I am clear that an institution has no business to do such a thing at the present time'.)[18]

15. C.P. Kindleberger, *The World in Depression, 1919–1939* (Penguin 1987), p. 155.
16. Kunz, *Battle*, pp. 99–100; Cairncross and Eichengreen, *Sterling*, p. 67; Williams, 'London', p. 528.
17. Kunz, *Battle*, p. 122.
18. D. Moggridge, *Maynard Keynes: an economist's biography* (Routledge 1992), p. 529.

> There are few Englishmen who do not rejoice at the breaking of our gold fetters. We feel that we have at last a free hand to do what is sensible. The romantic phase is over, and we can begin to discuss realistically what policy is for the best.
>
> It may seem surprising that a move which had been represented as a disastrous catastrophe should have been received with so much enthusiasm. But the great advantages to British trade and industry of our ceasing artificial efforts to maintain our currency above its real value were quickly realised.[19]

Before the abandonment of gold, it could be said that Britain had two main economic/financial policies; to maintain the parity of sterling and to balance the budget. Afterwards, although balancing the budget continued as an important aim, the abandonment of gold made it possible to ease some policies and to contemplate fresh ones.

Interest rate policy

The first relief came in the form of interest rate policy. The defence of sterling had necessitated comparatively high interest rates since the return to the gold standard, in comparison with Paris and New York. This was now no longer necessary. Although Bank Rate had been raised to 6 per cent on the day after suspension of the gold standard, as a defence against an anticipated large rush out of sterling, this proved an unnecessary precaution. It was rapidly reduced in several stages, coming down to 3 per cent on 21 April 1932. Since, apart from a brief period in 1930 (March–July) it had never been below 4 per cent since 1923, this was a great change.

The period of 'cheap money' now inaugurated, which was to last until after the Second World War, was bound up with a further aim – the reduction of the sums paid by the government in debt interest. The conversion of old loans to lower rates of interest would be easier if interest rates came down further, so the authorities continued to lower Bank Rate. In June 1932 it was reduced to 2 per cent. The subsequent conversion operation was a great success; by the end of September all but 8 per cent of £2,086 million of 5 per cent War Loan stock had been converted into a new 3.5 per cent stock. Further conversion operations on the National Debt reduced the debt charge on the main part of the debt by £55.5 million annually by 1936. The general level of interest rates followed Bank Rate downwards; ultimately, mortgage rates also fell.

A measure accompanying the conversion, which was designed to safeguard the supply of internal capital, and thus to assist in keeping interest rates low after the introduction of cheap money, was the embargo on overseas capital issues imposed on the Stock Exchange. How necessary this restriction was in the trough of a depression when there were neither borrowers nor lenders is debatable, although it was a safeguard against the effects of any future expansionary monetary policy.[20]

19. *New Statesman*, 27 September 1931; reprinted in J.M. Keynes, *Essays in Persuasion* (1931; Hart-Davis 1951), p. 281.
20. H.W. Richardson, *Economic Recovery in Britain, 1932–39* (Weidenfeld & Nicolson 1967), pp. 187–90.

The managed exchange rate

The most radical development was of a policy to manage the exchange rate. This came in the form of the Exchange Equalisation Account, announced in the Budget of 1932. Designed to insulate the domestic economy from short-term fluctuations in the exchange rate, through intervention in the foreign exchange markets, it came effectively to mean that the exchange rate was stabilised in the short run. This did not mean that it did not change; after September 1931 it fell sharply, then rose. After April 1933, when the USA also left gold and devalued, the pound–dollar rate returned to slightly above its gold standard level. In practice, as British capital flowed back across the exchanges in the later 1930s, much of the effort of the Account went into keeping the rate down rather than having to sustain it – a far cry from the years after 1925.[21]

Budgetary policy

The abandonment of the gold standard thus freed policy from several financial or monetary constraints. In so far as the depressed state of much of industry in the 1920s could have been attributed to these constraints, it could be said that it augured well for recovery. At this point, proto-Keynesians might have argued that conditions were right for an expansionist policy, and that (for example) a large programme of public works could be undertaken without endangering either the exchange rate or the stability of the state's finances. But this was not a course of action favoured by the government, which still favoured balanced budgets. This was evident in the Budget of 1932, which, presented by the new Chancellor of the Exchequer, Neville Chamberlain, was highly orthodox. The cuts implemented in the Budget of the previous September, the most politically sensitive of which had been the cut in the standard rate of unemployment benefit by 10 per cent, were maintained. Snowden had sought to bring his Budget into balance at around £851 million; Chamberlain's Budget was intended to balance at £848 million.[22]

In fact, neither Snowden nor Chamberlain succeeded in balancing their budgets. The published statements of budget balance contained a good deal of 'window dressing' which concealed much of the deterioration in the financial position in the depression. When all categories of revenue and spending are accounted for, the budget deficit in 1931–32 was about £46 million, and in 1932–33 about £50 million.

However, on paper, the budget was balanced, and conventional financial opinion placated; Britain had not followed other countries along the road of substantially unbalanced budgets during the depression. But, it has been argued, this conceals the fact that the balancing of a budget during such a sharp depression is really highly deflationary. Since tax receipts can be expected

21. N.F. Hall, *The Exchange Equalization Account* (Macmillan 1935); L. Waight, *History and Mechanism of the Exchange Equalization Account 1932–39* (1939).
22. Mallett and George, *Budgets*, pp. 450–3.

to fall and government expenditure to rise in a depression (via the operation of unemployment benefit), the budget balance will automatically deteriorate as national income falls. In this situation, to attempt to balance the Budget is to exert a further deflationary pressure on economic activity. A more realistic exercise involves calculating what the ratio of government tax and spending would have been in relation to the national income had employment remained constant. This, the 'constant employment budget balance' has been used to demonstrate that, by (nearly) balancing the Budget superficially, the government was in reality imparting a further dose of deflation to an already depressed economy. Use of this procedure suggests that, beginning in 1929–30, a 'full employment surplus' developed which reached a peak in 1934–35 of £174 million. The most contractionary period was between 1929–30 and 1933–34, when the ratio of the full employment surplus to national income rose from 0.4 to 4.2 per cent; in other words, the government was running a budget surplus of around 4 per cent of the national income.[23]

Protection

Thus the occasion of devaluation, although permitting new financial and monetary policies, did not lead to budgetary experiment. Devaluation apart, the most striking change in the economic environment was the adoption of protection. While protectionist devices had been tried since 1915, the abandonment of free trade was politically unfeasible before the formation of the National coalition government. The Conservative Party, which dominated the coalition, had a strong protectionist element, and protection was widely canvassed as the sole solution to the depression.[24] In November and December 1931, 'abnormal importations' duties had been imposed. In February 1932 an Import Duties Act came into force. This imposed a general tariff of 10 per cent, with the important exceptions of Empire goods, those covered by earlier protectionist legislation, and a large free list, including wheat, meat, and other foodstuffs, as well as all important raw materials. It was thus aimed essentially at manufactured goods from the non-Empire world.

The rates of protection in individual industries were to be recommended by an Import Duties Advisory Committee (IDAC). This reported in April, recommending a further increase of 10 per cent, making 20 per cent in total, on fully manufactured goods. Higher duties of 25 or 30 per cent in total were fixed for luxuries or semi-luxuries; the government accepted these suggestions. The IDAC made further recommendations for certain industries, the chief of which were iron and steel, in which certain products were dutied at 33.33 per cent, on condition that the industry should put forward a scheme of reorganisation. In 1935 the industry was to be granted a temporary duty of 50 per cent in

23. R. Middleton, *Towards the Managed Economy: Keynes, the Treasury and the fiscal policy debate of the 1930s* (Methuen 1985), pp. 81, 135, Table 7.4.
24. Compare the anti-protectionist conclusions reached by the team of economists in W. Beveridge (ed.), *Tariffs: the case examined* (Longmans, Green 1931).

order to improve its negotiating position while applying to join the European steel cartel.[25]

Protection also had external ramifications. The first was a series of attempts to negotiate bilateral trading agreements with other countries, in exchange for tariff concessions. Over the years, arrangements were made with Scandinavia, the Baltic states, Poland and Argentina. These had some success in providing export markets. Whereas between 1929 and 1937 the proportion of British imports coming from these countries remained almost stable, at around 17 per cent, the proportion of British exports going to these countries increased from 8.9 to 13.5 per cent.[26]

Less successful was the attempt to use protection as a basis for an expanded system of Imperial Preference. This was negotiated at Ottawa in July–August 1932. The idea was essentially the mercantilist one of the mother country finding markets for manufactures in an agrarian empire, and the latter selling food and raw materials to the mother country. But this concept was seriously out of date, since most of the Empire, especially the Dominions (Canada, Australia, New Zealand and South Africa) had long since developed their own 'infant industries' which they were determined to protect. Nor, since by then the government had decided to protect British farmers, was there much possibility of supplying a higher proportion of imported food from the Dominions. In the end, a series of bilateral treaties resulted, designed to increase Dominion exports to Britain by a system of quotas and licences. The Dominions responded, not by lowering tariffs to British exporters, but raising them against non-British exporters.

British tariffs against the rest of the world were further raised by the Ottawa duties. Imperial Preference was also extended to the colonial (i.e. non-Dominion) areas of the Empire, and the Irish Free State. In the event, the system benefited Britain less than the other countries, although Britain had started in a more favourable position. In 1924–29 the UK had on average taken 26.8 of its imports from the Empire, and had sent 35.2 per cent of its exports to the Empire. By 1937, the UK took 37.3 per cent of its imports from the Empire, but the proportion of UK exports going to the Empire had risen only to 39.7 per cent (trade with the Irish Free State is excluded).[27]

Since the principle of protection for industry had been established, it could hardly be denied to agriculture. For the first time since the repeal of the Corn Laws in 1846, farmers were now given substantial protection by the state. This eventually came in a variety of forms. In crops, the most important development was the Wheat Act 1932, which subsidised wheat growing via a 'standard guaranteed price' (i.e. minimum price). This was a recognition of the parlous financial position of wheat growers, following the fall in the wheat price from

25. J.H. Richardson, 'Tariffs, Preferences and Other Protection', in British Association, *Britain in Recovery* (Pitman 1938), pp. 127–9.
26. T. Rooth, *British Protectionism and the International Economy: overseas commercial policy in the 1930s* (Cambridge UP 1993), pp. 314–21, Apps C, D.
27. Richardson, 'Tariffs', p. 139.

an average of 9s. 10d. per hundredweight in 1929 to 5s. 9d. in 1931. The success of the policy was not in doubt; the wheat acreage of Britain rose from a 1930s low point of 1.247 million acres in 1931 to 1.873 million acres in 1935.[28] For other crops (barley, oats, horticultural products and potatoes) import duties were levied under the Import Duties Act 1932.

The third form of agricultural protection came in the form of marketing arrangements. These were designed, by combining producers together, to strengthen their economic position in relation to consumers and importers; in principle, a move towards some of the arrangements and advantages of cartelisation. The first Act to this effect was the Agricultural Marketing Act 1931; the only industry to take action under it was the hop industry.

The Agricultural Marketing Act 1933 was more successful, since it now authorised producers to control output as well as the prices of their products, and the government could bolster any scheme by giving it a tariff. Marketing boards were established for potatoes, milk, bacon and pigs. The most successful was the Milk Marketing Board (MMB), which survived until 1994; those for bacon and pigs had virtually broken down by 1936. The MMB weekly milk cheque was the financial salvation of many small farms in the later 1930s. The final form of assistance from the state was the provision of a subsidy on fat cattle in 1934, replaced by a new subsidy system under the Livestock Industry Act 1937.[29]

SIGNIFICANCE OF THE CRISIS

It remains to consider the significance of government financial and economic policy during the early years of the depression and the crisis of 1931, culminating in the policy changes of 1932. There seems no doubt that the twin aims of the government – to stay on gold at the existing parity and to balance the budget – made the depression worse, in that they constrained exports, reduced home demand, and encouraged the fall in prices. On the other hand, such policies were the common prescription of governments everywhere, and the more comprehensive and generous British scheme of social security served to protect the living standards of unemployed people. For those employed, there was even the gain of a higher real wage, as the cost of living fell.

However, once it had become apparent that the basic policy aims of 1925 could no longer be achieved, they were abandoned rapidly. After the crisis, the novelty and variety of new policies was most striking. The markets had slaughtered the sacred cow of the gold standard; the government used the moment to adopt substantial protectionist measures – import duties, a new

28. C.S. Orwin, 'Agriculture: grain and other crops', in British Association, *Britain in Depression* (Pitman 1935), pp. 94–5; Ministry of Agriculture, *A Century of Agricultural Statistics: Great Britain 1866–1966* (HMSO 1968), pp. 82, 98.

29. Orwin, 'Agriculture: grain and other crops'; A.W. Ashby and W.H. Jones, 'Agriculture: the milk industry' and 'Agriculture: the livestock and meat trade', all in British Association, *Britain in Recovery.*

version of Imperial Preference, a managed exchange rate, restriction of overseas lending, cheap money, the protection of agriculture and the cartelisation of agricultural marketing.

In this situation, the impact of policy and policy changes was mixed. The significance of the events of 1931–32 would appear to be threefold.

First, in spite of the trauma of the crisis, it was not taken as the opportunity to develop a coherent policy to achieve economic recovery. The gold standard had been reluctantly abandoned. Afterwards, it seems to have been assumed that no radical overhaul of internal policy was needed; the need to balance the Budget was still seen as paramount. However, the abandonment of gold allowed the formulation of a cheap money policy, which was to make a substantial contribution to economic recovery after 1932.

Second, the abandonment of gold, and the various devices such as protection and the managed floating of the pound, served to insulate the economy against further external shocks. The lessened outflow of new investment overseas in the 1930s also served to relieve pressure on the exchange rate, and made the task of the Exchange Equalisation Account easier.

Third, the international effects of British decisions in 1931–32 helped to spread the depression internationally. Thus eventually twenty-five countries followed Britain's example and went off gold, largely in the Empire, Scandinavia and eastern Europe, as well as Argentina, Egypt and Portugal. The scene was set for competitive devaluation, as countries scrambled to obtain a price advantage. The same was true of protection; prior to this, only the USA had raised its tariffs (in 1930); now the world followed. Partly as a result, the world economy did not recover completely in the 1930s. The volume (= value at 1980 prices) of the exports of the thirty-two leading exporters in the world, accounting for the great bulk of world exports, was still some 18 per cent below the 1929 level in 1938.[30]

CONCLUSIONS

The financial crises of 1931 had their origins in the world depression which had begun in 1929. The subsequent strains in the international payments mechanism, and the volatile flow of funds across frontiers, were bound to have an effect on the British position. Britain was vulnerable to such financially induced crises, since it had an overvalued exchange rate, a weak balance of payments, a growing budget deficit, and a Labour government. The last two elements were particularly likely to panic holders of sterling.

In the event, it was the growing budget deficit, and the quasi-political speculation which it spawned, which caused the final run on sterling. In retrospect, much of the near-hysteria was overdone. The budget deficit could have been absorbed into the rest of the National Debt without much difficulty. Even if, for example, sterling had been devalued within the gold standard system, and

30. A. Maddison, *The World Economy in the 20th Century* (Paris, OECD 1989), Table D4.

the budget deficit had been as large as the May Report guessed it would be, there is in retrospect no reason to think that the government's credit and the internal purchasing power of the pound would have collapsed. In other words, Britain in 1931 bore no resemblance to Germany in 1923. But the actions of sterling holders suggested that such an outcome was what they were anticipating. In that sense, the British crisis of 1931 was unnecessary. But the abandonment of the gold standard was accompanied by the development of new policies, some of which were to be of material help in the economic recovery of the 1930s.

CHAPTER 13

ECONOMIC RECOVERY AND GROWTH IN THE 1930s

ECONOMIC GROWTH

The negative image of the 1930s persisted, as far as economic historians were concerned, until the 1960s, when a reappraisal took place. It was then pointed out that in spite of substantial unemployment and lost export markets, the home economy recovered quickly after 1932, that there was something of a boom in important industries such as building and steel, and that the pace of growth in large sections of the 'new' industries such as motor vehicles, and in service trades, was impressive. The national income rose substantially above the pre-depression level, both in total and in per head terms. While unemployment rose substantially in the early 1930s, it had diminished by 1937 to the level of 1929. Thus by comparison with the 1920s it could be said that considerable economic progress had been made. On the other hand, such a reappraisal has been in danger of being carried too far. For example, this approach ignores the substantial loss of output during the depression, and the use of terms such as 'boom' can be defended only with difficulty in a decade where the average level of unemployment was even higher than in the 1920s.

The extent to which economic recovery and subsequent growth took place in the 1930s may be examined by means of the national income statistics presented in the Appendix. From these calculations, it seems on a superficial view that economic progress in the 1930s was marked; GDP per head rose by about 11 per cent between 1929 and 1937, in spite of the depression of the early 1930s. However, a comparison with the 1920s is less favourable; between 1924 and 1929, GDP per head grew at 2.5 per cent annually; in 1929–37 it grew at 1.8 per cent; over the whole period 1924–37, it grew at 2.0 per cent. The comparison between the 1920s and 1930s can also be made visually on a semi-logarithmic graph, which gives a true picture of *rates* of growth, since on it lines of equal slope, wherever they are on the graph, represent equal rates of change; this property is not found on ordinary constant-scale graphs (see the Appendix).

Expressed in this way, the economic trends of the 1930s look less favourable; there is clearly much lost output in the recession of 1929–32, as there had been in 1919–20. Exhibiting the growth rate of output in this way also explains why some authors regard the 1930s as years of rapid expansion, since the rate of recovery in GDP per head from the trough of the depression in 1932 to the peak of the recovery in 1937–38 was at least as fast as the growth of output in the later 1920s. However, it must not be forgotten that the 1930s line in the graph represents recovery from a serious depression, while the 1920s line (after 1924) represents the 'normal' growth of the economy, apart from the loss of output caused by the General Strike. Thus comparisons of growth rates are to that extent inappropriate and can be misleading.

The possibility of misleading comparison raises the question of the definition of economic recovery. Economists have so far not given a satisfactory definition. For example, the Collins definition is 'a phase of the business cycle characterized by an upturn in the level of economic activity'. The word 'upturn' here means simply a rise; there is no indication that the 'recovery' may raise economic activity to the pre-depression level or higher – as presumably it should to constitute a recovery.[1] The most obvious definition is that an economy has recovered from a depression when its total output has recovered to the pre-depression level, and the general utilisation of productive capacity is similar to the pre-depression level. In terms of total output, the recovery had been achieved between 1933 and 1934. However, similar capacity utilisation (judging by the degree of unemployment) was not achieved until 1937. Thus it is not safe to employ the term 'recovery' until 1937. This must be distinguished from economic growth; as already noted, the rate of growth of national output in the 1930s was similar to that of the 1920s. The achievement of the 1930s was thus not the achieving of a particularly high rate of economic growth, but the near-maintenance, when all the years of the period are averaged, of previous growth rates even in the face of a severe depression.

UNEMPLOYMENT

While national output more than recovered during the 1930s, the record was less impressive in the two important indicators of employment and foreign trade. While total employment grew in the 1930s, as the population of working age rose, it grew insufficiently to reduce unemployment below the pre-depression level. In 1929 there were, in the UK, 19.48 million employed persons and an estimated 1.50 million unemployed persons; the unemployment rate of the insured population was 10.4 per cent. The alternative unemployment rate estimate by Feinstein, which is of the rate of unemployment in the whole working population (i.e. including the uninsured occupations) was 7.3 per cent.

By 1932, all these indicators were at their worst recorded level. The population employed had fallen to 18.43 million, the number unemployed was 3.40 million, the insured unemployment rate was 22.1 per cent and the unemployment rate in the whole working population was 15.6 per cent. There were thus

1. C. Pass and B. Lowes, *Collins Dictionary of Economics* (2nd edn, HarperCollins 1993).

over 3 million people unemployed, and the national unemployment rate was about one-sixth of the national labour force. Recovery began after 1932, and reached its peak in 1937, with 20.99 million employed, 1.78 million unemployed, an insured unemployment rate of 10.8 per cent (7.8 per cent for the unemployment rate of the whole working population). In 1938, the recession was briefly renewed, and unemployment rose to 2.16 million, the insured unemployment rate to 12.9 per cent, and the rate for the working population to 9.3 per cent (unemployment figures include those persons 'temporarily stopped').[2]

FOREIGN TRADE AND PAYMENTS

Foreign trade and payments also languished in the 1930s. The sharp fall in the value of exports, although offset by an improvement in the terms of trade, which meant that a given volume of imports could be purchased by a smaller volume of exports, was accompanied by a decline in invisible income. Thus the overall balance of payments, although improving after the high deficits of 1931–32, was in deficit for most of the decade (Table 13.1).

Table 13.1 UK foreign trade and payments, 1929–39 (£million)

	Exports and re-exports	*Imports*	*Trade balance*	*Invisible balance*	*Current balance of payments*
1929	854	1,117	–263	359	96
1930	670	953	–283	319	36
1931	464	786	–322	219	–103
1932	425	641	–216	165	–51
1933	427	619	–192	184	–8
1934	463	683	–220	198	–22
1935	541	724	–169	206	23
1936	523	784	–261	234	–27
1937	614	950	–336	289	–47
1938	564	849	–285	230	–55
1939	500	800	–300	50	–250

Source: C.H. Feinstein, *National Income, Expenditure and Output in the United Kingdom, 1855–1965* (Cambridge UP 1972), Table 37

After the sharp decline in exports and invisibles in the early years of the depression, and the corresponding large payments deficit, the balance was improved by a fall in the value of imports, as the terms of trade improved. By 1935 there was even a small payments surplus, as exports began to recover. But by the end of the decade, exports were still worth less than in 1929. The invisible balance recovered steadily after 1932, but it also stayed well below the level of 1929. By 1938–39, rearmament was affecting the picture, as it led

2. Feinstein, *National Income*, Tables 57, 58.

Table 13.2 UK balance of payments as per cent of national income, 1900–38[a]

	Visible balance (%)	*Invisible balance (%)*	*Overall balance (%)*
1900–09	–5.8	+9.9	+4.0
1909–13	–4.0	+12.2	+8.3
1920–29	–3.8	+5.9	+2.1
1930–38	–5.4	+4.6	–0.8

Note: a Per cent of GDP
Source: Feinstein, *National Income*, Tables 10, 11, 82

to a rise in imports, and diverted some capacity away from the export industries. Invisibles also declined sharply, so that 1939 saw a very large deficit.

Consideration of trade values might be misleading, in view of the large changes in the relative prices of exports and (especially) imports in the 1930s. In volume terms, exports fell sharply to a low of 62 per cent of their 1929 level, in 1931 and 1932. Thereafter they rose steadily but slowly, but even at their peak in 1937 were only 80 per cent of their 1929 level. Net import volumes fell more slowly in the early years of the depression after a sharp rise in 1930, when importers had tried to forestall the imposition of import duties. By 1933, imports were 90 per cent of their 1929 level, peaking in 1937 at almost exactly the 1929 level, before falling back in 1938 due to the renewed recession. It is not unlikely that only the improvement in the terms of trade in the early years of the recession prevented further balance of payments crises after 1932.[3]

The deterioration in the balance of payments on current account in the 1930s was part of a longer-term process, which by the Second World War had left the British economy with the fundamental weakness of a chronic tendency to a balance of payments deficit (Table 13.2 above).

As Table 13.2 indicates, and as already suggested in respect of the 1920s (Chapter 6), the greatest reason for the deteriorating foreign payments position since 1914 had been the deterioration on invisibles account, and this remained so in the 1930s. By 1938, the surplus was, in current values, only about two-thirds of that of 1913. The greatest loss had been on the shipping account, although investment income had fallen also (Table 13.3 opposite).

The recovery of the 1930s was essentially based on the home market. Exports, as had been noted, did not recover, and the continued growth of the economy meant that they became much less important in the national income; whereas they had amounted to 20.4 per cent of GDP in 1929, by 1938 they were worth only 11.4 per cent of GDP. The contribution of property income from abroad also fell, from 5.8 to 3.9 per cent of GDP in between the same years.[4]

3. B.R. Mitchell, *British Historical Statistics* (Cambridge UP 1988), pp. 519, 527.
4. Feinstein, *National Income*, Tables 6, 37.

Table 13.3 UK invisible account surplus, 1913–38 (£million)

	1913	*1920–29*	*1930–33*	*1934–38*	*1930–38*
Overseas investment income	210	216	165	188	178
Shipping earnings	94	53	10	20	15
Financial services	25	43	23	21	22
Other	10	27	24	2	12
Total invisibles surplus	339	339	222	231	227

Sources: 1913: M.D.K.W. Foot, 'The Balance of Payments in the Inter-War Period', *Bank of England Quarterly Bulletin* 12 (1972), p. 359
1920–38: Feinstein, *National Income*, Table 84

INTERNATIONAL RECOVERY COMPARISONS

In view of the recovery of the UK economy, it is salutary to compare this with the degree of recovery in other industrial societies. There are difficulties in doing so. Not all countries entered or left the recession at the same time; populations grew at different rates; policies differed, and all had their own particular problems. But it seems useful to make some comparisons. Between 1929 and 1937, the greatest rise in national income in Europe (GDP) was seen in Germany, whose GDP rose by 41 per cent; then came Sweden (26 per cent) and Denmark (20 per cent). The UK's GDP rose by 18 per cent. At the other end of the scale, Austria's GDP was still 5 per cent below that of 1929, and France's was still 4 per cent below that of 1929. The GDP of the USA had risen by only 6 per cent. The UK thus had a rather favourable record in comparison with some other industrial nations in Europe and the USA, although it was less successful than Scandinavia and Germany.[5]

THE COURSE OF RECOVERY

The chronology of the recovery was not smooth. The trough of national output was reached in 1931. A slight expansion was perceptible in 1932. The next year was one of strong recovery; building expanded rapidly and in August retail sales rose for the first time since 1930. In 1934, expansion slowed down, to reaccelerate from the spring of 1935. Consumer and capital goods industries were especially buoyant. In 1936 the recovery continued, although to some extent of a different character; residential construction slackened, and industrial building rose. The heavy industries expanded rapidly, and this was reflected in a rise in raw material prices. In 1937, the recovery was checked; exports, which had been rising, began to fall again, there were sharp rises in raw material prices, and industrial profits and investment fell. The brief recession of the next year was largely confined to exports and consumer durables,

5. D.H. Aldcroft, *The European Economy 1914–1980* (Beckenham, Croom Helm 1978), p. 81.

although previous orders and the influence of rearmament served to cushion building, engineering and shipbuilding. In 1939, the influence of rearmament orders was even more marked, and output continued to rise until the outbreak of war in September.[6]

SECTORAL AND INDUSTRIAL RECOVERY

A broad view of the impact of the recession, and the extent to which the different sectors of the economy recovered in the 1930s may be obtained by splitting national income (GDP) into its main sectors (Table 13.4).

Table 13.4 Sectoral income components of UK GDP, 1929–37 (1929 = 100)

	1929 (£m)	*1929 (%)*	*1932 (%)*	*1937 (%)*
Agriculture, forestry, fishing	164	100	91	101
Mining and quarrying	151	100	77	108
Gas/water/electricity	98	100	107	127
Manufacturing	1,177	100	80	121
Building and construction	189	100	87	121
Transport and communication	406	100	84	109
Distribution and services	1,600	100	95	116
GDP (income measure)[a]	3,967	100	88	112

Note: a Imputed income from the ownership of dwellings has been excluded. Total GDP is not the sum of its parts, due to unallocated income and stock appreciation.
Source: Mitchell, *Statistics*, pp. 823, 846–7

The depression was most severe in mining and quarrying, closely followed by manufacturing, then transport and communications, and building and construction, and agriculture. The important service sector, accounting for about 40 per cent of national income in 1929, showed only a slight fall. The only sector to expand in 1929–32 was gas/water/electricity. The final (1937) output levels are highest for this sector, closely followed by manufacturing and building. However, agriculture, mining and transport failed to rise as much as the national income. Much of the apparent superior performance of services was due to the existing secular tendency for this sector to expand between the wars, and latterly to the expansion of defence and public administration.

The search for the salient economic sectors behind the recovery therefore is restricted to (gas/water/electricity and) manufacturing and building/construc-

6. H.W. Richardson, *Economic Recovery in Britain, 1932–39* (Weidenfeld & Nicolson 1967), pp. 27–34; G.D.A. McDougall, 'General Survey 1929–1937', in British Association, *Britain in Recovery* (Pitman 1938).

tion. In the case of building, there is strong evidence that the residential sector led the way in the recovery process; in 1929 there had been 228,000 houses built in the UK. Although this fell slightly, to 208,000 in 1930, the trend thereafter was continuously upward; by 1932 there were 223,000 houses built, and the movement accelerated after this; by 1936, at the peak, 366,000 were built, mostly by private enterprise. The building sector as a whole had recovered its 1929 level of output by 1933.[7]

In the case of manufacturing, a sharp distinction must be drawn between those industries which did not recover as fast as the national economy, and those which outperformed it. The principal industries of slow or negative growth were coal-mining, textiles and shipbuilding. Coal-mining was particularly hit by the decline in exports, which outlasted the inital depression period; in 1929, some 256 million tons had been mined, of which 82 million were exported; in 1932, exports had fallen to 57 million tons, and total output was down to 209 million tons. Even by 1937, when output had recovered to 240 million, exports were only 56 million tons. Thus, although a slight rise in home consumption was recorded, it was insufficient to offset the fall in exports.[8] (These exports include coke, manufactured fuel and bunker coal as well as coal *per se*, and are thus higher than those in Mitchell.)[9]

Cotton was badly hit by the decline in exports; piece goods exports, which had been 3,765 million linear yards in 1929, fell to 1,790 million in 1931, and although briefly reaching 2,302 million in 1932, fluctuated at or around 2,000 million yards until 1938, when they sank to a new low of 1,448 million yards. Yarn exports, which had been 167 million lb in 1929, fell less, and by 1937 had recovered to 159 million lb. The decline in exports was reflected in the overall figure of raw cotton consumed, which, having been 1,498 million lb in 1929, reached its trough in 1931, at 985 million lb. Thereafter there was some recovery, and the 1937 figure was 1,431 million lb. The drop in exports was not offset by a switch to artificial fabrics; exports of rayon products drew in an average of only £3.1 million a year in 1930–37, compared with £64.4 million of cotton manufactures.[10] (Continuous statistics of cotton cloth production did not begin until 1941; until then, there are only intermittent estimates such as those of the Census of Production (1907, 1913, 1924, 1930, 1935), and estimates of the pre-1941 output of the industry use the consumption of raw cotton as a proxy.) The woollen industry was also hit hard by the decline in exports; exports of woollen and worsted cloth fell from 155 million yards in 1929 to a low of 82 million yards in 1932, recovering in 1937 to 123 million yards. Yarn exports, having been 47 million lb in 1929, fell to 35 million in 1931, and then recovered to 43 million in 1933, before falling away again to

7. H.W. Richardson and D.H. Aldcroft, *Building in the British Economy between the Wars* (Allen & Unwin 1968), p. 62.
8. B.E. Supple, *The History of the British Coal Industry, vol. 4, 1913–46: The Political Economy of Decline* (Oxford, Clarendon 1987), p. 273.
9. Mitchell, *Statistics*, p. 257.
10. R. Robson, *The Cotton Industry in Britain* (Macmillan 1957), Tables 1, 2, pp. 333–5.

32 million lb in 1937.[11] For textiles as a whole, the picture was not so grim; the output of all textile industries grew between 1929 and 1937 by 26 per cent, as lost export markets were replaced to some extent by the home market.[12]

The greatest sufferer from the decline in foreign trade was shipbuilding. In 1927–29, output had averaged 1,398,000 gross tons a year; in 1930–37, it averaged 630,000 tons a year. The lowest point was reached in 1933, when output was a mere 133,000 tons, and it was only 1,030,000 tons in the decadal peak in 1938, under the stimulation of the government's 'scrap and build' policy. Most of this decline reflected the drying up of home rather than direct export orders; on average, foreign orders accounted for 20 per cent, and in 1930–37 22 per cent of all output (chiefly due to some high foreign orders in 1930–31), but the decline in home demand was closely linked to the state of world and British trade.[13]

One other major 'staple' industry deserves note as in relative decline during the 1930s – mechanical engineering. This is a protean grouping, whose main components were 'prime movers' (i.e. power sources), constructional engineering, and textile and marine engineering. The latter two were badly hit by the decline in exports and shipbuilding. Steam engine building was not a buoyant market at home or abroad, and only constructional work maintained its position during the depression. Over the whole period 1929–37, the output of the mechanical engineering industries rose by only 6 per cent, which was much lower than the expansion of manufacturing as a whole.[14]

The decline or slow growth of these major industries was offset by the rapid growth of a wide range of other industries in the 1930s. The result was a rapid expansion of manufacturing output as a whole, even when the problems of the laggard industries is taken into account. A listing of the major industries will make this clear (Table 13.5 opposite).

Electrical engineering had been growing rapidly since the late nineteenth century. In the depression, it was noticeable that its output fell only slightly (by 4 per cent in 1931), and thereafter resumed strong expansion. By 1935 its output was estimated at £107 million, having been £88 million in 1930. It was buoyed up by the expansion of electricity supply via the national grid, the growing industrial and domestic use of electrical power, and the use of new appliances such as the radio. The housebuilding boom of the 1930s gave it fresh impetus, and the reducing price of electricity expanded the market.[15]

11. Mitchell, *Statistics*, p. 362.

12. Richardson, *Economic Recovery*, p. 73.

13. L. Jones, *Shipbuilding in Britain: mainly between the two world wars* (Cardiff, University of Wales Press 1957), p. 64.

14. Richardson, *Economic Recovery*, p. 73; T.R. Gourvish, 'Mechanical Engineering', in N.K. Buxton and D.H. Aldcroft (eds), *British Industry between the Wars* (Scolar 1979), p. 133; E. Allen, 'The Engineering Trades', in British Association, *Britain in Recovery*.

15. Feinstein, *National Income*, Table 115; R.E. Catterall, 'Electrical Engineering', in Buxton and Aldcroft, *British Industry*, p. 254. See also A. Plummer, *New British Industries in the Twentieth Century* (Pitman 1937), ch. II.

Table 13.5 Increase in manufacturing industries' output, 1929–37 (per cent)

Electrical engineering	82	Timber	29
Vehicles	66	Textiles	27
Non-ferrous metals	58	Building and construction	26
Metal goods, n.e.s.*	47	Paper and printing	21
Ferrous metals	41	Precision instruments	20
Building materials	40	Tobacco	20
Food	39	Clothing	15
Leather	34	Drink	9
Chemicals	33	Shipbuilding	7
		Mechanical engineering	6

Source: Richardson, *Economic Recovery*, p. 73
* n.e.s. = not elsewhere specified

The motor vehicle industry suffered more in the depression. Output of private cars fell in 1929–32 by about 11 per cent, and that of commercial vehicles by about 12 per cent. However, the numbers of both types on the roads continued to grow, although more slowly than before, during the depression. In 1929 there had been 981,000 private cars and 330,000 goods vehicles in use in Britain. In 1932 the figures were 1,128,000 and 370,000, and, in 1937, 1,798,000 and 479,000. The total of vehicles produced had been 238,805 in 1929; by 1937 it was 507,749. In both cases demand was encouraged by continuous technical improvement and price reductions, together with the improvement of the road system and the growth of suburban housing. On the side of production, economies of scale were being achieved by amalgamations of firms and consequent large production runs; by the early 1930s the industry was dominated by Ford, Morris and Austin.[16]

Non-ferrous metal industries also expanded rapidly. None of them was new; the newest, aluminium, had been manufactured by the British Aluminium Co. since 1894. By 1927–29 the average British output was about 9,000 tons. The uses of aluminium were expanding rapidly in aircraft, vehicle and electrical industries, as well as replacing earthenware and iron in household cooking vessels, and tinfoil in the wrapping of cigarettes and chocolate. The expansion of the Royal Air Force after 1936 further stimulated the use of aluminium (as 'duralumin') in the new generation of all-metal military aircraft such as the Spitfire; by 1937, British aluminium output was 19,000 tons. The other major non-ferrous metal to benefit from the changing technologies of the era was copper, chiefly as wiring for electricity in factories, houses and vehicles; the average British production had been 18,600 tons in 1927–29; by 1937 it was 128,000 tons.[17]

16. Mitchell, *Statistics*, p. 557; M. Miller and R.A. Church, 'Motor Manufacturing', in Buxton and Aldcroft, *British Industry*, p. 181. Production figures are from L.F. Duval, 'The Motor Industry', in British Association, *Britain in Recovery*, p. 394.
17. Plummer, *New British Industries*, ch. IV (i); Mitchell, *Statistics*, p. 310.

The iron and steel industry was the only example of a major exporter suffering severely from the depression, and yet growing subsequently far above the pre-depression level. Between 1929 and 1931 the output of steel in Britain fell by 46 per cent (to 5.2 million tons) and between 1929 and 1932 the output of pig-iron fell by 53 per cent (to 3.6 million tons), but by 1937 steel output was 35 per cent, and pig-iron output 12 per cent above the 1929 level.[18] Demand was encouraged by the building boom, the highly protective import duties after 1931, the rise of motor vehicles (which by 1937 may have been consuming about 1 million tons of iron and steel a year) and the beginning of rearmament (which on one estimate may have taken as much as 3 million tons in 1937).[19]

THE MONETARY AND FISCAL ENVIRONMENT OF RECOVERY

The recovery took place in a different monetary and fiscal environment from that of the late 1920s. The most significant changes were the devaluation of sterling in 1931, the policy of 'cheap money' and the tariff. Budgetary policy, however, remained firmly wedded to the idea of the balanced budget.

The depreciation of 1931 improved British export competitiveness, making British prices lower by 13 per cent than those of a composite index of 28 countries. In spite of the efforts of the Exchange Equalisation Account to hold the pound down, the rate drifted up, and by the end of 1936 it was back to its pre-devaluation level in respect of these currencies. The short-term gains from devaluation may have been considerable; it has been suggested that it may have improved the trade balance in 1931–32 alone by £80 million.[20]

The monetary policy ensured that interest rates remained low. The long-term rate, as represented by the yield on Consols (long-term government bonds), which in 1926–31 had averaged 4.5 per cent, came steadily down to a low of 2.9 per cent in 1935 and 1936, before gradually rising to 3.7 per cent in 1939. Short-term rates came down more sharply. The rate on best six-month commercial bills, which had been between 4 and 5 per cent per year in 1928–29 fell to an average of 0.6 per cent per year in 1937. Bank Rate remained at 2 per cent between 30 June 1932 and 24 August 1939.[21]

The tariff began with the Abnormal Importations Act of November 1931, passed to stem the flood of opportunist importing provoked by the anticipation of protection. It imposed duties of 50 per cent *ad valorem* on a range of manufactures. The Act was replaced in February 1932 by the Import Duties

18. Mitchell, *Statistics*, pp. 286, 289.
19. British Association, *Britain in Recovery*, pp. 310, 371–2.
20. J. Redmond, 'An Indicator of the Effective Exchange Rate of the Pound in the Nineteen-Thirties', *EcHR* XXXIII (1980), p. 87; S.N. Broadberry, *The British Economy between the Wars* (Oxford, Blackwell 1986), pp. 125–9.
21. Mitchell, *Statistics*, pp. 678, 682; F. Capie and M. Collins, *The Inter-War British Economy: a statistical abstract* (Manchester UP 1983), p. 105.

Act, which imposed a basic duty of 10 per cent *ad valorem* on manufactured imports. Previous higher duties ('McKenna', 'Key Industry' and 'Safeguarding' duties) were retained. Duties under the 1932 Act could be raised above 10 per cent on the recommendation of an Import Duties Advisory Committee. The IDAC recommendations, accepted by the government, imposed a further 10 per cent on fully manufactured products, making 20 per cent in total. Higher total duties of 25 or 30 per cent were fixed for semi-luxuries and luxuries, total tariffs of 33.33 per cent were proposed for bicycles and certain chemicals, while some raw materials were to be dutied at 15 per cent total. The iron and steel industry got special treatment, the duties on some products being set at 33.33 per cent total, while some received 20 per cent total.[22]

Budgetary policy remained tight. The National Government had been elected, it was assumed, to produce a balanced budget, and it tried hard to do so. Superficially, the two budgets of 1931–32 and 1932–33 produced small deficits, averaging (–)£48 million, and in 1933–34 to 1936–37 there were small surpluses averaging £22 million. However, it has been pointed out that these figures are misleading, since the economy was in a depression for much of the period, and thus government spending was necessarily higher, and receipts lower, than if activity had been normal. In these circumstances, to balance the Budget in an accounting sense was in fact severely deflationary. Middleton suggests that the Budget was in effect in substantial surplus in the early 1930s. At the peak of this notional budget surplus in 1933–34, it was equivalent to 4.2 per cent of GDP. These results have been disputed by Broadberry, who used alternative techniques to arrive at the conclusion that budgetary policy was broadly neutral in the 1930s. Whichever school of thought is adhered to, it can at least be said that budgetary policy did not become expansionary in the early 1930s, and that substantial deficit budgeting did not occur until the rearmament surge after 1937. In effect, therefore, budgetary policy can not be said to have changed in a positive direction after 1931 (see also Chapter 12).[23]

REGIONAL DIFFERENCES IN RECOVERY

There were regional differences in the extent of the depression and of the recovery. At the trough of the depression, the rates of unemployment for insured persons were in all regions roughly double those of 1929. By 1937, in most regions, unemployment rates had fallen back to, or near, their 1929 levels, although there were some regional variations. Whereas the midlands and the north-east somewhat improved their position in 1937 compared with 1929, unemployment in Wales, Scotland and Northern Ireland in 1937 was still noticeably higher than in 1929 (Table 13.6 overleaf).

22. British Association, *Britain in Recovery*, pp. 127–9.

23. R. Middleton, *Towards the Managed Economy: Keynes, the Treasury and the fiscal policy debate of the 1930s* (Methuen 1985), p. 135: Broadberry, *British Economy*, pp. 151–2; see also the discussion by Middleton and Broadberry in *EcHR* XXXVII (1984), pp. 95–106.

Table 13.6 Regional insured unemployment rates, 1929–37

	1929 (%)	*1932* (%)	*1937* (%)
London	5.3	12.9	6.0
South-east	5.6	14.3	7.2
South-west	8.3	17.2	8.3
Midlands	9.2	29.6	7.1
North-east	14.1	28.8	11.4
North-west	12.3	25.6	14.4
Northern	—	—	19.4[a]
Scotland	12.3	28.2	17.4
Wales	19.9	36.8	24.2
Northern Ireland	14.0	25.7	24.6

Note: a Created out of parts of the north-east and north-west
Source: Mitchell, *Statistics*, p. 125

Unemployment rates do not tell the whole story; there was quite substantial internal migration during the depression and recovery. Between 1931 and 1936, London and the home counties together gained about 358,000 people via migration, and Wales and the north-east lost a total of about 231,000 people. While not all the migrants can have found jobs, even in such modern and expanding industries as motor vehicles, these movements affected the regions concerned, and help to account for the fact that regional employment growth in the recovery was very different. Between 1929 and 1937, the four major expanding regions (London, south-east, south-west and midlands) showed employment growth of 21 per cent on average, while employment in the five remaining regions grew by only 5 per cent on average.[24]

EXPLANATIONS OF THE RECOVERY

Explanations of the economic recovery of the 1930s are hard to disentangle. In broad terms, commentators have divided into those emphasising demand and those emphasising supply factors. In addition, there are controversies surrounding specific items – devaluation, 'cheap money', the tariff, the building boom, business confidence, 'new' industries, government employment policy and rearmament.

Demand and consumption

On the demand side, there is no doubt that most of the recovery was due to internal rather than external forces. The peak year for exports was 1937, when they totalled £521 million, which was much below the 1929 figure of £729

24. H. Makower, J. Marschak and H.W. Robinson, 'Studies in Mobility of Labour: analysis for Great Britain, part I', *OEP* 2 (May 1939), p. 77; Richardson, *Economic Recovery*, p. 270.

million. What has to be explained therefore is why a depression which was, at least initially, due to a foreign trade slump, was counteracted by domestic forces. An important point here is that domestic consumption was well maintained during the slump, thus providing a 'floor' from which recovery could occur, as well as mitigating the short-term effects of the slump. In fact, the average propensity to consume of the UK population rose in the recession years. In 1929, consumers' expenditure (net of taxes) had been £3,507 million, or 78.0 per cent of GNP; in 1932 it was £3,193 million, or 81.6 per cent of GNP. This leeway was permitted mainly by the deterioration in the balance of payments and a sharp drop in domestic investment and stockholding.[25]

The buoyancy of consumer demand was aided by two other factors – real incomes (of those in work) rose, and the terms of foreign trade improved. Real incomes rose because money wages and salaries did not change very much (although there was an increase in short-time working) and the cost of living fell sharply. The extent to which the latter fell is uncertain; the Ministry of Labour (working-class) cost of living index showed a fall of 15 per cent between 1929 and 1933, when prices ceased to fall. This is probably an overestimate; the index was based on household budgets collected as long ago as 1904, in which most family expenditure went on food. Since the price of food fell more than other items of popular consumption in the 1930s, this overstates the reduction in the cost of living.[26] An alternative index derived from the spending of all consumers (not merely the working class) shows a smaller cost of living fall, of 11 per cent.[27] Thus for those in work, if they maintained their money incomes, real incomes rose. One estimate is that the real incomes (including short time) of all wage-earners rose between 1929 and 1933 by about 8.5 per cent.[28]

A boost was also given to consumption by the improvement in the foreign terms of trade. The unit prices of many imported items (especially food and raw materials) fell more than the unit prices of British exports (chiefly manufactured goods), so that a given volume of exports now bought more units of imports than previously. As well as helping the cost of living to fall, this eased the balance of payments constraint which might otherwise have impeded the recovery. Between 1929 and 1933, the net terms of trade improved by 25 per cent. Although they declined thereafter, they remained in the range of 11–20 per cent higher than in 1929.[29]

Finally, consumption was encouraged by continued government spending, which largely represented a transfer from the better-off to the less well-off. In 1929–30, such transfer payments had been £501 million, rising to £551 million

25. Calculated from Feinstein, *National Income*, Table 9.
26. N. Branson and M. Heinemann, *Britain in the Nineteen Thirties* (Weidenfeld & Nicolson 1971), pp. 154–6.
27. R. Stone and D.A. Rowe, *The Measurement of Consumers' Expenditure and Behaviour in the United Kingdom 1920–1938*, vol. II (Cambridge UP 1966), p. 114.
28. Mitchell, *Statistics*, pp. 171–2.
29. Ibid., p. 527.

in 1932–33. Since the interest on the National Debt fell in this period, a greater proportion of these payments went to the working classes, who had a higher propensity to consume than the middle and upper classes, thus further boosting popular consumption.

It is not known how the average propensity to consume (APC) among different income groups varied during the depression. Colin Clark suggested that the rich maintained their consumption by running down their capital. The propensity to consume of the unemployed was presumably almost 100 per cent; the rise in the national APC noted above may indicate that those in work were taking advantage of the rise in real incomes to consume more.[30]

Thus consumption was maintained at a high level during the early years of the depression, providing a 'floor' to the slump, and a stimulus (actual and potential) to producers and entrepreneurs. Unlike in some other economies such as that of the USA and Germany, the confidence of entrepreneurs had not been almost entirely destroyed. Thus there was a potential market to be tapped, provided that the right products at the appropriate prices could be supplied. This leads to a discussion of supply factors.

Supply factors

On the side of supply, the foremost technical innovation was the continuing development of electricity. Crucial in this respect was the completion of the national grid, which began operation in 1933, at the depth of the slump. Thus the way was paved for a truly national system of electricity distribution, and sales of electricity rose almost as fast in the 1930s as in the 1920s; from 3,707 gigawatt hours in 1920, to 9,169 in 1930 and 20,404 in 1938. By the latter date, industrial usage accounted for 51 per cent of all sales, and the proportion of factories using electricity, which had been 70 per cent in 1929, had risen to 84 per cent. The average price came down steadily: 2.48d. per kilowatt-hour in 1921, 1.38d. in 1929 and 1.04d. in 1938.[31] (A kilowatt-hour (1 kWh) is 1,000 watts per hour; a gigawatt-hour (1 gWh) is 1 million kWh.)

The expansion of electric power gave a substantial boost to a wide range of industries, both old and new. Even in cotton spinning, the use of electrical power rose from 1,484 million kWh to 1,819 kWh between 1930 and 1937, although electricity accounted in 1937 for only 18 per cent of the power consumed.[32] In the coal industry, electricity made possible a substantial expansion in the proportion of coal cut by machinery, which rose from 29 to 58 per cent between 1929 and 1938.[33] Even in 1930, about 61 per cent of all power used in manufacturing had been electric, and the total industrial consumption

30. C. Clark, *National Income and Outlay* (Macmillan 1937), pp. 141, 253.
31. L. Hannah, *Electricity before Nationalisation* (Macmillan 1979), pp. 121, 428, 430–1; Plummer, *New British Industries*, p. 37.
32. Political and Economic Planning (PEP), *The British Fuel and Power Industries* (PEP 1947), p. 386.
33. Supple, *Coal Industry*, Table 7.7, p. 317.

of electric power rose between 1930 and 1938 from 5,355 gigawatts to 10,320 gigawatts.[34]

As the numbers of domestic consumers rose, the wider use of electricity led to further cost reductions, permitting manufacturers to engage in longer production runs, and reap the benefits of economies of scale. By 1938, the numbers of households connected to a power supply, which had been only about half a million in 1919, had risen to about 8 million, and represented about two-thirds of the total housing stock in Britain. In many years of the 1930s the number of houses newly wired exceeded 600,000, partly due to the rapid pace of new construction, but also due to wiring of older dwellings. This undoubtedly underpinned the expansion of the 'wireless' (radio), of which 9 million sets were in use by 1939. The only other major electric utensil in common use was the electric iron, of which there were some 6–7 million in use by 1939, accounting for 77 per cent of consumers. By the end of the 1930s, about one-quarter of domestic consumers used electric fires, and there were 1.5 million electric cookers in use. A late though rapidly growing market was that for vacuum cleaners; after 1934, with the advent of cheaper models, sales peaked at 400,000 a year, and by 1939 there were some 2.3 million in use. But only 16 per cent of consumers had electric kettles, and only 14 per cent had electric cookers.[35]

Increased efficiency and lowered costs were also at the forefront of the expansion of the motor vehicle industry. During the slump, productivity rose at the same time as materials prices fell; iron and steel prices fell by 9 per cent between 1929 and 1932. Concentration of production first began to make its effects felt during the 1930s. The number of car producers had fallen from eighty-eight in 1922 to thirty-one in 1929, and by then the 'big three' (Morris, Austin and Singer) accounted for 75 per cent of production. They were joined by others; Ford's plant at Dagenham opened in 1932; Vauxhall, Standard and Rootes all grew in relative importance. By 1938, these six firms (excluding Ford, which made mainly commercial vehicles) produced 90 per cent of all cars. The reductions in price made possible by the slump and mass production outlasted the recovery in the general price level which began in 1933. The average price of a private car fell from £206 in 1930 to £156 in 1932 and approximately £130 in 1935–36. In this process, a notable innovation was William Morris's rebuilding of his Cowley works (at Oxford) in 1934, incorporating for the first time the moving assembly line pioneered by Ford (in 1912).[36]

Price reductions also boosted another 'new' industry – rayon. Even in the

34. M. Compton and E.H. Bott, *British Industry: its changing structure in peace and war* (Lindsay Drummond 1940), p. 243; Mitchell, *Statistics*, p. 264.

35. Hannah, *Electricity*, pp. 188–9, 193–5, 208; PEP, *The Market for Household Appliances* (PEP 1945), ch. 1; PEP, *British Fuel*, p. 246.

36. G. Maxcy and S. Silberston, *Motor Industry* (Allen & Unwin 1959), pp. 14–15; Plummer, *New British Industries*, p. 87; P.W.S. Andrews and E. Brunner, *The Life of Lord Nuffield: a study in enterprise and benevolence* (Oxford, Blackwell 1955), p. 197.

1920s, the policy of the major producer, Courtaulds, had been to pass on lower costs to the customer. The slump accentuated this policy, since it forced half of the producers to close down. In 1933, Courtaulds announced substantial price reductions, and the other firms (the largest was British Celanese) were forced to follow suit. For the remainder of the decade, rayon prices fell faster than those of cotton or wool, and boosted a demand which was in any case growing strongly. Between 1929 and 1939, British production of rayon yarn and staple fibre rose from 56,000 million lb to 180,000 million lb. By 1937 the value of rayon piece goods production was, at £20.5 million, almost as large as that of worsted piece goods (£22.0 million), and almost one-third of those of cotton piece goods (£63.7 million).[37]

Thus the slump was counteracted in certain industries by increases in efficiency of supply. A more general 'supply-side' point is that, as the economic recovery proceeded, the price level began to recover, and this rise was not matched by rises in money wages. The (working-class) cost of living index of the Ministry of Labour (1914 = 100), having fallen from 164 to 140 between 1929 and 1933, then rose steadily, to 156 in 1938.[38] Thus the rise in real wages which had occurred in the early years of the depression was almost wiped out. This loss of the previous gain in real wages, it is contended, spurred the recovery after 1931 by raising industrial profitability. This thesis is reasonable *a priori*, in that there is no reason to doubt that real wage reduction aided the rise in industrial investment which took place after 1931, and thus the recovery in general. However, there is still debate as to whether the recovery was mainly due to this reduction, or proceeded largely via a revival of demand.[39]

Specific Causes

Turning to specific elements of the 1930s which may have assisted recovery, the most striking change from the 1920s is the abandonment of the gold standard, and the associated devaluation of the external value of the pound sterling. In the long run, the greatest impact of these events was the unhitching of economic policy from the exchange rate; in future it was to be monetary policy which determined the exchange rate, not the other way around. Gone was the somewhat obsessive repression of the domestic economy in the cause of defending the exchange rate.

Apart from the longer-run consequences, the foreign trade position benefited

37. J. Harrop, 'Rayon', in Buxton and Aldcroft, *British Industry*, p. 283; H.A. Silverman, *Studies in Industrial Organization* (Methuen 1946), pp. 306–7, 318, 336–9.

38. Mitchell, *Statistics*, p. 739.

39. This 'supply-side' view is in M. Beenstock, F. Capie and B. Griffiths, 'Economic Recovery in the United Kingdom in the 1930s', in *Bank of England: Panel of Academic Consultants, papers presented at the 23rd meeting, 27 January 1984* (Bank of England 1984); see also M. Beenstock and P. Warburton, 'Wages and Unemployment in Interwar Britain', *ExEH* 23 (1986). A contrary view is expressed in N.H. Dimsdale, S.J. Nickell and N. Horsewood, 'Real Wages and Unemployment in Britain during the 1930s', *EJ* 99 (1989).

greatly in the short term. This benefit was not to be had from trade with the countries whose currency was tied to sterling (broadly, the Empire and Dominions, accounting for about one-third of all British exports). But that it improved the position in relation to industrial countries is not in doubt. By 1932, the sterling rate had fallen by 28 per cent against both the US dollar and the French franc. In 1933 the dollar was devalued, and in 1936 the French franc, so that these gains were shortlived. But wider measurements of exchange rate comparability indicate that the effect was more long-lasting than the official bilateral rates indicated (Table 13.7).

Table 13.7 Sterling exchange rates, 1929–38 (1929 = 100)

	1 *£/$*	*2* *£/French franc*	*3* *Effective exchange rate*	*4* *Average exchange rate*	*5* *Real exchange rate*
1929	100	100	100	100	100
1930	100	99	100	100	98
1931	93	93	100	94	94
1932	72	72	87	75	81
1933	87	68	91	77	83
1934	104	62	96	75	82
1935	101	60	95	74	82
1936	102	67	97	78	86
1937	102	100	101	85	92
1938	101	138	105	87	92

Source: Broadberry, *British Economy*, Table 12.4

In this formulation, an index number of less than 100 shows that the sterling exchange rate had fallen, and thus British competitiveness improved; a figure higher than 100 shows the opposite. The nominal (official) franc and dollar rates (columns 1 and 2) show that the advantage of devaluation against these currencies was wiped out when the USA and France devalued. The other rates in this table relate to all the major British trading partners, and thus measure general British competitiveness. The effective exchange rate (column 3) shows that this more general advantage of the 1931 devaluation lasted until 1937. The indices of average and real exchange rates, which best measure general British competitiveness in manufactures, show that the competitive advantage gained in 1931 was maintained to some extent throughout the rest of the decade. It can thus be concluded that the devaluation of 1931 was beneficial to the British external position.[40]

It has been estimated that the depreciation of 1931–32 may have raised exports by 12.0 per cent and reduced imports by (–)4.5 per cent (both by

40. The rate in column 3 is derived from Redmond (1980); those in columns 4 and 5 from Dimsdale (1981); see Broadberry, *British Economy*, p. 125.

volume), resulting in a boost to national income in that year of about 3 per cent. Thereafter, the moves to protection in the UK and elsewhere make direct estimate of the benefits of devaluation problematical.[41]

The other major change in policy was the pursuing of 'cheap money'. Between 5 March 1925 and 12 December 1929, Bank Rate had varied between 4 and 6 per cent. Between 30 June 1932 and 24 August 1939 it remained at 2 per cent. Other interest rates, both short and long, followed this downward trend. Thus the 1930s was a decade of easy credit, a fact reflected in the rise in the supply of money in the banking system. Between 1932 and 1938, the measure of 'broad money' (M3) rose by about 25 per cent, whereas in 1925–29 it had risen by only 5 per cent. (M3 is defined as the sum of cash in the hands of the public, till money in banks, bankers' balances at the Bank of England, and the value of current and deposit accounts.) While this might be rather a reflection of economic expansion than a cause of it, it remains the case that lack of credit was not allowed to impede the recovery. There is little doubt that, had a commitment to defending the exchange rate been the main concern of policy, as it had been in 1925–31, interest rates would not have been allowed to decline, and credit would have remained as tight after 1931 as before.[42]

The direct influence of cheap money on the recovery is harder to identify. For firms making losses, lower interest rates on bank overdrafts may have eased the impact of the recession. On the other hand, bank interest rates fell more slowly than did Bank Rate, and there was a 'floor' to bank rates of about 4.5 per cent, so that direct borrowing of this sort was only marginally cheaper than under the previous regime.[43]

Indirectly, cheap money had favourable, if unquantifiable, effects. The high security (i.e. shares and bond) prices ruling (a corollary of the low interest rates) made it expedient for firms to sell their gilt-edged bonds, and use the proceeds either to pay off bank overdrafts and loans or to finance their own investment. Thus the banks were financing industry indirectly, since they themselves were heavy purchasers of the gilt-edged securities thus released on to the market.[44]

The cheap money regime also helped to revive the capital markets such as the new-issue market and the markets in existing securities provided by the Stock Exchanges. The reasons for this were various. Share prices were boosted by the fall in the costs of industrial investment and the rise in investor confidence following the easing of monetary policy. The reduced interest rates made borrowing by means of debenture or preference shares more attractive. The rise in gilt-edged prices induced investors to move out of gilt-edged securities and into industrial shares (either ordinary or fixed-interest). These sentiments

41. Broadberry, *British Economy*, pp. 129–30.

42. Mitchell, *Statistics*, pp. 674, 682.

43. D.H. Aldcroft, *The Inter-War Economy: Britain, 1919–1939* (Batsford 1970), p. 338.

44. E. Nevin, *The Mechanism of Cheap Money: a study of British monetary policy 1931–1939* (Cardiff, University of Wales Press 1955), pp. 250–1.

were reflected in the rise in share prices; in 1932 the London and Cambridge Economic Service's index number of industrial share prices had been 40 per cent lower than in 1929, but by 1936 it was 16 per cent above the 1929 level.[45]

The capital market did not revive immediately. Total new issues had been £315.5 million a year in 1927–29, the main components of the market being 'industrial' issues of UK securities (£138.5 million), and overseas issues (£136.1 million). Total issues fell sharply in the depression, reaching their nadir in 1931, at £94.5 million; UK industrial issues had fallen to £32.9 million, and overseas issues to £49.6 million. While the UK capital market eventually recovered, the overseas market did not. By 1936, total new issues had risen to £244.6 million, of which £165.6 million was for UK industrial issues, but overseas issues were only £32.4 million.[46]

That the market took several years to revive may be explained partly by the initial boost to the financial position of firms consequent on selling their gilt-edged securities, and partly by a lag in investors' perception that the recession was over, and that the prospects for industrial profitability had improved. While there is no reason to doubt the beneficial effect of cheap money in this revival of the capital markets, it can not be disentangled from the effect of the rise in the marginal efficiency of capital (i.e. profits) during the recovery.[47]

The capital market, even in its revived form, was a declining source of funds for industry and trade, and to that extent the influence of cheap money on the recovery was weakened. As in other periods of economic recovery, such as 1921–24 and 1926–29, firms had survived the recessions by drawing down on their reserves, and now needed to rebuild them. In addition, replacement and extension of plant was now required, and thus firms tended to use a higher proportion of their cash-flow for internal finance. *The Economist*'s series of firms' profits (from 2,095 firms on average in 1929–38) indicated that firms paid out 60 per cent of their net profits in ordinary dividends in 1929, and 61 per cent in 1930; between 1934 and 1938, the figure was only about 52 per cent. There were some notable examples of self-financing among the expanding industries, such as Morris Motors and Courtaulds. The increased reliance on internal funds affected the banks; failing to find profitable industrial and commercial outlets for their deposits, they were forced to invest in gilt-edged stock on a larger scale; between 1929 and 1938, their ratio of investments to deposits rose from 14.3 to 28.0 per cent.[48]

That cheap money made some direct contribution to the building boom is clear, but it was not a large effect. Interest rates were irrelevant to the local authority housing schemes. Most of the boom, however, was in the private

45. Aldcroft, *Inter-War Economy*, p. 339; London and Cambridge Economic Service, *Key Statistics of the British Economy, 1900–1964* (Times Publishing Co. 1965), Table G (index of ninety-two industrial companies).
46. Mitchell, *Statistics*, p. 685.
47. Nevin, *Cheap Money*, p. 222.
48. W.A. Thomas, *The Finance of British Industry 1918–1976* (Methuen 1978), pp. 89, 107; Richardson, *Economic Recovery*, pp. 193, 201.

sector. This had begun even before the depression, so that cheap money can not be credited with initiating it. Moreover, it took six years for average mortgage rates to fall from 6 to 4.5 per cent (1929–35). By that time, the reduction in building costs was probably more important in sustaining the boom than the decline in mortgage rates. On the other hand, by then an increasing proportion of building was for investment, and the existence of low interest rates at a time when rents showed no tendency to fall made housing investment attractive. The fact that building societies kept up their rates on deposits and shares attracted more funds, and enabled the societies to provide finance for purchasers on a large scale.[49]

The contribution of the tariff to recovery is perhaps the most difficult of all to assess. This is partly because it coincided with many other changes, notably devaluation, cheap money, and the improvement in the terms of trade. In addition, there are difficulties in selecting appropriate years for comparison. Until recently, historians were sceptical about the influence of the tariff on recovery, although recent work rehabilitates the tariff to some extent.[50]

Prior to the imposition of the general tariff in 1932, about 83 per cent of British imports came in free of duty. After the tariff and Ottawa arrangements of 1932, this was reduced to 25 per cent. Yet average tariff levels were still not high by international standards. Most non-Empire and Dominion foodstuffs, and all important industrial raw materials, came in free, and the bulk of the duties fell on manufactures, on which the average general tariff rate has been calculated at 13.2 per cent *ad valorem* in 1932.[51]

Whether these relatively mild rates were responsible for the subsequent decline in imports of manufactured goods is still a matter of debate. Whereas the import volume of food remained stable, and those of materials and fuel had more than recovered their 1929 level by 1936, this was not true of manufactures, which, although recovering, were still 26 per cent below their 1929 level. The volume of imports of manufactures expressed as a proportion of the volume of domestic demand for manufactures (i.e. import propensity) had been 12 per cent in 1931, and fell sharply in 1932 to 8 per cent, at which level it remained for the rest of the decade. The reduction in imports affected both the newly protected industries and other industries to a very similar degree. On the other hand, the decline in manufactured exports was also a world affair; between 1929 and 1937, the volume of world trade in manufactures fell

49. M. Bowley, *Housing and the State* (Allen & Unwin 1945), p. 278; Nevin, *Cheap Money*, pp. 276–9.
50. Richardson, *Economic Recovery*, ch. 10, and F. Capie, *Depression and Protectionism: Britain between the wars* (Allen & Unwin 1983), are the chief sceptics. M. Kitson and S. Solomou, *Protectionism and Economic Revival: the British interwar economy* (Cambridge UP 1990) take a more sanguine view. The latter base much of their conclusions on their view that the 1930s exhibited a rise in the secular (i.e. long-term) rate of British economic growth; this view is not supported by the present author.
51. Aldcroft, *Inter-War Economy*, p. 286; Kitson and Solomou, *Protectionism*, pp. 65–6.

by 13 per cent, so some of the reduction in import penetration is explained on more general grounds.[52]

Reduction of manufactured imports was one thing; whether such reduction contributed much to recovery was another. It has not escaped notice that the building industry, one of the main industries associated with the recovery, did not benefit from the tariff. On the contrary, it received 'negative protection', i.e. was disadvantaged by having to pay more for its imported materials. It has also been suggested that the use of the concept of the 'effective rate of protection' (essentially, stripping out the tariff's negative effect on industries which had to import dutiable materials or goods) demonstrates that the steel industry effectively received light protection only – about 8 per cent, as opposed to the nominal 33.3 per cent selected by the Import Duties Advisory Committee. Also, the general nature of the tariff meant that industries whose contribution to recovery was slight or negative, such as cotton textiles, also received protection. Nor were all ailing industries protected; shipbuilding was subject to a degree of 'negative protection' in the same way as building.[53]

Protection was also given to agriculture. In 1932, tariffs were imposed on imports from foreign countries of wheat, dairy produce, and eggs. However, since Ottawa countries' produce was let in free, the British farmer received no net protection. But the farmers would have benefited from the quantitative regulation of imports of beef and mutton which was also adopted. Of greater assistance to rebuilding the financial position of the industry were the measures of internal protection, which began with the Wheat Act 1932, guaranteeing a minimum price to British farmers for growing wheat. Thus fortified, wheat acreage in Britain rose from 1.29 million to 1.70 million acres between 1932 to 1935. A further policy decision was that the sugar-beet subsidy, timed to end in 1935, was continued indefinitely, although applied on a limited volume of production. The addition of marketing schemes, notably for milk, completed the range of measures which boosted agricultural income; by £47 million in 1932, and by £69 million in 1938.[54]

The effects of the tariff are probably impossible to isolate satisfactorily. What can be said is that to a considerable extent it excluded manufactures which otherwise would have been imported, and thus protected the profits of the British companies concerned, which in turn contributed to the general upswing in domestic trade and business confidence. Whether in the long run all such industries should have been protected is more debatable.

The one clear case of an industry closely connected with the recovery is building. This was chiefly a matter of housebuilding. This had remained at a

52. Aldcroft, *Inter-War Economy*, p. 246; Kitson and Solomou, *Protectionism*, p. 20 and Table 5.4; H. Tyszinski, 'World Trade in Manufactured Commodities, 1899–1950', *ManS* XIX (1951), p. 282.

53. Capie, *Depression*, Table 8.1.

54. Feinstein, *National Income*, Table 23; Ministry of Agriculture, *A Century of Agricultural Statistics* (HMSO 1968), Table 46; British Association, *Britain in Recovery*, pp. 140–5.

high level in the late 1920s, at around 200,000 a year. Briefly dipping in 1930, it then rose rapidly every year, to peak at 366,000 in 1936. The bulk of the building was private, the Chamberlain subsidy being withdrawn in 1930, and the Wheatley subsidy in 1933. Thereafter, the main contribution of policy was the slum demolition and replacement programme of the 'Greenwood' Act 1930 (and later ones on similar lines), whose effects were not felt until 1935. In 1930–39, a total of 2,723,000 houses were built in England and Wales, of which 2,079,000 (76 per cent) were privately built; for the UK, the ratio was 75 per cent. Yet the true scale of the building boom was even greater, since housebuilding accounted for only about 70 per cent of all building, and non-residential building was also expanding rapidly after 1934. All forms of building in total accounted for £203 million of investment in 1930, and this peaked at £272 million in 1937.[55]

The reasons for the building boom are various. Generally, there was still a housing shortage, estimated at 1.2 million to 2.0 million in 1930. In addition, standards were rising, in official circles and in the wider market. The continuing rise in real incomes, which accelerated in the early years of the depression, provided a further impetus. Building costs also fell substantially. The average capital cost of a three-bedroom, non-parlour house is estimated at £416 in 1929, and fell to £361 in 1934; although costs then rose again, it was not until 1937 that the 1929 figure was exceeded. Taken in conjunction with the direct and indirect effects of cheap money, the weekly cost of buying a house fell by about 20 per cent between 1929 and 1934. Finally, the building societies liberalised their terms, extending the length of life of mortgages, and in the later 1930s devising methods such as the 'builders' pool' by which the initial deposit could be reduced substantially. Altogether, building societies lent £1,034 million on mortgage between 1930 and 1939, as opposed to £433 million in the previous decade.[56]

Although building employed only 6–7 per cent of all insured workers in the 1930s, it accounted for about 30 per cent of the rise in the number of employed insured workers between 1932 and 1937. Whereas it had accounted for about 27 per cent of national capital formation in the 1920s, it accounted for 34 per cent in the 1930s. Taken in conjunction with the derived demand for furniture, household fittings and equipment, there is no doubt that building was an important feature of the economic recovery of the 1930s.[57]

The question of 'business confidence' may also be considered. This was continually being used in argument by economists, business people and politicians in Britain and elsewhere in the 1930s. It had constituted one of the main objections made by the Treasury to the extension of public works schemes in the 1920s. It did so also in the early years of the depression, although in a

55. Bowley, *Housing*, App. II, Table 2; Richardson and Aldcroft, *Building*, pp. 62, 67.
56. Bowley, *Housing*, App. II, Tables 1, 6; Richardson and Aldcroft, *Building*, pp. 204–6.
57. Richardson and Aldcroft, *Building*, p. 276; G.D.A. McDougall, 'General Survey, 1929–1937', in British Association, *Britain in Recovery*, p. 42; see also (Sir) H. Bellman, 'The Building Trades', in the same volume.

more flexible form. It had been a powerful force behind the Labour government's deeply felt need to act conservatively in economic and (especially) financial policy during the crises of 1931. It is also likely that the perceived need to maintain it was a powerful, if seldom expressed, motive behind the government's reluctance to consider any further radical reshaping of economic policy after 1931–32. Booth considers that the basis of the Treasury's opposition to deficit finance in the 1930s was 'the very legitimate fear that a [budget] deficit would produce a disastrous flight from sterling and a cumulative economic catastrophe'.[58]

In practice, business confidence may have been something of a shibboleth; business opinion accepted demurely such radical changes as the abandonment of gold, the devaluation of sterling, the Exchange Equalisation Account, and the general tariff, without suffering a crisis of nerve. In retrospect, the surprising thing about business confidence in the depression was that in practice it was so little affected. Between 1929 and 1933, total gross fixed domestic capital formation (excluding dwellings) fell from £309 million to £206 million, a fall of 33 per cent. At constant prices, the fall was only 28 per cent. Although this was a sharp fall, it was much less than in the USA, where total gross domestic fixed investment (excluding dwellings) fell by 63 per cent (at constant prices) between 1929 and its trough in 1933. An earlier estimate of 'producers' goods' (i.e. investment goods) output was that it had fallen by the third quarter of 1932 by 76 per cent in the USA, 48 per cent in Germany, but only 28 per cent in the UK (1925–29 = 100).[59]

After 1933, the price level recovered, and with it the level of business profits, thus permitting industrial and commercial investment to recover. The gross trading profits of companies had fallen by 34 per cent between 1929 and 1932; thereafter they rose steadily, and exceeded the 1929 level in 1936. Fixed investment recovered more rapidly; excluding dwellings, domestic fixed capital formation (chiefly plant, machinery, and non-residential building) in 1936 was 12 per cent above its 1929 level.

It remains to discuss the contributions to recovery which are sometimes suggested as deriving from the expansion of the 'new' industries, government employment-creation policy, and the rearmament drive of the later 1930s.

Assessing the contribution of the 'new' industries is fraught with difficulty. There is no generally accepted definition of what industries the term should encompass. Nor is the use of the concept free from tautological error; if the recovery was more marked in certain industries than others, this does not explain the recovery, but merely draws attention to the rapidly growing industries – which may or may not be caught by an appropriate definition of what the 'new' industries were.[60]

58. A. Booth, 'Britain in the 1930s: a managed economy?', *EcHR* XL (1987), p. 514.

59. Mitchell, *Statistics*, pp. 859–60; London and Cambridge Economic Service, *Key Statistics, 1900–1964*, Table I; L. Robbins, *The Great Depression* (Macmillan 1934), Table 9, p. 211.

60. J.A. Dowie, 'Growth in the Inter-War Period: some more arithmetic', *EcHR* XXI (1968), p. 104.

The broad outlines of recovery were indicated above; the laggard sectors were agriculture, mining/quarrying and transport. Apart from manufacturing, the above-average growth sectors between 1929 and 1937 were gas/water/electricity, distribution, services, and building. The latter three do not fit most definitions of 'new' industries. Thus if the influence of 'new' industries is to be discerned, it is to be found in manufacturing and gas/water/electricity. Within manufacturing, the only 'new' industries with above-average growth rates were vehicles and electrical engineering, to which may be added the rayon industry (Table 13.8).

Table 13.8 'New' industries' growth in output and employment, 1924–37

	1924–29	*1929–37*
OUTPUT (% pa)		
Vehicles	5.6	6.6
Electrical engineering	4.0	7.8
Rayon	42.4	35.6
Gas/water/electricity	5.8	6.0
EMPLOYMENT (% pa)		
Vehicles	3.3	2.6
Electrical engineering	4.8	5.6
Rayon (inc. silk)	11.7	1.0
Gas/water/electricity	2.9	3.0

Sources: Dowie, 'Growth in the Inter-War Period', Tables 1, 3, 4; rayon output from Mitchell, *Statistics*, p. 353

Thus, while growth in these sectors was usually rapid in the interwar period, it can not be said that there was a marked acceleration for this group as a whole in the 1930s; indeed, the tendency in vehicles and rayon, as in any new industry, was for the rate of growth to slow as the market grew. Nor was it the case that the new industries grew so rapidly in the 1930s as to represent a break with the trends of the 1920s. Finally, it must not be forgotten that the new industries also suffered from reductions in employment and investment during 1929–32, although not on the same scale as the older industries. There is a strong case for saying that, while resources had been transferred from the old to the new sectors in the 1920s, this process was interrupted during the recession of 1929–32.[61]

Attempts by the government to create employment directly were notable by their absence. Prior to the depression, the major direct effort by the government was the Unemployment Grants Committee. Although spurred into renewed

61. N.K. Buxton, 'The Role of the "New" Industries in Britain during the 1930s: a reinterpretation', *Business History Review* 49 (1975).

activity in 1929–31, it effectively lapsed with the demise of the Labour government. Schemes amounting to some £77 million were sanctioned between August 1929 and December 1931, which on the basis of £1.0 million providing 2,500 'man-years' of employment, may have found work for some 192,000 men over these two years.[62]

Apart from that, there was the Industrial Transference Scheme, which had begun in 1928. The high point of this was in 1929, when 32,000 single men and 2,850 families were moved. However, between 40 and 50 per cent of persons transferred from Lancashire, south Wales and Scotland during 1928–31 returned home, and by 1933 the scheme was almost defunct, with only 8,000 single men and 605 families transferring, as the general demand for labour in all regions fell. The scheme was complemented with Transfer Instructional Centres in 1929, allegedly to retrain men who found physical work too demanding after prolonged unemployment. In practice the element of retraining was largely absent, and the men were put merely to a variety of muscle-toughening labouring tasks.

The nearest approach to a positive long-term employment-creating policy in the early 1930s was the creation of four Special Areas (south Wales, north-east England, west Cumberland and Clydeside) at the end of 1934. This was designed to meet the criticism that the government was not doing enough about unemployment. It was thus essentially a public relations exercise, and was not designed to be a new direction in policy. The government's Chief Industrial Adviser in September 1935, described the overall employment policy as 'restoration of general business confidence, cheap money, fiscal policy etc. . . . nothing must be done to shake confidence or check business development'.[63] The Commissioners of the Special Areas were given limited funds (£2 million in the first instance), were debarred from assisting any undertaking established for profit, and could only spend on projects satisfying very strict conditions. These conditions were soon relaxed, and development boards in the Special Areas were allowed to establish trading estates, notably at Team Valley (Newcastle), Treforest (south Wales) and Hillington (Glasgow). Although the most visibly successful of the regional unemployment measures, they had only a limited effect. By May 1939, 273 factories were in production, employing just over 8,500 people. Unemployment in the special areas in July 1939 stood at 226,193.[64]

The origins of the rearmament programme began in 1932, when the Chiefs of Staff dropped the 'ten-year rule' (which had postulated that there would be

62. U.K. Hicks, *The Finance of British Government, 1920–1936* (Oxford 1938; 1969), pp. 194–9, Table I.

63. Ibid., pp. 199–205; W.R. Garside, *British Unemployment 1919–1939: a study in public policy* (Cambridge UP 1990), pp. 241–6, 250. The labour camps are criticised in W. Hannington, *The Problem of the Distressed Areas* (Gollancz 1937), and given a more balanced treatment in D. Colledge, *Labour Camps: the British experience* (Sheffield Popular Publishing 1989).

64. Garside, *British Unemployment*, pp. 257–8.

no need to anticipate a major war within ten years), and set up a committee 'to prepare a programme for meeting our worst deficiencies'. This affected policy finally in the Statement Relating to Defence published in March 1935. Subsequently, rearmament could be said to have begun, although slowly at first. In 1934, expenditure on the three armed services had been about £108 million, of which £37.2 million went on military equipment; by 1937, the total had risen to £186.7 million, of which £104.2 million went on equipment. So far, the extra expenditure had been met through taxation. The programme was then much increased; spending of £1,500 million in the next five years was agreed. Resort was therefore had to increasing the National Debt. Under the Defence Loans Acts 1937 and 1939, a further £64.9 million was raised in 1937–38, which had risen to £380 million by the time of the Budget in April 1940. In 1938–39 alone, total defence spending was, at £400 million, almost exactly four times that of 1933–34.[65]

Thus the bulk of the rearmament spending occurred after the national output had recovered in 1936–37; in 1936, the extra spending had been only about £29 million above that of 1934. But the programme had made some contribution to reducing unemployment; it has been estimated that defence-induced civilian employment in 1936 was 226,000 higher than that of 1935; in 1937 it is estimated at 578,000 more than in 1935. However, given the enormously enhanced spending after 1937 it is difficult to escape the conclusion that the main economic effect of rearmament was to render the recession of 1937–38 shorter and milder than might have otherwise been the case.[66]

CONCLUSIONS

The 1930s was a decade full of economic paradoxes. The economy suffered a severe slump, yet recovery occurred in a few years. The maxims of conventional economic wisdom were abandoned, yet disaster did not occur. The pound sank, yet rose again. The government refused to increase the National Debt to pay for unemployment programmes, yet did so with alacrity only a few years later to counter the military threat from Germany. Exports did not recover, yet the economy still grew. In retrospect, the decade appears as one in which the average pace of economic growth barely altered, in spite of large losses of output during the depression. Technical change continued to underpin the rise of the newer industries, and the modernisation of the older ones. What had changed was policy and attitudes to it. The hiatus of the 1920s was over, and it could be seen that the old policies had failed to provide the answer to the structural problems which had emerged after 1918.

65. Hicks, *Finance*, p. 380; M.M. Postan, *British War Production* (HMSO 1952), p. 12; Middleton, *Managed Economy*, pp. 106–7.

66. M. Thomas, 'Rearmament and Economic Recovery in the Late 1930s', *EcHR* XXXVI (1983), pp. 566, 570–1.

CHAPTER 14

UNEMPLOYMENT AND ECONOMIC AND SOCIAL WELFARE IN THE 1930s

THE GROWTH AND NATURE OF UNEMPLOYMENT

The depression of 1929–32 resulted in much higher unemployment than previously. In 1929, the average number of insured persons out of work had been 1,216,000. At the trough of the depression in 1932, the average in Britain was 2,745,000. Thereafter there was a steady decline, reaching a low point of 1,484,000 in 1937, before the short recession of 1937–38. The decade ended with the figure at 1,514,000 in 1939.[1]

In terms of numbers unemployed, unemployment in the 1930s was on average higher than in the 1920s. In a relative sense, the picture was not so gloomy, because the total occupied population (employed plus unemployed) was growing, and this helped relative unemployment rates to decline almost to the 1929 level by the end of the 1930s (Table 14.1 overleaf).

These rates, which are those usually quoted by historians, overstate the average propensity to unemployment of all the persons engaged in economic activity in the UK, since the insurance scheme was largely confined to manual employees and other employees earning less than £250 a year. In addition, for most of the 1930s, there were large numbers of manual and low-paid workers who were excluded from the insurance scheme – notably agricultural workers, who were first insured in May 1936, and domestic servants. An attempt has been made by Feinstein to incorporate the uninsured in a calculation of the unemployment rates of the total working population, based on the ratio of insured to uninsured unemployed revealed in the 1931 Census of Population. This estimate shows a much higher absolute figure of workless, but a relatively lower proportion than that shown in the employment insurance figures. This is because the uninsured occupations had lower rates of unemployment than the insured occupations. In addition, Feinstein's estimate includes employers and the self-employed, both of whom were excluded from the insurance scheme, and had lower unemployment rates than those of employees (Table 14.2 overleaf).

1. B.R. Mitchell, *British Historical Statistics* (Cambridge UP 1988), p. 127.

Table 14.1 UK unemployment rates of insured workers, 1929–39

1929	10.4	1935	15.5
1930	16.1	1936	13.1
1931	21.3	1937	10.8
1932	22.1	1938	12.9
1933	19.9	1939	10.5
1934	16.7		

Source: Mitchell, *Statistics*, p. 124

Table 14.2 UK working population and total unemployment, 1929–39

	1 *Working population*	*2* *Total unemployment*	*3* *Unemployment (col. 2 ÷ col. 1 × 100)*
1929	20,982,000	1,503,000	7.3
1930	21,494,000	2,379,000	11.2
1931	21,917,000	3,252,000	15.1
1932	22,153,000	3,400,000	15.6
1933	22,223,000	3,087,000	14.1
1934	22,294,000	2,609,000	11.9
1935	22,474,000	2,437,000	11.0
1936	22,770,000	2,100,000	9.4
1937	23,140,000	1,776,000	7.8
1938	23,582,000	2,164,000	9.3
1939	23,600,000	1,340,000[a]	5.8

Note: a Change of statistical basis
Source: C.H. Feinstein, *National Income, Expenditure and Output of the United Kingdom 1855–1965* (Cambridge UP 1972), Table 57

Whichever of these two procedures is adopted, the conclusion is that unemployment doubled, both relatively and in absolute numbers, within the first three years of the start of the depression. While the ultimate cause was clearly the economic depression of 1929–32 itself, analysis of the features of unemployment helps us to understand the nature of contemporary unemployment.

As emphasised earlier, the rate of unemployment did not refer to a static population. Thus a rate of, say, 10 per cent, could be compatible either with 10 per cent of the population in question being continuously unemployed for a year, for 100 per cent of the population being unemployed for 10 per cent of the year, or for any position between these two extremes. The experience of the interwar period occupies an intermediate position. Even before the 1929 depression occurred, a fairly high proportion of the labour force was liable to frequent, if shortlived, spells of unemployment. In 1923–26, it has been calculated, about 42 per cent of the insured population experienced at least one spell of unemployment during an average year, and, taken in all, these spells of unemployment would amount to about 27 per cent of the year. The impact of the

Table 14.3 GB sources of unemployment, 1923–36

	Rate of unemployment	*Average period of unemployment (days)*	*Proportion of year unemployed*	*Proportion of labour force unemployed within year*
1923–26	11.3	84.0	26.9	42.0
1928	10.7	84.3	27.0	39.6
1929	10.3	84.9	27.2	37.9
1930	15.8	99.2	31.8	49.7
1931	21.1	126.0	40.4	52.2
1932	21.9	129.8	41.6	52.6
1933	19.8	131.4	42.1	47.0
1934	16.6	117.9	37.8	43.9
1935	15.3	117.0	37.5	40.8
1936	12.9	111.1	35.6	36.2

Sources: M. Thomas, 'Labour Market Structure and the Nature of Unemployment in Interwar Britain', in B. Eichengreen and T.J. Hatton (eds), *Interwar Unemployment in International Perspective* (1988), p. 106

1929 depression was to increase the proportion of the labour force experiencing unemployment, and to extend the proportion of the year which it occupied (taking all spells of unemployment in the year in total) (Table 14.3 above).

Thus between 1929 and 1932 the average length of time spent out of work by the unemployed rose from some fifteen weeks to about twenty-four weeks (assuming a working week of five and a half days). These are minimum estimates, since the data do not carry on after the end of one year. But by 1932 it is safe to say that about half the insured population were experiencing unemployment at some time in the year. Thus the total number of people affected by unemployment in the course of the year was far higher than that in the monthly returns. At the end of 1933, when the insured unemployment figure was somewhat over 2.5 million, it was noted that about 6 million people (about half the insured workforce) had claimed unemployment benefit or transitional payment in the course of the year.[2]

Not all those registered as unemployed were 'wholly unemployed', in the contemporary official phrase. A certain number were returned as 'temporarily stopped', which indicated that they had a reasonable chance of being rehired by their former employers within six weeks; if this had not occurred by then, the person was reclassified as 'wholly unemployed'. In practice, a large proportion of the temporarily stopped were working part-time and claiming benefit. The rules allowed up to three days' work without benefit loss (although no more than half the full week's earnings could be paid), and any subsequent three days' periods of unemployment could be run together to count as continuous

2. J.A. Dale, 'The Interpretation of the Statistics of Unemployment', *JRSS* 97 (1934), pp. 85–6.

Table 14.4 GB duration of unemployment, 1929–36

	Per cent of all applicants unemployed for these periods[a]				
	0–2 months	*3–5 months*	*6–8 months*	*9–11 months*	*12+ months*
Sept. 1929	78.5	10.6	3.8	2.4	4.7
Feb. 1931	61.1	18.3	9.7	5.9	5.0
Aug. 1932	59.0	11.1	7.3	6.2	16.4
Aug. 1933	54.1	10.6	6.9	5.5	22.9
Aug. 1934	58.4	9.3	6.0	4.5	21.8
Aug. 1935	55.5	9.5	6.6	5.0	23.4
Aug. 1936	54.9	9.5	6.1	4.5	25.0

Note: a Percentage of all applicants (male and female) for unemployment benefit or allowance

Source: W.H. Beveridge, 'An Analysis of Unemployment, II', *Economica* IV, 13 (1937), p. 6

unemployment. This so-called 'OXO' system (O = work; X = leisure) was much resorted to in cotton and coal-mining. The proportions of temporarily stopped to the total unemployed rose sharply in 1930–31; in 1930, about 10 per cent of all registered unemployed were females thus stopped, and in 1931, about 16 per cent of all unemployed were males thus stopped. With the economic recovery, these proportions fell; by 1937 they were down to 5 and 9 per cent respectively.[3]

The rise in longer-term unemployment, which was a feature of the depression, altered substantially the characteristics of the unemployed population. The chief feature was the decline of short-term unemployment (less than three months), and the rise of long-term unemployment (twelve months or more). Intervening periods showed less marked change (Table 14.4 above).

Thus between September 1929 and August 1932, while the overall rate of unemployment of insured workers rose by 122 per cent, the proportion of those unemployed for one year or more rose by 249 per cent. Even so, at the trough of the slump, slightly over half of unemployment was still of less than three months in duration. But the most severe change had been the rise in long-term unemployment, which now accounted for one-quarter of all unemployment. Nor did the structure of unemployment revert to its pre-1929 pattern as the overall level of unemployment declined after 1932. In September 1929 there had been 45,100 of the long-term unemployed claiming unemployment benefit or allowance; in September 1936 there were 324,902.[4]

3. Mitchell, *Statistics*, p. 127; M. Thomas, 'Labour Market Structure', in B. Eichengreen and T. Hatton (eds), *Interwar Unemployment in International Perspective* (Dordrecht 1988), p. 136.
4. W.H. Beveridge, 'An Analysis of Unemployment, II', *Economica* IV, 13 (1937), p. 4; F. Capie and M. Collins, *The Inter-War British Economy: a statistical abstract* (Manchester UP 1983), p. 64.

The incidence of unemployment fell unequally on the labour force. Women had been less prone to unemployment than men in the 1920s; this continued to be the case in the 1930s. In 1927–29, the female rate had averaged 59 per cent of the male rate. In 1930 and 1931 this rose sharply, reaching a peak of 90 per cent of the male rate in 1931. However, this seems to have reflected not so much a genuine rise in female unemployment as it did the effects of the removal of the 'genuinely seeking work' qualification early in 1930. Consequently a large number of (presumably mainly married) women became entitled to benefit. This provision being removed by the Anomalies Act 1931, the female rate fell after October of that year. By 1932 it was down to 54 per cent of the male rate, and averaged 52 per cent of the male rate in the four years 1932–35.[5]

There were also gender differences in the length of unemployment periods. Women were more prone to short-term, and less prone to long-term unemployment, than men. An analysis of male and female unemployment at 8 June 1936 showed that 49.7 per cent of men claimants, but 67.6 per cent of women claimants, had been unemployed for less than three months. Whereas 26.5 per cent of the men claimants had been unemployed for more than a year, only 9.1 per cent of the women claimants had been.[6]

Finally, unemployment was affected by age. In the case of men, this had been so even in the 1920s, and the depression did not greatly alter the pattern. Samples of those claiming unemployment benefit in December 1930 and December 1932 showed that, while for workers aged over 34 the chances of being unemployed did not vary much with age, those aged 25–34 were less liable to claim benefit, and those aged 16–24 were more likely to claim benefit. After the age of 34, it was not so much that the chances of being unemployed varied according to age, but the older the worker, the longer the period of unemployment was likely to be. Thus in July 1935, whereas the proportion of insured men who had been unemployed for twelve months or more was 4.1 per cent, the proportion of men aged 55–59 unemployed for 12 months or more was 8.0, and of men aged 60–64 was 10.5 per cent. A study of working-class households sampled in the *New Survey of London Life and Labour* (1928–32) concluded that the risk of unemployment for adult males (aged 18 and over) was lowest for those aged 35–44, and greatest for those aged 55–59 and 25–29.[7]

REGIONAL UNEMPLOYMENT

The experience of unemployment was very much affected by regional disparities. These had emerged in the 1920s, and persisted into the 1930s (Table 14.5 overleaf).

5. W.H. Beveridge, 'An Analysis of Unemployment, I', *Economica* III, 12 (1936), pp. 358–9.
6. W.H. Beveridge, 'An Analysis of Unemployment, III', *Economica* IV, 14 (1937), p. 170.
7. Beveridge, 'Analysis, II', pp. 12–15; B. Eichengreen, 'Unemployment in Interwar Britain: new evidence from London', *Journal of Interdisciplinary History* XVII, 2 (1986), p. 348.

Table 14.5 Regional insured unemployment rates, 1924–38

	South-east	*South-west*	*Midlands*	*North-east*	*North-west*	*Scotland*	*Wales*	*GB*
1924–29	5.8	8.2	9.4	14.3	12.6	13.1	17.5	10.7
1930	8.0	10.4	14.7	20.2	23.8	18.5	25.9	15.8
1931	12.0	14.5	20.3	27.4	28.2	26.6	32.4	21.1
1932	14.3	17.1	20.1	28.5	25.8	27.7	36.5	21.9
1933	11.5	15.7	17.4	26.0	23.5	26.1	34.6	19.8
1934[a]	8.7	13.1	12.9	22.1	20.8	23.1	32.3	16.6
1935	8.1	11.6	11.2	20.7	19.7	21.3	31.2	15.3
1936[b]	7.3	9.4	9.2	16.8	17.1	18.7	29.4	12.9
1937	6.7	7.8	7.3	11.1	14.0	16.0	23.3	10.6
1938	8.0	8.2	10.3	13.6	17.9	16.4	24.8	12.6

Notes: a From 1934 to 1938, the figures exclude juveniles under the age of 16, and persons insured under the Agricultural Scheme, who first became insurable in September 1934 and May 1936 respectively.

b The administrative divisions were rearranged in August 1936, so that a new Northern division was created, taking areas from the former North-east and North-west divisions. The new Northern division does not appear here, but its presence makes it impossible to compare the North-east and North-west figures before and after 1936.

Sources: W.R. Garside, *British Unemployment 1919–1939* (Cambridge UP 1990), Table 4, p. 10; W.H. Beveridge, *Full Employment in a Free Society* (Allen & Unwin 1944), p. 47

The experience of the early years of the depression showed some general, and some particular regional variations. By 1932, the relative incidence of unemployment rates was still similar to that of 1924–29. The greatest relative deterioration had been in the south-east; in 1924–29, its unemployment rate had been 54 per cent of the national average; in 1932 it was 65 per cent. There had also been deterioration (although less marked) in the midlands, Scotland and Wales. The greatest fluctuation in the years between 1929 and 1932 was in the north-west; in 1924–29, its unemployment rate had been 118 per cent of the national average; in 1930 it shot up to 151 per cent, and then came down exactly to its 1920s level in 1932.

With the beginning of economic recovery in 1932, and the decline of unemployment, regional differences became much more marked. While the south-east, south-west and north-east rates had come close to their 1920s relative level by 1936, and the midlands position had improved considerably, those of the north-west, Scotland and (especially) Wales had deteriorated considerably.

The incidence of unemployment was also uneven within regions. This was true of regions with expanding or of contracting industries. Much depended on local conditions. Thus on average in 1936, London had an unemployment rate of 7.7 per cent, but this ranged from 4.6 (Greenwich) to 12.4 (Poplar). Cornwall's average of 16.2 per cent covered variations from 6.5 (Newquay) to 31.0

(Redruth). Even in Warwickshire, with an expanding workforce, unemployment varied from 2.3 per cent (Rugby) to 9.3 (Bedworth). Very wide disparities were found in coal-mining counties, since colliery villages provided little alternative employment. Thus Durham's unemployment rate in 1936 was 27.6 per cent, ranging from 7.6 per cent (Consett) to 48.1 (Bishop Auckland). South Wales showed a more extreme form of this pattern: in 1936, Glamorgan's average was 34.9 per cent, rising from 10.0 (Resolven) to 67.1 (Ferndale). In Scotland, the most extreme variation was in Ayrshire, from the low of 4.7 per cent (Dalmellington) to the high of Kilwinnig (38.5). (The percentages are those of all persons, insured and uninsured, aged 14 and over, registered as unemployed, as a proportion of all persons aged 16–64 in the general unemployment insurance scheme.)[8]

The emergence of greater regional disparities in unemployment after 1932 was largely due to the failure of the declining industries to expand their employment with the economic recovery. To some extent, the unemployment gap between the declining and the expanding industries was diminished by labour migration, so that the declining industries lost some of their potential workforce. Between 1928 and mid-1937, about 150,000 men and about 40,000 women were transferred out of the depressed areas under the Ministry of Labour's industrial transference scheme, which had revived as the recovery got under way. Of these, 50,000 men and 5,600 women were known to have returned home; there may have been others. But it is likely that many more migrated on their own initiative. In the eighteen months to mid-1937, although 30,000 men transferred under the scheme, more than twice as many unemployed men moved from the depressed areas on their own account. Between 1932 and 1936 alone, the south-east absorbed 72,000 additional workers from other regions, and the largest component of this (24,000) was from the depressed north-east.[9]

Regional disparities reflected above all the differing mixture of declining and expanding industries to be found within regions. The classification of an industry as declining did not necessarily indicate a higher than average unemployment rate; agriculture is the great example of this. But declining demand made it more difficult to maintain employment. Nor did expansion necessarily result in particularly low unemployment; the building industry had particularly high unemployment in the slump of 1929–32, and thereafter its unemployment rate hovered about the national average. But within broad limits, unemployment was a function of expansion or decline (Table 14.6 overleaf).

Examples of the rapidly growing industries in 1937 were such as vehicle, cycle and aircraft manufacture (4.8 per cent unemployment) or electrical engineering (3.1). Above-average-growth industries were the manufacture of bread, biscuits and cakes (8.6). Below-average-growth industries were chemicals (6.5) and general engineering (5.4). Declining industries were cotton (11.5), woollens (10.2) and shipbuilding (23.8). Among consumer service industries, the

8. Beveridge, *Full Employment*, App. B2.
9. Royal Commission on the Distribution of the Industrial Population; *Report* (1940), Cmd 6153, para. 316; B. Thomas, 'The Influx of Labour into London and the South-East 1920–36', *Economica* IV, 15 (1937), pp. 330, 335.

Table 14.6 GB unemployment rates by industry, 1937

	Insured persons, 1937 (million)	*Unemployment rate, 1937 (%)*
Manufacturing industries		
Rapid growth[a]	1.618	6.2
Above-average growth	0.855	8.4
Below-average growth	2.232	7.6
Declining	1.574	12.8
Services	3.407	9.2
Transport	0.530	19.1
Building	1.035	13.8
Coal-mining	0.868	14.7
National (GB) average		10.6

Note: a Rapid growth = Employment growing more than twice average
Source: Beveridge, *Full Employment*, Table 33

only high unemployment groups were entertainment (17.5) and hotel, restaurants, etc. (14.6). The high unemployment in transport was due to shipping (21.9) and docks (25.8).[10]

The previous concentration of industries in certain regions made for regional pockets of unemployment dominating the national picture. This was recognised in the government's designation of the 'Special Areas' in 1934; these were south Wales, the north-east coast, Cumberland and lowland Scotland. Although only accounting for 15 per cent of the insured population, they accounted for 45 per cent of 'excess' unemployment (any unemployment in excess of the national average).

The dependence on a local industry was seen to its greatest extent in south Wales, where coal-mining accounted for 52.7 per cent of all unemployment at the 1935 Census of Production. There were other regions where different local factors predominated. This was especially so for Lancashire, where the number of 'excess' unemployed in 1937 was 138,000, equivalent to 7.5 per cent of the total number of insured workers in the county; taking account of the large amount of short-time working in June 1938 would have been equivalent to a further 5.5 per cent of all cotton workers unemployed. In Dundee, where 38.5 per cent of the insured population were engaged on jute manufacturing in 1937, unemployment among jute workers amounted to 21.5 per cent even at the peak of the recovery in 1937. In Stoke-on-Trent, 47.1 per cent of all insured workers were in the manufacture of pottery in July 1937, and they accounted for most of the nearly 11,000 pottery workers unemployed nationally.[11]

10. Beveridge, *Full Employment*, Table 33.
11. M.P. Fogarty, *Prospects of the Industrial Areas of Great Britain* (Methuen 1945), pp. 6, 88, 138–9, 203, 325; Beveridge, *Full Employment*, p. 318.

Table 14.7 GB unemployment and employment in certain industries, 1929–37

	Insured unemployment			*Employment in 1937*
	1929 (%)	*1932 (%)*	*1937 (%)*	*as % of 1924*
Declining/slow growth industries				
Coal-mining	15.5	33.9	14.7	60.0
Cotton	13.1	28.5	11.5	76.6
Shipbuilding	23.8	62.2	23.8	76.7
Woollen and worsted	13.7	20.7	10.2	86.2
General engineering	9.6	29.1	5.4	114.1
Fast growth industries				
Chemicals	6.3	16.5	6.5	119.0
Building	12.2	29.0	13.8	146.0
Metal industries	8.0	19.3	6.0	162.7
Electrical engineering	4.4	16.3	3.1	167.2
Motor vehicles	7.1	20.0	4.8	179.5
Electrical equipment	4.8	12.7	5.2	247.3

Source: Beveridge, *Full Employment*, p. 47, Table 33

INDUSTRIAL UNEMPLOYMENT

The depression had hit all sectors of the economy. The industries which had shown rapid growth in the 1920s were not immune to higher unemployment at the trough of the depression, but they tended to shake it off more easily than slowly growing or declining industries (Table 14.7 above).

THE RELIEF OF UNEMPLOYMENT

By the middle of the 1930s, it was apparent that the failure of exports to recover their previous volume, and the continuing decline of coal, textiles and shipbuilding, meant that long-term unemployment was now a large-scale and intractable problem. This was reflected in the rise in the proportion of unemployment claimants who had been out of work more than a year, and the concentration of this population in the regions where those industries predominated. Thus in June 1937, out of a total of 301,850 claimants in Britain who had been unemployed twelve months or more, the largest proportions were from Scotland (21.4), the north-west (21.1), the north (17.2) and Wales (16.2). Taken together with the north-east, these regions, which may be labelled 'Outer Britain', accounted for 84.9 per cent of such long-term unemployment.[12]

The areas of long-term unemployment had a higher proportion of claimants receiving unemployment assistance rather than unemployment insurance benefit, since claimants could not have satisfied the minimum conditions for insurance

12. Beveridge, *Full Employment*, Table 9.

benefit, or, more likely, would have exhausted their right to insurance benefit, and would then be forced on to the 'transitional' scheme. On 19 April 1937, there were 458,826 men receiving benefit and 569,192 receiving assistance in Britain, so that assisted men were 55.3 per cent of the total; but the proportion of assisted men ranged from 27.0 in London to 72.7 in the northern region. For women, the assisted accounted for only 23.2 per cent of the total of claimants (insured and assisted together), and the range was from 8.7 per cent assisted (in the midlands) to 39.6 in Scotland. This was an important cause of the regional resentment towards the 'means test'.[13]

By the late 1920s, it was becoming apparent that the long-hoped-for recovery in world and British trade had not taken place. The ensuing trade depression further dashed these hopes. Yet official policy remained conservative; no initiatives of any great moment were mounted until the rearmament programme began in 1936. Until then, policy concentrated on the relief of unemployment via the system of unemployment insurance, relief outside the insurance scheme, and the Poor Law.

The formation of the National Government in August 1931 was followed immediately by efforts to reduce the cost of income support for unemployed people. The standard rate of unemployment benefit was cut in October by 10 per cent, from 17s. to 15s. 3d. a week for men, and from 15s. to 13s. 6d. for women, with proportionate cuts for young persons and children, and standard benefit was limited to twenty-six weeks. Transitional benefit (now renamed transitional payment) was to be administered by the Public Assistance Committees (PACs) of the local authorities, established in 1930. These were obliged to enforce a stringent household means test, by which the income of all members of the household (net of rent) would be assessed before deciding on the level of relief. While a case could be made for the reductions in benefit, both on grounds of national economy and on the fact that the cost of living had fallen since 1929, the use of the PACs, with their members' and officials' experience of administering Poor Law relief, and the resentment entailed by the use of their officials to investigate household means, was to leave a bitter social and political legacy. The scales of benefit under the PACs differed widely in different parts of Britain, thus adding injustice to demoralisation. Receipt of transitional payments via the PACs in effect (though not in name) put unemployed people back on the Poor Law.[14]

The final adjustments to the system of unemployment relief took place following the report of the Royal Commission on Unemployment Insurance, chaired by Holman Gregory, which had been established by the Labour government at the end of 1930 in order to answer Opposition charges of extravagance in handling unemployment. The essence of the Commission's final

13. Political and Economic Planning (PEP), *Report on the British Social Services* (PEP 1937), Table 24.
14. D. Fraser, *The Evolution of the British Welfare State* (Macmillan 1973), p. 180; E.M. Burns, *British Unemployment Programs, 1920–1938* (Washington, DC 1941), p. 368.

report in December 1932 was that the relief of those qualified under the insurance scheme should be separated from the relief of those whose right to benefit had been exhausted. The policy of separating insurance and outright relief commended itself to the government, which hoped thereby to use the process to detach unemployment relief from immediate political pressures in Parliament.

The Commission's work bore fruit in the Unemployment Act 1934. The relief of the insured was to be entrusted to a semi-independent body, the Unemployment Insurance Statutory Committee. At the same time, the insurance scheme was to be extended; the principal beneficiaries were the agricultural workers, whose insurance scheme came into force in 1936. After that, the chief uninsured groups remained domestic servants, nurses, civil servants and railway workers. Finally, the benefit rates were restored to their pre-October 1931 level. Those unentitled to benefit were to be catered for by an Unemployment Assistance Board. This would be responsible for the relief of all the uninsured able-bodied on a national basis. On one of two 'Appointed Days' it would assume responsibility for about 800,000 people maintained on transitional payments from the PACs; on the second of these days it would take on a further 200,000 currently in receipt of poor relief from the PACs. For the first time, relief scales were to be decided centrally, replacing the local determination of relief amounts by PACs.[15]

The Unemployment Insurance Statutory Committee had a fairly easy life; from its inception, unemployment was falling, and by 1937 it had built up a surplus of £60 million. Although its first chairman, Sir William Beveridge, insisted on keeping a large reserve, the committee was able to increase dependants' allowances in 1935, and reduce contributions in 1936, as well as introducing the new scheme for agricultural workers.

The Unemployment Assistance Board (UAB) fared less well. It had been designed to fulfil the radical task of implementing national scales of benefit (paid direct from the Treasury). This would have the virtue of eliminating local inequities, and its statutory existence meant that it would be subject neither to daily parliamentary pressures (in the manner of the insurance scheme in the 1920s) nor to local political pressures such as faced the PACs (which were composed of local councillors). A subsidiary motive in the formation of the UAB had been the desire of the Treasury to gain control over the cost of relief; by 1934, the cost of transitional benefit had risen to exceed that of the insurance benefit, whose cost had fallen with declining unemployment.[16]

But the start of the work of the UAB was marred by 'a political and social blunder of the first order' (M. Bruce). On publication of the proposed UAB benefit scales, it was found that, due to official ignorance of the very varied existing scales offered by PACs, most applicants would be worse off under the

15. M. Bruce, *The Coming of the Welfare State* (4th edn, Batsford 1968), pp. 269–71; Fraser, *Evolution*, pp. 181–2.

16. Bruce, *Welfare State*, p. 272; Fraser, *Evolution*, p. 182; Burns, *Programs*, App. IV, Table VII.

UAB than under the PACs. The resulting political outcry was serious enough to force the government to introduce hurriedly a 'standstill' Act (February 1935), under which applicants would have the right to receive either the rate under the proposed UAB scale, or what they would have got under the local PAC's rules – whichever was the higher. For almost the next two years, each applicant to the UAB had to be assessed twice; once according to the UAB regulations, and once in accordance with the scales for transitional payment which would have been applied by the local PAC had the UAB not existed. It was not until after new scales had been agreed, in April 1937, that the second appointed day could occur, and the able-bodied unemployed were not completely assimilated from the PACs until the summer of 1938.[17]

The Act of 1934, and the inception of the UAB, had a profound effect on the Poor Law. In 1936, an average of 285,000 individuals (including dependants) were being relieved by the Poor Law on account of unemployment; in 1937 this fell to 106,000. After 1937, when it lost almost all its able-bodied males, the Poor Law remained solely as a residual, last-resort service. Indoor relief still remained in the form of institutional care for children, old people, sick and mentally ill people, but the great majority of those relieved received out-relief; such categories as sick people, aged, widows, deserted wives and those unemployed still outside the scope of the UAB remained in the Poor Law out-relief system.[18]

THE EFFECTS OF UNEMPLOYMENT ON THE UNEMPLOYED

Incomes and earnings

The immediate effect of unemployment on unemployed people was a fall in income. The question of how far in the 1930s the incomes of unemployed people actually fell below what they might previously have been earning is fraught with difficulty. A reworking of the data on London working-class households assembled for the *New Survey of London Life and Labour* (1928–32) suggests that for both adult males and adult male heads of households, the earnings of unemployed people were lower than those of employed people by about 12 per cent. In the study made by the Pilgrim Trust of 933 long-term unemployed persons in six towns in November 1936, only 21 per cent of the men received allowances equivalent to 70 per cent or more of their normal wage. For those men whose income was mainly derived from unemployment assistance, the replacement rate (i.e. the ratio of income when unemployed to the income before unemployment) ranged from 45 to 66 per cent of the wages which the men might have reasonably have been expected to earn.

The only data on a national scale are those derived from two official samples of benefit and assistance claimants in 1937; the results of this suggest

17. Bruce, *Welfare State*, pp. 272–3; Fraser, *Evolution*, p. 182; N. Branson and M. Heinemann, *Britain in the Nineteen Thirties* (Panther 1973), pp. 45–7.
18. Fraser, *Evolution*, pp. 182–3; Burns, *Programs*, p. 356.

that the loss of income was more severe. Thus a replacement rate of 70 per cent or more was achieved, in the case of benefit claimants, by only about 11 per cent of males and about 10 per cent of females. The proportions of those on assistance with a replacement rate of 70 per cent or more were higher; some 31 per cent of both males and females; this higher rate is less surprising, since those on assistance tended to have lower earnings than those on benefit, and correspondingly higher replacement rates.[19]

The suggestion that about 90 per cent of those claiming benefit, and about 70 per cent of those claiming assistance, lost at least 30 per cent of their earnings when unemployed, is relevant to the debate on the causes of unemployment in the interwar period. What the actual average replacement rate was in the 1930s is still debated. Two estimates put it at 54 and 34 per cent respectively. The authors of the first estimate consider this such a generous proportion that it must have materially raised the numbers claiming benefit or assistance; the author of the latter considers it too low to have this kind of effect. Until it is known how individuals valued the leisure which unemployment brought them, such judgements are premature.[20]

That the rates of benefit were much less than wages is certain. From 1 July 1934 (when the 1931 cuts were abandoned) the rate for men was 17s. a week, and for women 15s. a week. Young men (18–20) received 14s., young women 12s. Boys and girls aged 16 and 17 received less. The wife or husband of the unemployed worker received 9s., and 2s. was payable in respect of each dependent child (raised to 3s. in October 1935). Thus a married couple, whose husband was unemployed, with an uninsured wife, would receive 26s.; the same couple with two children would receive 30s. (32s. after October 1935).[21] These rates may be compared with the average weekly wage rates estimated by Routh for 1935, which were 75s. 9d. for skilled men, 55s. 5d. for semi-skilled men, 52s. 4d. for unskilled men, and 34s. 3d. for agricultural labourers.[22]

Whether unemployment would throw a household into poverty depended above all on the existence of secondary earners apart from the main earner, and whether there were dependent children. While on a national scale, it is not known what proportions of unemployed people met these criteria, Eichengreen's work on London in 1928–32 suggests that low-earning households with children and/or without secondary earners were more likely than the

19. Eichengreen, 'Unemployment', p. 129; Thomas, 'Labour Market Structure', pp. 129–31; Pilgrim Trust, *Men Without Work* (Cambridge UP 1938), pp. 203, 118–19.

20. D.K. Benjamin and L.A. Kochin, 'Unemployment and Unemployment Benefit in Twentieth-Century Britain: a reply to our critics', *JPE* (1982), p. 426; D. Metcalf, 'Still Searching for an Explanation of Unemployment in Interwar Britain', *JPE* (1982), p. 388; Thomas, 'Labour Market Structure', p. 131.

21. Ministry of Labour, *Twenty-Second Abstract of Labour Statistics (1922–1936)* (1937), Cmd 5556, pp. 70–1.

22. G. Routh, *Occupation and Pay in Great Britain, 1906–60* (Cambridge UP 1965), pp. 88–104.

average to suffer unemployment. On the other hand, unemployed earners were very likely to have their wives also working. Thus it is relevant in assessing unemployment-induced poverty to concentrate on low-earning households with children; the average household with children in the London study had between one and two children.[23]

Thus unemployment of workers in insured industries led to substantial falls in income on average. However, this average applies largely to the manual workers, skilled and less skilled. On either side of it lay two further groups: those middle-class or upper-class persons (largely uninsured) who fell into unemployment, and those of the very low-wage occupations (whether insured or not). The fate of the middle-class worker suddenly thrown into poverty by prolonged unemployment, although presumably rare, deserves mention. An extreme case was that of the young Helen Forrester, whose family, comprising parents and seven children, was in 1931 thrust suddenly, due to her father's bankruptcy, from comfortable surroundings in Cheshire on to the Poor Law in Liverpool. After only a few months of extreme poverty and increasing squalor, malnutrition was beginning to affect the family's health. Another (anonymous) case was of an advertising agent formerly earning £1,000 a year, who, unemployed, found himself entirely dependent on his adult children, having failed in applications to the PAC and private charities.[24]

At the other end of the scale were those who were more or less as well-off under unemployment assistance as under their previously low wages. This would clearly apply to agricultural workers, unless of the skilled variety, as Table 14.7 indicated. The Pilgrim Trust's survey of the long-term unemployed studied the cases of 936 men, of whom 158 had four or more dependants; it was suggested that for the great majority of these, unemployment meant little reduction in the standard of life. For those (59) men with six or more dependants, it may have been advantageous to be unemployed, since income was now regular, whereas before it had been intermittent. On this slim basis, perhaps about one-fifth of those on unemployment assistance were as well off, or better off, than when employed. (The opinions are those of the Pilgrim Trust. The persons concerned were on unemployment assistance, not unemployment benefit; benefit lasted for 156 days only.)[25]

The unemployment figures do not allow firm statements as to the condition of those on short time or interrupted spells of work, such as in the coal-mines, docks, or cotton. For these, the working of the 'OXO' system meant a perpetuation of low incomes; of the 512,000 of unemployed people on 24 April 1934 who were 'temporarily stopped', it was estimated that 150,000 were working on an institutionalised system of short time, and 150,000–200,000 were working short time on an irregular, unsystematic basis. While there is little information on the length of the short week, in October 1931, when 15 per cent of

23. Eichengreen, 'Unemployment', pp. 353–5.
24. H. Forrester, *Twopence to Cross the Mersey* (Fontana 1981); H.L. Beales and R.S. Lambert, *Memoirs of the Unemployed* (Gollancz 1934), ch. 1.
25. Pilgrim Trust, *Men Without Work*, p. 120.

industrial workers were on short time, it was thought that the short-time week was less than the standard week by about twelve hours (about one-quarter of the week).[26]

Living standards

Reductions in income, which were undoubtedly the lot of the majority of unemployed people, entailed reduced living standards. The degree of reduction is not known, simply because the previous incomes of the unemployed workers are not known. The most that can be done is to examine the contemporary social surveys, and see what they tell us about the connection between unemployment and poverty.

The survey of Bristol by Tout in 1937, at the peak of the economic recovery, surveyed the city's working-class and lower-middle-class households (whose heads earned less than £5 a week), and found that, on a rather exiguous definition of needs (equivalent, for example, to 37s. 8d. a week, excluding rent, for a family of two adults and three children), 10.7 per cent of households were below the standard (i.e. in poverty). Unemployment was the largest single cause of poverty (32 per cent), followed by old age of the head of household (15.2), illness or incapacity (9.0) or insufficient wages with a large family (9.0).[27]

An earlier survey of working-class households in Sheffield at the trough of the slump, in 1931–32, took as its standard an even more exiguous line, equivalent for two adults, two schoolchildren and an infant to 24s. 11½d. (excluding rent); on this basis, the proportion of households in poverty was 15.4 per cent. Unemployment was the main cause of poverty by a large margin; 60 per cent of poverty was caused by unemployment, and a further 6.6 per cent by chronic unemployment (over five years); widowhood and old age accounted for only 16.8 per cent of poverty.[28]

In the Merseyside survey of working-class households (1929–32), a poverty line was adopted which was similar to that of Bristol, at 37s. 7d. for a family with one infant and two schoolchildren; on this test, 16 per cent of the families sampled were below the poverty line in 1929–30. Of all families below the poverty line, 39.9 per cent suffered from the unemployment of the chief earner, and 23.3 per cent from the casual employment of the chief earner. While these families constituted only 21.8 per cent of those sampled, they accounted for 63.2 per cent of the families below the poverty line.[29]

Southampton, a city which relied, like Merseyside, on dock and shipyard work for a large proportion of its employment, was also surveyed in 1928–31.

26. Dale, 'Interpretation', p. 89; Thomas, 'Labour Market Structure', p. 136.
27. H. Tout, *The Standard of Living in Bristol* (Bristol, Arrowsmith 1938), pp. 12, 20, 22, 25–6, 44.
28. Sheffield Social Survey Committee, *A Survey of the Standard of Living in Sheffield* (prepared by A.D.K. Owen) (Sheffield 1933), pp. 6, 19, 24, 29.
29. D.C. Jones (ed.), *The Social Survey of Merseyside, vol. I* (Liverpool UP 1934), pp. 150, 152, 166–70.

Adopting a standard based on Bowley's 1924 work, it was found that in the autumn of 1931, when unemployment had risen substantially, the proportion of working-class families below the poverty line was between 20.6 and 22.5 per cent; had unemployment still been at the relatively low level of 1929, the proportion in poverty would probably have been only about 14–15 per cent. Unemployment was by far the greatest cause of poverty in 1931, accounting for about two-thirds of the poverty of all the families below the poverty line.[30]

The final relevant social survey was that of Seebohm Rowntree, who repeated in York in 1936 his earlier survey of 1899. Like the early survey, that of 1936 was based on an exhaustive investigation of 'practically every working-class family in York' (the other surveys cited above used random sampling, but Rowntree seems to have been unaware of this technique). Rowntree's poverty datum line, based on more recent nutritional research than that employed in the other surveys (Sheffield excepted), worked out at 43s. 6d., exclusive of rent, for an urban family of man, wife and three dependent children. On that basis, or pro rata for different sized households, 31.1 per cent of the working-class population was below the poverty line. The largest single cause of poverty was inadequate wages of those in regular employment (32.8 per cent), followed by unemployment of the chief wage-earner (28.6) and old age (14.7).[31]

In 1899, Rowntree had made a further distinction, that of 'primary poverty', which was defined in relation to a bare minimum poverty line (the dietary constituent of which was 'even less generous than that allowed to able-bodied paupers in the York workhouse').[32] Should individuals fall below this, they would lack the bare necessities to secure physical (i.e. bodily) efficiency:

> Nothing must be bought but that which is absolutely necessary for the maintenance of physical health, and what is bought must be of the plainest and most economical description. Should a child fall ill, it must be attended by the parish doctor; should it die, it must be buried by the parish. Finally, the wage-earner must never be absent from his work for a single day.[33]

At 1936 prices, this bare minimum standard of 1899 worked out at 30s. 7d. for the five-person family. In 1899, primary poverty had affected 15.5 per cent of the working class; by 1936 this had fallen to 6.8 per cent. But the causes of

30. P. Ford, *Work and Wealth in a Modern Port: an economic survey of Southampton* (Allen & Unwin 1934), pp. 111, 114–18, 129–30.
31. The standard of poverty used by Rowntree in 1899 was used as a basis by Bowley (1925) and Owen (Sheffield 1933). Ford (Southampton 1934) was based on Bowley; Caradog Jones (Merseyside 1934) was based on Rowntree and Bowley. Llewellyn Smith (*New Survey of London*) relied on Booth's rather impressionistic standards in the original *Survey of London Life and Labour* (1902); C.A. Linsley and C.L. Linsley, 'Booth, Rowntree and Llewellyn Smith: a reassessment of interwar poverty', *EcHR* XLVI (1993), pp. 90–2; B. Harris, 'Unemployment, Insurance and Health in Interwar Britain', in Eichengreen and Hatton, *Interwar Unemployment*, p. 156.
32. B.S. Rowntree, *Poverty: a study of town life* (Macmillan 1901), p. 133.
33. Ibid., p. 134.

Table 14.8 Food values (after preparation) in standard diets

	BMA	*Stiebeling*	*League of Nations*
Calories	2,777	2,810	2,887
Protein (grams)	82	68	68 or 83[a]

Note: a Two interpretations of the instructions for preparation
Source: (Sir) W. Crawford and H. Broadley, *The People's Food* (Heinemann 1938), p. 151

primary poverty had altered. In 1899, the greatest cause had been the low wages of those employed (52.0 per cent); in 1936 the largest cause was unemployment (44.5 per cent). Although unemployment only accounted for 28 per cent of all poverty in the city, 44.5 per cent of the families in primary poverty existed on unemployment benefit.[34]

Nutrition

Poverty, from whatever cause, had implications for nutritional status. The assessment of the poverty datum line had developed over time; Rowntree's minimum standard, which was that just enough to sustain life, formed the basis also for Bowley's survey of 1913 and 1924, and the Southampton and Sheffield surveys. By the early 1930s, it was recognised that nutritional science had advanced to make a more comprehensive and substantial measurement necessary. This was done in 1933 by the British Medical Association (BMA), which recommended a minimum of 3,400 calories per man per day, and a supply of protein of 100 g, of which at least 50 g should be of first-class (i.e. animal) origin. The BMA costed the diet at 5s. 11d. per man, reducing to 2s. 8d. for a child under 2. The BMA was later criticised for underestimating the cost of the diet, but its recommendation caused consternation at the Ministry of Health, which strenuously denied for the rest of the decade that malnutrition was purely a matter of food intake, or that it could be clinically tested.[35] Later, slightly higher standard dietaries were worked out by Stiebeling, and the League of Nations, although the differences between the diets were not very great. They may have had the food values (after preparation) shown in Table 14.8 above.

In all cases where subsequent social investigations made use of these standards, it was shown that the population contained a high proportion of inadequately fed people. John Boyd Orr's survey of 1936 (using the Stiebeling standard) suggested that the diets of about 4.5 million people were below standard in every respect (calories, proteins, fat, vitamins and minerals); a further 9 million were more than adequately supplied with proteins, barely adequately in calories and fats, but were deficient in minerals and vitamins. It was particularly

34. B.S. Rowntree, *Poverty and Progress: a second social survey of York* (Longmans, Green 1941), pp. 28, 32, 39, 102, 110, 116, 150.
35. M. Mayhew, 'The 1930s Nutrition Controversy', *JCH* 23 (1988), pp. 450–2.

noticeable that the lowest 10 per cent of the population (4.5 million) consumed much less of the 'protective' foods than the top 10 per cent; 1.8/5.5 pints of milk a week; 1.5/4.5 eggs per week; 2. 4d./1s./8d. on fruit per week. Complete adequacy of diet was enjoyed by only half the national population.[36]

Boyd Orr's survey was based on a collection of 1,152 budgets made between 1932 and 1935; no special budget inquiry was made. But a special inquiry was made for the only national (England and Wales) survey of food consumption made in the 1930s, that of Crawford and Broadley between October 1936 and March 1937, which comprised 4,989 households in seven large urban areas, covering all income classes. (This is to exclude the survey by the Rowett Research Institute in 1937–39 which covered 1,352 families (7,920 persons) in England and Scotland. This would seem to be less representative of the total population than the Crawford survey, being more biased towards working-class families with children, and over-representing Scotland.)[37] The results, when expressed in broad national terms, were even more alarming than those of Boyd Orr. Adopting the BMA diet as the standard, and recosting it to take account of the 1936 prices actually paid by the respondents, it was estimated that some 36 per cent of the population (16 million individuals) were living in homes where the weekly expenditure on food per head was less than that needed to purchase the BMA diet. Some two-thirds of the survey's Class D (semi-skilled and unskilled employees, unemployed people and pensioners) fell into this category. If the League of Nations diet were to be used as the yardstick, then the number of individuals with expenditure less than required would rise to 23 million, and four-fifths of Class D would be in that position.[38] In general, it was concluded:

> A study of the foregoing charts and tables suggests that only half of the working class achieves the League of Nations requirements in calories and protein; while practically all its members fall very considerably short in their intake of calcium, phosphorous, iron and the vitamins. . . . The middle class, on the whole, are, according to League of Nations standards, adequately provided with calories, protein, and phosporous, iron and vitamin C, but are probably in need of greater quantities of calcium and vitamins A and B1. . . . In the wealthy class there is no real shortage, except in regard to vitamin A.[39]

While national nutritional inadequacy seems proven for the late 1930s, the connection with unemployment is less clear; the nutritional standards employed by social investigators after 1933 were higher than previously, and the nation as a whole experienced improved nutrition. But a large proportion of the poverty of the decade stemmed from unemployment, and poverty implied poor nutrition. Rowntree suggested that probably almost all the families in York living

36. J.B. Orr, *Food Health and Income: report on a survey of adequacy of diet in relation to income* (2nd edn, Macmillan 1937), pp. 27, 41, 55.
37. Carnegie United Kingdom Trust, *Family, Diet and Health in Pre-War Britain: a dietary and clinical survey* (Dunfermline, Carnegie United Kingdom Trust 1955).
38. Crawford and Broadley, *People's Food*, pp. 308, 320, 325–30.
39. Ibid., pp. 158–9.

below the minimum were undernourished. He studied the diets of twenty-eight families, of whom thirteen were below the poverty line; eleven of these families were badly underfed, and the underfeeding was particularly acute in the seven of these families who depended entirely on unemployment benefit. Dr M'Gonigle, the Medical Officer of Health in Stockton-on-Tees, surveyed the diets of employed and unemployed people on two housing estates in 1932, and found that both employed and unemployed groups consumed insufficient protein, but on both estates the unemployed families consumed fewer calories and less protein, fat and carbohydrate than their employed neighbours. A further survey of the food budgets of 126 families showed that both the calorie and first-class protein intake was below the BMA standard for all families whose income was less than 55s. An attempt to reconstruct working-class food budgets for Teesside in the 1930s suggests that the average diet contained only 2,587 calories and 51.7 g of protein per day; this, while probably sufficient to prevent actual malnutrition in the average adult, was insufficient for nursing and pregnant mothers, and members of large families, if living at home.[40]

Mortality and health

Boyd Orr had recognised that the standards employed in his investigations were those ensuring perfect health, and derogation from these levels did not necessarily imply starvation – 'or even such a degree of ill-health as is recognised in the term disease'. It can perhaps be agreed that the national statistics of mortality do not support the view that they were adversely affected by the depression. Lewis-Faning in 1938 examined the general mortality statistics in urban areas in England and Wales; while it was clear that they were higher in depressed areas, these differences were too long-standing to be attributed to 1930s conditions. Winter has examined infant mortality statistics (long held to be a sensitive indicator of social conditions) and concluded that the observed fluctuations between the wars were not to be decisively attributed to unemployment – although some of the deleterious effects of the 1930s depression on health were to be observed in the infant mortality experience of post-1945 mothers.[41]

Infant mortality statistics may be a rather blunt instrument to assess national deprivation, especially since, while regional and local differences abound, our knowledge of the full range of reasons for these differences is inadequate. To complicate matters, infant mortality was, in the long run, diminishing, and had been since before 1914. But two points may be made. The first is that the rate of decline of infant mortality slowed sharply in the 1930s (Table 14.9 overleaf).

40. Rowntree, *Poverty and Progress*, ch. VII; G.C.M. M'Gonigle and J. Kirby, *Poverty and Public Health* (Gollancz 1936), pp. 124, 248–63; K. Nicholas, *The Social Effects of Unemployment on Teesside, 1919–39* (Manchester UP 1986), pp. 64–8.

41. Orr, *Food*, p. 42; Harris, 'Unemployment', pp. 170–1; J. Winter, 'Unemployment, Nutrition and Infant Mortality in Britain, 1920–50', in Winter (ed.), *The Working Class in Modern British History: essays in honour of Henry Pelling* (Cambridge UP 1983), pp. 233, 254.

Table 14.9 GB infant mortality (deaths of infants under 1 year per 1,000 live births), 1900–60

	1900	*1910*	*1920*	*1930*	*1940*	*1950*	*1960*
England & Wales	154	105	80	60	57	30	22
Decadal decline (%)	—	32	24	25	5	47	27
Scotland	128	108	92	83	78	39	26
Decadal decline (%)	—	16	15	10	. 6	50	33

Source: Mitchell, *Statistics* (Cambridge UP 1988), pp. 58–9

The second point is that the interwar period as a whole showed a sharp widening of the gap between the infant mortality rates of the classes at the bottom and top of the social scale (Table 14.10).

Table 14.10 Infant mortality rate (per 1,000) in Registrar-General's social classes I and V, England and Wales, 1911–51

	1911	*1921–23*	*1930–32*	*1939*	*1951*
Class V	152.5	97.0	77.0	60.1	40.8
Class I	76.4	38.4	32.7	26.9	18.7
% excess, V/I	99.6	152.6	135.5	123.4	118.2

Source: Winter, 'Unemployment', p. 246

Thus the possibility is raised that the entire interwar period was one in which economic depression coincided (to put the matter no more strongly) with *relatively* poorer chances of survival for the poorest social groups.

Other evidence for worsening health in the 1930s is patchy.[42] Official indicators of malnutrition were based entirely on the subjective opinion of the local Medical Officer of Health, and are effectively useless as historical evidence. A large number of studies showed that the health of male unemployed workers was worse than those in work, but it is unsafe to conclude thereby that unemployment had produced the poorer health. Nicholas' study of Teesside suggests that the already established trend towards better health continued, even in the 1930s, although it may have been retarded by unemployment. There are also local studies which point to poor health in young children and the mothers of young children, and raise also the possibility that unemployment contributed to higher rates of maternal mortality. More recently, it has

42. The discussion as to the effects of the interwar period (especially the 1930s) on health may be followed in the work of Harris (1988), Mayhew (1988), Webster (1982) and Winter (1983). See also C. Webster, 'Health, Welfare and Unemployment during the Depression', *Past and Present* 33 (1985).

been suggested by Harris that children from the depressed areas suffered a stunting of growth, so that the heights of schoolchildren formed a kind of physical index of deprivation. Overall, Harris concludes that, while unemployment had some effect on health nationally, this effect was less marked in depressed regions, in which an already inferior diet was at least maintained by the operation of unemployment benefit and assistance.[43]

Psychological effects[44]

Even more difficult to demonstrate than the physical effects of unemployment, but none the less real, were the psychological effects. These developed from the initial shock to anger, shame, loss of social confidence, irritability, nervous depression, and finally apathetic resignation. Throughout, there was the fear that one's case might be referred to the Court of Referees, and the benefit or allowance reduced or stopped. There was also the strain of applying for non-existent jobs to satisfy the 'genuinely seeking work' proviso. Family unity was weakened by the means test, which also made it tempting for young people to use an accommodation address to give the impression that they were no longer living at home, and thus gain a higher rate of benefit. Perhaps the following quotation from a study of the south Wales colliery village of Brynmawr in 1929–32 may serve as a description of the life of unemployed people.

> Visits to the Exchange at most take up part of two half-days in the week. For the rest, some men stand aimlessly on the Market Square or at the street corners, content apparently with a passive animal existence, or with the hour-long observation of passers-by, varied by an occasional whiff at a cigarette. Others work on allotment or garden, tend fowls or pigs, or do carpentry in their backyard or kitchen. Others again stroll 'down the valley' or sit on the banks when the sun is warm. On wet days the Miners' Institute offers papers and a shelter, although shop doors and street corners satisfy many. At night, there are the pictures, and the long queues outside the 'Picture House' probably account for more of the pocket-money of the unemployed than do the public-house.
>
> In these and other ways the unemployed man drags out his time and, whether he expresses it lucidly or not, in almost every individual there is an abiding sense of waste of life.[45]

Sometimes the sense of being uprooted from normal life contributed to a nervous breakdown. Max Cohen, a young cabinet-maker who was made unem-

43. Harris, 'Unemployment', pp. 150, 161ff.; Nicholas, *Teesside*, ch. 3.
44. M. Cohen, *I was One of the Unemployed* (Gollancz 1945; EP Publishing 1978); Individual testimony on the effects of unemployment, usually covering the psychological effects as well as the physical, is plentiful. One of the most substantial accounts is that of Max Cohen. Less satisfactory, being composed of anonymous case histories, but covering a wider range of individual experiences, is Beales and Lambert *Memoirs*. The subject is also covered in Pilgrim Trust, *Men Without Work* (Cambridge UP 1938) and Carnegie Trust, *Disinherited Youth: a report on the 18+ age group enquiry* (Edinburgh 1943).
45. J. Jennings, *Brynmawr: a study of a distressed area* (Allenson 1934), pp. 139–40.

ployed in 1932, recounted the stages of his own (temporary) psychological disintegration: the immediate loss of self-confidence, then a feeling that the world was a surreally ludicrous place, and then a generalised state of fear:

> Eventually I lived under a menacing cloud of fear that darkened my whole existence. . . . There was no immediately obvious cause for it, no objective happenings or surroundings to which it could be immediately traced. It was a hellish brew, compounded of crushing despair, an abysmal sinking of the heart, and a mental distress so acute as to be well-nigh indistinguishable from physical pain.
>
> I grew to an attitude of life that was entirely morbid. I sank deeper and deeper into a vortex of fear, depression and despair.[46]

Poor food and psychological depression contributed to reducing the employability of the long-term unemployed. Little was done to obviate this; perhaps the most useful were the clubs for unemployed people which sprang up in the depressed areas, providing companionship and social recreation. Some of these had developed spontaneously in the late 1920s. After 1933 the movement received an impetus from the National Council of Social Service, and by 1935 there were said to be 400 of them, with a total membership of 250,000.[47] (Croucher estimates that there were 2,300 clubs in May 1934, again used by 250,000 people.)[48]

Retraining

A similar contribution may have been made by government training centres, which aimed to retrain workers, but the numbers involved were not great, amounting to a total of 58,465 entrants in 1930–36, of whom 38,894 obtained employment subsequently. On a larger scale, and aimed specifically at restoring the employability of unemployed men in depressed areas prior to their transference to other areas, were the Transfer Instructional Centres. These dated from 1929, but the Unemployment Act 1934 empowered the UAB officials to require unemployed people to attend the centres as a condition of receiving assistance. These residential centres, in remote spots, concentrated on outdoor work to toughen the muscles and re-instil mental and moral discipline, and were denounced as 'slave camps' by the National Unemployed Workers' movement. Between 1929 and 1938, 182,597 men passed through these camps, the peak year being 1934, when 32,788 attended. The 'instruction' provided was nugatory, complaints over food were frequent, and 'mutinies' were not unknown. The camps were for the long-term male unemployed. Women's training was confined to the courses in domestic service skills run by the Central Council on Women's Training and Employment, established during the war; the Home Training Centres run by the Council produced only 59,506 women who completed their courses in 1925–38. The lack of interest shown

46. Cohen, *Unemployed*, p. 165.
47. H.A. Mess, *Voluntary Social Services since 1918* (Kegan Paul 1947), p. 42.
48. R. Croucher, *We Refuse to Starve in Silence: a history of the National Unemployed Workers' Movement* (Lawrence & Wishart 1987), p. 165.

by unemployed women in being retrained as domestic servants continued to puzzle middle-class opinion throughout the interwar period.[49]

CONCLUSIONS

The unemployment of the 1930s was a cause of great economic loss and social and individual waste. Its impact was the more obvious and acute because it hit most severely those industries and regions which were already experiencing high unemployment in the 1920s. For the most part, the reduction of unemployment was left to the operation of market forces, the government having little to do with the process until rearmament began to have an effect on the labour market. The reluctance of the state to intervene was due to a variety of political and social considerations, not least the fact that the relatively generous unemployment benefit and assistance schemes in Britain reduced the political incentive for the government to act. Unfortunately, market forces proved inadequate to solve the unemployment problem. This also may be attributed partly to the relative generosity of the social security schemes, and partly to the high level of unemployment even in relatively prosperous regions, so that the chances of getting another job by moving residence were not perceived as particularly high by unemployed people. But even if the social security schemes had not existed, and labour had been abandoned to the unsoftened rigour of market forces, there were simply not enough jobs available to reduce unemployment further.

49. Croucher, *We Refuse*, p. 164; see also W. Hannington, *The Problem of the Distressed Areas* (Gollancz 1937), ch. VII; D. Colledge and J. Field, 'To Recondition Human Material: an account of a British labour camp in the 1930s', *History Workshop* 15 (1983), 161; J. Field, *Learning through Labour: training, unemployment and the state 1890–1939* (University of Leeds Studies in Continuing Education 1992), chs 5, 7; D. Colledge, *Labour Camps: the British experience* (Sheffield Popular Publishing 1989).

CHAPTER 15

REARMAMENT AND THE WAR ECONOMY, 1935–45

REARMAMENT: PACE, SCALE, FINANCE

The rearmament programmes of the later 1930s still bore some of the marks of the First World War and the 1920s. The most visible sign of this had been the 'ten-year rule', under which the Cabinet had laid down that for at least ten years to come no major war need be expected and prepared for. First adopted in August 1919, it had been reaffirmed in 1928. The mounting irritation of the Chiefs of Staff with the rule, under which, they said, all three Services had developed great deficiencies, induced the Cabinet to rescind it in 1932. It had been the Japanese aggressions against Manchuria and Shanghai which had moved the Chiefs to their final outburst against the rule. The accession of Hitler to power in Germany in 1933, and his policy of immediate military expansion, further crystallised strategic thinking; by 1934, all defence plans were focused on the Japanese and German dangers. Italian policy caused concern also, but not until 1937 did the Cabinet instruct the Service chiefs to include Italy in the list of possible aggressors.[1]

Uncertainty as to the identity of the possible enemy was not the only hindrance to rearmament. The domestic political unpopularity of rearmament was still evident until after the general election of 1935, when the National Government gained another term of office without making much of the rearmament issue. Thereafter, events such as the Italian invasion of Ethiopia (Abyssinia) in 1936, and Hitler's military occupation of the Rhineland in the same year removed much of the political hostility to rearmament. The same might be said for the outbreak of the Spanish Civil War in 1936, but this had a divisive effect on popular opinion; it was not until 1937 that the Labour Party reconsidered its position on defence, and stopped voting against the Estimates.

The final obstacles were economic and financial. The economic obstacle was that, while the rearmament programme had expanded greatly by 1936–37, the government was unwilling to control the process, believing that 'normal trade' ought not to be interfered with. Thus the programme was hindered; the

1. W.K. Hancock and M. Gowing, *British War Economy* (*HSWW* 1949), pp. 45–6, 63–4. This volume gives an overall view of the general history of the wartime economy.

Secretary of State for Air declared in September 1937 that such a policy of non-interference would postpone completion of the current aircraft programme for two years (from 1939 to 1941). The rule as to non-interference lasted from February 1936 until March 1938.[2]

The financial obstacle stemmed from the fact that, since a large programme could not be financed by taxation alone, borrowing by the government would be required. Borrowing was feared for various reasons. It might, the government thought, 'crowd out' private investment, and so retard economic recovery. It might lead to inflation, which might also retard recovery. Inflation of export prices might lead to a deterioration in the balance of trade, and thus downward pressure on the exchange rate. Finally, any of these consequences, and the general departure from orthodox finance which borrowing entailed, might frighten the owners of sterling assets, so that a crisis might ensue either in public finance or in the exchange rate – or both.

These fears were overcome only slowly. Inside the government, the idea of borrowing was accepted in December 1935, but was not proceeded with until the Defence Loans Bill of February 1937. By that time, a further rearmament programme totalling £1,500 million for the five years 1937–38 to 1941–42 had been agreed, and the borrowing envisaged under the Defence Loans Act for that period was set at £400 million; it was raised by a further £400 million in February 1939. These sums may be put into perspective by considering that central government expenditure in 1935 had been £785 million, and had risen only to £889 million in 1937. Thus financial orthodoxy had been jettisoned abruptly and on a very large scale. But the Treasury was always conscious of the need to reassure financial markets, and to diminish the possibilities of inflation. The main reason for the lag between the decision to borrow and the actual borrowing in 1937 had been the need to raise taxation in the interim, so that at least £170 million of defence expenditure was financed from taxation, this being the amount needed to cover the estimated annual debt charge once the programme was completed. Thus the programme could be financed with the minimum inflationary consequences.[3]

Thus rearmament transformed public finance, well before the outbreak of war, and this process accelerated after the Munich crisis of September 1938. In spite of increased taxes, the proportion of defence spending financed by taxation fell from 75.5 per cent in 1937–38 to 21.2 per cent in 1939–40,[4] in which year total defence spending at £1,118 million was slightly higher than total central government revenue (£1,049 million) (Table 15.1 overleaf).

British rearmament had begun later than that of Germany, but by September 1939 had gone far to catch up. In 1938, 7 per cent of the British national

2. Hancock and Gowing, *War Economy*, p. 70; G.C. Peden, *British Rearmament and the Treasury 1932–1939* (Edinburgh, Scottish Academic Press 1979), pp. 83–5, 153.
3. Peden, *Rearmament*, pp. 71–9; R. Middleton, *Towards the Managed Economy* (Methuen 1985), pp. 107–8; B.R. Mitchell, *British Historical Statistics* (Cambridge UP 1988), pp. 590–1.
4. Middleton, *Managed Economy*, p. 109.

Table 15.1 GB defence expenditure, 1935–36 to 1939–40

	1 *Total defence vote (£m)*	*2* *Borrowing under DLA[a] 1937, 1939 (£m)*	*3* *Total defence spending (£m)*	*4* *Total CGS[b] (£m)[c]*	*5* *Defence as % of CGS (%)*
1935–36	136.9	—	136.9	750.0	18.2
1936–37	186.1	—	186.1	802.9	23.2
1937–38	197.3	64.9	262.2	843.8	31.1
1938–39	254.4	128.1	382.5	940.0	41.0
1939–40	626.4	491.8	1,118.2	1,325.1	84.4

Notes: a DLA = Defence Loans Act
b CGS = central government spending
c Excludes 'self-balancing' expenditure on Post Office and BBC
Source: Central Statistical Office (CSO), *Annual Abstract of Statistics no. 84* (1935–46) (HMSO 1948), Tables 251, 253

product (i.e. net national product or NNP at factor cost), and 17 per cent of the German, had gone to military purposes; in 1939 the figures were 16 and 25 per cent; in 1940 they were 48 and 44 per cent, as the British effort exceeded the German for the first time. (Brown gives an early estimate of the economic effort of the belligerents during the war.)[5]

THE STRATEGIC BACKGROUND

The outbreak of an official war in September 1939 proved somewhat anti-climactical. Accepting that Poland could not be saved, the British military effort was limited to the expeditionary force in France, and the tightening of the naval blockade of Germany. Rearmament targets were raised much higher, but were designed to be fulfilled on a long-term basis. This 'phoney war' period came to an end with the German invasions of Denmark and Norway, the Low Countries and France in April–May 1940. Shortly afterwards, Italy entered the war as a German ally. Although the change of government in May 1940, when Churchill replaced Chamberlain as Prime Minister, promised more dynamic leadership, for the time being attention would have to focus on the defence of Britain.[6]

It was not until after the German invasion of the USSR in June 1941 that the world came near to a truly world-wide war; henceforth the Soviet Union and Britain were allies. The final strategic events were the Japanese attack on Pearl Harbor in December 1941, and Germany's subsequent declaration of war on

5. M. Harrison, 'Resource Mobilization for World War II: the U.S.A., U.K., U.S.S.R. and Germany, 1938–1945', *EcHR* XLI (1988), Table 3, p. 184; A.J. Brown, *Applied Economics* (Allen & Unwin 1947), ch. II.
6. Hancock and Gowing, *War Economy*, pp. 95–100.

the USA. Thus it was not until 1942 that what proved to be the final alignment of major forces was attained. Henceforth, the British and US economies were to be linked, with the ultimate aims of mounting an invasion of mainland Europe, and recovering the lost possessions in the Far East.

WAR ECONOMY AND WAR ECONOMICS

The strategic and political changes of the first year of the war had implications for the organisation of the war economy. On the outbreak of war, the government had taken all necessary powers to control economic affairs. Even before the war began, the Food (Defence Plans) Department had been given the status of a ministry. In September 1939, new ministries were established for Home Security, Economic Warfare, Information, Food and Shipping. The Ministry of Aircraft Production was set up in May 1940. The activity of all these was coordinated by the War Cabinet, via ministerial committees such as the Economic Policy Committee. Yet most civil ministers (except the Chancellor of the Exchequer) did not have a permanent seat in the War Cabinet, and central economic direction of the war was hesitant and uncoordinated, being concerned with finance rather than the mobilisation of real resources. The service departments were responsible for their own procurement of *matériel*, via the Ministry of Supply. Nowhere was the lack of positive overall direction more evident than in the field of labour mobilisation, where the Ministry of Labour was fearful of anything resembling industrial conscription, mindful of the labour troubles of 1914–18.

It was not possible to recast the central economic direction of the war until the political changes of May 1940. A start was then made with the appointment of new ministers such as Ernest Bevin, a prominent trade union leader, as Minister of Labour, and the inclusion of more economic ministers in the War Cabinet. The existing ministerial committees were reorganised, and their activities coordinated by a committee chaired by the Lord President of the Council. After a further reorganisation at the end of 1940, this committee (now under Sir John Anderson) emerged as the most powerful and permanent of the wartime administrative agencies. It was in effect the seat of the central direction of the war economy for the rest of the war. But it was not until 1941 that coherent central direction of the war economy can be said to have been achieved.[7]

Had the nature of the future military task been known in September 1939, and the economic mechanism to supply its wants been available, much inefficiency would have been avoided. But even in the phoney war period, the general principles of running a large-scale war economy were clear. Ultimately, the problem is one of mobilising real resources (labour, machinery, factory space, raw materials, fuel and foodstuffs) and services such as transport, and allocating them between competing uses. In peacetime this allocation is

7. Ibid., pp. 88–94, 216–20; D.N. Chester, 'The Central Machinery for Economic Policy', in Chester (ed.), *Lessons of the British War Economy* (Cambridge UP 1951); J.D. Scott and R. Hughes, *The Administration of War Production* (*HSWW* 1955), p. 415.

performed by the price mechanism; in war by government, whose actions largely supersede the price mechanism. But in a large war, the total demands made on the economy are greater than would be met by the normal free-market system. Two consequences follow: if the military needs are to be satisfied, there must be some corresponding reduction in non-military consumption, and, since non-military consumption is unlikely to be reduced immediately or adequately, there will be an inflationary tendency (overt and covert) in what remains of the price mechanism. Thus the financial problem is particularly concerned with the control of inflation, as well as with the traditional function of raising enough money by taxation and borrowing to pay for the war.[8]

LABOUR MOBILISATION

The allocation of labour was critical to the entire war economy; one of the great failures of 1914–18 had been the lack of coordination of military and civilian demands for labour. On the outbreak of war, military conscription was imposed on all males aged 18–40 years. At the same time, a Schedule of Reserved Occupations was used to protect civilian labour in essential industries from military service, although with the growing demand for military service this system was increasingly replaced by one of individual exemption after 1941. In the first nine months of the war, little was done to control the distribution of civilian labour, except that different agencies were entitled to different priorities, with the result that firms complained of shortages of skilled labour, and of 'poaching' of labour by rivals. It was not until the accession of Bevin as Minister of Labour that industrial conscription was politically or industrially feasible, and not until August 1940 that the national personnel requirements were fully surveyed for the first time. The critical decision was that taken, in March 1941, to limit the size of the Army to about 2 million men; only then could a rational national personnel 'budget' be evolved. However, the events succeeding Pearl Harbor upset the calculations, and it was not until July 1942 that an effective budget was drawn up.[9]

There had been some notable inefficiencies in the first nine months of the war – in particular, an excessive number of agricultural workers and coal-miners had enlisted, although in theory they were debarred. This changed in May 1940, with the almost limitless legal authority now given to the Ministry of Labour to impose industrial conscription, by which anyone in the UK could be directed to perform any service in any place. But it was recognised that persuasion was preferable to command; the ministry also used its powers of labour allocation to persuade firms to pay reasonable wages and provide

8. L. Robbins, *The Economic Problem in War and Peace* (Macmillan 1947); E.A.G. Robinson, 'The Overall Allocation of Resources', in Chester, *Lessons*; R.S. Sayers, *Financial Policy 1939–45* (*HSWW* 1956), ch. 1; M. Kalecki, 'What is Inflation?', in Oxford University Institute of Statistics, *Studies in War Economics* (Oxford, Blackwell 1947).
9. Hancock and Gowing, *War Economy*, pp. 143–50, 283–4, 438–43.

reasonable conditions, including works canteens. Opportunity was also taken to tie essential workers to their jobs, by the Essential Works Order of February 1941. Industrial conscription also extended to women. The National Service Act (No. 2) of December 1941 made women liable for service in the Women's Auxiliary Services or Civil Defence Force; the alternative was to accept in effect an industrial posting. The only major case of compulsory labour allocation regardless of the feelings of the workers concerned was in the coal industry under the 'Bevin Boys' scheme (October 1943).[10]

Mobilisation of labour, especially skilled labour, brought considerable problems. During the phoney war period, firms 'poached' skilled labour from one another, there were embarrassing losses to the services, and 'dilution' was negligible. After the fall of France, progress was more rapid, and a high proportion of the greatly expanded male labour force in munitions became skilled. By the end of 1943, over 1.1 million more women had entered the engineering and allied industries, and by 1944 about 85 per cent of all the women employed were skilled or semi-skilled. Shipbuilding presented unique problems; labour shortage was continuous throughout the war, and the strength of organised labour prevented any extensive resort to dilution. Throughout the war, progress in replacing the peacetime format of two skilled men per job by one skilled man and an unskilled mate was slow, and there were still districts at the end of the war which employed three-man riveting squads.[11]

The distribution of the national labour force had crystallised by the end of 1941, and altered little by the end of the war. Between June 1939 and June 1945, the number of men in the armed forces rose by 4.17 million, and women by 0.44 million. The number of persons engaged in munitions rose by 1.25 million, of whom 0.96 million were women. The labour force in the basic industries (agriculture, mining, government, public utilities and transport) rose by 0.51 million; this concealed a female incursion of 0.84 million and a male exodus of 0.34 million. The biggest losses were in the rest of the industrial and service sector, whose labour force fell from 10.13 to 6.75 million, a loss almost entirely of men. The national labour force was boosted by a fall in unemployment from 1.27 million to 0.10 million. With the expansion of the female labour force, and the reduction of unemployment, the national labour force rose from 19.75 million to 21.65 million.[12]

Thus by the end of the war, some 4 million men and nearly half a million women had entered the Forces. In addition, the female labour force at home had risen by almost half a million. From this should be deducted the 3 million men who had left civilian life, so that the rise in the national labour force, both civil and military, was about 2 million, most of which could be attributed to the greater employment of women. This was not a matter of finding women

10. Ibid., pp. 298–314; H.M.D. Parker, *Manpower: a study of war-time policy and administration* (*HSWW* 1957), pp. 253–5.

11. P. Inman, *Labour in the Munitions Industries* (*HSWW* 1957), ch. II, pp. 78–9, 140–1.

12. Hancock and Gowing, *War Economy*, p. 351.

without either employment or household responsibilities, and finding them wartime employment; the numbers of such women proved to be small. It was rather the natural buoyancy of the labour market, and the entrance of school-leavers into the labour force, coupled with shifts of labour from civilian into war industries, which effected this movement.[13]

FAILURES OF ECONOMIC MOBILISATION

There were some failures of economic mobilisation. Most of these occurred during the phoney war, when government action was not as strong or single-minded as it became later. One of the great problems was congestion of ports. The diversion of ships from east to west coast ports, to avoid enemy action, caused considerable confusion even before the fall of France, and the resulting congestion was estimated to have lost the equivalent of 10 per cent of all imports in 1941. There were serious personnel losses to the Forces at the start of the war. In agriculture, where the complete reservation of workers had been considered politically impossible, the industry was estimated to have lost some 50,000 workers in England and Wales alone by March 1940. In coal-mining, failure to exempt labour from military service cost the industry 80,000 men (over one-tenth of the prewar labour force) by July 1941.[14]

The greatest single failure was the coal industry. Total output fell steadily during the war, from 232 million tons in 1939–40 to 191 million tons in 1944–45. After 1942, there were continuous fears that production would be insufficient for war needs. The reasons lay partly in the losses of labour, and partly in a sharp decline in output per man-shift at the coal-face after 1941. This was itself partly due to the decline in labour, which had led to a disproportionate decline in coal-face workers. There was also the ageing of the labour force, a smouldering discontent over wages, and a decline in efficiency due to indiscipline consequent upon the introduction of the Essential Work Order of March 1941. As a result of the labour shortage, coal became notable for the most direct example of industrial conscription in the war; some young men liable for military service found in 1944–45 that, following a ballot, they were directed instead into the coal industry. In all, about 21,800 men thus became 'Bevin Boys', although only about 6,000–7,000 of them came to be employed at the coal-face.[15]

The other industry to give concern was the railways. The freight tonnage on the railways grew steadily. The passenger-miles almost doubled, from 18.9 million in 1938 to 35.2 million in 1945, as motoring was curtailed. There was

13. G. Ince, 'The Mobilisation of Manpower in Great Britain for the Second Great War', *ManS* XIV, 1 (1946), pp. 18–23.
14. C.B.A. Behrens, *Merchant Shipping and the Demands of War* (*HSWW* 1955), p. 128, App. XIX; K.A.H. Murray, *Agriculture* (*HSWW* 1955), p. 82; W.H.B. Court, *Coal* (*HSWW* 1951), p. 115.
15. Court, *Coal*, pp. 241, 304–5, 388, ch. 6; Hancock and Gowing, *War Economy*, pp. 470–1.

a shortage of labour, and little new capital equipment; whereas in January 1941, 3.7 per cent of the total stock of railway wagons was awaiting repair, the figure in June 1945 was 10.3 per cent. The movement of US personnel to Britain in 1943–44 had to be underwritten by the loan of 400 railway engines from the USA. As early as 1940–41, railway congestion threatened to become critical, partly due to air raids; at the peak of later dislocation, in January 1943, some 1,500 trains weekly were being cancelled due to unavailability of locomotives.[16]

FACTORY EXPANSION

Mobilisation of labour had to be matched by the expansion of factories. The armaments industry, together with the three historic Royal Ordnance Factories (Woolwich, Waltham and Enfield), had shrunk after 1918. A start in reviving the manufacture of armaments had been made in 1934, when the idea of 'shadow' factories was adopted, that is the extension of armament orders to firms outside the industry, usually in factories paid for by the government. But most of the wartime output came either from the much expanded number of Royal Ordnance Factories, or from the civilian armament industry (although usually from factories paid for by the government). Thus by March 1942 there were over forty Royal Ordnance Factories (with a labour force of 312,000), and at the peak of war production the Ministry of Supply operated over 170 'agency' factories. In the newest sector, aircraft, the industry itself was responsible for 88 per cent of total aircraft output between 1939 and 1945, although it had greatly expanded, from a labour force of 27,000 in 1936 to one of 250,000 in 1944; in 1945, the 'shadow' aircraft firms employed only 45,000.[17] All told, from the beginning of rearmament in April 1936 to September 1945, the government spent £1,029 million on fixed capital for war production, and some of this would have value in the postwar economy.[18]

RAW MATERIALS AND MACHINERY

Labour and factory space apart, two possible critical limitations on output were the supply of raw materials and machines. The former was adversely affected by the phoney war; it was not until the Lord President's decision in June 1940 to reduce civilian consumption that a serious attempt was also made to economise on raw materials. Thereafter, conservation proceeded on a broad front, from the spread of utility clothing to the reduction of production of matches from 22 million gross to 12 million gross to save timber, and the increasing use of salvaged materials (notably, public and domestic iron railings, but also scrap aluminium, rubber, paper and rags). A critical part was

16. C. Savage, *Inland Transport* (*HSWW* 1957), pp. 224–6, 409, Apps XVI, XXIV, Statistical App., Table 6.
17. W. Hornby, *Factories and Plant* (*HSWW* 1958), pp. 91–2, 154, 218, 222–3.
18. M.M. Postan, *British War Production* (*HSWW* 1952), p. 448.

played by the USA, from which only 8 per cent of raw material imports had been drawn in 1939; at the peak in 1941, the USA supplied 37 per cent of all raw materials imported.[19]

Machinery played a vital role. The most important products were the machine tools. In 1935, UK output had been 20,000 to 23,000 machines; by 1939 it had risen to 37,000. The peak of production was in 1942, when some 96,000 machines were produced, although considerable reliance had to be placed on imports from the USA in 1940–41. Over the entire war, total UK production was 411,048 machines, and US imports 126,572. The achievements of Machine Tool Control, from 1939 onwards, were signally impressive.[20]

FINANCIAL POLICY

Internal financial policy was faced with two main, interlocking tasks – to raise money for the war and to constrain inflation. Initially, the first task was approached in a cautious manner. The Treasury, still being concerned not to alienate the taxpaying public, proceeded in the historic manner by considering how to raise taxes. By July 1940, the standard rate of income tax had risen from 5s. 6d. to 8s. 6d. However, up to 1941, the yield from such direct taxes went up at a slower rate than that of indirect taxes.[21]

The traditional approach was jettisoned in the Budget of 1941. This was not only a response to criticisms of the inadequacy of the tax yield, but also an acknowledgement of the development of the 'national income' approach to tax policy, under the influence of Keynes. He argued that the right approach to the problem of finding resources for the war was first to look at the national output (including any capital inflows from abroad), then ask what proportion of it would be required to fight the war, and then squeeze civilian consumption as much as possible to make those resources available. Failure to do this would leave an inflationary gap, which would not call forth the desired resources (which were not in any case available), but lead merely to price rises, long queues and social disharmony.[22]

The use of national income analysis, which produced for the first time a White Paper (Cmd 6261) on the size of the national income, accompanying Kingsley Wood's Budget of April 1941, concentrated minds on the economic potential to wage war. The Chancellor's calculations indicated that most of the potential inflationary gap could be plugged by tapping the savings of the public, businesses and local authorities, and by some rise in taxes; out of an estimated £4,207 million of central government spending, only about £250 million would remain as an inflationary gap. Income tax was accordingly raised to 10s. in the pound, and other tax rates proportionately. A novelty of the Budget was the institution of a 'deferred pay' scheme, under which taxes

19. J. Hurstfield, *The Control of Raw Materials* (*HSWW* 1953), pp. 355, 359–60, 161.
20. Hornby, *Factories*, pp. 333, 330, ch. XII.
21. Sayers, *Financial Policy*, App. I (Table 4), App. II.
22. J.M. Keynes, *How to Pay for the War* (Macmillan 1940).

paid in wartime could be paid back to the taxpayer after the war, a further device to mitigate inflationary pressure in wartime.[23]

The most notable wartime tax innovation was Excess Profits Tax, introduced in the Budget of September 1939, and designed to make over to the Treasury the profits above prewar levels of the armament manufacturers. Set at 60 per cent initially, it was raised to 100 per cent in the course of the passage of the April 1940 Budget (during which the change of government occurred, and Kingsley Wood succeeded Simon as Chancellor). The impact was softened to some extent by a 20 per cent postwar credit on the tax paid.[24]

This apart, the most notable innovation was the introduction of 'Pay As You Earn' (PAYE), by which tax was automatically deducted from wages and salaries in the course of the year. It made tax collection much more efficient, and could even be said to be beneficial to the taxpayer, since income came net of tax, and there was not the fear of a tax bill from the Revenue at the year's end. Finally, purchase tax was much extended to raise revenue and counteract inflationary demand, especially for alcohol, tobacco and entertainments.

Changing tax policies permitted a continued rise in the total tax yield after 1941, and a steep rise in direct taxation. Central government revenue rose from £980 million in 1939 to £2,143 million in 1941, and to £3,265 million in 1945; the proportion of revenue produced by direct taxes rose from 52 to 63 per cent (1939–45).[25]

Even the largely increased tax yield could not fund all the war spending. Over the six financial years 1939–40 to 1944–45, total government spending was some £28.1 billion, but revenue was only £15.4 billion, thus covering only 55 per cent of expenditure.[26] The great bulk of the gap was filled by government borrowing: only £770 million was financed by the printing press (i.e. increasing the fiduciary note issue). The government, after a brief panic in August 1939, when Bank Rate was raised to 4 per cent, reduced it to 3 per cent as before, and was able to conduct a '3 per cent war'. On this basis, it made available a wide variety of investment outlets for large and small savers, via the 'National Savings' movement. For the small savers there were the Post Office and Trustee Savings Bank, and a series of National Savings Certificates and Defence Bonds. For the larger saver, there were National War Bonds at $2\frac{1}{2}$ per cent, and 3 per cent Savings Bonds. The idle balances of firms were lured with Tax Reserve Certificates. To attract the money lying in bank deposits, there were the existing instruments of Ways and Means advances at the Bank of England, Treasury Bills sold to the banks, and the new scheme of Treasury Deposit Receipts (TDRs).

23. R. Stone, 'The Use and Development of National Income and Expenditure Estimates', in Chester, *Lessons*, pp. 86–8; Sayers, *Financial Policy*, ch. III, App. II.
24. Sayers, *Financial Policy*, App. II; B. Sabine, *British Budgets in Peace and War* (Allen & Unwin 1970), pp. 162–8, 186.
25. Sayers, *Financial Policy*, pp. 99f., App. I, Table 4; Sabine, *Budgets*, pp. 241–3.
26. Central Statistical Office (CSO), *Statistical Digest of the War* (*HSWW* 1951), Tables 172, 173.

In all this panoply of devices, the government was concerned to split the market up, tailoring each financial instrument to the group which it was intended should buy the issue, and striving to avoid paying to all borrowers, past and present, a rate of interest as high as the current marginal rate. Thus the borrowing was done as cheaply as possible. A considerable help in this was the control of capital issues and the constraints on individuals' spending, so that surplus funds accumulated in the banking system. Total bank deposits rose from £2,730 million in 1939 to £5,551 million in 1945. The banks' lack of commercial outlets forced them to invest heavily in government paper; by the end of the war, the banks held TDRs alone equivalent to 38.6 per cent of bank deposits, and it could be said that the banks had changed into agents for the absorption of funds from the public for the use of the government.[27] Thus in effect, a large proportion of the national income became 'forced savings', either in bank deposits or in government paper instruments. The end result was a large increase in the National Debt, which rose from £7,111 million in 1938 to £21,473 million in 1945.[28]

INFLATION, RATIONING AND CIVILIAN CONSUMPTION

As well as raising money for the war effort, policy was directed to the control of inflation. This was partly done via financial policy. But there was also an attempt to limit inflation by more direct methods. Since inflation fed on itself, by the use of the cost of living index as a bargaining weapon by trade unions, it was decided to subsidise the prices of important components of the index. The first intervention came in December 1939, when a temporary subsidy to steady food prices was accepted. In the 1941 Budget it was accepted that subsidies should be used to stabilise the cost of living index in the range of 25–30 per cent above the prewar level. In addition to food, rents were controlled, and the government had powers to control the prices of coal, electricity and railway fares, but the largest subsidy cost was that of making good to farmers the difference between the market price and the official price of foodstuffs.

The subsidy policy succeeded broadly in its aim of minimising the rise in the cost of living. This success was to some extent deceptive, since the official (working-class) cost of living index calculated by the Board of Trade was ludicrously out of date, being based on expenditure patterns in 1904. It covered essentials only (food, rent, clothing, footwear, fuel and light) and certain important goods were not represented in it (notably drink and tobacco) (Table 15.2 opposite).

The contrast between the first and third columns in Table 15.2 illustrates the extent to which subsidies prevented the rise in wholesale prices from feeding through to the items covered by the official (working-class) price index. The

27. S. Pollard, *The Development of the British Economy 1914–1990* (Edward Arnold 1992), p. 176; Sayers, *Financial Policy*, chs V, VII.
28. CSO, *Annual Abstract of Statistics, no. 84 (1935–1946)*, Table 255.

Table 15.2 Price changes in Britain, 1938–45

	1 *Board of Trade cost of living index*	*2* *Prices paid for consumers' goods and services*	*3* *Board of Trade wholesale price index*
1938	100	100	100
1939	101	106	101
1940	118	124	135
1941	128	137	150
1942	128	147	157
1943	128	152	160
1944	129	156	164
1945	130	161	167

Sources: Cols 1 and 3 calculated from CSO, *Statistical Digest of the War* (*HSWW* 1951), Tables 190, 193; Col. 2 calculated from C.H. Feinstein, *National Income, Expenditure and Output of the United Kingdom, 1855–1965* (Cambridge UP 1972), Table 61

second column is a measure of the rise in the unit price of national expenditure; thus it covers the whole population and its buying patterns, and is the best guide to the impact of inflation on consumers as a whole. From this it appears that the true impact of inflation was much greater than indicated by the official (working-class) cost of living index, and, by the end of the war, not far short of the rise in wholesale prices.

In the effective mobilisation of national resources, a significant part was played by rationing of civilian consumption, which also helped to control inflation. It was not the case, however, that rationing was employed to *reduce* consumption. It was rather that, the decision to reduce consumption having been taken, rationing was subsequently employed in order to distribute the remaining supplies equitably, and in line with what was perceived to be the wartime interest.

The most notable example of rationing was of food. Food rationing preceded that of other commodities, the basic foods being rationed in 1940, and others being rationed under a 'points' system in 1941. Consumption levels fell thereafter, especially for meat and sugar. The supply of fresh and frozen meat fell by 27 per cent, and that of sugar by 35 per cent, by 1943 (when supplies were at their lowest) compared with the average for 1934–38. Butter was largely replaced by margarine, and the supply of eggs fell by over a half (by 1943). The supplies of certain basic foods were maintained. Bread was not rationed at all, the sale of milk rose by 44 per cent in 1939–45, and that of potatoes by 56 per cent by its peak in 1944 (over 1934–38).[29]

The task of food rationing was much eased by the outstanding contribution

29. CSO, *Statistical Digest*, Tables 67, 70.

made by home agriculture, which was the greatest single example of successful industrial mobilisation. Drawing on the experience of 1914–18, the government decided to plough up grassland on an unprecedented scale, and grow cereals and potatoes. The policy was administered by County War Agricultural Executive Committees, largely composed (as in the previous war) of farmers and landowners. The 'War Ags' helped to supply machinery, labour and fertilisers to farmers, who were further encouraged by generous guaranteed prices for their produce. Between 1939 and 1945 tillage in Britain rose from 8.3 million to 13.1 million acres. Combined with a policy of restricting food and animal feed imports, the relative degree of self-sufficiency rose sharply. Having after 1918 fallen to about 30 per cent, the effort in 1939–45 raised UK self-sufficiency (in calories) to 40 per cent. To this may be added a substantial but unknown amount of food produced in households and domestic gardens, spurred by the government's 'Dig for Victory' campaign.[30]

For non-food consumption, the government's target was to reduce supplies by one-third. Most of the restrictions fell on clothing, which was rationed on a points scheme. Later on, footwear, furniture, household textiles (i.e. carpets and curtains) and other household goods (e.g. pottery) were included. Supplies of clothing, already reduced before Pearl Harbor, were further cut in the spring of 1942. For the next three years, the volume of adults' clothing purchased was down to about half the prewar level; the volume of children's clothing was about 60 per cent of prewar; both these items were cut further after February 1945. Control was extended to a wide range of other goods – pottery, pencils, domestic electrical appliances, sports gear, mechanical lighters, fountain pens, umbrellas, and musical instruments (but a small supply of gramophone records and needles was made available to civilians).[31]

A notable innovation from 1942 was the use of 'utility' styles of clothing, furniture, hosiery and footwear. The idea was to reduce the diversity of consumer choice (and thus economise on materials and labour) by producing long runs of standardised, well-designed products, permitting useful economies of scale to be achieved. The schemes were successful, and on average about 80 per cent of total cloth production (for all purposes, including clothing) was of the utility kind. Hosiery was the most successful utility scheme; by the summer of 1943, 96 per cent of all hosiery, 99 per cent of women's stockings, 93 per cent of male underwear and 97 per cent of female underwear was utility. The UK was the only nation whose civilians relied on government-designed underwear in the Second World War.[32] The design virtues embodied in utility furniture have been noted recently.[33]

Apart from the rationed items, civilian consumption was cut down by other means. Private motoring was cut by an exiguous petrol ration, which vanished

30. Murray, *Agriculture*, pp. 242–8.
31. E.L. Hargreaves and M. Gowing, *Civil Industry and Trade* (*HSWW* 1952), p. 102; Hancock and Gowing, *War Economy*, pp. 493–5.
32. Hargreaves, and Gowing, *Civil Industry*, p. 434, Table 32, p. 463.
33. H. Dover, *Home Front Furniture: British utility design, 1941–1951* (Scolar 1991).

Table 15.3 UK consumers' expenditure at constant (1938) prices, 1938–45 (£million)

	1938	*1941*	*1942*	*1943*	*1944*	*1945*
Food	1,305	1,082	1,114	1,076	1,137	1,154
Rent, rates and water	491	502	497	498	503	506
Other services	483	411	373	350	343	369
Clothing	446	275	273	247	275	279
Alcoholic drink	285	288	267	269	274	297
Durable household goods	234	115	81	67	60	82
Fuel and light	197	205	199	187	193	197
Tobacco	177	196	206	204	205	225
Other goods	177	131	109	110	113	120
Travel	163	155	181	193	196	224
Private motoring	127	30	17	8	8	25
Other items	219	325	352	393	404	444
Total	4,304	3,715	3,669	3,602	3,711	3,922
Per cent	100	86	85	84	86	91

Source: CSO, *Statistical Digest of the War*, Table 186

altogether after March 1942. The consumption of alcohol and tobacco rose, but this was limited by sharp rises in price. Private services (notably domestic service) were curtailed simply by lack of labour. The supply of housing, although subject to rent control, was cut by bombing and population movements. The net result was a substantial squeeze on living standards (Table 15.3 above).

The volume of consumers' expenditure had fallen by about one-sixth by 1941–42. The largest fall was in private motoring, which almost disappeared. The next largest reduction was in durable household goods (61 per cent) and clothing (45 per cent); other household goods fell by 26 per cent. 'Other goods' fell by 38 per cent. 'Other services' fell by 8 per cent. Food consumption in volume terms fell by 18 per cent. There were slight reductions in alcohol and fuel and light, and a rather larger rise in tobacco consumption. The rise in entertainments was notable, at 39 per cent, as were travel and communication services; the former reflected the lack of alternatives, the latter the lack of motoring and the need to keep in touch by post in wartime. After 1943, some items rose, as imports were allowed to rise, and as industry was allowed to some extent to reconvert to civilian production.

THE EXTERNAL SECTOR AND NORTH AMERICAN AID

In no sphere of the war economy was the dependence on north America after 1940 clearer than in finance. Both the USA and Canada were the main suppliers to Britain of food, raw materials, and war *matériel*, for which substantial contracts were placed in 1939–40. Until the summer of 1940, policy was to husband foreign exchange reserves for a long war; it was thought in the

Treasury that the reserves might last for three years.[34] An attempt to eke them out by an export drive was made in 1939–40 without success.[35] The fall of France transformed the situation; not only was the strategic situation radically altered, but also Britain now took on responsibility for French contracts in the USA, which would have to be honoured in dollars. (They were estimated to be worth about $612 million).[36] The only feasible policy was now to spend all the gold and dollar reserves necessary, and hope that in due course the USA would intervene. In spite of gathering together private dollar securities in the USA and Canada and disposing of them, the gold and dollar reserves fell from £503 million in August 1939 to £108 million in December 1940.[37] On 8 December, Mr Churchill wrote to the newly re-elected President Roosevelt that: 'The moment approaches when we shall no longer be able to pay cash for shipping and other supplies.'[38]

The response of the US government was the Lend-Lease scheme, which commenced in March 1941. Referred to by Mr Churchill as 'the most unsordid act in history', it was an unparalleled example of national generosity, by which the USA supplied goods and services to the value of some $30,000 million to the British Empire ($27,000 million of which went to the UK) between March 1941 and September 1945. All of these supplies had to be paid for by US taxes or by the sale of US government bonds. While speculation as to what might have happened in history is fruitless, it may be suggested that, had such external financial assistance not been made available, the UK would have had to sue for peace with Germany.[39]

Essentially, Lend-Lease was a scheme whereby the materials of war and other essential supplies were provided from the US without being paid for in dollars; the right to demand payment at some stage was reserved to the US President. The USA, however, reserved the right to exact some 'consideration' for this agreement. In particular, Britain had to undertake that imports under the scheme should not be employed in subsequent exports. In making this condition, the USA had south America particularly in mind. The scheme also contained provision for the ending of discrimination in international trade, which reflected US suspicions of Imperial Preference.[40]

Financial assistance did not come solely from the USA. By the end of 1941, British commitments in Canada had amounted to roughly $700 million. It was agreed that this should be converted into an interest-free loan to the UK for the rest of the war, and a further $1,000 million was offered as a gift to the UK.

34. Sayers, *Financial Policy*, p. 366.
35. Hargreaves and Gowing, *Civil Industry*, ch. III (ii).
36. H.D. Hall, *North American Supply* (*HSWW* 1955), p. 149, App. II.
37. Sayers, *Financial Policy*, ch. XII (ii), App. I, Table 7 (Exchange Equalisation Account holdings of gold, and US and Canadian dollars).
38. Quoted in Sayers, *Financial Policy*, p. 373.
39. Ibid., pp. 375, 529–31.
40. Ibid., ch. XIII (iii), (iv); App. III ('Mutual Aid between the U.S. and the British Empire, 1941–45', by R.G.D. Allen).

This was followed by two 'mutual aid' appropriations and other credits; total Canadian gifts and free aids came to $3,468 million for the whole of the war.

In the Sterling Area, heavy military spending, the fall in UK exports to these countries, and internal inflation led to the building up of large unspent sterling balances, chiefly in India and Egypt. In effect, these were IOUs written by the British authorities to pay for the war, with the possibility that they would be presented for payment afterwards. At the end of 1939, the external liabilities of the UK had been about £550 million. By mid-1945 they had risen to £3,355 million, of which £2,723 million was due to the Sterling Area. At the official exchange rate of $4.03:£1, the increase in Sterling Area balances by 1945 was equivalent to about $11 billion, or about one-third of the total of Lend-Lease.[41]

The final source of overseas finance was the realisation of British-owned overseas assets. In August 1939, the Treasury took powers to requisition from British residents any securities 'likely to be marketable outside the United Kingdom', for the purpose of strengthening the British financial position. The owners were paid the market price (in sterling), and the proceeds went to the Treasury. These powers were exercised in regard mainly to the USA and Canada, but also to India. In effect, this was a process of repatriating overseas investment. The wartime total of this disinvestment came to £1,118 million, or about one-quarter of the prewar total foreign assets of Britain; about 38 per cent of the disinvestment occurred in north America, thus weakening the ability of the country to pay for north American exports after the war.[42]

The inflow of external assistance was offset by aid (military stores, petrol, food, services and construction) supplied by the UK and other Empire countries to the USA. For the whole war period, this amounted to £1,896 million from the UK (equivalent to $7.6 billion, or about one-quarter of Lend-Lease aid) and £379 million (about $1.5 billion) from the rest of the Empire.[43]

External assistance was essential if the much higher deficit in the wartime balance of payments was to be covered. In 1938, total UK imports had been worth £920 million, and exports worth £471 million. By 1943, imports had risen to £1,234 million, and exports fallen to £234 million; in volume terms, imports had fallen by 23 per cent, and exports had fallen by 71 per cent. As in 1914–18, war needs were responsible for the higher imports, and a combination of vanished export markets and diversion of the productive capacity of the economy to war work was responsible for the decline of exports.

In 1934–38, the current balance of payments had averaged a deficit of some £26 million a year; in 1939–45, the total deficit averaged £790 million a year, being £4,740 million in all. This was offset by sales of overseas investments (£1,118 million) and the increase in external liabilities of £2,879 million. Thus

41. Sayers, *Financial Policy*, ch. XI, esp. pp. 343f., 439, App. I, Table 13; Pollard, *Development*, p. 180.

42. Sayers, *Financial Policy*, pp. 257–9, 353–6; CSO, *Statistical Digest*, Table 177; Treasury, *Statistical Material Presented during the Washington Negotiations* (1945), Cmd 6707, App. III.

43. Sayers, *Financial Policy*, App. III, Tables 8, 9.

disinvestment and Sterling Area debts could be said to have covered most of the wartime payments deficit. However, this overlooks the fact that, especially in 1939–40, much of the disinvestment had already gone to pay dollar debts, and, most importantly, without north American aid, the flow of munitions and other supplies from the dollar area would have been still-born. Over and above these sums, net grants (i.e. after reciprocal aid from the UK) by the USA and Canada were valued at a total of £5,400 million in 1939–45. The total dollar cost of the war to Britain would have financed sixteen years of British imports from the USA at the 1938 level and at 1938 prices, taking no account of British exports or other dollar earnings.[44]

SOURCES OF THE REAL ECONOMIC EFFORT

There were several ways in which the financial and real resources of the nation were made available for the war of 1939–45. Consumption was squeezed; domestic investment was curtailed; depreciation was allowed to mount up; overseas investments were repatriated. Finally, a large addition to national resources was provided by Lend-Lease, which allowed the UK to utilise the resources of a much larger economy at no net cost to itself. The consequent redistribution of the national income is outlined here, for the period after the phoney war, when the national economy had been placed on a full war footing (Table 15.4 opposite).

Thus the sources of the 'real' effort of the UK can be discerned. The largest domestic source was the reduction in consumer spending, which at its lowest point made available about a quarter of the national income for the war effort. The next largest domestic contribution (line 4) was made by the repatriation of overseas investment (line 4). The last domestic resource was the neglect of new investment and maintenance (line 3). These relatively minor domestic resources were dwarfed by the contribution of Lend-Lease. The estimates of this in Table 15.4 are crude, since they do no take into account reciprocal Lend-Lease (from the UK to the USA), and the 'Maximum' entry is for Lend-Lease to the entire British Empire. But even on the 'Minimum' estimate, which is solely for the munitions and other goods shipped to the UK, it can be seen that the effect of Lend-Lease was enormous, contributing at its peak the equivalent of an extra one-fifth of national income to the UK (without incurring any foreign exchange or other financial cost). Finally, the Sterling Area debts, which were substantial, are omitted here.

Tapping these real resources (or the financial claims on them) enabled the British economy to shift over to war production on a very large scale. By 1941, over half the national income went on war purposes, and this figure was maintained until 1944, when policy was eased and the consumer goods industries permitted to expand slightly. By 1941, the current value of war ex-

44. Feinstein, *National Income*, pp. 112–13, Table 15; Sayers, *Financial Policy*, App. I, Tables 10, 14; A.S. Milward, *The Economic Effects of the World Wars on Britain* (Macmillan *SEH* 1970), p. 48.

Table 15.4 UK national income[a] and war resources, 1938–45

		1938 (%)	*1941 (%)*	*1942 (%)*	*1943 (%)*	*1944 (%)*	*1945 (%)*
Per cent of national income							
1 Government spending	war	7	52	52	55	54	46
	other	9	7	7	6	6	6
2 Consumers' expenditure		79	58	54	52	54	58
3 NDCF[b]		6	–5	–4	–5	–6	c
4 Net overseas lending		–1	–12	–9	–8	–8	–10
5 Total national income		100	100	100	100	100	100
Plus: Lend-Lease	maximum	n/a[d]	4	15	28	32	13
	minimum	n/a	2	8	14	19	7

Notes: a net national expenditure at factor cost
b NDCF = net domestic capital formation
c less than 0.5 per cent
d n/a = not applicable

Sources: Calculated from Hancock and Gowing, *British War Economy*, p. 347; CSO, *Statistical Digest of the War*, Table 178; Sayers, *Financial Policy*, pp. 491–2.

penditure was eleven times the prewar level (about seven and a half times in real terms). Thus the output of munitions grew enormously. An estimate suggests that, taking output in the last quarter of 1939 as 100, total munitions output rose to about 650 by the first quarter of 1944. The only published official wartime index was for aircraft production, and it is estimated that this rose to about 590 per cent in the same period.[45] (The latter index was based on a combination of airframe structure weight and man-hours per airframe; an index based solely on airframe weight gives a figure of 679 by the first quarter of 1944.)[46]

THE COSTS OF THE WAR

The costs of the war may be variously assessed. In what follows, it is useful to use the national income as a yardstick; this was around £5,000 million in 1938, and had risen to around £8,800 million by 1945. (UK national income estimates at current prices; 1938 GDP at factor cost = £4,932 million; 1938 GNP = £5,124 million; 1945 GDP at factor cost = £8,787 million; 1945

45. M. Harrison, 'A Volume Index of the Total Munitions Output of the United Kingdom, 1939–1944', *EcHR* XLIII (1990), p. 665; A. Robinson, 'Munitions Output of the United Kingdom, 1939–1944: a comment', *EcHR* XLV (1992); CSO, *Statistical Digest*, Table 132.
46. A. Cairncross, *Planning in Wartime: aircraft production in Britain, Germany and the USA* (Macmillan 1991), Table 6.3.

GNP = £8,867 million.)[47] Between 1938–39 and 1944–45, defence spending had totalled £23,101 million; almost all this may be regarded as due to the war, since prewar spending was comparatively low. Most of the war spending had been financed by borrowing. Borrowing at home in 1939–45 had amounted to £15,237 million, or the equivalent of between two or three times the annual average national income.[48] The total National Debt had risen from £7,130 million in 1939 to £21,366 million in 1945.[49] Thus a substantial burden of internal indebtedness had been created for future taxpayers.

Internal loss also resulted from hostile action; about 4.5 million houses were damaged, mostly by bombing in 1940–43, or by the later V-weapon attacks in 1944. Of the 4.5 million, 210,000 were totally destroyed, and 250,000 rendered uninhabitable. Total damage to property, domestic and industrial, was estimated at £1,450 million at 1945 replacement costs.[50]

Over and above the direct physical loss was that due to disinvestment in physical capital, by deferring all but the most essential repair and maintenance in industry, transport and housing. Between 1940 and 1944, the cumulative total cost of the industrial disinvestment alone was estimated at £885 million. This did not take account of the reduced quality of housing due to the near-cessation of even normal maintenance during the war.

External losses were also considerable. The greatest physical loss was shipping; 18.0 million gross tons of shipping were lost due to the war, and even a substantial building programme left the UK fleet at little more than three-quarters of its prewar size (15.9 million tons as opposed to 22.1 million tons) by the end of the war. The total cost of this loss (including cargoes) was about £700 million. (These figures include colonies' shipping, which was negligible.)[51]

Other forms of external loss were financial. The stock of overseas investment was much reduced, either through sales forced by the Treasury to raise foreign exchange, or through overseas debtors taking the opportunity of rising sterling payments in wartime to repatriate sterling debt. In the entire war, it was estimated that the proceeds of sale or repatriation of overseas investments amounted to £1,118 million, or about one-quarter of the prewar total British foreign investment.[52] (These estimates split as: Sterling Area, £564 million; north America, £428 million; south America, £96 million; Europe, £14 million; rest of world, £16 million.)[53] There was in addition the loss of foreign assets

47. Feinstein, *National Income*, Table 6.
48. CSO, *Statistical Digest*, Tables 173, 185.
49. CSO, *Annual Abstract of Statistics no. 84 (1935–1946)*, Table 255 (net total National Debt).
50. *Statistical Material presented during the Washington Negotiations* (1945), Cmd 6707, App. VIII; see also *Statistics Relating to the War Effort of the United Kingdom* (1944), Cmd 6564, Table 31.
51. *Statistical Material*, Apps II, VIII.
52. Ibid., Appendix III.
53. The total is from Royal Institute of International Affairs, *The Problem of International Investment* (1937).

through default, confiscation or physical deterioration, which may have added a further loss of £500 million or more.[54]

The investment loss was dwarfed by the increase of overseas debt. The net external liabilities of the UK rose by £2,879 million between August 1939 and June 1945 (from £476 million to £3,355 million). By the latter month, some 81 per cent of the total debt was owed to the Sterling Area (principally India, Burma and the Middle East).[55]

The loss of gold and dollar reserves was also due to the war; especially in 1939–41, the reserves were run down as required to pay for overseas supplies. By the end of 1940, they were, at £74 million, almost exhausted, having been worth £548 million at the end of 1939. Even the latter figure had been unusually low, since the reserves at the end of 1938 were £864 million. The stationing of large numbers of US troops in the UK in 1943–44 repaired the reserves to some extent, but they were still only £453 million at the end of June 1945. From September 1939 to December 1945, the net loss had amounted to £152 million.[56]

The total economic loss due to the war has been roughly computed (Table 15.5 below).

Since the prewar capital of the UK has been estimated as being worth about £30,000 million (at 1945 prices), then it could be said that the loss represented about one-quarter of the national wealth. Even this does not take into account the postponed cost represented by the future interest payments on the internal debt, the cost of making good the depreciation in the quality of housing, or of the reduction in household inventories. On the other hand, the cost was

Table 15.5 UK economic losses due to the Second World War

		£ million
Physical destruction	on land	1,450
	shipping (inc. cargoes)	700
Internal disinvestment in fixed capital		885
External disinvestment	realisation of capital	1,118
	increase in debt	2,879
	loss of reserves	152
	unallocated	49
Total		7,233

Sources: CSO, *Statistical Digest of the War*, Table 177; *Statistical Material Presented during the Washington Negotiations* (1945), Cmd 6707, App. VIII, p. 14

54. T. Balogh, 'The International Aspect', in G.D.N. Worswick and P.H. Ady, *The British Economy 1945–1950* (Oxford, Clarendon 1952), p. 477.
55. *Statistical Material*, App. IV.
56. Ibid., App. V; CSO, *Statistical Digest*, Table 177.

offset by the capital investment of £1,029 million made by the government during the war.[57]

THE POTENTIAL BALANCE OF PAYMENTS CRISIS IN 1946

The last instalment in the cost of the war was the prospective balance of payments deficit which would follow the cessation of Lend-Lease. This promised to be so enormous that, as Keynes wrote, it would be a 'financial Dunkirk'. It was due to the fact that exports of goods would take years to recover from their low wartime level, and the level of invisible income was now very much depressed, and looked to be so for the foreseeable future. The new factors in the situation were the reductions in income from shipping and overseas investments, and the low level of postwar gold and dollar reserves. Hanging over all this was the enormously increased debt, which could not be repaid to any noticeable extent for many years, although the Sterling Area countries were probably not going to press unduly hard for repayment. Even the Lend-Lease settlement had a sting in the tail, since supplies in transit when Lend-Lease was terminated, at 12.01 a.m. on 2 September 1945, a week after the Japanese surrender, had to be paid for.

But, even apart from debt, the position was grave. In 1936–38 the balance of trade deficit had averaged £388 million, substantially offset by invisibles of £352 million, leaving a mild balance of payments deficit on average of £43 million. The best prediction of the payments deficit for 1946 was £750 million. Although it was expected to decline thereafter, a cumulative deficit of £1,250 million for 1946–48 was predicted.

In the longer run, the only remedy for this was to increase the volume of exports, so as to fill the gap left by the decline of the invisibles, and thus pay for a larger proportion of imports than before the war. The Treasury considered that, to be on the safe side, the target should be a volume of exports at least 50 per cent, and preferably 75 per cent, higher than prewar. The date by which this might be accomplished could only be guessed. But in the meanwhile there was only one possible mitigation – a dollar gift or loan from north America, since the balance of payments crisis would be concentrated on dollar imports.[58]

Keynes' last great public service was to go to Washington to press for such an arrangement. He emerged with a not ungenerous settlement. The USA was to make available a 'line of credit' worth $3,750 million, carrying interest at 2 per cent a year (payable from 1951), repayable over fifty years. In addition, the value of Lend-Lease supplies shipped after the Japanese surrender ('in the pipeline') and of US government property in the UK – a joint total of $650 million – was to be added to the debt, on the same terms as the rest of it. All other Lend-Lease obligations, and any outstanding mutual obligations between the USA and the UK were finally cancelled. These terms were more generous

57. *Statistical Material*, p. 14.
58. Ibid., App. VII, pp. 5–6.

than might have been expected, although Keynes thought the loan should have been larger, and lamented his inability to persuade the USA to agree to an interest-free loan. But there were also strings attached; Britain had to undertake to reduce the sterling balances, and to apply the Bretton Woods terms of making sterling convertible within a year of the actual granting of the loan (i.e. by July 1947).[59]

In addition to the Washington negotiations, an agreement with Canada was concluded in the spring of 1946, under which Canada advanced to Britain a line of credit of $1,250 million, on similar terms to the US loan. In addition, it provided for the continuance until 1951 of the $500 million interest-free loan granted in 1942, and cancelled a debt of $425 million due to Canada.[60]

THE ECONOMIC LEGACY OF THE WAR

The economic legacy of the war was also seen in the state of the various industries afterwards. Some, which were expanding before the war, expanded still further during it, and continued to do so afterwards. These were mostly those which constituted the 'new industries' of the interwar years – steel, chemicals, motor vehicles, aircraft, aluminium, electrical equipment and goods (including radio and the new 'radar'). The engineering sectors which were linked to them also expanded, and the capital investment of wartime helped this expansion. But there were also industries which were essential for the war effort, which did not expand during the war, and found themselves at the end of it with overstretched capital and substantial arrears of maintenance to make up; such were the railways and coal-mining. However, some 'older' industries, such as agriculture and shipbuilding, were subject to substantial investment during the war, so that they (especially the former) emerged considerably more efficient and modern than before. Hornby gives the value of capital improvement schemes in wartime shipyards as £6.9 million.[61] Annual expenditure on farm machinery in the UK rose from £23.5 million in 1938–39 to £69.5 million in 1944–45.[62]

On the whole, though, the war was detrimental to the fixed equipment of the British economy. Estimates of the capital stock of an entire economy are very difficult to make; Feinstein's estimates of the net capital stock of the UK are shown in Table 15.6 overleaf.

At the average growth rate of net capital stock in 1920–38 (1.6 per cent a year), the value of the 1948 capital stock should have been 16 per cent higher

59. *Financial Agreement between the Governments of the United States and the United Kingdom dated 6th December 1945* (1945), Cmd 6708, pp. 2–7. See also Sayers, *Financial Policy*, App. III (by R.G.D. Allen); D. Moggridge, *Maynard Keynes: an economist's biography* (Routledge 1992), p. 816.

60. N. Crump, *The ABC of the Foreign Exchanges* (Macmillan 1951), pp. 263–4.

61. Hornby, *Factories*, p. 57.

62. Ministry of Agriculture, *A Century of Agricultural Statistics: Great Britain 1866–1966* (HMSO 1968), Table 32.

Table 15.6 UK net capital stock, 1920–48 (£000 million at 1938 replacement cost)

	Dwellings	*Other buildings and works*	*Plant, vehicles, ships, etc.*	*Total*
1920	1.90	4.48	1.54	7.92
1929	2.50	4.45	1.88	8.83
1938	3.51	4.56	2.16	10.23
1948	3.50	4.50	2.40	10.40

Source: Feinstein, *National Income*, Table 43

than in 1938, that is £11.87 billion; as it was, it was only about 1.7 per cent higher than in 1938. It could plausibly be suggested that the loss of capital, even after some years of reconstruction, was about 14 per cent of the 1938 total.

CONCLUSIONS

On balance, the Second World War was a period of great economic and human destruction for Britain, as for other belligerent countries. The losses of human life were less than in 1914–18; the losses of economic and financial capital were considerably greater. While both wars stimulated the growth of more modern and technologically advanced industries, they both entailed great losses in the international economic position of Britain. It could in truth be said that Britain had used up its stock of overseas assets in order to survive as an influential (in 1914) and independent (in 1940) nation. In 1938 Britain's external assets had exceeded its liabilities by about £4 billion. By 1945, its capital position had deteriorated by £4.8 billion and its liabilities now exceeded its assets.[63] The price had not yet been paid in full; the legacy of the Second World War was to be a weakness in the British balance of payments which persists to this day.

63. Economic Cooperation for Administration, *The Sterling Area: an American view* (London 1951), p. 177.

CHAPTER 16

CIVILIAN LIFE IN THE SECOND WORLD WAR

CIVILIAN LIVING STANDARDS

Living standards during the war were determined above all by the existence of full employment. The number of insured unemployed, which had still been 1,270,000 in July 1939, had fallen by about a half, to 645,000, a year later. In July 1941 unemployment was only 198,000. The wartime nadir was reached in July 1943, at 60,000. The average rate of unemployment in that year was 0.6 per cent of the insured population.[1] Truly it might have been said that 'over-full' rather than 'full' employment prevailed. In 1944, Beveridge was to suggest that the lowest rate of postwar unemployment compatible with 'full employment' would be about 3 per cent of the labour force.[2] (The 3 per cent is accounted for by short-term illness, people moving between jobs, and so on.)

The pressure of labour demand could be seen in the contrast between wage rates and earnings; whereas the index of wage rates had risen by almost exactly 50 per cent between October 1938 and July 1945, average weekly earnings for all industrial operatives rose from 53s. 3d. to 96s. 1d. (80 per cent).[3] Women's earnings rose by more than men's (by 94 per cent, as opposed to 76 per cent) and there was some narrowing of differentials between the unskilled and the skilled industrial workers. In 1938, the minimum time rate for engineering labourers was 76 per cent of the skilled fitter's rate; in April 1945 it was 83 per cent.[4] Engineering apart, the war saw some improvement in the relative wages of unskilled workers; the basic weekly rate of the agricultural labourer rose from 34s. 8d. in 1938–39 to 67s. 10d. in 1944–45.[5] Coal-miners

1. Department of Employment and Productivity, *British Labour Statistics, Historical Abstract 1886–1968* (1971), Table 116; B.R. Mitchell, *British Historical Statistics* (Cambridge UP 1988), p. 124.
2. W.H. Beveridge, *Full Employment in a Free Society* (Allen & Unwin 1944), p. 128.
3. Central Statistical Office (CSO), *Annual Abstract of Statistics no. 84 (1935–1946)*, Tables 140, 141.
4. P. Inman, *Labour in the Munition Industries* (*HSSW* 1957), p. 341.
5. Ministry of Agriculture, *A Century of Agricultural Statistics: Great Britain 1866–1966* (HMSO 1968), p. 65.

Table 16.1 Cost of living, 1939–45: social variations (1938 = 100)

	1939	*1940*	*1941*	*1942*	*1943*	*1944*	*1945*
INDICES							
Official WC	101	117.5	127	128	127	128.5	130
Actual WC	102	119	130.5	140	144.5	147.5	149
LMC	102	119	133	144	148	152	154
Average MC	103	120	136	146	153	157	164
UMC	103	121	139	148	157	160	170
Unofficial (Seers) national index							
	102	119	133	143	148	152	156

Notes: WC = working class LMC = lower-middle class
MC = middle class UMC = upper-middle class

Source: D. Seers, *The Levelling of Incomes since 1938* (Oxford, Blackwell 1951), pp. 10–13

and railway workers also recovered some of their lost wage advantage, and the boom industries in the war sector paid well.

Pressure of labour demand worked to the benefit of the employed in various ways. Those previously unemployed, employed part-time, or simply not considering themselves as part of the labour force (by reason of age, sex or marital status) could now experience full-time employment. There was continual upward pressure on wage rates. Those employed full-time had the chance of overtime work. Between 1939 and 1945, real (civilian) GDP per head rose from £60 to £68.[6]

This increase was not felt equally by all sections of the working population, since the cost of living rose unevenly. While the official (working-class) cost of living index, through subsidisation, had risen by only 30 per cent by the end of the war, the actual working-class cost of living rose more than that, and as one ascended the economic scale, the cost of living rose more steeply. A tentative estimate of the differential rises in the wartime cost of living has been provided by Seers (Table 16.1 above).

It should not be concluded that all sections of the working classes experienced rising living standards during the war. Inflation fell hard on those on low wages and with large families, especially in the early months of the war, when little action was taken to mitigate the effects of inflation on the poor. It fell hard also, for the whole war, on that class of 'newly poor' (Hancock and Gowing) – the wives and children of servicemen away from home, who struggled on inadequate income. Counting all allowances, the private soldier's wife with two children received only 32s. a week in 1939, rising to 43s. in 1942; these were the people who were most likely to run into debt. To make

6. C.H. Feinstein, *National Income, Expenditure and Output of the United Kingdom, 1855–1965* (Cambridge UP 1972), Table 42.

Table 16.2 Proportions of income retained after income tax and surtax, 1938 and 1945

Range of income (pa)	*% retained 1938*	*% retained 1945*
Under £250	99.8	96.7
£250–£500	97.1	85.5
£500–£1,000	88.9	73.1
£1,000–£2,000	83.0	63.4
£2,000–£10,000	71.1	47.6
£10,000 and over	49.4	18.8

Source: CSO, *Annual Abstract of Statistics no. 84 1935–1946* (1948), Table 275

matters worse, landlords and shopkeepers viewed service families as bad financial risks, and were reluctant to let them rooms or extend them credit.[7]

The rise in the relative economic position of the lower income groups was accentuated by wartime taxation. The rise of income tax thresholds and rates had a much sharper progressive effect by the end of the war (Table 16.2 above).

The tendency of wage-earners to improve their relative position was further enhanced by the changing balance of factor incomes in the national income. The main changes here between 1939 and 1945 were the rise in the relative importance of income from employment (from 58 per cent to 66 per cent of the national income), the decline in the proportion derived from rent (from 9 to 4 per cent), and the fall in the proportion derived from overseas property (from 3 to 1 per cent). Other types of factor income remained fairly stable. These changes resulted in a rise in the proportion of the national income going to the lower-paid groups in society, and those without investment capital.[8]

The relatively greater rise in the middle-class cost of living, the more progressive nature of income taxation, the reduction in income from property, and the sharp reduction in many essentially middle-class spending activities (notably employing servants, but also motoring and non-essentials generally), meant that, as Sidney Pollard wrote:

> In general, it would be broadly true to say that personal consumption was stabilized at the pre-war skilled artisan level, and that of other classes cut down to approach it.[9]

Not only was the average level of personal consumption reduced due to the exigencies of war, but the incomes of the upper income groups were actually

7. W.K. Hancock and M. Gowing, *British War Economy* (*HSWW* 1949), p. 169; R.M. Titmuss, *Problems of Social Policy* (*HSWW* 1950), p. 414; P. Summerfield, 'The "Levelling of Class"', in H.L. Smith, *War and Social Change: British society in the Second World War* (Manchester UP 1986), p. 196.
8. Calculated from Feinstein, *National Income*, Table 6.
9. S. Pollard, *The Development of the British Economy, 1914–1990* (Edward Arnold 1992), p. 186.

reduced in real terms, and this reduction persisted after the war. Thus in 1949, average real *wage* incomes were 20 per cent above those of 1938, but average real *salary* incomes (including the profits of sole traders) were 18 per cent below those of 1938. Professional incomes were down by 11 per cent. The most substantial long-term gainers were farmers, whose average real income had risen by 91 per cent.[10]

WAR WORK

The buoyant demand for labour attracted many people into 'war work'. In the first eighteen months of the war, this was largely unregulated; firms bid against each other for labour, and complaints of 'poaching' of skilled labour were frequent. By March 1941, some 910,000 more people were at work in the munitions industries than in June 1939. Most of this extra labour (491,000) was male. Thereafter, most of the expansion was of women workers; at their peak in June 1943, there were 1,367,600 more women in these industries than in June 1939, compared with a rise of only 738,200 men.

The enormous influx of (largely unskilled) labour posed problems, chiefly of training, adaptability and 'dilution' of work. Training was partly supplied through Government Training Centres, which, together with technical colleges running government-sponsored schemes, turned out nearly 300,000 workers between 1940 and 1945. For the rest, firms had to do the training, with greater or lesser efficiency. Adaptability was largely empirical, depending on the person and firm concerned. Dilution was often only reluctantly accepted by firms, under pressure from Ministry of Labour inspectors, who could vet demands for labour, or recommend the redeployment of skilled labour elsewhere. In the course of 1940, most trade unions accepted dilution agreements as a matter of principle, although the acceptance of women dilutees led to disputes, especially in the private engineering firms. Some activities, such as sheet metal working, and shipyard work in general, resisted female dilution until the end of the war.[11]

The introduction to factory work could be very painful, especially for women; one young woman from Andover (Hampshire), who volunteered to work in an Ordnance factory in Reading in 1941 when several of her workmates were directed there, found herself working an eleven-hour day, in conditions of extreme noise, lack of daylight, and boredom, conjoined with disorienting night shifts.[12] While the earlier female recruits into factories had been largely working class, with some industrial experience, later ones were accustomed to

10. D. Seers, *The Levelling of Incomes since 1938* (Oxford, Blackwell 1951), p. 54.
11. Inman, *Labour*, pp. 5, 48–62, 68, 71, ch. V. See also the comments on training in Mass-Observation, *People in Production: an enquiry into British war production, part 1* (John Murray 1942), pp. 111–17.
12. N. Longmate, *How We Lived Then: a history of everyday life during the Second World War* (Arrow 1973), p. 341.

a more gentle working environment, and this posed a problem for thoughtful managements. A personnel manager described one such problem:

> *January 16*: See two more girls sent down from London. A striking blonde from a beauty parlour and a brunette from a gownshop, both in the West End. Capstan shop foreman afraid to put them on his machines; said they were too good a type. I was seriously concerned myself as our factory is an old shabby place and its sanitary arrangements of a very low standard. . . . Mid-morning the blonde came to my office in tears almost and near breaking-point. The noise, the smell of oil, coupled with the nervous and emotional strain of the past day or two, had got her down.[13]

Another large wartime engineering factory, suddenly mushrooming with 1,000 workers in an old country town, had a twelve-hour day (8 a.m. to 8 p.m., with an hour for lunch, and two breaks of ten minutes), so that the workers (mainly young women) had little chance of a social life during the week, and felt isolated from the community.[14] On the other hand, especially for older women, the chance to escape from domestic chores and have the opportunity to mix with new people, made the experience thoroughly enjoyable.[15]

Wartime hours of work were longer than in peacetime. Before the war, the conventional limits on hours in engineering had been forty-seven, with overtime above that figure. The only statutory limits on hours were for women (forty-eight maximum) and young persons under 16 (forty-four hours). In the war, engineering and explosives firms were allowed to employ women for up to sixty hours a week, although in practice few women and young people worked more than fifty-seven hours. In practice, hours were determined at the factory level rather than centrally.[16] But there is no doubt that, especially with the pressure to produce early in the war, hours were very long. They were particularly long in aircraft factories, since the Ministry of Aircraft Production particularly favoured them; even in 1943, most firms were working their women between fifty-six and sixty hours a week.[17]

The average weekly hours for men and women manual workers together in the metal/engineering/shipbuilding industries had been 48.0 in 1938, but had risen considerably, to 54.1, by July 1943. After 1941, it was increasingly realised that full efficiency required some relaxation, and by January 1945, hours in general had fallen to 49.2.[18] But long hours were a strain, especially for married women who had also to stand in queues for food and do housework

13. Mass-Observation, *People in Production*, p. 164.
14. Mass-Observation, *War Factory: a report by Mass-Observation* (2nd edn, Gollancz 1943).
15. G. Braybon and P. Summerfield, *Out of the Cage: women's experiences in two world wars* (Pandora 1987), p. 197.
16. Inman, *Labour*, pp. 288–93.
17. H.M.D. Parker, *Manpower: a study of war-time policy and administration* (*HSWW* 1957), p. 444.
18. Department of Employment, *Labour Statistics*, Table 43.

as well; by 1943, 43 per cent of all women workers were married, compared to only 16 per cent at the 1931 census. These alternative pressures were to some extent responsible for the fact that women's absenteeism was substantially greater than that of men.[19]

Working conditions were also subject to the production pressures of war; something of this stress, combined with the use of inexperienced labour, may have been behind the rise of fatal industrial accidents reported, from 944 in 1938 to 1,646 in 1941, although they fell back to 1,003 in 1944.[20] But the expansion of war production was accomplished on the whole without deterioration in the quality of working conditions. That this was so was due to the Minister of Labour, Ernest Bevin, a prominent former trade union leader. Determined to protect conditions, he ensured that the Essential Work Order of March 1941, under which labour would be supplied (or withdrawn), specified that firms wishing to be registered as suitable to undertake essential work should satisfy the minister that the terms and conditions of employment were not below recognised standards, that welfare arrangements were suitable, and that where training was required the facilities were available. The Order was also extended to apply to the Merchant Navy, docks and building sites. By the end of 1944, some 67,000 undertakings employing about 8.5 million workers were covered by the Order.[21]

A particular emphasis was placed on the provision of canteens. In firms employing more than 250 workers, over 5,000 were in operation by 1944 (more than three times the pre-Order figure). In smaller factories, the numbers rose from approximately 1,400 at the beginning of 1941 to over 6,800 at the end of the war. Canteens were not necessarily popular; the mounting complaints about canteens run by commercial caterers were causing the ministry great concern by the end of 1942, and action was taken to remedy the defects. The number of industrial canteens before the war is estimated at 1,500, and 18,486 in December 1944.[22] But a survey of 2,573 canteens in 1944 showed that less than half the day-shift workers took a main meal in the canteen, although another report referred to the food in a factory canteen as being 'excellent', and noted that the menus had obviously been carefully planned by someone with a good knowledge of food values.[23]

The expansion of the war industries was accompanied by far-reaching restrictions on traditional civil liberties. The Orders by which the movement of labour was operated derived their legal force from the Emergency Powers

19. P. Summerfield, *Women Workers in the Second World War: production and patriarchy in conflict* (Beckenham, Croom Helm 1984), pp. 125–30, App. B3.
20. *Annual Report of the Chief Inspector of Factories for the Year 1944* (1945), Cmd 6698, Table I.
21. Parker, *Manpower*, pp. 137–8, Statistical App. Table XI.
22. Parker, *Manpower*, p. 418; Ministry of Food, *How Britain was Fed in Wartime* (1946), p. 43.
23. *Annual Report of the Chief Inspector of Factories 1944*, p. 84; Mass-Observation, *War Factory*, p. 74.

(Defence) Act. This, passed through Parliament in all its stages on one day (22 May 1940), allowed the Minister of Labour to direct any person to perform any service of which he/she was capable under terms and conditions which the minister would be authorised to prescribe. As the historian of manpower commented:

> In a matter of three hours the traditional liberty of British citizens to manage their own lives and property was, by the free vote of their Parliamentary representatives, surrendered for the duration of the war to the will of a Government statutorily vested with arbitary powers of direction.[24]

The administrative control of labour was in practice a matter of registration and direction. Registration (15 March 1941) of all men over age limit for military service (41 years) and of women aged 18–40 was followed by interview at the local office of the Ministry of Labour (actually the local Employment Exchange), at which, if not already in work of national importance, the interviewee would be offered one or two possible jobs which the ministry was anxious to see filled. In practice, most workers were willing to do what they were asked, since they were aware that compulsion was a possibility. Compulsion was used in the matter of direction of labour within industries; in the building industry in particular, labour was directed to large-scale projects, often in isolated areas, such as camps or airfields. Given the enormous numbers of persons in the war sector, and the frequent movements of workers, it is surprising that comparatively few directions were issued – a total of 1,086,698 for the entire war.[25]

A remarkable innovation came in December 1941, with the National Service (No. 2) Act, which extended conscription to single women aged between 20 (later 19) and 30. Mothers with children under 14 were exempt, as were certain women running households or taking care of other war workers. Women subject to conscription were in practice given the choice of war work or service in one of the women's auxiliary Forces.[26]

Munitions and associated products did not exhaust the categories of war work, although they dominated them. Many forms of war work were part-time and unpaid. There were the Air Raid Precautions (ARP) services, which employed 117,000 men and 16,000 women full-time at their peak early in the war (March 1940), and over three-quarters of a million people part-time for the whole war.[27] There was also the Women's Land Army, which grew to a peak of 87,000 (full-time) in August 1943.[28] In addition, there was the constant burden of 'firewatching' at night; a maximum of forty-eight hours a month

24. Parker, *Manpower*, p. 95.
25. Ibid., pp. 222–4.
26. D. Sheridan (ed.), *Wartime Women: an anthology of women's wartime writing for Mass-Observation 1937–45* (Mandarin 1991), p. 126.
27. CSO, *Statistical Digest of the War* (*HSWW* 1951), Table 16.
28. A. Armstrong, *Farmworkers: a social and economic history 1770–1980* (Batsford 1988), p. 207.

could in theory be required, and there were in theory 6 million firewatchers; in practice, many probably avoided the duty, thus making it more onerous for the conscientious. The Women's Voluntary Service for Civil Defence (WVS), founded in 1938, had almost 1 million part-time members by 1941, and undertook a multitude of tasks, such as escorting evacuated children, comforting the relatives of bomb victims, delivering essential supplies, ministering to passing contingents of servicemen, and supplying hot food and drink to aircrews between missions. Finally, there was the Home Guard (originally the Local Defence Volunteers), which was expanded finally to almost 1.8 million. Although not called upon to perform their original function, of repelling a German invasion force, some members did man anti-aircraft batteries. But Home Guard duty (made compulsory in 1942) was another spare-time burden for the (largely middle-aged) men who formed its ranks.[29]

INDUSTRIAL RELATIONS

Industrial relations during the war were undoubtedly not as peaceful as the government would have wished, since it was acutely aware of the need to avoid labour unrest on the scale of 1917–18. The number of industrial disputes and the number of days of work lost, having been comparatively low in the early years of the war, rose steadily, peaking at 2,293 disputes in 1945 and 3.7 million days lost in 1944. On the other hand, although the average number of disputes was much greater than prewar, the number of days lost was not dissimilar, and the prewar period had been one of comparative quiescence in labour relations. In 1935–39 the annual average number of disputes begun each year had been 863, with 1,977,000 days lost; in 1940–45, there were 1,625 disputes annually, and 1,984,000 days lost per year.[30]

The existence of strikes in wartime was in spite of the fact that they were subject to drastic legal restraint in the form of the Conditions of Employment and National Arbitration Order No. 1305 (18 July 1940). This set up a National Arbitration Tribunal (NAT) to which trade disputes had to be referred (unless alternative conciliation channels existed), and whose rulings were legally binding. Strikes and lockouts were prohibited unless the minister had failed to refer it to arbitration, whether of the NAT or other means, within twenty-one days of the matter being reported to him.

The effectiveness of such control is debatable. The most appropriate contrast is with 1914–18. In those years, there was an average of 814 disputes begun each year, with the loss of 5,360,000 working days per year. Although there were more strikes in the Second than the First World War, they were shorter and involved fewer people; in addition, there were far more people involved in the war economy in the Second World War than in the First,

29. Longmate, *How We Lived Then*, pp. 109–12, 135–6, ch. 30; CSO, *Statistical Digest*, Table 15. See also A.G. Street, *From Dusk Till Dawn* (Blandford 1945; Oxford UP 1989), a lightly fictionalised account of life in a rural Home Guard.
30. Mitchell, *Statistics*, pp. 142–5.

and there was the added potential irritation of direct controls on labour movement and wages. The working of Order 1305 suggested that fear of compulsory arbitration was a potent force in getting the parties in a dispute to agree; in the war, the ministry's conciliation officers helped to settle over 2,000 disagreements.

The largest strikes were in coal-mining, engineering and shipbuilding; only two other industries (road transport and docks) produced important strikes, both in 1943. Strikes in mining and quarrying (in effect, coal-mining) accounted for 43 per cent of all days lost in strikes during the war. Apart from the habitual poor industrial relations in the coal industry (the historian of wartime manpower described coal as being 'in a chronic state of unrest'), coal-miners protested against a basic wage rate which rose only slowly. The most serious stoppages were in the spring of 1944, in which a quarter of a million workers, chiefly in south Wales and Yorkshire, were involved, and nearly 1.75 million working days were lost. Other notable disputes were the strike of engineering apprentices in 1941, and of boilermakers on Tyneside in 1944, which involved an inter-union dispute over the operation of a new machine.[31]

Whatever else the wartime disputes demonstrated, they exposed the weaknesses in the official prohibition of strikes. This was shown most clearly in the Betteshanger (Kent) coal-mining dispute of 1942, in which 1,050 miners were prosecuted, and three union officials were briefly imprisoned. Only nine of the miners paid their fines, and although warrants for the arrest of the remainder were issued, they were not carried further. The three officials were released on the intervention of the Home Secretary. Prosecutions were in fact very rare. By January 1944 it was estimated that some 5,000 strikers (out of about 1.5 million) had been proceeded against under wartime regulations; the total number found guilty was 1,917. As the historian of 'manpower' observed: 'Where large numbers decided to take the law into their own hands, they could be fairly confident that no punitive measures could be effectively taken against them.'

By 1943, the Minister of Labour was convinced that a large number of disputes were politically motivated. The consequence was the passing of Regulation 1AA (17 April 1944), which made it illegal to instigate a stoppage of work in an essential industry. No prosecutions under the regulation were made, and it is likely that the minister was under a misapprehension, and that much of the increased number of disputes could be attributed to the irrationality which stemmed from simple fatigue and general war-weariness.[32]

The war led to a much larger role for trade unions, whose membership rose from 6,298,000 in 1939 to 8,803,000 in 1946. As in 1914–18, the growth in membership, the absence of union officials in the forces, and the pressure on local workplaces to produce led to a rise in the numbers and influence of shop

31. Parker, *Manpower*, ch. XXIV, App. V, Statistical App., Table XV, pp. 456–9; Mitchell, *Statistics*, p. 145.
32. Parker, *Manpower*, ch. XXV, pp. 457–71; K.G.J.C. Knowles, *Strikes: a study in industrial conflict* (Oxford, Blackwell 1952), p. 119.

stewards. The alienation of the stewards from the official leadership was a factor in some disputes, notably that of the Tyneside boilermakers in 1944. The continuing tension between the unofficial and official leadership did not prevent the official leaders playing a much larger role in the ordinary workings of industry, from the Joint Consultative Committee of employers and trade unionists advising the Minister of Labour, to the Joint Production Committees of labour and management, which began in the Royal Ordnance factories, and spread rapidly in engineering; by the end of 1943 there were about 4,500 of them, covering about 3.5 million workers. But they proved to be a hothouse growth, which withered away after the end of the war.[33]

HEALTH, HOUSING AND WELFARE

The effect of the war on the health of the civilian population presents some conflicting evidence. No unequivocal statement as to the overall level of wartime health can be made. The indirect evidence is that social conditions deteriorated early in the war, and improved after 1941. Infant mortality rates rose until 1941, then fell below prewar; that for England and Wales in 1945 was only 82 per cent of that of 1936–38; the Scottish figure was better, at 72 per cent of the 1936–38 level. Given the strains of the evacuation and the bombing of 1940–41, the surprising thing is that there was no greater or more long-lasting deterioration in public health in the early years.

The other remarkable feature of wartime health was the considerable reduction in the incidence of most major diseases. The negative achievement of the authorities in preventing a typhoid outbreak after bombing had cut water and sewage systems was considerable – although the number of cases of dysentery notified went up from 3,082 in 1939 to 21,110 in 1945. But considerable progress was made in overcoming diphtheria, where cases notified fell by 57 per cent, aided by a national immunisation programme which treated nearly 7 million children during the war. Mothers and children benefited from the more generous subsidised milk scheme (June 1940) and vitamin welfare scheme (December 1941), and the wartime diet may have been healthier than in peacetime – especially the war bread, which, being of a higher extraction rate, contained a higher proportion of essential nutrients. Even among middle-aged people, who did not benefit from special health schemes, the death rate fell. The only real black spot was tuberculosis, where the number of notifications rose from 53,834 in 1939 to a peak of 65,129 in 1943 (Scottish notifications rose by more than 50 per cent, and those in northern English industrial towns rose above the British average). But there was a substantial rise in short-term sickness; the national insurance scheme paid out £10.7 million in sickness benefit in 1939, and £18.7 million in 1945.[34]

33. Mitchell, *Statistics*, p. 137; Parker, *Manpower*, p. 464; A. Calder, *The People's War: Britain 1939–1945* (Panther 1971), pp. 459–61.
34. Titmuss, *Problems*, pp. 515, 521, 524–5, 528–9, 533–4; CSO, *Statistical Digest*, Tables 39, 42.

Wartime housing was a story of continuous deterioration. In the first week of war, the Ministry of Health instructed local authorities to stop their house-building and slum clearance schemes. Private building was restricted only slowly, through the controls on raw materials; no single authority was directly responsible for reducing private building. Only in October 1940 was there installed 'a proper system of building licences and a department to operate it'.[35] Under the system, building operations costing more than £500 needed a licence from the Ministry of Works; this limit was lowered to £100 in April 1941. Thereafter the number of houses built fell sharply: 221,756 had been built in 1939–40; this fell to 7,168 in 1942–43, and remained at roughly that level for the rest of the war.[36]

THE EFFECTS OF BOMBING

The existing stock of houses was severely damaged by bombing, chiefly in the 'blitz' of 1940–41, and the flying bomb (V1) and rocket (V2) attacks of 1944–45. The damage for the entire war has been estimated at some 222,000 houses (i.e. dwellings) destroyed or damaged beyond repair, and 4,698,000 houses sustaining various degrees of damage – some being rendered unfit for occupation for several years. Allowing for double counting (i.e. the same house being bombed more than once), some 3,745,000 different houses were either damaged or destroyed during the war. Thus about two houses in every seven were affected by enemy action.

London took more than half the damage or destruction. In the administrative county of London, only about one house in ten escaped damage of some kind. In the most blitzed area, the docks and East End, damage was greater. In Bermondsey, only about four houses in every hundred came through the war unscathed. But damage was not confined to London. Plymouth, for example, suffered the destruction of 8 per cent of its houses, and the rendering uninhabitable (until at least mid-1944) of a further 16 per cent. Thus about one house in four was put out of use, and a great many more were temporarily unusable. The standard to which houses were repaired by the local authorities' emergency services was very low: 'until the beginning of 1943 nothing more was usually attempted than wind and weather proofing, a rough patching up sometimes costing only a few pounds a house'.[37]

The effects of enemy action were not as bad as the doom-laden predictions of government and a multitude of 'experts' had envisaged in the 1930s. These had been nothing short of catastrophic, conjuring up a picture of mass casualties. When the Ministry of Health, in 1938–39, tried to compute the potential demand for hospital beds following air raids, its figures ranged from 1.0 million to 2.8 million, depending on the length of stay. The numbers of

35. Hancock and Gowing, *War Economy*, pp. 174–5.
36. Ibid., pp. 174–5; C.M. Kohan, *Works and Buildings* (*HSWW* 1952), p. 140; Mitchell, *Statistics*, p. 392.
37. Titmuss, *Problems*, pp. 295, 329–30.

graves and coffins required were expected to be so great that mass burials and burning of bodies in lime was thought unavoidable, as otherwise the demand for seasoned coffin timber would be unsupportable.

In the event, casualties from bombing were much less than this. Civilian deaths due to operations of war (mainly bombing) are estimated at between 60,595 and 62,464, to which can be added 86,182 persons seriously injured, and 150,833 slightly injured; these are all probably underestimates. It should not be forgotten that the civilians who served in the Merchant Navy had a much higher chance of being killed through enemy action. In 1938 there had been 131,885 serving British seamen; in the war, 25,864 were killed by enemy action (46 per cent of the crews involved in sinkings). But even ignoring the losses of life in the Merchant Navy, it remains true that it was not until after three years of war that the number of civilian war-related deaths was exceeded by the loss of life among members of the Armed Forces. For the whole war period, total British war deaths (including civilians) were 450,000.[38]

Bombing created some long-term, and much temporary homelessness. By the end of June 1941, roughly 2.25 million people in the UK had been made homeless for periods ranging from a day or so to over a month. Of this number, about 1.4 million belonged to the London region. While there is double counting in these figures, it may be said that about one person in six in the London region was rendered homeless at least once. Most people coped with this situation through the aid of friends and relatives; only about one in seven in the London region availed themselves of the official rest centres.

Institutions as well as houses suffered from bombing; nearly one-fifth of all elementary schools in England and Wales had been damaged by July 1941. Roads, sewage systems, gas and water supplies were seriously damaged, and the fire crews themselves were in great danger. But the enemy action had wider effects. Sleep was interrupted; the blackout made walking (and especially driving) after dark a dangerous business; nerves were frayed; children were more subject to accidents (for example 130 children drowned in static water tanks established for firefighting in 1941–45).

Bombing was a national affair. The East End of London took most of the damage (part of West Ham was so devastated that the Army used it for training its troops in street fighting), but the bombing extended to Liverpool and Glasgow, Coventry and Hull, Birmingham and Bristol. From 7 September 1940 to 16 May 1941, there were 127 major raids on UK cities and towns ('major' indicating that more than 100 tons of bombs were dropped), of which 71 were on London. South coast ports such as Plymouth, Southampton and Portsmouth were severely damaged; at the height of the Portsmouth raids, it was estimated that not more than one-quarter of the population was living in the city. In Clydebank (Glasgow), two severe attacks (13 and 14 March 1941) led to only 7 of the suburb's 11,945 houses remaining undamaged; 35,000

38. Ibid., pp. 13, 335, App. 8; C.B.A. Behrens, *Merchant Shipping and the Demands of War* (*HSWW* 1955), p. 157, App. XXVI.

people were made homeless. It is not surprising that in April the night population dropped from 47,000 to 2,000; it is not known where the 45,000 slept.[39]

During the worst of the bombing, a sort of 'mass trekking' developed, as thousands of urban dwellers tried desperately to find a place to shelter in the countryside. For about a fortnight after the first Plymouth raid the flow of people between town and country cannot have been less than 30,000; on 24 April it probably reached 50,000. During the Merseyside raids, on 10 May 1941, the trekkers probably numbered 40,000–50,000. In Southampton, the trekkers included the Mayor; the Town Clerk, benumbed by his experiences, proved ineffectual; the administration failed signally to come to terms with the situation after the raid, and in effect local government broke down. The 'Baedeker' raids of April–July 1942 (so named because it was alleged that the German Air Force chose its targets – some of the most historic and beautiful towns in southern England – from Baedeker's guidebook) were on towns of little industrial or military value – Bath, Norwich, York, Exeter, Canterbury – and their historic centres, with their medieval buildings, were severely damaged.[40]

On the whole, London suffered most; of the 146,777 serious or fatal casualties, London accounted for over 80,000. Throughout the war, it experienced 1,224 alerts in the central district, equivalent to 1 every 36 hours. It had a total of 354 attacks by piloted aircraft. It received 41 per cent of all the attacks by flying bombs, and 49 per cent of those by rockets. (There were in total 5,823 of the former and 1,054 of the latter.) But many other towns were bombed many times: next were Dover (125 attacks), Great Yarmouth (97), Folkestone (83) and Hull (76).[41] (These figures include cross-Channel shelling.)

Shelter from air raids was provided by the Anderson shelter (named afer the then Home Secretary, Sir John Anderson), which was a corrugated iron affair, designed to be semi-buried in the garden, and the Morrison, a heavy steel construction like a large table, for indoor use. These apart, there were domestic cellars, public shelters and, notably, the London Underground railway system, which was taken over by popular action; by 27 September 1940, 177,000 people were using the 'Tube' every night.[42]

EVACUATION

The spontaneous evacuation caused by bombing had been preceded by the largest short-term movement of the British population in recorded history, as the evacuation plans laid by the government were implemented in the early hours of 1 September 1939. Within three days, and before war had been declared on 3 September, the government's scheme removed 1,473,391

39. Titmuss, *Problems*, pp. 301, 313, 334; Calder, *People's War*, pp. 251–5; T.H. O'Brien, *Civil Defence* (*HSWW* 1955), App. IV.
40. Titmuss, *Problems*, pp. 307–8; T. Harrisson, *Living through the Blitz* (Collins 1976), pp. 143f.; O'Brien, *Civil Defence*, pp. 429–32.
41. O'Brien, *Civil Defence*, App. V (flying bombs and rockets); App. VI (towns raided).
42. Longmate, *How We Lived Then*, pp. 121–8.

persons, of whom 826,959 were unaccompanied schoolchildren, and 523,670 mothers and accompanied children, from the crowded cities of Britain. The whole operation was conducted without a single accident or casualty. In addition to this, about 2 million persons evacuated themselves, chiefly to western English counties and to Wales. While the response to the official scheme varied widely over Britain, the average proportion of schoolchildren evacuated from the sending areas was 47 per cent in England and 38 per cent in Scotland.

Evacuation was not confined to children; the population of hospitals was sharply reduced in expectation of mass casualties requiring beds. The hospital authorities emptied beds so zealously that many patients must have been discharged prematurely; 140,000 were sent home, including 7,000–8,000 tubercular patients, who may have contributed to the rise in the TB death rate in the first two years of the war.[43]

The reception accorded the evacuees varied from welcoming to resentful. Given that they were drawn from the overcrowded inner cities, and thus tended to be less well-off than the people with whom they were billeted, social tensions might have been expected, on both sides. Not all evacuees had happy experiences. One woman evacuee who returned home (to Greenford, Middlesex) wrote:

> We were treated like bits of dirt by the locals as though it wasn't bad enough going through what we did to get there. We started at 11 o'clock and did not get to Dunstable until 5 – after five changes by train and bus and standing on the curb at Luton for an hour and twenty minutes. We arrived at a skating rink and then were picked out [by locals offering accommodation] so you can guess what some poor devils were like who had four or five children. They were still there on the Sunday afternoon and then eight families were put in an empty house and different people gave them bits of furniture. I admit some of them were a bit much with their hair in curlers and overalls but we are not all the same.[44]

But the government was not prepared for the storm of resentment which welled up from the reception areas when it became apparent that an unexpectedly high proportion of the children had head lice, that bed-wetting was common (although more likely to have been induced by the stress of evacuation than being normal), and that some children were inadequately toilet-trained. Many children were just dirty, poorly dressed and shod.[45] Hostility was also directed at the perceived inadequacies of some of the mothers, although something may be allowed for class bias. R.C.K. Ensor, an Oxford history don, wrote in the conservative journal, the *Spectator*, that many of the mothers were 'the lowest grade of slum women – slatternly malodorous tatterdemalions trailing children to match'.[46]

43. Titmuss, *Problems*, pp. 101–3, 193–5, 524, App. 2.
44. Sheridan, *Wartime Women*, p. 64.
45. Titmuss, *Problems*, pp. 114–36. See also Women's Group on Public Welfare, *Our Towns: a close-up* (Oxford UP 1943), chs II, III.
46. Quoted in T.L. Crosby, *The Impact of Civilian Evacuation in the Second World War* (Croom Helm, Beckenham 1986), p. 34.

Yet the experiences of the evacuees were very varied. Some were smothered with affection; some were mistreated or ignored; some were bored in the countryside or in provincial towns; some responded lyrically to rural life; most must have been homesick.[47] Homesickness, coupled with the fact that the expected bombing did not materialise, led to a swift return of many evacuees; when a national count was taken in the reception areas on 8 January 1940, it was found that an estimated 59 per cent of all the official evacuees had returned home; the numbers of private evacuees who had done so is not known. The return to the cities was abruptly reversed with the blitz of 1940–41; in February 1941, the number of official evacuees rose to 1,368,700. The ending of the blitz saw another return, interrupted only briefly by the V1/V2 campaign in 1944–45, when the number of official evacuees rose to slightly over 1 million (September 1944).[48]

FOOD SHORTAGES, RATIONING AND NUTRITION

Among the many striking changes in civilian life in wartime, food shortages and rationing were outstanding in their effect, both on life at the time, and on the collective national memory. (Half a century after the end of the war, a series of BBC 2 television programmes, *The Wartime Kitchen and Garden*, described the privations of wartime eating, and the ingenious ways in which people coped with problems of food supply, rationing, and cooking. The series was associated with an exhibition at the Imperial War Museum on the same theme, October 1993 to August 1994.) Rationing began on 8 January 1940, for butter, sugar, bacon and ham. Meat rationing began on 11 March, tea and margarine rationing in July. The rationing of jams and other preserves (March 1941) and cheese (May 1941) completed the rationing edifice. All these foods were rationed by weight, except for meat, which was by value – an allowance of 1s. 10d. per person, which could be spent on beef, veal, mutton or pork in any desired (or obtainable) combination. Some of these amounts were relatively generous (bacon at 8 oz per week – more than the average prewar consumption), some nugatory (tea at 2 oz per person per week). The meat ration was equivalent to about 1 lb per week. The meat ration was lowered in January 1941 to 1s. 2d., at which level it remained for most of the rest of the war. This may be compared with the average price paid for meat by the consumers in the Ministry of Food's household expenditure survey (which began in July 1940); in 1943 and 1944 this was between 1s. 3d. and 1s. 5d. per lb.[49] The sugar ration began at 12 oz, but soon fell to 8 oz, which was a sharp reduction on prewar consumption. The cheese ration was the most

47. B.S. Johnson (ed.), *The Evacuees* (Gollancz 1969); Longmate, *How We Lived Then*, ch. 5; S. Isaacs (ed.), *The Cambridge Evacuation Survey* (Methuen 1941).
48. Titmuss, *Problems*, p. 544, App. 9.
49. Ministry of Food, *The Urban Working-Class Household Diet 1940 to 1949* (HMSO 1951), paras 66–7.

volatile; beginning at 1 oz (barely a mouthful), it rose to 8 oz at the end of 1942, but for most of the war was 3 oz.[50]

In addition to these basic ration schemes, 'points' rationing was introduced on 1 December 1941 for a wide variety of previously unrationed foods. This gave a certain number of points per person per week, which could be spent on a range of foods, each of which had an official points value. The latter was changed by the Ministry of Food, in accordance with variations in supplies and relative demand.[51]

The points schemes, which initially applied to such things as canned meats, fish and vegetables, but which also came to cover dried fruits, breakfast cereals, treacle and marmalade, could also be used to persuade the public to buy items with which they were unfamiliar. Thus, for example, points values were manipulated to deter the buying of tinned salmon, and encourage the buying of tinned US sausage meat. As well as providing an easy and flexible way of rationing a wide range of goods, the scheme had the virtue of restoring some element of choice to the shopper, and discouraged the mismatches of demand and supply so frequent in war, and so bad for public welfare and feeling. The originator of the scheme, a Principal Assistant Secretary of the Ministry of Food, Mr M.P. Roseveare, has well been described as an unrecognised genius.[52]

Finally, there were special schemes for milk and eggs, and for the supply of vitamins. The uptake of school milk was greatly increased, and a National Milk Scheme (July 1940) provided subsidised milk for pregnant women and children under 5 years old. The Vitamin Welfare Scheme, started in December 1941, was designed to make up for vitamin shortages caused by the lack of butter, eggs and fruit; it provided blackcurrant syrup and cod liver oil for children under 2 years. In April 1942 the blackcurrant was replaced by Lend-Lease orange juice. The main beneficiaries of these schemes were infants, schoolchildren and nursing mothers. For non-priority consumers (most adults), they meant a reduction in the milk and (especially) egg supply, and the substitution of dried egg on a large scale. Vitamin B1 was added to bread from June 1941 until the raising of the extraction rate to 85 per cent in March 1942 rendered it unnecessary. But flour was then given added calcium.[53]

But some foods were never rationed: principally bread, although its quality changed as the extraction rate rose substantially. Ernest Bevin, the Minister of Labour, complained that the National Wheatmeal loaf, at 85 per cent extraction, was inedible and gave him wind. Potatoes were unrationed and plentiful. Fish (when obtainable, which was rare), flour, oatmeal and fresh vegetables were also unrationed, and many people supplemented their diet by planting potatoes and vegetables on allotments or in their gardens, spurred by the government's

50. Ministry of Food, *How Britain was Fed*, pp. 56–7.
51. Ibid., p. 57.
52. J. Burnett, *Plenty and Want: a social history of diet in England from 1815 to the present day* (Pelican 1968), p. 328.
53. Ministry of Food, *How Britain was Fed*, pp. 47, 60–2.

'Dig for Victory' campaign. In addition, the overall supply of milk rose substantially. Finally, meals taken outside the home were not rationed, although a maximum of 5s. was to be charged for restaurant meals, and the great expansion of industrial canteens, 'British Restaurants' (to provide cheap meals for those away from home), and of the school meals service, helped to reduce the pressure on household budgets. There was even an official scheme (The Rural Pie Scheme) for supplying food for agricultural workers, who did not have access to canteens.[54]

There is no doubt that customary civilian food consumption was severely curtailed. By 1941, although the consumption of grain products, potatoes and milk had actually increased, there had been substantial reductions in butter and eggs (by 60–70 per cent), sugar (by 50–60 per cent), meat and tea (by about one-third) and cheese (by between one-quarter and one third). The calorie value of the national diet had declined by 6 per cent. The low point of the wartime diet was in 1941, when

> In some respects, and especially in regard to the consumption of such highly prized foods as fats, meat, eggs and sugar, the average working-class diet of 1941 compared unfavourably with that found among the poorer working-class families before the war.[55]

On the other hand, the energy value of the average diet had declined only slightly, and to some extent the losses of vitamins were already being made good through the raising of the extraction rate for flour, and the expansion of the government milk schemes. After 1942, the situation improved, and by the end of the war the supply of every principal food had risen above the 1942 level, with the exception of cheese.[56]

Shortages of usual foods led to searches for novelty; the Ministry of Food tried hard to popularise obscure varieties, especially of fish, which was unrationed, but the housewife was not impressed. The most unpopular was probably whale meat, although tuna ran it close. Dried egg became universal, and varieties of US tinned meats such as Spam (canned spiced ham) were freely available. Looking back, the shortages most remembered would probably be sugar, fresh fruit and onions. Onions were taken for granted until the German invasion of Brittany and the Channel Islands; the loss was then keenly felt.[57]

In the absence or large reduction in supply of important foods, households were driven to a variety of expedients, encouraged by the Ministry of Food, in the person of the minister, Lord Woolton, a publicist of great flair, whose phrase 'The Kitchen Front' was very successful. Meatless cooking recipes were promoted by the ministry, including the famous Woolton Pie, described as

54. Calder, *People's War*, p. 319; (Sir) N. Curtis-Bennett, *The Food of the People: being the history of industrial feeding* (Faber 1949), ch. IX; Ministry of Food, *How Britain was Fed*, p. 45.
55. Ministry of Food, *Urban Working-Class Diet*, para. 41.
56. Ibid., Tables 6, 8, 12.
57. Longmate, *How We Lived Then*, pp. 144–5.

'steak and kidney pie without the steak and kidney'. This suggested combination of potato, swede, cauliflower and carrot, covered with pastry, was his only great (and apparently inedible) failure.[58] (Consumer reaction to wartime food difficulties is described in Longmate.)[59]

The enforcement of food control proved surprisingly easy, chiefly because it had widespread popular support; the perceived equitable nature of rationing gave it popular validity. There is no doubt that without this support, the system would have crumbled rapidly. As it was, the Ministry of Food had, by the end of 1944, 550 local enforcement inspectors and 340 divisional inspectors.[60] While there is much anecdotal evidence of the existence of a 'grey' market, in the form of shopkeepers who could be persuaded to show favouritism, or force their customers to accept higher than legal prices, and there was undoubtedly a whole series of localised 'black' markets, these never coalesced to form a national black market. Apart from pilfered supplies which found their way into the hands of retailers, the only notable foods for which universal black markets can be said to have existed throughout the war were poultry and rabbits. These, though doubtless welcome to the urban consumer, were not major items in the national diet.[61] A study of prosecutions in north and east London and five provincial towns reveals more infringments of clothing control than food control.[62] The materials for a study of the black market are understandably lacking. A brief encounter with a household with access to the black market is described in the reminiscence of Lambert.[63]

In certain respects, normal standards of consumption were maintained. Tobacco consumption rose considerably; in spite of imports of the raw material being restricted, the war began with two years' stocks (one year was regarded as the minimum), and the tobacco companies proved adept at acquiring tobacco from the USA without spending dollars. Sales of cigarettes to the public rose from 73.8 million in 1939 to 93.3 million cigarettes in 1945; this was in addition to the tobacco supplied (cheaply) to members of the Forces. Tobacco was at the height of its public popularity, the public required it to 'calm their nerves', and the government was not disposed to argue. A further consideration was that the raw material came from the USA, and a severe reduction in imports would have seriously worsened diplomatic relations.[64]

58. Ministry of Food, *Food Facts for the Kitchen Front* (Collins n.d.) has this, and many officially suggested recipes.
59. Longmate, *How We Lived Then*, ch. 13.
60. Ministry of Food, *How Britain was Fed*, p. 40.
61. R.J. Hammond, *Food, vol. III, Studies in Administration and Control* (*HSWW* 1962), pp. 722–6.
62. E. Smithies, *The Black Economy in England since 1914* (Dublin, Gill & Macmillan 1984), ch. 4.
63. D. Lambert, *The Sheltered Days: growing up in war* (André Deutsch 1965), pp. 141–5.
64. G.F. Todd, *Statistics of Smoking in the United Kingdom* (4th edn, Tobacco Research Council 1966), Table 1.2; E.L. Hargreaves and M. Gowing, *Civil Industry and Trade* (*HSWW* 1952), pp. 26–33, 249.

CLOTHES AND CLOTHES RATIONING

Second only to food rationing, the civilian population felt the deprivation of clothes rationing. This began on 1 June 1941, using for a time the unused margarine coupons in the back of the food ration books. For the next twelve months, each person was to receive sixty-six coupons. Every item of clothing was given a points value, the most 'expensive' being, for a man, a lined raincoat or overcoat (sixteen coupons), and, for a woman, a raincoat or overcoat (fourteen) or dress (eleven). Underwear was rated at men's underpants (four) and women's pants (three). Children were treated more generously.[65]

In 1942–43 the ration was reduced, to an annual rate of forty-eight coupons. The authorities were hard pressed to fulfil even this ration, although they did so right until the last few months of the war; from February to August 1945, the rate was the equivalent of forty-one, and shortly afterwards the ration fell briefly to thirty-six coupons.

The 1942–43 ration in practice meant that a man could buy

> one pair of socks every four months, one pair of shoes every eight months, one shirt every 20 months, one vest and one pair of pants every two years, one pair of trousers and one jacket every two years, one waistcoat every five years, one pullover every five years, one overcoat every seven years, leaving about three coupons a year over for odd items such as handkerchiefs.[66]

From the start, clothes rationing was easier to evade than food rationing. The administrative controls were looser, and in spite of their progressive tightening, a black market in coupons grew up. Retailers did not have to register their customers (unlike food retailers), the coupons were valid for a year (two weeks for food) and there were no unrationed goods (again, unlike food) on the market to absorb the pressure of demand; the black-market price of a 1941–42 clothes ration book was at one time 2s. 6d., but the price in 1944 was more like £5.[67]

With the exception of certain industrial workers, who got an extra allocation on account of their jobs, use of the coupons was the only way for most people to clothe themselves. The stringency led to much 'make do and mend', and a variety of cloth was diverted from its official use; blackout cloth could be pressed into service as a black skirt; women's legs could be dyed to give the illusion of stockings; the occasional surplus Service blanket could be turned into a very hard-wearing winter coat or dressing gown; many people gave up wearing night clothes, and many women rediscovered the virtues of the nightdress (six points) as opposed to pyjamas (eight points). Shortages of shoes grew steadily worse as the war went on.[68] A particular problem was the disappearance of rubber after the loss of Malaya, and the consequent disappearance of

65. Longmate, *How We Lived Then*, p. 247.
66. Hargreaves and Gowing, *Civil Industry*, p. 315.
67. Ibid., pp. 315, 326–8.
68. Longmate, *How We Lived Then*, ch. 21.

Wellington boots and plimsolls (gym shoes) led to strain on other forms of shoes – plimsolls in particular had provided shoes for the poor before the war. Even though the output of children's shoes rose, it was not enough to meet the increased demand which was brought about by full employment. Wooden shoes were made in an effort to offset the shortages of crepe rubber soles – about 2 million pairs were made for women in 1944–45.

As well as being curtailed in quantity, clothing was restricted in style. The largest scheme was the 'utility' scheme, which aimed to reorganise production so as to produce long (and hence cheap) runs of standard cloth. From these cloths, approved designs of utility clothing could be made; these seem to have been well designed, and were received well by the public. The scheme also brought the price of clothing down; the price index number of clothing actually fell after the introduction of the scheme in August 1941.[69]

An additional twist of the knife was the 'austerity' regulations in spring 1942, which aimed to reduce wastage in clothing, in both utility and non-utility garments. They were very detailed, governing (for women) the number of pleats, seams, buttons and buttonholes in a garment, and (for men) the prohibition of trouser turn-ups, and restrictions on the length of shirts and socks. In addition, the range of styles was restricted – manufacturers of women's underwear, for example, were restricted to six designs for each article, and the styles of overalls were rigorously standardised. The prohibition of men's turn-ups caused a political storm, and had to be rescinded. On the whole, it is doubtful if the austerity orders were worth the bother.[70]

ENTERTAINMENT

One expanding sector in the war was entertainment. It was the finest hour of the BBC. The number of licences rose further, from 8.9 million at the end of 1939, to 9.9 million at the end of 1945. The Corporation became an essential source of news, and promoted a series of immensely popular programmes, notably the comedy show, *It's That Man Again* (ITMA), starring Tommy Handley, and the *Brains Trust*, with a bevy of notable 'experts', the most famous of whom was the philosopher, Professor C.E.M. Joad. An innovation was *Workers' Playtime*, which broadcast from factories. The Corporation's staff expanded enormously, from 4,900 to 11,500.[71]

Entertainment in cinemas and theatres was curtailed when the war began: the government had closed them down, fearing mass casualties due to bombing. Reopened after a short interval, they boomed. Cinema attendances rose from 19 million to 30 million a week between 1939 and 1945. A particular feature of the cinema was the improvement in quality of British films, notable

69. Hargreaves and Gowing, *Civil Industry*, pp. 433–4, 437, 491, 494.
70. Hargreaves and Gowing (ibid., p. 439) more or less admit this; Longmate (*How We Lived Then*, p. 249) is more caustic.
71. A. Briggs, *The History of Broadcasting in the United Kingdom, vol. III, The War of Words* (Oxford UP 1970), pp. 314–15, 318–20, 560–4, 564–6, 576, Apps A, B.

successes being *In Which We Serve* and *Henry V*. During the war, the proportion of British films being shown rose slightly, from 15 to 20 per cent of the total, and the film trade discovered that by 1945 people were attending a film because it was British; previously they had stayed away because the film was British.[72]

CRIME

There was a considerable increase in serious crime in the war. In England and Wales, the number of persons prosecuted for indictable crimes rose from 74,744 in 1939 to 110,073 in 1945; the number of persons proceeded against for non-indictable crimes fell from 597,117 to a wartime low of 291,096 in 1944. In Scotland, crimes rose from 60,104 to 86,075; miscellaneous (less serious) offences declined from 136,985 to 65,801 (both in 1939–45). There was a new category, of offences against the Defence Regulations, which spawned many prosecutions in the early years of the war, chiefly for infringing lighting regulations. The annual average number of prosecutions under the Defence Regulations in England and Wales was 188,000. What seems to have happened is that the normal causes of non-serious crime were in abeyance; chiefly motoring offences, which accounted for most of the decline in such crime. Drunkenness also declined, presumably because many of the serious drinkers were in the Forces, the supply of spirits was severely reduced, and wartime beer was weaker than before. But there was a sharp rise in burglary and stealing; how much of this is associated with attempts to circumvent the rationing system is uncertain.[73] Some of the increase was presumably due to the reduction of police personnel; the regular police fell from 57,012 in 1940 to a wartime low of 43,026 in 1943, and special constables declined from 25,220 in 1940 to a low of 12,951 in 1945.[74]

EDUCATION

Education was considerably disrupted in wartime. The greatest disruption was due to evacuation, when, in spite of promises to the contrary, schools' pupils were not kept together, but distributed among many local schools in the reception areas. Schools themselves were also damaged by bombing; 1,149 had been seriously damaged by the end of September 1942. The restoration of pupils to their home areas was seriously impeded by the requisitioning of their buildings by government departments (chiefly ARP). In June 1943, buildings which would have accommodated 150,000 children were occupied by government departments. On the other hand, there was a growing desire for more education, as evinced by the growing proportion of those aged 16+ taking the

72. P.M. Taylor (ed.), *Britain and the Cinema in the Second World War* (Macmillan 1988), p. 8; Longmate, *How We Lived Then*, ch. 33.
73. CSO, *Annual Abstract of Statistics, no. 84 (1935–1946)*, Tables 47, 48, 57, 58.
74. E. Smithies, *Crime in Wartime: a social history of crime in World War II* (Allen & Unwin 1982), p. 190.

School Certificate examination. The calling-up of schoolteachers was another difficulty, and the numbers entering training colleges and university departments of education fell sharply. The universities suffered a large reduction in full-time students, from 50,002 in 1938–39 to 35,648 in 1943–44, and some London colleges evacuated (usually to Cambridge); after 1942, arts students were not allowed to defer military service.[75]

TRAVEL

Wartime travel was difficult and exhausting – 'a nightmare' was a common judgement. Even apart from the military operations which demanded large numbers of special trains (538,000 over the whole war),[76] the enormous numbers of military personnel on leave meant overcrowded trains throughout the war. As early as 1941, some 50 per cent of all long-distance travel was said to be by members of the Forces, and the influx of US personnel from 1942 increased the strain. During the war, while the number of passenger journeys rose only slightly, the average mileage travelled rose from 16 miles (in 1938) to 25 miles (1944). Railways also suffered disruption through bombing, and the imposition of speed restrictions during air raid warnings.[77] The worst railway 'incident' in the war was the bombing of Sloane Square underground station on 12 November 1940, just when a train was leaving the station; there were seventy-nine deaths, three being 'missing presumed dead' (i.e. the bodies could either not be found, or not be found in recognisable form).[78] The blackout raised the tension of the travelling public further, and the lack of station signs (taken down for security reasons) increased the feeling of anomie.[79] The government tried to discourage civilian travel (the official slogan asked: 'Is Your Journey Really Necessary?') and 'cheap day returns' and other excursion tickets were withdrawn. Although discouraged, private citizens still tried to take holidays, although many seaside resorts were subject to military restrictions.

The abandonment of private motoring was almost total. Petrol rationing began on 23 September 1939. Gas propulsion for cars, using a rooftop balloon full of town gas, or the towing of a small trailer with a producer gas installation, proved only a partial solution. In September 1939 there had been 2,034,000 private cars licensed; by August 1943 there were 718,000. By October 1940 no more cars were being made for civilians, and the price of second-hand cars soared. Many cars were laid up by their owners until the end of the war. Headlights had to be severely masked, and the number of road deaths rose sharply in the last four months of 1939. The removal of road signposts was a potent cause of confusion. The only really useful innovation was the making

75. P.H.J.H. Gosden, *Education in the Second World War* (Methuen 1976), pp. 15, 65, 87, 105–15, Tables 1.1, 3.2, ch. 7.
76. F. Ferneyhough, *The History of Railways in Britain* (Reading, Osprey 1975), p. 173.
77. C. Savage, *Inland Transport* (*HSWW* 1957), pp. 196f., App. XXIV.
78. J. Simmons, *The Railways of Britain* (Macmillan 1987), p. 51.
79. Longmate, *How We Lived Then*, pp. 294–6.

compulsory of the white line painted down the middle of the road. In March 1942, the basic petrol ration for cars and motor cycles was abolished, although it was still available for those in essential occupations (e.g. doctors) or for health reasons. But thereafter any motorist had to prove when stopped by the police that the journey was really necessary – and that it was by the shortest possible route. The regulations' most celebrated victim was the composer Ivor Novello, who served four weeks in prison for his offence.[80]

Of more consequence to most people was the sharp reduction in bus services. Staff shortages followed from military conscription, and petrol and oil supplies were cut; within four months of the outbreak of war, 800 central London buses had been withdrawn; the number of bus stops was reduced to save petrol, and a 'bus curfew' was instituted. The blitz destroyed so many London buses that appeals had to be made for companies in other regions to lend buses to London. Before the war, boarding a bus had been a free-for-all, but queueing was made compulsory in April 1942. The shortage of labour and materials meant that bus seats were not upholstered, and were merely plain wooden slats. Most drivers remained male, but the replacement of the male bus conductor by the female 'clippie' was almost universal. The blackout made driving for a living hazardous and tiring. By 1942, however, the clippies themselves were in short supply, reflecting the general labour shortage in the country. The only really happy travellers were probably cyclists, who (at least in daytime) had safe travelling on roads virtually free of motor vehicles.[81]

THE LEVELLING OF INCOMES

The war also played its part in the levelling of incomes which has been a marked feature of social change in the twentieth century. While some of this was due to the political changes of 1945, it remains true that the war was a catalyst making for greater equality (Table 16.3).

Table 16.3 Distribution of UK post-tax incomes, 1938 and 1947

Proportion of incomes	*1938 (%)*	*1947 (%)*
Top 1%	14	11
2–5%	22	16
5%	28	21
10%	38	30
25%	54	48
50%	73	70
Bottom 50%	27	30

Source: Seers, *Levelling*, p. 39

80. Ibid., pp. 307–13; CSO, *Statistical Digest*, Table 168.
81. Longmate, *How We Lived Then*, pp. 313–20; Savage, *Inland Transport*, pp. 526–7.

This process has been described as the top strata ('broadly the rentiers, upper-middle class entrepreneurs and richer members of professions') losing their position relatively to the whole of the rest of the population.[82]

CONCLUSIONS

While for the economy, in its international setting, the longer-term consequences of the war had been entirely negative, for the civilians they were more mixed. The broad processes at work seem to have been, not merely a levelling down, but a levelling up. The levelling of living standards at the skilled artisan level, as a consequence of full employment, meant that, although the middle classes suffered real reductions in their standards of living, a much larger number of people from the ranks of the less skilled working classes experienced sharp improvements. It seems safe to say that malnutrition, which had undoubtedly existed in the 1930s, disappeared during the war. For the poorest third of the nation, the quality of the diet must have improved markedly. In addition, the government took great pains to provide nutritional supplements. The improved health of the people was perceptible in the falling infant mortality rate, and the reduction in the toll of some notable prewar diseases such as diphtheria. Against this had to be set the civilian deaths, which were unprecedented in British history since the Norman invasion in 1066. Even so, the collective memory of the war is one of stoical pride and faded excitement. For many civilians, the war stood out as one of the most exciting periods of their lives.

Finally, the war was notable as ushering in a period of considerable social reform after 1945. While the war was on, the government had accepted a commitment to a national health service, and reformed secondary education (the 'Butler Act' of 1944). Thus the frontiers of the 'welfare state', which had been delineated by Sir William Beveridge in his famous report of 1942, were pushed back politically even before the surrender of Germany. In this mood, a considerable part was played by the feeling that the 1930s had been a period of wasted human endeavour and economic resources, and that it was now time for government to play a more prominent role in popular welfare.

82. Seers, *Levelling*, p. 40.

CHAPTER 17

THE NATIONAL BALANCE SHEET, 1900–45

INTRODUCTION

In a little more than three decades, British society and the British economy had been subjected to immense strains and losses. The most obvious economic costs of this period were attributable to the two world wars, but the existence of mass unemployment meant that almost the entire interwar period had been one of wasted economic and human resources, and blighted individual lives.

In spite of these losses, the material welfare of the British people improved considerably between 1900 and 1945. This was due fundamentally to the continuing technological development which is a feature of all post-traditional societies. Technological development led to economic growth, which was powerful enough to more than offset the economic costs of wars and depressions. In addition, British society altered its social and political arrangements so as to benefit the poorer at the expense of the richer members of society. Thus the effects of economic growth on popular economic welfare were reinforced by a certain amount of redistribution of income and wealth.

In contrast to the picture of internal improvement, the external picture was one of almost continuous loss and relative decline. The British share of world exports declined considerably. The economy moved from a position in which the balance of payments showed a substantial surplus every year, to one in which huge deficits could be expected in the short run, and intermittent deficits thereafter. This deterioration was partly due to the loss of overseas investments sold to pay for the wars, partly to the loss of traditional sources of invisible income, and partly to the loss of export markets for goods.

The causes of the loss of markets were much discussed. While something must be allowed for the spread of industrialisation to other parts of the world, it can be said that in the long run British goods exhibited competitive weaknesses, which had been already apparent before 1914. Apart from the brief boom after 1918, conditions were, for the next two decades, unpropitious for manufacturers to make the necessary effort to overcome these weaknesses, and much capital and labour was immobilised in declining and loss-making industries. The comparative weakness of certain previously large exporting industries was a check on the rate of economic growth and on the improvement in living standards. Between 1899 and 1950, the UK share of world exports of manufactured goods fell from 31 to 24 per cent. But this latter figure was unsustainably high, since former trading rivals had as yet not recovered from the Second World War sufficiently to pose serious competition in export markets. By 1982, the proportion had fallen to 6.1 per cent.[1] In the circumstances, that economic growth was as high as it turned out to be was impressive by historical standards, and reflects the rapid growth of other industries and of the service sectors.

ECONOMIC GROWTH AND HIGHER LIVING STANDARDS

The conjuncture of economic growth and rising living standards *per head* has been expressed in quantitative terms by Feinstein (Table 17.1).

Table 17.1 UK real GDP per head, 1909–53[a]

	£		£
1909–13	46.8	1934–38	57.6
1914–18	52.6	1939–43	69.0
1919–23	45.4	1944–48	66.4
1924–28	49.0	1949–53	69.8
1929–33	50.8		

Note: a GDP is at constant factor cost per capita, at 1913 prices
Source: C.H. Feinstein, *National Income, Expenditure and Output of the United Kingdom, 1855–1965* (Cambridge UP 1972), Table 17

This indicates that GDP per head rose by 49 per cent between the first and last periods indicated here; the story has been continued until 1949–53 so as to arrive at a time when the economy had largely reconverted from its wartime structure. Thus, in spite of two world wars and the interwar depressions, the average real income per head in the UK had risen by almost one-half in four decades.

Measuring the rising standard of living by the increase in real income does not give a full picture of the improvements in this period, since it fails to take into account the qualitative changes in conventional living standards. In Sidney Pollard's words:

> Statistics fail to take full account of the difference made by electricity instead of candles, and gas cookers instead of coal or coke ranges, as standard equipment in working-class homes; of improved housing, including indoor water and sanitation; or of radio, the cinema and newspapers within almost everybody's reach.[2]

1. B.R. Mitchell, *British Historical Statistics* (Cambridge UP 1988), p. 524.
2. S. Pollard, *The Development of the British Economy 1914–1950* (Edward Arnold 1962), p. 293.

This list could be prolonged; George Orwell's famous attack on 'cheap luxuries' in the late 1930s can also be read as a testimony to the improvement of the quality of material life in the twentieth century for both unemployed people and those with jobs:

> Twenty million people are underfed but literally everyone in England has access to a radio. What we have lost in food we have gained in electricity. Whole sections of the working class who have been plundered of all they really need are being compensated, in part, by cheap luxuries which mitigate the surface of life. . . . It is quite likely that fish-and chips, art-silk stockings, tinned salmon, cut-price chocolate . . . the movies, the radio, strong tea and the football pools have between them averted revolution.[3]

REDISTRIBUTION OF INCOME AND WEALTH

There is little doubt that both income and wealth became more evenly distributed in the period, although substantial inequalities remained after 1945. Accurate estimates are hard to come by, and also suffer by being derived from the work of the tax authorities, which raises questions of coverage and evasion.

In spite of the uncomparable nature of the early estimates, the general impression is of a large reduction in income inequality, at least at the upper end of the national distribution, the process of redistribution being particularly marked after 1938.[4] Stamp estimated that in 1914 the top 1 per cent of income receivers obtained 30 per cent, and the top 5.5 per cent received 45 per cent of all national income; Seers estimated that in 1947 the share of the top 1 per cent had fallen to 11 per cent, and the share of the top 5 per cent had fallen to 21 per cent, of the national income. The reduction of income shares in the upper and middle echelons of society was clearly considerable.[5]

The proximate causes of this redistribution were various. A certain part was played by higher taxation, but the redistribution is not entirely explained by this. Thus, for example, between 1938 and 1949, the post-tax share of the national income accounted for by the top 10 per cent of income-earners fell from 33.6 to 26.9 per cent, but the pre-tax share fell also, from 38 to 33 per cent.[6]

More fundamentally, redistribution reflected the changing composition of the national income. The largest changes here were the growing importance of income from employment, the diminishing contribution from self-employment, and the decline of income from rent and foreign investment (Table 17.2 overleaf).

The growth of incomes from employment at the expense of incomes from self-employment and investment led to (or was a reflection of) a levelling of

3. G. Orwell, *The Road to Wigan Pier* (Gollancz 1937; Penguin 1962), pp. 80–1.
4. H.F. Lydall, 'The Long-Term Trend in the Size Distribution of Income', *JRSS* ser. A, 122 (1959), p. 32.
5. D. Seers, *The Levelling of Incomes since 1938* (Oxford, Blackwell 1951), p. 39.
6. Lydall, 'Size Distribution', p. 14.

Table 17.2 Factor incomes in UK national income, 1909–13 to 1949–53

Income from	*1909–13* *(%)*	*1949–53* *(%)*
Employment	50.5	63.6
Self-employment	16.3	10.9
Company gross profits	13.3	16.5
Public enterprise surpluses	—	2.5
Rent	11.5	4.3
Net property income from abroad	8.4	2.2
	100.0	100.0

Source: Calculated from Feinstein, *National Income*, Table 18

incomes, since the latter reflect the ownership of capital, which is much more unequal than the distribution of the earnings of employees. As well as the growth of employment income, there was also a tendency for the differential between wage and salary rates to fall. Finally, there was the change in the structure of employment, as the less skilled and lower-paid jobs declined, and were replaced by the comparatively more skilled employment in service trades, the 'new industries', and white-collar jobs generally. A signal part in this 'upgrading' process was played by the decline of female domestic service and male agricultural labour, both of which were before 1914 large employers of labour, and remained poorly paid throughout the period.[7]

The distribution of wealth was also changed. Measurements of this are beset by problems, both of definition and of source material. The evidence is usually derived from probate returns in respect of deceased person's estates, and thus continues to exclude a large proportion of the population. ('To this day . . . more than half the deceased adult population leaves no property at all at death which is caught by the probate net'.)[8] But attempts have been made to use the probate returns as a basis for calculation. These show a substantial redistribution of wealth (Table 17.3 opposite).

While these estimates are not ideal (they exclude the two important categories of state benefits and human capital),[9] they are the best available, and show a clear decline in the concentration of wealth-holding over this period, and particularly so for the period spanning the Second World War. On the other hand, it is clear that the distribution of wealth began as more unequal than that of income, and has gone less far than the latter. It also seems to be the case that most of the redistribution has been from the very rich to the middling rich; even by 1981, the top 50 per cent of wealth-holders accounted for an

7. Ibid., pp. 15, 21. See also G. Routh, *Occupation and Pay in Great Britain, 1906–60* (Cambridge UP 1965), Table 47.
8. W.D. Rubinstein, *Wealth and Inequality in Britain* (Faber & Faber 1986), p. 96.
9. A.B. Atkinson and A.J. Harrison, *Distribution of Personal Wealth in Britain* (Cambridge UP 1978), p. 4.

Table 17.3 Shares in total wealth, 1923–70

	England and Wales			*Great Britain*		
	Top 1%	*Top 5%*	*Top 10%*	*Top 1%*	*Top 5%*	*Top 10%*
1923	60.9	82.0	89.1	—	—	—
1930	57.9	79.2	86.6	—	—	—
1938	55.0	76.9	85.0	55.0	77.2	85.4
1950	47.2	74.3	—	47.2	74.4	—
1959	41.4	67.6	—	41.8	67.9	—
1970	29.7	53.6	68.7	30.1	54.3	69.4

Note: — = no data

Source: A.B. Atkinson and A.J. Harrison, 'Trends in the Distribution of Wealth in Britain', in A.B. Atkinson (ed.), *Wealth, Income and Inequality* (2nd edn, Oxford UP 1980), p. 218

estimated 78–82 per cent of all wealth.[10] In 1911–13, it is estimated that the top 0.9 per cent of wealth-holders had 67 per cent of all wealth, the top 3.9 per cent 83 per cent, and the top 11.7 per cent had 93.3 per cent of all wealth.[11] While to some extent the decline of wealth inequality has been a consequence of reduction in income inequality, a large part has been played by changes in taxation, principally the rise in rates of estate duty, which began in 1893 (in a small way).

RISE IN IMPORTANCE OF GOVERNMENT

One of the most notable features of twentieth-century British history is the rise in the importance of government. This process began before 1914, and has been a common feature of industrial societies. For the UK, it can be illustrated by taking the combined current spending of central and local government, comprising current expenditure on goods and services, subsidies, grants, and debt interest, and expressing the result as a proportion of current GNP (Table 17.4 overleaf).

On this formulation, after the temporary emergencies of the two world wars and the Korean War were over, public expenditure (central and local) settled down to about three times its relative level in 1910–13. It is of interest that the relative increase in public expenditure was greater in the decade spanning the First World War than in that spanning the Second World War; the first period saw the relative level double, while the second saw it rise by less than one-half.

10. Rubinstein, *Wealth and Inequality*, p. 97.
11. K.M. Langley, 'The Distribution of Capital in Private Hands in 1936–38 and 1946–47 (Part II)', *Bulletin of the Oxford University Institute of Statistics*, 13/2 (1951), p. 46.

Table 17.4 Current expenditure of UK central and local authorities as proportion of GNP, 1910–64[a]

	1 *Expenditure* *(£)*	*2* *GNP*[b] *(£)*	*3* *Expenditure/GNP ratio* *(%)*
1910–13	253	2,544	9.9
1920–24	1,049	5,094	20.6
1930–34	1,058	4,584	23.1
1940–44	5,222	9,399	55.6
1950–54	4,723	15,809	29.9
1960–64	8,618	29,180	29.5

Notes: a Excluded: public corporations, debt interest from local authorities to central government, central government grants to local authorities
b GNP is at current market prices
Source: Feinstein, *National Income*, Table 3 (col. 7), Table 14 (col. 11)

The above formulation may be criticised for including debt interest paid by central government, which, it may be argued, is not necessarily a long-term factor in the operation of government. However, the fact of debt after the major wars of the twentieth century has been very potent in determining economic and other policies. This was especially so after 1918, when deflation increased the real burden of paying for the war. It was not until 1932 that it was possible for the burden of interest payments to be reduced as a result of the decline in long-term interest rates and the debt conversion operation of that year. That this did not result in a lowering of the proportion of national income spent by government may be attributed to the higher cost of payments to unemployed people and their families during the depression of the 1930s. Conversely, after 1945 the persistence of inflation enabled the real burden of interest payments to be reduced in the long run. More basically, the greater financial efficiency with which the Second World War was financed left much more room (both politically and financially) for other forms of spending; in 1930, 33.2 per cent of government expenditure went on debt interest, but in 1956 only 13.7 per cent.[12]

The long-term rise in the proportion of the national income spent by government in the period under review was due to two movements. The first was a spreading of the conviction, among most shades of political opinion, and among a large number of social groups, that certain social arrangements were desirable – chiefly a more generous social provision expressing itself in payments to those with insufficient income for maintenance, and in improved medical and educational provision for the bulk of the population. In this sense, society as a whole was becoming more committed to more

12. Feinstein, *National Income*, Table 14.

generous social provision as the century progressed. The second movement was more short-term, consisting in sharp movements of political opinion, chiefly during and after the two major wars. As a result of these, the level and quality of public intervention in social welfare was suddenly raised. That these movements responded to the more long-term and general commitment to more generous and collectivist social policies is indicated by the fact that there was no retrogression following the alternations between Labour and Conservative administrations.

MORE GENEROUS SOCIAL POLICY

The more generous attitude to social provision was another long-term development in the twentieth century. Much of what this entailed has been described above. Notable advances were made in the provision of protection from the consequences of ill-health, unemployment and old age. In addition, the twentieth century had seen the entirely novel development of state responsibility for the housing of a large section of the population. The war of 1939–45 saw several substantial increments to this edifice. Most of these were foreshadowed in the report on social insurance services prepared by Sir William Beveridge at the request of the government, and published in 1942. Its general aim was to make the insurance system completely comprehensive, covering the entire population, with more generous treatment than hitherto for those who fell outside the scope of insurance. In order to cover all the known causes of the 'giant', Want, provision would be made for unemployment benefit, sickness benefit, disability benefit, workmen's compensation, old age, widows' and orphans' pensions, funeral grants and maternity benefit. While most of these were already available to some extent, the report aimed to make them universally available. This was a postwar matter, but the report was also based on the assumption that a comprehensive health and rehabilitation service (what was to become the National Health Service) was to be provided, and that all families would be paid children's allowances. These last two suggestions were accepted in principle before the end of the war, the latter being enacted in law in June 1945.[13]

The final element of social reform in wartime was the education policy enshrined in the Education Act 1944 ('Butler Act'). Apart from the administrative changes of the reduction in the number of local education authorities, and the conversion of the Board of Education into a full ministry, there were two major innovations. First, the principle of secondary education for all was propounded. This entailed the abolition of fees in secondary schools, which took place on 1 April 1945. Second, the school-leaving age was to be raised to 15. This was achieved in 1947; the aim of raising it to 16 was also stated. The 1944 Act thus took its place along with those of 1870 and 1902 as one of the central

13. *Social Insurance and Allied Services: Report by Sir William Beveridge* (1942), Cmd 6404, paras 17–19, 303–9; M. Bruce, *The Coming of the Welfare State* (4th edn, Batsford 1968), ch. 7.

planks of the educational system in England and Wales.[14] (Thom argues that the levelling effects of the Act were not as great as its proponents hoped.)[15]

THE COSTS OF WAR

The rise in living standards, the redistribution of income and wealth, and the move towards a more generous collective social provision were all achieved in the space of about fifty years, during which two major wars were fought. Their economic cost was an impediment to social amelioration which had to be surmounted. A rough estimate of the relative costs of the wars is that the First World War military spending took about 37 per cent of the GNP of the UK between 1913–14 and 1918–19. The Second World War military spending took about 48 per cent of the UK GNP between 1939–40 and 1945–46. In addition, both wars led to a substantial rise in the National Debt (Table 17.5).[16]

Table 17.5 UK National Debt/GNP ratios, 1913–46

	1 *GNP* *(at current prices)* *(£m)*	*2* *UK public debt* *(£m)*	*3* *Debt/GNP ratio* *(%)*
1913	2,322	625	26.9
1924	3,960	7,628	192.6
1936	4,625	7,784	168.3
1946	8,855	23,636	266.9

Sources: Mitchell, *Statistics*, pp. 602–3; Feinstein, *National Income*, Table 1

Relatively speaking, the rise in the National Debt was greater after 1914 than after 1939. This is reflected in the proportion of the national income going in debt interest; in 1924, after the price level had stabilised, debt payments of central government, at £315 million, amounted to 7.9 per cent of GNP, while in 1950, at £507 million they amounted only to 4.3 per cent of GNP.[17] (Debt payments include payments to foreign governments.) This relatively lesser burden reflects the lower interest rates at which the second war was financed,

14. S.J. Curtis, *History of Education in Great Britain* (7th edn, 1968), ch. XI; G.A.N. Lowndes, *The Silent Social Revolution* (2nd edn, Oxford UP 1969), ch. XV.
15. D. Thom, 'The 1944 Education Act', in H.L. Smith, *British Society and the Second World War* (Manchester UP 1986).
16. E.V. Morgan, *Studies in British Financial Policy, 1914–1925* (Macmillan 1952), Table 7 (military spending for the First World War); Feinstein, *National Income*, Table 1 (col. 11) (GNP at current factor cost); Central Statistical Office, *Annual Abstract of Statistics 1935–1946, no. 84* (military spending in the Second World War); Mitchell, *Statistics*, pp. 602–3 (National Debt).
17. Feinstein, *National Income*, Table 1 (GNP); ibid., Table 12 (debt payments).

as well as the different experiences of deflation and inflation after the two conflicts respectively. But the sums involved were sufficiently large to worry Chancellors of the Exchequer; in the whole period 1914–36, interest payments came to £5,825 million, or something more than the entire GNP of 1936. The large war debt of the twentieth century has been a potent influence on the long-term rise in the incidence of taxation, and thus on economic and social policy in general.

THE ECONOMY IN HISTORICAL PERSPECTIVE

In historical perspective, the growth of the British economy may be illustrated by looking at the growth rates of GDP per man-year, thus taking changes in the population into account (Table 17.6).

Table 17.6 UK real economic growth rates, 1856–1973 (%)

	Growth rate of real GDP per man-year		
	(%)		*(%)*
1856–73	1.3		
1873–99	1.2	1873–1913	0.9
1899–1913	0.5		
1913–24	0.3	1913–37	0.7
1924–37	1.0		
1937–51	1.0	1937–73	1.9
1951–73	2.4		
		1856–1973	1.2

Source: R.C.O. Matthews, C.H. Feinstein and J.C. Odling-Smee, *British Economic Growth, 1856–1973* (Oxford, Clarendon 1982), Tables 2.1, 2.2, 2.5

In the long run, the century since the mid-1850s splits into three phases. Initially, there were two decades or so of comparatively rapid growth, in which the 'mid-Victorian staples' of iron, coal and textiles were all developing rapidly, although perhaps less so than in the classical period of the Industrial Revolution in the first half of the nineteenth century. There then occurred a deceleration at some time in the last quarter of the century, whose exact turning point cannot be located with any precision. Thus the period from 1873 up to the First World War shows a decline in the rate of economic growth, which reaches its nadir in the period 1900–13. The interwar period brought substantial adjustments, which began to take effect at some time before 1937, and the economy entered a period of faster growth, which, with some interruption in the Second World War, continued into the postwar period.[18]

The economic history of the period with which this book is concerned may thus be seen as essentially a watershed. When the period begins, the economy

18. This is the essence of the analysis in Matthews *et al.*, *British Economic Growth*, pp. 26–9.

Table 17.7 OECD countries' economic growth, 1900–87

	Annual growth of real GDP per head			
	1900–13	*1913–50*	*1950–73*	*1973–87*
UK	0.7	0.8	2.5	1.5
OECD average	1.6	1.2	3.8	1.9

Source: A. Maddison, *The World Economy in the 20th Century* (Paris, OECD 1989), Table 3

was already growing more slowly than in the third quarter of the nineteenth century. This deceleration was enhanced by the losses of economic welfare due to the war of 1914–18, and the loss of export markets after 1914. By the later 1930s, although these markets had not been regained, domestic activity had revived, new industries had developed, and the terms of trade had improved substantially. Thus the underlying rate of economic growth, having declined in the late nineteenth century, was rising by the Second World War. More tentatively, it may be suggested that the underlying technological buoyancy of the 1940s played a part in permitting economic growth to continue after 1945.

It may be noted finally that the experience of the UK has not been entirely similar to that of other industrial countries. Here, the main differences are that the UK growth rate was already comparatively low before 1913, and that subsequent growth rates have not fluctuated as much in the UK as in other industrial countries. However, the acceleration of growth after the Second World War has been a common experience (Table 17.7 above).

THE ECONOMY IN INTERNATIONAL PERSPECTIVE

If the story of economic growth was one of retardation followed by acceleration, this was not the case for the position of the UK in the international economy, where it was one of continuous relative decline (Table 17.8 opposite).

That relative decline should be the main theme was not in itself surprising, since industrialisation and thus the exporting of manufactures spread around the world in this period. The rapidity of the relative decline after 1950 has caused much heart-searching. However, it may be noted that this recent decline is to some extent illusory, since between 1914 and 1945 the growth rate of world trade in manufactures was much reduced, but the industrialisation of other countries proceeded relatively unchecked. There was thus the potential for a rapid fall in the British share of world exports when the disruptions of wars had been overcome and trade restrictions reduced. Seen from this point of view, the British share in 1950 was unhistorically and unsustainably high. But even so, by 1973, the British share had fallen below that which could have been predicted by extrapolating pre-1939 trends.[19]

19. Matthews *et al.*, *British Economic Growth*, pp. 435, 466–7, Table 15.3.

Table 17.8 UK share of world exports of manufactures, 1881–85 to 1973

	UK (%)	*USA* (%)	*Germany* (%)	*France* (%)	*Japan* (%)	*Sweden* (%)
1881–85	43	6	16	15	0	1
1899	34	12	17	15	2	1
1913	32	14	20	13	2	2
1929	24	22	15	12	4	2
1937	22	20	16	6	7	3
1950	25	27	7	10	3	3
1964	14	20	20	8	8	3
1973	9	15	22	9	13	3

Note: Figures have been rounded
Source: Matthews *et al.*, *British Economic Growth*, Table 14.5

Table 17.9 UK foreign trade and payments: percentage ratios to GDP

	Balance of trade deficit (%)	*Net income from services* (%)	*Net property income from abroad* (%)	*Balance of payments* (%)
1891–1913	–6.1	4.3	6.8	5.0
1921–29	–5.1	2.2	5.1	2.2
1930–38	–6.0	0.9	4.2	–0.9
1952–64	–0.9	0.2	1.3	0.6
1965–73	–1.0	0.6	1.3	0.9

Source: Matthews *et al.*, *British Economic Growth*, Table 14.7

The financial results of exposure to the international economy were much less favourable at the end of the period than at the beginning (Table 17.9 above).

Before 1913, there was a substantial visible trade deficit, more than offset by the 'invisible' income from services and previous foreign investment ('net property income from abroad'). In the 1930s, exports fell substantially as a proportion of national income. Imports fell less; that this did not lead to greater balance of payments deficits was due to the improvement in the terms of trade. The greatest deterioration in the interwar period was in the invisibles, especially services. The need to make up for an even larger fall in invisibles after 1945, due largely to the reduction in the overseas capital stock, led to the export drive of the late 1940s. The relative success of this policy went some way to counteract the balance of payments weakness of the 1930s. After 1945, there was a much smaller visible trade gap, but it was barely covered by invisible income, leaving a much smaller balance of payments surplus than before 1913. In summary, it may be said that the weaknesses in the external position caused by the changes of 1914–24 were largely unremedied before the Second World War, but have been successfully counteracted since then. The result has been a new international equilibrium for the UK, with a smaller balance of payments surplus, and a lesser importance in the international economy.

CONCLUDING REMARKS

The decades with which this book is concerned were of great historical importance for the British economy and British society. The strongest underlying force was the continuing technological development which made all economic and most social change possible. Thus in the long run the British people could look forward to the higher living standards which follow, in a free society, from the improvement in scientific knowledge. Superimposed on this were the economic and social forces already in being before 1914: chiefly the rise of newer industries and forms of transport and communication, and the tendency to a more egalitarian distribution of social and economic welfare. These forces were substantially encouraged by the two world wars, which had the result both of stimulating technological development and of leading to a more equitable social policy.

However, the effects of wars tend to be sudden. The first war and its consequences were to be responsible for the blight of the former large exporting industries. This haunted the entire interwar period, and wasted human and other economic resources on a very large scale. That economic growth was as buoyant as it turned out to be (even in the 1920s) was a tribute to the enterprise displayed in many of the older, as well as the newer industries, and in the service sectors. The second war led to a much more favourable international environment, and stimulated the newer industries to a much greater degree than in 1914–18. Thus the stage was set for making up the losses of the interwar period.

In the long run, the picture was optimistic; economic growth persisted, not being suppressed for long even during the major depressions, and eventually rising above the rates of the early years of the century. The losses due to war had been mainly external. The greatest of these losses had been the losses of exports during both wars, and the loss of the huge stock of overseas investment which in 1913 had provided the UK with an extra 7 per cent of its national income. This stock, which derived its momentum from the early industrialisation of Britain, had been built up by the exertions of several generations of careful (and lucky) investors.

Lancashire cotton, Clyde and Tyne shipbuilding, and south Wales coalmining had come, gone, and been largely replaced with other industries by the 1960s. But once gone, previous foreign investment did not come back. After 1945, less reliance could be placed on the accumulated wealth of the past; more work had to be done by the contemporary generation. If the UK economy had shown some of the features of the comfortable *rentier* in 1913, it was in 1945 more akin to the younger son of an impoverished upper-class family, sent out into the world to earn a living.

APPENDIX: ECONOMIC GROWTH RATES IN THE UK, 1870–1948

The measurement of the rate of economic growth of a society is clearly critical to its economic and social history. In the case of the UK, the data are available in the work of C.H. Feinstein, *National Income, Expenditure and Output of the United Kingdom, 1855–1965* (Cambridge UP 1972), on which this Appendix is based.

Measurement of change in the rate of economic growth is based on estimates of change in the national income over time. The national income may be defined in various ways. One of the most widely used concepts, which is the one used here, is that of the Gross Domestic Product (GDP), which is the total money value of all final goods and services produced in an economy in a one-year period.

The first step in calculating economic growth rates is to estimate the size of the total national income at current prices over the period in question. However, this may be changed by two things – the size of the population, and the general price level. Neither of these changes indicates that the rate of economic growth has altered.

These confusions are avoided by performing two more operations on the national income estimates: dividing them by the total population, to give an estimate of current national income per head, and converting the estimates of national income to some constant price standard. What remains is an estimate of *real national income per head* over the period in question. This most closely depicts the changes in the rate of economic growth of a society.

This procedure has been followed in deriving the estimates below of UK GDP per head at 1900 prices. The levels of GDP per head at the decadal years are shown in Table A.1 overleaf. This series works out at an average rate of growth over seventy-five years (1870–1945) of 1.25 per cent per year.

Presentation of such data in tabular form encounters the problem of periodisation, that is, the problem of selecting appropriate years between which to make comparisons. The main problem is that the level of economic activity alters, sometimes markedly, from year to year, because of the working of the trade cycle, and because there may be large and erratic booms and slumps, whether linked to the trade cycle or not. Thus one could not (e.g.) use the decadal years in Table A.1 with any confidence to indicate changes in rates of

Table A.1 Levels of UK real GDP per head (decadal years)

	£		£
1870	35.06	1920	46.54
1880	38.62	1930	52.48
1890	40.84	1940	70.04
1900	46.99	1945	68.00
1910	48.56		

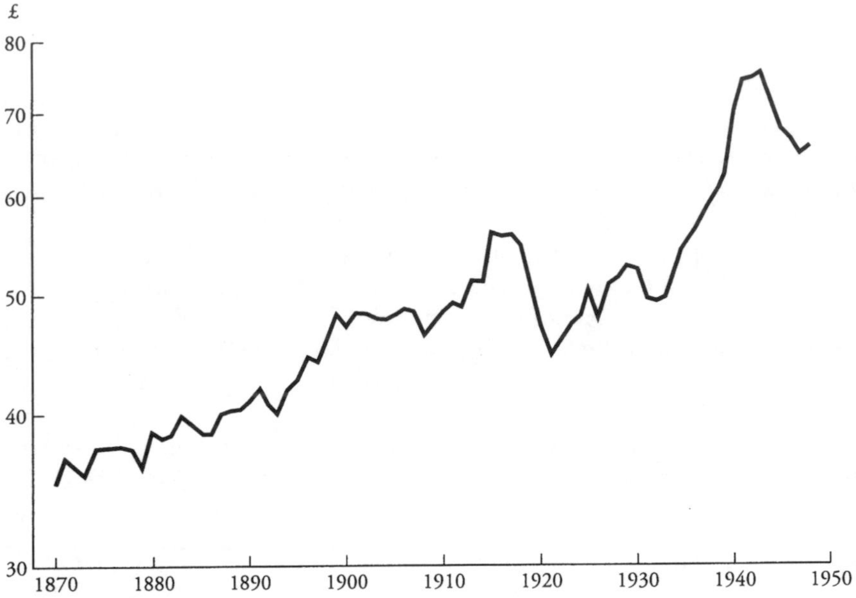

Figure A.1 UK Gross Domestic product per head at constant (1900) prices

economic growth in these sub-periods. These problems are especially acute for the years 1918–39, which not only experienced two major slumps, but also were a period in which a high proportion of labour and capital was unemployed or underemployed, so that it is not comparable with the period before 1914, when labour and capital were more fully utilised.

These problems may be avoided by presenting the economic growth series in visual form. The graph (Figure A.1) is that of GDP per head at 1900 prices. The use of a logarithmic scale on the vertical axis means that, at any point on the graph, lines of equal slope represent equal rates of change. Thus if the slope of the line changes, one can be sure that the rate of growth has changed.

This graphical presentation suggests certain conclusions:

1 Economic growth from 1870 to the late 1890s was faily rapid and steady.
2 The rate of economic growth was near zero in the first decade of the

twentieth century, most of the economic growth of 1900–13 occurring in the years 1910–13.

3 The growth of output per head was particularly rapid in both world wars, although it fell subsequently.
4 The interwar period was marked by unprecedented economic depressions, in 1919–20 and 1929–32.
5 Although the recovery of the 1930s was rapid, it was not much more rapid than that of 1920–25, nor of the upward phase of most pre-1913 trade cycles.
6 In spite of the sharp fluctuations of 1919–39, economic growth in the interwar years was more rapid than in the first decade of the century.

The graph (Figure A.1) is based on the data shown in Table A.2.

Table A.2 UK GDP and GDP per head at 1900 prices

1870–1913	*GDP* (*£m*)	*Total population* (*'000*)	*GDP per head of total population* (*£*)
1870	1,096	31,257	35.06
1871	1,164	31,556	36.88
1872	1,155	31,874	36.23
1873	1,150	32,177	35.74
1874	1,217	32,501	37.44
1875	1,232	32,839	37.52
1876	1,246	33,200	37.53
1877	1,259	33,576	37.49
1878	1,265	33,932	37.28
1879	1,239	34,304	36.12
1880	1,337	34,623	38.62
1881	1,334	34,935	38.18
1882	1,354	35,206	38.46
1883	1,413	35,450	39.85
1884	1,399	35,724	39.16
1885	1,390	36,015	38.59
1886	1,399	36,313	38.53
1887	1,463	36,598	39.97
1888	1,486	36,881	40.29
1889	1,514	37,178	40.72
1890	1,531	37,485	40.84
1891	1,587	37,802	41.98
1892	1,557	38,134	40.83
1893	1,547	38,490	40.19
1894	1,630	38,859	41.95
1895	1,678	39,221	42.78

Table A.2 Cont'd

1870–1913

	GDP (*£m*)	*Total population* (*'000*)	*GDP per head of total population* (*£*)
1896	1,757	39,599	44.37
1897	1,761	39,987	44.04
1898	1,862	40,381	46.11
1899	1,965	40,773	48.19
1900	1,934	41,155	46.99
1901	2,010	41,538	48.39
1902	2,018	41,893	48.17
1903	2,018	42,246	47.77
1904	2,031	42,611	47.66
1905	2,065	42,981	48.04
1906	2,111	43,361	48.68
1907	2,115	43,737	48.36
1908	2,041	44,124	46.26
1909	2,108	44,520	47.35
1910	2,181	44,916	48.56
1911	2,232	45,268	49.31
1912	2,225	45,436	48.97
1913	2,341	45,649	51.28

1913–48

	GDP (*£m*)	*Total population* (*'000*)	*GDP per head of total population* (*£*)
1913	2,341	45,649	51.28
1914	2,359	46,049	51.23
1915	2,596	46,340	56.02
1916	2,592	46,514	55.72
1917	2,605	46,614	55.88
1918	2,559	46,575	54.94
1919	2,335	46,534	50.18
1920	2,179	46,821	46.54
1921	1,967	44,072	44.63
1922	2,036	44,372	45.88
1923	2,098	44,596	47.04
1924	2,161	44,915	48.11
1925	2,269	45,059	50.35
1926	2,164	45,232	47.84
1927	2,314	45,389	50.98

Table A.2 Cont'd

1913–48	*GDP* *(£m)*	*Total population ('000)*	*GDP per head of total population (£)*
1928	2,354	45,578	51.65
1929	2,410	45,672	52.77
1930	2,407	45,866	52.48
1931	2,284	46,074	49.57
1932	2,291	46,335	49.44
1933	2,317	46,520	49.81
1934	2,474	46,666	53.01
1935	2,566	46,868	54.75
1936	2,646	47,081	56.20
1937	2,759	47,289	58.34
1938	2,841	47,494	59.82
1939	2,952	47,761	61.81
1940	3,378	48,226	70.04
1941	3,582	48,216	74.29
1942	3,617	48,400	74.73
1943	3,684	48,789	75.51
1944	3,517	49,016	71.75
1945	3,300	49,182	68.00
1946	3,280	49,217	66.64
1947	3,201	49,519	64.64
1948	3,283	50,014	65.64

Notes: Southern Ireland is included up to and including 1920

For 1915–20 and 1939–48, the estimates of total population include the Armed Forces serving overseas. For all other years, they are of the total population actually in the UK.

GDP: 1870–1913 at 1900 prices; 1913–48 in original table at 1938 prices; here linked to the 1870–1913 series by multiplying by 2,341, and dividing by 4,591, in accordance with the different figures for 1913 GDP given in Feinstein, Table 5, col. 8

Source: Feinstein, *National Income*, Table 5: Gross Domestic Product, by category of expenditure, at constant (market) prices, 1870–1965

Table 55: Mid-year home population of Great Britain and Ireland, 1855–1965

A GUIDE TO FURTHER READING

The political history of these years is presented with masterly aplomb by the late A.J.P. Taylor, in his *English History, 1914–45* (Oxford, Clarendon 1965). An earlier history of the interwar period, C.L. Mowat's *Britain between the Wars, 1918–1940* (Methuen 1955) is a penetrating and comprehensive survey of British life; the treatment of social and economic history is excellent, and it is still worth reading.

On more specifically economic and social history, two notable and substantial recent contributions repay fuller exploration. The second edition of R. Floud and D. McCloskey, *The Economic History of Britain since 1700* (Cambridge UP 1994, 3 vols, 1700–1860, 1860–1939, 1939–1992) has the virtues of its predecessor, in that it attempts to incorporate the recent findings of 'quantitative' economic history. It has also expanded to give greater coverage of the twentieth century, and particularly to social history since 1900. The other major work is already referred to in this text: *The Cambridge Social History of Britain, 1750–1950*, edited by F.M.L. Thompson (Cambridge UP 1990, 3 vols): vol. 1 Regions and communities; vol. 2 People and their environment; vol. 3 Social agencies and institutions). A review of *CSH* by G. Stedman Jones, *EcHR* XLIV, 4 (1991), places it in the wider context of the recent development of social history. Although weighted to the pre-1900 period, most of the *CSH* essays have something of relevance to say about the twentieth century. The editor's essay on 'Town and Country' in vol. 1 is superb. A particular virtue of the collection is the attention given to Wales and Scotland (although not to Northern Ireland).

Both of these collective works have extensive and up-to-date bibliographies, which form the essential starting points for further reading and research.

The best and most substantial single-volume economic/social histories are still S. Pollard, *The Development of the British Economy 1914–1990* (Edward Arnold 1992), the fourth edition of a book first published in 1962, and the older S. Glynn and J. Oxborrow, *Interwar Britain: a social and economic history* (Allen & Unwin 1977). The best single-volume social history is J. Stevenson, *British Society, 1914–45* (Penguin 1984). To these may be added P. Johnson (ed.), *20th-Century Britain: economic, social and cultural change*

(Longman 1994). Mention may also be made of the series of excellent studies published by Macmillan, in association with the Economic History Society, *Studies in Economic and Social History (SESH)*. These brief volumes aim to summarise recent research on a wide variety of topics; they are of high quality, and contain excellent bibliographies.

The more purely economic aspects of British history may be approached in R.C.O. Matthews, C.H. Feinstein and J.C. Odling-Smee, *British Economic Growth 1856–1973* (Oxford, Clarendon 1982). A more succinct treatment is in the issue of the *Oxford Review of Economic Policy* devoted to 'Long-Run Economic Performance in the UK' (4, 1, spring 1988). The post-1945 period is best approached in N. Crafts and N. Woodward (eds), *The British Economy since 1945* (Oxford, Clarendon 1991), which analyses developments up to the late 1980s. The wider view of the British economy in the world is provided as part of J. Foreman-Peck, *A History of the World Economy: international economic relations since 1850* (2nd edn, Harvester Wheatsheaf 1994), and of S. Broadberry and N. Crafts (eds), *Britain in the International Economy, 1870–1939* (Cambridge UP 1992).

The position of the entrepreneur, in the context of British long-term relative economic decline, continues to fascinate. An early assessment was by D.H. Aldcroft, 'The Entrepreneur and the British Economy, 1870–1914', *EcHR* XVII (1964–65). The most notable of the optimistic school is D.N. McCloskey, in (e.g.) 'Did Victorian Britain Fail?', *EcHR* XXIII (1970), and his *Enterprise and Trade in Victorian Britain* (1981). The pessimists are such as N.F.R. Crafts, 'Victorian Britain did Fail', *EcHR* XXXII (1979). The main proponent of the 'cultural failure' thesis is M.J. Wiener, *English Culture and the Decline of the Industrial Spirit, 1850–1980* (Cambridge UP 1981). The debate so far is summarised and assessed in masterly fashion in S. Pollard, *Britain's Prime and Britain's Decline: the British economy 1870–1914* (Edward Arnold 1989), which contains an extensive bibliography. The most recent contributions are by W.D. Rubinstein, *Capitalism, Culture and Decline in Britain 1750–1990* (Routledge 1993) and M. Dintenfass, *The Decline of Industrial Britain 1870–1980* (Routledge 1992).

Some views on how economic policy evolved (or failed to do so) are in R.W.D. Boyce, *British Capitalism at the Crossroads, 1919–1932* (Cambridge UP 1987), P. Clarke, *The Keynesian Revolution in the Making* (Oxford, Clarendon 1990) and A. Cairncross and N. Watts, *The Economic Section, 1939–61: a study in economic advising* (Routledge 1989). Of the major economists, only J.M. Keynes has attracted much biographical attention; to the impressive, but rather hagiographical book by Roy Harrod, *The Life of John Maynard Keynes* (Macmillan 1951) may now be added Donald Moggridge's definitive study, *Maynard Keynes: an economist's biography* (Routledge 1992). The best treatment of the gold standard from the standpoint of economic history is in B. Eichengreen (ed.), *The Gold Standard in Theory and History* (Methuen 1985), especially in the very thorough editorial introduction, and his more recent book, *Golden Fetters: the gold standard and the great depression,*

1919–1939 (Oxford UP 1992). There is a good brief formulation of how the gold standard worked in D. Winch, *Economics and Policy: a historical study* (Hodder & Stoughton 1969), pp. 83–4.

The most up-to-date statistical source is B.R. Mitchell, *British Historical Statistics* (Cambridge UP 1988), an enormous work of some 900 pages, with data from the fourteenth century to the 1980s. It is, however, fairly user-friendly, and repays browsing as well as more directed research. It is an essential source of evidence, although, as in all statistical compilations, the reliability of the figures cannot be assessed except by recourse to the original sources.

R. Pope (ed.), *Atlas of British Social and Economic History since c.1700* (Routledge 1989) provides a visual illustration of many of the themes of the present book.

Technological and scientific changes are most easily found in C. Chant, *Science, Technology and Everyday Life 1870–1950* (Routledge/Open University 1989), a masterly exposition, with a substantial bibliography. A wider world-view and a longer historical perspective are provided in Donald Cardwell, *The Fontana History of Technology* (Fontana 1994).

The most recent discussion to date of the causes of the world depression in 1929 is in B. Eichengreen, 'The Origins and Nature of the Great Slump Revisited', *EcHR* XLV (1992), bringing the discussion up to date since the publication of P. Fearon, *The Origins and Nature of the Great Slump* (Macmillan 1979), and in Eichengreen's book, *Golden Fetters* (referred to above). The most satisfactory extensive survey of the 1930s is still that of C.P. Kindleberger, *The World in Depression, 1929–1939* (rev. edn, Pelican 1987). All these publications contain extensive bibliographies.

The financial crises of 1931 have been much discussed. An early treatment is R. Bassett's *Nineteen Thirty One* (Macmillan 1958). C.P. Kindleberger has a chapter on them in his *The World in Depression*, putting them in the international context. The most useful recent contributions are A. Cairncross and B. Eichengreen, *Sterling in Decline: the devaluations of 1931, 1949 and 1967* (Oxford, Blackwell 1983) and D.B. Kunz, *The Battle for Britain's Gold Standard in 1931* (Beckenham, Croom Helm 1987).

Early examples of the reappraisal of British economic development in the interwar period (and especially the 1930s) were by R.S. Sayers, 'The Springs of Technical Progress in Britain, 1919–1939', *Economic Journal* 60 (1951) and H.W. Richardson, 'The New Industries between the Wars', *Oxford Economic Papers* 13 (1961). Lengthier treatments are in H.W. Richardson, *Economic Recovery in Britain, 1932–39* (Weidenfeld & Nicolson 1967) and D.H. Aldcroft, *The Inter-War Economy: Britain, 1919–1939* (Batsford 1970). The most recent general treatment (by an economist) is S.N. Broadberry, *The British Economy between the Wars: a macroeconomic survey* (Oxford, Blackwell 1986), which is less inclined to be enthusiastic about the achievements of the 1930s. The historiographical volte-face is described in P.K. O'Brien, 'Britain's Economy between the Wars: a survey of a counter-revolution in economic history', *Past and Present* 115 (1987).

General strategic/military histories of the Second World War abound. Two of the best recent books are R.A.C. Parker, *Struggle for Survival: the history of the Second World War* (Oxford UP 1989) and P. Calvocoressi, G. Wint and J. Pritchard, *Total War: the causes and courses of the Second World War* (2nd edn, Penguin 1989, 2 vols).

The two world wars continue to fascinate historians. Paul Fussell's *Wartime* (Oxford UP 1989) explores the personal experience of US and UK participants in 1939–45. The Mass-Observation archive at Sussex University has yielded some notable personal histories, notably in D. Sheridan, *Wartime Women: an anthology of women's wartime writing for Mass-Observation, 1937–45* (Heinemann 1990). Some of the same period is covered in the product of another social survey archive, R.J. Wybrow, *Britain Speaks Out, 1937–87: a social history as seen through the Gallup data* (Macmillan 1989). D. Thoms has written usefully on the industrial midlands in *War, Industry and Society: the midlands 1939–1945* (Routledge 1989). The recruiting of mass armies in 1914–16 is explored in P. Simkins, *Kitchener's Army: the raising of the new armies, 1914–1916* (Manchester UP 1988). Corelli Barnett has produced a general (and controversial) treatment of the second war, in *The Audit of War: the illusion and reality of Britain as a great nation* (Macmillan 1986). A more balanced work, which is the nearest thing to a general global history of the first war, is T. Wilson, *The Myriad Faces of War* (Oxford, Blackwell 1986).

There are many local accounts of air raids, listed in the books by Calder and Longmate. A local account, which gives a detailed account of a Baedeker raid, is that of J. Banger, *Norwich at War* (Norwich, Wensum 1974). John Strachey, *Post D: some experiences of an air raid warden* (Gollancz 1941), writes vividly of the effects of the raids. Tom Harrisson, *Living through the Blitz* (Collins 1976), provides a comprehensive national survey of the bombing, based on contemporary Mass-Observation reports. Angus Calder has supplied a corrective to some of the more cosy historical generalisations in *The Myth of the Blitz* (Pimlico 1991).

In spite of much writing on Scottish and Welsh economic and social history, it has yet to be gathered into a single satisfactory volume covering this period. Meanwhile, some approaches are provided in C. Harvie, *No Gods and Precious Few Heroes: Scotland, 1914–1980* (2nd edn, University of Edinburgh Press 1993), which has a usefully up-to-date bibliography, and C. Baber and L.J. Williams (eds), *Modern South Wales: essays in economic history* (Cardiff, University of Wales Press 1986).

The expansion of women's history has been the most striking historiographic development of recent decades. However, much of this has been concerned primarily with social or cultural attitudes towards women. This concern is rather peripheral to the economic and social developments which form the central themes of this book. There is as yet no satisfactory treatment of the *economic* role of women in twentieth-century Britain. The nearest approach to this is E. Roberts, *Women's Work, 1840–1940* (Macmillan *SESH* 1988). To this may be added the same author's *A Woman's Place: an oral history of working-class women, 1890–1940* (1984) and J. Lewis, *Labour and Love: women's experience of home and family, 1850–1940* (1986). M. Pugh, *Women and the*

Women's Movement in Britain, 1914–1959 (Macmillan 1992) provides the wider political background to the movement for female emancipation. There is no comprehensive history of the largest female occupation in the first half of the twentieth century, domestic service. There are some individual histories in J. Burnett, *Useful Toil* (Pelican 1977) and M. Glucksman, *Women Assemble* (Routledge 1990).

Adequate economic and social histories of most articles of popular consumption have yet to be written. A notable recent contribution is J.K. Walton, *Fish and Chips and the British Working Class* (Leicester UP 1992).

The form of, and distinctions between, the usual English (or Welsh) and Scottish housing types may be obtained from S. Muthesius, *The English Terraced House* (New Haven, CT and London, Yale UP 1982) and F. Worsdall, *The Tenement: a way of life* (Chambers 1979).

The social and occupational structure of Britain may be examined in G. Routh, *Occupations of the People of Great Britain, 1801–1981* (Macmillan 1987), which uses the population censuses as its basis. D. Cannadine, *The Decline and Fall of the British Aristocracy* (New Haven, CT, Yale UP 1990), takes a pessimistic view towards the ability of the top social classes to survive the twentieth century; this view is countered by F.M.L. Thompson, notably in his series of Presidential Addresses to the Royal Historical Society, reprinted in the *Transactions of the Royal Historical Society* for 1990–93. At the other end of the social spectrum, J. Benson, *The Working Class in Britain, 1859–1939* (Longman 1989) provides an excellent summary. P. Johnson, *Saving and Spending: the working-class economy in Britain, 1870–1939* (Oxford UP 1985) provides some answers as to how the working class survived. J. Burnett, *The Autobiography of the Working Class* (Brighton, Harvester 1984–89, 3 vols) provides some more. The scope of the recent work of R. Floud, K. Wachter and A. Gregory, *Height, Health and History: nutritional status in the United Kingdom, 1750–1980* (Cambridge UP 1990) is suggested in the title, and opens up an interesting line of research.

Recent works on education are few. A survey of a neglected area is G. Avery, *The Best Type of Girls: a history of girls' independent schools* (André Deutsch 1991). A.L. Rowse, *All Souls in my Time* (Duckworth 1993), is an affectionate memoir by a long-time don. The most important new addition is M. Sanderson, *The Missing Stratum: technical school education in England, 1900–1990s* (Athlone 1994), which fills a notable hole in the present work. There is a new history of the LSE by a former director of the school, Sir Ralf Dahrendorf, *The London School of Economics* (Oxford UP 1994).

Finally, there is a clutch of recent industrial histories, adding to the growing armoury of business histories deployed by the modern historian; R. Church, *The Rise and Decline of the British Motor Industry* (Macmillan *SESH* 1994) and T. Barker and D. Gerhold, *The Rise and Rise of Road Transport, 1700–1990* (Macmillan *SESH* 1993). G. Jones, *British Multinational Banking, 1830–1990* (Oxford UP 1993) is a useful addition to a hitherto-neglected area of history. E. Sigsworth, *Montague Burton: the tailor of taste* (Manchester UP 1990) studies a high street success story of the interwar period. R. Davenport-Hines and J. Slinn, *Glaxo: a history to 1962* (Cambridge UP 1992), J. Bamberg, *The History of the British Petroleum Company, vol. 2, 1928–54* (Cambridge UP 1994), P. Chalmin, *The Making of a Sugar Giant: Tate & Lyle, 1859–1989* (Churchill, Ont., Harwood Academic 1990) and T. Gourvish and R. Wilson, *The British Brewing Industry, 1830–1980* (Cambridge UP 1994) are also welcome additions to the literature.

BIBLIOGRAPHY

The great majority of these works are already referred to in the text of the book. Some are not, but are included in this bibliography because they provided useful background reading or fruitful lines of enquiry.

The journals referred to are usually obtainable in college and university libraries. If not, the inter-library loan service run by local libraries may prove helpful in supplying journal copies or off-prints of articles.

Since most academic monographs go out of print after about five years, most of the books listed below can be found only in libraries. Not all of them are obtainable, even in university libraries. The only certain places are the national copyright libraries: the British Library (London), Bodleian Library (Oxford), Cambridge University Library, National Library of Wales (Aberystwyth), National Library of Scotland (Edinburgh) and Trinity College (Dublin), which acquire copies of most books on publication. Otherwise, recourse may be had to second-hand bookshops (notably those at Hay-on-Wye) or to the various dealers in second-hand books who conduct their business by post. The best way to find the postal dealers currently active in the relevant subject is probably to enquire at the nearest antiquarian or good second-hand bookshop, or to ask the librarians at the local college, university or town library.

Place of publication is London unless otherwise stated
n.d. = no publication date given
UP = University Press

Abbreviations of journals/collected works:

CSH	*Cambridge Social History of Britain*
EcHR	*Economic History Review*
EJ	*Economic Journal*
ExEH	*Explorations in Economic History*
HJ	*Historical Journal*
HSWW	*History of the Second World War (Civil Series)*
HWJ	*History Workshop Journal*
JCH	*Journal of Contemporary History*
JEEH	*Journal of European Economic History*

JPE	*Journal of Political Economy*
JRSS	*Journal of the Royal Statistical Society*
ManS	*Manchester School of Economic and Social Studies*
NIER	*National Institute Economic Review*
OEP	*Oxford Economic Papers*
OREP	*Oxford Review of Economic Policy*
PS	*Population Studies*
SEH/SESH	*Studies in Economic/Social History*
SJPE	*Scottish Journal of Political Economy*

1 GENERAL ECONOMIC AND SOCIAL HISTORY

Aldcroft, D.H., *The Interwar Economy: Britain, 1919–1939* (Batsford 1970)

Aldcroft, D.H., *The British Economy between the Wars* (Deddington, Phillip Allan 1983)

Aldcroft, D.H., *The British Economy, vol. 1, The Years of Turmoil 1920–1951* (Brighton, Harvester Wheatsheaf 1986)

Aldcroft, D.H., 'The Entrepreneur and the British Economy, 1870–1914', *EcHR* XVII (1964–65)

Alford, B.W.E., *Depression and Recovery? British economic growth 1918–1939* (Macmillan *SEH* 1972)

Beenstock, M., and Warburton, P. 'Wages and Unemployment in Interwar Britain', *ExEH* 23 (1986)

Branson, M., and Heinemann, M., *Britain in the Nineteen Thirties* (Weidenfeld & Nicolson 1971)

British Association, *Britain in Depression* (Pitman 1935)

British Association, *Britain in Recovery* (Pitman 1938)

Broadberry, S., *The British Economy between the Wars: a macroeconomic survey* (Oxford, Blackwell 1986)

Broadberry, S., 'The Emergence of Mass Unemployment: explaining macroeconomic trends in Britain during the interwar period', *EcHR* XLIII (1990)

Broadberry, S., 'The Impact of the World Wars on the Long-Run Performance of the British Economy', *OREP* 4, 1 (1988)

Capie, F., *Depression and Protectionism: Britain between the wars* (1983)

Dintenfass, M., *The Decline of Industrial Britain, 1870–1980* (Routledge 1992)

Dowie, J.A., 'Growth in the Inter-War Period: some more arithmetic', *EcHR* XXI (1968)

Dowie, J.A., '1919–20 is in Need of Attention', *EcHR* XXVIII (1975)

Eichengreen, B., 'The Origins and Nature of the Great Slump Revisited', *EcHR* XLV (1992)

Eichengreen, B., *Golden Fetters: the gold standard and the great depression* (New York, Oxford UP 1992)

Feinstein, C.H., 'Economic Growth since 1870: Britain's performance in international perspective', *OREP* 4, 1 (1988)

Floud, R., and McCloskey, D., *The Economic History of Britain since 1700, vol. 2, 1860 to the 1970s* (Cambridge UP 1981)

Glynn, S., and Oxborrow, J., *Interwar Britain: a social and economic history* (Allen & Unwin 1977)

Hatton, T.J., 'Institutional Change and Wage Rigidity in the UK, 1880–1985', *OREP* 4, 1 (1988)

Howkins, A., *Reshaping Rural England: a social history, 1850–1925* (HarperCollins, 1991)

Kindleberger, C.P., *The World in Depression, 1929–1939* (rev. edn, Pelican 1987)

Kitson, M., and Solomou, S., *Protectionism and Economic Revival: the British interwar economy* (Cambridge UP 1990)

Liberal Industrial Inquiry, *Britain's Industrial Future, being the Report of the Liberal Industrial Inquiry of 1928* (Ernest Benn 1928; 1977)

Lomax, K.S., 'Production and Productivity Movements in the U.K. since 1900', *JRSS* A122 (1959)

McCloskey, D.N., 'Did Victorian Britain Fail?' *EcHR* XXIII (1970)

Maddison, A., *The World Economy in the 20th Century* (Paris, OECD 1989)

Matthews, K.G.P., *The Interwar Economy: an equilibrium analysis* (Edward Elgar 1986)

Matthews, R.C.O., Feinstein, C.H., and Odling-Smee, J.C., *British Economic Growth 1856–1973* (Oxford, Clarendon 1982)

Mowat, C.L., *Britain between the Wars 1918–40* (Methuen 1955)

O'Brien, P.K., 'Britain's Economy between the Wars: a survey of a counter-revolution in economic history', *Past and Present* 115 (1987)

Oxford Review of Economic Policy, 'Long-run Economic Performance in the UK', 4, 1 (Spring 1988: entire issue)

Pigou, A.C., *Aspects of British Economic History, 1918–1925* (Macmillan 1947)

Pollard, S., *The Development of the British Economy 1914–1990* (4th edn, Edward Arnold 1992)

Pollard, S., *Britain's Prime and Britain's Decline: the British economy 1870–1914* (Edward Arnold 1989)

Richardson, H.W., *Economic Recovery in Britain, 1932–39* (Weidenfeld & Nicolson 1967)

Robbins, L., *The Great Depression* (Macmillan 1934)

Royle, Edward, *Modern Britain: a social history, 1750–1985* (Edward Arnold 1987)

Rubinstein, W.D., *Capitalism, Culture and Decline in Britain, 1750–1990* (Routledge 1993)

Sayers, R.S., 'The Springs of Technical Progress', *EJ* 60 (1950)

Stevenson, J., *British Society, 1914–45* (Pelican Social History of Britain, Penguin 1984)

Tawney, R.H., 'The Abolition of Economic Controls, 1918–1921', *EcHR* XIII (1943)

Thompson, F.M.L. (ed.), *The Cambridge Social History of Britain* (Cambridge UP 1990, 3 vols)

Wiener, M.J., *English Culture and the Decline of the Industrial Spirit* (Cambridge UP 1981)

Worswick, G.D.N., 'The Sources of Recovery in UK in the 1930s', *NIER* 110 (1984)

2 STATISTICAL SOURCES

Agriculture, Ministry of, *A Century of Agricultural Statistics: Great Britain, 1866–1966* (HMSO 1968)

Board of Trade, *Statistical Abstract of the United Kingdom, 1905 to 1919* (1921)

Board of Trade, *Statistical Abstract for the United Kingdom, 1911 to 1925* (1927), Cmd 2849

Capie, F., and Collins, M., *The Inter-War British Economy: a statistical abstract* (Manchester UP 1983)

Central Statistical Office, *Annual Abstract of Statistics, no. 84 (1935–1946)* (HMSO 1948)

Chapman, A.L., and Knight, R., *Wages and Salaries in the United Kingdom 1920–1938* (Cambridge UP 1953)

Department of Employment and Productivity, *British Labour Statistics, Historical Abstract 1886–1968* (HMSO 1971)

Feinstein, C.H., *National Income, Expenditure and Output of the United Kingdom 1855–1965* (Cambridge UP 1972)

Halsey, A.H., *Trends in British Society since 1900: a guide to the changing social structure of Britain* (Macmillan 1972)

Labour, Ministry of, *Twenty-Second Abstract of Labour Statistics (1922–1936)* (1937), Cmd 5556

London and Cambridge Economic Service, *Key Statistics of the British Economy, 1900–1964* (Times Publishing Co. 1965)

Mitchell, B.R., and Deane, P., *Abstract of British Historical Statistics* (Cambridge UP 1971)

Mitchell, B.R., and Jones, H.G., *Second Abstract of British Historical Statistics* (Cambridge UP 1971)

Mitchell, B.R., *British Historical Statistics* (Cambridge UP 1988)

Stone, R., *The Measurement of Consumers' Behaviour in the United Kingdom 1920–1938*, vol. I (Cambridge UP 1954)

Stone, R., and Rowe, D.A., *The Measurement of Consumers' Expenditure and Behaviour in the United Kingdom, 1920–1938*, vol. II (Cambridge UP 1966)

Todd, G.F., *Statistics of Smoking in the United Kingdom* (4th edn, Tobacco Research Council 1966)

3 CONTEMPORARY SOCIAL SURVEYS

Bunn, M., 'Mass Observation: a comment on people in production', *ManS* XIII, 1 (1943)

Carr-Saunders, A.M., and Caradog Jones, D., *A Survey of the Social Structure of England and Wales as Illustrated by Statistics* (Oxford UP 1927)

Carr-Saunders, A.M., and Jones, D.C., *A Survey of the Social Structure of England and Wales as Illustrated by Statistics* (Oxford, Clarendon 1937)

Carr-Saunders, A.M., Jones, D.C., and Moser, C.A., *A Survey of Social Conditions in England and Wales as Illustrated by Statistics* (Oxford, Clarendon 1958)

Ford, P., *Work and Wealth in a Modern Port: an economic survey of Southampton* (Allen & Unwin 1934)

Jones, D.C. (ed.), *The Social Survey of Merseyside* (Liverpool UP 1934, 3 vols)

Marsh, D.C., *The Changing Social Structure of England and Wales 1871–1961* (Routledge & Kegan Paul 1958)

Rowntree, B.S., *Poverty: a study of town life* (Macmillan 1901)

Rowntree, B.S., *Poverty and Progress: a second social survey of York* (Longmans, Green 1941)

Smith, (Sir) H.L., (ed.), *The New Survey of London Life and Labour* (P.S. King 1930–35, 9 vols)

4 REGIONAL ECONOMIC DEVELOPMENT

Baber, C., and Williams, L.J. (eds), *Modern South Wales: essays in economic history* (Cardiff, University of Wales Press 1986)

Flinn, M., 'Exports and the Scottish Economy in the Depression of the 1930s', in W.H. Chaloner and B.M. Ratcliffe (eds), *Trade and Transport: essays in economic history in honour of T.S. Willan* (Manchester UP 1977)

Harvie, C., *No Gods and Precious Few Heroes: Scotland since 1914* (new edn, Edinburgh UP 1993)

Law, C.M., *British Regional Development since World War I* (Newton Abbot, David & Charles 1980)

Lee, C.H., *British Regional Employment Statistics 1841–1971* (Cambridge UP 1979)

Lee, C.H., *Regional Economic Growth in the United Kingdom since the 1880s* (Maidenhead, McGraw-Hill 1971)

Lenman, Bruce, *An Economic History of Modern Scotland, 1660–1976* (Batsford 1977)

Levitt, Ian, *Poverty and Welfare in Scotland, 1890–1948* (Edinburgh UP 1988)

5 THE FIRST WORLD WAR

Aldcroft, D.H., 'Control of the Liquor Trade in Great Britain, 1914–21', in W.H. Chaloner and B.M. Ratcliffe (eds), *Trade and Transport* (Manchester UP 1977)

Beveridge, W.H., *British Food Control* (Oxford UP 1928)

Board of Trade, *Report on the State of Employment in all Occupations in the United Kingdom* (unpublished 1914–20)

Bowley, A.L., *Prices and Wages in the United Kingdom, 1914–1920* (Oxford, Clarendon 1921)

Braybon, G., *Women Workers in the First World War* (Routledge 1989)

Bryder, L., 'The First World War: healthy or hungry?' *HWJ* (1987)

Dewey, P.E., *British Agriculture in the First World War* (Routledge 1989)

Dewey, P.E., 'Military Recruiting and the British Labour Force during the First World War', *HJ* 27 (1984)
Kirkaldy, A.W., *Industry and Finance* (2nd edn, 1920)
Middleton, T.H., *Food Production in War* (Oxford, Clarendon 1923)
Ministry of Munitions, *History of the Ministry of Munitions* (n.d., 12 vols)
Morgan, E.V., *Studies in British Financial Policy 1914–25* (Macmillan 1952)
Salter, J.A. *Allied Shipping Control* (Oxford, Clarendon 1921)
Simkins, P., *Kitchener's Army: the raising of the new armies, 1914–1916* (Manchester UP 1988)
Turner, J. (ed.), *Britain and the First World War* (Unwin Hyman 1988)
Turner, J., *British Politics and the Great War* (New Haven, CT, Yale UP 1991).
Wall, R., and Winter, J., *The Upheaval of War: family, work and welfare in Europe, 1914–1918* (Cambridge UP 1988)
War Office, *Statistics of the Military Effort of the British Empire 1914–1920* (HMSO 1922)
Wilson, T., *The Myriad Faces of War* (Oxford, Blackwell 1986)
Winter, J., *The Great War and the British People* (Macmillan 1985)
Wolfe, H., *Labour Supply and Regulation* (Oxford, Clarendon 1923)

6 THE SECOND WORLD WAR

Barnett, Corelli, *The Audit of War: the illusion and reality of Britain as a great nation* (Macmillan 1986)
Behrens, C.B.A., *Merchant Shipping and the Demands of War* (*HSWW* 1955)
Cairncross, A., *Planning in Wartime: aircraft production in Britain, Germany and the USA* (Macmillan 1991)
Calder, A., *The Myth of the Blitz* (Pimlico 1991)
Calder, A., *The People's War* (Panther 1971)
Calvocoressi, P., Wint, G., and Prichard, J., *Total War: the causes and courses of the Second World War* (Penguin 1989, 2 vols)
Central Statistical Office, Statistical Digest of the War (*HSWW* 1951)
Chester, D.N. (ed.), *Lessons of the British War Economy* (Cambridge UP 1951)
Court, W.H.B., *Coal* (*HSWW* 1951)
Crosby, T.L., *The Impact of Civilian Evacuation in the Second World War* (Beckenham, Croom Helm, 1986)
Dover, Harriet, *Home Front Furniture: British utility design, 1941–1951* (Scolar 1991)
Food, Ministry of, *How Britain was Fed in Wartime* (1946)
Food, Ministry of, *The Urban Working-Class Household Diet 1940 to 1949* (1951)
Fussell, Paul, *Wartime* (Oxford 1989)
Hall, H.D., *North American Supply* (*HSWW* 1955)
Hancock, K.J., and Gowing, M., *British War Economy* (*HSWW* 1949)
Hargreaves, E.L., and Gowing, M., *Civil Industry and Trade* (*HSWW* 1952)
Harrison, M., 'Resource Mobilization for World War II: the USA, UK, USSR and Germany 1938–1945', *EcHR* XLI (1988)

Harrison, M., 'A Volume Index of the Total Munitions Output of the United Kingdom, 1939–1944', *EcHR* XLIII (1990)
Harrisson, Tom, *Living through the Blitz* (Collins 1976)
Hornby, W., *Factories and Plant* (*HSWW* 1958)
Hurstfield, J., *The Control of Raw Materials* (*HSWW* 1952)
Ince, (Sir) G., 'The Mobilisation of Manpower in Great Britain for the Second World War', *ManS* XIV, 1 (1946)
Inman, P., *Labour in the Munitions Industries* (*HSWW* 1957)
Isaacs, S. (ed.), *The Cambridge Evacuation Survey* (Methuen 1941)
Johnson, B.S., *The Evacuees* (Gollancz 1969)
Keynes, J.M., *How to Pay for the War* (Macmillan 1940)
Kohan, C.M., *Works and Buildings* (*HSWW* 1952)
Longmate, N., *How We Lived Then: a history of everyday life in the Second World War* (Arrow 1973)
Madge, C., *War-time Pattern of Saving and Spending* (Cambridge UP 1943)
Mass-Observation, *People in Production* (John Murray 1942)
Murray, K.A.H., *Agriculture* (*HSWW* 1955)
O'Brien, T.H., *Civil Defence* (*HSWW* 1955)
Oxford University Institute of Statistics, *Studies in War Economics* (Oxford, Blackwell 1947)
Parker, H.M.D., *Manpower: a study of war-time policy and administration* (*HSWW* 1957)
Parker, R.A.C., *Struggle for Survival: the history of the Second World War* (Oxford UP 1989)
Peden, G.C., *British Rearmament and the Treasury 1932–1939* (Edinburgh, Scottish Academic Press 1979)
Postan, M.M., *British War Production* (*HSWW* 1952)
Robinson, A., 'Munitions Output of the United Kingdom, 1939–1944: a comment', *EcHR* XLV (1992)
Saunders, C.T., 'Manpower Distribution 1939–1945: some international comparisons', *ManS* XIV, 2 (1946) P/C
Savage, C.I., *Inland Transport* (*HSWW* 1957)
Sayers, R.S., *Financial Policy 1939–45* (*HSWW* 1956)
Scott, J.D., and Hughes, R., *The Administration of War Production* (*HSWW* 1955)
Sheridan, D. (ed.), *Wartime Women: an anthology of women's wartime writing for Mass-Observation 1937–45* (Heinemann 1990)
Smith, H.L. (ed.), *War and Social Change: British society in the Second World War* (Manchester UP 1986)
Smithies, E., *The Black Economy in England since 1914* (Dublin, Gill & Macmillan 1984)
Smithies, E., *Crime in Wartime: a social history of crime in World War Two* (Allen & Unwin 1982)
Taylor, P.M. (ed.), *Britain and the Cinema in the Second World War* (Macmillan 1988)
Thoms, David, *War, Industry and Society: the midlands 1939–1945* (Routledge 1989)

Titmuss, R.M., *Problems of Social Policy* (*HSWW* 1950)
Treasury, *Statistical Material Presented During the Washington Negotiations* (1945), Cmd 6707

7 ILLUSTRATIONS

Condell, D., and Liddiard, J. (eds), *Working for Victory? Images of women in the First World War, 1914–18* (Routledge & Kegan Paul 1987)
Donaldson, Frances, Introduction, in *Those were the Days: a photographic album of daily life in Britain 1919–1939* (Dent 1983)
Minns, R., *Bombers and Mash: the domestic front 1939–45* (Virago 1980)
Symons, Julian, *Between the Wars: Britain in photographs* (Batsford 1972)

8 POPULATION

Abrams, M., *The Condition of the British People, 1911–1945* (Gollancz 1945)
Banks, J.A., *Prosperity and Parenthood: a study of family planning among the Victorian middle classes* (1954)
Barker, T., and Drake, M. (eds), *Population and Society in Britain, 1850–1980* (1982)
Campbell, F., 'Birth Control and the Christian Churches', *PS* 14 (1960)
Census of England and Wales 1931: *Preliminary Report* (1931)
Census of England and Wales 1931: *Industry Tables*
Census of England and Wales 1931: *General Report*
Census of England and Wales 1931: *Housing Report* (1935)
Census of England and Wales 1951: *Housing Report* (1956)
Census of Great Britain 1951: *One per cent Sample Tables*
Census of Scotland 1911: *Report*, vol. II
Census of Scotland 1931: vol. III, *Occupations and Industries*
Census of Scotland 1931: *Preliminary Report* (1931)
Census of Scotland 1931: *Report*, vol. II, Housing
Census of Scotland 1951: *Preliminary Report* (1951)
Logan, W.P.D., 'Mortality in England and Wales from 1848 to 1947', *PS* IV (1950–51)
McKeown, T., Record, R.G., and Turner, R.D., 'An Interpretation of the Decline of Mortality in England and Wales during the Twentieth Century', *PS* XXIX (1975)
McLaren, A., *A History of Contraception: from antiquity to the present day* (Blackwell 1990)
Peel, J., 'The Manufacture and Retailing of Contraceptives in England', *PS* XVII (1963–64)
Royal Commission on Population, *Report* (1949), Cmd 7695
Royal Commission on Population, *Papers, vol. I, Report of an Inquiry into Family Limitation and its Influence on Human Fertility in the Past Fifty Years*, by J. Lewis-Faning (HMSO 1949)
Teitelbaum, M.S., *The British Fertility Decline: demographic transition in the crucible of the Industrial Revolution* (Princeton, NJ, Princeton UP 1984)

Tranter, N.L., *Population and Society, 1750–1940: contrasts in population growth* (Longman 1985)

9 WOMEN IN SOCIETY

Anderson, Gregory (ed.), *The White-Blouse Revolution: female office workers since 1870* (Manchester UP 1988)
Braybon, G., *Women Workers in the First World War* (Beckenham, Croom Helm 1981)
Braybon, G., and Summerfield, P., *Out of the Cage: women's experiences in two world wars* (Pandora 1987)
Gittins, D., *Fair Sex: family size and structure, 1900–1939* (Hutchinson 1982)
Glucksmann, M., *Women Assemble: women workers and the new industries in inter-war Britain* (Routledge 1990)
Humphries, S., *A Secret World of Sex* (Sidwick & Jackson 1991)
Martindale, Hilda, *Women Servants of the State 1870–1938: a history of women in the Civil Service* (Allen & Unwin 1938)
Pennington, S., and Westover, B., *A Hidden Workforce: homeworkers in England, 1850–1985* (Macmillan 1989)
Pugh, Martin, *Women and the Women's Movement in Britain 1914–1959* (Macmillan 1992)
Roberts, E. (ed.), *A Woman's Place: an oral history of working-class women, 1890–1940* (1984)
Roberts, E., *Women's Work 1840–1940* (Macmillan *SESH* 1988)
Summerfield, P., *Women Workers in the Second World War: production and patriarchy in conflict* (Beckenham, Croom Helm 1984)
Taylor, P., 'Daughters and Mothers – Maids and Mistresses: domestic service between the wars', in J. Clarke, C. Critcher and R. Johnson (eds), *Working-Class Culture: studies in history and theory* (Hutchinson 1979)
Titmuss, R.M., 'The Position of Women: some vital statistics', in M. Flinn and T.C. Smout (eds), *Essays in Social History* (Oxford, Clarendon 1974)
Weeks, J., *Sex, Politics and Society: the regulation of sexuality since 1800* (1981)

10 MIGRATION

Carrier, N.H., and Jeffery, J.R., 'External Migration, 1815–1950: a study of the available statistics', *Studies on Medical and Population Subjects* 6 (1953)
Frankel, H., 'The Industrial Distribution of the Population of Great Britain in July, 1939', *JRSS* CVIII (1945)
Friedlander, D., and Roshier, R.J., 'A Study of Internal Migration in England and Wales: part I', *PS* XIX (1966)
Makower, H., Marschak, J., and Robinson, H.W., 'Studies in Mobility of Labour: analysis for Great Britain, part I', *OEP* 2 (1939)
Makower, H., Marschak, J., and Robinson, H.W., 'Studies in Mobility of Labour: analysis for Great Britain, part II', *OEP* 4 (1940)

Royal Commission on the Distribution of the Industrial Population, *Report* (1940), Cmd 6153

Thomas, B., 'The Movement of Labour into South East England, 1920–32', *Economica* 1 (1934)

Thomas, B., 'The Influx of Labour into London and the South East, 1920–36', *Economica* 4 (1937)

11 SOCIAL AND OCCUPATIONAL STRUCTURE

Cole, G.D.H., and Cole, M., *The Condition of Britain* (Gollancz 1937)

Frankel, H., 'The Industrial Distribution of the Population of Great Britain in July, 1939', *JRSS* CVIII (1945)

Halsey, A.H. (ed.), *Trends in British Society since 1900: a guide to the changing social structure of Britain* (Macmillan 1972)

Leser, C.E.V., 'Trends in Women's Work Participation', *PS* XII (1958–59)

Routh, G., *Occupation and Pay in Great Britain 1906–60* (Cambridge UP 1965)

Routh, G., *Occupations of the People of Great Britain 1801–1981* (Macmillan 1987)

12 INCOMES, WEALTH AND CLASS

Atkinson, A.B. (ed.), *Wealth, Income and Inequality* (2nd edn, Oxford 1980)

Atkinson, A.B., and Harrison, A.J., *Distribution of Personal Wealth in Britain* (Cambridge UP 1978)

Barna, T., *The Redistribution of Incomes through Public Finance in 1937* (Oxford UP 1945)

Bowley, A.L., *Wages and Income in the United Kingdom since 1860* (Cambridge UP 1937)

Bowley, A.L., *Studies in the National Income, 1924–1938* (Cambridge UP 1942)

Chapman, A.L., and Knight, R., *Wages and Salaries in the United Kingdom, 1920–1938* (Cambridge UP 1953)

Clark, C., *National Income and Outlay* (Macmillan 1937)

Feinstein, C.H., 'Changes in the Distribution of the National Income in the U.K. since 1860', in J. Marchal and B. Ducros (eds), *The Distribution of National Income* (1968)

Hope, R., 'Profits in British Industry from 1924 to 1935', *OEP* I (1949)

Jackson, A.A., *The Middle Classes 1900–1950* (Nairn, David St John Thomas 1991)

Langley, K.M., 'The Distribution of Capital in Private Hands in 1936–38 and 1946–47', *Bulletin of the Oxford University Institute of Statistics* 13 (1951)

Lydall, H.F., 'The Long-Term Trend in the Size Distribution of Income', *JRSS* 122 (1959)

Lydall, H.F., *British Incomes and Savings* (Oxford, Blackwell 1955)

Marley, J.G., and Campion, H., 'Changes in Salaries in Great Britain, 1924–1939',

JRSS CIII (1940); also in A.L. Bowley, *Studies in the National Income 1924–1938* (Cambridge UP 1942)

Massey, P., 'The Expenditure of 1,360 British Middle-Class Households in 1938–39', *JRSS* CV (1942)

Routh, G., *Occupation and Pay in Great Britain, 1906–1960* (Cambridge UP 1965)

Rubinstein, W.D. (ed.), *Wealth and the Wealthy in the Modern World* (Croom Helm 1980)

Rubinstein, W.D., *Wealth and Inequality in Britain* (Faber & Faber 1986)

Seers, D., *Changes in the Cost-of-Living and the Distribution of Income since 1938* (Oxford, Blackwell 1949)

Seers, D., *The Levelling of Incomes since 1938* (Oxford, Blackwell 1951)

Stamp, (Sir) Josiah, *Wealth and Taxable Capacity* (P.S. King 1922)

Sturmey, S.G., 'Owner-Farming in England and Wales, 1900–1950', in W.E. Minchinton (ed.), *Essays in Agrarian History, vol. 2* (Newton Abbot, David & Charles 1968)

13 INDUSTRIAL STRUCTURE AND LOCATION

Allen, C.R., 'The Growth of Industry on Trading Estates, 1920–1939 with Particular Reference to the Slough Trading Estate', *OEP* III (1951)

Compton, M., and Bott, E.H., *British Industry: its changing structure in peace and war* (Lindsay Drummond 1940)

Florence, P.S., *The Logic of British and American Industry* (rev. edn, Routledge & Kegan Paul 1961)

Fogarty, M.P., *Prospects of the Industrial Areas of Great Britain* (Methuen 1945)

Gordon, L., *The Public Corporation in Great Britain* (Oxford UP 1938)

Hannah, L., *The Rise of the Corporate Economy* (2nd edn, Methuen 1983)

Labour, Ministry of, *Report of Investigations into the Industrial Conditions in Certain Depressed Areas* (1934), Cmd 4728

Leak, H., and Maizels, A., 'The Structure of British Industry', *JRSS* CVIII (1945)

Political and Economic Planning (PEP), *Report on the Location of Industry* (PEP 1939)

Prais, S.J., *The Evolution of Giant Firms in Britain: a study of the growth of concentration in manufacturing industry in Britain 1909–70* (Cambridge UP 1976)

Silverman, H.A., *Studies in Industrial Organization* (Oxford UP 1946)

14 INVESTMENT, CAPITAL AND FINANCIAL INSTITUTIONS

Balogh, T., *Studies in Financial Organization* (Cambridge UP 1947)

Committee on Finance and Industry (Macmillan Committee), *Report* (1931), Cmd 3897

Feinstein, C.H., *Domestic Capital Formation in the United Kingdom, 1920–1938* (Cambridge UP 1965)

Grant, A.J.K., *A Study of the Capital Market in Postwar Britain* (Macmillan 1937; Cass 1967)
Gregory, T.E. (ed.), *Select Statutes, Documents and Reports relating to British banking 1832–1928, vol. 2, 1847–1928* (Cass 1929; 1964)
Sheppard, D.K., *The Growth and Role of U.K. Financial Institutions, 1880–1962* (1971)
Thomas, W.A., *The Finance of British Industry 1918–1976* (Methuen 1978)
Worswick, G.D.N., and Tipping, D.G., *Profits in the British Economy 1909–1938* (Oxford, Blackwell 1967)

15 FOREIGN TRADE, PAYMENTS AND INVESTMENT

Atkin, J., 'Official Regulation of British Overseas Investment 1914–1931', *EcHR* XXIII (1970)
Baldwin, R.E., 'The Commodity Composition of Trade: selected industrial countries, 1900–1954', *Review of Economics and Statistics* 40 (1958)
Chang, T.C., 'The British Balance of Payments, 1924–1938', *EJ* 57 (1947)
Corner, D.C., 'Exports and the British Trade Cycle: 1929', *ManS* XXIV (1956)
Feinstein, C.H., 'Britain's Overseas Investments in 1913', *EcHR* XLIII (1990)
Foot, M.D.K.W., 'The Balance of Payments in the Inter-War Period', *Bank of England Quarterly Bulletin* 12 (1972)
Foreman-Peck, J., *A History of the World Economy: international economic relations since 1850* (Hemel Hempstead, Wheatsheaf 1983)
Hall, N.F., *The Exchange Equalization Account* (Macmillan 1935)
Kahn, A.E., *Great Britain in the World Economy* (New York, Pitman 1946)
Lewis, W.A., 'World Production, Prices and Trade, 1870–1960', *ManS* XX (1952)
Maddison, A., *The World Economy in the 20th Century* (Paris, OECD 1989)
Maizels, A., *Industrial Growth and World Trade* (Cambridge UP 1971)
Platt, D.C.M., *Britain's Investment Overseas on the Eve of the First World War: the use and abuse of numbers* (Macmillan 1986)
Platt, D.C.M., *Mickey Mouse Numbers in World History: the short view* (Macmillan 1989)
Redmond, J., 'The Sterling Overvaluation in 1925: a multilateral approach', *EcHR* XXXVII (1984)
Redmond, J., 'An Indicator of the Effective Exchange Rate of the Pound in the 1930s', *EcHR* XXXIII (1980)
Royal Institute of International Affairs (RIIA), *The Problem of International Investment* (RIIA 1937)
Saul, S.B., *Studies in British Overseas Trade 1870–1914* (Liverpool UP 1960)
Scott, M.Fg., *A Study of United Kingdom Imports* (Cambridge UP 1963)
Tyszinski, H., 'World Trade in Manufactured Commodities, 1899–1950', *ManS* XIX (1951)
United Nations, *International Capital Movements during the Interwar Period* (Lake Success, NY, United Nations 1949; Arno 1978)
Ware, R.G., 'The Balance of Payments in the Interwar Period: further details', *Bank of England Quarterly Review* 14 (1974)

Woodruff, W., *Impact of Western Man: a study of Europe's role in the world economy, 1750–1960* (Macmillan 1966)

16 LABOUR HISTORY AND TRADE UNIONS

Armstrong, A., *Farmworkers: a social and economic history 1770–1980* (Batsford 1988)

Benson, John, *The Working Class in Britain, 1850–1939* (Longman 1989)

Bienefeld, M.A., *Working Hours in British Industry: an economic history* (Weidenfeld & Nicolson 1972)

Clarke, J., Critcher, C., and Johnson, R., *Working Class Culture: studies in theory and history* (Hutchinson 1979)

Clegg, H.A., Fox, A., and Thompson, A.F., *A History of British Trade Unions since 1889,*
vol. I, 1889–1910 (Oxford, Clarendon 1964)
vol. II, 1911–1933 (Oxford, Clarendon 1985)
vol. III, 1934–1951 (Oxford, Clarendon 1994)

Croucher, R., *We Refuse to Starve in Silence: a history of the National Unemployed Workers' Movement, 1920–46* (Lawrence & Wishart 1987)

Fitzgerald, R., *British Labour Management and Industrial Welfare, 1846–1939* (Beckenham, Croom Helm 1988)

Hopkins, E., *The Rise and Decline of the English Working Classes, 1918–1990: a social history* (Weidenfeld & Nicolson 1986)

Jeffreys, J.B., *The Story of the Engineers, 1800–1945* (Lawrence & Wishart 1945)

Johnson, P., *Saving and Spending: the working-class economy in Britain 1870–1939* (Oxford 1985)

Jowitt, J.A., and McIvor, A., *Employers and Labour in the English Textile Industries, 1850–1939* (Routledge 1988)

Klingender, F.D., *The Condition of Clerical Labour in Britain* (Martin Lawrence 1935)

Knowles, K.G.J.C., *Strikes: a study in industrial conflict* (Oxford, Blackwell 1952)

Labour and National Service, Ministry of, *Annual Reports of the Chief Inspector of Factories for the year . . . 1939 to 1944*

Lockwood, D., *The Blackcoated Worker* (Allen & Unwin 1958)

Lovell, J., *British Trade Unions, 1875–1933* (Macmillan *SEH* 1977)

Morris, M. (ed.), *The General Strike* (Penguin 1976)

Pelling, H., *A Short History of British Trade Unionism* (Pelican 1963)

Phelps Brown, H., *The Growth of British Industrial Relations: a study from the standpoint of 1906–14* (Macmillan 1959)

Phelps Brown, H., *The Origins of Trade Union Power* (Oxford UP 1986)

Phillips, G., and Whiteside, N., *Casual Labour: the unemployment question in the port transport industry, 1880–1970* (Oxford, Clarendon 1985)

Wrigley, C.J. (ed.), *A History of British Industrial Relations, vol. II, 1914–1939* (Brighton, Harvester 1987)

17 ECONOMIC POLICY AND ECONOMIC THOUGHT

Beveridge, (Sir) W. (ed.), *Tariffs: the case examined* (Longmans, Green 1931)

Beveridge, (Sir) W., *Full Employment in a Free Society* (Allen & Unwin 1944)

Booth, Alan, *British Economic Policy 1931–1949: was there a Keynesian revolution?* (Harvester 1990)

Boyce, R.W.D., *British Capitalism at the Crossroads 1919–1932* (Cambridge UP 1987)

Cairncross, A., and Eichengreen, B., *Sterling in Decline: the devaluations of 1931, 1949 and 1967* (Oxford, Blackwell 1983)

Cairncross, A., and Watts, N., *The Economic Section, 1939–61: a study in economic advising* (Routledge 1989)

Clarke, Peter, *The Keynesian Revolution in the Making 1924–1936* (Oxford, Clarendon 1990)

Clay, Henry, *The Post-War Unemployment Problem* (Macmillan 1929)

Collins, M., 'Unemployment in Interwar Britain: still searching for an explanation', *JPE* 90 (1982)

Cross, R., 'How Much Voluntary Unemployment in Interwar Britain?', *JPE* 90 (1982)

Dimsdale, N.H., 'British Monetary Policy and the Exchange Rate 1920–1938', *OEP* 38 (1981), supplement

Eichengreen, B. (ed.), *The Gold Standard in Theory and History* (Methuen 1985)

Eichengreen, B., *Golden Fetters: the gold standard and the great depression, 1919–1939* (New York, Oxford UP 1992)

Falkus, M.E., 'United States Economic Policy and the Dollar Gap of the 1920s', *EcHR* XXIV (1971)

Financial Agreement between the Governments of the United States and the United Kingdom dated 6th December 1945, together with a joint statement regarding settlement for Lend-Lease, Reciprocal Aid, Surplus War Property and Claims (1945), Cmd 6708

Glynn, S., and Booth, A. (eds), *The Road to Full Employment* (Allen & Unwin 1987)

Gregory, T.E. (ed.), *Select Statutes, Documents and Reports Relating to British Banking 1832–1928, vol. 2* (Oxford UP 1929)

Hancock, K.J., 'Unemployment and the Economists in the 1920s', *Economica* XXXVII (1960)

Hancock, K.J., 'The Reduction of Unemployment as a Problem of Public Policy 1932–29', *EcHR* XVI (1962–63)

Howson, S., *Domestic Monetary Management, 1919–1938* (Cambridge UP 1976)

Howson, S., 'Slump and Unemployment', in Floud and McCloskey, vol. 2

Howson, S., and Winch, D., *The Economic Advisory Council, 1930–1939* (Cambridge UP 1977)

Jones, M.E.F., 'The Regional Impact of an Overvalued Pound in the 1920s', *EcHR* XXXVIII (1985)

Kahn, R.F., 'The Relation of Home Investment to Unemployment', *EJ* XLI (1931)
Keynes, J.M., *The Collected Writings of John Maynard Keynes* (Macmillan/Cambridge UP for the Royal Economic Society 1971–89, 30 vols); vols XV–XVIII were edited by E. Johnson, all other volumes by D. Moggridge.
Keynes, J.M., 'The Colwyn Report on National Debt and Taxation', *EJ* XXXVII (1927)
Kunz, D.B., *The Battle for Britain's Gold Standard in 1931* (Beckenham, Croom Helm 1987)
Lloyd George, D., *We can Conquer Unemployment* (Cassell 1929)
McKibbin, R., 'The Economic Policy of the Second Labour Government 1929–31', *Past and Present* 58 (1975)
Memoranda on Certain Proposals Relating to Unemployment (1929), Cmd 3331
Metcalf, D., 'Still Searching for an Explanation of Unemployment in Interwar Britain', *JPE* 90 (1982)
Middleton, R., *Towards the Managed Economy: Keynes, the Treasury and the fiscal policy debate of the 1930s* (Methuen 1985)
Miller, F.M., 'The Unemployment Policy of the National Government, 1931–1936', *HJ* 19 (1976)
Moggridge, D.E., *The Return to Gold 1925: the formulation of economic policy and its critics* (Cambridge UP 1969)
Moggridge, D.E., *British Monetary Policy 1924–1931: the Norman Conquest of $4.86* (Cambridge UP 1972)
Moggridge, D.E., *Maynard Keynes: an economist's biography* (Routledge 1992)
Moggridge, D.E., 'The 1931 Crisis: a new view', *The Banker* (1970)
Nevin, E., *The Mechanism of Cheap Money: a study of British monetary policy 1931–1939* (Cardiff, University of Wales Press 1955)
Ormerod, P.A., and Worswick, G.D.N., 'Unemployment in Interwar Britain', *JPE* 90 (1982)
Peden, G.S., *Keynes, the Treasury and British Economic Policy* (Macmillan *SEH* 1988)
Peden, G.S., *British Economic and Social Policy: Lloyd George to Margaret Thatcher* (2nd edn, Deddington, Phillip Allan 1991)
Pollard, S. (ed.), *The Gold Standard and Employment Policies between the Wars* (Methuen 1970)
Rooth, T., *British Protectionism and the International Economy: overseas commercial policy in the 1930s* (Cambridge UP 1993)
Skidelsky, R., *Politicians and the Slump* (Macmillan 1967)
Skidelsky, R., *John Maynard Keynes* (1983, 1986, 2 vols) *vol. 1, Hopes Betrayed, 1883–1920* (Macmillan 1983)
Specific Agreements Regarding Settlement for Lend Lease, Reciprocal Aid, Surplus War Property and Claims (1946), Cmd 6778
Williams, D., 'London and the 1931 Financial Crisis', *EcHR* XV (1962–63)
Winch, D., *Economics and Policy: a historical study* (Hodder & Stoughton 1969)
Wright, J.F., 'Britain's Inter-War Experience', in W.A. Eltis and P.J.N. Sinclair,

(eds), *The Money Supply and the Exchange Rate* (Oxford, Clarendon 1981)

18 SOCIAL POLICY

Abrams, M., 'The Failure of Social Reform, 1918–20', *Past and Present* 24–26 (1963)

Beveridge, W.H., *Social Insurance and Allied Services, Report by Sir William Beveridge* (1942), Cmd 6404

Bruce, M., *The Coming of the Welfare State* (4th edn, Batsford 1968)

Crowther, A., *British Social Policy, 1914–1939* (Macmillan *SEH* 1988)

Crowther, M.A., *The Workhouse System 1834–1929: the history of an English social institution* (Routledge 1983)

Fraser, D., *The Evolution of the British Welfare State* (Macmillan 1973)

Gilbert, B.B., *British Social Policy, 1914–1939* (Batsford 1970)

Macnicol, J., *The Movement for Family Allowances, 1918–45: a study in social policy development* (Heinemann 1980)

Mess, H.A., *Voluntary Social Services since 1918* (Kegan Paul 1947)

Political and Economic Planning (PEP), *Report on The British Social Services* (PEP 1937)

Rose, M.E., *The English Poor Law, 1780–1930* (Newton Abbot, David & Charles 1971)

Webb, S., and Webb, B., *English Poor Law History, part II, The Last Hundred Years, vol. I* (Longmans, Green 1929)

19 PUBLIC FINANCE

Committee on the National Expenditure ('Geddes Committee'), *Third Report* (1922), Cmd 1589

Committee on National Debt and Taxation ('Colwyn Committee'), *Report* (1927), Cmd 2800

Hicks, U.K., *The Finance of British Government, 1920–1936* (Oxford 1938; 1970)

Mallett, Sir G., and George, C.O., *British Budgets*
– *Second Series, 1913–14 to 1920–21* (Macmillan 1929)
– *Third Series, 1921–22 to 1932–33* (Macmillan 1933)

National Expenditure, *Committee on National Expenditure: Report* ('May Committee') (1931), Cmd 3920, PP 1930–31, XVI

National Expenditure, *Memorandum on the Measures Proposed by His Majesty's Government to Secure Reduction in National Expenditure* (1931), Cmd 3952, PP 1930–31, LXVIII

Peacock, A.T., and Wiseman, J., *The Growth of Public Expenditure in the United Kingdom* (Weidenfeld & Nicolson 1961)

Sabine, B.E.V., *British Budgets in Peace and War, 1932–1945* (Allen & Unwin 1970)

Stamp, (Sir) J., *Taxation during the War* (Oxford UP 1932)

20 EDUCATION AND YOUTH

Board of Education, *The Education of the Adolescent: Report of the Consultative Committee* ('Hadow Report') (1927)

Board of Education, *Report of the Consultative Committee on Secondary Education* ('Spens Report') (1938)

'Bruce Truscott' (pseud.), *Red-Brick University* (1943)

Curtis, S.J., *History of Education in Great Britain* (7th edn, University Tutorial Press 1967)

Gosden, P.H.J.H., *Education in the Second World War* (Methuen 1976)

Green, V.H.H., *The Universities* (Pelican 1969)

Harte, N., *The University of London 1836–1986: an illustrated history* (Athlone 1986)

Lowndes, G.A.N., *The Silent Social Revolution: an account of the expansion of public education in England and Wales, 1895–1965* (2nd edn, Oxford UP 1969)

Mountford, J., *British Universities* (Oxford UP 1966)

Ree, H., *Educator Extraordinary: the life and achievement of Henry Morris 1889–1961* (Peter Owen 1985)

Sanderson, M., *Educational Opportunity and Social Change in England* (Faber & Faber 1987)

Sherington, G., *English Education, Social Change and War 1911–20* (Manchester UP 1981)

Stocks, M., *The Workers' Educational Association: the first fifty years* (Allen & Unwin 1953)

Tawney, R.H., *Secondary Education for All: a policy for Labour* (Allen & Unwin 1922)

Tropp, A., *The School Teachers: the growth of the teaching profession in England and Wales from 1800 to the present day* (Heinemann 1957)

Wilkinson, P., 'English Youth Movements 1908–1930', *JCH* 4 (1969)

21 LEISURE

Brunner, E., *Holiday Making and the Holiday Trades* (Oxford UP 1945)

Delgado, A., *The Annual Outing and Other Excursions* (Allen & Unwin 1977)

Durant, H., *The Problem of Leisure* (George Routledge 1938)

Gilbert, E.W., 'The Growth of Inland and Seaside Health Resorts in England', *Scottish Geographical Magazine* LV (1939)

Holt, R., *Sport and the British: a modern history* (Oxford, Clarendon 1989)

Howkins, A., and Lowerson, J., *Trends in Leisure, 1919–1939* (Sports Council and Social Science Research Council 1979)

Jones, Stephen G., *Workers at Play: a social and economic history of leisure, 1918–39* (Routledge 1986)

Kelly, T., *A History of Public Libraries in Great Britain, 1845–1975* (Library Association 1973)

McKibbin, R., 'Working-Class Gambling in Britain, 1880–1939', *Past and Present* 82 (1979)

Mason, T. (ed.), *Sport in Britain: a social history* (Cambridge UP 1989)
Mass-Observation, *The Pub and the People* (1943)
Pimlott, J.A.R., *The Englishman's Holiday* (Faber & Faber 1947)
Political and Economic Planning (PEP), *The British Film Industry* (PEP 1952)
Prynn, D., 'The Woodcraft Folk and the Labour Movement, 1925–70', *JCH* 8 (1983)
Walton, J.K., *The Blackpool Landlady: a social history* (Manchester UP 1978)
Walton, J.K., *The English Seaside Resort: a social history 1750–1914* (Leicester UP 1983)
Walton, J.K., and Walvin, J. (eds), *Leisure in Britain 1780–1939* (Manchester UP 1983)
Wild, P., 'Recreation in Rochdale, 1900–40', in J. Clarke, C. Critcher and R. Johnson (eds), *Working-Class Culture: studies in history and theory* (Hutchinson 1979)
Williams, G.P., and Brake, G.T., *Drink in Great Britain 1900–1979* (Edsall 1980)
Wilson, G.B., *Alcohol and the Nation* (Nicholson & Watson 1940)

22 INDIVIDUAL INDUSTRIES AND ENTREPRENEURS

Alford, B.W.E., *W.D. & H.O. Wills and the Development of the U.K. Tobacco Industry, 1786–1965* (Methuen 1973)
Andrews, P.W.S., and Brunner, E., *The Life of Lord Nuffield: a study in enterprise and benevolence* (Oxford, Blackwell 1955)
Bowley, M., 'Fluctuations in Housebuilding and the Trade Cycle', *Review of Economic Studies* 4 (1937)
Burn, D., *The Economic History of Steelmaking, 1867–1939: a study in competition* (Cambridge UP 1940)
Burnham, T.H., and Hoskins, G.O., *Iron and Steel in Britain, 1870–1939* (Cambridge UP 1961)
Buxton, N.K., and Aldcroft, D.H. (eds), *British Industry between the Wars* (Scolar 1979)
Carr, J.C., and Taplin, W., *History of the British Steel Industry* (Cambridge, MA, Harvard UP 1962)
Church, Roy, *Herbert Austin: the British motor car industry to 1941* (Europa 1979)
Coleman, D.C., *Courtaulds: an economic and social history, vol. 2, Rayon* (Oxford UP 1969)
Committee on Industry and Trade ('Balfour Committee'), *Survey of Metal Industries* (1928)
Corley, T.A.B., *Domestic Electric Appliances* (Cape 1966)
Daniels, G.W., and Jewkes, J., 'The Crisis in the Lancashire Cotton Industry', *EJ* XXXVII (1927)
Davenport-Hines, R.P.T. (ed.), *Business in the Age of Depression and War* (Cass 1990)
Fine, B., 'Economies of Scale and a Featherbedding Cartel? A reconsideration of the interwar British coal industry', *EcHR* XLIII (1990)

Gourvish, T.R., and Wilson, R.G., *The British Brewing Industry, 1830–1980* (Cambridge UP 1994)
Haber, L.F., *The Chemical Industry 1900–30* (Oxford, Clarendon 1971)
Hannah, L., *Electricity before Nationalization* (Macmillan 1979)
Jones, L., *Shipbuilding in Britain: mainly between the two world wars* (Cardiff, University of Wales Press 1957)
Jowitt, J.A., and McIvor, A.J. (eds), *Employers and Labour in the English Textile Industries, 1850–1939* (Routledge 1988)
Keynes, J.M., 'The Position of the Lancashire Cotton Trade', *The Nation and Athenaeum* (13 November 1926)
Kirby, M.W., 'The Lancashire Cotton Industry in the Inter-War Years: a study in organizational change', *Business History* (1974)
Kirby, M.W., *The British Coalmining Industry 1870–1946: a political and economic history* (Macmillan 1977)
Lewchuk, W., *American Technology and the British Vehicle Industry* (Cambridge UP 1987)
Lorenz, E.H., *Economic Decline in Britain: the shipbuilding industry 1890–1970* (Oxford, Clarendon 1991)
Mackintosh, R.M., 'A Note on Cheap Money and the British Housing Boom, 1932–37', *EJ* 61 (1951)
Maxcy, G., and Silberston, A., *The Motor Industry* (Allen & Unwin 1959)
Minchinton, W.E., *The British Tinplate Industry* (Oxford, Clarendon 1957)
Overy, R.J. *William Morris, Viscount Nuffield* (Europa 1976)
Parkinson, J.R., *The Economics of Shipbuilding in the United Kingdom* (Cambridge UP 1960)
Peebles, H.B., *Warship Building on the Clyde: naval orders and the prosperity of the Clyde shipbuilding industry, 1889–1939* (Edinburgh, John Donald 1987)
Political and Economic Planning (PEP), *The Market for Household Appliances* (PEP 1945)
Political and Economic Planning (PEP), *Report on the Supply of Electricity in Great Britain* (PEP 1936)
Political and Economic Planning (PEP), *The British Fuel and Power Industries* (PEP 1947)
Plummer, A., *New British Industries in the Twentieth Century* (Pitman 1937)
Pocock, R.F., *The Early British Radio Industry* (Manchester UP 1989)
Reader, W.J., *Imperial Chemical Industries: a history* (Oxford UP 1970–75, 3 vols)
Richardson, H.W., and Aldcroft, D.H., *Building in the British Economy between the Wars* (Allen & Unwin 1968)
Richardson, K., and O'Gallagher, C., *The British Motor Industry 1896–1939* (Macmillan 1977)
Robertson, A.J., 'Clydeside Revisited: a reconsideration of the Clyde shipbuilding industry, 1919–38', in Chaloner and Ratcliffe (1977)
Robson, R., *The Cotton Industry in Britain* (Macmillan 1957)
Royal Commission on the Coal Industry (1925), *Report, vol. I* (1926), Cmd 2600
Sandberg, L., *Lancashire in Decline* (Columbus, Ohio State UP 1974)

Slaven, A., 'British Shipbuilders: market trends and order book patterns between the wars', *Journal of Transport History* 3 (1982)

Slaven, A., 'A Shipyard in Depression: John Browns of Clydebank 1919–1938', in Davenport-Hines, *Business in the Age of Depression and War* (1990)

Supple, B.E., *The History of the British Coal Industry, vol. 4, 1913–46: the political economy of decline* (Oxford, Clarendon 1987)

Sturmey, S.G., *British Shipping and World Competition* (Athlone 1962)

Sturmey, S.G., *The Economic Development of Radio* (Duckworth 1958)

Tolliday, Steven, *Business, Banking and Politics: the case of British steel 1918–1939* (Camb, MA, Harvard UP 1987)

Warren, K., *Consett Iron 1840 to 1980: a study in industrial location* (Oxford, Clarendon 1990)

Whetham, E.H., *The Agrarian History of England and Wales, vol. VIII, 1914–39* (Cambridge UP 1978)

Whiting, R.C., *The View from Cowley: the impact of industrialization upon Oxford, 1918–1939* (Oxford, Clarendon 1983)

Wilson, J.F., *Ferranti and the British Electrical Industry, 1864–1934* (Manchester UP 1988)

Wilson, C., *The history of Unilever* (Cassell 1954)

23 RETAILING

Bushell, S.M., 'The Relative Importance of Co-operative, Multiple and other Retail Traders', *Economica* (1921)

Jeffreys, J.B., *Retail Trading in Britain, 1850–1940* (Cambridge UP 1954)

Mathias, P., *Retailing Revolution: a history of multiple retailing in the food trades based upon the Allied Suppliers group of companies* (Longman 1967)

Rees, G., *St Michael: a history of Marks & Spencer* (Weidenfeld & Nicolson 1969)

24 UNEMPLOYMENT

Bakke, E.W., *The Unemployed Man* (Nisbet 1933)

Beales, H.L., and Lambert, R.S., *Memoirs of the Unemployed* (Gollancz 1934)

Benjamin, D.K., and Kochin, L.A., 'Searching for an Explanation of Unemployment in Interwar Britain', *JPE* 87 (1979)

Benjamin, D.K., and Kochin, L.A., 'Unemployment and Unemployment Benefit in Twentieth Century Britain: a reply to our critics', *JPE* 90 (1982)

Beveridge, W.H.

'An Analysis of Unemployment I', *Economica* III, 12 (1936)

'An Analysis of Unemployment II', *Economica* IV, 13 (1937)

'An Analysis of Unemployment III', *Economica* IV, 14 (1937)

Beveridge, W.H., *Unemployment: A Problem of Industry* (Longmans, Green 1930)

Burns, E.M., *British Unemployment Programs, 1920–1938* (Washington, DC 1941)

Carnegie United Kingdom Trust, *Disinherited Youth: a report on the 18+ Age Group* (Edinburgh, Carnegie Trust 1943)
Clay, H., 'Unemployment and the Wage Rate', *EJ* XXXVIII (1928)
Colledge, D., *Labour Camps: The British Experience* (Sheffield Popular Publishing 1989)
Constantine, S., *Unemployment in Britain between the Wars* (Longman 1980)
Croucher, C., *We Refuse to Starve in Silence: a history of the unemployed workers' movement* (Lawrence & Wishart 1987)
Dale, J.A., 'The Interpretation of the Statistics of Unemployment', *JRSS* 97 (1934)
Dimsdale, N.H., 'Employment and Real Wages in the Inter-War Period', *NIER* 110 (1984)
Dimsdale, N.H., Nickel, S.J., and Horsewood, N., 'Real Wages and Unemployment in Britain during the 1930s', *EJ* 99 (1989)
Eichengreen, B., 'Unemployment in Interwar Britain: New Evidence from London', *Journal of Interdisciplinary History* 17 (1986)
Eichengreen, B., and Hatton, T.J. (eds), *Interwar Unemployment in International Perspective* (Dordrecht, Kluwer 1988)
Eichengreen, B., 'Interwar Unemployment in International Perspective', in Eichengreen and Hatton (1988)
Eichengreen, B., 'Unemployment in Interwar Britain: Dole or Doldrums', in N. Crafts, N. Dimsdale and S. Engerman (eds), *Quantitative Economic History* (Oxford, Clarendon 1991)
Garside, W.R., *British Unemployment 1919–1939: a study in public policy* (Cambridge UP 1990)
Hannington, Wal, *The Problem of the Distressed Areas* (Gollancz 1937)
Ormerod, P.A., and Worswick, G.D.N., 'Unemployment in Inter-War Britain', *JPE* 90 (1982)
Pigou, A.C., 'Wage Policy and Unemployment', *EJ* XXXVII (1927)
Pilgrim Trust, *Men Without Work* (Cambridge UP 1938)
Royal Commission on Unemployment Insurance:
– *First Report* (1931), Cmd 3872
– *Final report* (1932), Cmd 4185
Unemployment Grants Committee, *Final Report* (1933), Cmd 4354

25 HOUSING AND TOWNS

Ashworth, W., *The Genesis of Modern British Town Planning* (Routledge & Kegan Paul 1954)
Becker, A.P., 'Housing in England and Wales during the Business Depression of the 1930s', *EcHR* (1950–51)
Bowley, M., *The British Building Industry* (Cambridge UP 1966)
Bowley, M., *Housing and the State* (Allen & Unwin 1945)
Brennan, T., *Reshaping a City* (Glasgow and London, House of Grant 1959)
Burnett, J., *A Social History of Housing, 1815–1970* (Newton Abbot, David & Charles 1978)
Chapman, S.D. (ed.), *The History of Working-Class Housing: a symposium* (Newton Abbot, David & Charles 1971)

Cleary, E.J., *The Building Society Movement* (Elek 1965)
Cole, G.D.H., *Building and Planning* (Cassell 1945)
Daunton, M.J. (ed.), *Councillors and Tenants: local authority housing in English cities, 1919–1939* (Leicester UP 1984)
Daunton, M.J., *A Property-Owning Democracy? Housing in Britain* (Faber & Faber 1987)
Durant, R., *Watling: a survey of social life on a new housing estate* (P.S. King 1939)
Elsas, M.J., *Housing Before the War and After* (2nd edn, Staples 1945)
Health, Ministry of, *Report of Overcrowding Survey of England and Wales* (1936)
Jackson, A.A., *Semi-Detached London* (Allen & Unwin 1973)
Jevons, R., and Madge, J., *Housing Estates* (1946)
Lewis, J.P., *Building Cycles and Britain's Growth* (Macmillan 1965)
Marshall, J.L., 'The Pattern of Housebuilding in the Inter-War Period in England and Wales', *SJPE* (1968)
Mass-Observation, *An Enquiry into People's Homes* (1943)
Muthesius, S., *The English Terraced House* (New Haven, CT, Yale UP 1982)
Ravetz, A., *Model Estate: planned housing at Quarry Hill, Leeds* (Beckenham, Croom Helm 1974)
Reiss, R.L., *Municipal and Private Enterprise Housing* (Dent 1945)
Rodger, R. (ed.), *Scottish Housing in the Twentieth Century* (Leicester UP 1989)
Rubinstein, A., Andrews, A., and Schweitzer, P., *Just Like the Country: memories of London families who settled the new cottage estates 1919–1939* (Age Exchange 1992)
Simon, E.D., *How to Abolish the Slums* (Longmans, Green 1929)
Simon, E.D., *The Anti-Slum Campaign* (Longmans, Green 1933)
Sutcliffe, A. (ed.), *Multi-Storey Living: the British working-class experience* (Beckenham, Croom Helm 1974)
Swenarton, Mark, *Homes Fit for Heroes* (Heinemann 1981)
Townroe, B.S., *The Slum Problem* (Longmans, Green 1930)
Worsdall, F., *The Tenement: a way of life* (Chambers, 1979)
Young, T., *Becontree and Dagenham: a report made for the Pilgrim Trust* (Becontree Social Survey Committee 1934)

26 HEALTH AND HEALTH SERVICES

Abel-Smith, B., *The Hospitals, 1800–1948* (Heinemann 1964)
Acton Society Trust, *Hospitals and the State* (1955)
Harris, B., 'Unemployment, Insurance and Health in Interwar Britain', in Eichengreen and Hatton (1988)
M'Gonigle, G.C.M., and Kirby, J., *Poverty and Public Health* (Gollancz 1936)
Political and Economic Planning (PEP), *Report on British Health Services* (1937)
Webster, C., 'Health, Welfare and Unemployment during the Depression', *Past and Present* 109 (1985)
Winter, J., 'The Impact of the First World War on Civilian Health in Britain', *EcHR* XXX (1977)

Winter, J.M., 'Infant Mortality, Maternal Mortality and Public Health in Britain in the 1930s', *JEEH* 8 (1979)

27 DIET

Burnett, John, *Plenty and Want: a social history of diet in England from 1815 to the present day* (Pelican 1966)
Carnegie United Kingdom Trust, *Family, Diet and Health in Pre-War Britain: a dietary and clinical survey* (Dunfermline, Carnegie Trust 1955)
Crawford, (Sir) W., and Broadley, H., *The People's Food* (Heinemann 1938)
Mayhew, M., 'The 1930s Nutrition Controversy', *JCH* 23 (1988)
Orr, J.B., *Food, Health and Income* (2nd edn, Macmillan 1937)
Webster, C., 'Health, Welfare and Unemployment during the Depression', *Past and Present* 109 (1985)
Winter, J., 'Unemployment, Nutrition and Infant Mortality in Britain, 1920–50', in J. Winter (ed.), *The Working Class in Modern British History: essays in honour of Henry Pelling* (Cambridge UP 1983)

28 MEDIA

Aldgate, A., and Richards, J., *Britain Can Take It: the British cinema in the Second World War* (Oxford, Blackwell 1986)
Boyce, G., Curran, J., and Wingate, P. (eds), *Newspaper History from the 17th Century to the Present Day* (Constable 1978)
Briggs, A., *The History of Broadcasting in the United Kingdom:*
– *vol. I, The Birth of Broadcasting* (Oxford UP 1961)
– *vol. II, The Golden Age of Wireless* (Oxford UP 1965)
– *vol. III, The War of Words* (Oxford UP 1970)
Pegg, Mark, *Broadcasting and Society, 1918–39* (Beckenham, Croom Helm 1983)
Political and Economic Planning, *Report on the British Press* (1938)
Richards, J., *The Age of the Dream Palace: cinema and society in Britain 1930–1939* (Routledge & Kegan Paul 1984)
Richards, J., and Sheridan, D. (ed.), *Mass-Observation at the Movies* (Routledge 1987)
Royal Commission on the Press 1947–1949, *Report* (1949), Cmd 7700
Scannell, P., and Cardiff, D., *A Social History of British Broadcasting, vol. I, 1922–1939* (Oxford, Blackwell 1991)
Steed, H. Wickham, *The Press* (Penguin 1938)

29 MEMOIRS AND PERSONAL ANTHOLOGIES

Cohen, M., *I Was One of the Unemployed* (Gollancz 1945)
Forrester, H., *Twopence to Cross the Mersey* (Fontana 1981)
Orwell, G., *The Road to Wigan Pier* (Gollancz 1937; Penguin 1962)
Osborne, J., *A Better Class of Person: an autobiography 1929–1956* (Faber & Faber 1981)

Peel, (Mrs) C.S., *How We Lived Then: a sketch of social and domestic life during the war* (John Lane, Bodley Head 1929)
Priestley, J.B., *English Journey* (Heinemann/Gollancz 1934)
Roberts, Robert, *The Classic Slum: Salford Life in the first quarter of the century* (Manchester UP 1971)
Rowse, A.L., *A Cornish Childhood* (Cape 1942)
Strachey, J., *Post D: some experiences of an air raid warden* (Gollancz 1941)
Tawney, R.H., *The Attack and Other Papers* (Allen & Unwin 1953)
Wybrow, R.J., *Britain Speaks Out, 1937–87: a social history as seen through the Gallup data* (Macmillan 1989)

30 TRANSPORT

Aldcroft, D.H., *Studies in British Transport History, 1870–1970* (Newton Abbot, David & Charles 1974)
Barker, T. (ed.), *The Economic and Social Effects of the Spread of Motor Vehicles* (Macmillan *SEH* 1987)
Barker, T., and Robbins, M., *A History of London Transport, vol. II, The Twentieth Century to 1970* (Allen & Unwin 1974)
Dyos, H.J., and Aldcroft, D.H., *British Transport: an economic survey from the seventeenth century to the twentieth* (Pelican 1974)
Foreman-Peck, J., 'Death on the Roads: Changing National Responses to Motor Accidents', in T. Barker (ed.), *The Economic and Social Effects of the Spread of Motor Vehicles*
Freeman, M., and Aldcroft, D.H., *The Atlas of British Railway History* (Beckenham, Croom Helm 1985)
Savage, C.I., *An Economic History of Transport* (Hutchinson, 1959)
Walker, G., *Road and Rail* (2nd edn, Allen & Unwin 1947)

31 BOOKS AND PUBLISHING

Briggs, A. (ed.), *Essays in the History of Publishing* (Longman 1974)
Kelly, T., *A History of Public Libraries in Great Britain 1845–1965* (Library Association 1973)
Morpurgo, J., *Allen Lane, King Penguin: a biography* (Hutchinson 1979)
Orwell, G., *England Your England and Other Essays* (Secker & Warburg 1954)
Watson, C., *Snobbery with Violence: English Crime Stories and their Audience* (Eyre Methuen 1979)

32 LIVING STANDARDS AND EXPENDITURE

Bowley, A.L., and Hogg, M.H., *Has Poverty Diminished?* (P.S. King 1925)
Florence, P.S., 'An Index of Working Class Purchasing Power for Great Britain, 1929–35', *JPE* (1936)
Jones, D.C., 'The Cost of Living of a Sample of Middle-class Families', *JRSS* XCI (1928)

Labour, Ministry of, 'Weekly Expenditure of Working-Class households', *Labour Gazette* (December 1940)

Linsley, C.A. and C.L., 'Booth, Rowntree and Llewellyn Smith: a reassessment of interwar poverty', *EcHR* XLVI (1993)

Llewellyn Smith, H. (ed.), *The New Survey of London Life and Labour* (1930–35, 9 vols)

Massey, Philip, 'The Expenditure of 1,360 British Middle-Class Households in 1938–39', *JRSS* CV (1942)

Nicholas, K., *The Social Effects of Unemployment on Teesside, 1919–1939* (Manchester UP 1986)

Orr, J. Boyd, *Food, Health and Income* (2nd edn, Macmillan 1937)

Reeves, M.S., *Round about a Pound a Week* (Bell 1913; Virago 1979)

Rowntree, B.S., *Poverty and Progress* (Longmans, Green 1941)

Rowntree, B.S., *The Human Needs of Labour* (Nelson 1918)

Sheffield Social Survey Committee, *A Survey of the Standard of Living in Sheffield* (by A.D.K. Owen) (Sheffield Social Survey Committee 1933)

Tout, H., *The Standard of Living in Bristol* (Bristol, Arrowsmith 1938)

Working Classes Cost of Living Committee ('Sumner Committee'), *Report* (1918), Cd 8980

33 RELIGION

Brown, C.G., *The Social History of Religion in Scotland since 1730* (Methuen 1987)

Currie, R.B., Gilbert, A., and Horsley, L., *Churches and Churchgoers: patterns of church growth in the British Isles since 1700* (Oxford, Clarendon 1977)

Gilbert, A.D., *The Making of Post-Christian Britain: a history of the secularization of modern society* (Longman 1980)

Hastings, A., *A History of English Christianity, 1920–1985* (Collins 1986)

McLeod, H., *Religion and the People of Western Europe, 1789–1970* (Oxford UP 1981)

Norman, E.R., *Church and Society in England, 1770–1970: a historical study* (Oxford, Clarendon 1976)

Wilkinson, A., *The Church of England and the First World War* (SPCK 1978)

34 CRIME AND POLICING

Humphries, S., and Gordon, P., *Forbidden Britain: our secret past 1900–1960* (BBC 1994)

McClintock, F.H., Avison, N.H., and Rose, G.N.G., *Crime in England and Wales* (Heinemann 1968)

Mannheim, H., *Social Aspects of Crime in England between the Wars* (Allen & Unwin 1940)

INDEX